*Ethics and Bigness:
Scientific, Academic,
Religious, Political,
and
Military*

THE PAPERS included in this volume were prepared for and discussed at the sixteenth meeting of the Conference on Science, Philosophy and Religion in Their Relation to the Democratic Way of Life, which was held at The Jewish Theological Seminary of America in New York City, on August 29, 30, and 31, and September 1, 1960. The Conference theme was "Challenges to Traditional Ethics: Government, Politics, and Administration." Harold D. Lasswell was Chairman, with Harlan Cleveland and F. Ernest Johnson as Co-Chairmen. Other papers written for the 1960 Conference appear in the companion volume, *The Ethic of Power: The Interplay of Religion, Philosophy, and Politics*. Each paper represents only the opinion of the individual writer. The authors of papers and comments are listed on pages 491 to 493.

Symposia of the Conference on Science, Philosophy and Religion are listed on pages 495–496. A report on the Conference as a whole is given in Appendix II.

This is a Jacob Ziskind Memorial publication.

ETHICS AND BIGNESS

SCIENTIFIC, ACADEMIC, RELIGIOUS, POLITICAL, AND MILITARY

Edited by

HARLAN CLEVELAND
ASSISTANT SECRETARY OF STATE,
FORMERLY DEAN, MAXWELL GRADUATE SCHOOL OF CITIZENSHIP AND
PUBLIC AFFAIRS, SYRACUSE UNIVERSITY

and

HAROLD D. LASSWELL
EDWARD J. PHELPS PROFESSOR OF LAW AND POLITICAL SCIENCE, YALE UNIVERSITY

PUBLISHED BY THE
CONFERENCE ON SCIENCE, PHILOSOPHY AND RELIGION
IN THEIR RELATION TO THE DEMOCRATIC WAY OF LIFE, INC.
NEW YORK

1962

DISTRIBUTED BY
HARPER & BROTHERS
NEW YORK

All rights reserved including the
right of reproduction in whole or
in part in any form.

Library of Congress Catalog Card Number: 41-1640

COPYRIGHT, © 1962
BY THE CONFERENCE ON SCIENCE, PHILOSOPHY AND RELIGION
IN THEIR RELATION TO THE DEMOCRATIC WAY OF LIFE, INC.
3080 BROADWAY, NEW YORK CITY
Printed in the United States of America

Table of Contents

Preface, *Alan M. Stroock* ix

Introduction xiii
    Moral Complexity and the Next Step, *The Editors*

    The Blurred Line between "Public" and "Private," *Harlan Cleveland* xxiii
        COMMENT BY:
        Paul H. Appleby xlv

    Moral Bases of Agreement and Cooperation in a Pluralistic Society, *Charner Perry* xlvii
        COMMENT BY:
        Robert C. Angell lxiv

PAPERS

I. Responsibility in Political Organization
    1. A Comparative Investigation of the Norms of Official Conduct, *Wayne A. R. Leys* 3
    2. The Ethical Problems of an Elected Political Executive, *Stephen K. Bailey* 21
        COMMENTS BY:
        Paul H. Appleby 36
        Bernard Mandelbaum 37
    3. Ethics and Practical Politics, *James MacGregor Burns* 39
    4. Moral Dimensions of Politics, *Eugene J. McCarthy* 45
    5. Ethical Challenges in Practical Politics, *Charles P. Taft* 53
    6. Popular Evaluations of Government: An Empirical Assessment, *Donald E. Stokes* 61
    7. The Management of Pressures and Opinion, *David Finn* 73
        COMMENT BY:
        Wayne A. R. Leys 80

II. Responsibility in Big-Scale Scientific and Academic Organization

8. Moral Judgments in Academic Structures, *James A. Perkins*   85
9. Big-Scale Scientific Research, *Karl K. Darrow*   99
10. Organizational Structure and Professional Ethics in a Government Laboratory, *C. M. Herzfeld*   105
11. "We Are Here as on a Darkling Plain," *Robert B. Livingston*   123

III. Responsibility in Big-Scale Religious Organization

12. The Cultural Background of American Religious Organization, *Talcott Parsons*   141
13. The Catholic Church and Modern Bigness, *Robert J. Dwyer*   169
14. The Organizational Dilemma in American Protestantism, *Robert Lee*   187
15. Large-Scale Organization in Jewish Religious Life, *David W. Silverman*   213

IV. Responsibility in Executive Organization in Big-Scale Government

16. Diversity in the Public Interest: Two Cases in Metropolitan Decisionmaking, *Paul N. Ylvisaker*   235
17. The Unsettled Limits of the American Presidency, *Rowland Egger*   259
    COMMENT BY:
    Paul H. Appleby   297
18. Ethics and the Federal Regulatory Agencies, *Louis J. Hector*   299
19. Congressional-Executive Responsibility, *Thomas K. Finletter*   311
20. The Proper Place of the Political Executive in the Governmental System, *William C. Foster*   329

V. Modern Organization of Civil-Military Relationships

21. The American Military Mind in a Strange New World, *Sidney F. Giffin*   341

Contents

22. Representativeness, Efficiency, and the Dual Problem of Civil-Military Relations, *William T. R. Fox* — 351
23. The Separation of Powers and National Security, *Edward L. Katzenbach, Jr.* — 363
    COMMENT BY:
    Quincy Wright — 381

VI. Fusion of Ethics and Organizational Considerations

24. Some Questions on the Measurement and Evaluation of Organization, *Kenneth E. Boulding* — 385
25. Prolegomena to Ethics for Administrators, *Nathan D. Grundstein* — 397
26. The Ethical Challenge of Modern Administration, *Ordway Tead* — 421
    COMMENT BY:
    Paul H. Appleby — 434
27. Irresponsibility as an Article of Faith, *Don K. Price* — 435
    COMMENTS BY:
    Paul H. Appleby — 467
    David B. Truman — 467

APPENDICES

I. First Lyman Bryson Lecture: Ethics and Politics, *Richard McKeon* — 469

II. Report on the Conference on Science, Philosophy and Religion — 489

Contributors to "Ethics and Bigness" — 491

Publications of the Conference on Science, Philosophy and Religion — 495

PROGRAMS

Sixteenth Conference on Science, Philosophy and Religion, August 29, 30, and 31, and September 1, 1960 — 497

"One World—One Ethics?", August 31, September 1, and 2, 1959 — 513

Index — 523

Preface

By ALAN M. STROOCK

The Conference on Science, Philosophy and Religion seemed a bit remote and ivory-tower to me during my early years at the bar when my father was Chairman of the Board at The Jewish Theological Seminary of America. But as I became more active on that Board and more knowledgeable about the Conference, that impression proved incorrect. Participation in its sessions, study of its papers, and acquaintance with its members have been an especially rewarding aspect of my association with the Seminary; as the relationship between it and the Conference has been especially important to their institutional development.

Scientists, philosophers, and theologians, feeling a profound sense of responsibility for the crisis of Western civilization, met at the urging of Rabbi Louis Finkelstein in September, 1940, in a large tent erected for the purpose in the Seminary quadrangle. That meeting initiated the attempt to talk across the barriers that traditionally separate disciplines—to confer, in the fullest meaning of that word. Speaking of that first gathering, Van Wyck Brooks wrote: "We see the passing of ancient sanctions and the collapse of traditional loyalties. . . . We know that democracy exalts the individual, but that individualism as an end in itself means anarchy. We know that tradition can make slaves of men, but that the lack of historical perspective and rootage in the past makes their lives thin and unheroic."

From its beginning, the Conference has attempted to strengthen our democratic institutions by bringing to bear upon them the collective thinking of leaders from a wide variety of disciplines. Over the years, it has developed techniques that facilitate this corporate thinking, and the participants have learned to respect each other in a way which transcends any mere technique as a basis for cooperative thinking.

Through meetings and publications, the Conference has demonstrated repeatedly that such thinking can be creative, productive, and effective. The kind of problems that the group is facing today—problems which accept the fact and validity of difference—is an indication of the strides which have been made.

Preface

As Chairman of the Seminary Board I was gratified that after twenty years the Conference returned to the quadrangle where it began, and as citizen rejoiced that the participants included scientists, philosophers, theologians of various denominations, and leaders from both government and industry.

The general outline for discussion advanced at the first session was particularly striking because it seemed to me to contain by implication the reason for the Seminary's involvement in this program: the fact that it is extraordinarily difficult to apply the sanctions and standards of traditional ethics to the problems posed by large-scale organizations in our complex world.

Remarkable consensus among the participants showed that not only was such discussion valid, but that through the medium of the Conference on Science, Philosophy and Religion has come a greater appreciation of one another's concerns and approaches to the many problems which beset our country and the free world.

Although an independent institution, chartered by the State of New York, since its preliminary discussions in 1939 the Conference has been supported by the Seminary's Institute for Religious and Social Studies which continues to house and maintain the Conference administration and to underwrite its publications.

If the search for truth is a valid goal for the Seminary—and it is; if Judaism (like other religions) with its respect for the sanctity of the individual and his right to approach God in his own way, has been a catalyst, bringing men and women together in this important venture —and it has; then the goals of the Seminary are in no small part fulfilled by its relationship to the Conference on Science, Philosophy and Religion.

Other members of the Seminary Board and of the Faculty share my hope that we may be privileged to help so the work and influence of the Conference will be deepened, yet expanded, to focus on fundamental philosophic and spiritual issues the wisdom of Africa, the Middle East, and the Far East, as well as Europe and both Americas.

Adlai E. Stevenson speaking at a recent meeting on behalf of this effort has given pithy expression to our goals. "I am proud and grateful to be identified with such healing scholarship.... I see a great opportunity here to further the search for those enduring values which transcend the divisive frictions between nations. While each country supports its national interests through an ethical rationalization, human progress can only be achieved if a way is found to identify the ethical ideas which are the basis for long range goals helpful to all men."

June 28, 1961

Introduction

Moral Complexity and the Next Step

By THE EDITORS

I

In one way or another, more and more people seem to be disturbed by a feeling that our twentieth century civilization lacks a commonly accepted moral philosophy. In times past, it is felt, societies developed and for practical purposes "adopted" systematic ways of thinking about the problems they collectively faced. In a more recent era the idea became current that societies could thrive in the presence of several such systems of thought, that the engine of civilization could run on a wide variety of doctrinal fuels. American democracy was, in fact, a political expression of the idea that market competition of philosophies was more likely than any one philosophy to produce practical answers to the questions thrown up by daily life and work. In ethics as in political loyalties, protected pluralism became the order of the day.

In the now global marketplace of ethics, a variety of traditional ways of thinking about the nature of man and man's relationship to society have competed for attention. Some of them are organized religions, rich inheritances from an ancient past—Roman Catholicism and the various forms of Protestantism, Eastern Orthodoxy, Judaism, and more recently the effort to apply Hindu, Buddhist, Moslem, and Confucian ways of thought to modern problem solving. Other strands were the contribution of secular philosophies, from the ancient Greeks to those of 1960.

The world to which we are trying to adapt this rich philosophic and religious tradition is, however, not cooperating very well. The pace of events accelerates every year; scientific discovery and technological innovation are sudden and worldwide in their impact, while our capacity to exercise social forethought grows with more deliberate speed. And as men attempt to marry discovery to purpose, they often find in traditional ethics more of comfort than of stimulation. At other times they find more of gloomy prediction than of eager confidence for an unknown future. Discussions of "ethics" thus take on a lugubrious tone, as men more clearly see the trouble new forces may cause than the opportunities they may present.

The challenge to traditional ethics is not so much whether any particular religious or philosophical inheritance is "right," as whether it is relevant. . . .[1]

Part of the Sixteenth Conference on Science, Philosophy and Religion was concerned with "ethics" in government. In American government we have to a striking degree blurred the distinctions that were once much sharper, in our theory if not in our practice. One is the distinction between what is "public" and what is "private." When private interests are directly represented both in the legislative committee structure and in the executive bureaucracy, where is the line to be drawn between representativeness and corrupt practice? How are we to reconcile free-and-easy access by "the people" to all levels of government with the need for efficiency and responsibility in complex and highly organized public agencies?

The other fuzzy boundary is that between the executive and legislative functions, in a governmental system so fluid that the executive initiates most of the legislation and legislators busy themselves with the executive process. How do we reconcile the need for wise and representative determinations of general policy with the efficient conduct of the people's executive business?

In these circumstances, what are the effective norms of conduct in Government in the United States, at State and local levels as well as the Federal? What trends are discernible in the popular image of "public ethics"? How do American norms of official conduct compare with those in other societies? Are the norms of conduct for party politics different from those for the "policy politics" of government operations? What are the ethical implications of our new proficiency in "the engineering of consent"?

The Conference first tackled these questions in the contexts of the chronic civilian-military tussle, the government of metropolitan

---

[1] From background statement by the editors and their Co-Chairman, F. Ernest Johnson, calling the Sixteenth Conference on Science, Philosophy and Religion.

areas, the structure of executive-legislative relations, and the growing importance of Congressional investigations.

We then turned our attention to selected problems of the executive process in the Federal Government: the unsettled limits of the Presidential Office; the proper place of the political executive in the governmental system; and the responsibilities of "independent" commissions, commissioners, and executive agencies.

The recurring theme in these discussions was a worry—or a sense of discovery and excitement, depending on one's attitude, experience, and temperament—about the consequences of modern big-scale organizations for moral responsibility.

Voices are often raised these days to deny that modern large-scale organization is compatible with freedom and individual human dignity. The questions that arise are not only those of policy and morality, but also those of fact. Does large-scale organization place more and more power in fewer and fewer hands? Does large-scaleness imply tighter or looser forms of organization and administration? What kinds of challenge does the modern behemoth present to individual and group responsibility?

II

The papers published in this volume are replete with illustrations of the complexity now faced by the American public executive— whether he is elected to office, or as an appointed "expert," or indeed is outside the government performing functions affected with the public interest. However defined, he is faced from day to day with decisions, not about what public policy should be, but about what action he will take on specific issues in the form and at the time in which they present themselves.

Again and again the suggestion is made, obliquely and by example, that the moral content of these issues is very great, and the issues are so manysided that they cannot be squeezed into the traditional two dimensional frame of "representativesness versus efficiency." In defense policy, in decisions about the mess our cities are in, in the eternal byplay between the Executive and Congress in our Federal Government, or in the crazy mixedup decisionmaking processes of some of the Federal regulatory agencies, one thing is clear: there seem to be no questions up for decision which present as few as two sides to the decisionmaker.

Can we derive from this wealth of intellectual raw material any propositions of general validity about ethics and big-scale organization? Perhaps we can. Some of them are here stated quite baldly, so that they will seem outrageous enough to be worth pondering:

1. The degree of moral complexity is very great, and is becoming greater all the time.
2. Public-interest decisions are always made by a complex process of multilateral brokerage among legislators, and public executives in and out of the public service. More and more of the "real" decisions (the irreversible steps that mold our collective destiny) are made by (among) the executives, often without benefit of formal legislative mandate until after the fact, if ever.
3. The problem for the individual executive is almost never to decide what is "right," since the choices mostly present themselves as choices between goods or choices among evils—or both at the same time.
4. Nor is the problem for the individual to perceive, develop, or assert a "consensus" (arrived at by relevant elites or people-in-general) as a guide to action.
5. The problem is rather to decide *what to do next* in the presence of too much information about the past and only the most primitive tools for perceiving all the angles of the present or foretelling the future. (We should keep trying to sharpen these tools, which range from social science to intuition; but meanwhile each person has to decide what to do next.)
6. The complexity of public-interest decisions is such that the public executive is forced back on his own moral resources. Before the public executive takes each "next step," there are no criteria for action more valid than those he has worked out for himself through study and experience. After the fact, his action may be subjected to partial review by "the public"; but the very complexity of the subject-matter is rendering this review very partial indeed. This appears to make life safer for the executive since the probability is diminishing of any relevant public being able to understand what the decision was about or what his part

Introduction xvii

in it was. But by the same token, when a judgment *is* rendered it is likely to be more unfair than might have been true in simpler days.

7. One result of this state of affairs is that the public executive's search for adequate power to go with his public responsibilities is self-justifying: If he really is acting in the public interest, the more power he can amass, the "better." Since no two public executives, or legislators, or external critics, have precisely the same concept of the public interest, there will always be enough competition in the marketplace of executive power to keep them honest, or at least to avoid undue concentration of authority in any one pair of hands. Without this new kind of "invisible hand" the implied doctrine of Rowland Egger and Richard E. Neustadt (in the latter's *Presidential Power*), whereby the President should always act so as to maximize his power, would indeed purchase efficiency at the expense of representativeness.

8. If the most relevant form of efficiency is the maximization of personal power by public executives, the most relevant form of representativeness is the interaction of these executives with each other, with legislators, and with executives responsible for "private interests" which may also be affected with the public interest.

9. If the above propositions are even half true, it is clear that general prescriptions, whether in the form of do's or don't's, are bound to be (as Louis J. Hector puts it) so general as to be useless or so specific as to be unworkable.

10. Reliance is rather to be placed on study and experience by the individuals involved in the multilateral brokerage system, and on the ability of enough of them to emerge as leaders and administrators—that is, as experts on the process of putting experts together to get the "next step" taken, and then the one after that.

If we thus, in mankind's most complex society to date, come back to the individual and his conscience, it seems that there is, after all, a place in modern political and administrative process for the religious traditions. But the Great Traditions must constantly re-earn this place, not by just being great (in the past) or traditional, but by addressing themselves relevantly to the kinds of contemporary issues actually faced by each individual carrying any form of public responsibility (which means, in some degree, all individuals). The key question is: To what extent can the organized religions, and will they, do so?

III

Introducing our general discussion, Harlan Cleveland considers the blurred line between "public" and "private," and sets out one way of thinking about the public interest in its relation to personal ethics. Charner Perry considers moral bases of agreement and cooperation in a pluralistic society, and indicates that the institutions which coordinate action in small communities are radically inadequate for achieving cooperation in the huge, pluralistic societies of recent times.

The eternal search for "objective" standards of public ethics is first pursued under the heading, "Responsibility in Political Organization," where Wayne A. R. Leys analyzes effective norms of official conduct in government. Thoughtful practitioners (Eugene J. McCarthy and Charles P. Taft) or expractitioners (Stephen K. Bailey, Paul H. Appleby, and James MacGregor Burns) of politics, scholars familiar with the ethical challenges in political careers, compare the norms of conduct for party politics with those for the "policy politics" of government operations and for civilian life. Employing the resources of The University of Michigan's Survey Research Center, Donald E. Stokes probes systematically trends discernible in Americans' attitudes to government, including the popular image of "public ethics." From inside Madison Avenue the ethical implications of our new proficiency in "the engineering of consent" are given expert airing by David Finn.

Analysis of "Responsibility in Big-Scale Scientific and Academic Organization" reveals the similarity of their problems to those of any huge agglomerate (Karl K. Darrow), but perhaps special tensions between the creative freedom required for basic research and the elements of control required in a large structure (C. M. Herzfeld), as well as the crucial need for wise, informed decisionmaking in science (Robert B. Livingston). James A. Perkins speaks for many areas when he describes the complex range of moral problems encountered and the need to adjust conflicting pressures to make proper judgments viable.

Not surprisingly, the chapters on "Responsibility in Big-Scale Religious Organization" provide striking similarities in various denominations. In the United States institutionalization of the value system has affected the socal structure, with—in turn—possibly a "secularizing" effect on the religions themselves, according to Talcott Parsons. Such secularizing appears a problem of overwhelming importance to Roman Catholic Bishop Robert J. Dwyer, who sees no insoluble problems in size itself. This is not altogether the case with contemporary Protestantism now undergoing particular strains because of its own organizational revolution (Robert Lee), but David W. Silverman thinks that, on the whole, American Judaism has benefited from institutionalization. Yet the four contributors to this section share great concern for the problem of community, for emphasizing and reemphasizing the long range goals of Religion.

If we are living in the era of blurred distinctions, between "public" and "private," between "executive" and "legislative" and indeed among the levels of government and between the political parties as well, one would expect the resulting disorientations to be visible across the whole spectrum of American government. Judging from the papers in Parts IV and V, they are. They can be seen in the contexts of the government of metropolitan areas (Paul N. Ylvisaker), the unsettled limits of the Presidency (Rowland Egger), the responsibilities of the "independent" commissions (Louis J. Hector), the structure of executive-legislative relations (Thomas K. Finletter), the proper place of the political executive in the governmental system (William C. Foster), and the chronic civilian-military tussles (Sidney F. Giffin, William T. R. Fox, and Edward L. Katzenbach, Jr.).

In the final section, Kenneth E. Boulding suggests that organization and "goodness" generally increase together, so development of a workable measure of organization would be at least a first step toward construction of an ethical calculus, while lack of such progress would impede progress toward solution of many problems including those in ethics. Varied approaches to a fusion of ethics and what Boulding has elsewhere called the Organizational Revolution are suggested by Nathan D. Grundstein and Ordway Tead. While Don K. Price pleads for "irresponsibility as an act of faith" he urges not Constitutional reform, but—as a fitting end to the discussion—greater discipline and higher moral standards within our historic traditions.

In the perspective these scholars encourage us to perceive, it becomes clearer and clearer that traditions, ways of thinking, points of view, and thou-shalt-nots are so deeply built into each of us that there is no sense in which they can be irrelevant. There is no sense in which we can decide to jettison everything that has gone before, and start over again because of the atom bomb.

One road to wisdom is that of specialists who want to erect their particular way of thinking about the world into a general principle that should govern everybody. Now we are coming to realize that we must find some other road to wisdom than that of specialized fact. Perhaps we can find it in the way wise men and prophets have always found it—in a more vigorous attempt to understand the situation as a whole.

IV

In grateful and affectionate memorial to Lyman Bryson, for many fruitful years Honorary President and Chairman of The Conference Executive Committee, The Conference on Science, Philosophy and Religion Lecture has been renamed for him. The First Lyman Bryson Lecture was presented by Richard McKeon on August 30, 1960. The editors are delighted that this notable paper, "Ethics and Politics," is included in this volume.

The editors express deep gratitude to their Co-Chairman F. Ernest Johnson and to all others who participated in the Conference program, to those who attended the sessions, to the authors of comments, and above all to the original writers, whose work formed the basis of the Conference meetings and the substance of this and its companion volume. In particular they record their indebtedness to Chancellor Louis Finkelstein of The Jewish Theological Seminary of America —also President of the Conference—the Seminary officers and staff, for its hospitality, both during the 1960 working sessions and at all other times. They again wish to thank Jessica Feingold for her indispensable help in every phase of the Conference program, including preparation of the printed symposia. It is not by any means too much to say that without her devoted assistance, the Conference itself could

Introduction

scarcely have been held and the volumes could not have appeared in their present form.

As indicated in the program at the back of this volume, papers had been expected from Clarence H. Faust, Muslih Fer, and Edward A. Shils, but they were prevented from completing manuscripts for publication. Conference Chairmen are most appreciative of the excellent studies by John R. Connery, S.J., Michal Polanyi with comment by Hannah Arendt, Bernard Schwartz, and Ruth Strang, which greatly stimulated discussion at the Conference sessions, but have been omitted from the resulting volumes for various reasons—such as prior publication and revised organization.

The oral proceedings of the sessions were recorded; they are available at the Conference offices to qualified students.

The present volume is intended to be a complete unit. However, all those concerned with contemporary challenges to traditional ethics will also wish to read the other study which emerged from the same Conference and the same editors: *The Ethic of Power: The Interplay of Religion, Philosophy, and Politics.*

August 29, 1961

Introduction

The Blurred Line between "Public" and "Private"

By HARLAN CLEVELAND

I

Several years ago, when Charles Van Doren was pretending to be an intellectual giant on television, he and his famous father Mark Van Doren were chosen as "The Father-and-Son Team of the Year" by the National Father's Day Committee. The grateful remarks that father and son made in accepting the award, heard now against the background music of Charles' later confession that his brilliance was a hoax, take on a quality of prophetic wisdom.

Father was the first to speak; our later hindsight leaves his words untarnished and wise:

> I claim no credit for (Charles') being what he is . . . people make their own intellectual and moral characters. If he was helped in making his by me . . . it was he who decided to accept the help. The decision in such matters is finally with ourselves. To say that responsibility begins at home should mean, I think, that it begins—and ends, too—in the individual. Sooner or later he must help himself. There are no alibis.

Charles Van Doren then rose to accept his public's accolade, and spoke of his father.

> . . . He has been able to move me, to laughter and to tears, for as long as I can remember.
>
> Both in public and in private—and that's of the greatest importance. For my father has been, to me, both a public and a private man. Oh, perhaps not as public a man as I have become recently. We have laughed about this, he and I. I doubt if anyone has had a better time than he in this strange and hectic last few months.
>
> But my experience has reminded me of something that he taught me—not consciously, I'm sure, but as an example. For the extraor-

dinary thing about my father is that his public face, and his private face, have been the same. He has been the same man to the world as he has been to his family. And that is harder than it sounds. It is the very definition of integrity, I suppose.

In modern society everyone faces in some degree the problem of making his public face the same as his private face.

How far any individual succeeds in this effort—which is indeed harder than it sounds—may be taken as a rough measure of "public ethics" for our time and place. Thus in an era of growing artificiality, of tinsel and packaging and makeup, and "falsies" of mind and body, the highest compliment that can be paid to a public man is paradoxically that he is made of the same stuff all the way through, inside and out. The more public responsibility he carries, the more important it is for him to have a private face that can without embarrassment be displayed in public.

In our time, more people carry more public responsibility than ever before—and the trend continues. The social fallout of science is an unimaginable increase in the numbers and kinds of new decisions that have to be made. A fine contemporary example is the explosive population increase and its economic, emotional, religious, military, and diplomatic ramifications. But in every field new kinds of decisions constantly need to be made: about H-bomb testing; about powerful insecticides; about the widespread use of tranquilizers and "lifters"; about the ethics of mass persuasion; about urban congestion; about food surpluses and mass starvation; about our involvement in the internal affairs of other nations; about Antarctica and the Moon. These new decisions are not generally a *substitute* for decisions that used to be faced by mankind. They are *additions* to the burden of public responsibility.

To get the expanding volume of decisions made, new social forms are developing. They tend to be large, complex webs of tensions, with power so diffused within them that the term "decisionmaking," which has been used and abused by a whole generation of political scientists is now quite misleading. Each "decision" about public affairs is now a complex process of multilateral brokerage both inside and outside the organizations primarily concerned. They are manned, these new style complex public/private organizations, by a relatively new breed of modern man, which I will call the Public Executive.

Introduction

It used to be possible to distinguish the public executive from the private executive by inquiring whether he worked for a "public agency." But nowadays all large organizations are in some sense public. The line between what is public and what is private can no longer be drawn between government organizations and nongovernment organizations. The line between what is public and what is private must be drawn within each organization, between its publicness and its privateness.

It is not hard to see how this has come to be so. The sheer size and influence of many private organizations—of corporations, and banks, and private foundations and universities, too—mean that these organizations are heavily affected with the public interest; indeed, the public responsibility of large private organizations has come to be a standard article of faith at businessmen's luncheons and other public occasions on which inspirational clichés are duly applauded.

Consider the reaction of all of us to the 1959 steel strike, in which it was perfectly clear that the two big private groups concerned were by no means all the parties whose interests were at stake. There was— we all felt it instinctively—an empty chair at the bargaining table, reserved for but not occupied by the general public. The issue was trilateral, yet collective bargaining is still, by antique tradition, bilateral.

The fence between "public" and "private" is being battered from both sides. Private enterprise has been pulling the organized public, which is to say the government, into its affairs to achieve legitimacy and to spread the risk of poor managerial judgment. Government, faced with public expectation that it will expand its functions but not expand its bureaucracy, freely farms out to private organizations staggering proportions of the public business.

In these circumstances it is evident that the "public executive" is marked not by his *affiliation* with a government agency but by his *attitude* toward the public responsibility he carries, whatever the character of the organization in which he carries it.

II

Compared to a generation ago, our private enterprise system is just as enterprising as ever, but not nearly so private. The growing sense of public responsibility in American business can best be seen as the search for legitimacy by managers who no longer are legitimated by ownership of the properties they manage.[1]

It is now commonplace to observe that the diffusion of property divorces ownership from control of the economic system. Managers of productive enterprises, and managers of pension funds, mutual trusts, bank-held trusts and funds, and other large-scale forms of organized "private property," are in practice answerable only to themselves—or, as David T. Bazelon puts it, to "history." These managers are "wealthy proletarians," owning personal assets and future rights that are closely connected with the success of the corporation. The "profit" line in the balance sheet no longer reflects the surplus generated for transfer to owners; ownership is, in most cases, merely a piece of paper entitling the holder to receive income if the managers decide he should have it. Most business earnings are in practice withheld from the "owners" and plowed into new investment (not necessarily in the same line of business as that which generated the new capital) under the control of the managers who decide to make the investment.

Thus if the question is, "Who owns Sears, Roebuck or General Motors?" the honest answer is so vague an entity ("the public") that it might better be rendered, "Nobody." A more sensible question might be: "Who is responsible for the actions of General Motors or Sears?" Here the answer is clear: their managers. What is not clear is the answer to the *next* question: "To whom are the managers responsible?"

In the absence of either settled purposes or processes of legitimation that are external to the organization itself, the true "ends" of business organization tend to be internal to the system:

　. . . to protect, diversify, and expand the organization
　. . . to "render a service"—which merely defines purpose by function
　. . . to make a "profit"—on the books, not for the "owners"

[1] The argument here follows pretty closely that developed by Adolf A. Berle, Jr., in recent writings. See, for example, Adolf A. Berle, Jr., *Power Without Property—A New Development in American Economy,* Harcourt-Brace, New York, 1959; *Economic Power and the Free Society,* Fund for the Republic pamphlet, December, 1957; Paul Harbrecht, S.J., *Pension Funds and Economic Power,* Twentieth Century Fund, New York, November, 1959; Harbrecht and Berle, *The Paraproprietal Society,* Twentieth Century Fund pamphlet, 1960; David T. Bazelon, "Facts and Fictions of United States Capitalism," *The Reporter,* volume 20, September 17, 1959, pp. 43–48.

Introduction xxvii

... to use most of the profit to protect, diversify, expand, and render service (*i.e.,* to perpetuate and enlarge the scope of the original organism under its existing management).

The growing crisis of legitimacy in business and finance is paralleled by the development of large-scale philanthropy, and nonprofit enterprise generally. In a Ford Foundation or an American Cancer Society or a private university, efforts are usually made to separate powers between a legislative board of trustees and a group of executive managers. But taking trustees and top managers together, they constitute for practical purposes a self-perpetuating oligarchy with effective control over and responsibility for the use of income from the productive sector of the economy. They are not really responsible *to* anybody—except "the public," which is to say their own sense of public responsibility. Circular reasoning? Precisely so.

Does it mean nothing to say that managers of private enterprise feel a responsibility to "the public"? On the contrary. At a minimum, the purposes internal to the system will not be served if too many people, or public regulatory bodies representing them, come to believe that the managers do not have the public's interest at heart. At a maximum, the managers find they can see goals and ideas better if the prospective customers feel that the faceless corporate bureaucracy is not interested in "mere profits" or at least does not regard profits and consumer satisfaction as mutually exclusive. The sense of being ultimately answerable to "people in general" is becoming the dominant philosophy of American business and nonprofit enterprise alike.

As a consequence the managerial control of large "private" organizations is exercised, says Berle, in relation to certain obligations. This is his list of the obligations of a business enterprise.

1. It should supply the want in the area of its production. (How far it should go in generating that want so that it can be supplied is another matter and is one of the interesting ethical questions of the day. Is any want that can be generated *ipso facto* valid?)
2. The price must not be considered extortionate. It must be "acceptable"—which doesn't necessarily mean fair or just.
3. It must provide at least some continuity of employment.
4. It must give a continuing attention to the technical progress of the art.

Bazelon renders the "imperatives of production" rather differently:
> Thou shalt not allow another Great Depression.
> Thou shalt produce fully and efficiently.
> Thou shalt compete globally with the Soviet Union.
> Thou shalt raise and spread the American standard of living.

The striking thing about both of these educated attempts to interpret the public philosophy of private business managers is the huge amount of discretion they leave to the managers. In Berle's list, how big is the "want," how high is "extortionate," how continuous is "some continuity," how fast is the "progress," on what technical aspects of the art? In Bazelon's list, how is a Great Depression avoided, by high interest rates or low, more government spending or less, more freedom for the managers to make their own decisions or less? How full is "fully" and who decides what "efficiently" means? How do we compete globally with the Soviet—by grants or loans, military or economic programs? What is the content of the American living standard which is to be raised? Which direction, indeed, is up?

In a public agency questions like these are no less pressing, no less inherent in day-to-day administration of the agency's affairs, no less difficult to answer. But they do not create the same sense of moral crisis because there is a legitimate, agreed-upon *procedure* for facing them. The opinion of people-in-general is ultimately consulted by counting votes in a general election or in a legislature which for the manager's purpose is defined as "representative" no matter how unrepresentative it may in practice be. But in private enterprise, profit and nonprofit, the public interest is not authoritatively determined. The ultimate source of legitimation is the managers' own self-perpetuating powers, the survival of their own purposes and functions as the managers define them. For private enterprise, the public interest is what the managers think it is—subject only in the very long run to a veto by the people-in-general.

The affected public can exercise this veto most decisively by making private managers responsible to the government, by a single act which both justifies and regulates the managers' power over large organizations affected with the public interest. Such decisions stretch in a long line from the nationalization of the post office through the public utility

Introduction xxix

holding company acts to the Federal Communications Act and the contemporary efforts to bring labor unions under governmental regulation. As Berle has described it:

> At every point in the individual history of large corporations there has been some moment of impact on the community when either the community felt the corporation was not fulfilling its obligations or, alternatively, the corporation realized it was up against a situation it could not handle. In every case the result has been either a friendly and orderly, or unfriendly and disorderly, hassle out of which a piece of planned economy emerged. Roughly two-thirds of American industry and much of American finance is now controlled by a formal or informal Federal industrial plan.

In nonbusiness enterprises we have not yet reached the point of Federal planning, but the straws in the wind are plain to see. The year-by-year growth of governmental participation in private higher education, expressed through subsidies for research, teaching, and fellowships, will eventually force public agencies to develop a philosophy about the extent and the proper method of Federal intervention in education. Activities which used to be mostly in the hands of churches and voluntary agencies, such as overseas relief, are now paralleled by massive Federal programs which dwarf the earlier private initiatives but which also help enlarge them in various ways by subsidies.

Voices have even been raised to contend that any tax-exempt organization is *ipso facto* subject to government regulation. After Congressman B. Carroll Reece had conducted an unfriendly investigation of some of the big foundations, he argued in his committee report that tax "exemptions are acts of grace by the Federal Government ... the Federal Government permits the equivalent of public money to be used by these foundations. Accordingly, it is justified in applying ... such conditions on the exemptions as may be calculated to prevent abuse of the privilege and to prevent the use of the exempted funds against the public interest."

To counter this doctrine the foundations could only invoke a vague constitutional protection and then argue that their own "high duty of public responsibility" was as effective a safeguard against abuse as any conceivable form of government regulation.

III

To avoid the embarrassment of restrictions on their freedom of action, the managers of American corporate enterprise and private nonprofit organizations are reacting in ways that blur the distinction between "public" and "private"—though this is not at all what most of the managers want to do or think they are doing. In fact, most of their protestations are to the opposite effect. Business managers usually think they are against government interference in business. Foundations and universities and churches seek jealously to preserve their status as private institutions. But if we hold aside the curtain of mythology, it is not difficult to see what is really going on:

First, the managers practice "collective leadership"—they diffuse power as much as possible. This is necessary for technological reasons anyway; growing bigness, growing complexity and more specialization of function multiply the interrelated decisions to be made and therefore diffuse the power to make them. But the diffusion of power equally serves the felt need to obscure accountability for acts which, because they are affected with the public interest, are vulnerable to public criticism. Corporate decisions of great moment are increasingly hard to pin on any individual: the process by which they are made is deliberately made complex by the erection of collective decisionmaking systems.

Thus in a typical corporation, the Board of Directors consists of top managers of the enterprise, together with some managers of other enterprises (industrial or financial) who share a similar view of society. Major decisions are usually taken by an Executive Committee; the effective head of an enterprise is quite often not called President but Chairman of an Executive Committee or Management Committee or even a Finance Committee or (in a publishing enterprise) a Board of Editors. No manager admits he takes any major move on his own responsibility—that would expose him to questions (asked not only by outsiders but in his own heart) about the legitimacy of the power he exercises. Burying his personal responsibility in committee decisions does not make an executive's power more legitimate. But an adequate complexity of process makes it less likely that the legitimacy of any individual's action will be opened to public criticism.

Introduction xxxi

Second, the managers maintain a drumfire of public relations, the primary purpose of which is to justify the managers' present and future actions in terms of some concept of the public interest. Just as a government agency spends a very large but necessary proportion of each year's appropriation trying to make sure it survives the next year's round with Congress, so a corporation has to spend much of the time and effort of its top managers on "corporate relations," "community relations," "stockholder relations," "employee relations," and "public relations." Some of this is merely an expression of personal vanity on the part of ranking managers who like to see their pictures in the newspaper. But most of it is a vigorous and relevant response to a growing public expectation that private organizations are ultimately responsible to the general public for the way they conduct themselves.

The heads of the major television networks made this clear during the Van Doren affair. "It is our responsibility," said N.B.C.'s Robert Kintner, "to make sure that these programs will be honestly conducted, so that the public can have confidence in all the programs it watches." Frank Stanton, President of C.B.S., was even more explicit: "We are responsible for what appears on C.B.S. We accept that responsibility. . . . We are only obligated to do one thing and that is to be responsible to the American people."

In spite of these efforts to achieve verbal legitimacy, the responsible executives both in government and in the networks evidently thought that a sharp line could be drawn between "public" and "private" by drawing it between the government and the networks. The networks did not reflect the publicness of their function in procedures designed to protect their consumers from fraud. The Federal Communications Commissioners felt so inhibited by tabus about "censorship," that they failed seriously to address their attention to the rapidly growing cultural monster over which they were appointed to watch.

The mimeographed protestations of public virtue by most large private organizations are far from phony: they describe a new attitude that pervades not only what they say but what they do. Sears, Roebuck & Company really believes that its corporate health depends on urban redevelopment, and has a whole staff of people in Chicago helping Sears store managers all over the country to become effective civic leaders. The Arabian American Oil Company is not merely talking when it describes itself as part of the Arab Nationalism movement; it throws itself with enthusiasm into the economic development of the Arabian peninsula and makes major concessions to local nationalism in its own operating policies (such as excluding Jews from jobs in the field). Over the past generation many corporate managers have found that verbal approval of unions led inevitably to allowing unions to organize their workers. As Emerson suggested, it is well to be careful in stating your intentions; destiny may take you seriously.

In a third response to an awareness of their own sense of public responsibility, the managers of private organizations arrange to bring the government into their affairs as the risktaking partner. The process is now so familiar that it scarcely requires detailed exposition. Consider atomic energy or housing and urban redevelopment or soil conservation, or the savings bank business. Consider the pleas by foreign investors for more foreign investment, followed by detailed proposals as to how that investment can be rendered risk-free. Consider the enthusiasm of farmers for price supports. Consider higher education: a major financial and budgetary crisis occurred on every major campus when Charles Wilson cut back research and development funds by five per cent just before he left office as Secretary of Defense; at the margin of precariously balanced budgets, every university business office was counting on those nonprofit profits for which the favored euphemism is "overhead." Consider, once again, the wide variety of activities now carried on under tax exemptions that advertise and confirm the interest of the public in the way they are conducted.

The trend is familiar, but its effect in blurring the public/private boundary is less widely noted. The "mixture of politically-legitimated power with the self-legitimated power of those who control property" increases the content of publicness of each major private enterprise. The consequent public expectations about the behavior of the "private" executives concerned leads them to act more like public executives. The new attitude has been well described by Marshall Dimock, paraphrasing the remarks of the public relations vice president of one of the country's largest corporations.

> The two things that can get a corporation into trouble fastest are slothfulness and gluttony, one of which results from unjustifiable complacency, the other from excessive power and lack of self-control. No institution . . . ought to set out to bribe and dominate another, as some business corporations sometimes treat government. When they

Introduction xxxiii

do they simply expose themselves to blackmail and lose their freedom and immunity which are their most precious birthrights. And no corporation should blow its own horn all the time, indulge in extravagant claims and advertising, because when the public gets wise to what is going on there will be a loss of public support. The policies of a corporation should therefore be determined with the question uppermost of what the public goodwill will be a generation or a century hence, for excessive gains in the short run are usually costly gains in the long run.[2]

Fourth, America's private managers are recognizing the growing publicness of their function by intervening more frequently and more vigorously in the processes whereby government makes up its democratic and collective mind. If business executives are responsible not only for running their own businesses, but for preventing depressions and competing with the Soviet Union, then they must participate in setting interest rates, controlling government spending, allocating government subsidies to the right interests, planning defense production, and managing foreign policy. If business firms are going to be held responsible for progress in their own urban communities, their managers had better interest themselves in the rehabilitation of "downtown" and the honesty of local government. If the State legislatures are going to regulate the insurance business, the managers of insurance companies had better try to regulate the State legislatures.

The process is ill described by the word "lobbying." There are, indeed, many effective devices for influencing legislation by influencing legislators. But with the growth of the government's technical function, most important legislation is now written and most policy is made in the executive departments of government. It becomes necessary for large private organizations to have surrogates inside the executive bureaucracy. We have already proceeded far along this road; as I have elsewhere suggested, we have institutionalized the inside track in government.[3]

Conscious efforts to affect the decisions made by government lead naturally to conscious participation in the politics of choosing the most

[2] Marshall Dimock, *A Philosophy of Administration,* Harper and Brothers, New York, 1959.
[3] Harlan Cleveland, "The Executive and the Public Interest," in Sidney Hyman, editor, *The Office of the American Presidency, The Annals of the American Academy of Political and Social Science,* volume 307, 1956.

influential public-policy brokers. Thus many business executives now sponsor Practical Politics Seminars, which are justified as a necessary corrective to political action by organized labor. In a period of a few weeks, the *New York Times* reported that Caterpillar Tractor Company had come out against the Forand old-age medical care bill, General Electric formally opposed the McNamara bill for school construction, McGraw-Edison Company assailed "the deep-rooted, documented corruption of our foreign aid program." Corporations find that selective forms of altruism and philanthropy pay off in public attitudes; one of the earliest definitions of corporate public relations was "good deeds, effectively advertised." Specialized staffs develop to handle public-affairs issues, distinct from the people who advertise and sell the company's products; Ford Motor Company has a public-affairs staff of fifteen in Detroit and eight regional public-affairs managers scattered around the country.

Here, then, are four trends:
- the development of "collective leadership" in private enterprise;
- the tendency to justify private actions in terms of public values;
- the universal yen to get the public to share in privately managed risk-taking, and
- the conscious participation of private managers in governmental decisionmaking.

All help to blur the distinction between what is public and what is private. We do not understand this very well because so much of our public debate so often sets government off *against* private business, or private education, or private welfare efforts, or even private philanthropy. The interest of large-scale private organizations and the public interest are not identical, in spite of Charles Wilson's famous effort to equate them. But they are now so mixed up with each other that managers of any large-scale enterprise cannot understand their own role without thinking of themselves as partly public executives.

IV

Aggression across the public/private frontier does not all come from the private side. The government frequently finds it advantageous to reach into the private sector and assume the risks of doing business, without actually taking on the business as a function of the bureaucracy.

Introduction xxxv

It is a cheap and administratively easy way to carry out a public responsibility in a hurry with a minimum of political risk and bureaucratic red tape.

The reasons for this trend, too, are straightforward enough. For the government is presented with two irreconcilable objectives.

On the one hand, we the people expect public agencies to take on many new or expanded functions, to do *as government* what is not being done enough or well enough in the "private sector," and to do some things (such as build a Strategic Air Command) for which responsibility cannot by its nature be delegated to private individuals or organizations. What we expect of government in our day is not so different from Lincoln's formulation, by which government would only do those things which people could not do, or do as well, for themselves. The problem is that growing social complexity, the product of scientific invention and technological innovation, has greatly increased the proportion of the world's work which the people cannot as well do for themselves. The growth of large aggregations of "private" power, notably the corporations, has partly filled this gap. But even the exercise of corporate power is often in practice the result of governmental initiative.

On the other hand, we the people all agree that, at least in the abstract, the growth of government payrolls is a Bad Thing, that government should not become a bloated bureaucracy. We laugh at the tendency of government to grow, and call it Parkinson's Law; but we worry about it, too.

Thus government, trying not to grow but also trying to carry the responsibilities placed on it by the people's expectations, freely farms out to private organizations (business firms, research organizations, nonprofit agencies, and the like) a very large part of the "public business." Most of the nation's taxes are now collected not by government but by private organizations, through the withholding device. Most of our military production is not undertaken, as it used to be, through government "arsenals," but through private corporations which do most or in some cases all of their business with the United States Department of Defense. A growing proportion, which may reach half before long, of the foreign aid program is farmed out to nongovernment contractors. The heavy use of the government's contracting power in such programs as atomic energy and space exploration suggests that major technological departures from now on, in our continuing Scientific Revolution, will normally be the product of government initiative with little or no private risk-taking. Another straw in the same wind is the fact that most of the nation's research and development expenditures are now ultimately financed by Federal revenues.

Note how contrary to existing mythology are the facts of the case. Mythology holds that government is responsible for law and order, and has recently assumed the additional function of succoring the weak and encouraging the fainthearted in the American economy. It is private enterprise which constitutes the cutting edge of our national economic growth—or so our mythology tells us. But the way our economy is actually working suggests that an equally good case could be made for the reverse of these propositions. Private organizations have taken on a very large share of the task of succoring the weak and encouraging the fainthearted (through featherbedding, tenure, contracts, locked-in pension plans, and permission for at least a few small-business enterprises to survive in every industry even though they may be relatively inefficient), whereas the cutting edge of our national economic growth is being developed and financed in major part by government agencies or government contractors, in fields like atomic energy, power, air transport, aluminum, housing, and the bulk of industrial research and development.

The heavy participation of the government in those sectors of the economy which will make or break our national economic growth is not undertaken merely for the benefit of private interests; indeed, some of the private interests involved are not too sure that the tendency is in their own long-run interest. (The General Electric Company, for example, is currently attempting to keep the government's share of its total business down below twenty-five per cent; a few years ago it was trying to keep that figure under twenty per cent.) But even if private enterprise did not tend to drag the government into risk-taking partnership, the dynamics of government and politics would move things in that direction. From the point of view of Congressmen and executives in government, it is a great advantage to prop up private enterprisers with subsidies and guarantees, and avoid the risk of political criticism that would attend any effort to handle a production function directly. This advantage is, indeed, so great that the government sometimes spawns a private corporation to which it can then give gov-

Introduction

ernment contracts to do public business under a private tent; a notable case is the Rand Corporation, established by the Department of The Air Force for Research and Development purposes, which has now become a thinking machine, in private corporate form, which has many different clients, including some outside of the government. Similarly, when the Department of Defense decided to set up a training program for the officers destined to staff its Military Assistance Advisory Groups abroad, it created a private corporation, staffed with retired military officers, as a more flexible administrative device than any government agency.

Illustrations of the trend are not all to be found in the Department of Defense. In the housing field, subsidies and guarantees to private builders and housing financers are better politics than "public housing" which is not only financed but managed by government officials. When the government is able to delegate administrative responsibility through the contracting device, it also helps insure that the inevitable administrative troubles which attend any large-scale undertaking will not redound to the discredit of the public officials involved, or the government agency they represent. How completely a government agency can seek to avoid responsibility for private activities undertaken at the government's risk was demonstrated by the Federal Housing Administration, when for several years after World War II it permitted speculative builders to overprice the apartment houses they built and make gigantic windfall profits on the inflated rents charged to the tenants of the new buildings. From the F.H.A.'s point of view, things were apparently going very well: impressive numbers of new dwelling units were being built, and a happy if mildly incestuous relationship existed between the government agency responsible for housing and the private enterprises in the housing field. It was a Congressional committee and the Comptroller General, not the Federal Housing administrator, who eventually raised the question that had been carefully ignored: whether gigantic windfall profits for the speculative builders were economically necessary or socially desirable in order to get F.H.A.-guaranteed housing built.

There are those who, observing that much of the marginal risk in our business system is now assumed by people-in-general through their government, leap to the conclusion that America is finding its way to socialism through the back door. This is, for example, the conclusion of Yugoslavia's economic planners, in a recent study of the United States economy. They argue that it is now unnecessary to have a cold war with the capitalists, since the capitalists are moving so rapidly toward socialism under their own steam. (The Yugoslavs are not equally impressed with the rapid movement toward the introduction of capitalist-type incentives in their own government-dominated economy.) Since so much of the risk and so much of the "ownership" of American business is being socialized anyway, perhaps it does not matter so much (it is being said) whether the next kind of missile is developed by a government laboratory or by the General Dynamics Corporation.

But doesn't it matter? The guarantee of freedom in our kind of society surely is closely connected with the degree to which power is diffused. From this point of view, it is surely better that even when enterprise has to be essentially public in its initiative and financing, its management and control should be widely dispersed into private managerial hands. The socialist countries have been learning, as have we, that it does not seem to matter very much who theoretically "owns" the means of production. The question is who controls them. In our society, we have bet on a system (for which no very good name has yet been invented) in which the management of the means of production is more and more widely diffused, both among organizations and within organizations. Our tendency to spread widely the responsibility even for functions recognized to be "public," helps to bring into play what Berle calls those "odd American notions that absolute power should not exist, that countervailing power ought to be maintained, and that legitimacy of any power must rest upon a popular base . . ."

The existence, side by side, of "private" and "government" organizations performing generally the same function, tends to produce pressures for the government to prop up the private organizations so that they can a. "compete" or b. "survive" in the face of the government's unlimited resources. In a situation where the government has to insure continuing economic growth, yet keep economic power diffused in many hands, the arguments about public policy and the political infighting that accompanies them have to do with just where the line will be drawn between direct government operation and indirect forms of public participation in private enterprise. We are used to listening to arguments on this subject in the productive, profitmaking sectors of the economy—the public power/private power issue, which generated the concept that the government would operate some electric power establishments for "yardstick purposes," has been a handy perennial in our politics. But it may be useful to note that similar issues arise in other fields where private profit is of little or no concern.

For example, Congress and some of the State legislatures are annually grappling with the issue of government aid for private, particularly parochial, schools. If people-in-general are going to take responsibility, through their government, for transporting children to public schools and feeding them hot school lunches when they get there, should not the government help transport children to private schools and feed them an equivalent lunch when they get there? The trend seems to be toward the government's assuming this kind of responsibility, presumably on the rationale that public schools should not put private schools out of business. Similar discussions are going on in the field of higher education, in connection with government aid to private universities. Here again, the trend is toward finding ways for the government to pump budget money into private universities without appearing to interfere with the control of private university administrators over academic matters.

When, after World War II, the government went into the overseas relief business in a big way, it was almost compelled to administer a part of the government relief through private organizations—both because the private organizations would otherwise have cried "unfair competition!" and because the private relief agencies had the personnel and the knowhow to handle overseas operations more effectively than the government, at least in the early days. Thus, when the governments sponsoring the United Nations Relief and Rehabilitation Administration decided to liquidate UNRRA in China, they also decided to turn over much of UNRRA's relief supplies to the Roman Catholic and Protestant relief agencies which had long existed in China. Similarly, when the United States government decided to use surplus agricultural commodities as a part of its foreign aid program, Congress provided that private relief agencies using these surplus foods in their own programs would get a subsidy from the government to help pay for the transportation of relief supplies to foreign areas.

The government also "uses" or "works through" private organizations in more informal ways. Government agencies regularly lean on private organizations for the collection of information needed by the government: the F.B.I. works with private detective agencies, our overseas embassies maintain close liaison with American businessmen, the United States Department of Agriculture and the State Agriculture Departments are closely tied in with private farm organizations such as the Farm Bureau, the Grange, and the Farmers Union. The Central Intelligence Agency and the Military Intelligence services often use private organizations as "cover" for covert activities abroad. (They also, as we learned in the case of the Space Agency's U-2 shot down over Russia, use civilian government agencies as cover.) Further, the government often encourages private organizations to engage in activities which are desirable but which the government for one reason or another cannot touch. A notable example was the decision in the Economic Cooperation Administration not to honor a request by the government of Burma for help to the Buddhist University in Rangoon; but the Ford Foundation was discreetly encouraged to take on the project, and subsequently built a large Peace Pagoda near Rangoon. Thus the United States derived some credit from the enterprise, without any executive official of the government having to explain to a Congressional committee why the taxpayers' money was being used to help Burma celebrate the 2500th Anniversary of the Gautama Buddha.

V

If a line cannot be drawn between "public" and "private" on the basis of who owns or sponsors an organization; if the reality is that the line between "public" and "private" is to be drawn *within* each organization, between its publicness and its privateness, no responsible executive can ignore the public responsibility he personally carries as an integral part of his function as an executive. He may be in or out of government, in business or in church, in foundation or association, but he is marked as a public executive by his consciousness of a responsibility to the public interest.

The public interest is, of course, by no means the executive's only touchstone of action and judgment; in the rarefied executive atmosphere of extreme moral complexity, it competes with organizational loyalty and family ties and "professional ethics" and personal ambition and personal health and an assortment of external expectations and internalized criteria, all interacting with a speed and subtlety which no imaginable computer could duplicate.

Is it possible to define the "public interest," to isolate it from the other considerations, at least for purposes of analysis? The answer is probably that it can be defined only:

> For each person by that person,
> For each situation in that situation.

In American society we find "the public interest" a difficult concept to grapple with, because we are searching for universal criteria, answers to the question "Why?" which will satisfy everybody rather than answers which will satisfy each of us individually. But the cultural pluralism and diffusion of power which are so characteristic of American society make it necessary to think of the public interest not as a code of ethics for the whole country, or even for an individual organization, but as a nontransferable way of thinking, developed by each individual for his own use.

To be sure, we get most of our "deep down" feelings about what is right and what is wrong in particular situations from the atmosphere around us—from family and church and school and the organizations with which we associate ourselves. But that is not at all the same as saying that there are collective or organizational ethics which we can adopt as a substitute for thinking about moral complexity ourselves. As Mark Van Doren said, sooner or later each individual must decide what to accept from the atmosphere he perceives around him. The wisdom of Van Doren père is still not widely accepted. "A group morality appears to be replacing personal codes of ethics. That is, you no longer refrain from doing something because you couldn't live with yourself—you refrain from doing something because you couldn't live with your neighbors. . . . A *Look* reporter found an extreme and ironic case of neo-moral conformity in Colorado, where a man who did *not* chisel on his income tax boasted that he did. To be well regarded by his friends, he pretended to be doing what he assumed the group considered smart."[4] The case of young Charles Van Doren was only an especially dramatic instance of an individual who thought he could transplant organizational ethics wholesale, and substitute

---
[4] William Attwood, "The Age of Payola," *Look Magazine*, volume 24, number 7, March 29, 1960; pp. 34–41.

them for a public responsibility concept of his own. Self-deception can be impressively complete at any age. One Federal executive, accused of unduly close relationships with some of the private organizations he was supposed to be regulating, protested that the phone calls he had made to his private-industry friends were all right because they were placed on his own time during his lunch hour! And Sam Snead discarded not only his own sense of right and wrong but the professional ethics of a golfer, when he found on the fourteenth hole of a televised golf tournament that he had one extra club in his bag and was therefore automatically disqualified. Instead of saying so forthwith, Snead finished out the match, but contrived to putt so badly that he lost. The show must go on, he felt; and the National Broadcasting Company agreed with him, because in full knowledge of Snead's curious way of disqualifying himself, the network subsequently aired the Snead match without warning the television audience that Snead had deliberately "taken a dive" in the last three or four holes.

In all these cases, and many more, the ultimate corrective turned out to be a sense of public outrage when the matter was brought to light. But we cannot draw from this the conclusion that a person should necessarily be guided by what he could get away with in terms of public opinion as it currently exists. In an age of mass communications, people-in-general can be corrupted almost as easily as small groups can be corrupted, although it costs a good deal more to do it.

No, for any individual in any situation, the public interest must ultimately be what he thinks it is. If this seems a peculiarly American answer to the question, "What *is* the public interest?" perhaps the answer demonstrates what free men we Americans really are.

For just as the essence of American democracy is that it is not anybody's business to say authoritatively what it is, so the essence of the public interest is that it cannot be authoritatively defined for any given individual in any given situation, except by that individual in that situation. It is not to be expected that everybody will arrive at the same definition, especially on matters of importance. The disagreements we call politics; or if they are violent enough, we may even call them revolutions. As in the evolution of law, precedents and precepts are some help. What was clearly the public interest in some historical situation, where we now think we know all the relevant facts, may aid in solving tomorrow's similar questions for ourselves, even though most of the surrounding facts are yet unknown. Wise sayings, from Mencius and Aristotle, the Bible and the Founding Fathers (not to mention our own parents), may likewise be useful, but hardly controlling; with a little help from Bartlett's *Familiar Quotations,* it is all too easy to find some pseudo-scriptural basis for whatever one really wants to do.

Since the public interest in social situations is, paradoxically, so intimately personal a decision, I cannot suggest a series of universal ethical principles, written on stone tablets or mimeographed in an operations manual. I can only suggest, for purposes of illustration, the frame that I myself find useful in making moral and political judgments about public affairs from day to day. Ultimately I try to relate what goes on in the world, in the nation, and in Syracuse to the basic wants of modern man. In the oversimplified terms we often reserve for our most fundamental ideas, I see these basic wants as four:

First, modern man wants *a sense of welfare*—a minimum standard of "enough" in material living. How much is enough will of course vary from society to society and from decade to decade. But at any moment in any society there will exist, even if it cannot be precisely measured, a practical definition of the minimum standard which the society will collectively guarantee to its every individual member.

Second, people want *a sense of equity*—the feeling that they are being treated justly, not as measured by some ultimate standard, but as measured against the treatment accorded to other people in comparable situations. (This does not, of course, mean *all* others, even in one's own society. Nobody in England seems to begrudge the provision in the national budget of a royal income for the Royal Family.)

Third, there seems to be a universal desire these days for *a sense of achievement*—man's feeling that he is getting somewhere, that the group of which he is a part is making progress in some generally accepted direction. For people in organized society, high morale depends not so much on what goals men choose as on their shared feeling of movement toward them.

Finally, modern man wants *a sense of participation* in deciding what those goals will be. He needs to feel that he has some control over his own destiny through taking part in a group or groups which can and do in fact influence the basic decisions on which his welfare, equity, and achievement depend—decisions about the state of the economy, the security of the person, the freedom of mind, and ultimately decisions about life and death, peace and war.

Three short comments on these "basic wants." First of all, they are not of course, statistically measurable, or empirically verifiable in general; they are all "feelings" or "senses" based on vague judgments about the relationship of the individual to the society in which he finds himself. Even for a small group at a defined time in a particular place, the judgments about adequacy, equity, achievement, and participation must be rough approximations, not "facts" that can in some sense be proved.

Moreover, this statement of the basic wants of modern man depends for its validity on an awareness by the individual of his relationship with society. They imply that he cares about this relationship; that his attitude is of one seeking to influence his destiny, not passively accepting what fate or the gods or his own family have provided in the way of environment. It hardly needs to be observed that this is a new state of mind for most of mankind, dating in the West from the Renaissance and the Reformation, spreading to the East through the colonial governors, district officers, navies, armies, missionaries, traders, and reformist politicians, all of whom stirred up ancient societies by providing new wants to want, and therefore, new enthusiasm for change.

Finally, these basic wants are appropriate to an era in which "we don't know where we are going, but we know we are going there fast." Rapid change is the dominant fact of our time, and presents problems which people in more static societies did not have to face. We know that an ever-higher standard of welfare is technically possible now— that greater equity can be achieved in a situation of growth. The very urge for a sense of achievement is evidence that change is the expected norm; both our aspirations and our actions are geared to it. The growing desire to participate in decisions affecting our own destiny stems from the conviction that things are certain to change, and that events must, therefore, be influenced in directions that are congenial to us.

If he measures his contribution to society against these basic desires for welfare, equity, achievement, and participation, I think a public executive can be said to have a standard of public responsibility more relevant to the world around him than most of his fellow executives.

Introduction

But, as I say, touchstones of conduct like these are ultimately subjective, personal, individual. The fact that each of us has both the freedom and the obligation to fashion his own ethical standards (taking into account the similar decisions of others around him) is I suppose an important part of what we mean by "the dignity of the individual."

If we cannot suggest an affirmative code of ethics, perhaps there is one universally useful thing we can suggest. It is not an answer, but a question, the kind of question that might be useful to any executive facing any situation in which he believes the public interest to be at stake. The question should highlight the desirability of making one's public face the same as one's private face. The question would compel each public executive to project *his own feelings* in the imagined event of critical public scrutiny of both the action taken and the procedure by which it was decided upon. The public executive should not therefore ask himself, "Will I be criticized?" If the executive is operating at all in the area of public responsibility, the answer to that question is always, "Yes."

He might better start by asking himself some such question as this: "If I am publicly criticized, will I still feel that this is what I should have done, and the way I should have decided to do it?"

Comment by Paul H. Appleby:

In general, what Harlan Cleveland says about the way in which public and private concerns are becoming interwined is certainly true. As understanding grows the visible content of problems grows, and as resources increase scope of solutions widens. We do, therefore, have to relate more and more things to each other, and this entails recognizing increasing public significance in private activities.

I do not believe, however, and think Cleveland does not mean to imply, that business folk all or in any common pattern are as aware of their public responsibilities as might here appear to many readers. They vary according to the present situation of their enterprises and their perceptions. There are still some highly self-centered businessmen, and the capital-gains economy offers particular place for heirs of Captain Kidd.

But what Cleveland says is true enough so that saying it helps speed the transformation. In a less justified instance in my more ignoble days as a young publisher in a small Midwestern town, I selected as the best of five a candidate for the Republican gubernatorial nomination. Week after week I predicted that he would carry our county. He did, but it was the only county of ninety-nine in the state he did carry. Cleveland's businessmen friends will be more publicly responsible than many others.

I question a sentence dealing with the farming-out of government functions to private concerns: "It is a cheap and administratively easy way to carry out a public responsibility in a hurry with a minimum of political risk and bureaucratic red tape." In my judgment there is—in terms of espoused programmatic objectives—a considerably higher percentage of waste in this method than there would be in a straight-line governmental action. The dollars cannot be traced, performance appraised, or accountability policed nearly as thoroughly or nearly so clearly. Some of this kind of expenditure is for goodwill purposes, some is done simply to hold down the figures covering public employment, some to *evade* responsibility, some to avoid definite action, and some for the record ("We had Such & Co. look into that matter"), while some is for the purpose of conforming to the principle or policy of "upholding and using private enterprise." The procedure often can be defended as either "cheap" or "effective" only if one attaches considerable importance to these other considerations, and relatively less to strictly programmatic achievements.

I enter a qualification, to which I am sure Cleveland would agree, to this sentenc- "The guarantee of freedom in our kind of society surely is closely connected with the degree to which power is diffused." Surely it is not intended to say that "Total diffusion of power provides total freedom." It would provide total chaos. Maximum desirable diffusion of power and minimum personal and social frustrations alike can almost certainly be achieved in a society more unified than ours, more coordinated by government than ours is.

And so I still think there is more special meaning in the term "public executive" than, for purposes of making the important points made in this paper, is acknowledged in it. There is a special and crucial function of somehow relating more things to each other and somehow making general sense out of a society in continual evolvement. This is importantly, even though not exclusively, and distinctly a governmental function.

Introduction

Moral Bases of Agreement and Cooperation in a Pluralistic Society

By CHARNER PERRY

How can people who do not know each other and have nothing in common discuss policies which may affect all of them, though in diverse ways, with some expectation of agreement? How can a Hindu scholar, a Mississippi sharecropper, a Japanese fisherman, an Egyptian bus driver, a Chicago banker, a school teacher from the African Gold Coast, a Russian mathematician, and an Irish priest communicate with each other about birth control, free trade, control of narcotics, rights of access to coastal waters, canals, and narrow seas, an international monetary system, rights of minorities, limitations of sovereignty by international law, treaties, or international agreement?

Perhaps the problem of such communication and minimum agreement differs only in degree from the ancient, ubiquitous one as to how a small group—say two men or a man and a woman—can by talking together establish a pattern of cooperation. But the degree of difference is enormous; and the problem has reached its present complexity only in very recent times. Since small groups, even groups of two, frequently do not achieve cooperation, living in discord or breaking up with violence, the larger problem must be approached with optimism or offhand declared obviously impossible of solution.

The present dimensions of the problem of communication may be roughly ascribed to two related changes. First, the size of constituencies, that is, of groups engaging in common political and social action, has expanded fantastically; and, second, the means or bases for establishing and maintaining patterns of cooperation have been radically changed.

As to the first, I shall briefly emphasize the fact without speculating about causes. For hundreds of thousands of years men lived in small groups. Barriers of water, mountains, deserts, or mere space provided relative isolation. Even small kingdoms and cities, though some seem ancient to us now, are recent achievements in human history. These cities, kingdoms, and empires involved great cumulative accomplishments in both technology and social arts; but except for the cities, where civilization was born, they were composed of local constituencies whose relations did not radically impair their social isolation.

Now, before any of the moderate size societies had elaborated adequate institutions for organizing cooperation among its citizens, we have mass societies, many of immense size, and the barriers between them have been so diminished that everywhere men are aware that they have a stake in actions and decisions across the world.

The changes in the bases of cooperation may be divided into four strands, though these overlap as well as interact.

First, it is a commonplace that social cooperation has been guided predominantly by custom. The word "custom," though it does not explain much, refers to the fact that patterns of behavior have developed gradually and have changed slowly, and that any generation acts largely through established behavior patterns, with only limited variations or adjustments. When, however, groups with different customs are thrown together, in the new group discrepancies and conflicts of customs occasion a gap, large or small, as to accepted social roles and lines of social action.

Second, enlightenment has spread over the world, and as it spreads, customs come to be regarded as obstructions, challenges, or the tentacles of an ignorant past, rather than as guides. Socrates was convicted of corrupting the youth of Athens, but he was a beginner who barely scratched the surface. Nowadays, not merely sophisticated young men in big cities, but farm boys in Arkansas and Africa, have heard that the old ways are probably wrong and certainly suspect. The old Dewey and Tufts *Ethics* asserted with approval that we are moving from customary morality to individual reflective morality. Enlightenment, ideally, leads each individual to think for himself about his actions, to decide for himself where he shall live and how, with whom he will associate and on what terms. Whether he makes thoughtful choices or flounders in confused anxiety his decisions must dovetail somehow with the reflective decisions of millions of other individuals.

Third, democracy, which our Founding Fathers considered with suspicion and diluted to representative government, has been almost universally accepted, albeit with widely varying interpretations, as an ideal. We are told that in the past social coordination rested on force and accepted authority, that control rested in the hands of elites, and that the effective constituency of a ruler was a small minority of his subjects. As democracy has spread, the constituency of rulers and politicians has been immensely extended vertically as well as horizontally. The number of people who expect to participate in the formation of policies, or at least to understand them sufficiently to consent, has been widened to almost all men and women.

Fourth, the tempo of change is always growing faster. Technological advances and mobility of populations, among other factors, present new problems before old ones are solved; and the area within which patterns of adjustment are unsettled becomes ever wider. Each policy which is settled occasions unforeseen consequences which must be brought under control.

The constituency for present formation of policy differs, then, radically from the town meeting, which is a symbol of democracy. Because of the rapidity of change and the diversity of groups, customs provide little in the way of a settled structure to which minor changes can be tried for fit. Because there are varieties of religion, tradition, and ethical conviction, it is difficult to find accepted premises from which discussion may proceed. Because men's interests depend to a considerable extent on what other men will do, even calculation of individual and group interests is, in an unsettled world, uncertain and confused.

Few men would today openly defend the view, ascribed with some justification to thinkers in the Age of Reason, that men, once free of superstition and tyranny, would see alike as to what is good and right. Yet many people seem to assume some such view. For instance, it is not unusual for men who are confident that we have the information, means of communication, and administrative procedures for managing a planned society, to suppose that a plan devised by impartial and reasonable experts would seem good to all enlightened men. And we are surprised that intelligent visitors to our country should criticize our ways and institutions. Perhaps many of us hold, as an examined article of faith, the conviction that rightminded men will see alike what is right or that, at least, calm, patient discussion will disclose fair and reasonable bases for agreement. Many intellectuals, however, whether social scientists or philosophers, contend that political convictions rest on feeling, taste, or custom, and that reason is neutral or value-free or, at most, instrumental, discovering means to ends determined by feeling, need, or desire. Whether or not enlightened men would attend only to arguments pointing out means to their given ends, enlightened men are still a negligible minority. Most men, we are told, think in terms of ideologies and myths.

Let me use these terms in wide and nonderogatory senses. An ideology may be roughly defined as explanation and defense of an institution which depend on at least some premises which would not be accepted by persons not participating in the institution. A myth may be defined as the projection into history of a dramatic pattern of action and feeling. Let me repeat, in the wide sense here given to these words, neither is derogatory. White supremacy is a myth, but so are equality, the rule of law, and romantic love. As to ideology, an explanation of an institution which depends on some premises not acceptable to nonparticipants might be better than an explanation which did not use such premises.

Ideologies and myths intertwine and overlap. Both shape and maintain institutions. An institution may grow to fit an ideology; and a myth may be actualized to a degree in institutions and customs. The rule of law is to a considerable degree fact in some parts of the world. According to R. M. MacIver, the myth of authority is a component of every actual government.

My first positive contention is that, at least in the foreseeable future, ethical and political discussion cannot rise above myths and ideologies. We cannot divest ourselves of myths and ideologies, nor can we expect other people with whom we need to agree to do so, and above all, we should not assume that our own myths and ideologies are plain sense, what everyone should plainly see.

In a small, likeminded community, the inability to dispense with myth and ideology need not impede discussion and agreement. It would rather facilitate it, since everyone might have more or less the same myths and ideology.

In a large society, however, or in different societies, we know as a fact that there is a diversity of both myths and ideologies; and my contention that political discussion cannot proceed on the high level of impartial reason may seem to rule out discussion and agreement.

Both speculatively and by appeal to history, however, we can see that, short of likemindedness, there are fruitful and effective procedures for cooperation and agreement. Such procedures must depend, to be sure, on a distinction of the problems and conditions of an extended society from those of a small, likeminded group.

Concomitant with the growth of societies and the increase of relations among them, there have developed institutions adapted to them. Indeed, without such development, social growth would, one might suppose, have been stifled by disorder and breakdown. Great societies have emerged because institutions appeared which made them possible; and an inquiry into the ethics of extended constituencies can at least begin, through an attempt to understand the institutions which have aided in the transition from the local community to the great society. This is only a beginning, because institutions have not been adequate, and because problems of communication and cooperation continuously become more complex.

At the risk of touching emotionally charged topics, let me begin with the market and economic transactions. A religious man may buy an automobile without inquiring into the beliefs of the dealer or of the men who made the car; buyers and sellers of cotton need not reach an agreement on politics. The ideal market is impersonal, with no real contact between the persons involved. Markets can organize cooperation on a large scale and in great complexity. Whatever the necessary conditions for, and limitations of markets may be, they provide an invaluable means for bringing about cooperation when less impersonal relations are impeded by conflicting beliefs or attitudes. In the family or in small groups, or in large groups which can be disciplined in some way, other modes of cooperation may be better; but in pluralistic societies or between societies, markets are highly useful if not indispensable. And our difficulties in understanding or accepting the working of markets derive in part from our reluctance to see the difference between the ethics of a small community and the ethics appropriate to the extended constituency of a vastly expanded society.

A second procedure for obtaining agreement and cooperation in the face of conflicting ideologies, myths, and interests is the working out of laws or patterns of action which may be accepted by different people for different reasons. A considerable part of politics does serve this function, with the politicians attempting, partly by trial and error, to find a formula, or a bill, or a deal which will combine appeals to many different kinds of people and give offense to few. Logrolling, compromise, and fence-straddling have their part in the process. Some people are surprised that an eloquent, closely reasoned speech by a Senator seems not to change many votes; but the surprise may rest on the assumption that one argument can be effective for many kinds of people. The Senator may need six different arguments, with variations on each; but to combine them in one speech might be awkward if not ridiculous. On the side of the public, many voluntary organizations operate to find a common denominator for groups whose members have diverse points of view. A pressure group can exert significant pressure only if it can concentrate on policies which run below the conflicting perspectives of its members.

Though no precise limits can be set to the process of achieving cooperation or agreement in action without agreement on values, it seems reasonable to suppose that a general and loose framework of action is more easily achieved than a tight, detailed scheme of organization. The system of markets and doctrine of limited government have played an important part in the development of modern democracies because they make possible large, complex societies with a minimum of consensus. The recognition that a state could exist without a common religion was one of the important steps in modern political development.

The ideal of a government whose primary internal task is the maintenance of law and order, the suppression of force and fraud, reflects the needs of a large expanding, diverse society. The achievement and maintenance of such a government is difficult. Groups will be continually attempting to capture its power, or part of it, for their own purposes or for self-protection. Other groups will attempt to limit its power to protect privileges or in fear of misuse. Reasons for supporting it, because general, may not exert a strong pull on anyone. The ideal, nevertheless, is a basic part of the ethics of extended constituencies.

It does not follow, of course, that a government should be limited to the maintenance of law and order. What else it might do would depend primarily on the extent to which wide or general agreement could be reached on objectives or policies. The ideal of a limited and neutral government posits, however, a necessary condition for the processes of discussion, voluntary association, adjustment, and political compromise which constitute the ethical resources of a pluralistic society.

The great difficulties in the way of achieving a limited government have been in part overcome by modern development of two ancient devices, courts and bureaucracies.

A court, conceived simply as a man having power to call other men before him, make decisions and issue decrees, and have the decisions and decrees enforced by armed men, is a formidable institution which might operate in many ways, to punish enemies, to collect tribute, or to maintain a ruling elite. Courts have, however, in some societies, been so placed in a context of legal institutions and supporting customs that they have been, to considerable degree, impartial and neutral, and more or less accepted as such as between groups with conflicting interests, myths, and ideals. How this has come about is difficult to understand in detail, but such a development was prominent in both the Roman and the British empires. The power of such an institution will be looked at with covetous eyes; and protecting it is not easy. The maintenance of such impartial legal institutions, which for brevity we may refer to as the rule of law, is an ideal demand of the ethics of extended constituencies.

A bureaucracy, defined loosely as a disciplined, hierarchical organization with developed procedures for performing specific tasks assigned to it, is also a powerful instrument which may be, and has been, used for various purposes. An organization to collect taxes might be used to enrich an elite or to establish political control of a society. Bureaucracies have, however, in some contexts been developed as more or less neutralized agencies. Their disciplined organization and their specialization to assigned tasks make them especially adaptable to the needs of a society with conflicting ideals. For the objectives that are generally agreed on and can be, within a degree, definitely specified so that their accomplishment presents merely technical problems, a disciplined organization may be an efficient and more or less neutral agency.

Objectives can never be so clearly specified and agreed on that administration and policymaking are sharply separated. Moreover, an organization effective for a specified objective may be highly useful for other purposes—a police force adequate for suppressing crime might be very helpful in controlling elections. Nevertheless it has been possible to orient bureaucracies to tasks sufficiently limited to be generally approved, and to neutralize them to an extent they are not feared as the instruments of special groups. This desirable condition has not always or even usually been attained; but its attainment at times has contributed greatly to the strengthening of government and the improvement of society. A society which has many of its basic and noncontroversial functions provided for by dependable and efficient bureaucracies may be able to take its time in dealing with more controversial matters. Moreover, controversies can be limited if a substantial part of the institutional machinery runs dependably in some independence of them.

Some thinkers have feared that bureaucracies would take over control of society; and others have hoped that they would. Still others have predicted that bureaucracies will become so large and complex that they will be blind mechanisms incapable of either controlling or being controlled. Either of these eventuations might, I suppose, occur; but neither seems likely. As to the latter, advances in organization techniques and resources have more than kept pace with increases in size of bureaucratic organizations; and, as Paul Appleby has noted, a large part of the increased complexity is more apparent than real— addition of a new bottom layer to a hierarchical organization multiplies the size several times without any great increase in complexity. In regard to the former, whether desired or feared, it is probable that needs of a large, complex society for institutional processes not congenial to bureaucratic organization operate strongly to maintain a balance among bureaucracies, markets, politics, and courts. The armed forces, which may fairly be called a bureaucracy, seem most self-sufficient and the most likely, in times of extreme danger, to dominate society; but actual developments in modern times do not seem to point in this direction.

So far I have written as if conflicting myths and ideologies were determinate structures, each of them being just what it is and differentiated from every other by whatever specific characteristics it has in contrast with others. This is, indeed, the proper and prudent way to approach the problems presented by conflicts of myths and ideologies. For people to whose lives they give shape and direction, the unique characteristics are real and vivid.

It is nevertheless true that below the surface of myths and ideologies there are significant common themes. Myths are similar to dramas—where, except from myths, should dramas draw their substance and their ability to grasp the emotions of the audience? In dramas, however fresh each may seem to an audience, the critic discerns recurring themes and plots. The materials and patterns of drama are, after all, limited; and this is true also of myths. Students of legend and folklore have been astonished by the discovery that in widely separated societies strikingly similar stories are found. They have wondered whether these similarities point to diffusion from a common source. Such diffusion has no doubt occurred at times; but in many cases the simpler explanation is that men working with limited material and similar problems have constructed stories and myths whose surface peculiarities embroider a few recurring themes.

Whatever the historical explanation, it is certainly true that in myths one may discover recurring themes and patterns. This fact provides basis for two ways of mitigating the conflict of myths. Given some desire for cooperation, people see or feel beneath the surface variety the patterns which are common to their competing myths. The conflict between good and evil, for instance, is a pervasive theme but one which is specified in many ways. Christians and nonChristians, Catholics and Protestants, Jews and gentiles, theists and humanists portray differently the drama of right against wrong. Nevertheless, because there is an underlying theme, a conference of Christians and Jews may enlist Catholics, Protestants, Jews, enlightened humanists, capitalists, and labor leaders in a common front against prejudice, discrimination, and selfishness.

Second, because myths are variations on themes, they are plastic. Existing myths are a challenge to creative minds to reconstruction. As societies grow and new problems arise, old themes are reshaped. Myths of world government and one world are produced when world government is a dream. Most of such myths are ephemeral because they do not succeed in synthesizing old myths and new opportunities, aspirations and facts, form and matter. In the profusion of myth construction, however, there may emerge new myths which project the old onto new circumstances in a proper and compelling pattern. Democracy is, perhaps, such a myth.

Ideologies, too, have common elements. Since they are attempts at rational justification or explanation, all of them have in common some aspects of rational structure. Though in content and detail ideologies have great variety, the possible structures within which justification or explanation might be attempted are quite limited. Indeed, it seems that they may all be adequately classified into three types. Perhaps a fourth type may be distinguished; but it has peculiarities, to be noted below, which might lead to its being considered a special case of one or more of the other three.

Institutions may be justified or explained in terms of their effectiveness in realizing ends of individuals or societies. The ends may be more or less explicitly indicated or they may be largely assumed and taken for granted. They may be subsumed under an ultimate or highest end such as "happiness." This type of rational structure would be related to the type of social action which Weber calls *"Zweckrational."*

Second, institutions may be justified or explained in terms of their conformity to, or exemplification of, principles, such as the principle of justice, fairdealing, or liberty. This kind of reasoning in social action Weber refers to as *"Wertrational."*

Third, reasoning may refer to, and rest upon, tradition, custom, or precedent; and the appeal to the authority of heroes, great men, or founding fathers may be regarded as falling under this type of reasoning. Weber recognizes traditional action as one of the kinds of social action though he does not label it as rational. For reasons which will be given below, however, the appeal to tradition is one structure of explanation and also of justification.

These three types of reasoning or justification are explicitly used in the *Federalist Papers* in the arguments in support of the proposed Constitution. The authors indicate they intend to show that the Constitution will be generally advantageous to citizens and specifically will contribute to safety from invasion, minimize domestic disorder, and promote trade and prosperity; that, second, it conforms to republican principles and especially the principle of liberty; and that, finally, it embodies the institutions and traditions long established in the governments of the several states.

That all three of these patterns of reasoning may be used in explaining institutions and that the first two may be used for justification seems obvious; but that the third, the appeal to tradition, is an authentic pattern of rational justification may seem questionable. That reasoning of this type is used, and used effectively, is hardly open to question; but that it provides rational justification has frequently, in an age of enlightenment, been denied. In considering this point, let me say first that I am talking of ideologies, that is, of attempts at justification which use some premises which need not be accepted by people who are not participants in the institutions being explained or justified. From this perspective, it seems plausible to suppose that any institution or society as a going concern involves some patterns of action which are taken for granted as resting on implicit acceptance or explicit agreement. Such patterns, to be sure, may be changed piecemeal; but they nevertheless have considerable stability. That appeal to tradition, precedent, or cherished institutions might not carry weight with an outsider or a detached observer is not here under consideration. It should be noticed, however, that the ends referred to or the principles assumed might also be rejected by an impartial outsider. Whether any justification of institutions, and any ideology, can avoid being a rationalization, can avoid, that is, dependence on some premises accepted because of participation in social activities is a difficult and much debated question. It will be considered later; but our concern now is with patterns of reasoning which may be common to different ideologies and which may provide bases for adjustment or agreement. Reasoning in terms of tradition and precedent is such a pattern; and it may be as cogent or "rational" as the other patterns to the extent that it rests on implicit acceptances and explicit agreements which actually are the case.

Any explanation or justification of an institution contains as content matters of fact and generalizations regarding human nature, the environment, and social processes. Such facts and generalizations stipulate the circumstances in which institutions develop; and such circumstances determine the possibilities for the development and maintenance of institutions. If knowledge of facts about man and the environment should establish the conclusion that in given circumstances only one kind of institution or constellation of institutions could possibly develop, then explanation and justification would forthwith be achieved. The attempt to show such inevitability or necessity might be regarded as a fourth rational structure. Since, however, reference to facts is made in any justification in order to determine possibilities, the difference between the limiting case in which there is only one possibility and other cases in which there are two or an indeterminate number would seem to be a difference as to the facts and their implications rather than a difference in the structure of the reasoning. Though emphasizing that the use of allegations of facts and interpretations of them to determine possibilities is an important process in ideologies, I conclude that the limiting case in which this use narrows the possibilities to one does not introduce a fourth pattern of reasoning.

I have argued that the many ideologies current in the world are limited to three basic types of rational structure. Moreover, a good case could be made out for asserting that in most, if not all, ideologies, some use is made of all three patterns of reasoning, though one or two may be emphasized. Even though ideologies with common patterns of reasoning have different contents, different premises, different allegations of fact, the fact that they have common structures of reasoning provides opportunity for discussion, argument, and even limited agreement.

Specifically, people who have different ends and traditions may be able to find principles held in common. People with conflicting principles and different traditions may find in common or related ends basis for limited cooperation. One of the main advantages of organization, of course, is that it facilitates such cooperation; and, conversely, market relations are likely to seem inadequate or unsatisfactory where principles or tradition are important. Finally, we may note, without running through all the possible combinations, that a common strong tradition may provide adequate basis for social action despite a diversity of both ends and principles.

It should be noted next that in regard to ends, principles, and traditions, it is possible to move up or down in terms of specificity and generality. One may move from the details of a tradition to its "spirit," or one may move from a local tradition to a national one, to the traditions of Western Civilization, and even to the traditions of civilization. Ends and interests are both conflicting and harmonious in many ways. Two groups have conflicting interests in regard to the distribution of the tax burden, but they may have a common interest in there being adequate revenue. In regard to principles, at least, it is not always the case that the maximum agreement occurs at the highest level of generality. People might disagree about abstract principles of justice and yet agree on what is just in many specific cases.

We should remember, as stated before, that myth and ideology are

Introduction

intertwined and overlapping. A myth is likely to have or acquire an ideology or several of them; and an ideology may generate a myth or at least help in shaping it. Usually the two are continuous, so that it is impossible to say where one ends and the other begins. They are rather opposite poles, myth being dramatic interpretation of men's situation, or aspects of it, and projected patterns of response, ideology being the rational explanation and justification of institutions. Myth is carried by symbol, ritual, ceremony, art, poetry, and oratory; ideology is presented in sober, reasoned discourse. Ideology, however, may be dependent on myth, or on commitment and participation, for the meaning of some of its terms and for the plausibility of its premises. That this relation exists between, say, religion and theology has often been asserted, and not usually with any derogative intent. Intellectuals have sometimes assumed that from all commitment and participation they might escape to impartial detachment. It would be presumptuous to deny that this might be achieved; but moderate skepticism, especially in regard to one's own efforts, is not inappropriate.

In any case, for most men myth and ideology provide complementary and to some extent alternative bases for agreement and cooperation. It has been said the cricket fields contributed to the winning of many of England's battles and also that parliamentary procedure and rules of order have been an important factor in the development of democratic government. Parliamentary procedure, at least in actual operation, is a myth involving ceremony and ritual. It is indeed a powerful one, though perhaps not self-contained or complete by itself. A few myths, even lowly ones lacking in glamor, especially if they include MacIver's myth of authority, can do much to maintain the orderly processes of society when there is diversity of ideologies and even of other myths.

Our problem, however, is how agreement and cooperation may be achieved in societies with many ideologies and myths and even between societies still more diversified. In relation to this problem, what needs emphasis is the multiple basis afforded by myths and ideologies for limited agreement and especially for cooperation in action. It is especially important to notice that cooperation in action may far outrun any doctrinal agreement. A socialist or even a communist may do fairly well buying his groceries at the A. & P. pending social change; and a capitalist may find it convenient to use the co-op. Some institutions, though not all, are concerned primarily with the organization of action; and the fact that cooperation in action can extend much further than agreement in doctrine or belief is of crucial importance.

Since the other side of multiple bases of agreement is that there are multiple sources of disagreement, it would seem to be the case that the utilization of sources of agreement depends in large part on there being appropriate institutions for maximizing the results of limited agreement and for minimizing the disruptive effects of disagreement. In the first part of this paper, I have argued that various modern societies, especially those that might be called pluralistic, have actually hit upon institutions of this type; and that the development of such institutions has been one of the conditions necessary for the vast expansion of societies. Such institutions may arise from interaction of people without being planned or even understood. I have specified, though cursorily, some of these institutions: limited government, market organization, bureaucracies specialized to definite functions, the rule of law, various democratic political processes, such as logrolling, the two party system, pressure groups, political compromise. No doubt such institutions can be improved and perhaps they may be replaced or supplemented by others—we still do not understand them very well; but I think I have stated the main requirement regarding institutions in a pluralistic society: the requirement, namely, that they should be such as to extend cooperation beyond the limits of achieved doctrinal agreement and that they should be capable of utilizing for limited agreement the points of coincidence among the multiple strands of diverse myths and ideologies, and that they should be such as to minimize the bad effects of disagreement.[1]

Having surveyed briefly the various resources of a pluralistic society for achieving agreement and cooperation, we come now to the last and most troublesome question: How are such agreement and forms of cooperation rational or moral? How can we make judgments that some institutional arrangements are better than others? How can we tell when we are making progress and when we are slipping backward?

The first answer is that myths and institutions are justified by ideolo-

---

[1]Though I have not been able to develop this last requirement, it is of great importance. A part of its meaning is that the penalties or disabilities resulting from being in a minority should be decreased as much as possible.

gies. They may be justified as providing effective means for achieving ends, as embodying established, ancient, and pervasive traditions and ideals, as conforming to principles and thereby being beautiful, just, or appropriate to human nature. These justifications may supplement and perhaps strengthen each other when they to some extent coincide. An institution may be justified as at once effective for the achievement of ends, as just, and as resting on and strengthening prior agreements and accepted institutions. Perhaps the convergence of different ideologies on certain institutions might strengthen the justification of such institutions. Also, the factual component of ideologies, the assertions about the environment, man and social processes, about what has happened and is happening, may be improved and the interpretations and generalizations based on it more carefully constructed and tested.

This answer may, however, seem to beg the question, or at least, to leave it partially unanswered. Tradition, precedent, and established institutions are merely historical fact reflecting the ignorance and prejudices of our ancestors; ends are simply given by the tastes and desires which people happen to have; principles are conflicting and elusive and are merely accepted by the people who do happen to accept them.

The second answer is that the patterns of justification interact; and that if we admit for other men the intellectual competence we assume for ourselves in making judgments of better and worse, we might presume that such interaction has produced improvement in justification. Institutions and traditions have to some extent been tested in regard to their utility for satisfying men's needs and desires and they have to some extent been shaped by principles. Interests have been disciplined and perhaps enlightened by established institutions and by accepted principles. Since ideologies attempt to convince, the competition among them to find principles which would be widely accepted might, unless we assume that both the producers and consumers of ideologies are stupid, select principles which are more and more acceptable. Granted that conditions and problems are rapidly changing and that ideologies are conflicting and incomplete, we might nevertheless argue that existing ideologies provide considerable basis for judging existing institutions and for planning new constructions on the more solid parts of them.

This second answer still seems not quite adequate. Though it does not assume that whatever exists is right, it does seem to assume that what exists, in myth, institutions, and ideologies, is a mixture of right and wrong without providing any guidance in distinguishing one from the other. One might against this argue that inadequacies in institutions, myths, or ideologies will occasion problems—suspicions that institutions are not as effective as they might be in satisfying interests, disputes about their justice, or conflicts between precedents and traditions; and that each solution of such a problem will be an improvement, a step forward. But, then in reply, one may ask how we know when a problem is solved. If we move in the wrong direction, may not the resulting problems be met by a series of expedients which make everything worse and worse? May not errors be cumulative, at least over a very long period, as the decline of societies might suggest?

Let us see if the analysis can be pushed further. The three structures of justification can more clearly be established as rational. Reasoning in terms of the means-end schema is presupposed in any action directed to the environment. Action involves some specification of objectives or ends and some consideration of alternative means for attaining them. Ends, however, despite considerable overlapping and possible organization, are diverse and incommensurable. The fact that ends are diverse and conflicting sets limits to the possibility of justifying institutions in terms of their utility; and these limits are, I think, narrower than we usually recognize. Within these limits, however, institutions may be judged as better or worse in terms of their utility in relation to ends.

Also, action is possible only for agents, whether individuals or groups, having a character or constitutions of some stability. Actions are considered or chosen in relation to an existing structure of habits, customs, dispositions, ideals which constitute the agent. Judging actions and institutions in terms of this established character does provide conclusions as to what is better or worse. Such judgments are, however, limited by the fact that different individuals and groups have different characters, customs, traditions, and precedents which reflect their histories and peculiar circumstances. As previously suggested, the character of an individual will to some extent reflect the customs and traditions of a society; and the customs and traditions of a society may belong to a larger family of tradition, so that we may perhaps significantly refer, as did Sidgewick, to the moral standards of Christendom or we might

Introduction lxiii

go farther and appeal to the traditions and ideals of civilization. Nevertheless, this basis of judgment is limited, especially in a period of rapid change, by the diversity and instability of customs and traditions.

Finally, principles may be established as presupposed in human activities, individual or social. I think that this is indeed the case and that principles, in contrast with ends and traditions, might even be called universal in the sense that they are necessary ingredients of various human activities. The principles of efficiency and economy seem to be presupposed in any action directed to the external world; and the principles of logic are presupposed in thinking, whether directed to action or to belief. Social activity in general and kinds of social activity seem to presuppose principles or ideal norms through the operation of which the activity comes into existence. Social relations do not exist until a distinction between persons and things is made by the operation of a normative principle relevant to persons and not to things. The imperative, "Treat persons as ends, not merely as means," is a hazy reflection of such a principle. Law as an organized human activity could not occur without principles by which acts are imputed to agents and authority is distinguished from force; and as law developed, other principles were necessarily operative as norms. Communication cannot occur unless the persons involved share principles which define and guide it.

In short, there are principles which are presupposed in activities; and one may attempt to discover them by analyzing activities. Principles, however, are elusive—it is notoriously difficult to state the principles of logic—and perhaps when they are disentangled from content, they may seem so abstract and empty as to be insignificant and useless. Consequently it is not easy to exhibit them and not profitable to attempt to bring them directly to bear on conflicting ideologies. If we reduce the principle of identity to the formula "P is P," we will not be able to use it as a premise nor find it helpful in deciding between conflicting doctrines.

The presence and implicit acceptance of principles in institutions is witnessed by the fact that characteristic human activities—art, law, science, government, technology—have some rationale, some norms of success or failure, some guidance by ideals which reflect, though they do not fully grasp, universal principles. Through our participation in the institutions of civilization, we become disciplined by principles and such discipline may enable us to become artists, scientists, judges, engineers, or statesmen.

Principles elude us when we attempt to state them because, perhaps, they are schema or forms of activity which cannot exist or be perceived in abstraction from the content of action but which nevertheless shape it. They are not directly accessible as common premises for people of different traditions and ideals. Disputes about doctrinal or even scientific issues are not likely to be settled by appeal to the principles of logic; but discussion of such issues cannot occur without implicit acceptance of such principles.

Principles, then, are common to all people insofar as basic types of activity are engaged in by everyone. They are used rather than known, and are so embedded in the content of actions and institutions that they cannot be separated.

Through them, however, we can to some extent understand myths and institutions other than our own. Because they are operative, we can be confident that myths and institutions embody values, however imperfectly, and have some sense and direction, and that ideologies are not always and entirely rationalization. They establish the possibility that through understanding our own institutions and others we can construct ideals which to some extent extend the limits imposed by tradition and interest. Such ideals, though narrow in scope, would help us distinguish more clearly between progress and change.

Comment by Robert C. Angell:

Although I find the analysis in Charner Perry's paper very suggestive because of his novel perspective on myths and ideologies, it seems to me that his preoccupation with communication leads him to leave out of consideration one very important moral basis of agreement and cooperation in a pluralistic society. The omission is one to which a sociologist is peculiarly sensitive.

What seems to me to be omitted are the dynamic possibilities of new social linkages between the segments holding different myths and ideologies. Mr. Perry's only treatment of the possibility of greater consensus comes in his consideration of discussion based on common patterns of reasoning. But surely we are not all philosophers. Most of our changed orientations come not from mere symbolic communication but from experiences in new social groupings. Young Southerners have testified to the influence on their racial attitudes of service in integrated armed forces. The work camps of the American Friends Service Committee have had similar effects on class and national ethnocentrisms. There are already in our society several forms of association that cut across the pluralistic lines. Surely these need to be pointed to as integrators of our so-

Introduction

ciety. This, not only for the sake of scientific completeness, but because by intelligent planning we might be able to multiply such forms of association and thus give our society a broader basis of agreement and cooperation.

But it is when we come to face the world of international relations that Mr. Perry's omission is particularly serious. Although it is still possible to keep societies at arms' length in family and community matters, it is not possible in the politicoeconomic sector. Communism and democracy are meeting head on all around the world. Nor does it seem likely that the moral basis for better cooperation will come from communication and discussion. Convictions are so deep that appreciation of underlying similarities is very difficult to attain. To a sociologist at least it seems probable that a gradually enlarging web of social structures will be absolutely indispensable to the growth of moral consensus. Not travel, not international sporting events, not even study abroad, but rather serious and lasting linkages such as are found in international secretariats, multinational research projects, and international nongovernmental organizations—these are what it will take to build an integrated yet pluralistic world society.

I. Responsibility in Political Organization

CHAPTER I

A Comparative Investigation of the Norms of Official Conduct

By WAYNE A. R. LEYS

MANY AMERICAN citizens expect their public officials to be controlled by higher ethical standards than the common standards of nongovernmental employment. Outstanding public officials have agreed that this is a reasonable expectation. But citizens and officials are not clearly in agreement regarding the nature of the "higher" ethical standards.

Legislators and editors, speaking for the citizenry, frequently say to judges and administrators: "You ought to be more scrupulously *honest* than men in private life." Public administrators typically say: "We ought to hold ourselves to a higher standard of *wisdom* than the average citizen." The spokesmen for "the public" say: "We are proposing stricter *rules* for you to follow." Representative men in government reply: "Good government is not secured by mere adherence to rules. Responsible performance means wisdom in judging the means to desirable ends, and this is more difficult in public life than it is in private life."

The first conception of the "higher morality" of public service is typified by the pronouncements of Senators Paul H. Douglas and Jacob K. Javits (please note the bipartisan reference) and numerous proposals to legislate a "code of ethics." The second conception of the more exacting norms of official conduct is found in numerous articles in the *Public Administration Review* and plans for improving the educational qualifications of office.

I shall try to show that superior *honesty* and superior *wisdom* are not alternative answers to the same question, *viz.*, "In what respect are the norms of official conduct more rigorous than the standards of private life?" Rather, conformity to the stricter rules regarding honesty,

Ethics and Bigness

etc., is a requirement for the solution of one kind of problem, *viz.*, how to secure action in the most controversial, nonrevolutionary society of our time. And the development of higher standards of wisdom contributes to the solution of another kind of problem, *viz.*, how to assure the morale and self-respect of our public officials.

A Few Preliminary Doubts

At the outset I must confess to a measure of sympathy with the administrators who look upon legislated "codes of ethics" as negative and formal. I believe that many citizens share their doubts. Will officials, who comply with all of the proposed rules and restrictions, achieve the ends and purposes of government?

Our uneasiness about this kind of "morality in government" comes possibly from our awareness that viable governments in other places and times have operated without such stringent rules. The avoidance of conflict of interest, for example, was not characteristic of our own government during most of the nineteenth century, and it seems Utopian when we look at the governments of many Latin, Arab, and Far Eastern nations.

Although our theory of government tends to be moralistic, government is always recognized as a power phenomenon. Even in our idealistic literature, which contrasts private and public administration,[1] the most important controls on public administration are often represented as political power. I am not referring merely to the extreme Machiavellians and their glorification of *raison d'état*. I also refer to such moderate men as Judge Learned Hand. In his testimony before the Douglas subcommittee on June 28, 1951, Judge Hand said,

[1] J. D. Barnett, "Public Agencies and Private Agencies," *American Political Science Review*, 18, February, 1924, 42–46.
W. B. Donham, "Governmental and Business Executives," *Public Administration Review*, 6 (spring, 1946), 176.
Paul Appleby, *Big Democracy*, Alfred A. Knopf, Inc., New York, 1945, p. 7.
Harold D. Smith, *The Management of Your Government*, McGraw-Hill Publishing Co., Inc., New York, 1945.
Josiah C. Stamp, "The Contrast between the Administration of Business and Public Affairs, *Journal of Public Administration*, 1 (1923), 162. Although my paper deals almost exclusively with recent American thinking, I include a few British references because of similarities in British and American standards.

Investigation of the Norms of Official Conduct

I hope you will not think that I am slack in my morals when I say that in judging public conduct we should always remember that it has to pass muster with the voters or it will be an idle gesture.[2]

Another reason for our uneasiness about legislated "codes of ethics," perhaps, is that they are aimed primarily at high offices. We want responsibility and self-regulation in the men who exercise managerial and policymaking powers: the judges, the men who award contracts, the legislators, the inspectors, the bureau chiefs, the men who prepare budgets. But from most of the 10,000,000 Americans on public payrolls we expect no more than we expect from their counterparts in private enterprise. They will be controlled by supervision, by the threat of prosecution and, to a limited extent, by competition.

I have chosen to preface the comparison of official norms and nonpublic norms with these skeptical reflections for two reasons. The first reason is that inquiries into occupational ethics sometimes lose sight of the nonmoral forms of social control. However urgent we may believe the adoption of ethical standards to be, we should not expect self-regulation to be the only means of securing desirable behavior. The second reason for these initial reminders of skepticism is that Americans are making demands upon their public officials which go beyond what most peoples have expected from their governments. The demands go beyond what American citizens expect from themselves and, as I shall try to show, the demands strike many officials as somehow missing the most important problems of government. The tensions produced by the demands indicate, in my opinion, the need for a revision of our understanding of government.

The Imposed Codes of Ethics

The standards, which have been urged upon American officials with increasing insistence in recent decades, call for honest, selfless, nonpartisan devotion to the public interest. The popularity of these standards is attested by the success of muckraking political commentators.[3] It is evidenced by the now almost continuous staging of legisla-

---
[2]Testimony reprinted in Irving Dilliard, *The Spirit of Liberty, Papers and Addresses of Learned Hand*, Vintage Books, Inc., New York, 1959, p. 172.
[3]The muckraking of Lincoln Steffens, conveniently summarized in his *Autobiography*

6   Ethics and Bigness

tive inquiries and exposés of corruption.[4] And if there were no widespread popular interest in these standards, it is unlikely that legislators would be proposing so many bills to establish a "code of ethics."

The proposals to legislate and codify ethical standards vary in detail, but what is conspicuous is their overall similarity. Whether introduced at the federal, state, or local level,[5] they generally say about the same thing. What is even more remarkable is the fact that many of

---

(Harcourt Brace and Co., Inc., New York, 1936), helped to establish a pattern for newspaper and magazine condemnation of official misconduct. The *Autobiography*, of course, was written after Steffens' conversion to Communism and, therefore, includes some interpretations that are atypical of American muckraking. Here are a few references to more scholarly literature:

David Loth, *Public Plunder, A History of Graft in America*, Carrick and Evans, New York, 1938.

Donald Kingsley, *Representative Bureaucracy*, Antioch Press, Yellow Springs, 1944.

Callender and Charlesworth, editors, "Ethical Standards in American Public Life," *Annals of the American Academy of Political and Social Science*, volume 280 (March, 1952). B. McGill, "Conflict of Interest: English Experience 1782–1914," *Western Political Quarterly*, 12 (September, 1959), 808–827.

[4]The brilliant staff work of Louis Brandeis in the Ballinger investigation during Taft's administration undoubtedly helped to set a pattern. Other landmarks were the Teapot Dome scandal investigation in the 1920s and the work of the Douglas committee in 1950 and 1951 (concerned with the Reconstruction Finance Corporation and the Internal Revenue Service). See *Ethical Standards in Government: Report of a Subcommittee of the Committee on Labor and Public Welfare*, United States Senate, 82nd Congress, 1st Session, 1951.

For a comparison with interpretations of more recent investigations, see Bernard Schwartz, *The Professor and the Commissions*, Alfred A. Knopf, Inc., New York, 1959; "The Furor over Gifts in Washington," *U.S. News and World Report*, 44 (June 27, 1958).

R. Dugger "What Corrupted Texas?," *Harpers Magazine*, 214 (March, 1957), 68–74.

[5]H. Con. Res. 43, 85th Congress, 1st Session, "Code of Ethics for Government Service," introduced by Representative Katherine St. George (New York), January 5, 1957.

S. 4223, A Bill to Promote Public Confidence in the Integrity of Congress and the Executive Branch, introduced by Senator Francis Case (New Jersey), August 1, 1958.

S. 658, A Bill to Establish a Code of Ethics for the Executive and Legislative Branches of the Government, introduced by Senators Jacob K. Javits and Kenneth B. Keating (New York), January 23, 1959.

Report of Committee on Ethics and Standards, The Council of the City of New York, February 3, 1959.

The Code of Ethics adopted by the Texas legislature has such provisions as the following: "No officer or employee of a state agency, legislator or legislative employee shall accept any gift, favor, or service that might reasonably tend to influence him in the discharge of his official duties" (section 3a).

Investigation of the Norms of Official Conduct

the proposals merely repeat prohibitions that already have legal sanction.[6]

The typical introduction is a general exhortation to serve the public interest. This is followed by more specific rules against practices which increase the temptations to sacrifice the public interest. The practices that are most frequently mentioned are:

> the acceptance of gifts and favors;
> the acceptance of offers of private employment (especially, if this involves representation of the employer before a governmental agency within two years after termination of government service);
> failure to disqualify oneself in a matter affecting some enterprise in which one has a personal investment;
> unofficial and secret communication with favored partisans.

It appears that widespread efforts are being made to lay upon all officials the kind of norms that were adopted (in 1924, after controversy) for judges.[7] In order to merit the trust that is reposed in public officials, the officials are expected to restrict not only their financial operations but also their social life. It begins to sound like Plato's discipline for the ruling class in the ideal state.

Voluntary Norms of the Trades and Professions

Now, let us turn our attention to the norms for nongovernmental trades and professions and to the standards that public officials propose for themselves. These norms are articulated in voluntary codes of ethics (though it must be admitted that many of them were adopted to prevent or to minimize hostile legislation and public regulation). They are also interpreted in a diffuse literature, much of it fugitive.[8]

---

[6] The conflict of interest rules of the United States Criminal Code, for example. See Title 18, Sections 281, 216, 284, 434, and 1914. These statutes are not regarded as perfect and have been under study by a special Committee of the Association of the Bar of the City of New York. There are, of course, sharp differences of opinion on this subject. Some proposals to "remove loopholes" are regarded as proposals to weaken existing statutes. See Hearings before the Antitrust Subcommittee of the Committee on the Judiciary, House of Representatives, 86th Congress, 2nd session, on H.R. 1900, H.R. 2156, H.R. 2157, H.R. 7556, and H.R. 10575. Serial number 17. Government Printing Office, 1960.

[7] *The Canons of Judicial Ethics,* The American Bar Association, 1957.

[8] See B. Y. Landis, editor, "Ethical Standards and Professional Conduct," *Annals of the American Academy of Political and Social Science,* volume 297, January, 1955.

Except for a few professions, the codes do not antedate 1900, and the great majority have originated since 1918.

Devotion to the public interest, honesty, and the avoidance of conflict of interest are among the subjects that are discussed in the voluntary codes.[9] But the voluntary codes emphasize something else, something that is only barely mentioned in the codes that are imposed upon public officials. The voluntary codes, almost without exception, lay emphasis upon the practice and the improvement of an occupational art, the maintenance of technical standards, and the cultivation of such relations with other craftsmen as will preserve and perfect the quality of performance.

The medical code expects contributions to the advancement of the healing arts and the avoidance of the kind of competition that might ruin the arts. The teachers' code is poetic in its references to children and the need for cooperative relations with other adults who are concerned with child development. The accountants' code is built around the central theme of securing accurate financial reporting. Industrial trade associations usually stress the improvement of the manufacturing arts and the economic health of a useful industry.

E. L. Heermance, *Codes of Ethics,* Free Press Printing Co., Chicago, 1924.
Annual Reports, Federal Trade Commission, Washington, D.C.
Temporary National Economic Survey Monograph, number 18, "Trade Association Survey," Senate Committee Print, 1941.
Robert Storey, *Professional Leadership,* Associated Colleges, Claremont, 1958.
J. Fletcher, *Morals and Medicine,* Princeton University Press, Princeton, 1954.
T. V. Houser, *Big Business and Human Values,* McGraw-Hill Publishing Co., Inc., New York, 1957.

[9]Conflict of interest is the subject of both legal and voluntary rules for bankers, lawyers, union officials, transportation and power company directors, and certified public accountants. See, especially
The AFL-CIO Codes of Ethical Practices.
H. Drinker, *Legal Ethics,* Columbia University Press, New York, 1953.
W. M. Trumbull, *Materials on the Lawyer's Professional Responsibility,* Prentice-Hall, Inc., New York, 1957.
J. Stone, *Legal Education and Public Responsibility,* Association of American Law Schools, Columbus, 1959.
M. T. Copeland and A. Towl, *The Board of Directors and Business Management,* Harvard University Press, Cambridge, 1947.
John L. Carey, *Professional Ethics of Certified Public Accountants,* American Institute of Certified Public Accountants, New York, 1956.

Voluntary Norms of Public Administrators

The same positive note is struck by public administrators when they develop voluntary codes and state their ideals. The 1924 code of the International City Managers' Association calls for belief in the worth of governmental services and relates integrity, courtesy, etc., to the tasks to be performed, the good to be achieved. The Washington State Chapter of the American Society for Public Administration had this positive accent, too, mentioning not only efficiency but also conservation as proper objectives.

The literature produced by public administrators and teachers of public administration has shifted, during the past half century, from preoccupation with technical efficiency[10] to wise decisionmaking as the goal of good administration.[11] But nowhere does the reader find the

[10]See Woodrow Wilson, "The Study of Administration," *Political Science Quarterly*, 2, 1887, 197–222.
Dwight Waldo, *The Administrative State*, Ronald Press Co., New York, 1948.
The early ideals of the public administration movement are well stated in the Federal Creed of Service, promulgated by the United States Civil Service Commission:

> We as members of the civil service accept our obligation and our opportunity to serve the American people well and in full measure, doing our best to further the free and democratic institutions of our country. We believe that it is our duty to carry out loyally the will of the people as expressed in our laws, serve the public with fairness, courtesy, integrity and understanding, help improve the efficiency, economy, and effectiveness of our work . . . and thus do our part in performing the great services of the Government.

[11]During the long emergencies of the Great Depression and the Second World War the ideal administrator came to be pictured less as an efficient technician and more as a wise decisionmaker. See
Paul Appleby, *Morality and Administration in Democratic Government*, Louisiana State University Press, Baton Rouge, 1952.
Gordon Clapp, "A Credo for the Public Service," *Public Personnel Review*, 12 (January, 1951), 14.
H. Emmerich, "Ethics in Public Administration," in Conaway, editor, *Democracy in Federal Administration*, United States Department of Agriculture Graduate School, 1956.
Wayne A. R. Leys, "Ethics and Administrative Discretion," *Public Administration Review*, 3 (winter, 1943), 10.
David Lilienthal, *TVA—Democracy on the March*, Harper and Brothers, New York, 1944.
P. Monypenny, "A Code of Ethics," *Public Administration Review*, 13 (summer, 1953), 184–187.
W. Mosher, J. Kingsley, and O. Stahl, *Public Personnel Administration*, Harper and Brothers, New York, 1950, chapter 17.
W. Sayre, "Trends of a Decade in Administrative Values," *Public Administration Review*, 11, (January, 1951), 1–9.

10   *Ethics and Bigness*

avoidance of bribery and conflict of interest as the *main* ethical problem.

In numerous conferences and seminars I have observed that federal administrators (above the grade of GS 11) crave an opportunity to talk over, not the simple cases of venality, but the puzzling situations where it is difficult to identify the public interest. They would like to solve problems, but they are not sure that they have an adequate view of the problem. They wonder whether they have anticipated all of the criteria by which the problem will be judged to have been solved or bungled.[12]

The standards to which public administrators aspire resemble the standards which most of the trades and professions adopt for themselves. They are standards of practical wisdom. They are the criteria by which to judge the performance of a task, the solution of a problem, the realization of a good.

By contrast, the conflict of interest rules, which are imposed upon public officials by legislation, are legalistic and negativistic. They are not principles of *wisdom*. They are not guarantees that specific goods will be achieved. The man who has never accepted the promise of a retirement job or even a free lunch, may still be failing to meet an important public need. The man who has never had secret communication with any of the contending parties before his agency, may still be unjust and prejudiced.

The Conflict-Resolving Function of Government

The only way that I can make sense of the negativistic pressure for the avoidance of conflict of interest is to recall that government is different from other institutions. Government is, of course, a service in-

---

E. S. Redford, *Ideal and Practice in Public Administration,* University of Alabama Press, University, 1958.

Y. Willbern, "The Broadening Concerns of Administrators," *Public Administration Review,* 17 (autumn, 1957), ii.

[12]The kinds of problematic situations, here alluded to, are collected in Harold Stein's book, *Public Administration and Policy Development,* Harcourt Brace and Co., Inc., New York, 1952, and in similar case studies more recently published by the University of Alabama Press for the Inter-University Case Committee. Typically, they present choices that involve conflicts of values: the efficiency of a service versus the security of some group, the strict enforcement of law versus the survival of an agency, the protection of health or safety versus minimizing the risks of trouble.

Investigation of the Norms of Official Conduct

stitution, solving some problems and taking action to achieve certain goals. But government is also the institution, *par excellence,* for adjudicating disputes. Government is the institution which makes it possible for action to occur, despite lingering disagreements. Even the service functions of government (postal service, fire protection, etc.) are political, insofar as they require taxes that are levied on everyone whether or not the taxpayer prefers to spend his money for a given service and whether he agrees with the effective majority concerning his share of the cost.

When government acts to settle a dispute or to set things in motion despite lingering disagreement, there is obviously no complete agreement on the merits, on the appropriateness of means to ends, sometimes even on the problem to be solved. What distinguishes a lawful government from a dictatorship is agreement on the procedure to be followed in reaching a decision. In recent decades, the agreement on procedure has included the conflict of interest rules. The contending parties cannot agree on the wisdom of officials, but they can and do agree that no official is going to decide between them or spend their tax money if he has accepted favors from one of them.

What the public calls "ethics in government" is thus comparable to the Civil Service Commission regulations and the Hatch Act,[13] which prohibit political party activity by most of the federal employees. The ethical codes are comparable to the loyalty oaths and the investigation of officials for the purpose of making sure that they are not subversives. They are comparable to the requirements of the Administrative Procedures Act (concerning notice, hearing, and judicial review).[14]

---

[13]See 18 *United States Code Annotated,* Section 16.
United Public Workers *v.* Mitchell, 91 L.Ed. 509, 67 S.Ct. 556 (1947).
Oklahoma *v.* United States Civil Service Commission, 91 L.Ed. 537, 67 S.Ct. 544, (1947).
 Ex parte Curtis, 106 U.S. 371 (1882).
McAuliffe *v.* New Bedford, 155 Mass. 216, 220, 29 N.E. 517 (1891).
See also O. Kirchheimer, "The Historical and Comparative Background of the Hatch Law" in *Public Policy,* volume 2, Harvard University Press, Cambridge, 1941

[14]Pub. Law 404, chapter 324, 79th Congress, 2nd Session, June, 1946. In this connection I should mention the results of an investigation conducted by Charner Perry and myself in 1958–1959. We found that many social scientists and philosophers conceived of "the public interest" as the result of a procedure rather than as an aggregate of interests. See *Philosophy and the Public Interest,* Committee to Advance Original Work in Philosophy, Chicago, 1959.

See also the forthcoming symposium of the American Society for Political and Legal Philosophy (Nomos V, edited by C. J. Friedrich, to be published by the Liberal Arts Press, probably in 1961).

Loyalty oaths are inefficient means of catching subversives. Compliance with the Hatch Act scarcely eliminates partisanship. And keeping clean of conflict of interest is no guarantee that an official will serve the public interest in the sense of wisely choosing the best means of attaining universally accepted ends.

It is because of the increase in disputes that are settled without substantially universal agreement on the merits, that judges and administrators are subjected to stricter procedural tests: no conflict of interest, no party activity, no subversive connections. You cannot hope for general agreement that Bidder A should be awarded a certain television channel, but the channel is going to be awarded. And the decision will be accepted if the award is made by a properly appointed commission, the members of which have not done various things that are forbidden by the conflict of interest rules, if they have at least gone through the motions of hearing evidence, etc.

This is why the conflict of interest type of norm is not an alternative to the efficiency and wisdom type of norm that public administrators themselves, like the tradesmen and professionals outside of government, seek to establish. The conflict of interest type of standard is added to ordinary professional ethics, when a man enters government service.[15]

The Troubled Conscience of Public Officials

Those who are familiar with philosophical ethics will recognize that I have so far agreed with some of the British intuitionists who say that not all obligatory standards can be deduced from "the good" or shown to be means to good ends.[16] To some extent, Utilitarianism and the other classical systems of teleological ethics break down.

I cannot come to rest with the British intuitionists, however, because it seems to me that they describe a predicament without thinking very

---

[15]The public officials who feel abused because they are held to "higher" standards than businessmen, farmers, and labor leaders, do not, in my opinion, fully appreciate the dispute-settling function of government.

[16]H. A. Prichard, "Does Moral Philosophy Rest on a Mistake?" in *Moral Obligation*, Clarendon Press, Oxford, 1949.
W. D. Ross, *The Right and the Good*, Clarendon Press, Oxford, 1930.

> Some of the recent "analysts," despite their homage to common sense and ordinary language, go far beyond the reasonable skepticism of Prichard and Ross. Pursuing casuistical skills to academic limits, they give the impression that every moral generalization disintegrates upon close inspection, leaving everyone on a case to case basis, dependent on pure native wit as embalmed in the historical accidents of the English language.

much of what one is going to do about it. A live public official will sometimes be unable to resign himself to a mechanical compliance with procedural regulation. If he sees some great public good that is not being served, his conscience as a citizen will bother him.

To point up the official's dilemma, let us mention a few of the situations in which politically safe, procedurally correct conduct is an alternative to aggressive pursuit of an objective which the official believes to be in the public interest:

1. An office, a school, or a city in which racial discrimination can be reduced more rapidly than the law, as interpreted by the Supreme Court, requires;
2. A legislative session during which a strong stand might possibly secure a more nearly adequate appropriation for education, defense, public health work, or some other service that the official believes to be urgently needed;
3. The enforcement of a safety regulation that has become a dead letter because it hurts the business of a politically powerful group;
4. The reassessment of property values for tax purposes, where low valuations have been "legitimatized" by long custom and usage;
5. The selection of candidates for a position requiring high ability but no specific qualifications, when the less competent candidate has strong political backing.

"Perfectionism" and "Realism"

In such situations public officials perceive themselves as subject to contrary demands: a. to meet the procedural requirements of their office but do the politically safe thing; b. to be goal-oriented and assume some risks in trying to solve a problem. There are two mistaken attitudes to which officials may be attracted: "perfectionism" and "realism."

The perfectionists are inclined to say that because not all public actions can be taken on the merits (as they judge the merits), their entire official performance is worthless. They talk about Schweitzer and Thoreau and how to get out of the rat race. Seeking all of their personal satisfactions in their job, they find their work unsatisfying. They are attracted by antipolitical and antilegal doctrines, whether they actually get out of public life or half-heartedly and guiltily continue to go through the motions of office.[17]

The opposite extreme is "realism." The realists are impressed by the fact that somehow controversies get settled, regardless of disagreement on the merits. Somehow, they go on to the conclusion that any action "that can be made to stick" is right.[18] This means that an action is right, if the official and his agency can take it and survive. An outward appearance of satisfying the conflict of interest rules becomes coupled with a readiness to sacrifice the public interest (in the sense of generally desirable goals) to the official's convenience.

Both perfectionism and realism as generalized attitudes assume the possibility and the rationality of a general solution. From the standpoint of feasibility, each seems to require the support of a factual judgment, *viz.*, "All of the actions of government are possible only on the basis of agreement to settle disputes by some test other than the merits of the action as seen by the disputants . . . *i.e.*, by leaving the decision to some arbitrator or by making the decision through a test of political strength."

The foregoing factual assumption, however, sometimes strikes an official as false. He sometimes believes that action on the merits (the official now judging the action as a citizen) can be agreed upon or that it can be brought about in spite of some disagreement.

Even if the official judges action on the merits to be impossible, he may feel a duty to "try the impossible."

In the latter instances, the official may stay in office and risk political

---

[17] E. Homrighausen, "No Monopoly in Theological Education," *Christian Century*, 74 (April 25, 1957), 514.

Hannah Arendt, *The Human Condition*, Doubleday and Co., Anchor edition, New York, 1959, chapter 2.

E. Brunner, *Justice and the Social Order*, Harper and Brothers, New York, 1945.

N. W. DeWitt, *Epicurus and his Philosophy*, University of Minnesota, Minneapolis, 1954.

[18] Glendon Schubert, Jr., "The Public Interest in Administrative Decision-Making," *American Political Science Review*, June, 1957, especially section on "Realists."

T. V. Smith, *The Legislative Way of Life*, The University of Chicago Press, Chicago, 1940.

E. Lefever, *Ethics and United States Foreign Policy*, Meridian Books, Inc., New York, 1957.

Wayne A. R. Leys, "Machiavelli in Modern Dress," *Christian Century*, 76 (November 11, 1959), 1308.

Investigation of the Norms of Official Conduct

suicide, or he may leave government service and become a citizen-partisan.[19]

The classical systems of philosophical ethics cannot make the official's decision for him, any more than the proverbial wisdom can. To this extent the recent philosophical skeptics are correct. But the skeptics overlook a most useful function of philosophical systems and traditional proverbs. That function is to remind a man, while he is deliberating, of the alternatives, the rival values among which he may choose.[20]

I am contending that there are some moral generalizations that make sense. For an alert and perceptive public official, these generalizations cannot function as unexceptionable imperatives. But they can serve as critical and deliberative questions. They help the official, as they help anyone else, to "ask the right questions."[21] They increase the chances that deliberation, prior to choice, will anticipate judgment after the action. They enlarge the scope of deliberation and assure consideration of more values that may be revelant to the impending decision.

---

[19] There appear to be many persons in public life who have given hostages to fortune. They have a family to support and mortgage payments to make, and they are not Gandhis, ready to sacrifice their family on the altar of public service. If the idea of returning to private life is inconceivable to them, they really have very little choice. Such officials may engage in breastbeating, trying to figure out how they can do heroic things and avoid all risks; but they are too dependent on their jobs to face alternatives. If courage is esteemed a virtue in a public servant, it might be well to make the transition to nonpublic employment less difficult by such measures as making pension rights transferable.

[20] The Socratic and Kantian value of consistency thus challenges the man who is preoccupied with Hobbesian self-preservation, and vice versa. The Benthamite criterion of future results thus challenges the man obsessed by Scholastic standards of authorization and legitimacy, and vice versa. The Hegelian appreciation of institutions and loyalty challenges the person who is thinking only about individual rights, and vice versa. The Stoic regard for peace of mind and self-respect challenges the decisionmaker who has been able to think only about desired results, etc.

[21] This interpretation of ethical standards is elaborated in my 1952 book, *Ethics for Policy Decisions* (Prentice-Hall Inc., New York). It should be obvious that I follow the tendency of twentieth century philosophers to be skeptical about the generality of Kantian, Benthamite, and other classical formulations of moral principles. Whereas skepticism in the nineteenth century was based on anthropological findings that not all human societies accepted the same principles, skepticism in the twentieth century is based upon administrative findings that the sweeping moral generalizations are not accurate summaries of what reasonable men will find to be right and good under various circumstances. I emphasize the survival of these sweeping generalizations as hypotheses, reminders, questions, possible tests, etc.; whereas the more fashionable emphasis in philosophical ethics has been upon the breakdown of Utilitarian formulas, etc., as unexceptionable rules.

Ethics and Bigness

Higher Standards of Honesty; Wisdom More Difficult

From an antiPlatonic, Madisonian viewpoint in political philosophy, public officials are morally obligated to give due consideration to two general types of questions, principles, values, criteria, or norms. One sort is represented in the legislated codes regarding honesty, no conflict of interest, loyalty, nonpartisanship, etc. These requirements are part of the fundamental agreement in society for securing orderly controversy, the settlement of disputes, and the making of political decisions. These norms undoubtedly impose upon public officials a "higher" morality than the public imposes upon itself. However irksome and inadequate these procedural rules may appear in the official's mind, they are sanctioned by a widespread desire to prevent destructive deadlock and to maintain peace.

The second general type of norm, the standard of wisdom, seems to me to be no "higher" for the public official than it is for the citizen. When the official asks himself what he should do to serve the public interest (in a substantive sense), he will be guided, to a large extent, by the insights and levels of aspiration of physicians, engineers, economists, personnel administrators, or whatever occupational group he may belong to. What distinguishes the official's quest for wisdom is the fact that he is working in a more difficult environment than his nongovernmental counterpart. The official must meet needs, perfect the arts and sciences, and solve problems in areas where there is political conflict. He must stay within the limits imposed by the rules of ritualized conflict.

The peculiar moral tensions of public service arise because there is no necessary connection between satisfying the comparatively rigorous standards of honesty, etc., and meeting (under difficulties) the ordinary demands for wisdom.

Bibliography

I *Books*

Paul Appleby, *Big Democracy,* Alfred A. Knopf, Inc., New York, 1945.
———, *Morality and Administration in Democratic Government,* Louisiana State University Press, Baton Rouge, 1952.
Hannah Arendt, *The Human Condition,* Doubleday and Co., Anchor edition, New York, 1959.

Investigation of the Norms of Official Conduct 17

E. Brunner, *Justice and the Social Order*, Harper and Brothers, New York, 1945.

John L. Carey, *Professional Ethics of Certified Public Accountants*, American Institute of Certified Public Accountants, New York, 1956.

M. T. Copeland and A. Towl, *The Board of Directors and Business Management*, Harvard University Press, Cambridge, 1947.

N. W. DeWitt, *Epicurus and his Philosophy*, University of Minnesota Press, Minneapolis, 1954.

Irving Dilliard, editor, *The Spirit of Liberty, Papers and Addresses of Learned Hand*, Vintage Books, Inc., New York, 1959.

H. Drinker, *Legal Ethics*, Columbia University Press, New York, 1953.

H. Emmerich, "Ethics in Public Administration," in Conaway, editor, *Democracy in Federal Administration*, United States Department of Agriculture Graduate School, Washington, D.C., 1956.

J. Fletcher, *Morals and Medicine*, Princeton University Press, Princeton, 1954.

E. L. Heermance, *Codes of Ethics*, Free Press Printing Co., Chicago, 1924.

T. V. Houser, *Big Business and Human Values*, McGraw-Hill Publishing Co., Inc., New York, 1957.

Donald Kingsley, *Representative Bureaucracy*, Antioch Press, Yellow Springs, 1944.

O. Kirchheimer, "The Historical and Comparative Background of the Hatch Law," *Public Policy*, Volume 2, Harvard University Press, Cambridge, 1941.

E. Lefever, *Ethics and United States Foreign Policy*, Meridian Books, Inc., New York, 1957.

Wayne A. R. Leys, *Ethics for Policy Decisions*, Prentice-Hall, Inc., New York, 1952.

David Lilienthal, *TVA—Democracy on the March*, Harper and Brothers, New York, 1944.

David Loth, *Public Plunder, A History of Graft in America*, Carrick and Evans, New York, 1938.

W. Mosher, J. Kingsley, and O. Stahl, *Public Personnel Administration*, Harper and Brothers, New York, 1950.

H. A. Prichard, *Moral Obligation*, Clarendon Press, Oxford, 1949.

E. S. Redford, *Ideal and Practice in Public Administration*, University of Alabama Press, University, 1958.

W. D. Ross, *The Right and the Good*, Clarendon Press, Oxford, 1930.

Bernard Schwartz, *The Professor and the Commissions*, Alfred A. Knopf, Inc., New York, 1959.

Harold D. Smith, *The Management of Your Government*, McGraw-Hill Publishing Co., Inc., New York, 1945.

T. V. Smith, *The Legislative Way of Life,* The University of Chicago Press, Chicago, 1940.

Lincoln Steffens, *Autobiography,* Harcourt Brace and Co., Inc., New York, 1936.

Harold Stein, *Public Administration and Policy Development,* Harcourt Brace and Co., Inc., New York, 1952.

J. Stone, *Legal Education and Public Responsibility,* Association of American Law Schools, Columbus, 1959.

Robert Storey, *Professional Leadership,* Associated Colleges, Claremont, 1958.

W. M. Trumbull, *Materials on the Lawyer's Professional Responsibility,* Prentice-Hall, Inc., New York, 1957.

Dwight Waldo, *The Administrative State,* Ronald Press Co., New York, 1948.

II *Periodicals*

J. D. Barnett, "Public Agencies and Private Agencies," *American Political Science Review,* Volume 18 (February, 1924).

Callender and Charlesworth, editors, "Ethical Standards in American Public Life," *Annals of the American Academy of Political and Social Science,* Volume 280 (March, 1952).

Gordon Clapp, "A Credo for the Public Service," *Public Personnel Review,* Volume 12 (January, 1951).

W. B. Donham, "Governmental and Business Executives," *Public Administration Review,* Volume 6 (Spring, 1946).

R. Dugger, "What Corrupted Texas?", *Harpers Magazine,* Volume 214 (March, 1957).

"The Furor over Gifts in Washington," *U.S. News and World Report,* Volume 44 (June 27, 1958).

E. Homrighausen, "No Monopoly in Theological Education," *Christian Century,* Volume 74 (April 25, 1957).

B. Y. Landis, editor, "Ethical Standards and Professional Conduct," *Annals of the American Academy of Political and Social Science,* Volume 297 (January, 1955).

Wayne A. R. Leys, "Ethics and Administrative Discretion," *Public Administration Review,* Volume 3 (Winter, 1943).

———, "Machiavelli in Modern Dress," *Christian Century,* Volume 76 (November 11, 1959).

B. McGill, "Conflict of Interest: English Experience 1782–1914," *Western Political Quarterly,* Volume 12 (September, 1959).

P. Monypenny, "A Code of Ethics," *Public Administration Review,* Volume 13 (Summer, 1953).

W. Sayre, "Trends of a Decade in Administrative Values," *Public Administration Review*, Volume 11 (Winter, 1951).

Glendon Schubert, Jr., "The Public Interest in Administrative Decision-Making," *American Political Science Review*, Volume 51 (June, 1957).

Josiah C. Stamp, "The Contrast between the Administration of Business and Public Affairs," *Journal of Public Administration*, Volume 1 (1923).

Y. Willbern, "The Broadening Concerns of Administrators," *Public Administration Review*, Volume 17 (Autumn, 1957).

Woodrow Wilson, "The Study of Administration," *Political Science Quarterly*, Volume 2 (1887).

III *Pamphlets, Reports, Legal Documents*

The AFL–CIO Codes of Ethical Practices.

Annual Reports, Federal Trade Commission, Washington, D.C.

The Canons of Judicial Ethics, The American Bar Association, 1957.

Ethical Standards in Government: Report of a Subcommittee of the Committee on Labor and Public Welfare, United States Senate, 82nd Congress, 1st Session, 1951.

Philosophy and the Public Interest, Committee to Advance Original Work in Philosophy, Chicago, 1959.

Report of Committee on Ethics and Standards, The Council of the City of New York, February 3, 1959.

Temporary National Economic Survey Monograph, Number 18, "Trade Association Survey," Senate Committee Print, 1941.

CHAPTER II

The Ethical Problems of an Elected Political Executive

By STEPHEN K. BAILEY

ANY ATTEMPT to construct what John Buchan once called "an essay in recollection" is fraught with ethical puzzles. When such an essay is addressed, upon commission, to the moral dilemmas of a political experience of some years ago, ethical issues are piled crazily one on top of the other. And they are nudged into further disarray by the tricks which rationalization and memory play upon all autobiographers. In view of the number of friends whose good names must be protected against my possibly accurate reporting of their (and my) occasional moral lapses; in view of the impossibility, six to eight years after events, of my recapturing the precise pattern of considerations which shaped the matrix within which decisions were made; and in view of the inscrutability of many of the ethical issues with which I, as mayor of a city of 30,000 had to deal, it is clear that this essay must be content with the perennially probable rather than the historically precise.

Insofar as I refer specifically to experiences in Middletown, Connecticut, during the years when I was mayor of that city, I hope that friends there will show me the same charity that Huckleberry Finn showed Mark Twain. Referring to *The Adventures of Tom Sawyer,* Huck commented, "That book was made by Mr. Mark Twain, and he told the truth, mainly. There was things which he stretched, but mainly he told the truth. That is nothing I never seen anybody but lied one time or another, without it was Aunt Polly. . . ." And Huck Finn was perceptive in spotting the moral flaw in Aunt Polly and in her old maid sister, Miss Watson: a flaw of self-righteousness so hideous that when Huck learned that Miss Watson was living "so as to go to the good place," Huck could "see no advantage in going where she was going," so he made up his mind he wouldn't try for it.

I have worried far more about the ethical consequences of my decisions as mayor since leaving office than I ever did as an incumbent. And perhaps this is the first point to be made. Most elected executives find that there is an ethics of *action* which is normally far more compelling than the urge to balance with precision the ethical niceties of pressing public issues. There are times when the good of the community demands firmness and decision at the expense of marginal injustice. Those who would make justice the sole criterion of the good society are not only, in my judgment, myopic in their ethical vision, they establish an impossible operating norm for administrators. Justice, in the sense of "just desserts," presumes omnipotence and omniscience. An elected mayor in a "weak-mayor" form of government, alas, has neither. He may desire to be just, but occasions arise when justice is not the highest ethical priority. If a local hospital, which has run a countywide ambulance service for years, suddenly decides for budgetary reasons to disown this responsibility, it may be unjust to make the taxpayers of a single city in the county pick up the check for keeping the countywide ambulance service going on an emergency basis. But, here, what is necessary overrides what is just.

And emergency actions by an authorized executive have meaning and value quite apart from the justice or injustice of any decision taken by the executive under his emergency authority. The justification for the emergency powers of the public executive are, I believe, not only in the necessities of organization under stress; there is a most significant social therapy in the public's sense that "somebody is in charge." The sight of Winston Churchill making his way through the rubble of blitzed London and barking orders to subordinates had the effect of strengthening resolve and dissolving fear among the affected public. Even lowly political executives at times perform this valuable emergency role.

But even when an emergency does not exist, there are frequently statutory deadlines or political deadlines—budgets, elections, schedules of compliance established by a higher level of government—which precipitate executive decisions largely uncomplicated by labored ethical considerations. Deadlines are great strengtheners of the resolve to choose. Those who would build theories of decisionmaking removed from the context of the clock and the calendar know nothing of the inner life of a political executive. And, even then, no executive in public life is free from having his life arbitrarily and often whimsically scheduled by real or fancied immediacies which are superimposed upon the clock and calendar, no matter how carefully the latter have been anticipated.

In brief, although almost every issue with which an elected executive must deal is charged with ethical dilemmas, it is rare that the executive has either the time, the context, or the liver for constructing balanced ethical judgments. He does what he must. Ethically, elected executives tend, like successful fighter pilots, to "fly by the seat of their pants." Speed is the enemy of deliberation, and in administration, speed—in the sense of dispatch—is often the condition of maintaining a tolerable if ineffable balance among those interests, obligations, and necessities which crowd the world of the elected executive.

All of this is not meant to suggest that ethical considerations are somehow peripheral to an elected executive's life. It is only to say that ethical issues are rarely trotted out for leisurely inspection and deliberate choice. This may be unfortunate, but my guess is that if ethical considerations were always carefully and honestly articulated in decisionmaking, the ensuing chaos—moral and administrative—would be impressive.

If we are talking about the real world, then, we are talking in large measure about the *inarticulate* moral premises of the office holder—the ethical signposts which a harried political executive catches out of the corner of his eye.

With this statement, of course, the essay could well end. Any attempt to list all of the precepts, proverbs, fables (and their rationalized versions) which conscience picks to guide or to justify actions, would lead to an endless and formless recitation of the obvious and the inscrutable. And ultimately such a recitation would tell us nothing about conscience itself, that ego-tempered temperer of egos; that culturebound transcender of culture; that ultimate sorter of ethical ambiguities. It gets us nowhere to suggest that all of the Philosophy 1-2 classroom stumpers are present in political life—as they are in all life. Should a cancer specialist be honest or kind? Ultimately, is it more honest to be kind or more kind to be honest? Is a half-truth a worse enemy of the truth than a falsehood? Should promises be kept if the situation changes (and when doesn't it change)? Should friends be reported if you know them to be mostly good and you know that they probably will not do it again? Should you subject someone to the consequences of wrongdoing if you are reasonably sure that the penalty is sufficiently harsh and inelastic as to be inequitable?

To pretend that there are clear religious, moral, or legal answers to such questions is to fly in the face of all sensitive moral inquiry.

How difficult the means-ends questions of living really are is known by every parent who ponders such matters. After a generation of permissiveness in raising children, we are finally returning to a belief that metes and bounds backed by sanctions are ultimately kinder to the growing child and the society than uninhibited license. But how many sanctions? How extensive the metes and bounds? Someone once commented that the Lord had left the two most difficult and important jobs in the world to amateurs: citizenship and parenthood. Elected political executives, at least most of them, are also amateurs, and their jobs may be no less difficult or important than the others mentioned. What is common to the life of all of these amateurs is that the value questions are extraordinarily complex, and the chances of adequate time for deliberation are slim.

But are there not peculiar ethical risks run by elected political executives? Surely, most people are not faced frequently with questions of bribery, spoils, corruption, favoritism. The difficulty is, neither are elected political executives and even when venality raises its head, it rarely looks to the responsible political executive as ugly as it appears in newspaper cartoons or Sunday sermons. Venality, like virtue, is rarely unambiguous. G. K. Chesterton wrote perceptively when he suggested that the error of Diogenes "lay in the fact that he omitted to notice that every man is both an honest and a dishonest man. Diogenes looked for his honest man inside every crypt and cavern. But he never thought of looking inside the thief. And that is where the Founder of Christianity found the honest man. He found him on a gibbet and promised him paradise."[1]

When the nicest people have rationalized their selfishness with a tactical deference to the public interest, elected political executives are often grateful that they are too preoccupied to be ethically astute. Even where venality seems clearest, as in the rare case of an attempt at straight bribery ("Mayor, here's $1,000 in five-dollar bills if you get

[1] G. K. Chesterton, *Charles Dickens: A Critical Study*, Dodd and Mead, New York, 1906, p. 222.

Ethical Problems of an Elected Political Executive

that easement through the council"—the political version of "payola"), the ethical issues may not be self-evident. Let us make some assumptions: suppose that the mayor knows that the easement will go through "on its merits" (begging what *that* slippery phrase means). Suppose further that the mayor knows that the party needs money not only to run the forthcoming election but to pay debts on a past election. Suppose the mayor knows further that the voting public has not responded favorably and positively to the appeal of the American Heritage Foundation for everyone to give to the party of his choice. Suppose finally that the mayor believes that a working two-party system is the nation's and the community's greatest safeguard of democracy and freedom. If it could be proved to the mayor's satisfaction that the lack of $1,000 at the moment could do irreparable damage to the two-party system in the area, would it be a higher principle in a naughty world for the mayor to accept the money on behalf of the party, or to refuse the money?

Stated this way, the issue is still not very complex for most people. "They've known what's right and wrong since they've been ten." You do not accept bribes, period; and you most certainly do not compound evil by cheating the briber. This is all very clear. But is it, really? There are ways of playing slight variations on this theme which would remove from the sternest Presbyterian moralist any burden of guilt. The briber has made a number of contributions to the party over the years. The latest thousand is simply another indication of his belief in the great principles of the party. On the easement question, every party member on the council, including the mayor, attempts to examine the issue on its merit. But a "will to believe" has set in—a subtle coloration of the problem. Good old Joe is a friend who provided all the favors for the party picnic. Isn't it fortunate that the merits of the easement case are on his side?

And bribery can take so many forms: money, favors, flattery, help in time of trouble, influence in building status. To pretend that bribery is a simple and easily spotted phenomenon is naive. To pretend it takes place only in politics is silly. I have seen the egos of older university professors successfully bribed by astute and ambitious instructors; I have seen great institutions bribe men into conformity with promises of promotions or demotions. I have seen them kill, spiritually, those who resisted. I have received threats that unless such and such happened, I'd be voted out of office at the next election. Is this not attempted bribery? Is money any more a thing of value than power or status or re-election? If there are clear moral distinctions here, they escape me, even though our cultural inheritance sanctions certain kinds of bribery and frowns on others.

I once asked a municipal judge in Middletown to tell me what pressures were most constant in trying to influence his impartial administration of justice. He thought a minute and then said, laughingly, "The university deans and the town clergy." But why should he have laughed? Certainly few would question the motives of deans and clergy in attempting to save the reputations of individuals known to them, and under their keep, who have been accused of wrongdoing. But what of the wrongdoer who has no "friend in court"? Anyone who has ever watched a municipal court in action over a period of time knows that "political influence" is frequently a corrective for the partial justice that results from the rich litigant's capacity to purchase superior legal talent. Middleclass justice is not always equitable to the poor. This is not to condone political influence in courts of law, it is to suggest that without political influence certain inequities might be greater than they are, and that those inequities need as much attention as overt or covert political influence.

I was never asked to fix a traffic or parking ticket in Middletown; but I cannot swear that tickets were not occasionally fixed while I was mayor. And I am not sure that under certain circumstances (*e.g.,* a hectic woman delayed in buying her six children school clothes) I would not have paid the dollar fine myself rather than penalize her for something beyond her effective control. Nothing is more unjust than unexceptional law except law that is all exceptions. Surely, one of the most difficult ethical problems in all governance is the drawing of lines between rules and exceptions. That the lines, to be moral, must be drawn near the rules end of the spectrum I do not question. But that exceptions are never warranted seems to me the most callous of all moral judgments.

To the moralist, words like bribery, favoritism, spoils, patronage, graft, are as clear and as evil as though bottled and marked with skull and crossbones. To those with political responsibility, on the other hand, it occasionally seems clear that poison can be therapeutic. The fact that poison is labelled with a skull and crossbones and placed back on a high shelf of the medicine closet may not mean that it is never to be used; only that it is to be used with care and in small doses. It is possible that if an elected executive had infinite time he might be able to discern ways to achieve his goals without using morally uncomfortable means—although the question of where rationalizations begin and end with this sort of game plays hob with moral certainty. But if an unskilled city job to a not-incompetent nationality-group representative might make the difference between winning or losing on an urban renewal referendum of vast benefit to the entire city for years to come, I know few elected executives who would boggle over making such an appointment even if the executive was convinced that someone else might do the unskilled job better.

George Bernard Shaw once wrote what many politicians must at times have felt. Shaw learned that a Labour candidate named Joseph Burgess had refused to compromise on some issue and had thereby lost his seat in Parliament. Shaw commented bitterly:

> When I think of my own unfortunate character, smirched with compromise, rotted with opportunism, mildewed by expediency—dragged through the mud of borough council and Battersea elections, stretched out of shape with wire-pulling, putrified by permeation, worn out by twenty-five years pushing to gain an inch here, or straining to stem a backrush, I do think Joe might have put up with just a speck or two on those white robes of his for the sake of the millions of poor devils who cannot afford any character at all because they have no friend in parliament. Oh, these moral dandies, these spiritual toffs, these superior persons. Who is Joe, anyhow, that he should not risk his soul occasionally like the rest of us?[2]

I was once confronted with a possible kickback on a fire truck purchase. The party representative reminded me that it cost money to run elections; that generosity from firetruck manufacturers to those who had the insight to see the need for public safety in their communities was rather standard; and that no one would really suffer. The gift would come as a preordained slice of the salesman's commission, who would give of his own income because "he believed in the principles of the Democratic Party." I drew myself up to my maximum height, stared at my good friend, and said in what I am sure must

[2] Hesketh Pearson, *G. B. S.*, Harper and Brothers, New York, 1942, p. 156.

have been the most patronizing of tones, "If the party needs $400 or $500, I shall be happy to try to raise the money personally; but I shall not do it that way." I then went a step further. I called the poor firetruck salesman into the office and made him add about $400 worth of extra equipment to the fire truck at the bid price he had quoted. In a swift double blow I had proved my moral worth and defended the taxpayers' interests. I had proved that at least in one American community "public office is a public trust."

I had also proved that it is easy to be moral when the pressure is not really on. Suppose the party coffers *had* been empty? Suppose my confident bluff to raise "$400 or $500" for the party had been called? Suppose the alternative to a Democratic re-election was the election of a rather disreputable Republican gang who would have practiced "boodle" with more frequency and with infinitely less flair than the Democrats? What then? And why should we refuse to accept money for the imperative cause of political party machinery, almost regardless of source, when the so-called "good" people of the community would not be caught dead giving to their political party—to the system of options which does far more than the Constitution to guarantee freedom and democracy?

I could not be a partner to a kickback, not because I had carefully weighed the moral issues, but because my moral viscera told me it was wrong. Unfortunately, my moral viscera are not always right. If they were right in this particular case, they were right for reasons removed from the issue at hand. They were right because, without sufficient time and eloquence, I could not have explained any contrary action— if forced to by the local newspaper or an official inquiry—to the satisfaction of the adult public whose moral viscera are quite as dogmatic as mine. I thereby would have undercut the public's faith in my honesty, and would have damaged that most priceless of all public executive resources: the public's confidence. There would then have been an unhappy and unproductive feedback into everything else I did or tried to do as an elected official. The moral dilemma remains however: for I am confident that if I had had the insight to have taken the kickback and the time and eloquence to have explained to the public why I had done it—describing to them the impossible position they put politicians into by their not assuming disinterested responsibility for financing party campaigns—they would have seen the point and respected me for my action. They even might have taken the lesson to heart and decided to give to their party as frequently and as richly as they give to other causes they value—such as community chests and churches.

The only serious ethical struggle I had with party leaders in Middletown dealt with a request for a zoning exception. Here I was firm, morally aroused, and dogmatic, and would be to this day. The story is quickly told. A contractor, who had contributed liberally to both political parties locally, hired a leading Democratic lawyer to plead for a commercial spot zone in a strictly residential area. The people of the area were almost solidly opposed to the change. Even if they had not been, nothing can ruin the orderly and esthetic development of a growing city like politically inspired spot zoning in contravention of a general plan. The members of the zoning committee, to their credit, said to me, "Mayor, there's a lot we'll do for the party, but we won't do this." The final showdown on this case took place in the lawyer's office with all major party leaders present. I walked in swinging. I made it quite clear that if the plumbing broke down in city hall, I would hire a licensed Democratic plumber over a licensed Republican plumber any day of the week; that if the law did not force us to go to bid, I would buy insurance from a Democratic rather than a Republican insurance agent; but that when it came to what Edmund Burke once called "the permanent forces" in the community, I was ready to do battle. I suggested that although there was much in politics that one rendered to Caesar, almost without qualms; city planning was rendered only to God. A few party leaders were upset; but most of them were understanding; and the lawyer in question, who over the years has been one of the most brilliant as well as constructive forces in the community and state, had the grace to accept my position without rancor.

But I have already dwelt far too long on such matters. In my two years as mayor, these kinds of party issues could not have represented more than one-fiftieth of my working time. Contrary to what many people seem to believe, the hard ethical issues of public life rarely concern party politics. Party decisions tend to roll according to pre-set patterns. Every elected executive works out a few obvious benchmarks for relationships with political leaders (for example, "consult party leaders on all appointments, but solicit their help in trading little appointments to the party for big appointments to you"). In any case, to suggest that most party officials are frequently ethical "problems" is to distort their normal role beyond recognition. For every occasion when a party leader asked me for a favor that disturbed my conscience, I can think of a dozen times when *that very same party leader* helped me defend the public interest against the importunities of non-party pressure groups.

Upon reflection, it is my firm belief that insofar as party politics interferes with the pursuit of the public interest, it is largely a result of the necessities of campaign finance. Most venality in public life could be abolished or reduced to insignificance if the public would assume responsibility for broadly based campaign financing and would insist upon the public auditing and disclosure of all campaign gifts and expenditures. This would not eliminate corruption entirely, for wherever power and money converge some venality will be found. But our present method of financing political campaigns is, in my estimation, the single most corrupting factor in our political life—local, national, and especially, state.

If what have been discussed so far are not the major ethical issues of the elected executive, what are? To the man who is ethically sensitive, the hairturning issues are those which involve impossible choices among contending interpretations of the public interest. Again, the necessity of dispatch is psychologically therapeutic; but the drain on energy and conscience is substantial nonetheless. Take ten or a dozen problems which faced me as mayor, and which are typical of perhaps a hundred which I faced in two years as an elected executive.

1. A peacock farm on the edge of town kept neighbors awake for a month or so a year during the peacock mating season. The City was asked by the neighbors to see to it that the birds were quieted. Ethical question: is a temporary irritation—including loss of sleep—for ten families worth the destruction of a hobby and a partial livelihood for one person?

2. A leading department store on Main Street said it had to have a rear access service garage on Broad Street or it would be forced to leave town. Broad Street was zoned residential. Ethical question: would

Ethical Problems of an Elected Political Executive

the loss of the department store be a greater loss than a break in the city's zoning pattern?

3. The best detective on the chronically underpaid police force is suspected of taking protection money from some local two bit gamblers. The evidence is too vague and unsubstantial to stand in court. Ethical question: is the *possibility* of the evidence being correct important enough to warrant a substantial investigation, with a consequent probable loss in efficiency and morale in the police department during and long after the investigation, a certain loss in public confidence in the whole force; and the ever present possibility that the rumor was planted by a crank? And out of the many pressing issues coming across the mayor's desk, how much time and effort does such an investigation warrant from the mayor himself?

4. The whole scheme of volunteer fire departments is looked upon by the chief of the city's only paid department as wasteful, inefficient, and dangerous to the public safety. The volunteers claim that their firefighting record is topnotch, that they save the taxpayers money. Ethical question: if neither side can be proved incorrect, how does one weigh the values of volunteer community endeavors against marginal inefficiencies in operation of a vital service?

5. Many years ago, one department store was farsighted enough to have bought up some land for offstreet parking. This offstreet parking gave the store quite a competitive advantage. The city, in a new municipal parking program, needed a portion of the private parking lot assembled by the department store years before. When established, the municipal lot might destroy the store's competitive advantage. Ethical question: at what point does the public interest demand that private farsightedness be penalized?

6. Two mayors in four years happened to have lived on Wyllys Avenue. Wyllys Avenue desperately needed repaving. But so did some other streets in the city. Ethical question: should Wyllys Avenue be paved, granted a heavy presumption that many citizens would claim that the mayor had "taken care of himself?"

7. A federal grant-in-aid cut in half the city's welfare load, making a sinecure out of one of the two city welfare positions. The holder of the sinecure was a Negro appointed by the opposition party. Ethical question: should work somehow be "made" for the Negro, or should he be dropped? (For anyone who knows the problems of status, morale,

and upward mobility among Negroes in a largely white community, the political questions posed by this case are easy compared to the long-range ethical questions.)

8. The virulent opposition of a local printer-publicist might be tamed on a few key issues with the proper placing of a few city printing contracts. Ethical question: obvious.

9. Buying of tires in wholesale lots would save the taxpayers $300 a year—about one cent per citizen per annum. A score of little Middletown tire merchants would lose ten dollars or more in income. Ethical question: how does one balance one cent each for 30,000 people versus ten dollars each for twenty merchants?

10. Parents concerned with the safety of their children on the way to and from school are constantly demanding increased police protection and more sidewalks. A more legitimate demand would be hard to imagine. But there are limits. Ethical question: granted that *total* safety never can be assured, what grounds beyond obvious necessity and "the squeaky wheel gets the grease" can be found for awarding or denying protection?

11. A health officer is technically qualified and conscientious, but egregiously officious. Ethical question: is the damage done to the city government's relations with its citizens by the meticulous and unfeeling enforcement of ordinances likely to be sufficiently serious to warrant the health officer's dismissal?

12. There is a likelihood that one of the major industries in town will have to close down a sizable slice of its operations. This may mean 2,000 unemployed. A steel company is looking for a New England site for a steel mill. It finds an "ideal" location in Middletown. That "ideal" location is a stretch of the Connecticut River which is unspoiled and is deeply treasured by small boat owners and by nature lovers. Ethical question: is the provision of employment for 2,000 people worth the destruction forever of natural beauty?

These are samples of the tough ones. And in most cases, the ethical values are sufficiently balanced so that no matter which side the mayor takes, half the concerned citizens in the community will charge him—and with considerable justification in their own minds—with having sold out. This is one of the reasons for the low image of politicians in our society: the fact that the losing cause in public policy generally

Ethical Problems of an Elected Political Executive 33

has substantial merit on its side, with the consequence that the loser can see nothing but venality or partiality in the elected official's decision. People get sore at politicians for the same reason they throw pop bottles at umpires: the disagreements always come on the close ones. If only citizens could pause on occasion to realize that the issues really are complex; that most elected officials do the best they can to be fair; that the peaceful resolution of conflict is a vast service to humankind, and is a most difficult art; that Solomon himself was perplexed by some of the issues posed by communities of men.

If I should be asked today how I resolved, in my own mind, the ethical dilemmas posed on the preceding pages, I should not know how to answer. Most of the dilemmas were not mine to resolve alone. Other people shared official power with me, and many citizens without official power assumed substantial unofficial responsibility for community decisions. There is not the loneliness and, perhaps, terror in executive decisionmaking at the local level which I assume there must often be at higher executive levels in American government. Consequences of errors in judgment are far less apocalyptic.

But insofar as I had to make up my mind by myself, or felt that my judgment might be determining in the minds of others, I did repair to two or three very general propositions for ethical guidance. In practice, the propositions were never articulated, but in retrospect, I know that they were there. All of them had been woven into my life by parental, religious, and academic influences—in most cases by all three. My father, although never a minister, was a Professor of Religion and a firm believer in the Social Gospel. My studies at Oxford had brought me close to Immanuel Kant and Jean Jacques Rousseau. Ideas like "the categorical imperative" and "the general will" were connected in my mind with such biblical injunctions as "Let justice roll down as waters; and righteousness as a mighty stream." I had nothing in my system that told me what was right; but I did have something in my system that told me to search for what was right. The most helpful single question I could ask myself seemed to be, "What do you want Middletown to be like ten years from now?" Against this, many things fell into place. I wanted more beauty, fewer slums, less bigotry, more recreation, more community spirit, a more sustained sense of public responsibility, a more dynamic and prosperous economy, better education, a stronger and more truly competitive two-party system, and a heightened sense of personal dignity for all. These were some of the benchmarks against which specific ethical issues were measured or rationalized. They were not my marks. They were the marks of the civilization of which I was a miniscule and clouded reflection. As Carl Becker once wrote:

> To have faith in the dignity and worth of the individual man as an end in himself; to believe that it is better to be governed by persuasion than by coercion; to believe that fraternal goodwill is more worthy than a selfish and contentious spirit; to believe that in the long run all values are inseparable from the love of truth and the disinterested search for it; to believe that knowledge and the power it confers should be used to promote the welfare and happiness of all men rather than to serve the interests of those individuals and classes whom fortune and intelligence endow with temporary advantage—these are the values which are affirmed by the traditional democratic ideology. . . . They are the values which since the time of Buddha and Confucius, Solomon and Zoroaster, Plato and Aristotle, Socrates and Jesus, men have commonly employed to measure the advance or decline of civilization, the values they have celebrated in the saints and sages whom they have agreed to canonize. They are the values which readily lend themselves to rational justification, yet need no justification.[3]

There are, perhaps, two other matters which ought to be touched upon in an essay of this nature. The first has to do with the effect of power upon personality. Acton is quite explicit that "All power corrupts and absolute power corrupts absolutely." This I cannot gainsay. I remember one evening when I was returning with political friends from a television performance. For a half-hour they told me what a brilliant performance mine had been. By the end of the half-hour I was aware only that a new political star had been born on the horizon: namely, myself, and that I could not long deny the people of the State of Connecticut the chance to vote for me either for Governor or at the very least for United States Senator. It was not until I got home that my wife—with that wonderful sixth sense of a level-headed and thoughtful woman—reminded me that my performance had, in fact, been a little on the mediocre side—but that she was sure

[3]Carl Becker, *New Liberties for Old,* H. Milford, Oxford University Press, London 1941, pp. 149 f.

I had just had an off night. The most devastating traps of public office are the ones set to catch the ego. It is so easy to forget that the tribute is to the office, not to the person. Even a mayor stands out a little: fathers bring up their daughters to "shake the mayor's hand"; the mayor sits at head tables; he officiates; he is often the central figure in ceremony. All this inflates the sense of personal worth and waters the thirsty garden of vanity. The consequences are often pathetic, often silly, sometimes dangerous. But Acton was wrong in suggesting that the only flowers in the garden of vanity are the weeds of corruption. Power may corrupt, but it also can ennoble. The sense that you, and the office you hold, are widely valued, often creates a heightened sense of responsibility, a desire to live close to the public expectation, a wish to become a kind of community example. Too few people appreciate the ennobling effect of public office. I have seen men utterly transformed by a judgeship. A politician—an old pro in western Connecticut—once confided to me that he hated all judges. "What are they but some hack lawyers who happened to know a politician?" And he went on, "After you've made 'em, what do they do? They turn around and kick you in the teeth! They draw their robes around them as though they was Solon or something! You can't touch them! Who the hell do they think they are?" The fact is that they think they *are* Solon; they suddenly realize that instead of petty politicians they are an essential part of the fabric of civilization —a fabric which can last only so long as there is a widespread public belief that judges in courts of law will try to be just. And what is true of judges is equally true of elected executives.

The ennobling effect of public office is one of its greatest psychic dividends. Those who believe that men seek to hold public office only because it gives them power and status do not appreciate the importance to many men of simply feeling that the job they hold makes them better members of the human race. The heightened capacity for doing good in the world is one of the key attractions of political power, and from my limited observations is a far more fundamental factor in determining the direction of men's ambitions than the baubles and tinsel of temporary status and deference.

This brings me to my final point. All ethical questions ultimately revert to propositions about the nature of man. The underlying complexity of ethical questions stems from the fact that man is morally ambiguous and teleologically inscrutable. Perched precariously on a whirling planet, blind to his origins, blind to his reasons for being, beset by the terrors of nature and of his own creation, man wobbles drunkenly between a certainty that he is nothing and an occasional, blinding revelation that he has a transcendent dignity and perhaps destiny. When man feels alienated from his universe, he may huddle in fear with his fellow men; but he cannot reach them with that fullness of feeling, that intenseness of identity, which is suggested by the Christian concept of love, or by the civil concept of community. I am not a mystical person, but I sense strongly that my best moments as mayor came when I felt—in an almost religious way—that what we were attempting to do in Middletown had meaning beyond itself. I remember Fred Smith, the editor of the local paper, once writing me an intimate note when I was particularly discouraged about the public response to some issue. "Never," he wrote, "lose faith in your neighbors." And he went on to explain, not that they were perfect, but that he had known them for a long time, and that they would ultimately respond to the good if they could be shown the good.

Surely this is the ultimate ethical postulate in a democracy: not that man is good, but that he is capable of good; not that he is wise, but that he is capable of valuing wisdom; not that he is free from corruption, but that he is desperately sick of it; not that he has fashioned the good society, but that he has caught an unforgettable glimpse of it. Ultimately the ethical problems of the elected executive are what they are for all human beings: the struggle to discover ends and means which heighten man's sense of individual worth in an ever more meaningful, extensive, and inclusive community.

Comment by Paul H. Appleby:

In some ways, similar problems in larger cities would probably be tougher, in other ways perhaps not so tough because of having less intimate personal involvements. At the national level of government I think the ethical problems posed by parties and their leaders are still less frequent, and probably more manageable while the problems posed by interest groups of other sorts are probably more complicated and in mass absolutely larger. An interest group with several millions of members somehow partakes more of a "public-interest" group—or seems to—than an interest group of a few hundreds.

Stephen K. Bailey may yield a little too much to Acton's dictum about the corrupting effect of power before he goes on to its ennobling effects. Under democracy,

Ethical Problems of an Elected Political Executive

where a two-party system is real, it is my observation that much vested power results *only* in ennobling him in whom it is vested. I am fond of quoting a thoughtful and eminent civil servant who served the national government for forty-two years. He declared it to be his observation that every President attempted progressively less exercise of power the longer he was in office, the more he reserved it for especially needed and important use.

Comment by Bernard Mandelbaum:

In a most admirable effort to deal with the specifics of the practical problems that face the government official, Bailey seems to bend backward in denying the tremendous force of a seemingly impractical notion, "doing what's right."

There is a second trap into which, I believe, Bailey's statement falls. One of the most devastating rationalizations for irresponsible behavior in contemporary society is the cry that time does not permit the more thoughtful, meaningful, ethical decision and action. Usually the result is that time is lost by the time "saved" in making the wrong decision, which then requires retracing one's steps—not to talk of the pain and anguish that follow in the wake of wrong decisionmaking.

Bailey indicates, validly, that ethical decisions are arrived at with the help of an intuition rooted in a pattern of character that is "woven into . . . life by parental, religious, and academic influences . . ." This pattern, the roots of decision, has its own roots, namely, a conception of the universe where right and wrong—although not always simply determined—is as true about the nature of the world as any law of nature. This law of righteousness, although elusive in the specific configurations of daily events, is unequivocally clear often enough.

Our times demand a radical change in our approach to the standards of behavior. Elements of such a radical change, which can be derived from the influence of the scholar and academician, include: reflection before action (patience), concern for detail (sacredness of the individual), working for long-range results (another form of patience). I would have wanted to see greater stress on these virtues in Bailey's analysis of good decisionmaking in government.*

*For comment by David B. Truman, see pp. 467–468.

CHAPTER III

Ethics and Practical Politics

By JAMES MacGREGOR BURNS

TWO YEARS AGO, when I was running for Congress, a prominent businessman invited me to stop in to see him the next time I was in his city. When I did so he told me that he liked the campaign I was conducting and wanted to make a substantial contribution. There was only one hitch. Since he was in business and had to deal with Republicans as well as Democrats, it would have to be an unreported contribution, or given to me through circuitous channels. But this of course was standard operating procedure in politics, he added, and the money, in cash, was waiting for me if I would stop by the bookkeeper on the way out.

I told him that I could not accept the contribution under those circumstances. Under the law, contributions had to be reported, and I did not care for the circuitous methods. He was surprised by this reaction—and more than a little hurt. He argued mildly that most financial contributions were handled this way, including those to the most honest and devoted officeholders, several of whom he mentioned. After a short and awkward discussion, I left.

I would like to report that I look back on the incident as a great stroke for virtue. Actually I look back on it with some discomfiture. The man who offered the contribution was one of the most civic-minded men in the city. His wife was also active in a number of good causes. I knew enough about him, and enough about myself, to be sure that there would be no strings attached. I doubt that there was anything he would want from the federal government. From his standpoint, he was trying to play the role of the good citizen contributing, as good citizens are supposed to do, to the operation of politics. On my side, the net effect was to deprive me of some money that would have helped me accomplish, through newspaper advertising or radio, my main objective of taking the issues to the people.

I relate this incident because it illustrates the two main contentions

I will advance here on the relation of ethics and practical politics: first, that the practical ethical problems faced by politicians (a word I use here without invidious connotation) are usually too complex to be settled by reference to simple norms of conduct; and second, that practical politicians cannot be expected to take leadership in establishing and maintaining norms of conduct—we can hope at most only that they will observe those that are established.

It is hard, I think, for most people to understand the circumstances under which men seek to gain or retain office. If the office is a substantial one, a man dedicates himself, his family, his friends, and often his savings and reputation to a great leap in the dark. Unlike almost every other endeavor, there is no second place. A businessman may come off second best to a competitor in a given year and still may turn a good profit; for the politician 50 per cent of the vote minus one vote means utter failure, and no matter how well conducted his campaign may have been, he will get little credit for his effort. Indeed, the rivals in his own party will take some satisfaction from his defeat because it will clear the way for their own efforts to get the nomination in the next campaign.

Politically the candidate conducts his operations on a darkling plain; ethically the situation is even more confused. For one thing, rumors float about that his opponent is up to all sorts of nefarious activities. Even though he discounts some of these reports, enough truth may remain in them for him to wonder why he should follow high standards of conduct—for example, in his attacks on the opposition, use of whispering campaigns, handling of money, distortion of his opponent's record and position on issues, and so on—when his adversary is resorting to all kinds of devious methods. He has the nagging feeling that the worst thing of all would be an election outcome that would seem to vindicate shady dealings. Far better for him to make some minor departures from propriety so that the more decent candidate will win—and have a chance to raise his standards when finally in office. From this nagging feeling it is a short distance to the conclusion that any expediency is permissible to defeat his opponent and keep the scoundrel out of office. What could be worse, the candidate concludes, than to let people see that improper conduct actually enables the bad guy to win out. Far better to make a few concessions now in order to show that evil cannot be triumphant.

Ethics and Practical Politics

And since the other candidate may be going through somewhat the same train of thought, it is easy for the campaign to deteriorate.

The practical ethical problems that a candidate faces are not easy to resolve. I am not talking about outright violation of the law, but of the more complex problems that rise in a campaign. For example, how much should the opponent's record or position be distorted? Not at all, one may reply; but the politician is engaged in a highly competitive operation in which he cannot even arouse interest of the voters unless issues are simplified and differences sharpened. After all, the billboards and magazine advertisements promoting toothpaste and cigarettes grotesquely exaggerate the virtues of their product—why should the candidate not do the same? His great problem is the apathy of the people; but they cannot be aroused, it is clear, by a rational and specific discussion of the issues, and the precise differences between the position of the two candidates. In a world dominated by Madison Avenue techniques of persuasion, the candidate will follow the herd.

The problem is intensified by the absurd standards set in some of our election laws. This is especially true of financial requirements. The limits set on campaign receipts and expenses by most state and national laws have long been recognized as utterly unrealistic. People allow the cosmetic, tobacco, and other non-essential industries to spend hundreds of millions advertising their products, but for some reason the candidates trying to sell themselves and their ideas are to be restricted to a pittance. Since most candidates simply cannot begin to engage the interest of the voters on such pittances, and since many of the laws were passed tongue-in-cheek, by and large the only candidates who observe financial limitations are those in a noncompetitive election situation. To be sure, it was the politicians in office who passed the election laws, but in most cases they acted in response to moralistic impulses of the people—impulses that had no relation to a realistic assessment of the task facing candidates for the more important offices.

The candidate, moreover, tends to become the slave of his own campaign forces. More than any other competitor, I think, the politician tends to become surrounded by people who support him uncritically and egg him on to questionable practices. Some of these supporters are simply self-interested—they are trying to prove their loyalty and devotion by advocating what they think the candidate wants advocated. Others become so fanatically devoted to the candidate in the fervor of the campaign that they, even more than he, lose their critical capacity. More and more the aim becomes victory regardless of the means used.

In a broader sense, the electoral groups supporting the candidate tend to give him blind support. This tendency has been well documented, I think, in the case of James M. Curley in Boston. His brushes with the law never seemed to hurt his standing among his large personal following; perhaps they strengthened his standing. One of his most enthusiastic receptions from Bostonians came on his return from prison. The sociological or psychological reasons for this situation are well known; Curley had a kind of Robin Hood aroma; he had been attacked by outside forces (in Washington); the attack was perceived as directed against his personal supporters as well as against Curley; the in-group was resisting the out-group. In a nation of sub-nations this means that local groups will adopt their own ethical standards as weapons to resist the standards (or claims) of the nation as a whole.

It is this situation—less dramatic, perhaps—that the candidate faces at every kind of hand. In twenty-five years of active politics, I have never known a voter to turn against a man he personally knows and likes because of his known violation of norms of conduct. The capacity to rationalize is a mighty thing.

Two examples will illustrate my point. A few years ago, a congressman was indicted and convicted on income tax charges. One would think that this was about the most heinous crime a man could commit —as a congressman he had raised taxes that he himself then tried to evade. But this congressman was triumphantly renominated by his party and re-elected to office. In my own campaign, on a much smaller scale, more than one person told me that he thought I was the better candidate, but my opponent had fixed a traffic ticket, or had had a suspended license returned. The vivid, vital favor that my opponent had done was far more important than the other hazy and general considerations about the candidates' backgrounds and positions on issues, or about the propriety of an almost mechanical procedure whereby state legislators fix penalties for highway offences. And in a way I could not blame the voter.

Because of all this I do not think we can expect the politician to take leadership in establishing higher norms of conduct. He is struggling too hard to stay in office, to defeat his adversary, to cope with the host of little problems that come along. The more idealistic or ethical his approach to politics, the more likely that the wrong man will win and hence make ethics and idealism appear to be handicaps in the world of practical politics.

But the game is not lost. The thing that mainly motivates a practical politician is the quest for victory, and that quest is not always unrelated to ethical standards. The extent to which a candidate observes such standards turns on his estimate as to how powerfully they are operating in his district. Just as candidates are abnormally sensitive to what their opponents are doing, or are reputed to be doing, so they are even more sensitive to the attitudes of ostensibly neutral observers —especially newspaper editors and nonpartisan groups like the League of Women Voters.

A case in point was Franklin D. Roosevelt's experience in his quest for the Democratic nomination in 1932. At a certain point in the preconvention struggle it became apparent that the Roosevelt forces were trying to bring about a change in the rules in the middle of the game. It seems doubtful that Roosevelt or anyone in his entourage were very much concerned with this as an ethical principle, as compared with what they could gain from making the change. But once the opposition made this into an ethical problem, the Roosevelt forces beat a hasty retreat. For editors and other keepers of public morals were picking the issue up and making it into a *cause célèbre*.

Where ethical standards are as thin and hazy as in this country, where they vary so much from group to group, the politician will be at a loss to improve them. The groups opposed to him will attack his norms of conduct no matter what he does, and his own groups will support him no matter what he does. He operates in an anomic campaign situation. But he is always concerned, too, about the "independent" voter who may lie athwart the crucial 49 per cent to 51 per cent of the voting spectrum. These people, rightly or wrongly, are considered to be especially responsive to the independent observers standing outside the candidate's supporters or his opponent's. It may well be that the keepers of public morals do not have nearly the influence that some suppose. But the same confusion and darkness that envelop political operations and foster impropriety also serve to exaggerate the power of the supposedly neutral outsider. Editors and ministers and teachers may have more influence than they realize.

Some moral philosophers have concluded that it may be wrong or at least illusory to ask the combatants in an arena to follow any guide other than the pursuit of victory. Nation-states, instead of trying to inflict their moral principles on the rest of the world, might better restrict themselves to maintaining their own integrity and role in a limited orbit. Businessmen, instead of trying to represent themselves as guardians of the national economy and polity, might better restrict themselves to competing sensibly for markets and profits. The theory is that people who indulge in ordinary, everyday, pragmatic competition are operating in a relatively restrained, rational, and predictable fashion, and hence reasonably conceived self-interest is not always a bad principle of conduct. The same may be true of the politician. We might like to put him on a higher level, because his struggles for votes so closely affect the nature of our ultimate rulers, and because the character of our rulers in turn closely affects the kind of laws we pass—which in turn are supposed to incorporate ethical standards. But as in the case of the nation-state and of the businessman, we may be putting an impossible burden on the shoulders of the politician. Let him compete—and let the rest of us try to establish the ethical framework within which competition can be as moderate and honest as possible.[1]

[1] For comment by Wayne A. R. Leys, see pp. 80–81.

CHAPTER IV

Moral Dimensions of Politics

By EUGENE J. McCARTHY

THE ETHICAL NORMS of men who hold public office have been the concern of thoughtful men throughout history. Aristotle assumed that the true politician is he who has "studied virtue above all things." In a *Federalist* paper attributed to Alexander Hamilton, he asserts that "the aim of every political constitution is, or ought to be, first to obtain for rulers men who possess most wisdom to discern, and most virtue to pursue, the common good of society; and in the next place, to take the most effectual precautions for keeping them virtuous. . . ."

This ideal, of course, is rarely reached; there is, rather, a tendency to be cynical about morality in government. In an article on "Corruption," Peter Odegard in the 1937 edition of the *Encyclopaedia of Social Sciences* observed that among the great modern nations, the United States had the least enviable record with regard to the probity of its public officials. Another critical judgment was passed by Senator J. W. Fulbright who in commenting on the investigation of the Reconstruction Finance Corporation in 1951 said:

> As our study of the RFC progressed, we were confronted more and more with problems of ethical conduct. . . . How do we deal with those who under the guise of friendship accept favors which offend the spirit of the law, but do not violate the letter? What of the men outside government who suborn those inside it? . . . Who is more at fault, the bribed or the bribers? . . . One of the most disturbing aspects of this problem of moral conduct is the revelation that among so many influential people, morality has become identical with legality.

Today the findings of congressional and of executive investigations, as well as reports on state and local governmental officials, indicate that public officials in 1960 are not very clearly different or better than they were in 1937 or in 1951. Men who have attempted to defend themselves have revealed through their explanations that their standards of conduct are extremely flexible, personal, and generally quite inadequate.

The explanation of the present state of public morality or immorality is not to be found in a simple one-cause explanation. Neither is it to be found in sweeping generalizations regarding the inevitable corruption in democratic government; nor is the final answer to be found in a study of techniques and procedures of government. We must look to more complex and fundamental causes: first, the general level of morality prevailing in the United States; second, the level of morality in public business and in the legal profession, as well as in other professions directly bearing on political life; and third, the lack of a strong tradition of political responsibility and of the honor of public office in the United States.

Let us look first at the general level of morality in the United States. It is a matter of common knowledge, sustained by statistical record, that this level is not as high as we might like it to be. This is not wholly the result of indifference to principles. On the contrary, part of our difficulty arises from confusion about values. Philosophical and religious beliefs do affect conduct; ideas do have consequences. When a leading scholar declares that "the seat of ethics is in the heart"; when it is acceptable to assert that the only absolute is that there are no absolutes; when religious and philosophical leaders lend their name to a declaration of their faith in man's ability "to make his way by his own means to the truth which is true to him"; we should not be surprised to find some government officials making up rules which may be convenient to their own purposes. Since in a democracy there is a carryover of influence from the general level to the government and since men who are a part of the general populace become office-holders, standards observed and accepted by the people will be reflected in the conduct of the officials of the country.

The conduct of public officials is likely to be affected even more directly by the standards of conduct accepted in business and in those professions more closely associated with government. It is significant that in almost every case in which an accused public official has attempted to defend himself, he has argued that his actions were fully within the bounds of accepted practices in the business world or of the professional group to which he belonged. It is not fair to say that selfishness is the only motive in business or in a profession, but

Moral Dimensions of Politics

there is evidence that personal gain is given too much consideration. The recent exposures regarding television and radio indicate that economic advantage seems to be sufficient justification, or at least the reason to explain action. In the business world the opportunist and the sharp dealer have not been eliminated or generally discouraged. There are the high pressure artists, the dealers of influence, and the public relations men, some of them following the philosophy of one who explained that his work was simply to find "doubt" and to expand it—which could be stated from the opposite point of view as finding the truth and contracting it as the case demanded. All of these disciples of Hermes have been given a place, and oftentimes they sit if not at the head of the table, at least on the right hand. The term *free enterprise,* which has a good and defensible meaning, has been abused. For many it has been the excuse for a sweeping rejection of social responsibility and of social justice. It has encouraged a rejection of the traditional idea of justice and has made it for many a thing of purely academic or historic interest and has made legality the watchword for too many.

The third general cause of the diminished sense of morality in our government is the lack of a strong tradition of the responsibilities and the honor of public office. In the beginning of our national existence, we cut ourselves away from the aristocratic traditions of the old world and adopted an egalitarian political philosophy. Every citizen was given a share in the political power, whereas in the old order this power was restricted to the nobility. In transferring to each citizen political rights we somehow, it seems, failed to transfer the corresponding sense of responsibility which the old traditions and institutions had with some success imposed upon the nobility. We failed to develop a new institution and a new tradition of directly attaching obligations and responsibility to political office as a substitute for the system which fixes such responsibility to birth and class.

What can be done to bring about an improvement in the public attitude toward government? First, the general level of morality in the United States must be raised. This is, of course, basically an individual and personal problem, though it is also related to churches and schools.

Second, ethical standards in business and in the professions must be raised, primarily for the sake of business and the professions, but also because improved standards in these fields will affect public morality as well as morality in government.

Third, we must take immediate action to develop in the United States understanding and acceptance of the special responsibility of public office and to lay the foundations upon which we can build a tradition of the high order and responsibility of government service.

The effort to establish effective norms of conduct in American government is complicated by a number of factors and conditions.

There is, for example, the question of the size and complexity of government activities. Measured in terms of revenue and expenditures, the federal government is an $80,000,000,000 a year operation. In addition, the combined state and local governments spend and collect approximately $40,000,000,000 a year. Initiating and supervising operations of this magnitude dwarf any other problems of professional ethics.

Functions and responsibilities vary greatly and effective norms of conduct must be developed for various situations. In the federal government alone there are three constitutionally distinct branches: the legislative, the executive, and the judicial, and a fourth, extra-constitutional or postconstitutional branch made up of the independent regulatory agencies like the Interstate Commerce Commission, the Federal Power Commission, the Federal Communications Commission. These agencies combine legislative or policy decisions with executive and quasijudicial functions. In many instances the jurisdictional lines between these branches are not clear.

The press within recent years has been filled with phrases such as "violation of the principle of separation of powers," or "upsetting the balance of powers," or "legislation by the courts," or "usurpation of legislative function by the executive," "congressional interference with executive operations," and the like. More effective norms of conduct are needed for all divisions of government, but especially in these gray areas of jurisdiction where even conscientious public officials do not know clearly where to draw the lines.

The judicial branch of government at both federal and state levels has done most to establish an effective set of rules for the conduct of its courts and of the officers of the courts. The area of operation is, of course, limited and defined, and consequently the work of estab-

Moral Dimensions of Politics

lishing norms of conduct is made easier. Judges generally are above scandal, and courts are most careful to insure due process for all.

In the legislative branch of the government, each body—the House and the Senate—is responsible for its own proceedings and is the final judge of the fitness of its own members. The seating of members is occasionally challenged, but the disposition on the part of Congress is to respect the action of the voters of a congressional district or of a state. Censure or condemnation has occasionally been voted in the Congress, but only after extreme provocation.

The question of conflict of interest between the private interest of individual members of the Congress and legislation under consideration is occasionally raised, though it has been suggested that members refrain from voting on matters involving personal advantage to them. Occasionally members do refrain in committee. For the most part the gain to the individual congressman includes advantage or the advancement of an interest which is shared by many other persons, including constituents. Consequently all of these would be unrepresented and would suffer if the individual member refrained. Criminal actions involving such things as kickbacks on the part of employees, income tax evasion and the like have been exposed and carried through the courts. Within recent years, one member of Congress was re-elected while serving out a sentence for income tax evasion.

It is generally accepted, however, that the thorough public examination which goes along with campaigns for election to the House and to the Senate and continuous surveillance by the press constitute a thorough and continuous discipline of the House and of the Senate and makes specific regulations unnecessary.

It is within the executive departments and in the independent regulatory agencies that the most serious problems arise, and it is in these offices that conflict between public duty and private interest is most likely to occur and most likely to go undiscovered or unchallenged.

The problems and involvements are of many kinds. Often there are circumstances and questions of intention which make it difficult to pass judgment on the legality of the relationship and likewise on its morality. For example, conversations or discussions between petitioners and government officials are often necessary preliminaries to decisions, but when these discussions are held during weekends at resort hotels at the expense of petitioners, the question of undue influence or improper influence inevitably arises. The issue of conflict of interest is clearly involved when a person holds government office and at the same time has an active interest in a business directly affected by government policy or procurement. Conflict of interest is not so clear when the government official is a former employee of a firm doing business with the government. An additional complication arises when future employment possibilities are involved.

There are in a democracy, I believe, two forces which can be effectively brought to bear on public service: one, the force of public opinion, and two, the force of laws and regulations.

Ultimately and basically the force of public opinion is demonstrated at the ballot box. Turning the rascals out is a time tested procedure in democratic government. Voting, however, is not an automatic guarantee of good government. The power of public opinion and attitude must be strong between elections, as well as during campaigns and on election days.

An alert press is essential as is an active and responsible opposition party. For either press or opposition to be effective, it is important that channels of information be kept open. In the federal government in recent years, there has been an increase in the use of executive privilege as a basis for withholding information. The right of the public to know must be carefully safeguarded. Knowledge of the facts is essential to sound judgment. No measure of goodwill will make up for the lack of such knowledge.

A second effective force for morality in government is that of regulations and laws. There are limits, of course, to the effectiveness of these devices, but they are not wholly ineffective. Lindsay Warren, as Comptroller General of the United States, testified before the Douglas committee as follows:

> For a long time I thought that no code of ethics or morals would insure a high standard of conduct of the Government's business. I have felt that moral integrity is something innate, the result of a person's conscience, upbringing, and education and not something controllable by regulations, no matter how rigid. . . . Without good administration the best written codes will fail. However, the things I have seen in my 25 years in Washington, especially the shocking disclosures of the war and postwar period, have made me more receptive to an offi-

Moral Dimensions of Politics 51

cial moral code. In the first place, I no longer feel that we can rely on the moral training of all those who come into or deal with the government.[1]

Although individual offices and agencies have provided some guidance for their employees, there is no broad code of ethics for federal government officials and no comprehensive set of laws with penalties covering official conduct. Legislation is needed to clarify and to set broad limits of what is proper and what is excluded. A subcommittee of the Senate, of which Senator Paul H. Douglas was chairman, has held hearings pursuant to establishing a Commission on Ethics in Government.[2] The Association of the Bar of the City of New York, with assistance of funds provided by the Ford Foundation, has made a valuable study of the problem of conflict of interest.[3]

These studies furnish a basis for the difficult process of establishing a code of public conduct which will be a guide to responsible action and act as a deterrent to violation of public trust.[4]

[1] Hearings before Douglas subcommittee, June 19, 1951, pp. 10–11.

[2] *Cf.* Hearings, 82nd Congress, 1st Session, on Senate Concurrent Resolution 21, Committee on Labor and Public Welfare, June and July, 1951.

[3] *Cf.* study prepared for the public hearings before the Antitrust Subcommittee of the Committee on the Judiciary of the House of Representatives, February, 1960.

[4] For comment by Wayne A. R. Leys, see pp. 80–81.

CHAPTER V

Ethical Challenges in Practical Politics

By CHARLES P. TAFT

IN THE CONTEXT of this Conference, with its careful definition of the area for each paper, the writer must resist the inevitable temptation to spread into byways, relevant, but assigned to someone else.

The exact area assigned to me ought to be well circumscribed by reference to a good sample of the efforts of practical reformers to establish in codes, standards of political life. That of the Cleveland Citizens League (Autumn, 1959) seems to serve. My headings are in most cases a paraphrase rearranged from their nine points, and from my own experiences.

1. "No special consideration to persons, asked for or given." This principle has a biblical tinge, which is a good atmosphere in which to begin. Ethics in politics can well acquire a scriptural foundation—minus cant and hypocrisy. The Bible is a textbook for realists as well as theologians.

Fixing traffic tags is standard operating procedure in most places. A businessman supporter of our Cincinnati reform movement in 1926 found the new administration would not fix his tag and he went back permanently to the old machine. Fixing tags or none is a good test of your city government. It is the basic political favor for the eager citizen.

But something even more common than requests and agreement to fix tags is administrative inertia in dealing with an aggrieved citizen in shabby clothes. As a councilman or even as one with a good many other relationships to government departments, I get complaints at regular intervals from persons who seem to have a good case, but can get no action. Because it seems so outrageously unethical, nothing is more annoying to me than to get immediate action on my call, action to which the person was entitled in the first place, now granted as a favor simply because I took it up or raised Cain about it.

A really difficult ethical question is in a third situation for the slightly more serious traffic offense (*i.e.,* moving violations). A busy man may be perfectly ready to plead guilty and pay, but the last thing he wants is to spend a morning in traffic court listening to other similar offenders before his case is called. There probably is a way, a legal way, and proper, to do this, but it takes some knowing. Most people don't know it, or don't know of its existence. Is the businessman justified in taking advantage of it?

Weight with that the Cleveland principle: "What is done for one is done for all—in the same kind, in the same amount, in the same manner." Clearly the way of avoiding nuisance, while paying up, ought to be well publicized.

2. "Public compensation ought to be related to the amounts paid for comparable jobs in outside employment." This looks like a simple enough principle, even when complicated by such jobs as firemen and policemen who generally have no local counterparts.

But the public legislative body has a wide variety of employee pressures, including those of unions which don't like wage differentials, and want a standard rate for a plasterer or carpenter without stepups for merit and experience. For a different reason political machines want a high uniform scale for all their political jobholders (which usually means all jobholders except a very few technicians). Every precinct worker and every ward leader is just as necessary as every other worker or leader, and all have to have a good middleclass income, no matter what the job. So the same levelling effect appears, and just differentials for merit in the job are hard to maintain.

In both cases, unions and political machines, there is opposition to pay for supervisory positions in any way comparable to private industry. What management insists on, politicians pass up. Part of their reluctance, especially in state employment, grows from the popular smalltown feeling among both union members and farm communities against high executive salaries. In Kentucky under their constitution, until a few years ago, no public salary could be paid over $5,000 a year to anyone in the public service. When O'Neil, Governor of Ohio, in 1957, largely to justify what he had to pay to get a topnotch highway director, put through a general and proper increase in top state salaries, public and political pressure was largely responsible for a repeal within five months of all but the highway

Ethical Challenges in Practical Politics

director's pay scale. His scale disappeared, too, with a change in administration.

Yet the political machine can go to the other extreme when it is strongly entrenched, like the Democrats in New York City. Salaries are paid like private business, and go to at least many incompetents, with perquisites like Cadillacs to a fantastic degree.

This widespread political fact of life makes a farce of the demand of business for efficient and economical government. Not only do businessmen concerning themselves with local and state politics do little about this, but they accept the destruction of the merit system, and incidentally of any real democracy, which is involved in the city machine based on the political work of jobholders. The merit system required in states and cities by statute or constitution is almost universally avoided by calling employes "deputies," or by failing to create any eligible lists, and then making all appointments "temporary" for an indefinite period. That is the equivalent of appointment "during good behavior," as interpreted by the boss who controls the patronage selection committee. This is usually associated with a 2.5 per cent assessment for party funds based on the salary. The jobholders' machine has no relation, or little, to basic questions of national or state policy. National patronage provides some special plums, but not daily bread. State patronage has a good many jobs especially in the highway department, but is particularly important in providing agencies for distributing sales tax stamps or automobile license tags. These, widely distributed geographically in a city, are a potent political agency, and a percentage of the agent's fee, 5 per cent to 25 per cent, goes to party funds.

This kind of organization becomes inevitably more interested in jobs than in principle and is essentially unethical and unmoral.

It does not produce votes in any hotly contested election. My brother nearly lost in Ohio in 1944 (plurality 17,000) because he relied on the county political organizations who are now so reverent of his memory. Sheriffs and auditors and other important local officials with patronage, ran ahead of him even in his own county. In 1950 he had his own man in every county.

The standard method for election work is to pay for work at the polls. This is generally, in the big cities, money down the drain. In 1950 my brother's supporters in Cuyahoga County raised special money and paid the expenses of 100 women who were trained like Fuller

Brush salesmen to do a door to door job in the suburbs, where of course Bob was more likely to be strong. It was extremely effective, and in general people visited reported they had never been approached that way by anybody before.

The businessman who contributes does not like to face facts like these. He is even less willing to look at what is likely to develop from a jobholders' machine. It may frequently move to special treatment for liquor permitters, for friends with a real estate valuation problem, building inspection "oversights," or food inspection for special payola, into outright racketeering connections and even control.

The businessman's answer is likely to be:

1. He just hasn't time to do anything about it; it involves not only more continuous supervision than he thinks he can give to it, but it involves a fight and publicity he doesn't want, with perhaps in the back of his mind the possibility of uncomfortable retaliation; or 2. you can't apply his own standards in his own business to politics; it is something different.

This is nonsense. There is politics in a big business, or a big church, or a big university or school system, wherever there are people in relation to each other. There are difficult questions of ethics in all of them and public politics is no different in principle. Public pay ought to be for public work only, and it should be so adjusted that a person is not at any disadvantage, financial or psychological, by going into the public service.

3. "No citizen, public official or public employe should request or permit the use of government owned vehicles, equipment, materials, or property for personal convenience or profit, except where such services are available to the public generally."

This is pretty obvious, though in many places I hear about, it needs emphasis. Our own Cincinnati experience does not add much to what you read in the papers.

4. "Every citizen has the duty of reporting violations of law—and also evidences of fraud, theft or attempts to use improper influence in the conduct of public business."

This is even more obvious, but every public prosecutor will tell you that people in this area are very difficult, even church people.

As a city councilman I get frequent complaints about what somebody else is doing, and I am supposed to stop him without revealing who made the complaint. A fine churchwoman objected to a zoning violation near her home, but was unwilling (on her husband's insistence, I must say in fairness) to take any step or even testify herself. Witnesses to criminal violations (or automobile accidents) are notoriously skittish, and distrust the time it takes to appear in court.

But essentially it is a shyness in standing up to say, "This is wrong!" They know that there is plenty of cynicism and don't want it directed at them, or perhaps even retaliation.

This is associated with a very widespread belief, even among educated people, that everybody in the City Hall is a crook. Perhaps I should add that this attitude is also aimed at the rich and powerful and, in fact, at almost anybody who appears in the papers. I remember polling my precinct many years ago and meeting through the screen door, the wife of a master plumber. She was virulent on the subject of our City Manager because the city had just taken over the furnishing of all water meters (at cost) from the plumbers. But she was not registered to vote, and said there was no use voting anyway, since all the city officials were crooked. Lincoln Steffens did his work thoroughly, or at least he documented this basis of normal human prejudice.

Not a 5¢ cigar, but the courage to stand up and say to neighbors and bystanders what you think, is what this country needs most.

5. "Outside employment is generally incompatible with fulltime public service."

"Public officials should avoid even the appearance of conflict between their private interest and the public welfare."

"No citizen should offer, no public official or employe should solicit or accept any gift or special service or privilege, in relation to transaction of public business."

Conflicts of interest exist in many walks of life. Generally they are obvious, and most people who run into them know what is right and what is wrong. The trouble usually is the bystander's lack of such a sense, and in his advice, eagerly accepted by a bad conscience, that everybody is doing it.

Furthermore, the newcomer in politics may well be impressed by the political nogoods who try to tell him that politics is different from the business world he comes from. Again, Nonsense! Amorality is not sustainable anywhere.

Our most recent example was a man in charge of the city's off-street parking program who took a finder's fee or real estate commission from a broker with whom he had been surreptitiously employed while on the city payroll, on a piece of property bought by the city for the program. He did not make the decision on the purchase, but reported on the property. A county chairman, as his lawyer, advised him it was all right to do so. He is now under conviction awaiting sentence. Judgment or advice like that has lost all personal or legal ethics.

But gifts are very difficult. Senator Douglas, I think it was, limited gifts to a $1.75 necktie. A former judge in our county never took more than a cigar. I've taken ashtrays. One suggested rule of thumb was nothing accepted that could not be consumed in twenty-four hours. The rules at the head of this section applied with common sense are about as good as the ordinary person can do.

But what if King Saud gives the United States Secretary of State a gold watch, an embroidered robe, and a suitcase to carry it in? Or of course what of the gift of a rug and substantial hotel accommodations? Foolish as it may seem, the rules of thumb just suggested perhaps have real merit, with the added provision of a museum in which to put all gifts of unique quality, and a public auction process for the rest.[1]

These may all seem somewhat piddling samples of ethical problems in politics. But they are the day to day points of impact of the basic question: "How does one apply moral principles to daily living?"

Advise and Consent gives the frequent answer, and clearly the wrong one: absolutist morality is impossible; therefore a particular immoral practice may be accepted without thinking or resisting. Reinhold Niebuhr's title sums it all up, *Moral Man and Immoral Society*. The Archbishop of Canterbury claimed that Niebuhr's philosophy simply amounted to giving excuses for sin. Perhaps.

But here is the dilemma of the man with religious convictions who must realize they are worthless unless they can be guides for living in a world with plenty of evil, including evil in himself.

Clearly he must stand for the real validity of his principles. Clearly

---

[1] An excellent study appeared in August, 1960, by Professor Bayless Manning of Yale and a Committee of the Association of the Bar of the City of New York headed by Roswell Parkins, *Conflict of Interest*, Harvard University Press, 1960, Cambridge, which seems likely to be implemented by Congress under the stimulus of President Kennedy.

Ethical Challenges in Practical Politics

he must see that at any point he may be faced with limited choices of action or no-action, and that all of the choices may include some elements of evil. Clearly his moral obligation is to choose what in his careful analysis is the best choice. No choice, no-action is in itself a choice. A Christian cannot avoid the lesser of two evils.

But each choice must be made with a full consciousness—and remorse—that it does include evil. There cannot be the thoughtless and unresisting choice of evil, without rapid deterioration, both of one's ethical sensitivity, and of one's influence with others.

Two areas of application deserve quick comments in conclusion.

A candidate's (or businessman's) organization is described as tough and competent, and as riding roughshod and ruthlessly over the opposition. The strong man lays down the conditions of surrender and the weak man takes them. Toughness is not immoral. I am not justifying all means; I am simply saying that this is a competitive world, and that if the objective is sound, one cannot occupy one's worrying capacity over the competitor who for his own ineptness or incompetence cannot keep up with the procession. One may provide ways and means for him to rehabilitate and strengthen himself, but one shouldn't hold his hand in order to help him run faster. It is no favor to him to do so.

The second area is more difficult. Does one lie, as in the "cover story" for the U-2?

A political leader of stature is primarily motivated by patriotism, in the broadest sense. I am afraid I cannot rule out the possibility that an outright lie may be "patriotic" and necessary on rare occasions, but it is a narcotic and very dangerous. There are several alternatives.

The first is to say nothing. I have often been in political jams of various sorts, and I never have found damage from keeping my mouth shut, at least for a number of long breaths. Patience is a great political virtue.

The second alternative is to open your mouth wide and say a lot that is either meaningless or seems internally contradictory. This takes much greater skill, but it is often a very useful skill.

The third is to say something which is entirely true but partial, leaving your opponents to fool themselves. This also is a useful skill, but again takes intelligence.

The lie calls for a lot of other lies to cover it up, and when you are caught out in one, every future declaration is suspect. Perhaps I should add that there is a kind of false representation that everybody knows to be false at the time, like the disavowal of a spy who is caught. This does considerably less harm than the lie which is intended to be believed.

Finally to wind this up, I repeat that ethical challenges in practical politics are very little different from ethical challenges in practical business or practical church organization. They are better publicized, that's all. In this world of many good things and many evil things, we do better to cling to what is good, and preserve a sensitive remorse and repentance for what is not.

CHAPTER VI

Popular Evaluations of Government: An Empirical Assessment

By DONALD E. STOKES

I

ALTHOUGH THE IMPORTANCE of evaluations of government formed by large-scale publics is widely seen, only the most fragmentary information is available on these evaluations in actual political systems.[1] Certainly accounts of American attitudes toward government are largely impressionistic. We know from the election returns that negative feeling about governmental ethics is at times a strong force in American party politics; the practice of throwing the rascals out is as old as our party system. But it is far from clear what ethical values enter this feeling and what relation they have to other tests by which a party in office may be evaluated. Does the electorate have distinct ethical criteria that it applies to public conduct? Or are its ethical judgments imbedded in much more general attitudes toward an administration in office?

Nor is it clear what attitudes the public has toward politics or government as a whole. It is one thing to throw the rascals out by changing parties. It is quite another to reject the party system itself—to want to throw the rascals out by inducing fundamental change in the political order. Most observers who have treated this aspect of American politics assume a basic acceptance of the system. But unfavorable at-

---

[1] A fact that is itself widely noted. For some empirical matter and suggestive discussions of this problem in the context of American and other cultures, see Morris Janowitz, Deil Wright, and William Delany, *Public Administration and the Public—Perspectives toward Government in a Metropolitan Community*, Institute of Public Administration, University of Michigan, Ann Arbor, 1958; National Opinion Research Center, *The Public Looks at Politics and Politicians*, University of Denver, Denver, 1944; Edward C. Banfield, *The Moral Basis of a Backward Society*, The Free Press, Glencoe, 1958; and Klaus A. Lindemann, *Behoerde und Buerger*, Eduard Roether Verlag, Darmstadt, 1952.

titudes toward government and politics are a familiar element of our political culture, and popular favor has at times been given to attacks on government that reach well beyond normal partisan infighting. The savage feeling associated with the McCarthy movement raises pointed questions about attitudes toward government held by parts of the electorate. The truth is that these are matters on which little careful evidence is at hand.

Several streams of contemporary political thought draw attention to the importance of basic evaluative orientations toward government and politics. Orientations of this sort play an important role in theories of mass society and of the latent support for totalitarian mass movements. The tendency of these theories is to assert that the weakening of the social fabric in which the individual is held produces psychological stresses from which he will seek release by identification with authoritarian political movements. If this is true, latent support for movements of this sort in a democratic society would be indicated by the presence of strong negative attitudes toward the existing regime, attitudes that are bound into more general feelings people have about their life circumstances.

Popular evaluations of government also play an important role in theories of politics as group conflict. Marxian and nonMarxian conceptions of group competition to control the machinery of the state imply that attitudes toward existing government may differ substantially between major groups in the social structure. The more central and enduring the group basis of conflict and the more the state is an instrument of the dominant social forces, the more extreme will be the differences in the attitudes different groups have toward government. Certainly examples are plentiful enough of societies in which deep hostility toward the regime has developed in racial or class or ethnic groupings that feel themselves lastingly cut off from political power.

Both these currents of thought are related to the problem of the meaning of nonparticipation in democratic politics. By the standards of some Western democracies the rate of nonvoting in the United States is high. But the meaning to be given the level of participation clearly depends on the motives of the nonvoter. If the millions of people who are free to vote yet do not are politically indifferent in a partisan sense but positively oriented to the system itself, nonvoting is a relatively benign phenomenon. Indeed, some writers have argued that a large reserve of occasional voters with little emotional involvement in politics is useful to the political system; such a group keeps political divisions from going too deep and, by entering the electorate from time to time, provides the majorities for needed policy changes.[2] But if the millions of people who fail to participate in the electoral process are hostile to the political system, their nonvoting carries a far different meaning.

II

As part of its program of electoral research, the Survey Research Center at The University of Michigan has examined the nature of the evaluations Americans have made of their national government over the past decade. This research has sought to describe two main types of attitude. First, an effort has been made to describe evaluations of the parties as agents of government, particularly the party holding office. Second, an effort has been made to examine the feelings Americans have toward government more generally, to learn what criteria of evaluation go into these feelings and to learn something of the causes and consequences of basic orientations toward government.

A first conclusion to be drawn from this research is that the public's evaluations of government are exceedingly diffuse. This quality is illustrated well by the reactions of the electorate to the record of the Truman Administration. The responses given by a nationwide sample in the Presidential election of 1952 showed that the actions of the Democratic Administration had left the public with a profound sense of moral and ethical wrong. But this impression was largely devoid of detailed content. The public had neither a general understanding of the problem of ethics in government nor particular information about the misdeeds that had been done. The Truman Administration had not been held up by the public to well defined standards of ethical conduct and found wanting.

What is more, there was not in 1952 a sharp distinction in the electorate's mind between the *ethical* misconduct of the Democratic

[2]This essentially is the view of Bernard R. Berelson, Paul F. Lazarsfeld, and William N. McPhee in *Voting*, University of Chicago Press, Chicago, 1954, chapter 14, "Democratic Practice and Democratic Theory."

Administration and its other errors. The "mess in Washington" carried great motivational significance for the vote, but its scope was much broader than simply the moral and ethical shortcomings of some Democratic officeholders. As it formed in the perceptions of the mass public, the mess in Washington was compounded of personal dishonesty, inefficiency, bad administration, and serious mistakes of policy, particularly in the field of foreign affairs.

Apparently the same diffuse quality characterizes the public's positive and negative feelings about government generally. In order to probe these feelings more adequately, the Survey Research Center asked a nationwide sample in November and December of 1958 a series of questions designed to tap basic evaluative orientations toward the national government. The criteria of judgment implicit in these questions were partly ethical, that is, the honesty and other ethical qualities of public officials were part of what the sample was asked to judge. But the criteria extended to other qualities as well, including the ability and efficiency of government officials and the correctness of their policy decisions. The possibility was deliberately left open that these qualities would not be distinct in the public's mind but would rather be incorporated in a single dimension of feeling.

The reality of such a dimension was borne out by the internal coherence of the responses to the several questions. An analysis of the responses showed that the questions could be merged into a single scale;[3] that is, a single dimension of attitude toward government was found to embrace the various criteria of evaluation implicit in the questions asked. With this empirical warrant, the persons in the sample were placed in several categories of a single scale of positive and negative feeling toward government.

The global nature of the dimension of feeling that emerged from these interviews suggests that the electorate's sophistication in evaluating government is commonly overestimated. Indeed, most discussions of popular reactions to ethics in government are probably carried on at a level that is far removed from the public both in the concepts used and the information presupposed. Yet the public's positive and

[3]The responses to several of the questions were found to cohere in the sense of satisfying the requirements for a one dimensional cumulative scale, as these have been defined in the work of Louis Guttman and others.

Evaluations of Government: Empirical Assessment

negative feelings toward government are of immense significance. However poor their content, these orientations have farreaching consequences for a nation's politics. Their composition across social groups, their relation to other psychological orientations to politics, their role in prompting or inhibiting participation—each of these things holds a key to understanding a political system in which public opinion is a principal force.

III

Do the evaluations Americans have of government differ markedly between social groups? Apparently not. One of the most arresting features of our empirical results is the similarity of these evaluations across a very wide range of social groupings in the United States. Persons of strong negative feeling toward government are not concentrated in particular elements of the population; American society does not have important social groups that are alienated from government. By the same token, positive feeling is not centered in particular groups, but is diffused throughout the population.

It is especially noteworthy that hostility toward government is not pronounced in any disadvantaged solidary groupings. Whereas the French or Italian working class is largely alienated from the regime, the American working class is not. And whereas racial and religious minorities in many societies are disaffected from the political order, the great minorities of this society—Negroes, Catholics, Jews, the southern and eastern European ethnic groups—do not show a tendency of this sort. In fact, the desire to accept and be accepted is vigorous enough that Americans who are foreign born or of recent immigrant stock tend to be more favorable to government than are those whose forebears have been Americans for three generations or more.

But if attitudes toward government do not follow deep social fissures in the United States, these orientations are not entirely divorced from social aspects of the individual's life experience. Two connections of this sort deserve mention. First, the disposition of the individual to take a favorable stance toward government seems to depend somewhat on the extent of his education. As the entries of Table 1 indicate, the greater an American's educational background, the more likely he is to view government positively, although the relation is weak enough that education is by no means to be taken as a sovereign explanatory factor.

Table 1
Relation of Orientation to Government to Education

	Extent of Education		
Attitude toward government[a]	Grade School (N = 505)	High School (N = 892)	College (N = 369)
Negative	22%	14%	12%
Intermediate	57	66	64
Positive	21	20	24
Totals	100%	100%	100%

[a] The scaling procedure used to measure attitude toward government established the *relative* favorableness of each respondent toward government, but it did not yield a "zero point" of neutral feeling that could be used to separate those who were in an absolute sense favorable from those who were unfavorable. As a result, the terms "positive" and "negative" are applied here only to respondents close to the ends of the scale, whose direction of feeling is clear from the face content of their responses. Undoubtedly the point of neutral feeling, if it could be identified, would fall somewhere in the interval of the scale that is termed "intermediate" here.

Second, an American is more likely to be favorable to government if he lives in urban rather than rural surroundings, as Table 2 suggests. Although the difference in attitude between our urban and rural populations is not great, someone living in a city of medium size or in one of our great metropolitan centers is more likely to be favorable to government than is someone living in a small town or in the open country. And this difference does not disappear when the educational disparity of urban and rural people is taken into account.

The main conclusion to be drawn from the similarity of response to government in different social groupings is that the American attitudes toward government are influenced relatively little by group conflict. Almost certainly the subcultural differences found by educational level and place of residence do not reflect group conflict in any important way. These attitudes seem instead to rise from other sources.

In the search for other determinants, a relation of central interest

Table 2
Relation of Orientation to Government
to Size of Place of Residence

Attitude toward government	Population Size of Place of Residence	
	Under 10,000 ($N = 798$)	10,000 or over ($N = 842$)
Negative	20%	13%
Intermediate	62	65
Positive	18	22
Totals	100%	100%

is the connection between attitude toward government and the degree of influence the individual feels he has on government. People differ widely in their sense of the power that they and persons like themselves have over the course of public affairs. Of course the individual who thinks of himself as actually affecting public affairs is exceedingly rare. But some people do feel that the opinions of citizens like themselves count for something, whereas others do not, and this difference can be shown to have important consequences in the motivation of political behavior.[4]

When the individual's sense of political efficacy is compared with his positive or negative attitude toward government, it is apparent that a sense of ineffectiveness is coupled with feelings of hostility. This relation is more than a tautology. In other cultures or other historical eras a sense of ineffectiveness might well be associated with positive feeling. But in the context of democratic values, feelings of powerlessness toward public authority tend to create feelings of hostility toward that authority. As is shown in Table 3, the proportion of people strongly negative to government is much less among those who feel a high sense of political efficacy than it is among those who feel they are without influence over the course of government.

This relationship takes on added meaning when it is further seen

[4] Reports of the use of measurements of this sense of political efficacy appear in Angus Campbell and others, *The Voter Decides,* Row, Peterson and Company, Evanston, 1954, pp. 187–194, and Angus Campbell and others, *The American Voter,* John Wiley and Sons, New York, 1960, pp. 103–105.

Table 3
Relation of Orientation to Government to Sense of Political Efficacy

		Sense of Political Efficacy			
Attitude toward government	Low (N = 140)	Low Medium (N = 102)	Medium (N = 371)	High Medium (N = 241)	High (N = 130)
Negative	29%	26%	16%	13%	7%
Intermediate	56	59	66	63	55
Positive	15	15	18	24	38
Totals	100%	100%	100%	100%	100%

that the individual's sense of efficacy toward politics and government is rooted in a highly general sense of effectiveness or ineffectiveness the individual has in coping with his personal environment. There are wide differences in the extent to which people feel they are able to manipulate their surroundings to achieve their goals. Some persons feel they are masters of their fate; others feel buffeted by capricious external forces.[5]

Apparently this general sense of personal competence plays a substantial role in forming the individual's sense of efficacy toward politics and government. As a result, the positive or negative color the individual imparts to government seems to be linked to the degree of mastery he feels over his environment. This pattern of association is shown by the entries in Table 4.

Table 4
Relation of Orientation to Government to Sense of Personal Competence

	Sense of Personal Competence			
Attitude toward government	Low (N = 378)	Low Medium (N = 233)	High Medium (N = 352)	High (N = 706)
Negative	24%	23%	13%	11%
Intermediate	61	64	64	64
Positive	15	13	23	25
Totals	100%	100%	100%	100%

[5] For a discussion of this sense of personal effectiveness see Angus Campbell and others, *The American Voter*, pp. 516–519.

IV

The fact that general feelings of ineffectiveness toward the political and social environment can produce negative feeling toward government suggests that the political participation of those who are hostile to government will be qualified and incomplete. Two important types of evidence bear this out. First, it can be shown that negative attitude toward government is associated with rejection of the party system. For some years the Survey Research Center has measured the party loyalties of the electorate by asking individuals in nationwide samples to locate themselves on a dimension extending from strong Democratic commitment through independence to strong Republican commitment. Most Americans freely place themselves on a psychological dimension of this sort, but a small minority does not. This is not the difference between partisans and independents; it is rather the difference between partisan and independents on the one hand and those apolitical citizens on the other who do not think of themselves as having any relation to the party system. When the attitudes of the latter group are compared with the attitudes of independents and party followers, as they are in Table 5, it is clear that the apolitical group is extraordinarily hostile to government. And an intensive case analysis of these individuals shows that a very large proportion have deep feelings of ineffectiveness in dealing with political and personal affairs.

A second important type of evidence showing the limited participa-

Table 5
Relation of Extent of Party Identification
to Orientation to Government

Extent of Party Commitment

Attitude toward government	Apoliticals (N = 52)	Independents (N = 349)	Party Identifiers (N = 1373)
Negative	42%	16%	15%
Intermediate	48	66	62
Positive	10	18	23
Totals	100%	100%	100%

tion of the politically disaffected is found in reports of voting turnout. The difference in frequency of voting between those who are hostile to government and those who are not is seen most clearly among the less well educated, where normative sanctions against nonvoting are weaker, but this difference appears at least in attenuated form in all social strata, as Table 6 suggests for voting in our Presidential elections.

Table 6

Relation of Orientation to Government to Frequency of Electoral Participation

"In the elections for President since you have been old enough to vote, would you say that you have voted in . . ." [a]

Attitude toward government, within educational groups	All of them	Most of them	Some of them	None of them	Totals	Number of cases
Grade School						
Negative	24%	31%	30%	15%	100%	91
Intermediate	37%	25%	25%	13%	100%	238
Positive	40%	29%	20%	11%	100%	88
High School						
Negative	49%	30%	14%	7%	100%	80
Intermediate	46%	29%	19%	6%	100%	369
Positive	62%	23%	10%	5%	100%	104
College						
Negative	62%	20%	18%	0%	100%	34
Intermediate	64%	25%	10%	1%	100%	138
Positive	60%	28%	12%	0%	100%	65

[a] To limit this examination to persons who had been of voting age long enough to permit some variability in their voting behavior, only persons thirty-five years of age or older are included in the table.

V

As they emerge from this empirical assessment, the properties of American attitude toward government deserve close attention. It may be surprising, even to the knowledgeable observer, that evaluations of government formed by the general public are so largely undifferentiated, combining ethical issues, the ability of public officials, the soundness of government policy, and other evaluative criteria into a single, generalized dimension. It may be surprising, too, that the position of different social groups on this dimension is so much the same, that attitudes toward government do not change markedly across class or ethnic or racial or other group boundaries, despite the familiar tendency to explain politics in group terms. In these data a source of positive and negative feeling toward government is more easily found in psychological antecedents occurring in many social strata: it is the individual who feels little mastery over personal affairs and little effectiveness in his role as citizen who is the least likely to develop an acceptance of government. Lacking this acceptance, he is more likely to dissociate himself psychologically from the party system and to withdraw from participation in the electoral process.

To be sure, these findings ought to be taken with some reserve. Several of the relationships cited are of very moderate strength, and several of the psychological measures used in this work have not been tested in repeated studies. What is more, it is clear that to assess the full significance of these findings for democratic politics further information of great importance is required. In particular, to judge the implications of these findings for our political system we would need further evidence on two points on which this research stands moot. First, we would need to know whether the development of American society is intensifying or lessening the psychological syndrome that apparently qualifies the individual's acceptance of government. And, second, we would need to know whether the individual who lacks this acceptance can easily be drawn into antidemocratic political movements.

Whether our social order is increasing or lessening the individual's self-confidence in dealing with his personal setting is a question that can evoke strongly contradictory views. On the one hand, the rise in educational level and occupational skills of our population, coupled with the greater ease of occupational and residential mobility, can be taken as evidence that Americans exercise steadily greater control over their personal affairs, participating to an extent unknown before in the decisions that shape their lives. On the other hand, the familiar patterns of mass industrial society—the shattering of the extended family and weakening of the primary family, the rapid transfer of populations, the increasing complexity and bureaucratization of economic life, the passive role of the audience of modern communications media—can be taken as evidence that the individual controls his environment less and less. A correct statement of the matter awaits far better evidence about the emotional qualities of life in contemporary America.

It is equally uncertain whether the individual who lacks a positive emotional tie to government can be induced to support antidemocratic political movements. Plainly we ought not to assume that the people expressing negative feeling toward government in this research were calling for fundamental change in the political order. To the contrary, the idea of such change was not spontaneously articulated and presumably would have very little meaning for many of these respondents. What they have in common is not a commitment to political change but simply an affective feeling toward existing government that is to some degree negative.

And yet the latent support for antidemocratic movements in this group cannot wholly be discounted. Electoral studies of large-scale publics repeatedly have shown that those who seek popular support are judged more by their stand on certain gross features of the past and present than by their detailed proposals for the future. And where extremist movements have won favor at the polls in Western nations they have done so more by capitalizing on popular discontent with the existing politics than by gaining approval for explicit programs of change. Indeed, it is likely that the implications of granting power to those exploiting this pure element of discontent have typically been unclear to the mass public, as they have often been unclear even to the extremist leadership itself. In view of this, an element of a democratic electorate that is negatively oriented to existing government must in some measure be seen as latent support that might be tapped by parties or factions or individual political leaders whose stance is hostile to the prevailing order.

CHAPTER VII

The Management of Pressures and Opinion

By DAVID FINN

THE POLITICAL ADVISER of a candidate for the office of President of the United States recently asked a leading public relations practitioner to work with him on his campaign. The latter was hesitant and explained that he hadn't made up his own mind how to vote. "Oh, that," said the adviser, "is your own private affair; this is purely business. We mean, of course, to pay you."

Shortly afterward, the same practitioner was approached to work for the other side. This time, he was asked to volunteer his services because it would look bad (would be "bad public relations") if it became known that Madison Avenue had been brought into the picture at an early stage of the campaign. However, there was plenty of money in the till, and he was told he would eventually be rewarded. The second candidate was more to his liking, and so he agreed to undertake the assignment.

A week later, the public relations expert was not a little amused when the candidate of his choice, his new client who would rather not have it known that he was a client, made a major speech denouncing his opponent for using public relations in his campaign, trying to substitute slogans for ideas, and the slick sell for honest debate.

This story exemplifies the cynicism, discomfort, and hypocrisy often involved in the effort to sell ideas in a mass society. And these attitudes and feelings make it difficult to deny that opinion management as it is now practised raises grave ethical problems.

If opinion management can be harmful to society, however, the harm done is not easy to identify. For the most part, present practices follow the traditional pattern of activity found in the marketplace and around seats of power. Eloquence, excitement, drama—these are the age old tools of salesmanship, whether aimed at one man or millions. To succeed in the world of affairs, one always had to win the respect of already powerful members of the community: today the techniques of accomplishing this are only more complicated because society is more complicated; they are neither more unscrupulous nor more ingenious. And the dangers of mass hypnosis, if they are to be judged by the record, are as remote as they ever were.

The modern public relations specialist recognizes that he is the successor to the unofficial adviser to men and causes who played important and worthy parts in many previous periods of history. Who encouraged Thomas Paine to write and then helped him publish *Common Sense?* Who thought of asking William Blake to illustrate *Paradise Lost?* Who helped Shakespeare implement his masterful sense of showmanship in creating excitement and expectation for contemporary audiences? Who helped Aristotle gain support for his teachings? Who helped Titian win his position of influence in his time?

In some cases, we know there was a specific individual who helped the great person achieve his just respect, or the great deed its just recognition. In other cases, we know the great man was his own public relations expert. But in all cases, the progress and enrichment of society was served by a well developed skill of getting things accomplished in a practical world where opinion plays a significant role.

Why, then, does the use of public relations, which follows in such a respectable tradition, make people uneasy? Before attempting to answer this, I would like to disagree with a number of explanations which have been given in the past.

1. It has been argued that people are afraid of the professional management of opinion because it is a new field of specialization, and that as people become more sophisticated, their fear will disappear. I do not agree with this, because many sophisticated people (like Presidential candidates) continue to worry; in fact, they may even worry more than the uninitiated. And the effort to influence opinion has been around too long for it to be considered a novelty. The first attacks against it in its modern form were published over fifty years ago.

2. Madison Avenue is supposed to have achieved its unique position in American life because of a marked ethical deficiency. Defenders say the diagnosis is inaccurate and the right kind of public relations program for the field of public relations (and advertising, motivational

The Management of Pressures and Opinion

research, etc.) would combat this mistaken impression. I do not agree with either of these ideas. True, the ethics of Madison Avenue leave something to be desired, but they are no worse than the ethics of any other business or profession. And the inhabitants of this famous street have not been as negligent in trying to improve their reputations as might be supposed. They have made many efforts to publicize their contributions to society—perhaps not as much as they should, but still enough to suggest that there is a basic fault which cannot be corrected by mere promotion.

3. Men who use public relations are said to be more pretentious about their virtues than others. I do not agree. Any man who tries to make a sale or win an argument presents his case in the best possible light. This is true whether he is plainspoken or eloquent, whether his phrases are clumsy and rough or slick and polished.

4. Public relations is considered a means by which power groups can exploit an unknowing public. As Bertrand Russell once put it, "If A desires B to act in a certain manner which is in A's interest but not in B's, it may be useful to A to keep B in ignorance of facts which would show B where his true interest lies." This is a more serious charge, for even though this approach is traditional in the marketplace, as common to the ancients as it is to us, its continuation cannot make the world a better place to live in. But I do not agree that this method of doing business is inherent in public relations; it is more common for the modern practitioner to induce his client A to modify his desires so that he can serve B's interest as well as his own. And this *can* make the world a better place to live in.

There is, I believe, a more realistic danger in the organized attempt to mobilize public opinion. The public relations practitioner is a mercenary, and as such, is expected to sell his knowledge and skill to anyone who pays the price. Thus he may be hired to secure votes for a political candidate he doesn't like; to convert people to a religion he doesn't believe in; to promote a theory of history he thinks is mistaken; to gain acceptance for a scientific or medical idea which fails to convince him; to win popularity for a school of art he dislikes; in short, to do anything which he may find personally distasteful, but which someone pays him to promote.

To put this in perspective, one must recognize that the professional soldier was in many traditions quite a romantic character, even though he was willing to fight for almost any cause. The physician treats many people he doesn't like. The engineer builds structures which may not appeal to his taste. The lawyer argues cases for reprehensible characters. And certainly, a salesman takes on products which he may consider to be inferior. However, a mercenary in the world of ideas differs from all these. By his efforts, he runs the danger of creating seeds of doubt in his own mind about the fundamental values of his culture. Ultimately, he can spread a disease of unbelief throughout the culture that can cause decay and degeneration.

To understand how this can happen, one must follow these considerations which underlie the business of persuasion.

The basic premise of professional salesmanship of ideas is that any cause must be aggressively sold to the public in order to gain public support. Human nature being what it is, most people don't reason carefully when weighing alternative choices on public issues. They respond to emotional appeals. And competitors for public support must make effective appeals if they want to win. Anyone who doesn't know how to make such appeals will not succeed. And in a mass society, if appeals aren't made loudly, they will not even be heard.

The problem of gaining a hearing for a new idea becomes more difficult as more people get more new ideas. When one person succeeds by shouting his selling message from a rooftop, everybody else follows suit and rooftops are finished as an effective platform. Then streamers in the sky are tried. And so on as the din gets louder and louder.

In selling products, promotion specialists reduce arguments to as few basic themes as possible. This is a simple matter, so long as a product can boast of a real performance innovation—a new washing machine incorporating a method to dry clothes as well as wash them, a new detergent making rinsing unnecessary, a new synthetic material retaining its shape after washing. But if a product has no such distinction, the theme has to be created through selling slogans or through the addition of a product feature which has little or no real value, but which gives the manufacturer something on which to hang a selling message. Thus a female hygienic product is sold just "Because. . . ." And a new automobile which performs no better or worse than its competitor's is designed with an upswing or a down-

The Management of Pressures and Opinion

swing or an inswing or an outswing, and whichever it is, it is touted as the basic ingredient of driving pleasure.

In the face of the mounting noise, with everyone promoting a single feature in the loudest possible voice, new methods are sought to break the sound barrier. Hidden desires or frustrations are investigated so that selling messages can be aimed beneath the surface where, it is hoped, the impulses are irresistible. A cigarette is successfully advertised by a man with a tattoo on his arm, suggesting that here is a secret formula for virility (until the manufacturer discovers that psychoanalysts consider tattoos a symbol of latent homosexuality which suggests that success is due to a different hidden desire than originally thought). Another cigarette is claimed to smoke cleaner (no cancer). A third is said to taste better (oral satisfaction).

As things get more and more competitive and complicated, the illogical, contradictory claims begin to look ridiculous. One cigarette is claimed to taste better because it *does* have a filter, another because it *does not* have a filter. Soon people begin to doubt all claims. Authorities are then sought whose endorsement still might have the power to be believed. This could be a well known personality (a famous movie actress uses the product to gain her perfect complexion); it could be the ordinary man on the street (Mrs. Jones, a housewife from Middletown, U.S.A., says the product works wonders for her); it could be a discriminating, highly respected type of person (more doctors choose this product than any other); or it might be a recognized authority whose job it is to make independent and presumably uninfluenced judgments of product qualities (journalists, scientists, educators). Eventually this technique defeats itself. The movie actress is openly paid for her kind words. Mrs. Jones becomes an obviously fictitious person. Doctors explain that when one product is as good as another, they use the product made by the manufacturer who gives them free samples. Journalists, scientists, and educators turn out to be subject to their own brand of influence which too often makes their judgment no more objective than others.

All grounds of belief about product virtues now become threatened. People can't believe what anyone tells them—whether he is claiming something for himself or for someone else. And as the advanced practices of promotion spread into government, religion, education, art, and science, convictions about fundamental values begin to drop by the wayside.

The major obstacle to the spread of this disease is the phenomenon of what Milton Mayer calls "self-selling ideas."

Self-selling ideas are found in the great religious and political principles that have become so deeply imbedded in the hearts of so many people that some kind of *natural* appeal can be assumed. They seem to satisfy a fundamental need which no master stroke of salesmanship can imitate.

Few people realize that the phenomenon of self-selling ideas also dominates the marketplace and the world of politics. Hula hoops did not spread around the world like a flash fire because a great salesman was behind them, but because they spontaneously caught the imagination of children. Perry Como's recording of "Far Away Places" and last year's best seller in Jonathan Logan dresses had the same kind of appeal. So did Harry Truman in the historic campaign of 1948 and the antiMcCarthy forces of 1956.

All the technique and skills developed by promotion experts cannot enable man to master his fate in the marketplace, any more than he can command his place in history. In the end, a product will sell, or an idea will win out, if it possesses the mysterious ingredient mystically called "IT." When something has this natural appeal, the specialist believes the right kind of promotion may help increase his success; if something doesn't have "IT," no amount of promotion in the world can help.

But this obstacle may not be strong enough to prevent the ultimate breakdown of values which can result from the work of idea mercenaries. While the secret of self-selling ideas may remain a mystery for quite a while, the promotion specialists *behave* as if they will one day be able to deliver to a client any kind of public support he wants. This creates an attitude in which public opinion manipulation is considered to be a good thing if only it could be arranged. And this means that whether or not it ever might be arranged, respect for people's right to have their own opinion is destroyed, as well as respect for the opinions themselves.

The cause of this ultimate cynicism lies in the economic and social structure of our society, not in the practices of promotion experts.

Conscience will not avert the evil; a change in the structure of our

The Management of Pressures and Opinion

marketplace may. Those engaged in influencing public opinion can be the bestwilled men in the world, but it is the competitive system, not their goodwill, which is the problem. All enterprises *must* have the support of promotion experts somewhere along the line if they are to succeed. It is unthinkable for them not to, for they must fight direct or indirect competition from other enterprises. And the experts must do their best to secure public support. The fact that they make this effort means, as can be seen from the considerations outlined above, that there is going to be trouble.

Though the villain is the competitive system, it is unlikely that a totalitarian system can be the hero. If competition were eliminated, contempt for public opinion would be even greater. A free competitive society saves us from an even greater evil. But this doesn't mean we should ignore the fact that the system is not benign, for it unleashes a savage part of human nature which brings on its own brand of danger. Competition can drive the most civilized and cultured man to violence, whether it is found among political candidates, educational institutions, cereal manufacturers, scientific research organizations, or even individual artists who do battle with each other. With the competitive spirit overwhelming us in all these areas, the forces which drive the public relations practitioner to divorce himself from an appreciation of the values of our culture are very great.

Is there any hope at all to avert this challenge to the rights of public opinion? I believe there is, but it can only come through a broad social change which would enable the community to limit the damaging effects of competition on ideas. As a promotion specialist myself, the only way I know this can be done is through the establishment of a more effective institution of independent criticism for all phases of contemporary life. This would place a more secure block against the effort to invade the public mind. It would indeed cause a revolution in the promotion world. The field of public relations might even suffer more directly than other fields, for its goal is specifically to obtain favorable comments about its clients from independent sources wherever possible. Nevertheless, I believe that aggressive criticism of business and other power groups provides the only possible escape from the trap of persuasion in a competitive society.

Institutions of public criticism now exist in a random and uncontrolled pattern in the mass media and to a certain extent in the scholarly, scientific, and artistic worlds. But as presently constituted, they are too weak and unstructured to withstand the pressures which inevitably are put on them. These institutions need to become strong and vital social instruments, if they are to be effective.

A mechanism of criticism that works well would guarantee the public that an effort will be made to evaluate objectively all appeals developed by an enterprise to further its own interests. This mechanism would not guarantee objectivity, and critics would disagree with each other as much as they do today. But the critics would be far better trained for their jobs than they are today. They might even be officially established as public servants, and hence, would be as free from the danger of influence as society can make them. Through them, the opportunity to arrive at an educated opinion about any subject would be protected. And since their judgments would be expressed in public, the right of private individuals to have opinions as well would continue to remain highly respected.

Only if critics increase their power of criticism in the same degree that promotion specialists increase their power to influence, will the war of the competitors being fought for the public mind be contained. The secret of self-selling ideas would still be pursued, but critics would stand perpetually on guard against the evils of manipulation. Promotion experts would turn their attention to helping clients meet ever higher standards of criticism, rather than use devices to catch momentary attention. Whatever new ideas in persuasion were developed would serve the progress which a healthy competitive system can generate, rather than the decadence which an uncontrolled competitive system threatens. And the management of public opinion can help bring richer and more rewarding experiences to masses of people, rather than destroy their capacity to have any worthwhile experiences at all.

Comment by Wayne A. R. Leys:

The ethics of partisanship is a difficult subject. Contemporary public opinion is ambivalent. The nineteenth century liberal belief in competition is not dead, but it is challenged by fears of partisan persuaders, not unlike the fears expressed by Rousseau and Plato.

Recently I have been trying to disentangle these divergent sentiments by means of role-theory. Suppose that offices and occupations are distributed in a spectrum from

The Management of Pressures and Opinion

the most partisan roles at one extreme to the least partisan roles at the other extreme.

The standards (voluntary and imposed) of these various roles should not be the same. Special pleading is allowed to the salesman, the politician, and the lobbyist, whereas strict truthfulness (on certain matters) is demanded of the C.P.A. and the scientist. There may be a few tabus of general application, such as the avoidance of secret agency. But, when a man lets people know that he has stepped into a partisan role, he is not held to the tighter restrictions of the nonpartisan roles.

Some roles are difficult to define in terms of partisanship. Top management in large corporations, clergymen, etc., are in some respects partisan; in other respects, they are nonpartisan.

Unless some such distinction is made, the more partisan role players may be forced into a very dangerous kind of hypocrisy, and the more nonpartisan role players will seem to be justified in dodging the special sanctions and restrictions of their office in what appears to be a general corruption of public morality.

*II. Responsibility in Big-Scale Scientific and
   Academic Organization*

CHAPTER VIII

Moral Judgments in Academic Structures

By JAMES A. PERKINS

THERE ARE MANY values with which an individual must be concerned. They originate in imperatives of his environment and his own image of his own nature. Moral complications derive from the fact that man is at one and the same time a family man, a community man, a religious man, a patriotic man, a professional man, and an institutional man. The institution with which he is identified, and which typically pays him an income, in turn can be so structured as to present a simple picture of his responsibilities; or it may be so arranged as to impose additional conflicting loyalties with which the individual man must be concerned.

The large-scale academic structure is in the latter category, because it embodies a number of distinctive features which complicate rather than simplify the task of making moral judgments.

The Discontinuous Hierarchy: The Statement

The first of these distinctive features could be called *the discontinuous hierarchy*. One has only to consider the difference between the straight line of authority that runs from trustee to president to business manager to power plant director and the discontinuous relationship between trustee, the president, the dean, and the assistant professor of economics. In the first case, there is a normal chain of command. Each person in the chain can identify his superior, can recognize him as such, and would have no difficulty in describing the relationship that existed between each level of this particular hierarchy. There is no basic ambiguity, and as a result power can be delegated and responsibilities assigned and accepted with relative clarity and precision. With respect to institutional decisions to be made by anybody in this chain, is can be said with some accuracy that the moral requirements are relatively clear. The business manager may be harassed, but his moral brow is relatively unruffled.

In the second chain of command, something quite different is involved. From the moment the trustee even begins to talk to the president about the assistant professor his tone of voice changes, because he is not talking with authority. He knows, if he knows anything about the academic world, that he is talking with a man whose relationship with the assistant professor is different from his own with his business manager. This is also true when the president talks to the dean about the assistant professor, and, of course, when the dean himself is talking to this end of the conversational chain. In short, there are two quite different authority relationships built into our academic structures. In one chain a directive will be accepted and understood. In the other, a directive would be a signal for a civil war. In the first, the hierarchy is continuous. In the second, it is discontinuous.

The discontinuous hierarchy presents enormous problems of moral judgment on the part of the participants. When authority is unclear, responsibility is unclear; when responsibility is unclear, it is impossible to hold people to account. And when people cannot be held to account for their actions, it means that one of the bases for moral judgment has been removed, both for the performer and for associates. (This situation is not unknown in other structures. The relationship between the Secretary of Defense and the general officer presents some of the same fascinating subtleties as does that of the relationship between the university president and the assistant professor of economics. It may be difficult for a Secretary of Defense to realize it, but probably his authority *vis-à-vis* the general officer is more clearly delineated than that of the university president *vis-à-vis* his economics professor. A comparison of these and similar relationships involving a discontinuous hierarchy would be an interesting exploration.)

The Discontinuous Hierarchy: The Case

An assistant professor is up for a tenure appointment. He is a controversial character, because he believes and indeed is publicly committed to the view that a rapid transfer of United States sovereignty to a world government is our only hope of survival. As an earnest of his belief he has written an article for a popular magazine urging an

Moral Judgments in Academic Structures

immediate transfer of the Strategic Air Command to the United Nations. His appointment to the rank of associate professor has been recommended to the president by his department chairman, and is to come up for approval by the board of trustees within a week's time. There is known to be strong opposition to this appointment by several board members who believe that the professor's political position borders on treason. The president has convened at his house a small group consisting of the assistant professor concerned, his department chairman, and one of the board members known to be in opposition to the appointment. What follows might be a digest of the positions presented by each of the four, and may serve to illustrate the moral confusion implicit in the discontinuous hierarchy.

The Assistant Professor

At the outset I wish it understood that this meeting itself is out of order. My views on world government are not a matter for proper review by university officials. My field is economics and political science, and I am the sole judge of what I teach and what I say on or off campus. The only question that is pertinent to my promotion is the effectiveness of my teaching and the solidity of my research. I appeal immediately to the doctrine of academic freedom and protest this discussion and the assumed right to consider my views as relevant to my promotion. My own moral problem is unambiguous. I must teach what I think is right. Difficulties such views present for a university are not my concern. Fellow scholars may attack me for inaccuracies or illogic. That would worry me. But I am an economist first and a member of this faculty second. It would be immoral for me to take any other position.

The Department Chairman

While I support the position of my colleague, his position is extreme. He has a right to his views and he has a moral duty to call his shots as he sees them. But I have institutional responsibilities also, and I have a right to weigh them and put his views on my own scales. In a large department I must be sure there is a proper balance of points of view. I cannot afford to have a faculty that is exclusively of the right or the left or of only one religious belief. If he denies my right and responsibility to have a balanced department, he is wrong, because the department must have such balance to allow students their fundamental right to hear various points of view.

As a matter of fact, my colleague's vigorous urging of his particular point of view has forced me to give even more serious attention to his own and other points of view than would normally be the case. He is thus in the strange position of forcing me to take the very notice of his views that he denies is my right.

However, there are those in the department who will offset his position, and therefore I can with clear conscience recommend his appointment. I suspect that the president and the trustees have problems presented by my colleague's views, but they involve institutional considerations that are not mine. In short, in my case I deny my colleague's insistence that I may not take his views into account. I must, and I have, and on the basis of having done so I make my favorable recommendation.

The Board Member

These are most interesting but disturbing presentations. They are interesting because I got a clear picture of the way in which members of this faculty view their job, but disturbing because of the anarchy these views imply. The professor says that no one has a right to take his views into account. The department chairman says he has that right but only for the limited purpose of departmental balance. Both would deny the right of any other faculty authority to concern itself with the content of their teaching. I know of no other organization where the individual members claim, with respect to their main activity, that they are not accountable to anyone else.

Theoretically, we trustees possess the ultimate authority. The charter so stipulates. It is unarguable that the central function of the university is the business of instruction and research. And yet it has become very clear that with respect to this central function the trustee attempts to exercise any authority only at his own peril.

If I have responsibility, then I do not see how I can refuse to make judgments with respect to the primary functions of the university, and if this is the case, I must surely render judgments on the key decisions—namely, the appointment to tenure on the part of members of this faculty. But I would be the first to admit that I am not prepared to make such a review. But should I so prepare myself? Is it my responsibility to bring to the judgment considerations as to the overall good of the institution and the views of society as to the value of the prospective contributions of various faculty members? The charter would suggest an affirmative answer. My role in other organizations surely says yes. But the faculty denies the existence of a continuous hierarchy. If this is so, my moral duty is fudged and I cannot act responsibly.

If I withdraw from any decisionmaking function with respect to faculty appointments, who then exercises such judgment? I'm back to my previous point—namely, that no one makes any critical judgment on the content or knowledge of the teacher.

The President

And this is where I come in. The positions of all three parties have been stated with ample clarity. Collective institutional responsibility cannot be exercised in the academic realm by a lay board without changing its composition, its background, and its time on the job. Collective institutional responsibility will also not be exercised by the faculty. At least not when it involves review of individual performance. Both have withdrawn from this central matter and have left it to the office of the president.

No university president can fill this vacuum. He can only accommodate. He can protect the faculty from those who would restrict its freedom. He cannot protect it from the incompetence of its individual members, because the faculty will not concede to the president rights of review it will not give its fellow members. So my role in this review presents as grave a dilemma as that of the trustee. Except in one particular, it is worse—I am supposed to represent the good of the institution as a whole, even though denied the right to review the functioning of a part.

I came from a small college presidency, and there it seemed to me far more essential for members of the faculty as well as trustees to think in institutional terms that included the rights and responsibilities of the others. The larger the institution, the more narrowly these responsibilities are conceived, and the more onerous and opportunistic the job of the president. This is particularly true because, with respect to faculty and curricular matters, a line of authority does not exist. It is for precisely this reason that a case like this makes my conversations with the business manager about the director of the power plant seem so pleasant.

Dual Loyalties: The Statement

The second substantial and distinguishing characteristic of the academic structure is the dual loyalty of the faculty member: to his institution and to his profession. Often his standards of performance are dictated more by his associates in his field than by his colleagues in his university. He will continually have to weigh time for students against time for research. The weights he will assign will vary, depending upon the field of his work and his own interests and capacities. Some fields are more professionally cohesive than others, and in these noninstitutional considerations will loom large. But in some measure both loyalties will be felt by every faculty member, and his judgments about allocation of time and the importance of specific activities will require him to weigh these conflicting responsibilities.

Once again it can be said with some measure of certainty that the larger the institution the more likely it is that the member of the faculty will feel more strongly identified with his profession and less with the institution as such. At some small colleges members of the faculty are involved in decisions as to whether to allocate additional tuition income between scholarships, faculty salaries, or physical improvements. In large-scale institutions no such discussion could conceivably take place. The larger the institution, therefore, the more likely it is that the loyalty of the individual faculty member will stop with his department. His moral choice will involve weighing departmental loyalties against professional loyalty, and both may be mobilized against matters that are put to him as of general institutional concern.

This problem is enlarged not only because of the increased size of our institutions but also because of greater faculty mobility and the broadened range of their outside opportunities. A professor of public administration must consider not only his students and his research work but also the demands put on him by the state planning commission, the Bureau of the Budget in Washington, and perhaps a variety of private organizations that put forward strong claims for his time.

But it is not only in allocating time that these differing responsibilities complicate the individual's judgment. They also come forcibly to his attention when he comes to develop, and more particularly communicate, his ideas. The nutrition expert in a state university in a dairy state who feels strongly that margarine has been unfairly treated in the state legislature may find a lively moral question in his lap when he comes to testify or to lecture or to write his next article. He has a variety of audiences in mind—not only the dairy farmers on the committee of the legislature, but also colleagues within and without his own institution who will be drawing their own conclusions of his integrity from what he says or from what he does not say. Chances for conflicts of loyalties are increased by the extent to which the professor is engaged in controversial matters and the extent to which he has identified himself with his field as well as his institution.

Dual Loyalties: The Case

A professor of psychology has just been made chairman of his department. For years his department has been split between the social and experimental psychologists. This schism has resulted in bad morale and poor teaching of the dwindling number of students who are taking psychology. It is believed by everyone that the new chairman, whose plans for the department have just been approved by the president, will lift the department. It will take several years of hard work, however, and thoughtful professional decisions before this task can be accomplished.

At the end of the first year the professor is invited to fill the most distinguished chair of psychology in the country. His income will not be substantially increased, but the prestige of the position will put the departmental chairman at the front rank of psychologists. Furthermore, he will have access to and indeed control of several important research facilities and research income that will make it possible for him to become once again a productive research scholar.

At a faculty luncheon table he is discussing his problem with some of his friends inside and outside his department.

It is clear that he owed a great deal to this university, he acknowledged. He had been promoted faster than the average, had received generous leaves of absence, and had, apparently, the full confidence of the dean and the president. He admitted that prospects for reshaping the department would be seriously reduced if he left. There was no one else who has the full confidence of both branches of the psychology department. This would have ramifications outside psychology itself, and would affect the university's effort to develop a more consolidated program in the general field of the behavioral sciences. From an institutional point of view there is a cleancut case, the professor said. "I owe the university much, and the university expects much of me."

However, he continued, psychology is a field of knowledge, and he had obligations to contribute to it. In the new post he could work in the area of his specialty with undreamed of financial support. His area was a critical one dealing with the learning process. His research, if successfully accomplished, might have a substantial effect on some of the central assumptions of current educational theory.

Finally, to complicate his problem further he said that his last remark showed that the two responsibilities of course interacted. Successful research would eventually affect the material taught at this university and so the institution would be an ultimate beneficiary. On the other hand, a successful reorganization of the department would produce better trained psychologists, some of whom might make equal or more substantial contributions.

Where does duty lie? Will he be driven back to having the decision turn on housing, climate, and the relative geographical proximity to his married daughter?

It will have to be reported that he got little help from his luncheon companions. A colleague in his department was appalled that he would consider moving in the face of the immediate past history of his department. But this man was a student-oriented professor, so this reaction might have been anticipated. Another took the position that professional and institutional loyalties were so evenly balanced that it was proper to consult personal factors and make the decision on them. On this basis he urged the psychologist to stay because he

Moral Judgments in Academic Structures

could not sail his fifteen foot boat where there was no water. But this man was known to have developed deep community roots both inside and outside the university, and while he was a first class professional man he had some years ago decided that he would finish his professional career at the local university. These roots and the social contacts and chances for service now played a large part in his life. He, in short, was instinctively against movement. The basic dilemma was no longer his chief concern.

The third person at luncheon was a young assistant professor only several years out of graduate school. He was completely absorbed in the emerging field of plasma physics which dominated his life. As might be expected, he had a hard time bringing into focus the position of his other colleagues. He heard the words but he could not feel them, so he strongly urged the professor to return to a life of research as the only occupation that could exact a legitimate first claim on a scholar.

The professor decided to leave and take the new post, but even he would be hard put to identify with any certainty the factors, moral and professional, that contributed to his decision. The institutional and professional conflict was basic, but he suspected that his final decision rested on the simple fact that he was really happier when he was alone with his own work.

The Unstructured Student: The Statement

The third distinguishing feature of the university is the unstructured role of the students within the academic community. From an organizational point of view their role is highly ambiguous. They are the overwhelming majority in numbers, but they have an essentially passive role. (The fact that they exercise minor responsibilities for student behavior only sharpens the essential picture.) They are between the ages of seventeen and twenty-one and are, therefore, not fully adult but no longer children. Their reactions are unpredictable and are only partially responsible. Many are away from families for the first time and are not clear on the extent to which the dean is supposed to take over the responsibility of the father. (Neither is the dean.)

The environment provides the student's most compulsive values. Traditions of behavior, the habits and mores of his fellow students, the habits brought from his previous environment—all these form a series of value structures that determine his conduct.

But the main purpose of the university concerns only part of his interests and activities—his intellectual growth—so his relations with the adult world are only partial. Institutional requirements that are specific but partial are continually balanced against factors of personal growth that are general and personal.

This dichotomy in the unstructured role of the student provides the main substance of the moral conflicts for the student and university faculty and administration when they must deal with each other.

The Unstructured Student: The Case

The local student debating society has invited a most controversial figure to the campus for a public appearance. This personage has recently been found guilty of perjury on matters having to do with the public interest of the United States. However, the invitation has been extended and accepted. The matter has come up for review. The issue before the president is whether to overrule the student debating society on grounds of damage to the reputation of the institution. He has convened in his office the chairman of the student organization, the dean of students and the vice president for public affairs (including fundraising and alumni relations).

The Student

The student made his case somewhat as follows: Essentially the members of the debating society were curious to see at first hand a man who had aroused such national controversy. Since the case had entered the political literature of the United States and since the question of the man's veracity was one of the central points at issue, they wanted a chance to make up their own minds on this score. They felt they were mature enough young men to be able to withstand an evening's exposure without damage.

The student went on to say that he recognized that the issue had been posed in terms of damage to the institution rather than damage to the students. He asked why the university should be identified with anyone who happened to be on the campus. It certainly would not pretend to validate the positions taken by its professors or hold itself responsible for the action of its alumni. It was his impression that a university campus was the one place where students could develop close contact with people and issues about which they were studying. Deny them this and their world is a restricted one indeed. The student ended by saying that for the life of him he could not understand what the shouting was all about. Why were people so excited about what this exgovernment official would or would not say? He confessed to being astonished at what he had read in the papers and in the alumni letters indicating the amount of heat that had been generating. In short, what gives? Not that an answer was relevant to his rights to invite the visitor, but he sure was curious.

The Dean of Students

The dean of students pointed out that the student position had been accurately presented. He went on to say that he viewed the matter as one of necessary student education, and that he was glad that the reaction had been forthcoming because without it the students would have missed the relevance of the case which made the visitor a controversial figure. In short, for the first time the students had come directly up against the beliefs and passions of the nonuniversity adult world. He wanted to point out that while the benefits were as he had stated them, the problems for student judgment were complicated by the fact that they had had no direct contact with the world of controversy surrounding the prospective visitor. In short, their lack of experience made it impossible for them to make a decision with the same range of considerations in mind that would be in the scales of a mature person, were he a university official, an alumnus, or merely an interested spectator. Since they could not know of the anger and passions surrounding this case they obviously could not weigh them. The student judgment was, therefore, bound to be deficient with respect to the net effect of their invitation. And this was inherent in a student body made up of young men who talked mostly with each other, cut off from adults for substantial periods of time, and resident at the university for only a few years. Their experience was bound to be partial, and their concern for the institution or even the adults in it was likely to be low on their scale of values.

The dean pointed out that it was his job to try to inject these other considerations where possible, but his own position was complicated by the crosscurrents of his role of acting father with that of defender of the students' right to grow and, therefore, to make mistakes. He had, in all honesty, to point out that the sensitive process of assisting in the maturing of young adults was a matter for which his training was sparse at best. Furthermore, he was constrained to point out that his colleagues on the faculty were really only properly concerned with the process of intellectual development and were not likely to participate effectively in the consideration of the dean's problems. Indeed, one of his difficulties was in getting members of the faculty to consider that the broad problem of student maturity was their concern at all.

The Vice President for Public Affairs

The vice president for public affairs had difficulty in maintaining silence during these two expositions. When his turn came he exploded, saying that there was an overriding consideration, namely, the right of the institution to survive or at least to protect itself from mortal wounds. In this case a student action would damage the university, and the finding of damage was obviously not the responsibility of the student nor that of the dean of students.

He recognized the importance of the theory of freedom of discussion on the campus, but contended that this should not cover activities beyond the faculty and the students themselves. The right to speak on the campus was not absolute and in weighing the right of the institution as a whole against the right of the students he was in this case strongly for the institution. Surely, he complained, there was an obligation of community citizenship which all should recognize.

The President

During this discourse the president, of course, had to weigh both arguments as well as silently count to himself the votes pro and con he was likely to receive in his board of trustees. He had been deeply disturbed at the reaction of some of his most friendly and influential alumni, whose point of view had been expressed by his vice president

Moral Judgments in Academic Structures

for public affairs. But for him it was not a matter of weighing the institution against students. In the end it was deciding whether in this particular instance the institution would be more severely damaged or more greatly strengthened by the decision to review or not to review. For this he had to take into account the nature of the invited speaker and his culpability, the morale of his faculty, the experience of his students, his relations with his board, his own personal commitment to the idea of free speech, his own personal horror at the damage done to free speech by the visitor himself. His was the loneliest role of all because no one on the board, faculty, in the administration, or of the alumni was prepared to make his decision in the light of the same range of values. It may be that in the end his decision not to review the student case was based upon the opinion of his fellow university presidents and his belief that they would expect him in this case to support the students.

Conclusion

It would seem that some of the essential features of the large-scale academic structure complicate the problem of moral judgments. It would seem that as a result the administrative coordinating task primarily involves adjustments of conflicting pressures rather than considerations of institutional purpose.

Perhaps the central question to raise is whether or not internal administrative and structural arrangements can be so modified as to simplify the problem of moral judgment. This writer believes they will have to be if leadership in our academic institutions can function with a higher content of educational purpose than is now the case. There are no simple solutions and no pat formulas. Some directions for improvement could be:

1. An increased knowledge about education on the part of board members and an increase in the number of educators on the board.
2. A continued selection of academic administrators who show signs of strong educational purpose.
3. A positive view of administration by members of the faculty, and by positive I mean a realization that governance, management, and administration are essential purposes to the survival and

growth of educational institutions and require the encouragement and support of members of the faculty.

4. A recognition that some of these tensions are inherent and cannot be permanently eliminated, and that any effort to do so would bring disaster.

CHAPTER IX

Big-scale Scientific Research

By KARL K. DARROW

SCIENCE IS INDEED a big-scale enterprise, absolutely and as compared with what it was in the memories of men yet living. It has been estimated that more than one-half of all the scientists who have ever lived are living and active today. Gone are the times when a young Newton worked out the laws of mechanics in the remoteness of his mother's Yorkshire farm, a Cavendish explored the laws of Nature in his private laboratory and a Darwin assembled the evidence for evolution in the study of his country home. A theorist might yet work in isolation, but he would be likely to need a great library if not the stimulus of associating with his fellows. An experimentalist almost always needs equipment and a laboratory environment which are expensive and may be colossal, and he may be compelled to be a member of a large team.

As I understand it, I am supposed to write of the moral problems of big-scale science. Unfortunately I think of no important ones that are peculiar to the big scale. The major problems appear to be those that have always existed, intensified by the number of people who encounter them.

The greatest commandment to the scientist has always been "Report your observations truthfully." A deliberate violation of this commandment would be considered practically an unforgivable sin. Rarely indeed is anyone accused, even by innuendo, of such a violation. I call to mind only one such case, and in that case (which did not occur in this country) the man's supervisor issued a statement that he was mentally irresponsible.

There are a couple of aspects of this commandment that merit attention. It is felt that a physicist must not only report his observations truthfully, but must describe his procedure accurately so that any other capable physicist could repeat his experiment and discover any honest mistake that he might have made. I do not think that a man who neglected this part of his duty would be considered to have sinned; I do think that his publications would come to be disregarded and that editors would soon refuse to publish what he wrote. Another type of situation arises when an observer must decide which of many observations are the most reliable. He may make a considerable number which are coherent with one another and with some reasonable theory, but among these there may be a few which are wildly at variance with the rest. He may suspect reasons for these deviations, but be unable to prove them absolutely. Shall he publish everything, or shall he select what he believes to be the reliable observations, trusting that he is sufficiently impartial to refrain from eliminating others because they contradict what he would like to prove? This is a question that no man can answer unless he be an expert in the particular type of experiment. A pertinent point is that if everybody published *every* observation, the already enormous literature of physics would become completely impossible.

Here is a moral problem which was posed by the French author Duhamel many years ago, and may have been posed elsewhere. Does one have the right to amuse oneself by exploring congenial researches in "pure" science, when there are so many practical questions waiting to be solved? I suspect that this question hardly ever occurs to any physicist. Even the general public is beginning to realize that "pure" researches may have the most dramatic and even terrific practical results, while investigations directed toward a specific goal may never reach it. One of the earliest illustrations of the first part of this statement is still one of the best. X-rays and radioactivity, the two best weapons against cancer next to the surgeon's knife, were discovered by physicists with no plans or expectations of making a contribution to medicine. And to illustrate the second part of the statement, think what gigantic sums are annually sought and given for research oriented directly to the cancer problem, and how far the world yet seems to be from the general solution! One such example as this allows anyone to feel that he may be doing the very best thing by following his own bent: and there are many such examples.

But while such a question hardly ever occurs to a working physicist, it must occur many times to a "director or research" and to the management of a great laboratory of industry, government, or even a

Big-scale Scientific Research

university. Sometimes the apparent sidetrack really is a sidetrack and not the main line, and sometimes the best way to attack a specific problem is to go straight at it.

My guess is that questions of this kind are solved partly by the judgment of the man higher up, partly by his feeling of what the ultimate source of funds—the stockholder, the Pentagon, the taxpayer—will "stand for." In terms of what was acceptable half a century ago, these ultimate sources will often "stand for" a great deal. There are, of course, limits. I should be surprised to hear that a great electrical company was financing a laboratory of bacteriology, or that a pharmaceutical company was paying for research in general relativity. But even as I write this sentence I am aware that I may some day hear just that.

(Parenthetically I return to the title "director of research." This title antagonizes many people who feel that what is called "research" is not really research unless it springs spontaneously from the mind of the uncontrolled investigator. It is a strange thing that some of the most eminent people who have borne that title have felt essentially that way about it. I knew well one of them who used to say that he considered that his duty was to find good men and then let them strictly alone. He was not unique. On the other hand, I would not dare to say that every "director of research" shares that view.)

Another moral problem that has been posed by nonphysicists is whether a person ought to take part in work that may lead to a discovery helpful to warfare. This seems to be of very little concern to physicists, probably for the following reason. Let us suppose that Dr. X were to announce "I will not enter such-and-such a field of research, for I might make a discovery useful in war." He would then be saying, in effect: "I think that there is a dangerous discovery waiting to be made in such-and-such a field of physics; I think also that I am the only person clever enough to make it, and so, if I get out of that field, it will remain unmade forever." Such an assertion would be as ridiculous as it sounds, and furthermore it would be dangerous to the man's own country, in this era when brilliance in physics is by no means a monopoly of any one nation.

Another moral issue is whether a physicist should feel an obligation to tell the general public loudly and emphatically about the hazards resulting from such things as nuclear fission and its applications.

Those who read the *Bulletin of the Atomic Scientists,* and those who follow the press in the discussions of (for instance) fallout, know that there are many physicists who deem this a serious obligation, and some of the most eminent are among these.

An issue on another plane is afforded by patent rights. When I became an employe of a great industrial laboratory many years ago, I was given one dollar in exchange for assigning to the company all rights to all patents that I might subsequently make. This dollar was a total loss to the company, for I never made a patent. There were many of my colleagues who made valuable patents, and it is to be presumed that these had some effect upon their salaries. But there also may have been employes of this or other companies, who would have become multimillionaires if they had made their inventions as independent investigators in laboratories of their own; and such a man may rue the day when he accepted the dollar. This patent policy may be regarded as a sort of leveling process, in which the most ingenious man gets less and the least ingenious man gets more than they would have got if they had been independent.

Another issue is that connoted by the word "secrecy." Everyone agrees that if everything about the development of a new weapon were told to all the world, the knowledge could help other countries to attack us. Yet everyone, or at any rate most people, will agree that if everything that might help in the development of weaponry were kept secret, the development of weaponry itself might be slowed down for want of the contributions that might be made by people outside the closed circle of "cleared scientists," and so would be the peaceful applications of whatever may be developed. The question therefore is where to draw the line, and this is a technical question rather than a moral one. Nevertheless there is an associated issue which has ethical aspects. A scientist may be denied entry into the closed circle because of what are called "security reasons." This may hurt his prestige generally, and also his particular opportunities in a firm or a university which is engaged partly but not wholly in secret research. Grave injustice may be done in this way, and intense bitterness has been engendered in cases which are known to everyone who reads the newspapers. There are those who fear that if a university gets an appreciable part of its gross revenue from government to finance "contract research" (and for some institutions the part is not merely appreciable but considerable), its choice of staff and of research problems will be unduly influenced by other than academic motives.

Another issue that has paled of recent years is whether a young man who knows himself to be a good physicist should be a poor professor devoted to pure science or a richly paid employe of industry devoted to something less noble. This has been attenuated partly by a rise in the salary scales of professors, partly by the policy of great companies already mentioned in these pages, whereby the physicists whom they employ can do good work in interesting fields and publish it in the literature of physics. Nobody could affirm either that physicists in the major universities are generally of lower caliber than physicists in industry, or that the latter generally do second-grade work. Though there is a flow of established physicists from university into industry, there is also a counterflow from industry into university. It must be admitted that in the first year after the Ph.D. is attained, the difference between what a young man can get in industry and what he can get in a university may be very large. What I have said in this paragraph continues to be true in the main if for "university" is substituted "government laboratory."

There are a few problems which are definitely correlated with the big scale of contemporary physics. Rivalry among the young has become much more intense, now that the announcement of a new type of experiment or a new ramification of theory may result in immediate attempts to repeat and to develop it in dozens of institutions. Shall a physicist withhold his new observation until he has double-checked and triplechecked it and refined his method, or shall he rush it to the editors at the risk of having to try to stop the presses to pull it out again and finding that he has waited too long to do so? I fear that an increasing number of young men are doing the latter, and it is useless to tell them that Cavendish waited years to publish some of his results and never published others at all, for they can correctly reply that neither the social standing nor the economic situation of Cavendish would have been impaired in the least if he had never published anything. Another question is how the credit for a piece of work done by a team or group of investigators shall be distributed among its members. In this country at least, the problem is usually solved in what is commonly miscalled the "democratic" way: everybody gets his name in the byline in alphabetical order: I have seen a short article of which the byline comprised sixteen names (!) much to the distress of indexers, and I doubt whether even this is the record. Another question is how far the physicist should go in referring to previous work in the field of his paper. This is generally solved by going to the extreme of deference. I have seen short notes in which the references to prior work constituted more than one-quarter of the wordage. If there is anything of which physicists in general *cannot* be accused, it is insufficient acknowledgment of the work of their predecessors and their rivals!

CHAPTER X

Organizational Structure and Professional Ethics in a Government Laboratory

By C. M. HERZFELD

I. *Introduction*

IN THIS PAPER I shall attempt to examine how the structure of a large research organization (particularly in the case of a government laboratory) affects, and is affected by, the professional ethics of its members.

We shall begin with an examination of the relation of the *structure* of a research organization to its *goals,* then explore the interaction of *structure* and ethical *behavior,* and finally seek some clarification of the ethical problem posed.

These problems are quite complex and not very well defined. Furthermore, while most scientists have opinions or feelings about them, these latter are not well articulated, and sometimes not even very reasonable.

Two comments must be made right away. One is, that *any* social structure can and will raise certain problems having ethical dimensions, merely because it is a structure and involves the relations of human beings. We shall try to concentrate on those problems which are characteristic of structures of *research* organizations. The second comment is, that it may be thought unusual to classify some of the problems under discussion as ethical. Our point of view here is that any human action which has an element of "oughtness" about it has to that extent an ethical dimension. As we shall see, the number of such types of actions in a research organization is surprisingly large. We shall not discuss those "ordinary" ethical problems which arise in everyday life and which have no relevance to the special topic at hand.

II. The Problem of Structure of a Research Organization

To a certain extent the idea of a structure imposed "from the outside" on a research organization violates the idea of freedom and independence inherent in research. Even the expression "research organization" suffers from this intrinsic contradiction. Let us look at this difficulty more closely because it is close to the center of concern. Research is a "search" for truth, knowledge, insight (in our context, in the physical sciences). We must distinguish two levels of research: Basic research, whose motive is the new knowledge itself, and applied research, whose motive is the accomplishment of certain definite goals whose existence is known or suspected beforehand. Clearly, the extent to which one can "organize" research differs for basic and applied research. More precisely, the type of organization possible differs.

It is clear that even an institution devoted entirely to basic research can have (indeed must have) a minimal structure. A department in a university may be a good example of such minimal organization.[1] The nature of basic research (and the characteristic element here is its motive) then determines the nature of the organization and its structure. The principle of organization is one which gives complete independence and autonomy to every individual who has demonstrated that he has the ability and the motive to do basic research. The function of the organization is limited to providing this individual with the resources he needs. In return, the individual is expected only to contribute his own research, his activity as "master" of the "apprentices" (direction of research of graduate students and teaching of courses). The role of the professor as teacher (in the sense of lecturer, divorced from, or at least separated from, researcher) has been generally overemphasized and this unbalance is obviously one of the factors contributing to the general mediocrity of higher education.[2] The

---

[1] We shall ignore here as irrelevant that a university has an "applied" motive also, namely, the training of students. The great institutions of higher learning are characterized precisely by the proposition that the best training can be given by apprenticeship in research which is done solely for the sake of knowledge itself.

[2] It is clear that contemporary university life is complicated by the need to get contracts, to serve on committees, etc. Some of this is obviously detrimental to the exercise of the primary functions of the university. Some of it may, however, involve the necessary relation of the university to the whole of society. This relation, complex and not well understood, goes certainly beyond the "turning out" of research and of students.

ideal structure of the university department is consistent with its function. It is quite loose, there is no direction given by a department head, except that which he gives by his outstanding example as scholar. Decisions which affect the whole department are made by the faculty as a whole. This includes such things as budgets, the hiring of new staff, etc.

This paper is devoted to another kind of research institution where the primary aim is applied research, *i.e.,* where it is possible (indeed required) to set some definite goals. These goals are, however, assumed to be so broad that it is impossible to deduce from the goals a complete program. Hence most of the applied research is applied only in the sense that the *area* of the research can be specified in advance. Furthermore, such an institution must always devote a significant fraction of its effort to basic research, *i.e.,* research motivated principally by the desire to advance scientific knowledge.

Many government research institutions are of this type.[3] They have statutory missions which are often sufficiently broad or vague that the management can (and must) make many decisions to limit the activities of the institution. This in turn affects the freedom of the members. How does the structure of the institution affect the making of such decisions? What are the ethical dimensions of this interplay between goals, structure, and decisionmaking?

It is clear that an institution devoted to applied research of the type here envisioned must have some definite structure. The broad statutory mission must be translated into a more narrow mission with definite emphasis on certain areas of work, and must further be translated into a program. Decisions must therefore be made about the allocation of (always scarce) resources such as manpower, funds, equipment, space. Such processes involve the elements of control and responsibility. These must be vested in certain definite individuals

[3]This is the approximate situation at the National Bureau of Standards. The primary mission of the National Bureau of Standards is to provide the United States with a complete and consistent system for all physical measurements. The other activities are more or less dependent on this. This is a very definite goal in a certain sense. It specifies unambiguously that certain lines of research *must* be pursued. But the goal is not sufficiently precise that one can deduce from it the whole program. Particularly today, where the demands of science and industry on this system of measurement change very rapidly, and are becoming constantly more severe, it is necessary to insist on a great deal of flexibility in the program, making it quite similar to a basic research program in certain concrete ways.

who must be responsible for the fulfilment of the statutory mission. The structure also facilitates the expression of ideas, of consent, disagreement. At the same time, because of the nature of the institution (which involves both some direction and a great deal of uncertainty) it is essential that there be a large element of freedom for the seasoned and responsible scientist. It is he who is usually the best judge about these questions: What needs to be done in a given field (*e.g.,* temperature standards), and how it should be done? The first function of management is therefore to determine the main fields which need attention. Then the responsible scientists' advice must be obtained on what should be done in these fields. Finally, management must decide which of the many promising and sound approaches are to be taken. The first decision is usually made on the basis of national needs, the second on the basis of the scientific judgment and personal interests of the senior scientists. The third decision is usually a compromise between many attractive (and even urgent) possibilities and the limited resources. The structure must make it clear that these three tasks need to be accomplished, and how and when each member of the organization is to make his contribution.

The three steps of deciding the program are of course not neatly separable. Rather all three run in parallel and should involve a continuing process. But it is essential that at some regular intervals each component of the organization be required to go through this process explicitly.[4]

The precise form of the structure is probably less important than most suppose. There are several reasons for this. For one thing, it seems really impossible to construct a thoroughly logical structure for an institution of the type under consideration. Both the technical structure and the power structure of an organization appear to follow certain *informal* lines of organization, which do not always coincide with the formal lines. The formal lines become obsolete through many technical and personal developments which involve shifts in the relations of programs and the interactions of people. Thus, a structure

---

[4]Unfortunately this is usually only done at budget time, say, once a year. This is a mistake. At budget time everyone is likely to confuse the desirable with the possible, and concentrate on the latter. This habit dilutes the estimates of the objective needs in a given situation and results often in complete inability to determine the real needs. To be sure the last step of the decisionmaking must involve budgets, but it is probably a mistake to bring budgetary considerations into the picture before this last step.

Structure and Ethics in a Government Laboratory 109

which is logical today will inevitably be less logical tomorrow. Rather than strive for the perfect system, it seems desirable to have a two-axis structure. One axis (conventionally taken as vertical) is like a chain of command. A is the boss of B who is the boss of C, etc. This vertical structure should be the locus of the formal responsibilities of management. It should approximate the scientific structure of the program moderately well, and should not change rapidly.[5] The second axis (horizontal, say) should be designed to follow the present day technical problems. Its function is primarily to coordinate, to stimulate. It should be fairly independent of the vertical axis, and should be flexible and quite loose. It should be temporary, and easily done away with, to be replaced by a new coordinating scheme more perfectly adapted to the later scientific and human situation.[6]

If an organization has two such independent (and "opposite") types of structure with comparable real significance, then management has a tool for the stimulation and development of the staff, of the program, and of the whole institution, which cannot be found in *either one* of these structures. At the same time the staff of the institution has a strong lever to affect management. This interplay involves some ethical problems; they are dealt with below. It should be noted that such an arrangement will strike many persons as unworkable, and irrational. It is certain that such an arrangement does not make for simple and obvious relations between persons, and may often frustrate and confuse. This is inevitable. Strictly orderly procedure is possible only in a morgue. A research organization, on the other hand, is a living organism which undergoes constantly the analog of mutations. A static structure will always fail, and will only produce peace by stagnation. It should be further noted that the horizontal structure is only a generalization of what every imaginative administrator does anyway, namely, to go outside the formal structure (here the vertical structure) to get ideas, advice, reactions.[7]

[5] These vertical elements resemble the conventional "Divisions" of a large organization.

[6] The horizontal elements resemble coordinators or coordinating committees which cut across the "Division" lines. It is my contention, however, that in any such institution as considered in this paper, two quite distinct and in a certain sense opposing (or-thogonal) systems are desirable and possible, *i.e.,* that the same two *types* of structures should exist (officially or not) on *every* significant level of organization.

[7] For an excellent discussion of this phenomenon on the largest scale see *The Coming of the New Deal,* A. M. Schlesinger, Jr., Houghton Mifflin, Boston, 1959, chapter VIII.

Ethics and Bigness

So far we have discussed the structure of a research organization by looking at the types of technical goals and their effect on the structure. So far no explicitly ethical questions have arisen, except the general one of controlling (in some sense) the uncontrollable act of scientific creation in research. This question is, of course, the basic one, from which most of the others arise.

III. Some Ethical Problems Arising from the Organizational Structure

1. *The problem of the control of creative freedom*

The most basic ethical problem which arises is undoubtedly the following: The scientist is expected to do creative research, to search for the truth, yet, in some way or other he is told where to search, and in some measure, how to search. By what right does anyone tell another that he must think about certain problems? How can this in fact be done? This is of course no different, in one sense, than the usual employer-employe relationship. But the general problems arising there are here amplified greatly because the activity of the "employe" is so highly creative. Any direction of this activity therefore penetrates much more deeply the interior life of the person being directed than is the case for less creative activities. The creative scientist gives very much more of himself than someone in a less creative activity. This element of giving of oneself makes the scientist particularly vulnerable.[8] There would, perhaps, be no problem if all research were done by wealthy individuals (as was often the case in the eighteenth and nineteenth centuries) who do precisely as they please, and provide their own resources. But today two factors operate which produce the problem. On the one hand, many research problems require large financial and physical resources. High energy nuclear physics, large nuclear accelerators, and the IGY come to mind. Hence large organizations are required for the solution even of many *basic* scientific problems. On the other hand, the vast majority of scientists must work for a living. Hence this vast majority of creatively

---

[8]The situation is not very different from that of a creative artist who is "employed" to do a "job." One can detect here the same incongruity of such a situation, and its inherent dangers, as in the case of the creative scientist.

active people must accept many conditions of employment to be able to practice their art. For the scientist the ethical problem is to keep his own integrity while accepting work in a larger framework, and on problems which are not wholly of his own choosing. The ethical problem of the administrator is to accomplish the task assigned him without violating the freedom of the scientists engaged in the task.

Several comments are required here. First, the scientific task may be given to the administrator by someone else, or it may be a task which he has created, *e.g.,* the solution of a scientific problem which he has discovered. He may therefore have the role of the manager or of the scientific leader or a mixture of the two. Second, there is a wide range in the amount of freedom of the individual scientist. This amount depends perhaps most on his experience and stature, rather than who his employer is. It is largest (usually) in the universities organized on the American plan. But even here government contracts for research may make a problem.[9] In government or industrial laboratories this problem is much more serious, because of the demands made by their goals and missions. If the institution has a definite goal which requires that certain objectives be met, but if these objectives are so complex and so difficult to meet that a large element of basic research with its type of creativeness is required, then the problem of reconciling creative freedom with meeting the goals is particularly acute. I should observe that we concentrate here on the ethical problem of controlling creative freedom. But it is also important to remember that one of the most serious effects of violating the creative freedom of the scientist by improper control is the loss (or impairment) of his creativity. This impairment occurs precisely to the extent that the intended task is basic research. The more basic the intended approach, the more vulnerable to control are the scientist and his productivity.

2. *The problem of responsibility for decisions made by management*

The problem of creative freedom arises in still another form: How much moral responsibility do the scientists "in the ranks" have for the decisions of management? This has two aspects. One, the decisions

[9] J. C. Weaver, "What Federal Funds Mean to the Universities Today," *Annals*, American Academy of Political and Social Science, Philadelphia, January, 1960, p. 114.

about the way in which the scientific work is done, and what is to be done. This has been raised above. The second aspect is, what to do with the scientific results, their social use. The most spectacular example is surely the debate over the use of the atomic bomb in 1945. The scientific community attempted to affect the decision to use the bomb chiefly through the Franck report, but the managers on the national level, *i.e.,* the President and his advisers, certainly did not pay real attention to this problem.[10] The same problem arises in a less spectacular way every day in industrial and government laboratories. The scientific community is widely split on this issue. Some believe that the issue of the use of scientific discoveries has no ethical dimension at all, at least not for the scientist. They assert that all they are morally responsible for is their work. What is done with it is none of their business. The other side believes that they are completely co-responsible with the users of their work, and find that they cannot collaborate, even remotely, with any enterprise where they have no determining voice in the major decisions.

It is not clear how to resolve this. Some comments are attempted below. But in any case, this issue is quite real.

3. *What kind of decisions may management make*

This problem is really related to the previous one, but arises in a different context. Concretely, may management make decisions which will surely affect the future development of an institution, both on the human and the technical level? Indeed, must not management make such decisions? The precise point is this: How much consultation is needed for a major decision? (We are not concerned at all in this paper with the practical "political" question: How much consultation is required to be able to persuade everyone to put the decision into effect without excessive annoyance by the staff, to avoid a rebellion, etc. We are here interested in the questions of right and wrong. Thus it is quite conceivable that a particular move would not upset anyone significantly, and thus could be "brought off," but would still violate important rights of the staff members.)

Such problems are quite acute when an institution with a definite mission but a basic approach must plan for the future. Such plans

[10] M. Amrine, *The Great Decision,* Putnam, New York, 1959.

Structure and Ethics in a Government Laboratory   113

always arise from a mixture of experiences, hunches, and guess work based on incomplete information. Yet when implemented they do (and must) deflect the activities of large portions of the staff. They may change the climate and tone of the institution. Does it follow that all such major changes must be approved by the staff in a formal and explicit way, or even that they must originate *only* with the staff?

Occasionally, decisions must be made quickly which have such farreaching effects, and there is no chance for extensive consultation. Must, therefore, no such quick commitments be made?

Another way this problem arises is at the appointment of supervisors and administrators. How much consultation with staff at the same level, at lower and higher levels, is required before an appointment can be made? Such an appointment will affect many persons directly. What voice should they have in this process?

4. *The giving and taking of scientific advice*

Closely related to problem 3 is this: How can one operate in a situation where one disagrees with basic policy? This is a common problem in government, but has some special features in a research organization. The added complication arises from the fact that policies are generally decided on the basis of broad "political" and "strategic" considerations while the advice of the scientist to the policymaker is at least in part based on scientific facts and arguments. Usually the scientific adviser will (unconsciously) exaggerate the degree to which his advice is based on scientific considerations and underestimate the same base in the thought of the policymaker (particularly if his advice is not taken). Hence the conflict looks like "politics" versus "science" to the scientist. On the other hand, the same situation looks to the policymaker often as special pleading by the scientist. This problem arises on all organizational levels, in fact whenever purely scientific considerations must be superseded by others. This happens when budgets are prepared, staffing plans made, in other words, in almost every managerial act.

How can the scientist work with someone who apparently disregards scientific evidence, follows his hunches rather than the experience of the scientist, etc.? Conversely, how can the manager or policymaker use scientific advice, why, indeed, does he bother with it?

Clearly, the advisee has the right not to take the advice given, but what about explaining his decision to his adviser? Usually the advisee feels no ethical compulsion to do so. But does the person who gets scientific advice have a greater obligation to his adviser when disregarding scientific advice precisely because it is (to some extent) scientific? Conversely, what about the responsibility of the adviser not to "dress up" his advice, not to use science as a weapon or as camouflage, especially with a layman?

5. Rebellion in the ranks and the control of humans

Scientists cannot be made to have ideas, nor can they be forced to work. Hence scientists have a potentially powerful tool to defend themselves. This is rarely used intentionally or deliberately, mostly because such "rebellion" can only be achieved at the cost of professional growth. Scientists apply this force indirectly, however. They simply do not work under certain conditions. Thus, as long as there is a shortage of really good scientists, they can force important changes in the conditions of employment. This has resulted in salaries for scientists which are usually much higher than those of nonscientists with comparable stature. It has also resulted in an increase in the support for basic research in government laboratories, because competent people cannot be hired unless they can spend a significant fraction of their time pursuing their own interests.

The ethical problem arises because this process is based to some extent on selfish interests, and to some extent on the inherent demands of the scientific enterprise. At what point does this process cease to work for the good of science and begin to be a subtle form of blackmail? Conversely, opposition to these trends may be a matter of justice, or of provincialism. When is it one, when the other?

Closely related to this problem is one involving the operations of management. Promotions, awards, special recognition are standard components of the managerial tool box. They are said to "reward" to "underscore special achievements" to "recognize" outstanding work. To what extent does such a system result in the gradual enslavement of the staff? On the literal level such a suggestion sounds absurd, but is it really so at deeper, less obvious, levels? Certainly all such systems allow managers to create an ambiguous relation of excessive dependence of the staff members. Again, this situation exists in any organized relationship, but it is particularly difficult to understand in the subtle interplay involved in the "controlled" creative freedom of the research laboratory.

IV. *Possible Guides for Ethical Behavior*

In this section we shall attempt to see how it may be possible to construct a guide for consistent ethical behavior in a research laboratory. We shall not attempt to provide solutions to these problems posed in Section III here, but shall attempt to use these problems as test cases to examine what may be a useful approach to the general situation.

First let us say what we shall require of any acceptable system of ethical behavior. It must have some general principles which are understandable and potentially acceptable to a very large fraction of the persons involved, and it must have some reasonably definite ways of formulating practical rules of behavior based on these principles which are usable in specific circumstances.

It seems clear that the usual formulations of the traditional systems of ethics do not meet the requirements we have just made.

Let us examine this further. For definiteness let us concentrate on the traditional JudeoChristian systems of ethical behavior. Neither the Decalogue nor the Sermon on the Mount provides us with a system adequate for our needs. They do not provide us even with all of the required principles. There is little to be learned there about the basic problem under discussion in this paper, namely, the conflict between creative scientific freedom and the requirements of social usefulness. Certainly the most basic imperatives of justice and of charity (love) are found in the traditional religious systems and we certainly require these for ethical behavior in the laboratory. But the gap between these principles and their application is exceptionally wide. (Is this related to the relative indifference of the scientist toward the traditional religions?) As we have pointed out just above, there are some new principles required before the most basic imperatives can be applied meaningfully.

This calls for an extended analysis of the problem of freedom and usefulness in society, surely one of the most basic problems of modern society. But this analysis must be relevant to the context of the research organization. There exist various attempts within the Judeo-Christian framework to extend the basic religious principles in a rational way so that they can be applied to practical problems in society. These attempts suffer (in our context) from having been made long ago, long before the concrete problem in view arose. They are not very helpful, as far as this writer can see. Their basic strategy to arrive at usable results, however, may be useful here: 1. Let us accept the basic moral imperatives. 2. Let us analyze the concrete nature of the broad problem (here, the problem of the freedom of the creative scientist in its relation to social usefulness), and try to see what concrete principles of behavior are relevant with respect to the concrete situation and consistent with the basic moral imperatives. 3. Let us see if one can formulate these concrete principles of behavior so that they may be effectively and unambiguously communicated and "held" within the environment.

Obviously the whole task required here goes far beyond the scope of this paper. It may, however, be useful to point out certain ideas which are germinal and suggestive. What is required most is a program for further thought on our problem rather than concrete suggestions for the solution of concrete difficulties. The basic need is for better understanding of the relation between the creative scientist and society. We have only stated the problem in a fragmentary way. It would be most interesting to analyze it with the method used by Richard McKeon[11] to illumine the larger problem of freedom in general.

In the meantime it may be useful to suggest certain revelant ideas which may add perspective to our view.

A. The personal position of the scientist must be made clear. In particular, the contribution which he makes precisely *because* of his freedom must be explained. This contribution is much like that of the artist. Camus has said[12] that "The work of art, by the mere fact that it exists, denies the conquest of ideology." Similarly, the creative scientific idea (and the "creative" is essential here!), by the mere fact that it exists, denies the "social usefulness" interpretation of science as an ideology. The analogy between the two situations is, in fact, extremely

[11] R. McKeon, *Freedom and History*, Noonday Press, New York, 1952.
[12] A. Camus, "The Artist as Witness of Freedom," *Commentary*, December, 1949.

close. The scientist is also a witness to freedom, and like the artist, can never be completely committed to any ideology. (If he tries, as many do, and also is a man of conscience and sensitivity, he involves himself in the sharpest interior dilemma imaginable.) In a certain sense, his science must always "come first."

This freedom of the scientist means that, in the long run, he is an overturner of society, a revolutionary, a prophet. The role science has played in the history of ideas demonstrates this. Perhaps the usual interpretation of science as socially useful (by improving living conditions, giving mastery over environment, etc.) suffers chiefly from nearsightedness, and perhaps the long-range revolutionary effect on thought, together with the constant witness to human freedom is the most significant contribution. The scientist is committed to society first of all through his commitment to freedom, and this is his most important social contribution by far.

The importance of creative freedom lies in the fact that it is a prerequisite for the act of basic discovery as was pointed out in Section III, 1. Hence this creative freedom is strictly necessary if the scientist is to make his most important contribution to society, his contribution as a "prophet."

Also, if this prophetic function of the scientist is understood, the problem of his responsibility for the use, or misuse, of ideas (discussed in III, 2) becomes transformed. The most profound ideas probably have an influence of their own which is quite incalculable, and which may well be beyond the power of anyone to pervert by immoral use.

B. A certain conception of basic research popular among scientists in universities may be based on lack of historical perspective. This is the idea that basic research flourishes best when separated from all connection with application. Certainly, in the great schools devoted to basic research today it is often considered demeaning, "second-rate," to take problems in applied science seriously, and this mystique is carefully instilled into the graduate students. I believe that a subtle confusion is involved here, between the freedom to proceed on scientific problems according to the internal logic of research (which freedom is essential for basic research), and the question whether the basic research at hand has other, "inferior," connections. The history of science seems to show that many great discoveries were made by scientists either while working on applied problems, or by scientists who worked on applied problems part of the time.[13] In fact, a good case might be made that basic science thrives by contact with applied problems, *provided* the freedom necessary for basic research exists. It is not at all easy to be very concrete about this point. In the practical situation an indefinable, delicate balance seems to be involved in this creative symbiosis, and the extremes of complete isolation of basic from applied research, on the one hand, and the complete subordination of basic to applied research, on the other hand, are much easier to define and to embody in a mystique and an organizational structure. If such a symbiotic relation exists, the research organization most productive of new ideas may well be one with some "applied" side interests. How to guarantee the necessary freedom, how to gauge the desirable degree of involvement, etc., are unsolved problems.

C. A precisely located though very complex sociological problem is unsolved. It is the following: How is the sociology of science affected by changes in the method of science? It seems to be becoming more evident that the method of science is changing with time, as science progresses. The formal method, the "scientific method" does not seem to have changed very much since the contributions of the Copenhagen school to the interpretation of quantum mechanics (we leave aside here the "causal" controversy). But what about the informal method, the art of doing science? It is my contention that this has changed very significantly since 1925. As it became clear in the period from 1926 to 1940 that quantum mechanics and the special theory of relativity were "good" scientific theories which had great power to predict and to systematize, the informal scientific method, the art of doing science changed. The principal effect appears to be to make today's informal method much more deductive than the formal method would lead one to think possible. This is not the place to elaborate on this. But does it not have considerable effect on the sociology of science, *i.e.,* on the way in which the society consisting of those who do science is organized and how it operates, on its value systems? One obvious effect is this: It is much easier now for an administrator or a senior colleague to discourage by a theoretical argument a line of investigation than it was, say, thirty years ago. How many discoveries are *not* made

[13]This point is discussed in several articles in *Roots of Scientific Thought*, edited by P. P. Wiener and A. Noland, Basic Books, New York, 1957.

because of this phenomenon? (Indeed how many are not made because the investigator talks *himself* out of the idea?) It is well known that almost all theoreticians of note thought that nothing interesting would come of the first parity experiments (except, of course, Lee and Yang who proposed them).

This increasingly deductive feature of the informal method traps the scientist and it also changes the balance of power between him and the "organization."

D. The nature of the adminstrative activity is often given an excessively simplistic interpretation. To be sure there exist certain methods and principles of administration, though these are not easy to formulate in an unambiguous way. But it seems to me that administration (distinguished from "caretaking") is a creative art. The medium of this art form is uncommonly rich and complex. It involves people, their ideas, their interests, it involves resources, relations between very different types of activities and demands. There are differences between administration and more conventional art forms. In the former, the work of art is even less finishable than in the others, and hence the frustration of the "artist" correspondingly greater. Two aspects of this interpretation of administration are particularly relevant here. One, that it *is* an art form, and that therefore all attempts to make its principle explicit are bound to fail eventually. Two, that the "work of art" is never really finished. This means that the usual criteria for successful administration, such as orderly procedure, reliable decisionmaking processes, etc., may be much less important than those elements which liberate the creative energies of the members of the organization.

It is imperative for creative activity in any art form to respect the materials, the medium. As we have tried to show, these "materials" have unusual properties if the art form is the administration of research. Only the administrator who understands and respects his "materials" will be able to understand what is required of him, will be able to elicit the potentialities of the medium.

E. Finally, it seems useful to consider a phenomenon which is well known, but whose significance in the present context seems to have been largely overlooked. Every institution has, in its bones, so to say, certain rules of behavior which are usually quite vaguely defined, but which exercise considerable influence over the behavior of the individuals involved, the *mores* of the institution. These mores are usually very difficult to make explicit, often they are most clearly noticed when they are offended against ("this is one of the things which one simply does not do, at least not around here"). But they do give in an informal way a statement of what is expected of everyone. It may be that this set of vaguely defined rules of behavior which differ from one institution to another may be the mechanism by which certain ethical principles can be made effective. Two things must be accomplished to make this so. First of all, the existence of the mores, and the fact that in a certain sense they are binding on the members must be generally known and their significance appreciated. So far, this does not really go beyond an institution having a strong esprit de corps. Second, the mores must be affected, if possible, in such a way that they really become helpful in providing everyone with a shared sense of ethical behavior. This means that thought must be given to "build into" the mores such reactions which reflect the various facets of the basic ethical problems, some of which have been examined above. But one cannot manipulate the mores of an organization without destroying it. Therefore, they can only be modified (or even clarified) by leadership on the moral plane. This seems to me to require that *all* participants approach the difficult concrete ethical problems with great clarity about their personal obligation to function on this moral plane. This also requires a systematic attempt to understand the concrete situation in which these problems arise.

V. *Conclusions*

We have seen that the central ethical problem is the balance between creative scientific freedom and the real or supposed requirements of the social usefulness of science.

To find a guide for ethical behavior with respect to this problem we have proposed a few general principles which may be operative in addition to the basic moral imperatives of justice and love found in the traditional religions. One of these principles is the social function of the scientist as a prophet, a revolutionary of the spirit. Another is the possibly stimulating symbiosis of basic and applied research, provided the basic freedom is not impaired. We have also pointed out that recent changes in the art of doing sciences may make improper control of science easier to achieve. But we have in addition called attention to the creative element in administration, which, with proper respect for the materials it works with, may forestall some of the major abuses usually encountered.

Finally, we have suggested that the mores of an institution may offer a suitable framework or vehicle for the general principles to become effective in the concrete context.

VI. *Acknowledgment*

Many colleagues have contributed to this paper with ideas, suggestions, and criticism. R. D. Huntoon has pointed out to me the relevance of the "mores" of an institution.

CHAPTER XI

"We Are Here as on a Darkling Plain"
Comment on Responsibility in Big-Scale Scientific and Academic Organization

By ROBERT B. LIVINGSTON

> *"And we are here as on a darkling plain*
> *Swept with confused alarms of struggle and flight,*
> *Where ignorant armies clash by night."*
> from *Dover Beach* by Matthew Arnold

Introduction

THIS PAPER is divided into two parts. Part I concerns the background of world issues in which science is a prime mover. Part II concerns the future, especially in relation to problems we face in this country with respect to decisionmaking. The paper concludes with a tentative proposal of an institutional safeguard to help in the matter of obtaining for the government more objective advice in relation to science and technology.

I

A. Assumptions Relating to the Chief Problem Facing Mankind

1. *Human needs and international anarchy*

Each human shares certain fundamental interests and objectives with all others: that it is better to be alive than dead, fed than starved, free than enslaved. No individual can safeguard fulfilment of these needs for himself, nor for any other. No social system can safeguard them for its own people, nor for any other. A condition of social anarchy is most threatening and perilous amongst the most inclusive social systems, nations, and confederations of nations. The peril is equal to the extinction of all life. Triggers for catastrophe are not under the confident control of any person, system, or combination of systems.

2. *The requirement for a new system of social integration*

The chief problem facing mankind is to establish a new system that is worldwide in its purview and sufficient to satisfy certain basic needs for all mankind. It remains to be seen whether we can meet the main requirement of our day, to establish some kind of world order under a just system of law, within whatever gap of time may be available. If we make our best effort, and yet fail in this attempt, we cannot lose anything not already lost.

B. Assumptions Relating to Possible Solutions

1. *Dimensions and requirements of the problem*

Mankind has become so much one family that there is no way to safeguard our lives or welfare without achieving the same for everyone else. Perforce creative thinking of ways to satisfy fundamental human needs and to arrange for the just settlement of disputes must be conducted on a global scale.

We need a fresh analysis of the role of institutions bearing directly or indirectly on the requirement for a world government to support universal maximum individual self-realization, that is, universal individual freedom and opportunity in the maximum possible degree. Then, we need research with the widest possible world base, to enlarge man's understanding and opportunities in relation to social integration. The wide base is recommended because it will encourage contributions toward modifying all institutions in the required direction, and it will provide the advantage of construction by the largest pool of creative thinking.

2. *The need for a world view*

The situation facing mankind can be improved by the encouragement and development of a world view in all these objectives and

"We Are Here as on a Darkling Plain" 125

undertakings; not a view to conquer the world, but to make it safer, and in other basic ways better for all mankind. Greatness, security, and welfare cannot any longer be secured on a merely national scale. We recognize this and put it into increasing practice in our foreign and defense policies, foreign aid, military aid, and mutual security programs. Something new has been added to nationalism, without detracting from a full and honorable national devotion and allegiance.

3. *Integration cannot be initiated unilaterally*

No nation or confederation of nations, acting unilaterally, can put a world government into effect. Thus, the only alternative to our present uneasy international anarchy seems to be to invite the broadest world base of creative social thinkers to undertake research and deliberations leading to the development of plans for an all-inclusive community of mankind. We have substantial reason to hope for progress in this direction through the application of the methods of science. Ultimately agreed upon research findings and the results of world based deliberations can be subjected to national recognition or rejection by referenda.

4. *Broad scale educational requirements*

The world situation will be improved by the encouragement and development of longer-range motives and aims, on the part of individuals, families, nations, and international confederations. Appropriate educational procedures will lead to the recognition and acceptance of enlarged freedom and self-realization as well as social responsibility, changes which can be realized only through safeguarded interdependence. Growth in opportunity and freedom for self-development is known to increase with each more inclusive level of social integration and will increase even more when that extends to the inclusion of all mankind.

5. *Our biological heritage includes mechanisms for cooperation as well as conflict*

These requirements are not contrary to human nature; they can be met merely by an extension of certain vital influences that have in the past secured the survival and welfare of the individual, family, nation, and international confederation.

However, for nearly a century, man has been swayed by a conviction that conflict is the principal fulcrum around which great issues are decided. Yet emphasis on conflict as the basis for individual and collective progress reveals only half our capability, half our opportunity, and half our responsibility. It de-emphasizes the importance of altruism, faith, and mutual trust throughout biological and social affairs.

6. *We live by faith*

In truth, biological survival and evolution, individual and social development could not have gone very far without there being sound biological foundations for cooperation and altruism. These are necessary for the reproduction and survival of most offspring and are recognizably farreaching in their social as well as internal satisfactions. We must now learn faith in mankind. We have to arrange institutions that will support and reinforce a new and broadened worldwide faith in man.

7. *Military efforts have provided a gap of time*

Partly because of the widespread philosophic acceptance given the notion of conflict in the solution of our most complex problems, and partly because it is always easier to discover how to destroy something than how to construct something better, mankind has been spending much energy and resource on instrumentalities for conflict. This has, however, yielded the world a gap of time. It is within this gap of time that certain crucial social adaptations must take place.

C. Bases for Confidence in the Feasibility of Universal Social Integration

The idea of a world government safeguarding universal maximum self-determination seems to offer an opportunity for survival, together with the most essential conditions for continuing survival. But as yet there is no general, worldwide acceptance of this objective.

1. *The conservation of ideas*

Traditional ideas and consistent forms of behavior preserve continuity. They bring us such comfort as attaches to the familiar. Yet, in the long run, such comfort may be illusory.

2. *Rational ideas, though novel, are realistic*

Mankind can look back with justifiable pride on a number of now widely accepted revolutions in attitude and behavior which grew out of an enlarged respect for human needs viewed increasingly objectively. We can expect traditional forms of thinking to reject and perhaps actively oppose research and discussion dedicated to the establishment of a system for the integration of mankind as a whole. Yet, if any lesson can be clearly drawn from recent history, it is that many ideas labeled only recently as visionary, idealistic, and unrealistic have already become the only tenable, practical, and realistic ones.

3. *Man is constructively adaptive socially*

Contrary to the reputation we declare for ourselves, we are by nature highly adaptive beings. The social, political, military, and economic changes that have affected our lives within this generation are eloquent testimony to the fact of change, of man's capacity for social adaptation, of the powerful effect of conscious dedication to constructive adaptation, and of the stimulating as well as disruptive effects of social change.

In brief, we can recognize that traditional ideas and traditional modes of action are susceptible to rational appeal and to modification, that human nature is not so fixed and rigid as we usually suppose, and that a conscious desire for constructive social adaptation is the main instrument for social progress.

4. *A worldwide pool of creative intelligence is needed*

The creative research and deliberations necessary for the solution of worldwide problems must be worldwide in empathy and should make extensive use of the world's cultural resources.

I do not wish, in any way, to underestimate the dimensions of such undertakings. The knowledge essential to a solution of many of these issues is lacking: therefore, considerable fundamental research needs to be undertaken. Like the problem of mental illness, the problem of international anarchy is so little understood that even the main lines of investigation to be pursued are poorly defined. I would, therefore, stress the breadth of research disciplines, the intensity and the extent of devotions needed to accomplish the research, to carry on the discourse, and to establish a charter for action that is as free as possible from dogma.

D. Assumptions Concerning the Potential Contributions of Science to This Problem

1. *Power expansion in scientific disciplines*

Problems that resist solution may be insoluble. Yet if one will believe the history of science, it is more likely that the means of approach being attempted are inadequate. Since World War I, the physical sciences have been dominant in generating and guiding engineering technology. By the end of World War II, the impact of the physical sciences had outstripped all other forces affecting business, law, and politics. An analogous transition took place in the field of agriculture and more dramatically in medicine during World War II. The social sciences have been slow to develop, because the subject-matter is vastly more complex than anything dealt with in biology or the physical sciences, and because there has always been a tabu against investigating social processes. The social sciences are now engaged in transition from an empirical to a theoretical science. Their capacity to provide insight and control relating to social behavior will ultimately dwarf the contributions of other scientific disciplines.

2. *The discipline and power of science*

Widespread acceptance of a new level of understanding in science is achieved through the examination of evidence that is made as free as possible from personal appeal, coercion, or fashion of thinking, and without recourse to authority external to science. Science is one of the few creative intellectual undertakings that is truly progressive. Further power comes from the scientists' attempt always to discover simpler and more inclusive relations. In this way neighboring disciplines come to dovetail and reinforce one another.

3. *Science can substitute for traditional conservatism in adequately safeguarding culture in times of transition*

Science has proved so useful in discovering and exploiting energy sources that its contributions through technology to the standard of living have been taken by many to be its chief social value. An even more impressive utilitarian value will attach to science when it becomes more effective in the comprehension of behavior. Yet perhaps the worthiest social value of science results from its contributions to the mainstream of human intellectual activity, to the philosophy of thought, to the vitality of ideas, and to the optimism as well as opportunities of the culture.

Despite natural tendencies favoring conservatism and operating against creativity, man has shown himself capable of farreaching intellectual accomplishments. This has been made possible largely through the cumulative power of education and science. The whole history of intellectual progress consists of a liberation from essentially reflexive behavior, from the limitations of immediate and imperious perception, judgment, and response, from common sense and from traditional ideas.

Important scientific achievement depends upon the fruitful combination of a group of essentially positive factors: some of these relate to the competence, self-discipline, and nimble imaginativeness of the scientist himself, and others concern his surroundings. The introduction of thinking which will change the entire character and direction of scientific pursuit, which will reformulate the nature of a problem or its solution, is not likely to occur except where circumstances are especially favorable for creativity. Improvement in social theory, increase in the grasp of social problems and their solution, will depend upon a few creative advances of this sort far more than upon the extension of concepts that now seem familiar. Every advance in social evolution must make this break with common sense. The history of the introduction of new and useful concepts makes obvious the requirement in scientists of a high level capacity for conceptual thinking, coupled with a capacity not to hold any concept too dearly.

The search for Scientific Truth (which can never be realized) becomes increasingly powerful as error is discovered in lesser scientific truths. Science, in contrast with many other callings, creates a zeal for integrity. The community of scientists has been international in professional character since long before nationalism became a force in human affairs. If scientists are invited to seek truths of advantage to mankind as a whole, they can probably outperform any other mode of approach to this problem. Because of these several facts, the best hope for accomplishment of worldwide social integration with, at the same time, preservation of universal maximum individual self-realization, lies in the cultivation of scientific research adequate to this objective.

4. We can make substantial progress toward constructive universal interdependence

Progress of insight and practice favoring more universal and longer-range aspects of human welfare is already considerable. The question is not whether such achievements can be made, but whether they can be made within the time available.

II

A. Assumptions Relating to the Future of Science in Relation to Society

1. Society is becoming increasingly dependent upon creativity

We are living in the beginning of an intellectual revolution which takes this form: science, operating through technology, has relieved man from much of his original burdens of drudgery, freeing his mind for other pursuits. Although he has mostly taken up interests and activities of ephemeral and superficial attraction, he has also tasted more enduring and cumulative experiences relating to science, the arts, and the humanities. This exposure and its farreaching cultural impact is taking place in every part of the world. The taste, once appreciated, is not lost. It is impossible thereafter to return to older, more provincial views. It is wrong to imply that man is interested only in utilitarian aspects of science, in applied arts, and in application of the wisdom of the ages. The impact of creative accomplishment, whether directly or vicariously experienced, is not dogmatic or coercive, it is instead liberating.

2. *The competition of science cannot be met by recourse to tradition*

Already science is outstripping all other forces affecting business, law, and politics. In the near future equally powerful influences will be felt throughout biological, psychological, and social affairs.

3. *Science will be increasingly appreciated for its cultural contributions*

Scientific discovery ultimately has a cultural impact upon the philosophy of thought and upon the vitality of ideas in the world community.

4. *Scientific disciplines will become more complementary to one another*

Science will become far more coherent and unified than any of us can presently appreciate. There will be an extraordinary expansion in the power and dimensions of science and in the dependence of society upon science. Perhaps the greatest cultural impact of science will be as a method for understanding.

B. Consequences for Moral Responsibility in Big-Scale Scientific Research

1. *The cultural interface relating science to society*

A research enterprise that depends upon the patronage of a democratic society depends upon a relatively broad understanding throughout the society of the values of science and of the conditions under which science can flourish or will languish.

The predominant system of values and conception of working conditions in our society (at this time) relate to the marketplace. The leaders of our society understand the values and conditions relating to successful business and political enterprise. This code is the primary cultural reference by which scientific activities are likely to be interpreted. A further general feature of the action interface among different cultural groups is that the predominant group not only evaluates the actions of other groups in the light of its own system of values, but that it actively exerts pressures to compel conformity of action in accordance with that system. Anything else seems "alien," "illogical," and "improper," according to the code of the predominant group.

2. *The poor articulation between science and society in the United States*

Two general features of cultural interaction, compelling judgment and conformity to a code based on entirely different principles, exert a powerful influence on the action interface existing between scientists engaged in research and the patrons of science.

3. *The indispensable requirement to attract the ablest scientists to a scientific organization*

There is no substitute for setting the highest standards, and for providing the greatest attraction possible, for key scientific personnel.

Without substantial provision for encouraging creative accomplishment and opportunities for creative individuals to fulfil their capabilities, a scientific institution is bound to languish. Without substantial *professional recognition* both inside and outside of the institution no other recognition is meaningful.

4. *Essential operating policies relating to science must be decided and controlled by scientists*

Policy needs to be determined by scientists according to standards of professional aspiration and professional discipline which they must assume responsibility for setting: no one else is suitably qualified; no one else has a higher stake in the continuing exercise or practices which will yield the most farreaching scientific accomplishments.

5. Professional responsibility relating to the decisionmaking process

The leaders of our society and the patrons of our scientific enterprises are dependent, in all of the complex and confusing decisions relating to science, upon an adventitious knowledge and judgment in scientific affairs which is contributed by scientists, consultants, and committees of scientists.

6. The articulation between science and society is culturally determined and is not arbitrarily fixed

One reason why science may appear to be so effective in the Soviet Union is that the Russians consider themselves to have a scientific society. Therefore they encounter no conflict between social, political, and marketplace criteria and the system of values and conditions essential for successful enterprise in science.

7. The ideal of professionalism in science

Our primary concern as scientists relates to growth in intellectual and creative power of ourselves and our colleagues, to the improvement of our mental grasp and understanding, particularly of the more general and comprehensive theories of science. What seems to be required is a restitution of an ideal of professionalism as practiced, for example, in the guilds.[2] By this is meant an increased sense of dedication, an enlarged sense of responsibility relating to one's own work and the work of one's colleagues, a greater sense of identification through individual and group accomplishments, an increased sense of pride in the mastery and exercise of professional skills, and an increased concern for the great moral issues raised by science and technology.

[2] This idea was first introduced to me by the philosopher Scott Buchanan. At first it seemed an unreasonable and alien analogy. But on further reflection and reading on this subject it seems to remain an example of dedicated professionalism to which we might, at least in part, aspire.

C. Decisionmaking in Science in Relation to
the Leadership Process in the United States

1. *Some problems of decisionmaking in science*

In previous sections we took note of the opportunities as well as problems science presents. Great errors can be made, by neglecting to recognize opportunities, or doing badly with them, or by neglecting to recognize problems, or doing badly with them.

It is a mistake to allow decisions relating to science to be made predominantly according to conflict considerations and according to marketplace criteria. Justifications made understandable and "logical" to the predominant culture become remote from scientific criteria and scientific evidence. At present scientific activities have to be explained and justified to a whole hierarchy of competing interests within a referring department or agency as well as competing interests within the entire executive branch of the government, prior to their ultimate justification before the Congress and the people. Skill in justification comes to rival or surpass merit of scientific performance.

2. *Safeguards lie in three directions*

The most advantageous articulation between science and its patrons would involve all three of the following safeguards. First, professional integrity on the part of the scientist responsible for the program, and his assumption of full and proper responsibility extending to the farthest imaginable limits of the implications of the scientific program and of its official justification; second, an understanding on the part of the decisionmaker of the potentialities and limits of science, the criteria of scientific evidence, the conditions essential to scientific enterprise, and the gulf in assumptions, outlook, and scale of values between himself and the operating scientist; and, third, institutional safeguards which should be built into the fabric of the institution, whether it be a university, foundation, corporation, or the federal government.

D. Some Requirements for Improved Safeguards in Decisionmaking in a Democracy

It can be shown with cogent and persuasive argument and in all sincerity and scientific honesty that if any of several channels of science are neglected our nation will fall behind in security, welfare, and prestige, and very likely be subject to ruin. The other side of the scientific coin is seductive. Science holds out many potential benefits. To neglect these is to neglect one's countrymen and their descendants.

These are heroic times. The choices before us are far larger than our means. The alternatives range from the best imaginable to the worst imaginable destiny. We are being sorely pressed by a society that considers itself to be more scientifically oriented than our own and which has vastly different decisionmaking processes. Perhaps the outcome will depend less upon the relative merits of the scientists and resources concerned, or the aspirations of the respective societies, than it will depend on the techniques for rendering major scientific decisions.

It is always easy to imagine something worth doing, but what is *most* worthwhile is very difficult to determine: yet, that more critical determination is principally what separates us from great achievements. We cannot dispense with budgets, but we can perhaps attend more conspicuously to more important things. Perhaps a wastage most to be regretted occurs as a result of pursuing justifiable research when more creative thinking might have suggested something far better.

Here are some of the problems faced by any federal decisionmaking operation:

> What should be the jurisdiction of the various scientific disciplines in the decisionmaking body? Should this be on the basis of present activities in science? Should this representation change with evolution of science? Should it be designed instead to express the major needs of the people? Should it be based on scientific representation from professional scientific societies, foundations, and universities?
>
> What powers should such a decisionmaking body have for effecting coordination within the vast and sprawling operations of federal and nonfederal activities in science and technology? How much duplication is necessary? How much desirable? How balance resources de-

voted to science as distinguished from technology? How balance programs of teaching, scholarship, and research?

How avoid overjustification of research and development proposals? How preserve scientific evidence to the decisionmaking level? How phase out programs no longer of equivalent value as compared with newly visualized programs? What to do with the associated personnel and facilities?

How avoid special interests on the part of the decisionmakers themselves? Should they themselves be involved in the scientific work? Or in its administration? Or is decisionmaking a full time job? Should they be allowed to represent their own programs under consideration? If the best scientists are chosen to perform the scientific work, can they also play a role in the pertinent decisionmaking? If not, can the decisions be made by less qualified people? What constitutes vested interests in science?

Should the decisionmaking body report only to one branch of the government? If it is to the President, where is the Congress to look for advice in these matters? It cannot look to the individual agencies for disinterested advice. Should the Congress have its own advisory institutions for scientific matters?

Where can the judicial branch of the government find objective, disinterested advice relating to science and technology? Science is continually providing new challenges to law through the development of new understanding. Consider the issue of insanity—of criminal responsibility—of punishment—in the light of new findings in medicine and psychology. At present, there is a great lag in the impact of science on judicial procedure, theory, and teaching, as well as law enforcement and punitive procedures.

Many aspects of science have implications extending far beyond the domestic jurisdiction of the United States. How should the United States formulate policies and decisions respecting science in relation to collective defense, international law, commerce, and health? What about scientific problems relating to the jurisdiction of nonterritorial resources, for example, the Antarctic continent, the oceans, the atmosphere, space?

What seems to be required involves a high level Science Commission for rendering opinions and advice to benefit all three branches of the government. The Commission should be made up of the most judicial scientific competences our nation can provide, and encompass a representative span of competences across several general frontiers of science. Appointment to the Commission should be, as it is with the Justices of the Supreme Court, for life, and for the same reason, namely, to secure as much detachment and objectivity as possible. The Commission should have access, at its invitation and with its consultative support, to the entire scientific and technological community and to other groups, as pertinent to a given issue. The Commission should have discretion as to what scientific issues it considers to be most cogent to the nation's welfare, and which it will undertake to study. The Commission would render *opinions* reflecting its considered appraisal of the scientific evidence pertaining to a given issue. Opinions might specify areas where additional knowledge is needed. Opinions rendered would be made available to the government, and, as appropriate, to the scientific community and public. They would *not* be binding in relation to policy or decisionmaking. They would simply represent the considered opinion of the Science Commission, on a given issue, as of a given date. The value and reputation of the Commission would depend in the long run on how wise and prescient its opinions turned out to be.

This suggestion is tentative, and is submitted in the hope of encouraging criticism and evoking a better plan. My main point is that *we should be prepared to encourage the evolution within our government of ways to accommodate the farreaching and profound demands and opportunities laid before us by achievements in science and technology throughout the world.*

III. Responsibility in Big-Scale Religious Organization

CHAPTER XII

The Cultural Background of American Religious Organization[1]

By TALCOTT PARSONS

IT IS WELL KNOWN that the Constitution of the United States contained the beginning of the development of what, at the time, was an altogether unique basis of religious organization for a society with a Christian religious heritage. Though its formal constitutional basis is restricted to the guarantee of religious freedom in the First Amendment, by interpretation and the general process of evolution of the society it has developed into a system with two primary characteristics, namely, the full separation of church and state, and the system of denominational pluralism.[2]

The essential meaning of the separation of church and state is the relegation of the organizational aspect of religion to the private sphere, with church membership for the individual an altogether voluntary matter, with no religious group enjoying particular protection by public authority, with financial support through voluntary contributions. To be sure there is the recognition that religious groups, along with the other two categories of educational and charitable ones, have a special place among private associations, the most important indication of which is the very important privilege of tax exemption. But political authority must be carefully impartial as between such groups, and no pressure from public sources put on any individual to affiliate himself with any one, or indeed any at all.

---

[1] In drafting this paper, I have been especially indebted, both for prior stimulation and for careful critical discussion to Robert N. Bellah and Johannes J. Loubser.

[2] I have outlined the main features of this system on the contemporary organizational level in the paper, "The Pattern of Religious Organization in the Contemporary United States," *Daedalus*, Summer, 1958. This essay is reprinted in the volume of my collected essays under the title, *Structure and Process in Modern Societies*, Free Press, Glencoe, 1960, chapter X.

Denominational pluralism essentially means that religious bodies, in the eyes of the law, are voluntary associations. There is, and is expected to be a considerable number of such groups which are equal before the law and stand in competition with each other. To persons familiar with the conceptions of church and sect as formulated by Max Weber and Ernst Troeltsch, it may be useful to contrast this conception of the denomination with both of them. Weber, for example, conceived the church as an *Anstalt,* which by its nature claimed religious jurisdiction over all persons fulfilling certain objective criteria and without reference to their personal wishes or beliefs. Apart from proselyting activity as through missions, then this primarily meant recruitment by birth and that the individual born within the jurisdiction of a church would as a matter of course be brought up in the church. It meant financing out of taxation. It clearly also meant that as an ideal, secular authority should enforce membership in and recognition of the normative order of the church within its territory. The conception of the Established Church in the historic Christian sense is the type case. Here the ordinary Christian layman is conceived as participating fully in secular society in ordinary ways, but the established church is the sole trustee and administrator of his religious interests.

By contrast with this the sect is a voluntary grouping of believers who place their religious commitment above all others, who therefore profess a totally religious way of life. They must therefore, in some sense parallel to that of the early Christians, live "in the world, but not of it."

The denomination, as I conceive this category here, shares with the sect the criterion of voluntary membership by act of personal commitment. With the church, however, it shares the expectation that its typical lay member will be a full participant in the life of secular society, that religion will, whatever its subjective importance to him, be only a part of his participating life, being restricted to his associational group participations with his fellow religionists—in the "church" in the relevant current American sense—and to entirely private contexts. The presumption, however, is that there are no "religious tests" for the important participations in secular social life, *e.g.,* holding public office, employment, educational opportunity, etc.

Cultural Background of American Religions 143

The denomination, as noted, expects to be one of an indefinite number of formally equal religious associations in the society.

Quite clearly American religious organization comprises a wide range of groups, including, in addition to those which most fully accept denominational status in the above sense, those which traditionally have been churches in the Weber-Troeltsch sense, and must hence live in some kind of compromise between the historical ideal and current reality, and those which have originated as, and to some degree still are sects in the above sense and, like the Mennonites, to varying degrees isolate themselves from the main secular society. Traditional Judaism belongs in still another category. It is, however, clear that the denominational group is the "ideal type" of the main pattern of American religious organization, and the bulk of this paper will be devoted to elucidating the background on which this has come to be the case. A few of the strains involved for certain groups will be briefly noted at the end of the paper.

It is thus clearly an important point that today the range of groups included within the broad religious consensus of the society is considerably broader than the "ascetic Protestants" who set the main historic pattern. The facts will be briefly noted here, and taken up again at the end of the paper.

In the contemporary American religious situation there are three main religious groups, Protestants, Catholics, and Jews;[3] all three of which are institutionally recognized as "authentically belonging" in the American picture, as also are people who prefer not to accept any positive organized religious affiliation at all, who in this sense are "secularists." Hence it would not be correct to speak of the American religious constitution at the present time as a Protestant one, or even a Christian one, since both Jews and secularists (where Unitarians belong is a special problem) are not merely "tolerated" in a negative sense but acknowledged as "belonging." The paradox is, in our opinion, resolved by making clear that there is an essential difference between the role of religion in the historical background of a value system and the range of religious orientations having a place in the resulting society at a later stage in its development.[4]

[3]*Cf.* Will Herberg, *Protestant, Catholic, Jew*, Doubleday, Garden City, 1955.
[4]We of course take it for granted that in cultural terms Christianity itself above

Ethics and Bigness

The bridging of the gap comes about through what we are calling a process of "upgrading" in one of its important aspects. This is the fact that with the process of structural differentiation there goes a process by which the operative level of values must be couched in progressively more highly *generalized* terms. This means dropping out many of the "particularities" of the cultural orientation from which the more generalized orientation has been historically derived.[5] At the same time it means the capacity to include under its conceptions a wider range than before, including some of the historical antecedents (or their derivatives) with which the originally paramount religious orientation once stood in conflict. Our present concern is with the cultural factors in the *genesis* of the American value system, not with the range of religious inclusiveness and exclusiveness which fits with its present and prospective form. The latter problem should be taken up independently.

It should be remembered that Christianity, in a sense not true of any other of the world religions, institutionalized the differentiation (as distinguished from the separation) between church and state, and that this differentiation came to be incorporated in the medieval synthesis which is the base line for the later Catholic position. This essentially meant that, in a sense which, for example, was not true of historic Judaism and still less of Islam, the secular sphere was granted autonomous independence from *immediate* religious tutelage. Our view here is that the Catholic position was, in this context, a halfway station in a process which Protestantism carried a major step farther.

As Troeltsch has made so clear, the medieval synthesis was the first version of the conception of a "Christian society," that is, of a secular society which was ideally infused with Christian values.

---

all originated from a synthesis of Judaism on the one hand, Greek culture on the other. To follow the cultural antecedents of American values back this far would, however, be beyond the scope of this discussion. It may be suggested though that there is a sense in which, just as American Jews fit within the broader contemporary version of what in our own national background was originally a Protestant value system, so many contemporary "secularists" are, in a certain sense, "neoclassical humanists" who therefore have a place in the broad cultural spectrum which is in certain respects parallel to that of the Jews: to refer to them simply as "irreligious" is in our opinion pejorative, certainly if by this is meant that they do not really have a place in the basic cultural framework.

[5]This proposition involves complex historical-sociological problems which cannot be entered into here, but will be extensively treated by the author on a later occasion.

Christianity was a transcendentally oriented religion; it was built about an inherent and fundamental tension between the divine order and the "world." But, as Weber points out, in its main trends it took the fundamental alternative of conceiving the world as the *field* for the exercise of Christian virtue rather than of withdrawal from the world in ascetic or mystical modes of action. The crowning of the Holy Roman Emperor by the Pope was the central symbol of this religious sanction of secular society, since, in medieval terms, the "state" *was* secular society.

The church, however, maintained a special set of controls over this society which, seen in the present perspective, constituted limitations on the full development of the idea of the Christian society. These controls were essentially two. First, the Catholic church did not abandon the conception, derived from its historic past, that there should be a fundamental category of persons whose lives embodied the highest Christian ideal, but who could do this only by virtue of segregation from the affairs of secular society; these were of course the religious orders. This essentially made full participants in secular affairs into a category defined in religious terms, as "second class citizens," including of course those in the positions of highest authority and prestige in secular contexts. In *religious* terms furthermore the secular priesthood remained in a position clearly and in principle inferior to that of the members of the orders, which of course were the heirs of the early church.

The second basic restriction on the automony of secular society was institutionalized in the role of the church itself, a role which in turn had two main aspects. One of these was the establishment of an area of reserved jurisdiction, the famous field of questions of "faith and morals"—similar to the reservation, by formerly colonial powers, in the process of relinquishing full control, of the fields of public order and foreign policy. This above all concerned, besides the constitution of the church itself, education, marriage, and the family. Furthermore, conformity in matters of faith and morals was enforced by the special Catholic version of the sacraments. Put rather crudely, the good Catholic deviated in questions in this sphere at the peril of the fate of his immortal soul, on terms set by the secular priesthood of the *visible* church.

It is not our concern even to sketch the main religious innovations introduced by the Reformation, but only to make clear certain of its consequences for values institutionalized in a society. Here two main points are crucial. In the first place the Reformation eliminated the religious basis for any *special* position on the part of a category of persons who led the religious life in the sense of *renouncing the world*.[6] Elimination of the celibacy of the clergy was a symbol of the change, in that even for the intermediate status of the secular clergy nonparticipation in normal "worldly" concerns was not treated as a source of religious status or merit. *In principle,* all secular positions became equal in basic religious standing, with each other and with any special "religious calling." The essential point is the establishment of equivalence; if monasticism was eliminated, it was equally true that "every man became a monk." It was a sharp upgrading of the religious evaluation of the life of the Christian layman.

The second change was the elimination of the special position of control held by the *visible* church, conceived as holding the Power of the Keys through the sacraments, as evidenced on the one hand in authority over the field of faith and morals and on the other in the special Catholic conception of the sacraments. So far as his ultimate religious status was concerned, this meant that the position of the individual was a matter of his direct relation to his God, without *any* controlling human intermediary. Even the enforcement of doctrinal conformity in the Reformation churches thus had to be treated in terms of "enlightenment"; it could not be accomplished through sacramental manipulation of the individual's state of grace.

Clearly this was a major step in the emancipation of the individual in secular society from ecclesiastical tutelage. *If* Christian values were to be institutionalized at all it had to be through the commitments of individual Christians to these values, commitments which were either

---

[6] It is a notable fact that there is, as noted by Harnack, and lately developed by The Reverend Father Paul Tufari, S.J. (unpublished manuscript), a notable progression in the development of types of religious order within the Catholic Church, away from exclusively devotional concerns in the direction of greater emphasis on the performance of function on behalf of the church in the secular world. Of the major orders, that of the Jesuits has gone farthest in this respect, but the little publicized "Secular Institutes" in continental Europe, have gone still farther in that they have given up the segregated communal pattern of life in favor of "living" in the world. They are, however, still subject to the authority of the Papacy and to the traditional vows of poverty, chastity, and obedience. The position of the Protestant layman could be considered as the very last step in this series.

Cultural Background of American Religions

Divinely wrought through Grace accorded to the individual, or willed by him through faith or some combination, but not "engineered" by a church. The main qualification of this statement, for the original Reformation churches, concerned the use of secular authority to enforce conformity, both in doctrine and in conduct. In this respect the institution of the Established Church was of course characteristic of both the Lutheran and the Calvinistic branches. The changes which will be our particular concern, however, involved the dropping of this connection, first through the development of religious toleration, then through the separation of church and state and the eventual institutionalization of denominational pluralism.

The very development, in medieval Catholicism, of the idea of the Christian society introduced a duality of aim into Christianity. It could be said that early Christianity, with its eschatological expectation, was concerned overwhelmingly with the salvation of the souls of individuals. Medieval Catholicism, on the other hand, acknowledged a dual concern, for the salvation of souls, and for the implementation of Christian ideals in secular life. Very broadly the same fundamental duality reappeared in altered form in the main structure of Protestantism. The Lutheran branch emphasized primarily the salvation, or "justification" of the individual, but through faith rather than "works" in the Catholic sacramental sense. The Calvinist branch, on the other hand, with which we are primarily concerned, took the other alternative and emphasized the ideal of the Christian society; the key conception was that of the Kingdom of God on Earth. Indeed in its radical form, through the doctrine of Predestination, Calvinism drastically excluded the problem of the salvation of the individual; action in this life could have meaning *only* as fulfilling the Divine Will through contributing to building of the Kingdom. In our theoretical terms it was a completely *instrumentalist* doctrine as contrasted with the consummatory emphasis, in the sense of the religious interests of the individual, of Lutheranism. It was on this ground that Max Weber spoke of it as *ascetic* Protestantism.

The ascetic branch of Protestantism thus established a fundamental orientation toward the "world"—it was *thisworldly* as distinguished from *otherworldly, not* in the sense of abandoning the transcendental basis of meaning and legitimation, but in the sense that action *in* the world, *i.e.,* in secular society, was the *field* in which the religious mission of the individual was to be carried out. But this individual was subordinated to religious normative considerations in a double sense. On the one hand, he did not pursue even his own consummatory religious interests but served as an instrument of the Divine Will, while on the other hand, his worldly mission concerned not a state for himself as an individual but a *good society,* the Kingdom of God *on Earth.* It was his *contribution* to the building of this good society which was the criterion of religious merit for him.

In our analytical terms, Calvinism thus gave a religious legitimation to a system-goal for the good society and made the contributions of individual persons and of other social units to this goal the basis of the religious meaning of their lives. This was not, however, the whole story of the "mandate" for human action of ascetic Protestantism. There were two other essential components, namely, the conception of the moral order within which this Divine mission was to be carried out and the conception of the "order of nature" or the conditions to which it was subject.

One of the most distinctive features of the JudeoChristian tradition has, from the very beginning, been the conception of the *Covenant.* This is to say that the conception of the transcendence and majesty of God has never stood alone, if by that would be meant the implication that man was simply a passive instrument of God, living only to be "manipulated" by Him. In spite of the fundamental difference of level between Divine and human the relation has resemblances to a kind of "treaty" in which there were certain obligations and undertakings on *both* sides.

In theological terms this clearly means an act of *self*-limitation on the part of the omnipotent sovereign God. But nevertheless *obligations* have been assumed on the Divine side which in some sense match those imposed on man. The element of *mutuality* of obligations involved in the conception of the Covenant marks the difference between man being subject simply to the Will of God, and being subject to a *moral order,* the main principles of which can be presumed to be stable in the sense of not being subject to arbitrary change for Divine reasons which are totally inscrutable to man.

This conception of a moral order eventually conceived to be binding on both sides is the conception from which the Jewish Law derived. Christianity emancipated the law from the ethnic particularism by

Cultural Background of American Religions 149

virtue of which it was specifically the law *for Jews* and made it in principle universal. The Jewish law was, to be sure, universal in that it was the law sanctioned by a universal God, but on condition that its adherents became Jews in the ethnic sense; in Catholic Christianity they must only become members of the Church; a much wider range of variability was open in secular contexts.

For ascetic Protestantism of course the tradition of such a moral law remains central; the essential difference from the Catholic case is that it is no longer under the special guardianship of a sacramental church. The tendency of Calvinism was, to be sure, to *authoritarian* interpretation and enforcement, but fundamentally on a Protestant basis on which acceptance of moral law is a matter of the Christian conscience. With the attenuation of authoritarianism a central connection emerged between freedom of conscience and the moral responsibility of the individual. We shall return to this problem.

It may be said that Calvinism drove the paradox of human freedom to a very sharp point. With the doctrine of Predestination, it carried the conception of the sovereignty of God to an extreme; yet for the person taking his religion seriously, this accentuated the profound urgency of his obligation to do God's Will. Both the heavy emphasis on collective action and the "elitist" component of predestination, however, tended to a kind of "legalism" in the sense that there was a strong tendency to prescribe acceptable conduct by authority, particularly since the unregenerate fundamentally could not be trusted with moral responsibility. For reasons which will be outlined below, this was a relatively unstable position, the breakdown of which led to that which immediately underlies American values.

The final component of basic religious orientation concerns the conception of the exigencies of social action, what ultimately becomes the conception of the order of nature. In Judaism, it may perhaps be said, conceptions in this area were relatively *ad hoc,* traditionalistic and commonsense. Christianity, however, incorporated the main traditions of Greek rationalism, albeit often with severe tensions. In medieval Catholicism this incorporation crystallized in the conception of Natural Law as formulated in the first instance by Aristotle, later by Thomas Aquinas. Here it may be said that the concept "natural" extended all the way from purely physical nature through the field of organic and "human" nature to that of secular society, above all as conceived in terms of secular law as that crystallizing in Roman Law, partly through Stoic influence. This was explicitly set over against Divine Law.

The medieval Catholic position, which reached its most definitive formulation in Thomism, thus involved a basic duality of the normative structure to which human action was subjected, namely, as between Divine Law and Natural Law. Divine Law regulated the conditions of salvation, the specifically religious functions of the Church, whereas by and large Natural Law regulated the principal affairs of secular society. There was, however, the difficult problem of their articulation, especially in matters of faith and morals; to what extent was there a responsibility of enforcement by secular authority and within what limits? (We should remember that heresy was a *civil* crime as well as a religious offense.)

The effect of the Protestant position generally was, however, to make this distinction essentially untenable. It tended to be reshaped to the distinction between matters of *conscience,* which were private to the individual and not a subject of institutionalized "legalization" at all in the sense of formal authoritative formulation—except in the Bible—or of formal coercive sanctions, and the *general sphere of law* which tended to be conceived as the law of the good society. Matching the subjectivity of conscience was the conception that the "true church" was the invisible church, the community of souls, and that the visible church was essentially human association, in no way wielding supernatural powers. If this meant a "downgrading" of the position of the visible church it was an upgrading of the position of the normative order of secular society, because in principle it was the embodiment of the ideal of the Kingdom of God on Earth. The result was essentially a fusion of Catholic Divine and Natural Law. There is only one coercively binding law for man, that of the good society.

Associated with this collapsing of the duality of the medieval conception of normative order was the tendency to pay more systematic attention to the empirical conditions which underlay the attempt to build a Christian society. For understandable reasons the *human* conditions stood in the forefront. The difficulties very naturally concentrated on the sinfulness of human nature, that very central Calvinistic preoccupation. The element of activism, however, is sharply emphasized by the fact that it was felt to be possible that even the unregenerate

Cultural Background of American Religions

majority could be effectively controlled by a sufficiently strong leadership of the presumptively elect, and be brought thereby into the service of building the Kingdom. In any case, the first major focus of the problem of the order of nature in this context is the conception of human nature in the context of Divine ordination. Clearly this was not in any sense a scientific psychology, but it was the matrix of religious ideas which had an important bearing on later psychology; first steps were made by Machiavelli and Hobbes, both of whom emphasized the elements of human nature which threatened social order, as did Freud, much later and in a different context.

It is our view that the version of English Puritanism from which American values are, on the religious side, primarily derived, developed by a process of differentiation from the Calvinistic base. The first major phase of the process concerned emancipation from the religious ascription which was above all expressed in the doctrine of Predestination. This concerned in particular the problem of religious freedom implicit in the idea of the Covenant, and revived the salvationist line of thought in ascetic Protestantism; a line which had been very much kept alive by some of the Baptist type of sectarian movements of the Reformation period; this circumstance made it possible to defend the interest in individual salvation without the implication of Lutheran subjectivism and social conservatism.

Given an instrumentally activist orientation, the corollary of religious freedom is that of *autonomous* responsibility. From being ascriptively obliged to implement the Divine will, whether he belonged to the elect or the damned, the implication came increasingly to the fore that the individual was responsible for contributions to the building of the Kingdom through fulfilling *his* part of the Covenant.

There is complete continuity in the basic conception that it is through Grace alone that, in the absence of the external pressure applied to the unregenerate, it is possible for sinful man to assume this responsibility. In the early, Predestinarian, Calvinism, the gift of Grace was enjoyed only by the elect. Gradually, however, through a series of stages the basis of access to Grace was broadened, a particularly important intermediate stage was the Federal Theology espoused by the early New England Congregationalists.[7] The end of this par-

[7] See Perry Miller, *Errand into the Wilderness,* Harvard University Press, 1956, chapter I.

ticular road was the Arminian theology which explicitly made Grace accessible to all who would only make the essential commitment of faith.

Apart from certain important but secondary tendencies, this never meant the development of a doctrine of salvation or justification by "works" so that moral or "righteous" conduct in worldly callings could be treated as the direct means of earning Divine Grace as a direct reward of morality. The conception was, on the contrary, consistently held to that only through "unconditioned" Grace was moral action possible. The change was from the conception that Grace would be given only to God's own predestined saints, in the direction of the conception that it was, through faith, accessible to *any* committed Christian. If he secured justification by his faith, then the gift of Grace would enable him to act righteously as a contributor to the building of the Kingdom on Earth. Only through this *double* relationship, between faith and justification on the one hand, grace and righteous action on the other, could true autonomous moral responsibility be given a religious grounding, on a basis which dispensed both with the moral tutelage involved in the historic Catholic position, and with the religious "subjectivism," which turned responsibility over to the secular authority rather than to the moral individual, of Lutheranism. It is a case of the institutionalization of "Christian individualism" at the farthest level of institutionalization in secular society yet attained in the history of Christianity.

The basic position is fundamentally Protestant in that it insists on the relation of immediacy between the individual man and Divinity without human intermediary. The "true church" then becomes the "invisible" church, the community of committed believers in Christ. The visible church is essentially a human association, among other associations, which, as the theological position progressed more from the Predestinarian in the Arminian direction, became eventually a fully *voluntary* association, one in which fellow-believers simply acted out the implications of their common religious commitments on the level of social organization. The church then is organized for teaching and worship, whereas the rest of secular society is the *field* in which the state of Grace of the individual is manifested by righteous action. So far as secular *social* organization is concerned then the ultimate motivation of participation and acceptance of responsibility is the

Cultural Background of American Religions

conscience of the individual. But in proportion as Christian values in fact come to be institutionalized, the dictates of conscience tend to enjoin action in accord with the normative, *i.e.,* the law, of the *good society.* The accord of this law with religious values is, however, *always* problematical and subject to test in the light of conscience.

Relative to the medieval Catholic position which is the primary base line for present purposes, then, it may be said that "Puritanism" accomplished a double emancipation or differentiation in the framework it provided for the institutionalization of Christian values in a good society. The first context of emancipation concerns the emancipation of the conscience of the individual from the moral tutelage, sanctioned by the sacraments, of a visible church. The second concerns the position of the church itself, which was changed from the status of a collectivity claiming direct implementive control of a major sector of the operative society to the position of an association responsible only for the cultural-religious interests of its members, without coercive authority in any phase of specifically societal matters. Since the "state" is, in every politically organized society on the relevant level, the supreme collective organ of societal responsibility, the "separation" of church and state constitutes the institutional definition of this new situation. A direct corollary is the voluntary basis of denominational membership which signalizes the final abandonment of the ascriptive basis of jurisdiction of the "church" in the Weber-Troeltsch sense.

Thus, in terms of our paradigm the emancipation of the conscience of the individual has a double reference. On the one hand, so far as human leadership was concerned, it made religious "support" for the collective goal of building the Kingdom of voluntary matter, essentially removing the basis of the *unquestioned* legitimacy of either traditionalist secular leadership—*e.g.,* hereditary monarchs—or the self-appointed type—*e.g.,* charismatic religious leaders like Calvin himself. It laid the groundwork for a democratic constitution both of secular authority and of church polity, democratic in the sense of legitimizing the contingency of support on the basis of conscience. One consequence of high importance was the enhanced emphasis on a secular moral order which must stand above the goal-specifications of particular leaders or groups.

The second part of the double reference is a further development of the undermining of the traditionalism which underlay the ascriptive occupational structure of earlier society. Thus the cultural parallel to the alienation of labor as a resource at the social system level. The individual's operative "contribution" to the Kingdom becomes a matter of voluntary commitment, through a kind of cultural "contract of employment." Above all this position undermines "legalism" through making the empirical situation, that is, in the first instance, the relevant aspects of the actual structure of the society itself, but also "technological" conditions, essential desiderata of choice in these matters rather than foci of authoritative prescription. It is in this context that the values of ascetic Protestantism could reinforce, among other things, the complex of economic individualism.

It can thus be seen that this step from religious ascription to the conception of the religious autonomy of the individual meant a fundamental differentiation between the cultural and the societal levels of reality.[8] The Kingdom, while it remained the religious conception underlying the development of secular society, was no longer thought of as directly implemented by the inspired action of the Elect, but as defining the religious meaning of the directionality of development toward the good society. This meant the abandonment of the ideal of a specific goal-state for the Christian society, in favor of a society conceived as the maximally favorable *environment* for the making of religiously valued contributions to the building of the Kingdom. So far as goals were concerned, this was the step from the conception of a single comprehensive societal goal, that of enforcement of the Divine will to that of stress on the valuation of the achievements of *units* of the society, particularly of individuals' achievements which, however, must always be conceived as contributions in the sense of instrumental activism.

The consequences of this autonomy of the individual are several. To elaborate the above statement a little, one is a step beyond the Calvinistic conception of the church itself. In Calvinism, it may be said, while the church did not as in the Catholic case directly control individual actions by sacramental sanctions, it did assume the primary responsibility for implementing the divine mission of the Christian

---

[8]This is parallel to the differentiation between familial and extrafamilial spheres of activity for the postoedipal child. *Cf.* Talcott Parsons and Robert F. Bales, *Family, Socialization and Interaction Process,* The Free Press, Glencoe, 1955.

Cultural Background of American Religions

community; as in the case of Calvin's Geneva the tendency was to a theocracy with the ministry acting as the moral supervisors of the secular authorities, if not directly preempting their responsibilities.[9] With the shift toward the Arminian position the church became primarily the association of believers who used it to reinforce their faith and as a source of teaching of the Word. It certainly legitimized the secular order, but at the level of *general* moral principles, not that of responsibility for specific collective action. Calvinism, it may be said, came close to jeopardizing the differentiation of church and state. Arminian Puritanism reestablished this differentiation in a pattern which was amenable to their future separation. This "withdrawal" of the church from secular functions may be said to be parallel to the decentralization of goal-orientation to that at the societal level, the latter became unit-achievement as guided by conscience, *i.e.*, in a "calling" in Weber's sense, which was the focus of the secular obligation of the Christian. The good society thereby assumed, by differentiation, *part* of the cultural meaning which the church itself had incorporated on an earlier basis.

The establishment of this autonomy, with the accompanying sharpening of the differentiation of function between church and "state," was associated with, partly stimulated by and partly encouraging, striking further changes in the conceptions of the patterns of moral order, on the one hand, of natural order, on the other. It is thus well known that Puritanism in England had a major influence on the development of the Common Law.[10] It is certainly not fortuitous that it was in this period (roughly the seventeenth century) that this development took place, and that it had to do above all with the complexes of property and contract—of which the Mosaic Covenant was, sometimes explicitly, made a prototype.

The seventeenth century was also the period of the great philosophical concern with Natural Law. It may be said to be the same period in which, as noted, the operative legal system of society came to be, very broadly, identified with the normative order of a redefined Natural Law, completing the process indicated above. Essentially the corollary and condition of leaving primary operative responsibilities to decen-

---

[9] Calvin's church thus had a certain resemblance to a modern totalitarian party.

[10] *Cf.* Roscoe Pound, "Puritanism and the Common Law," *American Law Review*, XLV (1911), pp. 811–829.

tralized independent units was the institutionalization of a normative order in society which could be understood as directly congruent with what was understood as Christian ethics. It would, however, be wrong to *identify* the legal order with that of Christian ethics as such. The difference of level between what we have called cultural and societal references is above all expressed in the formula that ethical conduct is a matter of conscience—for the individual—which is a *cultural* conception, whereas legal obligation is institutionally determinable and coercively enforceable and is part of the *societal* structure; something which can never be said of conscience as such. Thus was, above all, the version of the conception of Natural Law formulated by John Locke. It could be said to be the expression of the Puritan orientation in this sphere.

The other important context was that of the problems of Natural Law in the sense of the order of nature. Here the well known story of the relation between Puritanism and the development of science, above all as analyzed by Weber and Merton, is a central point of reference. Interest has, however, centered on the influence of Puritanism on the development of science. On analytical grounds we would treat this as independently derived from the essential religious premises; it is not a simple "manifestation" of Protestant *values*.

Granting this, the main present concern is with the fact that science became an integral part of the more general cultural orientation of which American values are an essential part. With respect to natural science in the present more technical sense the name of Newton of course stands preeminent. It is certainly of first rate importance that Newtonian physics came broadly to be accepted in the whole Puritan movement—far more readily than in either Catholic or Lutheran circles. For the American case perhaps the seal was put on this by the way in which Jonathan Edwards built Newton's principles (of method rather than content) into his theology; more generally the name of Locke is here again a central one.

It was suggested above that at the stage of Calvinism the order of nature was above all represented by a still largely theological conception of sinful human nature. The phase with which we are concerned seems to have been characterized by a double development. The first is the gain in the obviously technical quality of genuinely empirical knowledge—most conspicuous of course in the physical field.

Cultural Background of American Religions

The second was a process of differentiation between the fields of nature, above all as between the physical and the human.

In the latter field it is by no means fortuitous that the same seventeenth century, and again preeminently in Puritan territory, saw the first major development of a genuinely technical analysis of human action, specifically differentiated from the earlier apologetics for religious positions. With Machiavelli as a very special early forerunner, the foundations of the new human science were laid above all by Hobbes and Locke. The major early fruit was the classical economics. But the utilitarian movement as a whole represented a new level in the attempt at systematic *theoretical* understanding of human social behavior; notwithstanding all the defects which have become visible from the vantage point of contemporary social science. Utilitarianism clearly was the most important single matrix out of which the modern behavioral science disciplines have developed—German idealism was an important, but still definitely secondary current. Though the classical economics was its most immediate scientific fruit, utilitarianism also profoundly influenced the frame of reference of psychology, of law, and of Darwinian biological theory, and it provided the most important single intellectual basis for the rationale of political democracy.

Essentially this is to say that the phase of Western cultural development of which American values were a part definitely *included* certain main outlines of the Enlightenment; in this sense it was by no means purely "religious." Whereas much of continental European culture, including the aspect in Germany which most directly influenced Karl Marx, religion, and the "rationalism" of the Enlightenment tended to be treated as irreconcilably antithetical, in the Englishspeaking world rather generally and perhaps in America in particular, in spite of tensions the antithesis has never been driven to an extreme. It is from this point of view that not only New England Puritanism with all its many ramifications, but also the ideas of Jefferson and Franklin may be regarded as expressions of different facets of the same basic cultural tradition.

Let us try to sum up the main outline of the above analysis, in relatively formal terms and with special reference to the place of values in the cultural orientation, rather than the broader concern with the cultural tradition as a whole which has had to enter in above.

The transcendental orientation is of course common to all branches of Christianity, and a thisworldly conception of the field for carrying out the implications of Christian faith has always been one aspect of this religious complex. In Protestantism generally, however, the bridges toward an "internal" otherworldly alternative were greatly weakened, and within it, for ascetic Protestantism the consummatory (salvationist) alternative was definitely excluded. In old Calvinism this took the form of drastic exclusion of the salvationist problem from relevance to the conduct of the individual altogether. The goal of seeking salvation reappeared in the Arminian form, but this time in the form of access to the Grace which could motivate righteous conduct in the Puritan sense, a type of conduct which comprised neither devotions nor sacramental rewards but was conceived as ethical performance in "worldly" affairs.

The basic religious orientation of ascetic Protestantism was therefore the one we have called instrumental activism: it was "externally" oriented to action in the "world," action hence characterized by specificity of interest in achievement as distinguished from the "diffuseness" of a mystical or other state of "subjective" religious perfection, and it was instrumentally oriented in that the *functions* of the actor in contributing to a religiously meaningful state of the world took precedence over the gratification of *his* personal religious interests, a more affectively stressed alternative.

To match this mode of orientation of religiously committed individuals the modalities of the "world" as object had to be conceived in a certain manner, the one we have characterized as universalistic and performance-dominated. In the performance context the world is an object to be mastered by active shaping and control in the interest of a Divinely ordained plan—this is the conception of the Kingdom of God on Earth. One application of the element of universalism is given in the fact that the standards for attainment of the Kingdom are generally given in the Covenant in its later specifically Christian interpretation; it is not a set of prescriptions for a Chosen People, but for all mankind; the most important Puritan conception is that of "righteousness." (This element of universalism was of course present in Christianity from the beginning.)

Within the general context of types of religion there is a special set of reasons why values should assume special importance for ascetic Protestantism. Primacy of the salvationist interest for the individual

Cultural Background of American Religions

is clearly excluded, as is *any* primacy of internal specifically religious states. Then once the type of eschatological expectation, which made its appearance in the Reformation, for instance with the Anabaptists, was repudiated, the primary accent of religious legitimation *had* to be placed on types of conduct *in the world*.

A religious movement of this type necessarily constitutes a "moral community" in the sense that the expression of its orientation should be the *common* concern of a community of believers. Normative uniformities of righteous conduct constituted the definition of what primarily should characterize such a community. But if a community of righteous conduct is to be specified to the level of concrete action in the world, the first characteristic of such a system of action is a *society* which is valued. The premium is on building the good society and the primary criterion of actual righteous conduct is its bearing on the goodness of the society. This goodness, in turn, is constituted by the institutionalization of Christian values. Hence the general Christian concern, highly visible since medieval times, with the Christian Society, was given maximal emphasis in ascetic Protestantism.

We have outlined two stages of this process of institutionalization on the ascetic Protestant basis. In the first, the Calvinistic, the building of the Kingdom became a direct collective goal under the centralized direction of the putative members of the elect. Under the pressure, however, of the general individualistic strain in Christianity, the element of religious ascription in this orientation tended to break down and the autonomous responsibility of the individual for his own contributions to gain primary emphasis. This displaced the conception of "contribution" from the level of a collective societal goal to that of the goals involved in unit-achievements. The corollary of this goal-pluralism was the enhanced importance of a normative *order* within which the pursuit of unit-goals could ethically be carried out.

We may thus trace a series of steps in the specification of the orientation of instrumental activism, postulated at the beginning of this analysis, through all of which this basic *pattern* of orientation may be presumed to remain constant, as follows: 1. Within the cultural system, from basic religious commitment in terms of the grounds of meaning to primacy, among cultural components, of patterns of evaluation; the classic Puritan expression is the premium on righteousness of conduct. 2. From the cultural to the other subsystems of action in the primacy of the good society as the field for carrying out the values of righteousness and as the test-ground of religious commitment. For the individual (or other unit) the crucial concept here is that of *contribution* to the building of the religiously sanctioned good society. 3. Given the primacy of the society either over otherworldly religious concerns or over the interests of the individual as personality or organism, by specification from the accent on values at the cultural level we arrive at a *special* accent on the right institutionalized values at the societal level; rightness here being defined as conformity with the pattern of instrumental activism. 4. On the old Calvinist base, these values could be identified with direct implementation of the collective goal. The cultural differentiation marked by the Arminian trend, however, had its counterpart (by some process of mutual interdependence) in the displacement of goal-valuation from the societal to the unit level and with it the emerging urgency of an analytically distinct institutionalization of norms which are relatively independent of the societal values as such, though "governed" by their specification. The keynote here is goal-pluralism and the independent responsibility of the acting unit for specification of its own goals, and, under the norms, choice of means to their attainment. 5. A new level of positive concern for the order of nature as setting the principal exigencies to which human action is subject in attaining valued goals. The crucial point is the application of the standards of universalism and specificity (which also apply to norms, relative to value-commitments and goals) to the empirical knowledge on which action is to be based; knowledge, that is, should be objective, generalized, and detailed in reference. We have seen that both natural and behavioral science are involved. Instrumental activism here means an orientation to "mastery" over the cognitive problems of the empirical world.

Broadly, as we have seen, the displacement of the concept of building the Kingdom to the level of unit-contribution was associated with the differentiation between the cultural and the societal conceptions of religious community; this was the fruit on the cultural level of the institutionalization of the religious autonomy of the individual. The firm cultural basis for the institutionalization of an autonomous institutionalized normative order—preeminently in law—and of a new conception of the order of nature, was closely linked with another direction of cultural development, that primarily associated with the

Enlightenment, with its preoccupation with Natural Law in its existential as distinguished from its normative meaning.[11] The *relation* between the two was of course a special concern of the culture of both the seventeenth and the eighteenth centuries.

It may, finally, be pointed out that this kind of value system, with this kind of cultural base, is subject to what we have called the "paradox of institutionalization" in a particularly accentuated form. To put it very sharply, unless the enterprise of actually institutionalizing transcendentally grounded religious values is inherently meaningless, there is the possibility, however qualified and partial, of some *success* in this enterprise. If we define success in terms of institutionalization, this means a profound dilemma as to the religious concept of "the world."[12] Precisely that aspect of the world which has been influenced by religiously sanctioned human action becomes, *empirically,* in *some* sense an embodiment of religious values. What, then, becomes of the conception of the *inherent* evil of things worldly and the consequent basic tension between them and the transcendental basis of orientation?

Surely this presents an uncomfortable dilemma. It becomes impossible simply to deny *any* moral status to the institutionalized order of actual society, but on the other hand *full* approval would be equally unthinkable, since it still is "the world." It is our view that the American cultural system tends to resolve this dilemma through some version of the idea of progress. It would be altogether too damaging to the whole tradition of religious commitment to allege that the result of several centuries of sincere and competent effort was in no sense "good."[13] If the authenticity of previous record of moral achievement is not radically denied, however, then clearly the door is open to saying, yes, of course in some sense and to some degree it *is* good, but the important thing is that it is *not good enough!* There is hence a builtin impetus to going *further* in what in some sense is the same direction, a sameness which does not preclude changes of emphasis which, from a short-run point of view, may readily appear to be changes of basic direction, such as change from an emphasis on eco-

[11] *Cf.* O. H. Taylor, "Economics and the Idea of Natural Law"; "Economics and the Idea of 'Jus Naturale,'" *Quarterly Journal of Economics,* volume 44, pp. 1–39, November, 1929; pp. 205–244, February, 1930.

[12] *Cf.* Weber's quote from Wesley in *The Protestant Ethic,* p. 175.

[13] *Cf.* Talcott Parsons, in *Religious Perspectives in College Teaching,* Hazen Foundation.

nomic individualism to one giving much greater place to collective political action.

There is, however, at the same time a builtin tendency to *oscillation* between smug acceptance of the current state of society as embodying the values of righteousness, and, at the other extreme, agonized guilt and self-depreciation over the patently unacceptable features of the current situation. This tension between the moral sanctification of the *status quo* and allegation of "unprecedented" moral corruption constitutes perhaps the primary framework of ideological polarization in American society.

We have assumed at the start, as working hypotheses, that the basic American pattern of values has remained constant throughout the period of national existence, and that very broadly, it has been shared by the great bulk of the population—a proposition the evidence for which cannot be presented here. If this is the case, apart from some ethnic and other variants, the supposition is that the *main* conflicts which can be plausibly interpreted as those of values, should rather be treated as ideological; thus not so much as direct expressions of value-commitments, as apologies for or interpretations of the state of affairs and prescriptions for remedy. It is on the assumption that this is the case that we have suggested that the paradox of institutionalization as just stated constitutes the main axis on which American ideological views have been differentiated. On one side have been those who have tended to be satisfied with things as they are, to emphasize the accomplished goodness of the current "American way," to claim moral justification for it, and to try to combat threats to its integrity. On the other side have tended to be those who are primarily impressed by the gap between what we are and what we ought to be, and who are concerned with stimulating efforts to *change* the current state in the desirable direction.

Both sides would, in the nature of the case, be characterized by typical ideological selections and distortions. They can also be subdivided on various other axes. All these problems, however, belong in another connection. The present discussion has been concerned with elucidating the cultural basis which, broadly and with due qualifications, we feel to be the *common ground* on which the many varieties of more concrete orientation can be seen to make sense. However acute the current conflicts, the positions are, in our opinion, all basi-

Cultural Background of American Religions 163

cally variations of a single theme, the theme of instrumental activism. It is to provide a basis for this interpretation that it has been necessary to go as far as we have in setting forth the main cultural base of American values in such wide historical and comparative perspective.

Conclusion

Perhaps it is best to begin these concluding remarks by noting again the crucial distinction between the factors which account historically for the original establishment of an institutionalized pattern of values, and the way in which, once established, it can organize the relations of a contemporary constellation. The American religious system was primarily the creation of the postCalvinistic phase of ascetic Protestantism, working in interaction with the complex political and social circumstances of the New World. In the contemporary world it includes, as noted, with varying degrees of strain, several other groups which do not have a close fit with the historic denominational pattern as outlined, namely, the largest, the Roman Catholic, several Protestant groups such as Lutherans and members of sect groups which do not easily fit in as denominations, the Jewish groups which vary from a type of ethnic-religious community far removed from a denomination to, in the case of Reform Judaism, a type very close sociologically to the Protestant denomination.

As noted early in the paper, we do not feel that this inclusiveness would have become possible without a further step in the level of generalization of the value system beyond that of the original crystallization of the main pattern and a higher level of differentiation of the society within which it exists. On the negative side, it is the generalization of the English pattern of "dissent." *All* American religious groups are "dissenters" in that none of them is either in a majority (Protestants being split into many denominations) or in an institutionally or legally privileged position, certainly the *de facto* privileges of the older "prestige" Protestant denominations, like Congregationalists, Presbyterians, Unitarians, and Episcopalians, have substantially diminished in significance in the past generation or so.

Secondly, to a perhaps surprising degree there has been an implicit approximation to value consensus among many of the most important of the religious groups. Within the broad religious traditions represented there is of course a profoundly important common history. But within especially the nonProtestant groups it is perhaps not too much to say that elements relatively close to the ascetic Protestant orientation have been especially important in this country. Thus in the Catholic group the special role of the Irish is important on at least two counts. They of course have been the most important leadership group within American Catholicism. Irish Catholicism is both notably more "Puritanical," *i.e.,* morally rigoristic, than many other branches, an orientation which includes a certain special interest in the secular world. It is perhaps not fortuitous that the Jesuits, as the most "world-oriented" of the major orders have played a special role in it. It seems to me that the main line of Irish-American Catholicism both incorporates the tendency within Catholicism to institutionalize a secular but religiously based ethic more than do other Catholic groups, and that it has not been uninfluenced by its long association with Protestant England; in cases such as these bitter antagonism is not a measure of lack of relationship; it can often be the contrary. In certain respects the antiEnglish attitude of the Irish may have had the covert meaning of resentment at being treated as second class *Englishmen.*

Factors such as this seem to be involved in the generally widespread desire on the part of groups ethnically different from the early dominant ones to achieve full Americanization. The problems of social structure involved in fitting into the American denominational system have of course been obscured by the fact that the vast majority of American Catholics have, until relatively recently, been both fairly recent immigrants and hence in other respects than the religious only partially assimilated, and that they have been of relatively low socioeconomic status, and hence not to a very great extent exposed to some of the structural pressures inherent in the higher structural positions. The problem seems now to be coming into a new phase of adjustment which may prove a difficult one; the election of a Roman Catholic to the Presidency for the first time may in certain respects have brought it to a head. It is certainly likely to involve major changes from the main historic position of the Catholic church and it is very difficult to predict how fast and how far this change is likely to go.

The case of the Jews, with all its differences, has certain similarities. Of all the large nonProtestant groups they are the ones who have been most notably successful by all the usual standards within the Ameri-

Cultural Background of American Religions 165

can environment, especially in occupational advancement. This has not occurred without important changes in the character of the Jewish socioreligious community itself, most conspicuously shown by the drastic decline in the incidence of those Jewish groups which adhere to literal observance of the Orthodox Jewish law as practiced in Eastern Europe a half-century ago, notably those features emphasizing segregation from the Gentile community. The importance of the Reform movement in American Judaism is an important index; its radical character from a Jewish point of view is indicated by the fact that it is not recognized in the State of Israel.

This history of the Jewish group in the United States, both their success and their willingness to undertake the religious changes which have gone with it, indicate a set of values which are certainly congruent with the general American pattern of instrumental activism to a high degree, but this involves a variety of complex questions, which cannot be entered into here.

Whatever elements in the preexisting orientations of these groups may have favored fitting into the American pattern, there has also been a strong set of forces operating on the other side, namely, the very strong assimilative power of American society generally, a power which has been substantially stronger than that internal to most politically organized European societies. The most important factor here is one not familiar to common sense. It is the pluralistic character of the social structure which is an aspect of the high degree of structural differentiation of the society. This means that most of the important solidary groupings in the society are crosscutting so far as the memberships of classes of individuals are concerned. Thus with the recent substantial upward mobility of much of the immigrant and previously rural population of the early part of this century, religion, ethnicity, and social class no longer coincide in any clearcut way. Similarly, regional characteristics have, by the main criteria of social composition, been coming to be more rather than less uniform, and hence less a basis for social distinctiveness; the rapid industrialization and urbanization of the South is the largest-scale recent example of this change. Hence for the individual, the structural units with which he is affiliated, which we must remember are typically several, and increasing in relative number, do not all run together, but in terms of structured "interest," point in several directions.

This feature of American social structure comes to a head in the political system. Precisely because it is a pluralist society in the above sense, and at the same time one which has institutionalized a wide range of private autonomy relative to governmental authority, *i.e.*, it is a "liberal" society in the relevant sense, there is a minimum opportunity for religious or other special groups to "dig in" by consolidating their special positions in political terms—as for example for long the French Catholic group has done in Quebec or has happened in a number of European cases. For any one group to be politically effective it must form alliances with such a diversity of other groups, of a different character, and not only within its principal sphere of interests, but also in other spheres, that maintenance of a specially protected position for it becomes well nigh impossible; this is particularly true over a long period.[14]

It is undoubtedly likely that there will be many conflicts and strains over the American religious constitution in the coming generation. Perhaps the most acute focus of conflict will be the field of education. The general impression given by the current situation in the light of its history is, however, that the main pattern has come to be firmly institutionalized and is unlikely to be radically altered; I look much more to a gradual assimilation of the other groups to it (*i.e.*, those not predisposed to "denominationalism") than, vice versa, to the change of the pattern itself in the direction of their historic positions.

The Catholic church as historically a church in the Weber sense, the various sects, and the Jewish religiosocial community are all likely to be modified even further in the denominational direction. This prediction is based in the first instance on the consideration that I can see no prospect of a political coalition which would both be politically viable and also in a position to make deep inroads on the separation of church and state. And of course that any religious influence could reverse the general trend to pluralistic differentiatedness in the general structure of the society is almost unthinkable.

Some feel that this general trend to the extension of the institutionalization of denominationalism is a case of "secularization" in a

---

[14]This conception of a pluralist society is well set forth in William Kornhauser, *The Politics of Mass Society*. I myself have developed my interpretation in this field in a review article of this and another book in *World Politics*, October, 1960, and in " 'Voting' and the Equilibrium of the American Political System," in Eugene Burdick and Arthur J. Brodbeck, *American Voting Behavior,* Free Press, Glencoe, 1959.

sense incompatible with the deepest interests of religious groups. This problem involves technical questions which cannot be further entered into here. For what it may be worth, my own opinion is that, whatever the terms used, the general American pattern lies in the main line of development, not only of a narrow special movement within Protestantism, but of the main historic sweep of the JudeoChristian tradition in its relations to the structure of secular society.

CHAPTER XIII

The Catholic Church and Modern Bigness

By ROBERT J. DWYER

EARLY IN 1896 the eloquent and articulate Archbishop of St. Paul, John Ireland, published a collection of his papers and addresses under the title, *The Church and Modern Society*. It voiced his confidence that the Catholic Church, far from being an anachronism in the new age which was to be ushered in by the twentieth century, was in fact singularly adapted by her nature and constitution to cope with the problems which were implicit in the adumbrated developments. Without attempting a profound analysis of his thesis he nevertheless proclaimed his firm belief in the entire consistency of Catholicism with the democratic way of life, in its ability to meet and solve the conflicts of political and social change, and in its inherent power to reconcile religion and culture.[1]

Ireland in his time was one of the more prominent American advocates of a true marriage between democracy and traditional Christianity. He was one of the first to applaud Pope Leo XIII's advice to the French hierarchy, that it cease looking backward toward a theory of Christian kingship, whose disadvantages were at least equal to its advantages so far as the freedom of the Church was concerned, and seek instead to rally the faithful to an intelligent support of the democratic republicanism which had so evidently come to stay, both in Europe and in the New World. Without the least sacrifice of essential orthodoxy he was convinced that the Church could not only achieve a *modus vivendi* with the new political scheme of things, but would find in it a happier solution of her demand for freedom to function as a perfect society. In this, doubtless, he was echoing the urgings of earlier proponents of this marriage, of men like LaMennais and Lacordaire and Rosmini on the Continent, of Daniel O'Connell

[1] John Ireland, *The Church and Modern Society*, D. H. McBride and Co., Chicago and New York, 1896, pp. 85, 343.

170 *Ethics and Bigness*

and the leaders of the Young Ireland movement, and of Father Isaac Hecker and Orestes Brownson in America.

There is little question that Ireland spoke for the newer generation of Catholic leaders, clerical and lay, in the United States. Among his contemporaries in the American hierarchy there were some who questioned the forthrightness of his views or who reserved judgment on the completeness of his acceptance of the harmony of democracy and tradition, but it may be suggested that the controversy which at the time made so much noise in the public press was as much instigated by personalities as by conflicting philosophies. Most American Catholics, throughout the nineteenth century, were in full agreement that the Church in this country was committed to democratic republicanism and was indeed managing very well under the system. There was understandable hesitancy, nevertheless, on the part of some, to extend practice into the realm of theory. The question was complicated at the close of the century by rumors of an "Americanism" which aroused suspicions of heresy. As specified by the Holy Father in his letter to Cardinal Gibbons, *Testem Benevolentiae,* this tended in a moral way to exalt the "practical" virtues at the expense of the genuine spiritual life, and threatened to reduce religious authority itself to a mere democratic consensus. There is no reason to believe that such views were ever consciously held by any American Catholic leaders, and a balanced appraisal indicates that it was rather a sort of trial balloon set off by the European protagonists of the contemporary Modernist movement.[2] But if Ireland and his following at the turn of the century seemed to have been warned by Rome to proceed cautiously, it was by no means evident that the Holy See was of a mind to interfere with the exploration of the grounds of reconciliation. As the new century advanced it became entirely commonplace for American Catholic spokesmen to assert, with all confidence, that if the Church were made for America, America was made for the Church. This was the atmosphere in which Catholic America gave unquestioning support to the nation in the First World War, and which has become a characteristic of this large and growing religious minority.

[2]Thomas Timothy McAvoy, C.S.C., *The Great Crisis in American Catholic History,* H. Regnery Co., Chicago, 1957, p. 363.

The Catholic Church and Modern Bigness

Over the past half-century the gradual development of Catholic intellectual life in America has focussed an increasing attention on the problem of integrating the Church with the political and social democracy of America. Needless to remark, there are always Catholic liberals and Catholic conservatives, just as there were in the days of Archbishop Ireland, a point which would hardly require stress were it not for the fact that the popular criticism of the Church assumes that there is only one permissible Catholic viewpoint on any and all matters under the sun. It is not to be expected, therefore, that there should be a uniform development of Catholic thought in this area where freedom is sedulously preserved. Yet it is a fact that the overwhelming majority opinion of leadership and scholarship has been constantly and consistently pointed toward the basic harmony between American democracy and the Catholic Church. There are, to be sure, areas of dispute and points of conflict; papal and episcopal pronouncements affecting political situations of the past experience of the Church whose relevance to the actuality here and now need clarification; there is even an urgency for the recasting of accepted opinions which do not represent the final thinking of the Church in the whole field of her relations with the temporal order and with the state. American Catholic political philosophy, in rather sharp contrast with its social philosophy, has been somewhat tentative and uncertain in its growth.[3] Yet the broad lines of its direction are clear and unmistakable. It is impossible, for example, to read the series of annual Statements issued by the Administrative Board of the National Catholic Welfare Conference, representing the viewpoint of the American hierarchy, without recognizing the total and cordial commitment of American Catholic leadership to the spirit of American democracy.[4]

This, however, does not mean to say that American Catholics are in full agreement with specific phases of the democratic process as manifested in the nation. Separation of church and state, as Father Robert A. Graham, S.J., has reminded us, began with Our Lord's distinction between the things which are Caesar's and the things

[3]Thomas Timothy McAvoy, C.S.C., editor, *Roman Catholicism and the American Way of Life,* University of Notre Dame Press, Notre Dame, 1960; John Tracy Ellis, *American Catholicism,* University of Chicago Press, Chicago, 1955, *passim.*

[4]John Tracy Ellis, editor, *Documents in American Catholic History,* Bruce Publishing Co., Milwaukee, 1955, for text of "The Bishops' Program of Social Reconstruction, 1919."

which are God's, and was recognized explicitly by Pope St. Gelasius I in the fifth century.[5] Yet separation in the familiar sense of a "wall," a barrier of absolute impregnability, is, in Catholic eyes, an attempt to exalt a laicism, or a secularism, which experience has proved discredited and fallacious. To the extent that it is the conscious creed of other Americans, the Catholic minority is in vigorous dissent, not from the standpoint of demanding special privileges but of insisting that separation of the two powers need not and should not imply something very close to a mutual ignoring of existence. The Catholic analysis of the problem would suggest that there are ways and means of maintaining separation without secularism, on the one hand, and without clericalism, on the other. The area in which the debate is currently most acute is the field of education, where the Catholic minority, in undertaking a school system in which religion is taught and professed, is not convinced that it should therefore be deprived of the benefits designed to encourage all education in America.[6] Up to the present, however, the debate has had few political repercussions; whether it will remain out of the political arena is a question only the future will answer.

By and large, then, the Catholic Church in America, at this mid-passage of the twentieth century, finds itself in a reasonably relaxed posture so far as its relations with the state and with society as a whole are concerned. It confronts, therefore, the larger problems viewed by this Conference in its present discussions without too many of the distractions which would necessarily arise from such factors as political oppression or religious persecution, or even from an atmosphere charged with suspicion and the attribution of unworthy motives. The Conference has set itself to examine the challenges to traditional ethics manifested in government, politics, and administration. Specifically, the question is raised concerning modern big-scale organizations, and the consequences for moral responsibility. The purpose of this paper is an attempt to present a Catholic reaction to the total problem.

The first thing to remark, rather obviously, is that the Catholic

---

[5] Robert A. Graham, S.J., *Vatican Diplomacy,* Princeton University Press, Princeton, 1959, p. 4.

[6] "The Catholic School and American Education," *Annual Statement, Administrative Board, National Catholic Welfare Conference, 1956,* N.C.W.C., Washington, D.C., 1956.

The Catholic Church and Modern Bigness 173

Church is fairly well acquainted with the modern phenomenon of big-scale organization. She has herself been a big-scale organization for the better part of her corporate existence. For the past sixteen hundred years she has known what it means to operate as an international, indeed, a universal society, not merely in theory but in fact. Her constitution has proved applicable to the mathematics of her membership, not with absolute or unvarying success, but with a reasonable approach to it. Beginning as the *pusillus grex* of the time of the Apostles she entered, even before the close of the first century of her life, into the operational responsibility of exercising spiritual government over many thousands of adherents. Roman persecution hampered her growth and hindered the development of her administration, yet the publication of the Edict of Milan (313 A.D.) saw her marvelously prepared to assume a role which soon became hardly distinguishable from the political administration of the Empire.

The course of her subsequent history, whether in the East or the West, served to emphasize her administrative responsibility. The gradual clarification of the nature, authority, and extent of her centralized government, the papacy, and the flexibility and adaptability of her episcopal organization, emerged as the most successful venture in ecclesiastical polity that the world had known. There were mistakes and errors in abundance, but the marvel is that the system worked and endured. The tradition of papal authority even withstood the political and moral disruption of Italy during the tenth century, certainly the lowwater mark of her experience in the West, as the tradition of episcopal authority under the spiritual sovereignty of the Bishop of Rome survived the holy rivalry of the monasticism of the Dark Ages.

Very early in her corporate existence the Church became intimately aware of the tensions between her big-scale organization and the personal, individual problems of her adherents, whether ethical, doctrinal, political, or plainly social. This is to cite a truism of all human experience, and if the Church claims that she is divinely founded she makes no claim that she is or ever has been or ever will be exempted from these tensions. The problems of schism and heresy, however they may be studied as intellectual or theological disagreements, are invariably open to discussion as reflections of these same tensions between a vast administrative society and the individual components of it. And among the results of her innumerable difficulties, whether with Caesar or with the heresiarchs, there has been a recurring effort to purify as well as to strengthen her administrative structure.

We live in a society, religious and secular, which has been profoundly influenced by the Reformation of the sixteenth century. The decision of a large part of the Christian world to throw off the administrative control of the Catholic Church, together with portions of her accepted doctrine, created a fissure in society and a breakdown in moral unity. The Protestant revolt disrupted the organization of the Church over the bulk of northern Europe and substituted for it, broadly speaking, a system at the most national, at the least local, in character. With the passage of time this was to lead to the modern Protestant concern with the ethical and moral problems of big-scale organization.

In contrast, the Catholic Counter-Reformation was to essay two things: a rebirth of individual spirituality and a strengthening of the administrative unity and centralization of the Church. This was the work of the Council of Trent, and for an understanding of the success of that work it is essential that both objectives be given due value.[7] It is true that the papacy emerged from the Council with enhanced prestige and that the administrative organization of the Church generally was thoroughly overhauled, but it is equally true that minute and painstaking consideration was given to the religious life and the education of the laity. Whether the problem was foreseen in modern terms or only in the haze of the transition from the medieval world to the world we know, the Fathers of the Council seemed to sense its urgency.

The Church of the Counter-Reformation has been criticized as laying too great stress on administration, as creating bulwarks of defense against an embattled enemy, as sacrificing holiness to unity. There are, of course, elements of truth in this charge, yet it does not present a balanced picture. It has become a commonplace to represent the Society of Jesus, a typical Counter-Reform organization within the Catholic Church, as more interested in regaining lost territory and recapturing political strongholds than in saving individual souls. But surely this view suffers from radical distortion; the Jesuits who

[7] Léon Christiani, *"L'Église a l'Époque du Concile de Trente"* in (Fliche and Martin, *Histoire de l'Église,* volume 17), Bloud and Gay, Paris, 1948, *passim.*

The Catholic Church and Modern Bigness

campaigned to stem the incursions of the northern heretics were the same who introduced into Catholic society an enlightened piety and a tempered religious optimism.[8] The same remark holds true of the other religious orders and foundations which flourished from the sixteenth to the end of the eighteenth centuries, as well as of the older orders which enjoyed an amazing renaissance during the same period. They were concerned to build up the organizational strength of the Church, doubtless, but they were also deeply concerned to revive personal holiness in the vast body of the laity. The proliferation of saints who gave themselves endlessly to the work of individual sanctification is one of the cardinal characteristics of an era which a cursory view is apt to dismiss as wholly preoccupied with administrative strategy.[9]

In spite of serious setbacks, culminating in the storm of the French Revolution, the shape of the modern Catholic Church was becoming clearer. The authority of the Holy See was growing in acceptance, not merely as a remote theory, but as a matter of practical and constant application. There would be recurring difficulties with Catholic rulers over such matters as the appointment of residential bishops and governmental interference in the relationships of bishops with the Holy See, but it was observed that not even the intense Gallicanism of Louis XIV was able to turn the Church aside from her avowed purpose of achieving practical freedom in the administration of her affairs, regardless of political boundaries. Together with this phase there went on a steady growth in diocesan development, with the bishops insisting upon their single competence to govern their sees, subject only to the directives emanating from the Sovereign Pontiff.[10]

Thus, even before the Revolution there was steady pressure for ecclesiastical liberty and recognition of the right of the Church to govern her own house. The last attempts, during the eighteenth century, of royal absolutism to control or even to dismember the Church met with a growing and massive resentment. It is totally

---

[8]Pierre P. Pourrat, *Christian Spirituality from the Renaissance to Jansenism*, Burns, Oates and Washbourne, Ltd., London, 1927, volume 3, pp. 23-49.

[9]Joseph Lecler, *Histoire de la Tolérance au Siècle de la Reforme*, Aubier, Paris, 1955, 2 volumes; Edmond Preclin and Eugene Jarry, "Les Luttes Politiques et Doctrinales aux XVIIe et XVIIIe Siècles," in Augustin Fliche and Victor Martin, *Histoire de L'Église*, volumes 19 and 20, Bloud and Gay, Paris, 1955.

[10]*Ibid.*, volume 20, *passim*.

inaccurate to picture the hierarchy and clergy of, say, France and Spain, as flaccidly subservient to the interests of the crown. The suppression of the Jesuits, Josephism, and Febronianism, were at least as useful in warning the Church of her contemporary weakness as they were harmful in undermining her authority.[11] It is from this viewpoint that it is possible to endorse quite heartily the thesis that the Revolution was enormously beneficial to the Catholic cause. If Pius VI and Pius VII suffered the indignities of insult and imprisonment at the hands of the French invaders and Napoleon, they were at the same time freed from a bondage which had become intolerable. Shattered, but intact in her essential structure, the Church entered upon the nineteenth century.[12]

A broad view of the history of the Catholic Church during the past century and a half would necessarily place major emphasis upon the very points which are of concern to this Conference. This period has witnessed her astonishing numerical growth, both in the older nations of Catholic allegiance, in the New World, and in the vast missionary fields of Asia, Africa, and Oceania.[13] It has also witnessed the perfection, relatively speaking, of course, of her administrative system, its thorough and minute definition, along with the tardy conquest of freedom of operation within the framework of separation between Church and State. Finally, it has crystallized the problem of the relations of the masses to her traditional teachings and ethics.

There is space here only for casual reference to several of the more conspicuous events which have precipitated her reactions. In the first place it may be said that the Church, while welcoming the Restoration, was perfectly clear in her own mind that the revival of legitimacy did not mean a return to caesaro-papism. In other words, the lessons of the Revolution were not lost upon the Holy See and the hierarchy as a whole. Liberties gained, even partially, were more precious than privileges lost. This may not have been patient of exact formulation, but it was nevertheless a guiding principle of action. The Holy See

[11]Marie Henri Jette, *France Religieuse du XVIIIe Siècle*, Casterman, Paris, 1956, pp. 118–154.

[12]Jean Leflon, *Pie VII*, Plon, Paris, 1958; Bernardine Melchior-Bonnet, *Napoleon et le Pape*, Livre Contemporain, Paris, 1958.

[13]Kenneth Scott Latourette, *The Great Century in the Americas, Australasia, and Africa, A History of the Expansion of Christianity*, volume 5, Harper and Brothers, New York and London, 1937–1945.

The Catholic Church and Modern Bigness 177

protested, as was to have been expected, the rape of her territorial possessions as a phase of the unification of Italy, but there was an underlying sentiment among Catholics the world over that far worse calamities had befallen the Church. Its attitude toward liberalism was qualified less by a philosophical analysis of its tenets than by the painful experience of the worst phases of its anticlericalism.[14] What comes closest to the heart of the matter, however, was her realization, as the nineteenth century advanced, that in spite of her administrative achievement, in spite of her gratifying numerical growth, she was losing the proletariat. Other forces, other missionary enterprises, not Protestant this time, nor even Christian, were making steady inroads upon the presumed loyalty of the industrial masses.

This has been called the "tragedy of the nineteenth century." It is fruitless to question whether it could have been avoided because of the simple fact that it was not foreseen. By the time the Catholic Church, with her perfected administrative system, and the Protestant Churches, with their traditional dislike of administrative emphasis, came to see the situation as it was, it had gone too far for immediate remedy. It was Communism in one or another of its forms which rushed in to fill the vacuum and to create another and even more disastrous fissure in Western society. The slaughter of two successive Archbishops of Paris gave dramatic illustration of the extent to which the urban proletariat had been alienated from the Church. Her identification with the ci-devant aristocracy, the ultra conservative bourgeoisie, and with a peasantry lapsing gradually into religious indifference, emphasized the gravity of the situation.[15]

This was the Continental picture as the nineteenth century drew to its close. The picture elsewhere was far less uniform. In the burgeoning American Republic and throughout large areas of the British Empire the health and steady growth of the Church, separated from the State and free from its control, stood out in encouraging contrast. In Latin America, where the Church had lost her hold upon the education of the upper classes and was confronted with an enormous challenge of dealing with vast masses of illiterate peasants and primi-

---

[14]Edward Elton Young Hales, *The Catholic Church in the Modern World*, Hanover House, Garden City, New York, 1958; *idem, Pio Nono*, P. J. Kenedy, New York, 1954.

[15]Roger Aubert, *"Le Pontificat de Pie IX"* in Fliche and Martin, *Histoire de l'Église*, volume 21, Bloud and Gay, Paris, 1952.

tives, the demand was for a promptitude of action which, under the circumstances, fell short of realization in all too many instances.

Yet with the pontificate of Leo XIII, covering the last quarter of the century, hopeful signs of a sound Catholic reaction became manifest. Less burdened than his predecessor (Pope Pius IX) by the resentments and irritations of the politics of Italian unification, freed from the responsibilities of governing the former Papal States, his regime could give itself without distraction to the business of strengthening the Church, in her structure and in her operation, for the contest for the salvation of the modern world. Eminent among the accomplishments of the reign were the Catholic intellectual revival, marked by the return to her service of countless of the leading scholars and savants of Europe and the Empire, the rebirth of Catholic education, especially in the fields of higher study, a vigorous rethinking of the social problem, marked by the publication of Leo's epoch-making encyclical, *Rerum Novarum* (May 15, 1891), a general tightening of the discipline of the Church, universal and diocesan, and a resurgence of loyalty to the Church on the part of the laity, symbolized by a greatly heightened enthusiasm for the person and office of the Sovereign Pontiff. It was remarked by more than one observer outside the Church that the close of the century, which had witnessed the temporal decline of the Holy See, had brought its spiritual power and authority to unexampled summits.[16]

It might be well, at this point, to interrupt the historical sketch for a brief overview of the perfected discipline and administrative functioning of the Church in our times. It is the Catholic theological belief that these are inherent in her constitution, and are no more than the contemporary development of that which was always contained in the divine deposit of faith. It is nevertheless true that it has taken centuries to bring them to their present mode of operation.

The Catholic Church centers in the person of the Bishop of Rome, successor of St. Peter, the Bishop of all Bishops. His authority over the entire Church is universal, whether in defining doctrine, initiating legislation, or enforcing discipline. The appointment of bishops throughout the Church is solely the prerogative of the Holy See, and with the power to appoint goes the power to remove. As the supreme

[16]Edgar Hocedez, S.J., *Histoire de la Théologie au XIXe Siècle*, volume 3, L'édition Universelle, Brussels, 1947.

The Catholic Church and Modern Bigness

teacher of the Church the Pope has the right to insist upon the acceptance of his teaching anywhere and everywhere in the Church. His infallibility, though a correct understanding of this power emphasizes rather its negative aspect of freedom from error in matters of faith and morals than its more positive one of defining and publishing at will or at random, is uniquely for him a personal privilege. It is shared by the hierarchy only when acting in union with him. Clearly, the burden of the normal administration of the Church is far beyond the capacities of one man. For practical purposes, therefore, this is committed to the care of the Roman congregations, headed by the Cardinals in curia, who are answerable to the Pontiff for their day to day decisions, appointments, and disciplinary actions.

In intimate association with the Holy Father is the hierarchy of the Church throughout the Catholic world. Each bishop, as a successor of the Apostles, is the responsible head of his diocese, saving only the supreme jurisdiction of the Roman Pontiff. It should be well understood, however, that this is no mere "rubber stamp" arrangement. The local bishop, acting in union with the Holy See, possesses a wide discretion in the practical government of that area of the Church confided to him, both in temporal and spiritual matters. It is his business to supervise and promote the welfare of the Church under his jurisdiction, to make such decisions as are called for and as are consistent with the general discipline and spirit of the Church. Catholic education in its widest sense of preaching and instruction is his responsibility. As the man on the scene it is for him to enact particular legislation or even to emphasize particular points of Catholic doctrine. As steward of the temporalities of the Church he is given a broad competence in determining ways and means to provide for the needs of clergy and laity.[17]

Functioning as the direct assistants of the bishop are the priests of the diocesan clergy. This is a stable group of clergy in each diocese, generally entrusted with the cure of souls in the parishes but fulfilling other priestly functions consistent with their vocation at need. These functions may run the gamut from teaching to administrative appointments as members of the bishop's council. In a separate category are those priests bound together as communities living under vows of

[17] Charles Journet, *The Church of the Word Incarnate*, volume 1, Sheed and Ward, New York, 1955.

chastity, poverty, and obedience, organized, with either papal or diocesan approval, for a more intensive spiritual way of life as well as for the service of the Church in the particular fields of their choice, ranging from the work of education to the foreign missions. These priests (or brothers) owe obedience to their elected or chosen superiors, with due reference to the rights of the local bishops-ordinary.

The religious orders of women, not sharing the sacramental character of ordination, are nevertheless organized along the same lines as the religious orders of men. Again, their purposes, stated in their respective constitutions, stress certain special phases of the spiritual life within the general framework of the evangelical counsels, and the fulfilment of those services deemed useful for the Church. Here again, their obedience is vowed to their own superiors, with due regard for the normal diocesan rights of administration and discipline.

Out of this emerges an administrative and jurisdictional system which has proved to be applicable to all the temporal situations in which the Church finds herself. It functions efficiently in dioceses of extremely diverse size, importance, and ethnical nature. It goes without saying that inasmuch as the functionaries, from the Holy Father down to the lowliest fourth assistant in a large city parish, are human beings, there are always weaknesses and occasional breakdowns, yet it is a fact of plain observation that these are by way of exception, not by way of rule. It was doubtless this aspect of the operation of the Catholic Church which led an enterprising firm of administrative consultants, on the basis of their examination, to give her an extraordinarily high rating, even when compared with international business corporations which boast their efficiency. There is a certain humor in this, but it has its bearing on the theme of this Conference, and may be taken to answer at least one phase of the question. With her constitution working as it is at present, at least in the free world, the Catholic Church is not confronted by any particular administrative difficulty in its dealings with modern bigness.

The laity, as such, does not share in the administration or the jurisdictional operation of the Church. She looks back with strong distaste to the long quarrel over lay investiture which rocked the bark of Peter during the Dark Ages and the early medieval period, and has no intention of repeating the blunder. With a view almost as dim she recalls the unhappy experience of royal interference with papal and episcopal appointments, the various accommodations of the Pragmatic Sanction, and the assertion, on the part of the nobility and aristocracy of the old regime, of vested interests in the temporalities of her organization.[18]

It is nevertheless true that the Church is keenly aware of the necessity of a clearer and more viable definition of the place and role of the laity in her public life. To the "laicization" of Christian society which characterized the eighteenth and nineteenth centuries, she would counter with a "Catholic Action" defined by Pope Pius XI as the "cooperation of the laity in the work of the hierarchy." In place of the vacuum created by the disappearance from the scene of kingship and aristocracy, or even, in our day, of the "loyal bourgeoisie," she is fully intent upon developing a laity thoroughly instructed and organized. There is no question but that this is reflected in her increased concern for a program of Christian education to offset the inroads of a secularized system. It is noteworthy, too, that many of the leading Catholic theologians of the present are giving much thought and care to the formulation of an exact and comprehensive "theology of the lay state," and that the Holy See has cordially endorsed the foundation of the so-called Secular Institutes, which in many cases envisage a participation in the formal religious life by those whose occupations remain secular and who may even be in the married state.

Primary attention has been paid, thus far in this discussion, to the juridical and administrative preparation of the Catholic Church to deal with the problems of the present age and to meet their manifold challenges. This is an obvious approach, for it is generally conceded by friend and foe alike that the Church has developed an admirable organization and from that standpoint is in a position of strength. But organization alone, even the most perfect and coherent, would be a useless instrument without an informing spirit. And it is often alleged that the Church, in her anxiety to perfect her organization, has been indifferent to the development of a corresponding inner life. Now it must be said that it is much more difficult to substantiate this phase of Catholic life than to indicate the broad outlines of the other. This is no more than to say that the history of grace is far more elusive than the history of institutions.

[18]Yves Marie Joseph Congar, O.P., *Lay People in the Church*, Newman Press, Westminster, 1956.

Perhaps the clearest and most realistic answer that can be given is this: that the Church in our times has succeeded, better than ever before in her history, in holding the loyalty of her adherents, even under conditions of violence and extreme cruelty. Whereas in the past there are many instances recorded of wholesale abandonment of the Church or of the faith under the pressures of persecution or of political support of heresy, it is remarkable that the contemporary repetitions of these pressures have proved far less effective in alienating the faithful. This is not to say that many who were nominal Catholics before the victory of Communism have not succumbed to persuasion; it is merely to remark that the hard core of Catholic resistance has not by any means been dissolved, even after two generations of unspeakable hardship. Nor is this characteristic of only a few isolated groups, which might be compared to the Irish Catholic resistance to the Protestant Ascendency during the seventeenth and eighteenth centuries; it is sufficiently widespread to be indicative of a spirit which may properly be called Catholic.

It is a matter of observation, furthermore, that in the secularized West the predicted sweep of forces opposed to Catholicism have met with a definite stalemate. Where, as at the turn of the century in France, secular agnosticism seemed destined to reduce the Catholic body to an insignificant minority, the result has been something quite different, and an analysis of current trends would substantiate the strength of a vigorous Catholic reaction. These things are cited not so much because of their social or political interest, but as denoting an underlying Catholic spirit, working in enthusiastic support of the administrative structure of the Church and giving life to her organization.[19]

The inner life of the Catholic body, throughout the world, has been sedulously cultivated and enhanced by the leadership, example, and teaching of the Pontiffs of this century. From Pope St. Pius X to Pope John XXIII now reigning, the cardinal emphasis of the Holy See, shared by the hierarchy, has been spiritual, not political. The overriding anxiety has been to build in the clergy and laity a strong spirituality, based on the sacramental and liturgical life, coupled with a clear understanding of the teachings of the Church and the obligations of Catholic loyalty, both to Church and State. There are indica-

[19] André Desqueyrat, S.J., *La Crise Religieuse des Temps Nouveaux*, Spes, Paris, 1955.

The Catholic Church and Modern Bigness

tions that this approach has met with very considerable success, so that it is fairly characteristic of the Church at the peak of her administrative strength that her intellectual and moral life is in corresponding health.[20]

After this cursory examination of the development of the administrative structure of the Catholic Church, and of her spiritual preparation for the problems of contemporary bigness, the question remains whether the system is actually working (in distinction to the more technical sense of functioning), and whether it is equipped to confront the ethical challenges implicit in modern government, politics, and administration. It is a serious question; it goes without saying that Catholics themselves, from the Sovereign Pontiff down, have given it frequent and anxious scrutiny. Anyone, for example, who is familiar with the writings of the late Pope Pius XII, contained in his voluminous speeches, allocutions, and encyclical letters, must realize that it occupied a conspicuous place in the current of his thought.[21]

It is conceivable that the question is too vast, too complex, for a contemporary answer of any real validity. It has been indicated above that the Church seems to be reasonably satisfied with the operation of her administrative structure and reasonably confident that the underlying ethos or spiritual enthusiasm is genuine. She is aware of her weaknesses, more realistically than is perhaps credited. If an instance may be cited, it would inevitably reflect upon her present concern for her welfare in Latin America, where the need for a vigorous renewal of the normal discipline and action of the Church is extremely urgent, less because of any threat of Protestant proselytism than because of the danger of a wholesale lapse into a religious indifferentism which would be difficult to distinguish from sheer heathenism. In those areas of the world where she is estopped from performing her essential functions and where her administrative structure has been damaged if not destroyed, she, together with the other agencies of civilization and Christianity, can only hope for an amelioration which will permit her to resume her work, even on a more modest scale.

[20]Walter J. Burghardt, S.J., and William F. Lynch, S.J., editors, *The Idea of Catholicism*, Meridian Books, New York, 1960.

[21]A definitive edition of the late Pontiff's writings has not yet appeared; it is urgently needed. A fairly convenient source for his later pronouncements, etc., is the quarterly publication, "The Pope Speaks," John O'Neil, editor, Washington, D.C.

The great concern of the Church in the free world, however, is that congeries of philosophies, opinions, and prejudices lumped together under the convenient heading of secularism. The reader of the contemporary Catholic press is intimately aware of the frequency with which secularism is denounced by prelates and priests, by editors and zealous laymen. But like many nouns which are the names of things, it needs careful and discriminating definition. For there is a sense in which we are all secularists, we who live in this world and are expected to use it as a vehicle in the process of salvation. The secularism which disturbs the Catholic Church, as it must disturb all Christians and religiouslyminded men, is the exclusive emphasis on worldliness, leading to the conclusion that the concerns of religion are without public interest. To the extent, and it is unquestionably considerable, that this viewpoint has won acceptance in the affairs of government, politics, and big business, it does present a threat to the traditional ethics espoused by the Church. It does this only rarely as a philosophy, and is not particularly formidable when it attempts to vest itself in that toga; it is much more subtle and effective when used as an undisputed and indisputable first principle of action. For it takes for granted that the ethics of the Judeo-Christian tradition are purely relative, have no eternal validity, and may be dispensed with at will.[22]

It is the secularist spirit, rather than bigness as such, which the Catholic Church identifies as posing the severest threat to her ethical teaching. There is reason to believe that she is more deeply concerned over its inroads into the conscious or unconscious attitudes of men than she is over the political and social victories of Communism. For the latter is at least identifiable, can be known and analyzed, whereas secularism only too often defies rational examination. It is easier, in a word, to combat an ideology than to exorcise an impression. The very formlessness, or lack of formulation, of the secularist spirit is its greatest strength as a solvent of Christian ethics and morality, to say nothing of Christian morale.[23]

Hence it is that in these middle years of the twentieth century, in spite of the efficiency of her administrative system and in spite of a

---

[22] John Cuthbert Ford, S.J., and Gerald Kelly, S.J., *Contemporary Moral Theology*, volume 1, *Questions in Fundamental Moral Theology*, Newman Press, Westminster, 1958; Adrien Dansette, *Destin du Catholicisme Française*, Flammarion, Paris, 1957.

[23] Hans Urs von Balthasar, *Science, Religion and Christianity*, Newman Press, Westminster, 1959, pp. 92 ff., 119–142.

The Catholic Church and Modern Bigness

relatively high degree of spiritual vitality in her members, the Church is gravely worried. For she finds that the popular mind, eroded by secularism, is rapidly losing faith and confidence in the Natural Law as a system of first principles of ethical behavior and moral judgment, and is tending toward an easy acceptance of governmental control of all phases of life. She recognizes this spirit in a multiplicity of movements which would substitute subjective standards for objective moral principles, and sentimentality for a reasoned Christian approach.

In the sixty years since Archbishop Ireland proclaimed his confidence in the future of the Catholic Church in America, and voiced his *Esto Perpetua!* in praise of the American system of a cordial separation of Church and State, a great many problems unforeseen in his day have arisen to complicate the admirable simplicity of his view. The Church in this country has achieved an administrative organization which in its efficiency of operation is outstanding, even by modern Catholic standards. It has built a school system which is the largest and most impressive venture in private education in the history of the West. It is developing, at long last, a strong program of lay activity and participation in the work of the hierarchy. But it has not found the means of persuading the nation of the universal validity of its ethical teachings, nor is it, in the present situation, at all sure that a satisfactory basis of agreement currently exists.

One reassuring reflection remains, that as a well organized minority, reasonably confident of the loyalty of her children and of their basic fidelity to her dogmatic and ethical teachings, the Catholic Church stands in a position of strength as a witness to the truth handed down from the Christian past. She is not afraid of modern bigness as such; she is gravely concerned, however, that as a juggernaut of secularism it may crush the spirit of modern man.

CHAPTER XIV

The Organizational Dilemma in American Protestantism

By ROBERT LEE

I

LIKE OTHER SOCIAL institutions on the contemporary American scene, Protestantism is deeply implicated in what Kenneth Boulding calls "the organizational revolution." In an age of large-scale organizations and centralized agencies in various spheres of life, churches too must organize on a similar basis if they are to be relevant to the new *Zeitgeist*—not to mention the strain toward survival endemic to the career of most organizations.

The elaboration of organizational apparatus in American Protestantism, later to be reviewed, brings in its wake many pressing issues; for it seems a truism that the virtues of religion can seldom be as well organized as its vices. One of these key issues, which I shall call the "organizational dilemma," goes to the very core of the faith and challenges its integrity. Unlike the rather commonplace dilemma of the gap between an individual's profession and his practice (which is less an intrinsic dilemma than a commentary on the givenness of the human situation of finite man), this dilemma, of which we speak, is structural; it is part of the very makeup of the church which exists in a particular social context and interacts with its surrounding culture.

The dilemma is simply this: on the one hand, if the church is to take seriously its obligation as a missionary and witnessing movement, it must maintain some semblance of continuity, stability, and persistence; it must develop appropriate organizational and institutional forms. Yet, on the other hand, the very institutional embodiments necessary for the survival of the church may threaten, obscure, distort, or deflect from the purposes for which the institution was originally founded. Thus it is hardly sufficient to say that the task of the church is to be obedient or to be faithful if obedience and faithfulness are detached from the question of institutional self-maintenance.

In a very fundamental sense, the critical problem of the church is the problem of community. And community always involves the rational organization of human resources and more or less defined patterns of group interaction governing the life of its members. We may speak heuristically (not literally) of the church and community problem by reference to this familiar aphorism: "After the doxology, comes the theology, then the sociology." After the initial religious experience or the original creative impulse (doxology), soon there sets in the need to define and formulate a systematic body of teachings, a codified and articulated set of doctrines (theology); then follows the necessity of preserving and perpetuating the original experience through the organization of a community (sociology).

After the spiritruled (charismatic) church of Pentecost, there soon develops the institutionalized church of early Catholicism. After the prophets come the priests. Or, in the much quoted words of Max Weber, with the passage of the charismatic leader, attempts are made to preserve the benefits of charisma, resulting in a "routinization of charisma." The holy must necessarily be related to the profane. Indeed, "we have this treasure in earthen vessels." There must necessarily be a *manifestation* of the *essence* of the church. And, in the very process, the instrumental purposes of organizations become exalted as ends. Paul Harrison states this dilemma cogently when he points out, "the results are paradoxical, since the goals which the organization was created to achieve tend to be displaced by the goal of organizational self-perpetuation."[1] And Philip Selznick pinpoints the dilemma by the term "organizational imperatives." The organization must satisfy its own self-generated needs before the group can attend to the goals for which it was established:

> We can say that once having taken the organizational road we are committed to action which will fulfill the requirements of order, discipline, unity, defense, and consent. These imperatives may demand

[1] Paul Harrison, *Authority and Power in the Free Church Tradition*, Princeton University Press, Princeton, 1959, p. 136.

Organizational Dilemma in American Protestantism

measures of adaptation unforeseen by the initiators of the action, and may, indeed, result in a deflection of their original goals.[2]

In other words:

> Running an organization, as a specialized and essential activity, generates problems which have no necessary (and often an opposed) relationship to the professed or "original" goals of the organization. The day-to-day behavior of the group becomes centered around specific problems and proximate goals which have primarily an internal relevance. Then, since these activities come to consume an increasing proportion of the time and thought of the participants, they are—from the point of view of actual behavior—substituted for the professed goals.[3]

At present there are several prominent efforts to avoid or escape from the organizational dilemma confronting churches. One such approach would define the church solely in terms of its essence, in terms which focus on the "invisible church," or on the "bride of Christ." (As D. T. Niles quips, "who wants to marry an invisible bride?") Hence the church is defined in terms of its being and not in its organization and action, as if God were involved in the former but not in the latter. Such a view is essentially maintained by Emil Brunner in his *Misunderstanding of the Church,* which, indeed, has misunderstood the church. For it makes of the church something of a disembodied spirit floating about, perhaps in outer space. According to Brunner, "The New Testament *Ecclesia,* the fellowship of Jesus Christ, is a pure communion of persons and has nothing of the character of an institution about it."[4] We would do well to remember, as Jacob Taubes reminds us, that "man is not content to let the heavenly city remain an abode in the clouds, but longs for an earthly setting."[5]

The other alternative, which does equal violence to the "reality of the church" is to focus exclusively on the institutional and organiza-

---

[2]Philip Selznick, *TVA and the Grass Roots,* University of California Press, Berkeley, 1953, p. 256.
[3]Philip Selznick, "An Approach to a Theory of Bureaucracy," *American Sociological Review,* VIII (1943), 48.
[4]Emil Brunner, *The Misunderstanding of the Church,* Westminster Press, Philadelphia, 1953, p. 17.
[5]Jacob Taubes, "Community—After the Apocalypse," in *Community,* edited by Carl J. Friedrich, Liberal Arts Press, New York, 1959, p. 113.

tional aspects of the church. For ecclesiastical structures, in Protestant thought, do not exhaust the Protestant conception of faith. Indeed, as H. Richard Niebuhr observes, "Protestant religion centers less in the ecclesiastical establishment than in the Bible and the proclamation of its message, and in the personal religious experiences and attitudes of its adherents."[6] To view the church simply as a social organization is already to judge it by a set of assumptions which is more often covert than explicit. Thus the American Institute of Management's 1955 study of the American Baptist Convention concludes with this professional appraisal: "Viewed against the background of the modern business corporation, the management practices of religious organizations are appallingly archaic."[7] Again the report states, ". . . Religious organizations may be compared to corporations which concentrate on product development to the virtual exclusion of executive development."[8]

Note that the Institute's first generalization is made after a study of a single Protestant group. But even if such a judgment were accepted at face value, there remains the problem of whether a religious organization can legitimately be evaluated solely "against the background of modern business corporations." Religion cannot be treated as a "product," a commodity to be developed, processed, packaged, shipped out, and sold by a band of super-salesmen-evangelists. To be sure, there is no excuse for wastefulness, slovenly work habits, and the like. But that a business corporation should be the model for a church to conform to is to forget the purpose of the church; it would be similar to the hazards involved if higher education were evaluated solely in terms of business standards without regard for educational goals and traditions.

In point of fact, the real danger of large organizational development in the churches does not inhere in the organizational structure *per se,* but rather in the ethos that often accompanies mass organizations. Religious groups not merely conform, but sometimes overconform to the worst features of a business ethos. For example, one Protestant agency has adopted the symbols of status of a corporation hierarchy

[6] H. Richard Niebuhr, "Religious Institutions—Protestant," *Encyclopedia of the Social Sciences,* volume 13, 1934, p. 267.
[7] *Management Audit of the American Baptist Convention,* American Institute of Management, New York, 1955, p. 1.
[8] *Ibid.*

Organizational Dilemma in American Protestantism

to the extent that there are four different shapes and sizes of desks, each of which is assigned to denote a particular status in the hierarchy of the organization. In another agency there is an unusually great social distance between those on the executive and those on the secretarial staff, so that it would be unthinkable for executives who bring their lunch to eat in the same room with the secretaries who bring theirs. It is interesting to note that the terms used to designate leaders of most ecclesiastical structures are adopted from the business world: executive secretary, executive vice president, treasurer, board of directors, board of managers, etc.

The seeds of the organizational dilemma are contained in the very institutional structure of the church as it interacts with the culture. This inescapable problem is not derived from the fact that churches attract to their ranks persons of prestige and power. Such a notion, advanced by Elizabeth Nottingham in her book, *Religion and Society*,[9] neither does justice to the complexity of the dilemma nor to persons of prestige and power. Even if church membership consisted of those of lowly estate, the organizational dilemma, as we have portrayed it, would still persist. Indeed, in some sect groups and lower class denominations and conventions, the dilemma is particularly acute.

Let it be clear that our remarks should not be construed to mean that organizational structures are evil in themselves. To hold that organizations and human institutions are inherently corrupt would be untenable both from the standpoint of theology and sociology. For rational forms of procedure may, indeed, enhance and facilitate the better performance of purpose and function; this is certainly their intention. And to focus exclusively on the dysfunctions of large-scale organizations surely neglects the ways in which such organizations are conducive to the realization of purposes in the modern world. Large-scale organizations usher in new possibilities for creativity, and at the same time new institutional vulnerabilities and hazards.

It would be a mistake to assume that the organizational dilemma is a new phenomenon. It is at least as old as the church itself. Indeed, the apostle Paul may be considered a remarkable church organizer and administrator, whose visits and letters constantly reminded Chris-

---

[9] Elizabeth Nottingham, *Religion and Society*, Doubleday and Company, Garden City, 1954, p. 56.

tian communities, particularly at Corinth, of the tension between the *kerygma* and communal response. But, for our day, the search for that theoretical point which will allow the church to remain true to its purposes and yet operate through viable institutional forms that will preserve its gains and extend its influence must be an ongoing, neverending quest. Although there can be no simple resolution of the dilemma, it may become easily obscured, or perhaps, misunderstood, so that equally truncated views are adopted—views which interpret the church only as an organization or as a spiritual entity devoid of organization.

II. The Organizational Revolution in Ecclesiastical Structures

Although essentially a perennial problem, the organizational dilemma today clamors for urgent attention because church organizations have expanded immensely in scope and size. Hardly any aspect of church life is immune from the impact of large-scale ecclesiastical structures. This applies, without exception, to the local parish, as we shall later examine in greater detail. Suffice it at this point to call attention to a recent editorial in the *Christian Century,* which traditionally represents "grassroots" sentiments, urging local pastors to save all the mail received from denominational headquarters over a three month period, weigh the total, and then weigh that portion which precipitated any new or decisive action. The editors are convinced that "the proliferation of boards and bureaus has produced a startling increase in undesired helpfulness from the Bigger Brothers who want to see the Programs Produce."[10]

In his provocative volume, *The Organizational Revolution,* Kenneth Boulding draws a comparison between the number of large-scale organizations in 1852 and 1952. He points out that a century ago one found practically no labor unions, employers' or trade associations, farm organizations; no American Legion, Department of Agriculture or Labor in the national government, few corporations and large businesses.[11]

---

[10]"Weigh All Your Mail From Headquarters," *Christian Century,* December 9, 1959, p. 1429.

[11]Kenneth Boulding, *The Organizational Revolution,* Harper and Brothers, New York, 1953, pp. 3-4.

Organizational Dilemma in American Protestantism 193

In the case of Protestant ecclesiastical structures, the picture is equally dramatic. One need only go back roughly half a century to see how far the organizational revolution has taken place in American Protestantism. For in 1900 there was no National Council of Churches, no Interchurch Center, no denominations actively discussing merger, no United States Conference for the World Council of Churches (indeed, no World Council of Churches and no International Missionary Council); there were few local councils of churches and a mere handful of state councils. In addition, there was no National Evangelical Association, no National Conference of Christians and Jews, no American Friends Service Committee; numerous other religious associations were not yet on the scene, such as the American Association of Theological Schools, the Church Peace Union, Religious Newswriters Association, Religious Research Association, etc.

It is true that prior to 1900 such organizations as the American Bible Society, the Sunday School Movement, the YMCA and YWCA, the Young People's Society for Christian Endeavor, and the Foreign Missions Conference in North America had already been founded; and most of the major denominations had long since formed missionary boards for overseas and home missions work.

But the overall picture is one of intensive and extensive growth of religious organizations in number and in size during the past fifty years. There are now nearly a thousand local councils, forty-four state councils (as contrasted to four in 1927), 2,157 councils of church women, 119 councils of church men, 2,255 local ministerial associations. Local councils alone involve some 500,000 lay people in leadership posts and spend over $10,000,000 annually.

The budget of the Federal Council of Churches in 1909, the year of its inception, was $9,000. In 1950 the Federal Council merged with seven other major interdenominational agencies to form the National Council of Churches, whose budget for 1959 was approximately $21,459,470. At present the National Council has thirty-three church bodies in its membership with a combined constituency of nearly 40,000,000.[12] Almost forty additional religious groups are "associate"

[12] The new and imposing "home" of the National Council at The Interchurch Center on Morningside Heights, adjacent to Union Seminary and Riverside Church, has prompted some fundamentalist critics of the Council to suggest that Morningside Heights ought to be renamed "Vatican Hill." *Cf.* G. M. Savery, "Do We Want a Giant Church?" *Christianity Today*, April 29, 1957, p. 9.

or "affiliate" members in one or more of the Council's seventy program units.

The two largest Protestant groups in 1959 are the Methodist Church, with 9,670,690 members, and the Southern Baptist Convention, which numbers 9,202,205. At the turn of the century, however, the Methodist Church was still split into three parties, the major division resulting from the Civil War controversies. It was not until 1939 that the Methodist Episcopal Church, Methodist Episcopal Church South, and the Methodist Protestant Church reunited to form the Methodist Church. Since 1906 the Methodist groups which reunited have just about doubled in membership; and the Southern Baptist Convention, which had numbered around 2,000,000, has more than quadrupled its forces.

Today there are ten Protestant denominations which claim a membership in excess of 2,000,000 as compared to three in 1906. Along with growth in size, of course, has gone the proliferation of denominational boards, bureaus, departments, and agencies for the performance of specialized functions. Some of these newer functions which bring to birth new organizations may be found in such areas as research and survey, television and radio broadcasting, publications and public relations, church extension, etc.

A number of sect groups have grown with remarkable speed. Thus the Assemblies of God (founded in 1914) increased from 6,703 in 1916 to 148,043 in 1936, and 505,552 in 1959. The Nazarenes grew from 6,657 in 1906 to 136,227 in 1936 and 291,036 in 1959.

One of the most significant organizational developments in American Protestantism is the organic mergers and reunions which have been consummated during the first half of the twentieth century. Since 1905 no less than sixteen mergers and reunions have combined many of the major Protestant groups and reduced their number from thirty-six to fifteen. This fact is all the more significant when one recalls that between 1870 and 1905, not a single instance of church union is recorded in the United States.[13] Merger negotiations cur-

[13]Samuel McCrea Cavert, "Christian Unity in America," *The Church Through Half a Century*, edited by Samuel McCrea Cavert and H. P. Van Dusen, Charles Scribner's, New York, 1936, p. 360. Excluded from our total of sixteen mergers and reunions are the countless consolidations of smaller groups and synods and the type of mutual recognition known as "inter-communion."

Organizational Dilemma in American Protestantism 195

rently in various stages of discussion involve at the very least an additional thirty religious groups.

Another index of institutional expansion is the economic value of church buildings. Of course, reliable figures are very difficult to obtain.[14] Relying solely on government sources, we may report that the estimated value of *new* construction of religious buildings for the single year 1958 was $863,000,000. While by no means a fair comparison, note that the Bureau of the Census report for the monetary value of *all* church edifices in 1890 was $679,426,489. The last and most reliable report on church property values is contained in the 1926 *Census of Religious Bodies* (more complete than the 1936 one). The 1926 Census sets the total value of church edifices at $3,840,000,000, which excludes such items as pastors' residences, investment property, school buildings, hospitals, etc. Although there are no reliable sources reporting the current value of all church edifices, we do know that in the past decade more than $4,000,000,000 were invested in new church building construction. And the Department of Commerce predicts that church construction for the year 1960 alone will exceed $1,000,000,000. To hazard a very wild guess, and this is no more than a guess, the present "replacement value" of church edifices may be somewhere in the neighborhood of $25,000,000,000 to $30,000,000,000.

Thus religious institutions, in sheer physical and financial proportions, tower as one of the great and significant institutional features of American life. Judging from the promotional and evangelistic literature of many denominations, this trend is likely to continue into the future. To quote from an official of one of the major denominations: "We believe that the next fifty years are going to be the glorious years of the ―――― Church. We believe that when we reach the year 2000, the United States will have a population of more than 275,000,000 persons, and the ―――― Church will have more than 25,000,000 members." Here are several other projections made by different denominations: "By the year 1975, the ―――― Church will be needing 589 new ministers every year; it will require 25% more active ministers than are now on the rolls to staff the expanded number of congregations."

---

[14] For data on the financial and investment policies and practices of Protestant groups, *cf.*, F. Ernest Johnson and J. Emory Ackerman, *The Church as Employer, Money Raiser, and Investor*, Harper and Brothers, New York, 1959.

"The ———— Church has about 15% of the Protestant church membership. This means we should have a net gain of 400,000 persons per year for the next ten years just to keep up with population growth."
"As the ———— Church reached another million milestone in church membership in 1958, several interesting facts were revealed. Since 1946, we have gained 1,000,000 in membership every four years. By comparison, it took us twelve years to advance from 3,000,000 to 4,000,000 members. . . . . . . a record unmatched by any other religious group in America. At our present rate of growth, we should more than double our present membership by the time our ———— Church is 150 years old."

These statements by denominational leaders remind us again of our problem of the organizational dilemma. For certainly the church must promote with an eye to the future; but promotion must not be confused with evangelism. There is always the risk that the "church as employer, moneyraiser and investor" may obscure the church as the "household of faith."

Before we attempt to assess the consequences of the organizational revolution (which, by now, we are tempted to call the "ecclesiastical revolution"), we shall conclude this section by lifting up certain principal trends which seem to be implicit in our discussion: 1. movement toward unity and consolidation, 2. movement toward coordination and centralization, 3. development of specialized leaders, 4. development of an "administrative top."

1. *Movement Toward Unity and Consolidation*

Although we have been noting the proliferation of religious organizations, an unmistakable trend toward unity and consolidation of smaller units must also be recognized. This is particularly noticeable in the drive toward organic merger and reunion at the denominational level. Denominational mergers are hardly ever easy ventures; for they involve careful negotiations, the loss of separate identities and "distinctives," and many residual institutional problems, such as pensions, properties, publications, debts, etc. Hence it is all the more wonder that so many significant organic mergers have been successfully consummated in recent decades.

At the local level, too, there are signs of unity and consolidation.

Organizational Dilemma in American Protestantism

Note the mergers of local churches, particularly in urban areas of transition or rural places of dwindling population. It is now the rule, rather than the exception, for churches to serve the entire community without regard for denominational background. Many of these communitycentered churches are formed through the practice of comity, which is a rational organizational device for cooperating denominations to allocate their resources by mutual planning and assignment of church sites.

Many factors operate to favor the trend toward unity and consolidation. They cannot be detailed here, but suffice it to call attention to a few of the social factors at work:[15] efficiency, or the better deployment of limited resources; economy, or the avoidance of wasteful competition and needless overlapping; institutional power, or the gain in institutional strength and ability to wield influence in relation to other religious groups and in relation to secular currents of society.

2. Movement Toward Coordination and Centralization

Closely allied to the first trend is what Robert C. Angell has called the "nucleation process," or the tendency for a group of independent associations to become affiliated or form parts of a larger network of operations.[16] This centralizing tendency, enabling joint appeals and joint policies, is marked in denominations which typically bring together what were once separate agencies pursuing specific causes —such as social action, religious education, higher education, home and foreign missions, etc. The interdenominational agencies which merged to form the National Council of Churches are another instance of the same process.

J. Milton Yinger puts it aptly when he says, "In a day when poultrymen, engineers, and physicians have joined together in their various organizations for a more effective pursuit of their interests, it is not surprising to find religious groups following the same pattern."[17] Churches which fail to elaborate large-scale ecclesiastical structures

---

[15] For a fuller treatment of this problem, cf., Robert Lee, *The Social Sources of Church Unity*, Abingdon Press, New York, 1960.

[16] Robert C. Angell, *Free Society and Moral Crisis*, University of Michigan Press, Ann Arbor, 1958, p. 58.

[17] J. Milton Yinger, *Religion, Society and the Individual*, Macmillan, New York, 1957, p. 293.

equivalent to those in other organized spheres of American life run the risk of failing to keep pace in a technical, highly organized society. Without these large-scale coordinating and centralized bodies, churches would present a picture of chaotic disorder and would be totally irrelevant and ineffective in fulfilling specialized demands and responsibilities. So just as we have "Big Government," "Big Business," and "Big Labor," it seems inevitable that we should have "Big Religion."

3. Development of Specialized Leaders

In order to integrate and coordinate their services, large-scale organizations require a bureaucratic structure. Bureaucracy is a rational process for promoting technical efficiency. Its well known features include hierachical leadership, clearcut responsibilities and communication channels, devotion to formal rules and regulations, division of labor, and specialization of functions.

The increasing demands for technical services and competence in church organizations call for specialized and technically trained personnel. Denominations and councils seeking faithfully to discharge their responsibilities must either recruit or train experts in such fields as social work, race relations, research, family counselling, fundraising, evangelism, mass communications, publicity, international relations, church building and architecture, urban and rural church, etc. In short, specialization calls for specialists.

An indication of the need for specialized leaders may be seen by a description of some of the functions performed by a single department, such as religious education. A division or department of religious education in a medium-sized city council of churches may be responsible for citywide *training institutes* for lay teachers; it may operate the Protestant *released time education program;* it may have separate commissions or subdepartments for *children's work, youth work, college work,* and *adult work;* it might have a department of *family life* or *marriage counselling;* a committee on *family worship* and *camping.* It will operate summer vacation Bible Schools, or perhaps sponsor a *summer camp program* for various age groups; it will have *audiovisual resources* for lending, and a *library* of *curricula materials* of several denominations for each grade; it will likely *coordinate a scouting* or *"Brownie"* program. It might have a special program for work with *handicapped children,* the aged, or juvenile delinquents. Of course, each of these programs calls for trained personnel with specialized competence. At the denominational and National Council levels, the division of labor and leadership specialization are apt to be more complex in religious education as in other functional areas of church work.

4. *Development of an "Administrative Top"*

Large-scale organizations typically have echelons of administrators. As one approaches the top of the pyramid, the number who occupy these command posts becomes fewer. Such concentration of power seems necessary for effective decisionmaking which leads to the initiation of policy and to its execution by those in lower levels of the administrative hierarchy.

The development of an administrative top in religious organization seems to be a logical outcome of the three trends we have all too briefly depicted. Now, perhaps more than ever before in the history of Protestantism, we have a sizable corps of "managers" of ecclesiastical institutions. We need not go so far as Herbert W. Schneider, who contends that religion in twentieth century America is "shifting from religious worship to 'service,' from altar to office."[18] But the status and influence of ecumenical and denominational administrative leaders, and the important role they are coming to play in American religious life cannot be doubted. Upon the question of whether the "administrative top" in religious circles are mere "managers," or whether they can be religious "statesmen" may well hang the future status of religion in America.

III. Some Consequences of the Organizational Revolution for Ecclesiastical Structures

In this section we return to our problem of the organizational dilemma by detailing in concrete ways some of the consequences of the organizational revolution in American Protestantism. Recall our

[18]Herbert W. Schneider, *Religion in Twentieth Century America,* Harvard University Press, Cambridge, 1952, p. 24.

earlier contention that the consequences are both positive and negative. If it appears that the following discussion gives undue weight to negative consequences, it is solely for the purpose of sharpening up the issues of moral responsibility.

1. *The Local Church*

We begin with the local church for two reasons. First, it has been largely overlooked in our discussion thus far. Second, like the problem of easily seeing the mote in another's eye, but overlooking the beam in one's own, it is very tempting for most ministers and laymen to sneer at the "bureaucracy" in their denominational headquarters (or in the National Council) without discerning it in their own local situation. For wherever a pastor has a secretary or a janitor, there is a bureaucracy. Indeed, Charles Page introduces the notion of a "one-man bureaucracy" even in small parishes:

> ... The small-town jack-of-all-trades, unlike his village predecessor of an earlier era, tends to become a one-man bureaucracy, much in the manner of the one-room school teacher. His life (and usually his wife's as well) becomes scheduled, divided, compartmentalized, routinized, bureaucratized. And if he resists this development too much, not only will he experience serious difficulties in carrying out his specialized tasks, but he is apt to be dubbed a "poor administrator" of church affairs.[19]

Although bureaucracy is usually associated with large-scale organizational structures, Page's point is well taken. For even in small-scale organizations one finds many bureaucratic characteristics, not all of which should be attributed to the proliferation of national bureaus and agencies. One of the most talked about issues among Protestant clergymen for some time has been the problem of the multiple roles of the modern minister and the increased demands being made upon his time merely to keep the organizational machinery in the local church running smoothly.[20] In fact, H. Richard Niebuhr has coined

---

[19]Charles H. Page, "Bureaucracy and the Liberal Church," *The Review of Religion*, volume XVI, March, 1952, p. 148.
[20]*Cf.*, Samuel W. Blizzard, "The Minister's Dilemma," *Christian Century*, April 25, 1956; S. W. Blizzard, "Role Conflict of the Urban Minister," *The City Church*, September–October, 1956, etc. Wesley Shrader, "Why Ministers Are Breaking Down," *Life Magazine*, August 20, 1956. W. H. Hudnut, "Are Ministers Cracking Up?"

a new term—"pastoral director"—which symbolizes the drift toward administrative functions assumed by the local pastor.[21]

Moreover, the increased development of church staffs which have multiple ministers, group ministries, and assistant pastors, ushers in many new and unexplored organizational problems. It would appear that in training and in value orientation, clergymen have yet to learn how to work together in a team relationship; for they bring a strong individualistic bent to the leadership of the church. In the case of assistant pastors, for example, there are sometimes strains in role relationships between the assistant and his senior colleague. Some of these familiar role strains are as follows: the assistant pastor is relegated errandboy chores; he is assigned a very specialized task so that his experience of the ministry is fractional; he is not involved in the formation of basic policies which he has the responsibility to carry out; he has no "grievance procedure" or court of appeal in the event of conflict with his superior, upon whom he is dependent for future job recommendations; he may constitute a threat to the status of the senior minister, who may be hostile to new currents of theological thought which he embodies. Lets listen as "an assistant speaks his mind":

> Sad to say, many senior ministers in a very crude and ungracious manner make a studied attempt to keep their assistants in their "proper place." To be the pastor or shepherd of a congregation is a very high and holy privilege. Such a privilege the average assistant minister also covets from time to time for himself, but his superior all too often jealously refuses to share such joys with his colleague. . . . Too many senior ministers thoughtlessly assign only menial and unpleasant ecclesiastical chores to their assistants. Unfortunately, there are too many men . . . [who] find it extremely difficult to have anyone on their staff who enjoys to an equal degree the respect and admiration of their congregation. They would be the last to admit it, but what they want are yes-men and hirelings.[22]

Christian Century, November 7, 1956. Joseph Sittler, "The Maceration of the Minister," *Christian Century*, June 10, 1959. According to Blizzard, the average minister apportions 38 per cent of his time to administration, 26 per cent to pastoral duties, 19 per cent as a preacher and priest, 12 per cent as organizer, and 5 per cent as teacher.

[21] H. Richard Niebuhr, *The Purpose of the Church and its Ministry*, Harper and Brothers, New York, 1956, pp. 79 ff.

[22] John Schott, "An Assistant Speaks His Mind," *Religion in Life*, volume XXIV, autumn, 1955, pp. 579–580. Also, *cf.*, George C. Vincent, "The Assistant Minister—His Problem and Ours," *Religion in Life*, volume XXIV, autumn, 1955, pp. 585–590.

Of course, there are many assistant pastors who have established a good working relationship with their senior pastor. And, we must remember that there are two sides to the story. The senior minister also has many legitimate complaints. In his eyes, many younger men cannot take criticism, are reluctant to make calls and visitations, spend their time in questionable ways, and are overly ambitious. In some instances the assistant pastor does constitute a real threat, or foments controversy, or in other ways works to undermine the status of the senior minister. These factors, which we have identified in the image of both the assistant and the senior minister, are latent sources of tension which contribute to role strains in the organizational life of the local church.

Thus it is not only the interdenominational administrator or denominational board secretary in some big city headquarters who has bureaucratic problems or who is "cut off from the people." Social distance also exists between pastor and parishioner, as administration supersedes ministration. With the increasing specialization and segmentation of the local clergyman's role there develops a gap between the man in the pulpit and the man in the pew, between leaders and rank and file members. In short, the organizational dilemma is a serious issue for the local church.

Perhaps nowhere is this dilemma more evident than in the large urban or metropolitan church. In terms of goal displacement, one is tempted to argue that these large congregations tend to make conventional Christians of their members, who increasingly become spectator-worshipers.

The large urban church is symptomatic of the shift in our society from a communal to an associational pattern. That is, segmental participation or partial involvement in many special-interest associations takes the place of a communitycentered focus. "This means," in the words of Robert T. Handy, "the church tends to get reduced merely to one of the many groups in which persons, detached from locality, associate together with segments of their personality. In this segmentation of culture, we find . . . the substitution of multiple moral standards for a single communal standard."[23] With increased specialization of roles and multiple ministerial staffs in our large urban

---

[23] Robert T. Handy, *Home Missions,* American Baptist Convention, New York, n.d., p. 9.

churches, face to face primary group relationships are weakened and replaced by associational relationships.

Martin Luther once defined the church as a sustaining fellowship of "mutual conversation and consolation" in which the members love one another and share one another's fortunes and burdens. Yet this is hardly possible in the modern situation in which the church is a part of mass culture. Like its urban ethos, impersonality, anonymity, and mass participation are prevalent in the large urban church. In tune with the rapid pace of urban culture, church members rush to church for a brief hour a week and then are just as quick in leaving its doors. The congregation on a Sunday morning is a sea of more or less impassive faces. Everyone is alone in the crowd, be it subway or sanctuary. Strangers they come and strangers they go.

For the most part, there are few available opportunities for "mutual conversation," except among the inner circle of members. Greetings and comments which do get exchanged are usually "fatuous sayings" employed in order to fend off any deeper involvement. Contacts are fleeting and superficial. As a rule, the larger the size of the congregation, the fewer the opportunities for interaction on a meaningful level. The church as *Koinonia* (community) is virtually lost sight of in concept and in practice.

In place of *Koinonia,* we have an association of duespaying members, the majority of whom are on the fringes of church life. These, then, are apt to be conventional Christians who may come and go, but whose Christian fellowship in any corporate sense is devoid of vitality. I suspect their numbers are legion. It may well be that the sheer size of many large urban congregations makes them "unassimilable."

With growth in size of membership, it is quite possible that churches reach an ecclesiastical "point of diminishing returns." Adopting an analogy from the growth of biological organisms, Boulding suggests that "as an organism grows it absorbs more and more of its environment, and eventually it uses up the more favorable parts of its environment, and the environment turns increasingly less favorable."[24] What Boulding calls the "principle of increasingly unfavorable environment" may well apply to human organizations. For as a church increases its size beyond a certain point, it becomes exceedingly diffi-

[24]Boulding, *op. cit.,* p. 22.

cult to maintain adequate communications between leaders and members and an adequate sense of community among the members. Since membership size is a symbol of "success" in our culture, it would appear that the large urban church is a victim of its own success. Thus the consequences of the organizational revolution for the church call into question the very meaning of church membership.

2. Transition from Sect to Denomination

In this paper we have not ventured into a discussion of a typology of religious organizations, since this topic receives extensive treatment elsewhere in the literature of the sociology of religion.[25] Yet one facet to this problem is particularly germane to our main concern. This is the dynamic transition from sect to denomination, which many sectarian groups experience in their adaptation on the American scene.

We would argue that the logic of organizational elaboration itself serves as an important catalytic agent for the transformation of sects. Once sects begin to develop more complex organizational patterns, they are on the way to becoming denominations. And if sects perform the positive function of bearing protest against the church by recovering a neglected aspect of faith or by keeping alive the tension between church and culture, then the fact that this function is minimized or forfeited when the sect becomes a denomination raises the question of whether ethical protest must give way in the face of organizational accretion.[26]

Our argument is relevant, of course, only for those sect groups which make the transition from sect to denomination. For not all sects are involved in this movement. Some groups may persist for generations relatively unchanged, such as the Dukhbors, Dunkards, Amish, and Hutterian Brethren. Others, like the Jehovah's Witnesses, will develop highly centralized administrative procedures, but still remain

[25] Ernst Troeltsch, *Social Teachings of the Christian Churches,* Macmillan Company, New York, 1931; Y. Milton Yinger, *op. cit.;* H. Richard Niebuhr, *The Social Sources of Denominationalism,* Henry Holt, New York, 1929; Liston Pope, *Millhands and Preachers,* Yale University Press, New Haven, 1941; Howard Becker and Leopold von Wiese, *Systematic Sociology,* John Wiley, New York, 1932; Nottingham, *op. cit.;* etc.

[26] Of course, sects also perform negative functions as well, such as schismatic differentiation, fanaticism, radical experimentation leading to antinomianism, etc.

hostile to, and separate from, the main stream of Protestantism. But our contention is illuminating for the more "established sects," which include the Church of the Nazarene, Seventh Day Adventist, Mission Covenant, Christian Missionary Alliance, some of the Pentecostal groups, etc. These established sects become contenders for denominational status, just as some of our solid denominations, like the Methodist and the Disciples of Christ, were once in a similar position.[27]

To a significant degree the transition of these sect groups is enhanced by their orientation to large-scale church organizations. A rough analogy may be drawn between underdeveloped nations which must rapidly industrialize in order to join the family of modern nations and sectarian groups which must develop complex organizational patterns if they are to join the "family of churches." This contention may become clarified as we examine a concrete case of transition. Let us take the Church of God of Anderson, Indiana.

Originating as the "Church of God Reformation Movement" in the 1880s under the leadership of D. S. Warner, the new sect was founded as a protest against the trend toward ecclesiastical centralization, the formality of organized Protestantism, and the cooling of religious ardor. It sought to restore primitive Christianity by stripping away the symbols of institutionalism and worldliness; it eliminated honorific titles (Rev., Dr.), forbade its followers to attend the theater, vote in public elections, wear neckties or costume jewelry. The "Church of God Reformation Movement" attacked the Federal Council of Churches and called the denominations "apostate" and a "cancerous growth on the body of Christ."

Then within a short span of a generation or two, radical changes completely transformed the group, until today it stands on the threshold of denominational status. Val Clear's intensive study of the movement indicates the extent of transition:

> The process of adaptation has led the Church of God to build church buildings of Gothic architecture, with divided chancel and other factors suited to sacramental churches rather than to the revivalistic "religion of the frontier" which has characterized the Church of God.

[27]*Cf.*, Earl D. C. Brewer, "Sect and Church in Methodism," *Social Forces*, 30, May, 1952, pp. 400–408; Oliver Read Whitley, *Trumpet Call of Reformation*, Bethany Press, St. Louis, 1959. Whitley's book is a case study which traces the sect to denomination transition of the Disciples of Christ.

Ethics and Bigness

Status and honorific religious titles have become current. "Reverend," "Doctor," and "Mr." gradually replaced . . . earlier designations. Originally regarded as a kiss of death, increasingly pleasure is taken when a position of prestige is offered one of the group by an interdenominational body.[28]

Not least among the pressures precipitating transition stands the process of institutionalization. It is possible to trace clearly the steps involved. Almost from the beginning, despite its own protestations, the group's expansion and its fulfilment of necessary functions called forth committees and boards and other rational organizational patterns. Even the relatively simple task of issuing its magazine, *Gospel Trumpet,* which began as a one-man operation by D. S. Warner himself, soon expanded to a complex affair manned by several hundred. At first the organizations were informal and staff personnel were largely volunteers. But it soon became obvious, as in the case of producing the magazine, that this setup was not reliable. Then followed the formal structure of boards and agencies manned by specialists who could coordinate and plan for the ongoing work of an expanding movement.

A trend toward centralization may also be noted. Almost from the outset officials and trustees had to be selected to purchase land in the group's name and to conduct business affairs. One of the decisive steps toward centralization occurred in the 1890s when an effort was made to secure clergy rates on the railways for Church of God ministers. The railroad's Clergy Bureau required that all ministers requesting special rates be endorsed by their central bodies. This led to the "Registrar's Office," which in turn led to the publication of a *Yearbook.* In effect, any minister not listed in the *Yearbook* failed to receive legitimate recognition by the group as a whole. At first there was token resistance; now no Church of God minister would hesitate to acknowledge that his denominational affiliation is "Church of God, Anderson, Indiana."[29]

With the establishment of central headquarters at Anderson, a steady growth of power, prestige, and control developed. Disbursement of funds is centered at Anderson, as are the boards and agencies

---

[28]Val Clear, "The Church of God: A Study of Social Adaptation," unpublished Ph.D. dissertation, University of Chicago, 1954, pp. 16 f.
[29]*Ibid.,* p. 88.

Organizational Dilemma in American Protestantism 207

for Extension and Home Missions, Foreign Missions, Women's Missionary, Christian Education, and World Service. Services rendered to local churches by these agencies function latently to strengthen centralization. Also the group's retirement fund, centered at Anderson, tends to increase dependence upon the central office, particularly on the part of the older ministers. Concerning institutionalization and centralization, Clear aptly notes in these striking words:

> Born in a setting of anti-organization, the movement in seventy-five years has developed to a point where the most recent *Yearbook* (1953) lists over 200 names of persons holding office in the national organization. It takes 38 pages to describe the activities of various national and regional organizations.[30]

As one might expect, the 1959 *Yearbook* of the Church of God takes sixty pages to describe these same national and regional organizations. Taken alone this fact would seem trivial, were it not the case that the movement was founded precisely on the premise of reaction against the overorganization of the established denominations. To be sure, a whole complex of other factors (*e.g.,* education and urbanization and passing of the frontier spirit) are involved in the group's movement from sect to denomination. But one can hardly deny that organizational and institutional incentives and imperatives played a prominent role.

Thus we return to our originating question of the attenuation of protest as a consequence of organizational elaboration on the part of sect groups which become denominations. Another instance of this goal displacement may be seen in the Disciples of Christ, a group which has already made the transition. The Disciples emerged in protest against the divided state of Christendom and against the worldliness of organized Christianity, but, in time, added a few schismatic splinters of their own. Founded on the impulse of Christian unity, the Disciples have been involved in a number of discussions about church union, but have never been able to carry out a successful union.

We must conclude this portion of our discussion with one observation and one question. The transition from sect to denomination is one of the unanticipated consequences of the organizational revolution as it impinges upon ecclesiastical structures. Yet, as sects become

[30]*Ibid.,* p. 361.

domesticated and abandon their original purpose, is the transition, at least in some cases, too great a price to pay?

3. The Effect on Charismatic Leadership

A third item in our accounting of the consequences of the organizational revolution for ecclesiastical structures is its impact on charismatic leadership. Charisma, as originally defined by Max Weber, is an "extraordinary quality possessed by persons (or objects) which give these persons a unique, magical power."[31] In recent sociological usage the term refers more broadly to a gifted leader with a dynamic personality, capable of commanding a following and usually exercising prophetic leadership.

A full exploration of the consequences of large-scale church organizations on the charismatic-prophetic *person* would be highly desirable, since this is an area of limited knowledge based on research. In addition, there is the problem of "institutional charisma." For Weber did not confine the concept of charisma to a single personality, but also spoke of the "depersonalization of charisma"—that is, the shift from a sense of an extraordinary personal gift to an impersonal capacity that in principle can be taught and learned.[32] Such an exploration might examine Weber's contention that "in institutional charisma the typical problem of deterioration is the drift of functionaries and their education toward specialized performance at the expense of personal inspiration of substantive rationality."[33]

More evidence is certainly needed before we can state categorically with Robert Michels that "bureaucracy is the sworn enemy of individual liberty, and of all bold initiative in matters of internal policy."[34] Michel's statement runs the risk of being a kind of slogan in which one can easily single out a highly visible target for attack. Yet when one views some of the top administrative posts in Protestant bureaucracies, one cannot help but be impressed by the truly charismatic qualities of the persons who hold these offices. Think of men like the late John R. Mott and William Temple; James A. Pike, Lesslie

[31] Reinhard Bendix, *Max Weber: An Intellectual Portrait*, Doubleday, New York, 1960, p. 301.
[32] *Ibid.*, p. 313.
[33] *Ibid.*, p. 314.
[34] Robert Michels, *Political Parties*, Free Press, Glencoe, 1949, p. 189.

Newbigin, W. A. Visser't Hooft, Truman B. Douglass, G. Bromley Oxnam, Hermann N. Morse, David W. Barry, Roswell P. Barnes, and others. Of course, it may be argued that these are the exceptional individuals and that scores of other top leaders and those in the "lower-upper" echelons of ecclesiastical leadership leave something to be desired in the way of prophetic and imaginative leadership.

In order to identify this problem more clearly, let me cite three examples of the failure of personal charisma and of institutional charisma. These examples should not be taken as conclusive evidence of the decline of charisma, but merely indicative of the possible consequences stemming from organizational preservation and elaboration.[35]

1. In their study of the clergymen's role during the Little Rock school crisis, Ernest Q. Campbell and Thomas F. Pettigrew show that when ministers are faced with an "idealistic" as contrasted to an "organizational" alternative, they will choose the latter to a degree that impairs a prophetic ministry.[36] Ministers tend to "ease out of this conflict" by appealing to various "reference systems." One of the chief forms of appeal is the "organizational reference system" in which a prophetic role is eschewed for the sake of maintaining organizational equilibrium or survival. Taking a leadership role may "rock the boat," alienate powerful contributors, or interfere with a building fund campaign, etc. For the sake of maintaining institutional stability, the clergy, by and large, played a passive role.

2. Individual action is increasingly geared to conform to expecta-

---

[35] The relationship between charisma and the rationalization or secularization of charisma is a complex one. It is tempting to suppose that there was a period in the life of the church of "pure charisma," a pneumatocracy. If one begins with this assumption, then the history of the church may be conveniently viewed as a decline of charisma. This is essentially the framework of Rudolf Sohm, from whose analysis Max Weber formulated his own concept of charisma. Here I would have to agree with Harnack that there are legal and "constitutional" elements mixed in with charismatic authority almost from the beginning. Thus history is not the arena for an inevitable decline of charisma, but rather the scene for a continuous interplay between law and spirit. For a further discussion and exposition of Sohm's conception, *cf.*, Walter Lowrie, *The Church and Its Organization*, Longmans Green, London, 1904; James Luther Adams, "Rudolf Sohm's Theology of Law and Spirit," *Religion and Culture: Essays in Honor of Paul Tillich*, edited by W. Leibrecht, Harper and Brothers, New York, 1959; and W. D. Davies, *A Normative Pattern of Church Life in the New Testament: Fact or Fancy?*, James Clarke and Company, London, n.d.

[36] Ernest Q. Campbell and Thomas F. Pettigrew, *Christians in Racial Crisis*, Public Affairs Press, Washington, D.C., 1959, p. 127.

tions of denominational leaders, who gain personal power either by ascription or by appropriation. Thus many local ministers become more interested in making a good statistical showing in reports to their denominational headquarters than in the nurture of souls or in a prophetic ministry. Conformity to denominational expectations may operate in very subtle ways. Consider the case of the local minister who is asked by his denominational executive to assume a particular responsibility (*e.g.*, chaplain for a family summer camp) which happens to conflict with a prior commitment he has scheduled for his church. If he should have several such conflicts, it is likely that he will gain a reputation as a "noncooperative" person in the eyes of the denominational official. Thus local men often feel compelled to "play ball" with denominational officers, who either have a power of appointment, should another position be available, or who can put in a negative word that has the power of blocking advancement to another post. In a sense, the local pastor is part of the "captive constituency" of the denominational administrators.

3. An example of the problem of institutional charisma is contained in the statement of a church building and extension secretary of a leading denomination. He stated very bluntly that in looking for men to staff the new so-called "high potential" suburban churches, his committee was "considering only the 'good organization men'— men who are middle-aged, who have a large barrel of sermons to draw from so they won't have to spend too much time in their studies, men who can build up a church so that it will be on a self-supporting basis before long, men who can begin from scratch and have at least two hundred members within the first two years." The search for such men is certainly along the lines of Weber's concern that there is a drift in leadership "toward specialized performance at the expense of personal inspiration or substantive rationality."

Conclusion

The organizational dilemma in American Protestantism cannot be simply resolved. Obligations stemming from organizational needs cannot in all cases be perfectly compatible with the obligations of religious vocation and commitment. What we can hope for is that the tension, which is implicit in the organizational dilemma, be kept alive.

Organizational Dilemma in American Protestantism

To obscure this tension is to court institutional inertia and ossification. It is to take over without criticism whatever organizational forms and devices happen to prevail in the culture. This does not mean that the church is to develop a strategy in its organizational patterns which is always "against the stream." Such action may prove fruitless and irrelevant when the tide is flowing the other way. But it does mean a frank and conscious recognition of the dilemma, an appraisal of the opportunities and hazards of organizational life, and a periodic reexamination of ecclesiastical structures which will allow for flexibility, experimentation, and new patterns to emerge.

One of the great needs of large-scale ecclesiastical structures is a builtin self-evaluation process, which encourages critical reappraisal of organizational means in the light of purposes and goals. This process should enhance institutional self-understanding and enable a degree of self-transcendence, which may save ecclesiastical structures from becoming ends in themselves, and, if necessary, transform them better to carry out the purposes of the church in the modern world.

I take it that this, too, is involved in Philip Selznick's thesis that preoccupation with questions of administrative *efficiency* does not lead to the knottiest and most significant problems of leadership in large organizations.[37] Instead of efficiency, the focus ought to be on leadership. Large-scale organizations are desperately in need of statesmen, of leaders who lead. The "absence of spirituality among spiritual leaders" does not enhance the quality of the institutional life of ecclesiastical structures.

We cannot escape or withdraw from the organizational dilemma in American Protestantism. The benefits derived from large-scale ecclesiastical structures cannot be minimized. Nor can the everpresent hazard of enslavement to the organizational imperatives be denied. To be sure, we may eliminate some of the unnecessary dysfunctions and mitigate some of the abuses of organizational life. Responsible as we must be for living within this dilemma, its final resolution is not of our own contrivance, but surely within the province of our hope.

---

[37] Philip Selznick, *Leadership in Administration*, Row, Peterson and Company, Evanston, 1957.

CHAPTER XV

Large-Scale Organization in Jewish Religious Life

By DAVID W. SILVERMAN

THE OPERATIVE DOCTRINES of a religion are specified in its organizational patterns and modes of conducting its collective life. This latter statement is particularly applicable to Judaism, where no set systematic creed is presented as the differentiating norm between Jews and nonJews. The imperative of Judaism can be looked upon as an increasing approximation of the biblical demand that an entire people should become "a nation of priests and a holy people." Within the framework of this general ideal, however, a number of different organizational patterns evolved. Moses, the teacher and prophet *par excellence* in the eyes of the normative tradition, might be called in current sociological parlance, a natural leader with "charismatic authority." He did not derive his leadership of the ancient Israelites from their will; he was elected by the voice in the vision of the burning bush. His leadership is only acknowledged by the people; they are not its source. His claim to leadership and obedience could be contested (the forty years of wandering in the desert could be justly named "the trials of Moses"!) but not granted by them. To meet the people's demands Moses had continually to "prove" himself. But even in the desert orderly procedures, bureaucratic organization, and functional rationalization obtruded themselves. A hereditary priesthood was designated, one whose mission was to safeguard and care for the physical structure of the tabernacle, to oversee the sacrificial system, and maintain the purity of the cult. Parallel with this structure, judges were appointed to hear the litigations of the people. Administrative delegation of authority, to relieve Moses of the burdens of office, was instituted. These two organizational patterns, originally instituted in the earliest days of Hebrew history were to continue in force for close to

214 Ethics and Bigness

fourteen centuries.[1] The priesthood's fortunes waxed and waned, but were never totally eclipsed until the destruction of the Second Temple in 70 C.E. The desert administrators in time became the Judges, the Kings, and finally, the Rabbis. Since charisma can never be fully institutionalized (it can only be domesticated or tamed, *i.e.,* permitted, but not encouraged) prophecy was a sporadic phenomenon, and one which, once the biblical canon was established, and rabbinic hegemony assured, eventually ceased.

From the days of the Temple's destruction, the chain of authority in Judaism became an authority of interpretative excellence, one which was "traditional" in character and which invested its bearers with few, if any, charismatic perquisites.[2] With the destruction of the central religious institution, the polity of Judaism became, due to the vision of the talmudic sages, intensely congregational. Each congregation was a miniature sanctuary, and partook partially if not completely, of the holiness of the Temple. Rabbinic authority was granted through the "laying on of hands"—the classic mode of ordination. Such ordination had several degrees, the highest of which was restricted to those scholars who had studied in the Palestinian academies. The Rabbi was not, until the Middle Ages, a paid religious functionary.

This lack of centralization both in the physical structure and the office of Rabbinic Judaism stands in interesting contrast to the pattern of organization of the Roman Church. Both Jews and Christians were widely distributed geographically in the Roman Empire. Both were persecuted minorities. But the persecution of the Christians was spo-

[1] *Cf.* Max Weber, *Ancient Judaism,* Free Press, Glencoe, pp. 411–415. Weber, however, tends to underrate the preservative and ultimately creative effect of the priests and rabbis. "The religion of Israel developed into a structure able to resist all disintegrating influence from the outside, and it lived in this form through history. This entire development would have been impossible without the intervention of prophecy" (*cf.* p. 263). The prophetic thrust was not incorporated into the very structure of the Jewish social order until the Rabbinic period. The achievement of the Rabbis in making prophetic ethics viable is recorded in the Talmud. Ezekiel Kaufmann, *The Religion of Israel,* University of Chicago Press, Chicago, 1960, pp. 238–240, makes a further distinction within the priestly ranks, between the Aaronides and the Levites, the latter being more loyal to Moses. "The new religion thus had two sacerdotal classes from the beginning. By the Levites the sacred service was newly acquired through kinship and loyalty to the prophet" (p. 240).

[2] *Cf.* Moses Maimonides, *Mishneh Torah,* Introduction (numerous editions) where the chain of tradition is listed in full. Maimonides, who is often accused of being non-historical, shows a lively sense of the vicissitudes of the transmission of oral tradition, and indicates the conditions, both social and political, underlying rabbinic enactments.

Large-Scale Organization in Jewish Religious Life 215

radic and shortlived; that of the Jews, intense, bitter, and well nigh devastating. The Roman pattern of hierarchical authority could be adopted by the Church; the rancor and bitterness that Rome left in the collective memory of the Jewish people, especially among those who lived in the Holy Land, militated against any assimilation of Roman patterns of organization.[3] The teaching and legislating episcopate which had been centrally established in Jerusalem was now a memory. With the demise of the Sanhedrin and the decay of classic rabbinic ordination, Jewish congregationalism became, theoretically, unlimited. Partly because of the diaspora character of Jewish life, with its consequent lack of facilities for communication and transportation, and partly for the historical reason cited above, congregational polity produced individual variations in liturgy, observance, and interpretation. The attempts to revive ordination or the centralized authority of the Sanhedrin all died aborning.[4] In the days of the Second Temple, the Synagogue, the Academies, and the courts (the three foremost institutions of Rabbinic Judaism) were characterized by a lack of institutional rigidity and a genuine creativity in the face of untoward circumstance.[5] Such was not the character of the Synagogue in the later Middle Ages. The burghers of the community, some of whom were elected by their fellow Jews, some of whom appointed by non-Jewish authorities, and still others self-appointed by reason of their wealth or influence with the contemporary powers, could and did limit rabbinic prerogative, despite their formal allegiance to the authority of the Talmud, as interpreted by the rabbi.[6]

A remarkable example of how religious organization was underwritten by the civil power is provided by the Council of the Four Lands, which flourished as the court of final authority for the Jews

---

[3] *Cf.* Talmud Bavli, *Tractate Avodah Zara*, 2b, where Roman claims for the advancement of civilization (the building of roads, bridges, and bathhouses) were pilloried by the Rabbis as founded on fraud and self-aggrandizement.

[4] *Cf.* Cecil Roth, *Short History of the Jewish People*, East and West Library, London, 1948, p. 280.

[5] *Cf.* Judah Goldin, "The Period of the Talmud" in *The Jews: Their History, Culture, and Religion*, Louis Finkelstein, editor, Harper and Brothers, New York, 1949, pp. 115–216; and Louis Ginzberg's magisterial essay, "The Significance of the Halachah for Jewish History" in *Jewish Law and Lore*, 1954, Jewish Publication Society, Philadelphia, pp. 77–127.

[6] *Cf.* Salo W. Baron, *The Jewish Community*, Jewish Publication Society, Philadelphia, 1942.

of Eastern Europe during the seventeenth and eighteenth centuries. What is striking about this Council is that it did not differentiate between religious and civil matters, between the spheres of the sacred and the profane. This in itself reflects the Jewish imperative to make religion coterminous with all of life. The Council, representing the Jews of Great Poland, Little Poland, Ruthenia, and Volhynia, was composed of thirty members, twenty-four of whom were laymen. It met semi-annually at the time of the Spring and Summer Fairs, and was always administered by a layman. Cecil Roth has painted a vivid picture of the force and scope of the Council's organization and authority.

> The Council, at its prime, was virtually the Parliament of Polish Jewry, with power nearly as absolute as that of any legislature. All the more important congregations sent their representatives—an honour contested eagerly among themselves. Plenary meetings of the Council were held each year, not only at the Spring Fair at Lublin, but also at that in the early summer at Jaroslaw, in Galicia. In cases of exceptional urgency, emergency assemblies would be held elsewhere. During the session of the Polish Diet at Warsaw, the Council would send an agent, or shtadlan—generally persona grata at court—to watch over Jewish interests. Internally, its authority was unquestioned. Besides apportioning taxation, it would assist in enforcing royal edicts; it passed sumptuary laws, to enforce moderation in dress and social life; it did all that lay in its power to prevent undue competition; it supervised the system of education; it acted as a court of appeal, and decided on matters which were in dispute between one congregation and another; it exercised a rigid control over Hebrew printing, prevented infringements of copyright, and, on occasion, protected local production by forbidding the importation of one work or another from abroad. All its regulations, however trivial, *could be enforced if the necessity arose by the power of excommunication, backed up by the authority of the state.* A system, similar in every detail prevailed (though on a smaller scale) in the provinces adjacent to Poland proper. Nowhere, ever since the decay of the Jewish centre in Palestine, had so complete an approach to autonomy existed [italics mine].[7]

Thus the Sanhedrin and the Council mark the high points of large-scale communal and religious organization within Judaism, the one a product of the autonomous forces operating within the Jewish re-

[7] Roth, *op. cit.,* pp. 293–294.

Large-Scale Organization in Jewish Religious Life 217

ligion, the other constructed in whole or in part to satisfy the demands of the secular nation-state's appetite for taxation. Due to the rebirth of antisemitic persecution, the Council's power was never regained in later Jewish life, and congregational autonomy, especially in the United States, became an absolute norm—a norm which has persisted to this very day, although (as we shall see in the body of this paper) slight but significant dents have been made recently in the supremacy of congregational autonomy.

For 1,800 years, Jewish communal and religious patterns of organization reflected two parallel and sometimes conflicting demands; an inner religious demand posed by the Torah, and an outer civic demand, to preserve the Jewish community and its faith against the onslaught (sometimes physical, but always economic and psychological) of a hostile environment. With the entry of the Jews into Great Britain's Thirteen Colonies, this situation remained unchanged. With the successful completion of the American Revolution and the passage of the Bill of Rights, an entirely new ethos came into being. The prime legal condition for the development of Jewish communal and religious organization in the United States was the separation of church and state embodied in the first amendment to the Constitution.[8] However it came to be interpreted with the passage of the decades, for Jews it spelled an intensification of "localism"—of the supremacy of the individual congregation. Such primacy had not in the past eventuated in the disruption or corruption of the sacred system, because of the pervasive presence of a religious framework amongst all members of Jewish society. But when the separation of church and state was combined with an economy which glorified the individual entrepreneur, unprecedented moral and religious problems were bound to arise.[9] We cannot treat within this context the dimension of how the various American Jewish religious denominations arose within the context of the two factors.[10] But the lack of moral responsibility involved in the

[8] *Cf.* Mordecai M. Kaplan, *The Greater Judaism in the Making*, Reconstructionist Press, New York, 1960, pp. 453 f.

[9] The discontinuities between business civilization and the Christian faith is perceptively treated in Alvin Pitcher, "The Significance of the American Business Creed for the Churches: A Summary and Interpretation," *Journal of Religion,* January, 1959, pp. 1–25. The other articles in this issue also revolve about the same problem, and are worth careful scrutiny.

[10] The best treatment of this theme is Marshall Sklare, *Conservative Judaism*, Free Press, Glencoe, 1955, especially the first eighty-three pages.

denial of community, and the affirmation of *laissez faire* in Jewish religious affairs resulted in near disaster.

> Chaos and confusion prevailed in the internal life of American Orthodoxy. Small celled congregations came into existence suddenly and in almost as short a time split up. This seemed to go on endlessly. The chief attraction of the Orthodox synagogue was its cantor, and only in rare cases, the spiritual leader; the Hebrew classes were conducted in dingy, unsanitary stores and cellars; the sale of religious objects was abused; kashrut [conformity to the dietary laws] was mismanaged.
>
> The first attempt at formal organization of the Orthodox congregations had taken place in 1879. Representatives of twenty-six congregations met to found a board of Delegates of Orthodox Hebrew Congregations. They planned to invite a chief rabbi from abroad who would set their house in order. The attempt failed for want of a proper candidate. Nine years were to pass before further action was initiated. Chief Rabbi Jacob Joseph (1848–1902) distinguished scholar of Vilna, consented to come to America. The tragedy that befell him and the shame and disgrace that resulted to the community were a painful reflection of the scandalous state of affairs. The salary of the rabbi was to be gathered from the tax that was attached to kosher meat. Despite severe warnings by friends among the Reformists and Conservatives, not to finance the office of the rabbinate through kosher food income, the Orthodox association insisted on its plan. The direst predictions were unhappily realized; the association was dissolved and the idea of an Orthodox chief rabbinate shattered on the rocks of irresponsibility.[11]

However, the necessity for united religious action during the First World War and the accelerating effects of Americanization began to curb the excesses of congregationalism, without impairing the principle of congregational independence. The social distance that had separated synagogues of the same type and theological orientation had begun to shrivel with the advent of the second decade of the twentieth century. Ethnic amalgamation had lowered the bars between Lithuanian, German, Galician, and Russian Jews, and "the evolving style of life of the group fell imperceptibly into the molds of American middle class culture, although retaining distinctive features derived from the

---

[11]Moshe Davis, "Jewish Religious Life and Institutions in America" in *The Jews: Their History, Culture, and Religion*, p. 390.

Large-Scale Organization in Jewish Religious Life 219

past."[12] The common American culture became the focus of solidarity rather than the country or even customary religious practice of one's origin. With the flattening out of linguistic distinctions (Yiddish, Polish, and Germanspeaking Jews became an exception rather than the rule) a more homogeneous religious constituency came into being, one which challenged some of the unexamined bases of division between the three religious denominations. Ethnic isolation which had decreed the unwritten prohibition of intermarriage between former East European and West European Jews resident in the United States, disappeared. Consensus within the Jewish community was fostered by the continuing process of identification with the common values of American civilization (freedom, democracy, success, among others) and by an ever increasing exposure to mass media, which in turn facilitated a uniform style of life. Underlying all of these factors is the nature of urban industrial civilization which conditions men toward adoption of large-scale organization, because of the interdependence and size of such a civilization. The effective pursuit of one's interest can only be done in concert with one's likeminded fellows within the Organized Society.[13]

The factors outlined above form the backdrop to our discussion of the effects of large-scale organization upon Jewish religious life. I shall limit my analysis to Conservative Judaism in the United States, and portray the organizational settings of the United Synagogue of America, the Rabbinical Assembly of America, and of a local synagogue with which I am intimately acquainted.

The moral problems to be outlined will all deal with "practical ethics"—situations of conflict and strain, of the clash of greater and lesser interest. My point of view is indicated by a preference both on religious and philosophical grounds for that course of behavior, whether institutional or personal, which acts in accord with the interest of the whole, rather than that of the part.[14] Beyond this skimpy treatment of a vastly important theoretical problem, I cannot go.

[12]Oscar Handlin, *Adventure in Freedom*, McGraw-Hill, New York, 1954, p. 254.

[13]For an excellent analysis of the effect of these factors on the religious life and organizational problems of contemporary Protestantism, *cf.* Robert Lee, *The Social Sources of Church Unity*, Abingdon Press, New York, 1960, especially pp. 49–75.

[14]The grounds for such a choice are analyzed in W. L. Reese, *Ascent From Below*, Houghton Mifflin, New York, 1959, pp. 236–243.

The United Synagogue of America

As of June 30, 1959, the United Synagogue of America, the association of Conservative congregations in the United States and Canada, numbered 650 affiliated congregations with a reported membership of 1,000,000 men, women, and children.[15] The phenomenal growth of the United Synagogue can be gauged by comparing its present membership to that of 1913, when at the founding of the organization twenty-two congregations banded together. The statistics listed in the *American Jewish Year Book* document the steady growth of this organization of congregations. In 1945, 260 synagogues were affiliated; in 1954, 184 more congregations had affiliated and by the time of the publication of this essay, the number will undoubtedly exceed 700. The purposes of the United Synagogue are plainly stated in its preamble:

> The advancement of the cause of Judaism in America and the maintenance of Jewish tradition in its historic continuity; to assert and establish loyalty to the Torah in its historic exposition; to further the observance of the Sabbath and Dietary Laws; to preserve in the service the reference to Israel's past and the hopes for Israel's restoration; to maintain the traditional character of the liturgy, with Hebrew as the language of prayer; to foster Jewish religious life in the home as expressed in traditional observances; to encourage the establishment of Jewish religious schools, in the curricula of which the study of the Hebrew language and literature shall be given a prominent place, both as the key to the true understanding of Judaism, and as a bond holding scattered communities of Israel throughout the world. It shall be the aim of the United Synagogue of America, while not endorsing the innovations introduced by any of its constituent bodies, to embrace all elements essentially loyal to traditional Judaism and in sympathy with the purposes outlined above.[16]

At its first convention, Solomon Schechter, the founder, made the following insightful statement. "Nothing in this country can exist without proper organization backed by a large constituency, composed of members capable of denying, when necessary, their individual am-

---

[15] *Proceedings, 1959 Biennial Convention, United Synagogue of America*, p. 140.

[16] "Questions and Answers about the Conservative Movement and the United Synagogue of America" (pamphlet). This is a handy summation of the major emphases of the United Synagogue, and contains its *Code of Standards for Synagogue Practice.*

Large-Scale Organization in Jewish Religious Life 221

bitions and advantages in submitting to the mandates of the majority."[17] The ethical task facing the organization is here thrown into bold relief—the transcendence of individual claims for the benefit of the whole. Unfortunately, Schechter's holistic vision was not to be translated into reality until the fifth decade of this century. We shall turn to this matter in a moment.

At present, the United Synagogue functions through twelve committees and commissions which deal with such diverse matters as summer camps for Jewish youngsters, social action, and the operation of a national academy for adult Jewish studies.[18] It is affiliated with eight other national organizations of the Conservative movement.[19] The growth in constituency has been paralleled by expansion of its administrative staff. The committees and commissions are guided by standards of efficient performance and thus inevitably resemble the behavior patterns of large-scale business, professional, and farm organizations. But there is one fundamental difference between the corporate structure of American business, for example, and that of the United Synagogue. The latter has not developed a roving interchangeable managerial class which is grafted on to the organization and then discarded. The lay leaders are products of the local Conservative synagogues, and the rabbis involved in the administrative tasks have, to a greater or lesser degree, occupied congregational posts. Although, inevitably, policy positions stem from the executive staff, the policy stances of the organization, are, in the main, reflections of the majority sentiment of the constituency, and divorce of control from ownership which is the regnant situation in American business, has not (or not yet) been operative in the United Synagogue. The complex national administrative machinery, born out of the need for functional coordination, and the possibility of rapid, mass communication and transportation is duplicated by the Reform, and to a lesser extent, by the Orthodox Jews.

An excellent example of the standardizing effect of the United Syna-

---

[17]*Proceedings, United Synagogue*, quotation by George Maislen, p. 121.

[18]A full list of these and their functions can be found in the *Proceedings, United Synagogue*.

[19]They are the Rabbinical Assembly of America, the Cantors Assembly of America, Educators Assembly of America, National Association of Synagogue Administrators, National Women's League, National Federation of Jewish Men's Clubs, Young People's League, and United Synagogue Youth.

gogue, in the dual sense of raising current levels and making them uniform on a national scale, can be seen in the operation of its Commission on Jewish Education. The Commission, headed by a professional Jewish educator, operates within four major areas of activity, each of which would have been beyond the bounds of competency of the local congregation. It develops objectives, standards, and curricula for congregational schools. It publishes textbooks, audiovisual aids, and other educational materials. In both of these areas Conservative, Reform, and Orthodox groups have used materials more or less interchangeably. I think, however, that with increasing ideological clarification and organizational centralization this interchangeability will, in time, diminish. The hours of instruction fluctuate so much from one denomination to the other, that varying levels of achievement will compel greater reliance on specific materials prepared by the institution itself. The Commission's third objective is to serve affiliated congregations with supervisory staff. Finally, it tries to promote on a national scale a congregational and community climate favorable to more intensive Jewish education. Each one of these areas involves the activities of specialists, and the development of such a cadre would not come about if undertaken by a local synagogue, or even by a local group of synagogues. The benefits of large-scale organization are here apparent. The fourth generation of American Jews may be more appreciative of its religious heritage than its second or third generation precursors, because of the activities of the Commission. What might be viewed in other religious contexts as an "organizational dilemma" is here really an organizational opportunity; for what can be done in the name of the United Synagogue could not have been done educationally, in the name of the local synagogue.[20]

The United Synagogue has also ventured into the uncharted realm of congregational standards. Recognizing that the local congregations were themselves increasingly being staffed with professional personnel (other than the rabbi) and that the interests of local congregations might clash either with the general community or with each other, after four years of debate the organization adopted a code of standards

[20] The problems inherent in congregational schools are fully discussed in A. Dushkin and U. Z. Engelman, *Jewish Education in the United States,* American Association for Jewish Education, New York, 1959, pp. 47–50 and 221–255.

for synagogue practice, and has under examination at present two more proposed codes, one relating to the status and functions of educational directors, the other to that of synagogue administrators.

In the code of standards firm attitudes were taken with regard to the basis for authority, the sabbath, kashrut, public functions, fundraising, moral dignity, relationships with other congregations and the general community, and violations of the standards.[21] Not all of these are of equal importance or delicacy. At present the most sensitive area is that of fundraising. Here there is often generated a dysfunction between the need for institutional stability and maintenance, and the spiritual demands of Jewish tradition. A test case is that of the use of gambling devices, *i.e.,* bingo to raise money for congregational maintenance. Because of its accessibility to the general public, its regularity, and its discontinuity with the ethical standards of Judaism, the United Synagogue sees in the use of bingo an immoral instrument for the attainment of a moral goal. It recently invoked the section of the code dealing with violations and suspended a congregation which had stubbornly insisted on its right and need to turn the synagogue into a gathering for gamblers once a week.[22] This effort to enforce the announced standards is being watched by the other Jewish denominations, who are eager to utilize the success of the United Synagogue Code as a precedent for maximizing congregational discipline in their own groups. It is also noteworthy that since the adoption of the code no cases involving litigation between or within Conservative congregations have appeared on the court dockets of the United States. All intra- and intersynagogue disputes regarding the hiring of personnel or the establishment of new congregations are handled by the Executive Council of the organization without recourse to the civil authorities. This achievement is consonant with the mainstream of Jewish communal life in the diaspora.

An organization is only as effective as its personnel. If localism is to be curbed and concern for the whole to be evident, synagogue leaders must be trained for their task. The realities and requirements of leadership must be made clear. Local conferences involving hundreds of lay leaders have already taken place, and rational preparation for

[21] "Questions and Answers," pp. 7–10.
[22] Gershom Jacobson in *National Jewish Post,* July 1, p. 1, and July 8, p. 1.

the shifting nature of urban neighborhoods, with all of its attendant problems, is being made by certain regions of the United Synagogue.[23]

And, beyond the area of scientific synagogue management, there lies the greater problem of commitment to the ideals embodied in the synagogue. I recently spoke to a group of thirty leading laymen representing ten congregations in the New York area who were convened under the aegis of the Westchester region of the United Synagogue. I explored with them the possibility of setting standards for congregational membership; standards that would be prerequisites for the payment of membership dues. Under the proposed standards, newly affiliated congregants would have to undergo intensive courses in adult Jewish education before being accepted as full members of the local synagogue. The proposal was received with hesitancy in regard to the present generation, but with the prediction of certainty for the next generation. Here, too, the impact of a large-scale organization is manifest. The United Synagogue can, after a certain point of stability is reached, remake its own constituency in terms of the religious, and not the sociological imperative. Finally, and not least important, the code has strengthened the hands of the local rabbi in resisting the sometimes importunate demands of his laity for a greater adoption of merchandising techniques in "selling" religion, and thus preserving the local synagogue. At one of the meetings of congregational leaders referred to previously, it was clearly indicated that standards of big business success are not, in principle, applicable to the synagogue.

> While the scope of its financial affairs has widened considerably, congregational lay leadership must constantly be aware of the synagogue's original purpose: worship and education. The synagogue is not big business! The distinction between business and congregation affairs must be maintained if we are to imbue the next generation with the importance of Judaism's spiritual values.[24]

The proliferation and elaboration of organizational forms, has had, on the whole, a morally tonic effect on the life of the individual synagogue, and indirectly on the life of its congregants. Organizational structure on a national scale has become an instrumentality for

---

[23]*Cf. The Reporter*, Metropolitan Council of the United Synagogue of America, volume III, number 3, June, 1960, pp. 1–4.

[24]Max J. Routtenberg, in *The Reporter*, p. 4, column 1.

inculcating moral responsibility. It has not turned into a self-existent structure such as that of the military establishment, or of some business enterprises whose entire rationale is continued existence, no matter what their original function might have been.

The Rabbinical Assembly of America

The original cause which prompted the creation of the Conservative movement was protestant in nature—protest against the radical revision of Judaism explicit in the Reform movement. The Jewish Theological Seminary of America was the first institutionalization of this protest. The second was the organization of an alumni association of the Seminary. It was only much later in its development that the alumni association became a truly national group by changing its name to the Rabbinical Assembly of America, and admitting to its membership qualified rabbis of other groups who desired to join. The original alumni association numbered fifteen, and came together in 1901. The Rabbinical Assembly now counts 700 members, two-thirds of whom are Seminary graduates. The composition of its membership has undergone an interesting transformation over the past two decades. Whereas many of its members were once drawn from homes of a decided Orthodox bent, it has become increasingly clear that its newer adherents are drawn from a Conservative home environment, and are a product of the institutional arrangements of Conservatism.

> All of the facts and trends discussed in this essay seem to point to one central conclusion: a new kind of Conservative rabbi, a product of the denomination itself, has now made his appearance, and the future almost certainly belongs to him. As yet, those of Orthodox background are quite clearly in the overwhelming majority in the Rabbinical Assembly and a bare majority in the Seminary student body, but the trend is in the other direction. . . . These newer rabbis owe their formal Jewish education primarily to the Conservative movement. They are for the most part products of its congregational schools, of its youth groups, and of the Seminary's various new preparatory courses. The future Jewish education of this type of Conservative rabbi is primarily dependent on whatever level of educational achievement Conservative Judaism as a whole will attain. The emerging new type of Conservative rabbi is of the denomination and at home within it.

The future of the Conservative pulpit is now clearly in the pews of the congregations.[25]

The original reference group of the associated rabbis was explicit in its first title—the Seminary was its point of orientation and origin. Despite the change in cognomen, this primary referent has remained the same. "The only effective bond that unites us and distinguishes us from other rabbinic bodies . . . is our common devotion to the Seminary."[26] But this bond is not an exhaustive one. The Rabbinical Assembly contains a large enough group of nonSeminary graduates to insure that the old school tie will not be the only mark of a Conservative rabbi! Furthermore, the rabbis are aware of the dependence of the Seminary's campaign for funds upon their efforts. "The Seminary can do nothing effectively without the help and the support of the Rabbinical Assembly. Much of the strength of our movement lies not in the central institutions, but in the lives and careers of individual men in local congregations and communities."[27] Nevertheless, the ambivalence remains. "I believe it fair to state that the organizational strength of the Rabbinical Assembly, its influence as a religious movement, its prestige in the Jewish world, stem largely and primarily from its association with the Seminary . . . the Seminary is the central body of Conservative Judaism and the Rabbinical Assembly is one of its arms. We would lose by amputation."[28] Although some rather wild-eyed psychological and sociological explanations[29] have been offered of the ambivalent relationship of the Conservative rabbinate to its Alma Mater, it seems to me that the size of the organization and the fact that most of its members are personally well known to members of the Seminary faculty, would maximize the intensity of the organizational relationships. A truly large-scale organization, operating through hierarchical levels of authority, seeks to maintain itself by working out minimal personal relation-

[25]Arthur Hertzberg, "The Conservative Rabbinate," *Essays on Jewish Life and Thought*, A. Hertzberg and J. L. Blau, editors, Columbia University Press, New York, 1959, pp. 331–332.
[26]Eugene Kohn, *Proceedings of the Rabbinical Assembly of America*, 1927, Barnes Printing Company, Asbury Park, p. 59.
[27]Max J. Routtenberg, "Sixty Years of the Rabbinical Assembly," *Proceedings of the Rabbinical Assembly*, 1960, in proof.
[28]*Ibid.*
[29]Sklare, *op. cit.*, pp. 186–189. Sklare extrapolates from a few somewhat bizarre quotations to the membership as a whole!

ships between its staff members; in the smallest social unit, the family, the fullest possible primary relationship is engendered. The relationship between the Seminary and the Rabbinical Assembly is still on a familial basis, with the degrees of familiarity varying according to the date of ordination of the individual men. When Seminary classes were small (during the thirties and forties) this maximal family relationship was at its peak. With the graduates of the fifties (when classes expanded considerably) the relationship between the two organizations is slowly but surely being stripped down to a minimal relationship. Hence, it is possible to predict that the Rabbinical Assembly will augment its organizational independence as time goes on.

The loyalties that rabbis feel toward their professional training school and toward their rabbinic association point up the problem of the clash of organizational demands. Fifty years ago, the rabbi owed his allegiance to God, the Torah, and his individual congregation. The Age of Organization has multiplied the rabbi's "reference points." He now numbers among his allegiances not only the above elements, but his neighborhood, his city, the local association of Conservative Rabbis, the citywide Board of Rabbis, the regional grouping of Conservative Rabbis, the various standing committees of the Rabbinical Assembly upon which he may be called to serve, and possibly national and fraternal Jewish organizations upon whose boards he may sit, or whose constituencies he may be elected to lead! Orbiting in such an organizational constellation in many instances leads to confusion, distraction, and conflict. The United Synagogue's original *Guide to Congregational Standards* (which is not binding on individual congregations) merely emphasized the dilemma when it said, "Reasonable opportunity shall be afforded by the Congregation to the Rabbi to serve the interest of the larger community, both Jewish and civic, whenever and wherever such service shall not interfere unreasonably with the performance of his congregational duties." The notion of "reasonable opportunity" is notoriously flexible and vague, and varies not only from one congregation to the next, but from one congregant to another. There is little or no rule-orientation provided by the above prescription; and if one of the definitions of organization is operation in accordance with set rules, little headway has been made here. The logic of organizational structure is such, however, that in time, the various roles that rabbis play will be codified into rules. The intolerable strain of being at one and the same time, priest, preacher, rabbi, cleric, rector, pastor, father, and parson,[30] will eventuate in either the training of ministerial specialists, who will become relatively expert in one of these areas, or in the retreat on the part of the organized rabbinate from one or more of the functions listed. Since the latter is unlikely, groups of rabbinic specialists will crystallize within the, at present, amorphous membership of the Rabbinical Assembly.[31]

One of the effects, therefore, of increased communal and rabbinic organization has been the profusion of rabbinic reference groups. The rabbi's primary reference is no longer just the local congregation, but he has the communal and denominational structure to conform to as a reference group. He has interfaith organizations and the proliferated organizations and institutions of the general community. His preserve is no longer the parish, but the body politic.

As an organization, the Rabbinical Assembly has professionalized the status of its members, to the same degree that the American Medical Association has curbed the vicious effects of *laissez-faire* competition upon doctors. The chaotic methods of rabbinic placement which were in vogue until 1947, were abolished at one blow by the adoption in that year of the Code of Procedure in Placement of Rabbis.[32] The dominance of the local congregation in its choice of rabbis was severely limited. Seniority, experience, aptitude, need, and congregational requirements were all to be used as guide lines for the selection of rabbinic candidates to a particular post. Underbidding,

---

[30] *Ibid.*, p. 177. This section is worth quoting: ". . . services in the Seminary synagogue serve as training for fulfilling the role of conductors of public worship, or *priests*. Training in homiletics is also given: students deliver addresses at the services and thus prepare themselves to serve as *preachers*. . . . However Conservative spiritual leaders must perform many other roles in addition to their duties as preacher-priest and rabbi, . . . they serve as clerics—as an arm of the state which has empowered them to perform certain rituals and requires them to record these ceremonies . . . many rabbis feel that in their capacity as *rectors,* administrators, they require specialized training. Since they give counsel, guidance, and assistance to individuals in meeting the crises of life, the rabbis function as *pastors* . . . Assuming the headship of congregations, in a psychological sense they serve as *fathers*. Lastly, since the spiritual leaders are personages of some consequence in their communities and are given membership on various boards, semi-public bodies, and agencies in the field of social welfare, they act as *parsons.*"

[31] In his last reportorial letter to the Rabbinical Assembly, Rabbi Isaac Klein, past president, announced the formation of a cadre of rabbis who would specialize in the granting of religious divorces. In 1952 efforts to create such an elite had foundered.

[32] *Cf. Code of Procedure in Placement of Rabbis,* pamphlet issued by the Rabbinical Assembly office, 1950.

covert bargaining, lobbying, and acquiescence in unsolicited invitations to preach were forbidden to the rabbis. The limitation of freedom in both directions, *viz.,* the congregation and the rabbi, had a salutary effect. Orderly procedure replaced occupational anomie. The feeling of helplessness and anxiety which rabbis incurred in changing their pulpits, was now replaced by feelings of relative security, *vis-à-vis* job placement. Although the contemporary Conservative rabbinate is a restless body of men,[33] its restlessness is not a byproduct of the efficiency of the Placement Commission of the Rabbinical Assembly. The Placement Commission, whose activities are directed by an Executive Vice President and his assistants (all of them rabbis) circulates lists of available positions to all rabbis desiring a change of pulpit, and is available for individual consultation with the men. The routinization of change of pulpit has proceeded to the point where standardized forms eliciting the nature (financial, physical, and religious) of congregations and the needs and abilities of rabbis are now being prepared. The preamble and the postlude to the code allude directly to ethical considerations in invoking its acceptance. "The following Code of Procedure [. . . is adopted] in order to assure the placement of rabbis in a manner which is equitable, dignified and ethical. . . . [the Placement Commission] . . . is a democratic instrument that seeks to serve on the highest ethical level the interest of Judaism and the calling to which you have dedicated your education, your gifts and your very lives."[34]

In one other area, the Assembly takes direct moral responsibility. It adjudicates ethical disputes between rabbis, or between congregational members and rabbis, against whom charges may have been placed. Such adjudication is the function of the Ethics Committee,

---

[33] *Cf.* Ephraim Greenberg: "The Rabbinate—A Restless Body of Men," *Conservative Judaism*, volume XIV, number 2, winter, 1960, pp. 17–29. "The rabbi is in great measure caught between the role for which he has been trained, to be the teacher of a unique *derekh*, a religious way of living, and his role as administrator of an institution whose functioning is dictated largely by what Nathan Glazer has described as 'the desire of laymen to acquire religious services more in keeping with their social status.' For a rabbi Judaism is the all-compelling *derekh*. But for most American Jews, even the synagogued, being an adherent of Judaism is often more an indication of their social and civic status than a definition of their religious commitment." It remains to be seen whether the growth of such groups as the Rabbinical Assembly and the United Synagogue will alter lay attitudes. I believe, that, in time, they will alter.

[34] *Code of Procedure in Placement of Rabbis.*

which deals with problematic situations that have little or no precedent in Jewish law. As a case in point, the varying responsibilities of senior rabbis, associate rabbis, and assistant rabbis, are not treated in the classic Jewish codes and commentaries because such offices simply did not then exist. They are a byproduct of the development of synagogue life in the United States. The nature of rabbinic office, with its undue emphasis on preaching, can lead to clashes of temperament and opinion, when two rabbis are denominated as leaders of the congregation. When one is subordinate to the other, a fairly detailed division of functions must be undertaken from the outset, in order to avoid later conflict.

Since there is no episcopate in Judaism, the Ethics Committee limits its deliberations to matters of professional functions, *i.e.*, "lack of good judgment or carelessness and unconcern in the conduct of one's professional duties" . . . and . . . "conscious and deliberate violation of the standards of professional ethics [*e.g.*, fixing fees for congregational members, advertising one's services, fee-splitting]." Beyond the area of professional ethics those ethical standards which are widely accepted by the current social order are affirmed as binding upon the behavior of rabbis, and deviation from which in flagrant and conspicuous fashion will be dealt with severely. The sanctions of the Assembly are the following: written reprimand, threat of suspension from membership in the Assembly, temporary suspension and, finally, expulsion. Expulsion is a serious matter not only psychologically; it severely limits the opportunities for rabbinic service. Most congregations will not accept as their spiritual leader a rabbi who is not a member of a rabbinic association. Expulsion from membership is therefore equivalent to disbarment for lawyers, or lack of a license to practice for doctors. Maximum emphasis is placed by members of the Ethics Committee upon "objective standards of conduct and behavior." In the delicate area of the rabbi's general deportment and the quality of his religious opinions, individual liberty reigns. Although there is continuing debate among members of the Assembly on the propriety of setting standards in these areas, the difficulty of drafting such codes of particulars, and the quick pace of modern life will in my opinion indefinitely defer its formulation.[35]

[35]Mimeographed copies of the Code of Rabbinic Ethics are available at the Rabbinical Assembly headquarters, 3080 Broadway, New York 27, New York.

The Individual Congregation

The most recent analysis of congregations affiliated with the United Synagogue shows that 138 or 21 per cent have a membership of under 100 families, 218 or 33 per cent have a membership of 100-249 families, 173 or 26 per cent have a membership of 25-499, 102 congregations or 16 per cent have 500-999 members and 27 congregations or 4 per cent of the total have more than 1,000 member families.[36] From personal experience in three of the five congregational populations listed above, I have decided reservations as to the extent the organizational revolution has penetrated the individual congregation. It could be said, with some justice, that few or no elements of functional or substantive rationality obtain in the financial operations of the synagogue. Synagogue administration, except where it is handled by a trained executive director, is in little better case. Because it is a congregational "family" to whom the rabbi is a father figure, administrative and organizational procedures, however important, can never be a prime concern. The synagogue does not exist to maximize a profit at the end of every fiscal year. What does exist are face to face relationships among the various boards and synagogue committees. Efficiency and product management are not thought of as valid congregational goals. The rabbi delegates his burden of administration insofar as possible to lay committees, but these, being composed of volunteer workers, are not amenable to job control.

The family aspect of congregational belonging is attenuated as the institution grows in size. The rabbi becomes a pulpit figure, distant and somehow unapproachable; the secretaries in the synagogue office grow in number; paid specialists manage different aspects of the congregation's affairs (*i.e.*, educational director, executive secretary, youth director), and an attitude of bureaucratic impersonality and "coldness" is felt by the members. When a congregation includes more than 700 members, there is always present a group who wish to close or limit further membership. A number of congregations within the Conservative and Reform groups have stopped their growth at 450 to 600 member families. This number seems to be the outermost limit for proper rabbinic ministration. As yet there is no comity be-

[36]*Proceedings of the United Synagogue*, p. 141.

tween Conservative congregations, but it seems likely that it will develop within the next decade.

The danger of the organizational revolution in our age is its voracious appetite for organizational maintenance and growth at any cost. The proper ends for which the organization exists are either neglected or lost sight of, in the excitement of continued expansion. With regard to the three areas discussed, no such condition has been operative. If anything, the Rabbinical Assembly, the United Synagogue, and the local congregation, exhibit—if somewhat opaquely—the "final conclusion" of Kenneth Boulding:

> The final conclusion, therefore, is that though organizations are here to stay and though the only solution to many of the problems which they raise seems to be ever more and larger organization, yet there is also no substitute for the Word of God—the sharp sword of truth in the prophetic individual, the penetrating moral insight that cuts through the shams and excesses of even the best-organized society. However clever we become and however far we move toward betterment through cleverness and skill, there is always a place for wonder, for humility, for reverence for sensitivity, to the still, small voice of the Creator of all men and all morals.[37]

[37]Kenneth Boulding, *The Organizational Revolution*, Harper and Brothers, New York, 1953, pp. 220–221.

IV. Responsibility in Executive Organization in Big-Scale Government

CHAPTER XVI

Diversity in the Public Interest: Two Cases in Metropolitan Decisionmaking

By PAUL N. YLVISAKER

I

MY CONCERN is the age old problem of finding a touchstone for relating one's own interests and code of behavior to the swirling interests and patterns of life around him—but in a context which may not be so familiar, the modern metropolis.

Touchstones have never been easy to find, and the metropolis, I fear, may have made the quest so difficult that many have been discouraged into abandoning it. For the metropolis compresses into an area where none may really escape it the full range of Diversity which has always been the great gremlin in man's efforts to achieve a common standard of behavior and an accepted criterion of a general interest. By confronting man with his differences, the metropolis assaults two of our ethical Shangri-las, 1. the idyll of a homogeneous community insulated by time and distance from conflicting value systems; and 2. the comforting notion of a public interest which like a completed jigsaw puzzle will unite self-interests into a rational whole while leaving the pieces severally intact.

II

These generalizations launch us too quickly into the blue. Let me start toward ground level with some supporting observations; these will in turn be brought down to the illustrative "facts" of two hypothetical cases.

1. The city has long stood as an expression of human diversity; its genius has been the ability to make neighbors of widely divergent—

even conflicting and otherwise incompatible—groups of human beings and ways of life.

2. The metropolis is this diversity of the city writ large.

3. But the difference between the city and the metropolis is not only this obvious one of size. It is also the historical one that individuals could in other times find alternative ways of life outside the city; today they have all but lost their option to live otherwise than as citizens of the metropolis. For the modern metropolis represents the farthest stage in the imperialism of urban culture. In its web of growth, it has captured, bled, and assimilated what we once knew as the city, and has reduced farming and the other elemental occupations to ancillary forms of business. These no longer offer real or lasting alternatives as ways of life. Subcultures there may be; but in our day, they must be transplanted, or as the central city survive, or as the suburbs be created, within the embrace of the metropolis.

The fact is, then, that diversity in the face-to-face of the metropolis is fast becoming our universal and inescapable habitat.

4. What is not so certain is whether man can live with diversity of the suddenness and scale of the metropolis. It was one thing for the city to succeed when men came to it slowly and more often than not as a matter of reversible choice. It is quite a different problem for the metropolis when, as now, exploding millions are driven to urban life by lack of an alternative.

5. Whatever the outcome, it is not surprising that men within the diversity of the metropolis—at least in the short run before the melting pot has brewed a new homogeneity—should have great difficulty finding a common code of behavior and criterion of the general interest. Their attempts to do so are really what the current metropolitan ferment is all about. So far, this rising concern has been contained within the limiting form of debates over tangible problems such as metropolitan government, urban renewal, and commuter transportation. Inevitably they must take on the ethical dimension which the theme of the Conference suggests, and rise to the plane of discussion where Plato long ago discovered the meaningful relationship between man and his urban environment.

6. It is not surprising, either, that men caught in the open of this flooding diversity called the metropolis would seek refuge in sheltered waters of their own tastes and self-interests.

Diversity: Cases in Metropolitan Decisionmaking 237

I confess that it is this characteristic of the modern metropolis which most intrigues and troubles me—its constant division into insulating compartments of life brought on by the unending efforts of its citizenry to break an almost incomprehensible diversity into understandable and manageable pieces of homogeneity. Whether this is the genius or the curse of the metropolis, I'm still uncertain; I could argue the case either way. The relevant point is that, good or bad, this unceasing fragmentation of the metropolis is what gives birth to the kind of problems—call them ethical or political—which are the theme of this Conference.

III

To make this even more specific, let me give some evident examples of how, in the metropolis, we set about escaping the full sweep and turmoil of our differences.

One is the process of political balkanization: first we divide the metropolis into suburb and central city; then we redivide both into ward, neighborhood, authority, and special district. In each case, we search for the nearer image of the public interest and succeed in creating at least the fiction of a limited and more manageable community.

Next we perfect social distinctions. Morris Lambie once suggested you could trace the social boundaries of the metropolis most simply by following the contour lines on an urban map—below x feet of elevation the lower class, mainly immigrants, and above the line those whose residence had climbed upward with their income. Today the metropolitan process of social distinction points outward more than up. True, an old guard of the elite still clings to the inner heights of the near downtown, and a new contingent is trying through urban renewal to regain some of the lost ridges; but this rare breed is all but lost in the accumulating host of newcomers and others of low income and status to whom the core city is but a staging area for the long march to suburban affluence.

Outward from this downgraded core one finds successively its most recent graduates—immigrants of the second generation or of speedier fortune, crowding and infiltrating the lower middle class whose most outward mobile have by now pushed on to the city's boundary; then the middle and upper middle class breathing easier in suburbia; and then once again, a small company of the happy few, conspicuously turning rural farms into bastions of exurban consumption.

Not only do income groupings shift as one moves outward along the metropolitan axis; so does the very process of social distinction. Close in, the basis for separatism is likely to stem from one's place of origin—hence the Little Italys, the Harlems, etc. Farther out, the process is one largely of income and taste, thus the Scarsdales, the Winnetkas, and the Main Line.

This shading in the process of social distinction is obscured by the color line which now divides central city from suburb. And make no mistake about it, a color barrier does exist. But it, too, is being eroded by the undercurrent of class and taste differentiation which flows beneath it; Negroes no less than whites aspire to the system of self-determined segregation which the suburb at heart represents. The ultimate in freedom and irony is reached when, as wrily noted by a perceptive Negro, his mother—a lone colored citizen of a white suburb—dissolved into despairing tears at the rumor that "the Negroes" were moving into her neighborhood.

A third way of dividing the diverse into the homogeneous is by casting the illusion of whole life around a fragment of metropolitan function and existence. "Business" is one such compartment in which men can enclose a whole lifetime and *cursus honorum* with but passing concern and experience of the broader community about them. Education can become another world unto itself which attains its own reasons-of-state and its own self-sufficient system of loyalties and rewards—the more so as its governors have persuaded the metropolitan citizenry of the value of education above and beyond politics, thereby escaping this more raw but powerfully equalizing milieu in which other public functions are asked to compete for their resources.

Church, neighborhood, profession, juvenile gangs, and increasingly home and family—these, too, are fragments of the metropolis through which citizens can shrink responsibilities of uncertain dimension to known and manageable size, and can reduce the confusion and unsettling chaos of the diverse to a limited world whose rules of order they can comprehend.

But as a citizen of the metropolis becomes loyal to one or the other of these smaller worlds, his ethical problems—and the wider com-

Diversity: Cases in Metropolitan Decisionmaking

munity's political problems—begin. For these smaller worlds must in the nature of life and the metropolis collide. What then becomes a noble and vitalizing solution for the body politic—compromise—becomes a painful and often enervating outcome for the individual, particularly in our society with its penchant for the categorical and heroic, and its identification of compromise with moral and political surrender.

Let me now dismount from the blue to illustrate, by means of two cases which are offered as the meat of this presentation. They are hypothetical only in their details; situations and decisions akin to these have arisen enough times and in enough metropolitan areas of this country during the past decade for these two episodes to be safely considered as realistic.

Both cases center on the point of collision among the smaller worlds within the metropolis, and on the self-revealing dilemmas of choice (call them ethical considerations) faced by those persons whose station in life puts them regularly in that spot. These are usually public officials; increasingly (for reasons well worth speculating upon) they include staff of nongovernmental agencies professing a public purpose.

The Case of Metropolitan Government

If the Good Lord and His executive angels were to engineer the change, Mayor James of Central City would resolve his doubts and come out publicly in favor of establishing an overall government for the metropolitan area—provided, of course, that when the system was installed, he would be left in charge as metro-mayor. As an idea, "Metro" made a lot of sense; government was about the only American enterprise these days that was not organized on at least a regional and more often a national basis, and if he were to continue as mayor of anything, he'd have to find some way of catching up with the more affluent citizens and taxable industries which were constantly moving just out of reach beyond his municipal boundaries.

But the trouble was, as Madison long ago discerned, the Lord's work on earth has to be done by mere mortals; instead of angels, there are only angles. Keeping a close eye on these almost guarantees that public officials and the electorate won't see or think straight—certainly, the logic of metropolitan government, being straight, can't be followed headlong by practicing politicians. The safer way is the devious route which circumscribes all the angles.

But back to the good Mayor's predicament. The idea of metropolitan government is in the air. Two years ago, all the normally otherwise occupied notables in the area—or as that new breed of academic interventionists has been calling them, the "decisionmakers"—began signing petitions, holding forums, listening to experts fetched from a distance, and in other ways acting as their wives in the League of Women Voters would have them act. These early months had been quite a honeymoon. Mayor James's natural instinct of waiting out all reforms until he saw the self-interests showing through, had helped him keep his balance and be quoted only in the most rolling of generalities. But he had begun to wonder whether politics had indeed entered a new age when at a massive luncheon assembled, representatives of every one of the community's warring and ignoring interest groups had signed a pledge of cooperation. This alliance had so impressed a prestigious foundation that it wrote a check for more money than any of the local factfinders dreamed would be theirs to play with, "to carry out the necessary research." Necessary? Well, yes—research was one of those rituals which sufficiently cleansed the political ground for those normally above politics to walk on it; and it added a mystique which confused the old pros long enough for some new voices and fresh ideas to be heard.

But that was two years ago; now the game was again being played for keeps. The armistice of research was over; in a month, the binding question of a new form of metropolitan government was coming to a referendum vote; and there was no avoiding it, the Mayor would have to say publicly whether he was for or against. The bliss of consensus had long since dissolved. All that had held it together was undefined apprehension and ambition, each group uneasily aware that the metropolitan community had grown beyond its comprehension, yet vaguely hopeful that if a new order could be established, it would be theirs to inherit. Now the fears and the ambitions had been defined; and the only common element was the familiar one of mutual suspicion and jockeying for position. Labor had been among the first to disengage. It had joined the coalition mostly because it couldn't afford the public posture of not doing so—and to keep an eye on this new

Diversity: Cases in Metropolitan Decisionmaking

political animal that just might develop into something substantial. But when meeting after meeting produced nothing immediately of use at the bargaining table, when it became apparent the coalition was too divided to forge strength out of its diversity, and as more and more of the political iceberg of metropolitan government became visible, labor's representative attended less and less frequently until sufficiently dissociated to refer openly to "Metro" as dominated by the business interests.

But "business" as a dominating monolith had long ago proved a myth. In the first place, the usual distressing number of its magnates had again displayed their amateur status in politics and public affairs. Despite their heralded record of civic participation, the coalition was their first working contact with career politicians from the ward and city committee. They were out of their element; they didn't know the names and numbers; and their radar—sensitive enough to the signals of the market—was jammed by the shower of uncertain messages which emanated from a world where the laws of social abrasion and aspiration displaced the accepted canons of efficiency and economy.

Still, more than political naïveté had stymied the business community. The truth was, it wasn't a community except tenuously and occasionally so in opposition to labor and taxes. It was split between absentee and locally owned enterprises; it was divided into big and small, into the socially registered and those not; it was bedevilled by old feuds and factions; and more relevant, it was torn between those committed to the core city and those who were accommodating very nicely to the suburban market. For example, the area's largest employment complex was entrenched in an industrial park which for a negligible cost to the companies concerned had traded local property taxes for the political hospitality of an outlying suburb; no siren call of metropolitan government could lure either the firms or the suburb from their protected enclave.

Mayor James was no stranger to this division in the business community; he had been embarrassed by it several times when "plugging the Chamber's line" only to find he had bought a factional plank—and he had exploited the same weakness on just as many occasions, dividing to conquer and even defying the local barons outright. For he knew what they and the ward politicians knew, that very few of the business leaders lived any longer in Central City; and since they no longer lived there, they couldn't vote there; and even if they could, there weren't enough of them to swing an election.

As a matter of fact, the Mayor often wondered whether the whole drive for metropolitan government wasn't basically a matter of ex-residents trying to have their cake and eat it—people who had moved to suburbia but still depended for their livelihood on white collar jobs, businesses, and investment in Central City, now trying to regain their vote and political influence by enlarging the city's boundaries. One of the Metro leaders had come dangerously close to letting the cat out of the bag by saying publicly he'd settle for a double vote for the commuter—one in the suburbs where he lived, and the other in Central City where he worked. He hadn't added the reciprocal of double taxation, nor would he. Representation without taxation—what an ironic twist, mused the Mayor, of that earlier rallying cry of the American revolutionary.

Though he knew all this, Mayor James took care not to say it. On the one hand (though the reporting staff would quietly have loved him for it), he'd be clobbered by the editorial writers and publishers of Central City's newspapers who managed to be true to both halves of their schizoid selves by touting the virtues of downtown while living in the suburbs and using the press to endorse and plead what they no longer could vote for.

On the other hand, to have gone to the hustings with such candor and perhaps oversimplification would have invited extremism and demagoguery. The city was tinderbox enough without touching a spark to it. Every year saw an accelerating turnover in population and a darkening of color. A decade ago he had been elected councilman from a ward with only a handful of Negroes in it; today, he was one of a handful of whites who still lived there. The rest had moved on, most of them beyond the Iron Ring of suburbia. They lunched with him to say thanks for staying to fight their battles, and to lay out the strategy and objectives for other campaigns they hoped he would lead; then they left him to forage for his votes among the other half who lived in the city at night.

He was, he felt more and more, a man between worlds—no longer a member of the society he had grown up with, nor yet and perhaps never completely at home among the newer constituency upon whose

Diversity: Cases in Metropolitan Decisionmaking 243

vote his political life increasingly depended. Each campaign, each budget, each bond issue found him swinging more and more into the orbit of the newcomers and the philosophy of government which responded to their needs. Why the shift? He still wasn't sure, even though he'd spent most of his term defending this growing liberality to his economyminded friends (now supporting council manager plans in their several suburbs—"a manager is for the homogeneous," he was fond of saying to the students who visited him in City Hall, "but it takes a mayor to preside over diversity") and to the cynics of precinct and city desk. Sure, he wanted to survive; what politician, or for that matter what industrial, labor, or other leader didn't? But it wasn't only that. Not out of preference but of necessity he had come to know the minority cultures of Central City—Negroes from the rural South, Puerto Ricans, hill folk from the Appalachians, and always the steady flow of immigrants from abroad. It had taken a long time to get rid of the stereotypes through which he and his generation of well assimilated immigrants had regarded these newest recruits to the city. Even now, lingering resentment could flicker within him when he reviewed the lengthening procession of unmarried mothers, juvenile delinquents, and relief cases with color and speech so clearly marked. The historian's reminder that it was ever thus, wasn't much comfort. It would still be his wearying job to defend these untouchables among whom he didn't belong to the well washed to whom he did; to explain again the need for understanding to a public which lived on stereotypes and through a press which gained readership by sensationalizing the deeds it condemned; to talk the language of civil liberties to a frightened citizenry and an underpaid constabulary who lived too close to acts of violence to see where noble sentiments fit in.

But these were his city's citizens; like them or not, their welfare was his responsibility and their votes were essential to his political program and future. And like them he did—the more so as he came to see the inner logic of their own codes of conduct (he had heard even the high rate of "illegitimacy" and A.D.C. payments explained in terms no less moral than the culture of affluence), and as he penetrated the veneer of exceptional and unfamiliar behavior to see beneath it an élan born of adversity which had long ago been dissipated in the wealthier climate of suburbia.

They were, thought the Mayor, more attractive than some of the leaders who rose to represent them. But politics were the lifeblood of these people. Collectively, it was their main legitimate means of redressing the social and economic imbalance between themselves and the Haves; for an individual, it was a way of achieving in one's own lifetime the social prominence and acceptance which by the route of other callings usually took three generations to attain. Not strange that their leaders should play Robin Hood, nor that they should seem at times to be intent on turning City Hall into Sherwood Forest—may the rich and the law beware.

Among this constituency of newcomers and their political chieftains, metropolitan government was making few converts. It seemed, or easily was made to seem, a gerrymandering tactic by the same suburban element which had abandoned the Central City—and their instinct for the jugular told them that if the suburbanite now wanted to resume these political ties, it must be with the hope of gaining some undisclosed advantage. Suspicious, they were jealous as well; for as their constituency grew and the older population left, they were fast becoming the majority rather than the minority. The political prospects were obvious and appealing; certainly now was not the time to dissolve their growing identity in the larger metropolitan population, nor to be led by the propaganda of increased efficiency and economy into an alliance which would divert what little resources the Central City could still command to the satisfaction of suburban needs.

And the Mayor—for all he disliked the demagoguery of the argument—had to admit that the prospects of the Central City gaining financially from a metropolitan system of government were pretty dim. The suburbs had reached the point where they had population enough to outvote the mother city; and they would hardly play Alphonse and Gaston with the city at the door of the public treasury. For all their wealth—more likely because of it—they were now deeper in the quicksand of financial need than the core city. In a binge of expenditures, they had built their public plant from scratch, yet their outlays were just beginning. The cost of suburban development had been vastly underestimated; trouble was, everybody had assumed the advertised price of houses was the total cost to the suburban taxpayer of his new community. Now the full bill was becoming evident; public health people, finding up to 40 per cent of the suburban water supply contaminated by septic tanks, were among those who could, if asked, tell what the final tab was likely to be.

Adding Central City's present and imminent charges for maintenance and renewal directly to the suburban bill via the proposed route of metropolitan government would hardly help the Mayor in his campaign for more revenue. It was tough enough prying new tax money out of city, state, and Washington, when, as now, he was under no obligation to tell John Q. Taxpayer what all the costs of urban government amounted to.

No rightthinking man, the Mayor often thought, could avoid concluding from this combined balancesheet that the United States had simply bought too much for its income—or if it managed to accumulate enough wealth to pay the bill, it would have a hard time internationally justifying its lavish way of life. For the country was discarding its central cities before they were fully used or paid for, and now was buying a new suburban plant on an instalment plan of staggering proportions.

That was where he began again to wonder whether metropolitan governments weren't the solution—not so much of the community's administrative problem of providing services more efficiently, but of its problem of public morals. For the metropolis as presently organized was a gigantic system of buckpassing, of avoiding difficult choices and unpleasant facts, of having your cake and eating it; a system of incomplete responsibilities which left everyone with an excuse for inaction or a justification of acting only to the convenient extent of self-interest; a system with opportune blinders, in which no one could be blamed for abjuring the role of Good Samaritan and Brother's Keeper, for the simple reason that one's neighbor or brother in need had been gerrymandered into the other fellow's jurisdiction. A system perfectly constructed for the Pharisee and the politician. A system he could play, as other Mayors had done before him, to his own advantage—talking about problems, making token stabs at solving them, appointing study commissions, blaming other jurisdictions for neglecting "their" responsibilities, and coasting with prosperity and the taxpayers' love of postponed action to a reelection or two and then higher office, where the whole hypocrisy could be practised again on the clean slate of a new set of problems and a new constituency.

The thought of higher office pulled him back to the realities of his choice. Next year—and not again—the gubernatorial nomination might be his if all went well, and "well" meant either a major coup of some sort or not rocking the boat. The odds against Metro's winning at the polls—judging from experience across the country—were more than 100 to 1; but since Sputnik, and the electorate's newly conditioned response in favor of experiment and invention, past history was no certain guide. Tote up the sides: For Metro—the League of Women Voters; central city newspapers, radio, and TV; the college educated, upper income, and commuting suburbanites; the managerial group, especially in the utilities; and a scattering of dissident, desperate, or aspiring politicians. Against Metro—the majority of Negroes in Central City; suburban and Central City officeholders, their families, friends, and relatives; suburban newspapers; the working and middle class with jobs and homes on the same side of the city's boundaries; taxpayers' associations in the better off suburbs; suburban industries; and most important, those of the party who controlled the nominations. Fill in the numbers, and it was pretty clear—the Noes had it, and only a gambling upstart would go for broke against such odds.

Damned if he supported Metro—would he be damned if he didn't? The newspapers and pundits would give him a hard time, but soon enough they'd be back in his corner—among Central City candidates they had little or nothing else to turn to. There would also be disaffection and disillusion among the reform element. Many of these he'd shed no tears for—the self-interest of such dogooders was hidden only from themselves. But he grieved genuinely when he thought of the few noble Romans he would cut the ground under by failing to endorse their campaign for Metro. These noble few were battling not for a disguised self-interest, nor for an unexamined panacea, nor for the mere love of battling; they were out to stretch the mind and vision of the metropolitan community, and to give that community room and reason to grow to political maturity, finding in Metro a reform symbolic of their purpose and worthy of the effort. These people, too, had only a shallow well of opportunity to draw from; they, like the Mayor, could risk their political equity only so many times before being pushed aside and their ideals discredited. They knew they were

Diversity: Cases in Metropolitan Decisionmaking

working against the odds, and they knew that the slim chance left to them depended on the Mayor's endorsement.

It would not be easy facing the disappointment of these noble few, less easy for the very fact they would be the most tolerant of his decision. More so than his own conscience, or whatever it was that kept echoing the categorical imperatives of his youth and his never quieted expectancy that someday, if he were to prove his mettle and integrity, he would have to play the statesman on heroic scale even to the martyr's finish.

But was Metro this occasion? He had the courage; what came hard was the conviction.

And even if he were convinced that Metro was the public interest incarnate, and his martyrdom a way of speeding its birth, was this courage or presumption? Who was he to say that a rational order ought to be imposed on this imperfect thing called man or that a procrustean logic of the moment replace the disguised order of the evolutionary process? The present disorganization of the metropolity could hardly be blamed for the lack of solutions to all of men's problems or of resolutions of all his differences; it might, in fact, be a protection society instinctively erected against the disillusion that would follow if all institutional defects were corrected and man left naked to face his inherent political impotence.

And why should he feel conscience or suffer choice at all? Was "the public interest" only a theologian's invention which veiled the essential amorality of the political process—a process simply and purely of equilibrium, in which social forces out of balance strained toward equality? One could not say whether one resolution was better than another except in terms of his own interests, one could in selfishness then react, or in dispassion describe, or out of a projected abhorrence of violence help to secure an orderly and peaceful succession from one state of equilibrium to the next. Heroic acts proceeding from moral certainty were either irrelevant, or dangerous interventions inviting violent reactions.

When Mayor James lapsed that far into philosophy, he knew he had lost his way; and by an instinct he long ago came to trust, he left off contemplating the universe and checked the specifics of the case before him, searching for the middle way out.

He found it where he should have looked at the outset, in the details of the proposal to be voted upon. It was, he saw, an attempt at compromise—a metropolitan authority for specified functions and with limited powers. As he took pen in hand, he wondered with as much amusement as he could muster what the reform element would say when they saw tomorrow's featured story:

> "Mayor Rejects Metro as Not Enough; Says Nothing
> Short of Full Consolidation of Area Governments
> Will Provide Needed Solution"

He knew, however, that the old hands among the politicians would smile and understand; and he turned to wondering whether Nancy, his wife, really meant it when she said she didn't want to move or whether she'd feel differently when ensconced in the Governor's mansion.

The Case of Urban Renewal

John Stewart hadn't taken his new job as executive director of Better City, Inc., without some misgiving. The son of a medical missionary, he had never felt comfortable working for anything less *pro bono publico* than government itself—and if it weren't for "the Transition" and the increasing frustrations of public employment, he'd still be happily at work in the Washington niche which World War II had opened for him.

Better City, Inc., was a new animal that both attracted and unsettled him. It had been formed by a group of civic leaders and downtown businessmen aroused by the "blight and flight" which threatened the life of the central city. It offered the advantages of a private corporation (twice his government salary and precious little of the red tape), the satisfaction of a public purpose, and a tightly knit executive committee whose clear purpose and consistent interest made working life a pleasure. But it was the clarity and consistency that bothered him. In his government job, his marching orders had borne the moral seal of the public interest; confused, inconstant, incomplete—true enough—but still the declared product of the machinery of state, with all interests having had their chance to participate.

Now he was working for a private agency which could assert a

Diversity: Cases in Metropolitan Decisionmaking

public interest but not validate it. That is, by any formal process of law. The irony was that working for the leading businessmen of the community brought him respect and a sense of power far greater than he enjoyed as a public servant. In fact, as public servant turned "private," he was treated at times like an errant soul returned to the state of grace. The social and business elite welcomed him to their luncheon clubs and rounds of golf with the same exaggerated smile of new found brotherhood he remembered seeing on the faces of the church elders when a prodigal or convert was brought to the fold.

But to others he was rather the renegade. His friends still in the public service ribbed him about his "sellout to the interests," and he knew their jest hid a reprimand. He noticed, too, that the welfare workers, planners, and other social technicians of City Hall, for all their cordiality (with so few working on the city's problems, the club of the *pro bono publico* couldn't afford to be too exclusive), still kept half a guard up when dealing with him.

Still he might not have noticed any of this if his own nicked conscience hadn't sent him looking for it. The closest thing to religion he had was his dedication to the public interest; he worried at it with all the doubt and concern his father had tried unsuccessfully to have him attach to the doctrines of the church and the voice of God. There *was* the equivalent of right and wrong in public affairs; some things were in the public interest and others were not. An open mind and accumulating experience had kept him from becoming dogmatic—the older he got the less sure he was about the substance of the public interest and the more devoted he became to the process by which it was declared to be. Precisely for that reason he kept debating with himself the character of his new job and commitments. As far as substance was concerned, the corporation's general purpose was as virtuous and tenable as any mandate he had been given by Congress and President. But he no longer could say he worked for the general public, only for a fragment of them.

And a fragment, by definition, with a limited—if not a special—interest. As stated in its articles of incorporation, Better City, Inc., was to promote a healthier economic climate and improved housing conditions in the core area of Central City. Its roster of sponsors was a veritable Who's Who of local businessmen, industrialists, publishers, broadcasters, and civic association leaders. That didn't quite tell the story; yet a more earthy account wouldn't have added much grist for a muckraker's mill. It was a familiar tale of community leadership waking up, admittedly late, to the ominous facts of Central City life —declining population, declining sales, declining valuations; increasing dependency, delinquency, deterioration, and tax rates. In short, the economic and social stalwarts of the community began by running scared; and to their credit, instead of panicking or fleeing they had dug in their heels "to do something about it."

If they stated their objectives in terms as unassailable as motherhood and virtue, it was not in cynicism or with motives consciously hidden. The pledge to wipe out slums was made because everyone, including the social workers and the clergy, agreed that blight was responsible for the city's demise. The pledge was not adopted as a gimmick to clothe economic wolves in the garments of civic innocence. Nor was the decision to work through a private corporation motivated by a desire to subvert or bypass the machinery of government. City Hall was party to the act, officially and privately welcoming the new agency as another badly needed ally in its program of urban renewal, and as a reassuring sign of civic support. Even more, Stewart had not been able to ferret out anyone on his governing board who was mouthing one thing and intending another. Self-interests, yes; but the men he worked for—Stewart felt sure—were in this because they firmly believed that self-interest and the community interest in this case lay in the same direction; and they were emotionally prepared not to quit before both were fully realized.

The rub was, that none of them stopped to ask whether his own interests and those of the public could so happily and nicely coincide. Stewart had spotted this submerged question his first days on the job, and had quickly decided it was not one to attack frontally but rather by indirection, patience, and education. Preaching, argument, and constant nagging about the eternal verities would accomplish nothing; they would only build up resistance and resentment in the very people he wanted to educate—and he was sure they could be educated.

His policy of the slow approach by and large was proving successful. Hardly a week went by that one or the other of his governing board didn't rub his civic eyes incredulously over what he had learned from this new exposure to the city he thought he knew. A walk through the slums—the oldest lure the sociallyminded knew to attract

Diversity: Cases in Metropolitan Decisionmaking

blindfolded citizens out of their complacency—had worked again. So had the shock treatment of converting quashable impressions into unassailable statistics—on the extent and rate of blight; on the incidence of rat infestation; on the rate of tenement conversions, single room occupancy, and rent extortions; on the competitive gains of suburban shopping centers over the central business districts; etc., etc. And when the shock of these disclosures had worn off, some subtler lessons began coming through—for example, the art of seeing woods rather than trees (as was necessary to understand that Better City's trends were no different from those which affected other metropolitan centers, and to appreciate the reasons, economic significance, and inevitable stages of assimilation of the new migrants to Central City); also coming to sense the satisfactions and fascination of working toward a public good.

And he had to confess that he, too, was learning. He looked back with real embarrassment on the stereotype of the businessman which he and his fellow bureaucrats had constructed; close up, he had found few who fit the description. All that stress on getting things done rather than talking about them which on the receiving end he had scorned as so much balderdash now had materialized in his favor; it kept him hopping, but as a working environment, he liked it. He missed the companionship of intellectual and articulate men with their concern over values and their clear expositions of points of view; but that was not to say that profundity and humanitarianism were lacking in those who now employed him. One had to look for these qualities in cruder form—perhaps cruder wasn't the word for it, "operative" might be more like it. For these business leaders never let themselves be paralyzed by logic or philosophical dilemma. They lived and acted in the short run, confident that the long run would be better strung together from these shorter and visible pieces of certainty than by the only other process which life seemed to offer, which was somebody else's projection of prejudice into the farther unknown. Stewart had begun to glimpse a humane rationale behind even the feature of business life he had decried the most—its conversion of every value into the currency of the market. For out of the diversity and ambiguity of the human animal, would anything get accomplished (including people being fed) unless someone imposed a will and a coherence upon them? And of all processes of cutting the

Gordian knot, each with cruelty in its cutting edge, the market demonstrably was among the more humane and productive.

But Stewart knew he couldn't solve all his doubts and his agency's problems by sweet soliloquy and an opening mind. At yesterday's meeting on the Barrington Hill project, the whole damned iceberg of urban renewal problems had tipped upside down; and no amount of rationalization would hide or reduce the scale of the moral and political issues which suddenly hove into view and had now to be resolved.

Barrington Hill rose just behind the central business district and commanded one of the better views of the harbor. Several generations ago, it had been the city's most exclusive residential area. The Barrington Mansion was still there, scowling like a gargoyle over the city below, and with it a scattering of other Victorian monstrosities which local antiquarians exclaimed over but had neither the heart nor the income to live in. Then one day there was a new era; people fathomed the change though they couldn't quite account for it; and the exodus from Barrington Hill to the next arena of invidious distinction was on. For a time, the great houses remained vacant—except for those where the proud and childless remained to die. Then the Immigrants arrived—first the Irish and Italians, then the East Europeans. Their occupancy of the Hill began at its base, then infiltrated the older houses, converting one after another into multiple family dwellings and building drab frame houses in between; and so on until it reached the ridge. First generations of these immigrants stayed to die; the more intrepid, ambitious, and rebellious of the second generation moved out; but still in the third generation some of each remained, tied to shops, friends, and memories of a bygone day. Now another cycle of occupancy was well on its way—Negroes attracted to the city and shorefront boom of the Second World War, crowding into whatever housing they could find and gain entry to.

Barrington Hill was once again alive—more alive, in fact, than it had ever been in the sedate and solitary style of its aristocratic period. It was jammed with people in the full cry of existence, in some cases one and even two families to a room. Families, that is, by census definition but not always by benefit of clergy—easily one-fifth of the seemingly endless procession of children were born out of wedlock. But not until they moved outside their world on the Hill would they

Diversity: Cases in Metropolitan Decisionmaking 253

come alive to the stigma, and not until the label was pinned on them would they call what they inhabited a slum.

Barrington Hill was a slum by the standards of those who had come to know better shelter and were housebroken to the ways of the urban middle and upper class. And since neither were much in evidence on the Hill, those who had come to know the better life and judged vitality largely by the condition of real estate, declared Barrington Hill a dying part of the city. Marked for clearance and redevelopment was the official language used by City Hall in its application to Washington for renewal funds. "For Sale" and "Condemned" were the words which appeared on windows of the Hill, until the vandals on their ugly own began Stage One of the job of demolition.

All that was *fait accompli*. City Hall had made the decision and was now off on the pathetic chase to locate the refugees whom in pious pronouncements it had promised to help relocate in facilities as good as the ones they were forced out of. At best, the city's humanitarians would register and "help" a third of those displaced; the rest would be too impatient, skeptical, shiftless, uninformed, or proud to seek assistance—or just plain aware that they'd better wait for no man if they were to latch on to the few remaining places open to Negroes. And as for equal facilities, the new apartment might have as many square feet; but as likely as not it would be in another "dying" sector of the city scheduled for redevelopment—the cycle would start soon enough again. Far more than likely, the new apartment wouldn't re-create what neighborhood and family ties had been left behind, or the new shop carry with it the assurance of an equally devoted clientele.

In such a permanent state of transition, Stewart wondered, how could these new citizens of the city achieve family and neighborhood stability, unless it was to be the stability of continuing frustration and dependency as known by other bands of refugees on the Subcontinent and in the Gaza Strip. But he and his agency had not made the decision; this was a public action, and in that arena the virtue of the process of representation was fast becoming evident. The Negroes were stirring; already the mayor and redevelopment authority were feeling the discomfort of countervailing power. The early days of unilateral action endorsed by the carefully selected Uncle Toms of the Negro community were over; and the pace of urban renewal was slowing down, while public hearings and behindscenes considerations of the "human impact" of clearance and redevelopment were multiplying in geometric progression.

That's why last night's meeting on the Barrington Hill project had been such an unpleasant one. The matter to be decided was whether the new apartments which were to rise on the cleared land of the Hill were to be open to Negroes or restricted. This was no longer a decision which could be conveniently foisted on the public authorities. Better City, Inc., which had privately rounded up the capital necessary for the redevelopment scheme, together with the developer who had taken title to the land from the city, would determine the outcome and bear the burden of public explanation.

One way out of the dilemma would have been to blanket the Hill with luxury housing, letting the economics of high rent exclude all but the handful of Negroes who could afford them. But a market survey had not shown enough prospective demand; the majority of units would have to be within the middle and lower middle income range—which was also in accord with the public rationale of the Better City program, to make Central City again attractive to its disappearing middle class. Yet at these lower rents, there were enough Negro families in the housing market to make it possible and even likely that a third or more of the Hill's new residents would be nonwhite.

This, if one could believe the reported experience of other projects in other cities, would have defeated one of the central ideas behind the renewal program—which was to halt the flight of whites from Central City. Let a neighborhood or an apartment go beyond 15 per cent to 20 per cent Negro, and it would "tip," becoming entirely colored within a matter of a very few years.

Whether or not the reports were accurate or the experience universal, the board of Better City, Inc., had shown last night that they needed no outside evidence to persuade them; almost to a man they were convinced that an occupancy ratio of less than ninety to ten whites to non-whites would "kill the project," and they were ready for the motion to apply the ratio as a governing quota. To Stewart, the idea of a quota was abhorrent; but he had been spared the agony of an immediate reaction thanks to a cautious board member who asked that the decision be deferred until "influential opinion" in the community was quietly sounded out and the legal question explored.

But Stewart knew he couldn't hide behind the delay, nor could he hide behind the unanimous action by his board which he saw coming. He'd have to come to terms with himself.

There was no escaping it, the loyalty of his employment was to the interests of his board; and in terms of their own interests, their case for a quota was an understandable and defensible one. Their whole way of life, socially as well as economically, was built on the middle class culture of a stable white community. None of them was blind to the inevitability of change; but change at the pace of the postwar exodus to the suburbs, as drastic as the shift from middle class white to low income Negro, so apparently a denial of the values they held dear, and offering such slender prospect that if left in alternative hands the city would do anything but deteriorate—change of this sort could not be suffered passively. If Central City were to become something more than a shambles, a sad commentary on American democracy, yes even a ghetto, some force had to assert itself to moderate and even reverse the trends now on the loose. Radical surgery was called for—he remembered the pain of finally accepting on his father's explanation the medical need to hurt in order to cure, and saw that he and others might have to steel themselves for a similar act of social injury to achieve a social gain. Out of this generation's travail might come the next generation's wellbeing. The quota was obviously a moral compromise; but the alternative was an exaggeration of those divisive forces—white fleeing to the suburbs and colored piling up in Central City—which might well destroy not only the chance of realizing the principle of racial harmony, but the possibility of compromise itself.

A compelling line of argument, but it was incomplete and Stewart knew it. It left out the telling fact that this was but one section of the community judging the present and attempting to order the future by their own lights and self-interests; and to carry out their will successfully, they would have to interfere with the workings of the market, whose freedom was the cornerstone of the system they were trying to preserve. For what was a quota but a refusal to supposedly free consumers to purchase and enjoy the housing of their choice? What subsidies were being paid to acquire, clear, and redevelop urban houses and land—which though old and untidy were serving their elemental economic function of sheltering human beings? Admittedly these shelters did not yield enough taxes to cover the costs of the public services they required; but to be honest, neither did the shiny new residences the sought after middle class was building in suburbia. Wasn't the whole effort to revitalize downtown a massive denial of the market mechanism—clearly, effective demand was moving away from Central City for reasons of such magnitude (and few of them related to the race issue) that it was folly to try to reverse them.

But the question which most hammered at his inner peace was again, "Who were these self-chosen élite of the community to judge and decide?"

It was, Stewart recognized, the eternal question of the Republic; neither he nor the Greeks had managed to find an abiding answer to it, and almost certainly, no mortal ever would. But to live with one's self, and with the decision he had already made to stay with his job and to accept the quota—at least one had to have a rationalization.

There was faith. Faith that behind his agency's and his society's dedication to material progress, to the better bricks and mortar which seemed always to displace some less fortunate or desirable, was an ultimate good, inscrutably working its way through interim cruelties to man's apprehension of its social value. Yet this was a straw at best; he had seen it break under his father's lifelong grasp, as medical missionary he had saved men's lives only to expand the scale of their misery and insure their eventual starvation.

On the other hand, there were more tangible arguments but few could make fast to them without being drawn to the dubious safety of cynicism and detachment. How long should he struggle with a conscience that was far more demanding than most; why should he search for the public interest on inaccessible mountain tops while others were satisfied with what they found far below? Wasn't the situation he was interpreting as a battle for principle merely a battle among the interests, each as self-centered as the next? Was the image of the minority simply a myth he and others equally compulsive or dissatisfied had created in their quest for something to defend or to use as a lash—an extension of their own egos, an illusion cherished for its selfish use? In real life there were Negroes and there were Negroes, like other human beings each aspiring to the heights where

Diversity: Cases in Metropolitan Decisionmaking 257

he could look down on others beneath him. One could not deny the discrimination which already existed within the Negro community, nor the quiet wish of many a Negro to escape the chains of identical treatment into which they had been locked by the single and accidental trait of color. And weren't he and his corporation already doing more than could reasonably be expected of them by admitting at least some Negroes, when they had the option of excluding Negroes altogether? Or worse, they could have done nothing at all, or turned to piracy and plunder—as the slum landlords had done—while the city rotted to its foundations.

So there would be a quota; and Stewart, his eye on a mountain few would discern and only a heroic handful in history would be given opportunity to climb, would oppose it only by the slow and undeclared war of education. Quietly he hoped the local chapter of N.A.A.C.P. would not spoil his chances by kicking up too much of a fuss. Or maybe it would be better if they would. He wasn't sure. He just wished for once he could turn off his inner voice and get back to the straightforward job of making certain that the necessary capital were subscribed and those new apartments built. Which was all anyone seemed to be asking of him.

CHAPTER XVII

The Unsettled Limits of the American Presidency

By ROWLAND EGGER

I

THE CHARACTERISTICS of the American system of government of primary significance in a study of the unsettled limits of Presidential power are three in number: first, it is a government of limited power operating within the confines of a written constitution; second, the powers of government—legislative, executive, and judicial—are vested in independent organs not directly beholden to each other in the performance of their constitutional duties; third, these organs are presumed to operate so as to maintain a sort of perfect and perpetual equilibrium, so that none is in a position to dominate the others.

These characteristics, in a superficial view at least, appear to contribute to a very precise definition of what constitutes executive power and, *pari passu,* to a very exact settlement of the limits of the Presidency. That this ostensible precision and exactness is not observable in political practice is, in turn, due to three countervailing influences: first, "executive power" as used in Article II of the Constitution is a term of very uncertain import; second, the powers of the national government are subject to continuing interpretation and expansion, and a substantial part of this expansion inures to the executive branch; third, the separation of organs in the Constitution did not establish a correspondingly rigorous separation of power, so that a very substantial interpenetration of authority amongst the legislative, judicial, and executive branches has grown up over the 170 years in which the Constitution has been in operation. All this has resulted in a considerable fluidity with respect to the metes and bounds of Presidential authority, and has led to the recurring definition and redefinition of the powers of the President largely in terms of his moral and political stature.

As has been frequently observed, Article II of the Constitution is the most loosely drawn chapter of a loosely drawn document. In its opening words it is laid down that "The executive power shall be vested in a President of the United States." What does this mean? Is it a sweeping grant of prerogative, or merely the designation of an office? If it is a grant of prerogative, the subsequent specific grants of power in the same article are superfluous. If it is merely the designation of an office the powers of which are defined in the subsequent specific grants, it is indeed a singularly modest Presidency which the Constitution establishes. It is worth noting that Hamilton, who listed "competent powers" as one of the four ingredients constituting energy in the Executive, argued his case on the grounds of the specific grants of power in Article II, which implies that he considered them competent.[1] Chief Justice Taft, in *Meyers v. United States* argued that the specific grants lend "emphasis where emphasis is appropriate."[2] As Edward S. Corwin points out, if this is a proper canon of constitutional interpretation, the "general welfare" clause of Article I confers plenary rather than enumerated powers and potentially converts the national government into one of unlimited jurisdiction.[3] He goes on to ask: "Yet if there is 'executive power' that has been found essential in other systems of government and is not granted the President in the more specific clauses of Article II, how is it to be brought within the four corners of the Constitution except by means of the 'executive power' clause?"[4]

Moreover, is the grant of executive power in Article II the sum total of executive authority recognized by the Constitution? The language seems to say so, but of what import then is the power granted to Congress to make "all laws which shall be necessary and proper for carrying into execution" the powers of the national government? Likewise, what is one to assume from the charge to the President to "take care that the laws be faithfully executed"—presumably by organs other than the Presidency itself? And if executive power is the only kind of power the President can exercise, how can he receive power from the legislature, which, confined within its own limits, can delegate nothing but legislative power, since this is the only kind of power it possesses?

[1] *Federalist*, Number 70.
[2] 272 U.S. 52 (1926).
[3] Edward S. Corwin, *The President: Office and Powers*, fourth revised edition, New York University Press, New York, 1957, p. 4.
[4] *Ibid.*

Unsettled Limits of the American Presidency

Nor is the enormous variation in the scope and finality of Presidential powers, especially when compared with Congressional powers within the same general premises, without significance. His veto power and his duty to inform Congress on the state of the Union involve the President directly in the exercise of legislative power. On the other hand, his pardoning power, power to receive foreign ambassadors, and like prerogatives, are apparently quite independent of the legislative power. But his power to recognize foreign governments implied in the power to receive ambassadors, as well as other implied authority, is undoubtedly more vulnerable to Congressional restriction.

One of the classic examples of the amplification of Presidential authority through constitutional interpretation occurred in the case of *U.S. v. Curtiss-Wright Export Corporation*.[5] In 1934 Congress passed a joint resolution authorizing the President, upon the finding of certain facts and the following of certain procedures, to declare an embargo on the shipment of arms to participants in the Chaco War. The President duly made such findings, followed such procedures, and proclaimed the embargo, which Curtiss-Wright violated by selling machine guns to Bolivia. In its defense, the Corporation protested the constitutionality of the joint resolution and of the power exercised by the President. In its decision the Supreme Court said:

> ... the investment of the federal government with the power of external sovereignty did not depend upon the affirmative grants of the Constitution. The powers to declare and wage war, to conclude peace, to make treaties, to maintain diplomatic relations with other sovereignties, if they had never been mentioned in the Constitution would have been vested in the federal government as necessary concomitants of nationality ... As a member of the family of nations, the right and power of the United States in that field are equal to the right and power of the other members of the international family. Otherwise, the United States is not completely sovereign ... Not only, as we have shown, is the federal power over external affairs in origin and essential character different from that over internal affairs, but participation in the exercise of the power is significantly limited. In this vast, external realm, with its important, complicated, delicate, and manifold problems, the President alone has the power to speak or listen as a representative of the nation. He *makes* treaties with the advice and consent of the Senate; but he alone negotiates. Into the field

[5] 299 *U.S.* 304 (1936).

of negotiation the Senate cannot intrude; and Congress itself is powerless to invade it. As Marshall said in his great argument of March 7, 1800, in the House of Representatives: "The President is the sole organ of the nation in its external relations, and its sole representative with foreign nations" (*Annals,* 6th Congress, col. 613 . . .).

The interpenetration of legislative, executive, and judicial powers is clearly evident throughout the operations of the federal establishment. Judicial administration, as Sir Josiah Stamp has properly remarked, is only a form of general administration "which has acquired an air of detachment."[6] Courts have for many decades engaged in performing such essentially administrative acts as liquidating bankrupt businesses in receivership, naturalizing aliens, etc. The tendency of the Supreme Court to legislate has been frequently remarked. But if the courts administer and legislate, it is not less true that the President judges, and then supervises the execution of his judgment. He also legislates, frequently far beyond merely filling in the "operational" interstices of legislation. In fact, the delegation of legislative power is perhaps the most remarkable characteristic of contemporary national lawmaking. Nor is the Congress lacking in its own imperialisms. Congressional penetration into the realm of executive power, largely through its control of appropriations, but through many other channels as well, has frequently transferred the real locus of administrative decisionmaking from the President or his agents to the committee rooms, and more especially to the committee and subcommittee chairmen, on the Hill. It would, moreover, be hard to deny that some Congressional committees, such as the subcommittee headed by the late Senator McCarthy, have gone a long way in arrogating to themselves judicial powers, oftentimes without the accompaniment of judicial procedure.

What the Constitution actually established was not a strict separation of powers but rather a differentiation of organs to serve as the foci for the operation of the legislative, executive, and judicial modes.[7] Indeed, if a complete separation of powers had been achieved, checks and balances would be impossible, since the several powers would never impinge upon each other. Thus the President influences the Congress

[6] Quoted in W. A. Robson, *Justice and Administrative Law,* Macmillan and Co., Ltd., London, 1928, p. 11.

[7] This point is clearly developed in Richard E. Neustadt, *Presidential Power,* John Wiley and Sons, Inc., New York, 1960, chapter III.

by the exercise of an essentially legislative act—the veto. Congress protects its position in many ways—through its approval of certain appointments, which is an essentially executive power, through approving treaties—another executive power—and through pushing its control of the purse into the realm of executive authority, through legislation or the initiation of constitutional changes which reverse Supreme Court decisions, etc. The Court asserts its authority against the Executive by holding unconstitutional an exercise of authority by the President or his agents. It sometimes protects the Congress against itself as well, by holding inadequate the standards of executive action under delegated legislation.

II

The Constitution of the United States of America, in sharp contrast to the constitutions of parliamentary regimes, combines the offices of Chief of State and Chief of Government. And since it also adds to the office of Chief of Government the offices of Commander in Chief and Chief of Foreign Relations, the essentially symbolic role of the President as Chief of State emerges as something quite different from that of a mere king or queen in a constitutional monarchy. George Fort Milton sums up the office in these words: "As our Chief of State, and as such the embodiment of the people's elective will, the President is clad with the prerogative of the office, and possesses more actual sovereign power than any British king since George III."[8] As Theodore Roosevelt once wrote to Lady Delamere, the job is "almost that of a king and prime minister rolled into one."[9] John Bright, an Englishman, described the American Presidency in these terms nearly a hundred years ago:

> We know what an election is in the United States for President of the Republic . . . Every four years there springs from the vote created by the whole people a President over that great nation. I think the whole world offers no finer spectacle than this; it offers no higher dignity; and there is no greater object of ambition on the political stage

[8] George Fort Milton, *The Use of Presidential Power*, Little, Brown and Company, Boston, 1944, p. 3.
[9] This is developed in Sydney Hyman, *The American President,* Harper and Brothers, New York, 1954, in an introductory chapter entitled "The President Reigns and Rules."

on which men are permitted to move. You may point, if you will, to hereditary rulers, to crowns coming down through successive generations of the same family, to thrones based on prescription or on conquest, to sceptres wielded over veteran legions and subject realms—but to my mind, there is nothing more worthy of reverence and obedience, and nothing more sacred, than the authority of the freely chosen magistrate of a great and free people; and if there be on earth and amongst men any divine right to govern, surely it rests with a ruler so chosen and so appointed.[10]

As Clinton Rossiter has correctly observed, the Lockian theory of prerogative has found a notable instrument in the American Presidency.[11] Locke stated this theory in the following words:

Where the legislative and executive power are in distinct hands, as they are in all moderated monarchies and well-framed governments, there the good of the society requires that several things should be left to the discretion of him that has the executive power. For the legislators not being able to foresee and provide by laws for all that may be useful to the community, the executor of the laws, having the power in his hands, has by the common law of Nature a right to make use of it for the good of the society, in many cases where the municipal law has given no direction, till the legislative can conveniently be assembled to provide for it; nay, many things there are which the law can by no means provide for, and those must necessarily be left to the discretion of him that has the executive power in his hands, to be ordered by him as the public good and advantage shall require; nay, it is fit that the laws themselves should in some cases give way to the executive power, or rather to the fundamental law of Nature and government—viz., that as much as may be all of the members of the society are to be preserved. For since many accidents may happen wherein a strict and rigid observation of the laws may do harm (as not to pull down an innocent man's house to stop the fire when the next to it is burning), and a man may come sometimes within the reach of the law, which makes no distinction of persons by an action that may deserve reward and pardon, 'tis fit the ruler should have a power in many cases to mitigate the severity of the law, and pardon some offenders: for the end of government being the preservation of

---

[10]Quoted in Clinton W. Rossiter, *The American Presidency*, The New American Library of World Literature, Inc., New York, 1956, p. 9.

[11]Clinton W. Rossiter, *Constitutional Dictatorship*, Princeton University Press, Princeton, Oxford University Press, London, 1948, p. 218.

Unsettled Limits of the American Presidency

all, as much as may be, even the guilty are to be spared where it can prove no prejudice to the innocent.

This power to act according to discretion for the public good, without the prescription of the law, and sometimes even against it, is that which is called prerogative. For since, in some governments, the lawmaking power is not always in being, and is usually too numerous, and so too slow, for the dispatch requisite to execution; and also because it is impossible to foresee, and so by laws to provide for, all accidents and necessities that may concern the public, or to make such laws as will do no harm if they are executed with an inflexible rigour on all occasions and upon all persons that may come in their way; therefore there is a latitude left to the executive power to do many things of choice which the laws do not prescribe.

This power, whilst employed for the benefit of the community, and suitably to the trusts and ends of the government, is undoubted prerogative, and never is questioned. For the people are very seldom or never scrupulous or nice in the point; they are far from examining prerogative whilst it is in any tolerable degree employed for the use it was meant, that is for the good of the people, and not manifestly against it. But if there comes to be a question between the executive power and the people about a thing claimed as a prerogative, the tendency of the exercise of such prerogative to the good or hurt of the people will easily decide that question.[12]

Theodore Roosevelt has given us perhaps the clearest, but by no means the earliest, exposition of the notion of the Presidential prerogative:

> The most important factor in getting the right spirit in my Administration, next to the insistence upon courage, honesty, and a genuine democracy of desire to serve the plain people, was my insistence upon the theory that the executive power was limited only by specific restrictions and prohibitions appearing in the Constitution or imposed by the Congress under its Constitutional powers. My view was that every executive officer, and above all every executive officer in high position, was a steward of the people bound actively and affirmatively to do all he could for the people, and not to content himself with the negative merit of keeping his talents undamaged in a napkin. I declined to adopt the view that what was imperatively necessary for the Nation could not be done by the President unless he could find some specific

[12] J. W. Gough, editor, *A Second Treatise of Government,* The Macmillan Company, New York, Basil Blackwell and Mott, Ltd., Oxford, 1946, pp. 81–82.

authorization to do it. My belief was that it was not only his right but his duty to do anything that the needs of the Nation demanded unless such action was forbidden by the Constitution or by the laws. Under this interpretation of executive power I did and caused to be done many things not previously done by the President and the heads of the departments. I did not usurp power, but I did greatly broaden the use of executive power. In other words, I acted for the public welfare, I acted for the common well-being of all our people, whenever and in whatever manner was necessary, unless prevented by direct constitutional or legislative prohibition. I did not care a rap for the mere form and show of power. I cared immensely for the use that could be made of the substance.[13]

III

Obviously, the unsettled limits of the Presidency are to be understood primarily in the actions of the Presidents who expanded the executive power, not those who contracted it. George Washington undoubtedly did more to set the tone in respect of protocol for the role of President as Chief of State than has any of his successors. But his major contribution seems to have been as the head of the administration and as leader of public opinion. Moreover, not all "strong" Presidents emphasized their institutional powers. Thomas Jefferson, for example, who was certainly a strong President in the sense that he was able to achieve his aims for the government, was in principle committed to legislative supremacy—and was in practice compelled personally to undertake the control of his unruly Republicans. Despite his undeniable domination of the government during his Administration, he added little to the institutional Presidency, and indeed laid much of the groundwork for the difficulty of Madison—a less astute politician—by reason of his skill in and preference for the manipulation of legislative leadership.

As Louis Brownlow has noted, "The eighteenth century concept of the Chief Magistrate ended with John Quincy Adams. Andrew Jackson was both the leader and the symbol of the democratic revolt that made the President the choice of the mass of voters at the polls and made the Presidency an instrument for the expression and enforcement

[13]*Theodore Roosevelt: An Autobiography*, Charles Scribner's Sons, New York, 1913, p. 357.

Unsettled Limits of the American Presidency

of the national will."[14] Andrew Jackson while he was in the White House won many victories which expanded the executive power. His actions in respect of the tariff and internal improvements and the destruction of the Bank of the United States were remarkable examples of legislative leadership. His action with regard to the Cherokee Nation was an impressive invocation of executive and military powers. But his victory over the South Carolina Nullificationists was his outstanding assertion of the prerogative.

John Caldwell Calhoun, one of the most frustrated aspirants in the history of American Presidential politics, was the high priest of the nullification doctrine—the notion that a state could set aside acts of the National Government which it deemed to infringe upon its authorities, rights, and liberties. The tariff acts of 1828 and 1832 were obnoxious to the South Carolina legislature, and in 1832 it called a Convention which passed an Ordinance of Nullification, holding the tariff acts unconstitutional, prohibiting citizens of South Carolina from obeying them after February 1, 1833, and threatening secession if the National Government sought to enforce the laws. The South Carolina legislature then implemented the work of the Convention with punitive laws against persons who sought to collect or to pay customs duties. The President could send troops into the state at the request of the Governor—an unlikely contingency in this instance—or to see to it that the laws enacted by Congress were faithfully executed. But the legislation covering the latter aimed only at violations by individuals; there was no provision which covered violations by the duly constituted public authorities. His only remaining recourse was the *posse comitatus*.

To meet this situation Jackson did three things: 1. He drafted legislation for submission to Congress in December, 1832, authorizing the use of the Army against the state authorities; 2. he encouraged the substantial body of South Carolina Unionists to prepare for overt acts of nullification, gathered arms for their use, and sent a warship and several revenue cutters to Charleston where he put Winfield Scott in command; 3. he issued a proclamation on December 10, 1832, enunciating the proposition that when a faction in a state attempts to nullify a constitutional law of Congress, or to destroy the Union, the people

---

[14]Louis Brownlow, *The President and the Presidency*, Public Administration Service, Chicago, 1949, p. 56.

of the Union have the right to coerce them to obedience. This proclamation drew the support of states from Maine to Louisiana, and by the prescribed date of nullification Jackson could have put a *posse comitatus* of 200,000 men in the field.

Meanwhile no overt act of nullification had occurred. Clay and Calhoun connived in the Senate to pass a compromise tariff bill which would to some degree save face for the nullificationists, and the President's force bill was put behind it on the legislative calendar. Both bills emerged March 2, 1833. The South Carolina Convention promptly reconvened, repealed its Ordinance, and claimed a complete victory. If by this maneuver the nullificationists were able to console themselves with the illusion that they had won the applause, it is no less true that Jackson unmistakably had won the ball game.

Of the eight Presidents who served between Jackson and Lincoln only one exhibited talents commensurate with the dignity of the office. Martin Van Buren, like a later incumbent, was a good administrator but the victim of a depression, and he exhibited about as little imagination as his later counterpart in coping with it. William Henry Harrison died three weeks after his inauguration. John Tyler was excommunicated from his own party by Henry Clay, and though he was a game fighter his battle was hopeless from the beginning. His single success was in smuggling Texas into the Union, by substituting a Congressional joint resolution, which he could get passed, for a treaty, which he could not. Where he was good, James Knox Polk was very good, and where he was bad he was horrible. He was confronted with the Mexican War immediately upon his accession, as a consequence of Tyler's legerdemain, but was never able to consolidate his position as Commander in Chief because his two senior commanders, Zachary Taylor and Winfield Scott, were both Whigs. His attempts to secure the authorization of a new lieutenant generalship for Thomas H. Benton, to take charge of the armies in the field, were frustrated by a Southern-Whig coalition. Although Polk did achieve his major objectives—tariff reduction, the freeing of the Treasury from Congressional control, settlement of the Oregon dispute, and the annexation of California (for which Benton was probably mainly responsible), in addition to demonstrating exceptional ability as an administrator, he contributed little to the enhancement of the Presidential prerogative. Zachary Taylor died before his bellicose assertions concerning his intention to defend the Constitution could be tested. Millard Fillmore, who aided the Compromise of 1850, did nothing to enhance either the Presidency or the National Government. Franklin Pierce was a failure in all aspects of the chief magistracy, and James Buchanan was an unmitigated disaster.

IV

That Abraham Lincoln raised the Presidential office to unprecedented and, in many respects, unequalled heights of power and prestige cannot be questioned. But the significance of his achievements in terms of precedents is more difficult to evaluate. A great deal has been said and written about the way in which Lincoln coupled his authority as the receptacle of the executive power with his authority as Commander in Chief to develop the notion of "war powers." But four wars have come and gone since Lincoln's administration in none of which authority of the sort which he asserted has been requested or exercised by Presidents.

Jefferson would have wept at Lincoln's ineptitude in manipulating the Congress. Martin Van Buren and James Knox Polk would have deprecated his clumsiness as an administrator. Jackson would have been disgusted with his frequent indecisiveness even as Commander in Chief. He never functioned as Head of the Party, and the success of his administration in foreign relations, especially in the Trent Affair, was mainly due to Adams and Ewing. Yet withal Lincoln emerges as the greatest figure in the history of the American Presidency.

The importance of Lincoln's contribution lies almost altogether in the establishment of the fact of the Presidential prerogative. The recognition of the prerogative, it should be remarked, comes hard to American jurisprudence. The Convention, the Federalist papers, and the debates of the State conventions on ratification, all seem to assume that no contingency could possibly arise in which the rulers of the country would have to look outside the language of the Constitution for their authorities. Even in 1866, while Lincoln's administration was still a glowing memory, the Supreme Court insisted:

> The Constitution of the United States is a law for rulers and people, equally in war and in peace, and covers with the shield of its protection all classes of men at all times, and under all circumstances. No

doctrine involving more pernicious consequences was ever invented by the wit of man than that any of its provisions can be suspended during any of the great exigencies of government. Such a doctrine leads directly to anarchy or despotism, but the theory on which it is based is false; for the government, within the Constitution, has all the powers granted to it which are necessary to preserve its existence . . .[15]

It is possible, of course, to read the Court's dictum as an assertion of the prerogative—as affirming that all of the actions taken by Lincoln were within the powers granted to the government which were "necessary to preserve its existence." On the other hand, some of the things Lincoln did were clearly and unequivocally contrary to express provisions of the Constitution, and neither the dignity nor the integrity of the Constitution is supported by the argument that it contains within itself the authority for its own nullification in the event this should prove necessary to its preservation. There are strong grounds for the assertion once made by Corwin that the decision in *Ex Parte Milligan* was an "evident piece of arrant hypocrisy."[16]

Lincoln was inaugurated March 4, 1861. On April 19, 1861, he proclaimed a blockade of the ports of the seceded states, an act which was contrary both to the Constitution and to accepted principles of international law except when the government was involved in a declared foreign war; it was, in short, an act open to a belligerent under the laws of war. But only a declaration of war can establish the rights of belligerency, only Congress can declare war, and Congress was not even in session, nor would it be until the following July 4. On April 20, Lincoln directed the Secretary of the Treasury to advance $2,000,000 of unappropriated funds to three private citizens of New York, who had not the slightest color of legal authority to receive the funds, in direct violation of Article I, Section 9, which provides that "No Money shall be drawn from the Treasury, but in Consequence of Appropriations made by Law . . ." This transaction, it may be noted, was not even communicated for the information of Congress until May 26, 1862. On April 27, Lincoln authorized the Commanding General of the United States Army to suspend the writ of habeas corpus in cer-

---

[15]*Ex Parte Milligan*, 4 *Wallace* 2 (1866).
[16]Edward S. Corwin, *The President: Office and Powers,* second revised edition, New York University Press, New York, 1941, p. 165. This hearty language has been omitted from the present edition.

tain areas, in complete disregard of Taney's holding in *Ex Parte Merryman* and contrary to the almost universal opinion that only Congress could make the determinations required in Article I, Section 9, which alone could justify the suspension.[17] On May 3, he appealed for 42,034 volunteers to serve for three years, enlarged the authorized size of the Army by 23,000 men and that of the Navy by 18,000; Article III, Section 8, paragraphs 12 and 13 confer exclusively upon the Congress the power to raise and support armies and navies. Moreover, as were revealed in Secretary Stanton's executive order of February 14, 1862, concerning the release of political prisoners, Lincoln closed the United States mails to "treasonable correspondence" and authorized the seizure and detainment by special civil as well as military agencies of persons suspected of engaging in or intending to engage in disloyal and treasonable practices.

Two other notable assertions of the prerogative were made by Lincoln. The first occurred in the Emancipation Proclamation. Lincoln apparently assumed, probably with reason, that Congress could free the slaves only by compensation to the owners. In his conception of the President's war powers, however, he thought he could free any or all of the slaves without compensation if in his judgment this step were necessary to the prosecution of the war. But Article V is unequivocal about due process and the taking of private property without just compensation, nor does it exempt the Commander in Chief from its prescriptions. The second was in connection with the readmission of states to the Union. In his Proclamation of December 8, 1863, he fixed the terms and conditions for the readmission of the rebelling states, except as to the seating of their representatives in the Congress, decision concerning which he conceded belonged to the House and Senate. The Radical Republicans were of a very different mind about the conditions of readmission or, for that matter, about the postwar government of the rebelling states generally, and passed the Wade-Davis Bill in 1864. Lincoln pocketvetoed the bill, explaining that he was "unprepared by a formal approval of the bill to be inflexibly committed to any single plan of restoration . . ." Article IV, Section 3, paragraph 1, gives Congress the exclusive power of admitting new states into the Union. If the rebelling states had been out of the Union, it would seem that only Congress had the power to admit them; if they had not been out

[17] *Federal Case Number 9487* (1861).

of the Union the Wade-Davis Bill was unconstitutional. But in any case, the Constitution hardly contemplated Presidential determination of the policy issue.

Lincoln also played fast and loose, but not tyrannically, with other constitutional limitations, notably civil liberties. Most of his acts were regularized, frequently *ex post facto,* by Congress, by tortured interpretations of the Constitution by the Supreme Court, or, as in the case of the creation of the State of West Virginia by the free consent of a representative body assembled in Richmond under the gleaming bayonets of a military occupation.

V

The assassination of Lincoln ushered in two decades of Congressional terrorism in the national government. For twenty years a cabal of the toughest and most ruthless figures in the history of American politics—men such as Zach Chandler, Oliver P. Morton, Roscoe Conkling, Ben Wade, James G. Blaine, and Henry Wilson—ruled the Republican Party and the Nation. Lincoln's successor, Andrew Johnson, far from providing Presidential leadership, was barely able to keep his office until the end of his inherited term. Grant was no more than the tool of the Radical group in the Congress. Hayes, who brought a shoddy and clouded title to the Presidency, was nonetheless a courageous and an honest man, but he was quickly "contained" by the oligarchy in almost everything except his removal of Conkling's minion, Chester A. Arthur, from the New York Customshouse. James A. Garfield, who was Hayes' successor, was assassinated after six months in office, during which he continued Hayes' assault on Conkling and the spoilsmen. Chester A. Arthur, whom the oligarchy had elevated to the Vice Presidency in consolation for his loss of the lucrative Customshouse, was a traitor to his sponsors, and followed policies substantially similar to those embraced by Hayes. It was during this period that the Pendleton Act was passed. The oligarchy retired Arthur to private life after a single term, despite general public approbation of his leadership, and simultaneously retired the Republican Party from the Presidency.

Grover Cleveland restored the Presidency to the White House, and successfully asserted its independence of the Congress. He was a great Chief Executive, although his first term was largely ineffectual except for the repeal of the Tenure of Office Act, which he secured. Harrison, his successor after one term, was a nonentity in the Presidency, and Cleveland returned to the White House for a strong second term in 1893. His major assertion of the prerogative was in connection with the Pullman strike in 1894 in which, without consultation with Governor Altgeld, he sent federal troops to Chicago to insure compliance with a Circuit Court injunction against the strikers and to assure the prompt movement of the mails and the uninterrupted flow of interstate commerce. This action was sustained by the Supreme Court in the famous case of *In re Debs*. In another important instance, however, Cleveland solidified and made explicit the prerogative in respect of the recognition of foreign states. The Committee on Foreign Relations entertained a Republican resolution to the effect that "the independence of the Republic of Cuba be and the same is hereby acknowledged by the United States of America." Richard Olney, Cleveland's Secretary of State, called in the newspapermen and told them bluntly:

> It is perhaps my duty to point out that the resolution, if passed by the Senate, can be regarded only as an expression of opinion by the eminent gentlemen who vote for it . . . The power to recognize the so-called Republic of Cuba rests exclusively with the Executive. A resolution on the subject is inoperative as legislation, and is important only as advice of great weight voluntarily tendered to the Executive regarding the manner in which he shall exercise his constitutional functions . . . The resolution will be without effect and will leave unaltered the attitude of this Government toward the two contending parties in Cuba.[18]

Cleveland was succeeded by William McKinley. McKinley became involved in a war he did not want. He acquired for the United States a Pacific empire which he did not know what to do with. He espoused a great diplomatic policy—the Open Door—which he did not understand. After four years, six months, and ten days in the White House, he died of an assassin's bullet. He was succeeded by Theodore Roosevelt, of whom Mark Hanna is reputed to have observed, "Now, look, that damned cowboy is President of the United States."

[18] Quoted in Walter Millis, *The Constitution and Common Defense*, The Fund for the Republic, New York, 1960, p. 26.

Ethics and Bigness

Theodore Roosevelt was a strong President, and talked a great prerogative, but his additions to the power of the Presidency were not significant. His only major venture in the expansion of Presidential power was his plan to take over and operate the anthracite mines of Pennsylvania when the hard coal strike of 1902 threatened the economy of the Atlantic and Middle Western states. The mine operators rejected Roosevelt's proposal for the arbitration of the dispute, whereupon he began preparations for sending troops into Pennsylvania, despite a decidedly weak constitutional position under the commerce clause as then interpreted. In the face of this persuasion, the operators capitulated, but insisted that the arbitration commission should consist of one engineer officer, one man with experience in mining, and one eminent sociologist. Roosevelt appointed a railway union man as an eminent sociologist, and the strike was promptly terminated. His grand strategy never saw the light of day, but there is not much doubt about what the Supreme Court of 1902 would have done to it if it had been put into effect.

Roosevelt repulsed overtures for the Republican nomination in 1908, and instead threw his support to William Howard Taft. Taft was a man whose approach to problems was invariably judicial—almost—and except for his domination of English syntax he turned out to be an Eisenhower President and great disappointment to Theodore Roosevelt. Roosevelt gave voice to his displeasure during the Taft administration, even bolting the Republican Party in 1912 to head the Progressive Party ticket, which insured the election of Woodrow Wilson. Afterward, Roosevelt in his *Autobiography* classified Taft as a "Buchanan" President, which drew from his fellow expresident the rather waspish observation that:

> My judgment is that the view of . . . Mr. Roosevelt ascribing an undefined residuum of power to the President is an unsafe doctrine and that it might lead under emergencies to results of an arbitrary character, doing irremediable injustice to private rights.[19]

And at another place in his book he said:

> I may add that Mr. Roosevelt, by way of illustrating his meaning as to the differing usefulness of Presidents, divides the Presidents into

[19] William Howard Taft, *Our Chief Magistrate and His Powers*, Charles Scribner's Sons, New York, 1925, p. 144.

Unsettled Limits of the American Presidency

two classes, and designates them as "Lincoln Presidents" and "Buchanan Presidents." In order more fully to illustrate his division of Presidents on their merits, he places himself in the Lincoln class of Presidents, and me in the Buchanan class. The identification of Mr. Roosevelt with Mr. Lincoln might otherwise have escaped notice, because there are many differences between the two, presumably superficial, which would give the impartial student of history a different impression. It suggests a story which a friend of mine told of his little daughter Mary. As he came walking home after a business day, she ran out from the house to greet him, all aglow with the importance of what she wished to tell him. She said, "Papa, I am the best scholar in the class." The father's heart throbbed with pleasure as he inquired, "Why, Mary, you surprise me. When did the teacher tell you? This afternoon?" "Oh, no," Mary's reply was, "the teacher didn't tell me—I just noticed it myself."[20]

VI

Woodrow Wilson carried the actual powers of the Presidency to far greater lengths even than those exercised by Lincoln. His contribution to the prerogative lies primarily in the demonstration of the degree to which Presidential power can be expanded when the President is concurrently strong as legislative leader, strong as head of the party, and strong as a leader of the nation. Unlike Lincoln, Wilson never openly flouted the Constitution, although in the Vera Cruz incident and the punitive invasion of Mexico he skirted the rim of unconstitutionality. During World War I, when his powers were at their maximum, he operated entirely under legislative authorizations plus his own entirely uninflated view of his powers as Commander in Chief. The most important sources of authority were a series of War Powers acts which empowered him to: 1. take over and operate the railway and water transport systems; 2. take over or regulate all shipbuilding facilities in the United States; 3. prohibit or regulate all exports; 4. raise an army by draft; 5. establish transportation priorities; 6. regulate and control the activities of enemy aliens; 7. take over and operate telephone and telegraph facilities; 8. reallocate functions in the executive branch; 9. regulate the foreign language press in the United States; 10. censor and control all communication with foreign coun-

[20] *Ibid.*, pp. 143 *et seq.*

tries. In addition, the Lever Act of August 10, 1917, empowered the President to: 1. regulate the importation, manufacture, storage, mining, and distribution of any articles essential to the prosecution of the war; 2. requisition food, fuel, and other supplies for public use in connection with national defense; 3. purchase, store, and sell certain foods; 4. fix wheat prices, in accordance with a statutory minimum; 5. take over and operate factories, mines, packing houses, pipe lines, and similar facilities necessary to national defense; 6. regulate the production, sale, distribution, and storage, and fix the price of coal and coke; 7. prohibit or regulate the use of food materials for the manufacture of alcoholic beverages.

Whether the Congress had the authority to confer powers plainly in contravention of the Constitution—to delegate to the President authority which the Congress itself does not possess—is beside the point. President Wilson's wartime leadership is as clear and convincing an assertion of the prerogative as is afforded by either English or American constitutional history. And if the prescriptions of DORA bore more heavily on our British cousins than did its American equivalents, this was merely a function of proximity to the theater of war.

Wilson was succeeded by Warren G. Harding, and Harding, who died after two years and five months in the White House, was succeeded by Calvin Coolidge. Coolidge did a great deal for the prerogative of the Governorship of Massachusetts during the Boston police strike, but he left no such comparable imprint on the Presidency. Herbert Hoover, who was elected in 1928, was an executive of great ability, but he was the victim of an economic depression and his own political philosophy. He lasted one term.

Franklin D. Roosevelt expanded the prerogative power of the Presidency in peacetime more extensively than any prior or subsequent incumbent to date. Like Wilson, he depended heavily on his authority as Congressional leader, leader of the party, and leader of the nation, to support his claims to power, and generally moved, until close to the end of his second term at least, in accordance with legislative authorization. But the assertion of the prerogative was no less significant by reason of his initial care in its exercise. Indeed, his *bête noire* turned out to be not Congress but the Supreme Court. During the Hundred Days, it is not too much to say that the President united in all save a formal sense the full executive and legislative powers in his own person. The Congress was a rubber stamp. The Congress knew it, the people knew it, and even the Republican floor leader in the House, Snell, urged his fellow Republicans to support the emergency banking bill because "the house is burning down, and the President of the United States says this is the way to put out the fire."[21]

Roosevelt's first major act after taking the oath was to close the banks—under authority allegedly derived from the 1917 Trading With the Enemy Act which remained on the statute books, despite a Circuit Court opinion that the section was "probably repealed." This went into effect at 1:00 a.m. on March 6, and not a single bank in the country opened its doors that Monday morning. He then called a special session, and the following Thursday he sent to Congress legislation for licensing the reopening of those banks with sufficient liquidity to operate. Just where Congress obtained this power over other than national banks is not clear, but in any case the power was delegated to the President before the sun went down that day. The next day he sent up, and was granted, a request for authority to cut government expenditures up to 25 per cent of appropriations. On March 16, he sent up the A.A.A. legislation, which Congress passed on May 12. On March 21, he sent up a public works bill calling for appropriations of more than $3,000,000,000, for the establishment of the Civilian Conservation Corps, and for relief grants to the states. On March 29, he sent up the Securities and Exchange Commission legislation. The National Industrial Recovery Act became law on June 16, 1933. These are a few of the major pieces of legislation enacted by Congress in accordance with the desires of the White House, practically all of which extended Presidential power to objects not hitherto touched by executive, or even national, authority. And although the honeymoon eventually ended, and Congress became less alert in responding to the President's requests, throughout his first term he managed to secure practically anything he desired.

It was the Supreme Court, which threw out large parts of the A.A.A. legislation and forced a radical revision of the President's plan for dealing with the agricultural segment of the economy, and which killed the N.I.R.A. outright—although the Blue Eagle was a sick bird long before the Court delivered its *coup de grâce*—that checked the extension of the prerogative. In the Hoosac Mills Case, invalidating the "Triple A" processor tax, the Court said Congress had invaded the

[21] Quoted in Milton, *op. cit.*, n. 8, p. 258.

reserved powers of the states. In the Sick Chicken Case, which threw out the entire N.I.R.A. code system, the Court said Congress had delegated power without erecting proper standards for its use.

Roosevelt's attack on the Court is regarded in some quarters as his major political failure. But the results hardly justify this evaluation. To be sure, he did not get the authority which he desired to bring the Court into the twentieth century by appointing additional justices with modern ideas, but he did get a retirement system for judges which, within a very short time, gave him enough new appointments so that the Court no longer imposed an obstacle to the peaceful revolution he was seeking to bring about. Like the South Carolina Nullificationists, the defenders of the status quo for the Court may have won the applause, but the President won the ball game.

It is interesting to note that during the early years of the Roosevelt Administration the Court, speaking through Chief Justice Hughes, attempted to formulate a concept of emergency power that, while clinging to the notion of constitutional omnicompetence, did seek to square the facts of what the Congress and the President were doing—with the full assent of the electorate—with judicial theory. In *Home Building and Loan Association v. Blaisdell,* the Court said:

> Emergency does not create power. Emergency does not increase granted power or remove or diminish the restrictions imposed upon power granted or reserved. The Constitution was adopted in a period of grave emergency. Its grants of power to the federal government and its limitations of the power of the states were determined in the light of emergency and they are not altered by emergency. What power was thus granted and what limitations were thus imposed have always been, and will always be, the subject of close examination under our constitutional system.
>
> While emergency does not create power, emergency may furnish the occasion for the exercise of power. "Although an emergency may not call into life a power which has never lived, nevertheless emergency may afford a reason for the exertion of a power already enjoyed." Wilson v. New, 243 U.S. 332, 348. The constitutional question presented in the light of an emergency is whether the power possessed embraces the particular exercise of it in response to particular conditions. Thus, the war power of the federal government is not created by the emergency of war, but is a power given to meet that emergency. It is a power to wage war successfully, and thus it permits the harness-

ing of the entire energies of the people in a supreme cooperative effort to preserve the nation. But even the war power does not remove constitutional limitations safeguarding essential liberties. When the provisions of the Constitution, in grant or restriction, are specific, so particularized as not to admit of construction, no question is presented. Thus, emergency would not permit a state to have more than two Senators in the Congress, or permit the election of President by a general popular vote without regard to the number of electors to which the states are respectively entitled, or permit the states to "coin money" or "to make anything but gold or silver a tender in payment of debts." But where constitutional grants and limitations of power are set forth in general clauses, which afford a broad outline, the process of construction is essential to fill in the details . . .[22]

The opinion of the Court is ingenuous but not convincing. "Two" Senators, in Article I, Section 3, is specific, but "The powers not delegated . . ." in the Tenth Amendment is only a broad outline. This position is difficult to sustain.

In the immediate preWar period Roosevelt was less careful about legislative authorization and clear constitutional sanction for what he considered acts of necessity. While his experience in dealing with the domestic emergency had produced an extraordinarily wide range of discretionary powers, of which he was never reluctant to make the broadest possible reading, they were by no means equal to some of the maneuvers he undertook in getting the country ready for the inevitable war from the invasion of Poland in 1939 to the day of infamy in 1941. His first important act following the invasion of Poland was the declaration of a "limited" national emergency. The notion of a "limited" national emergency was a Rooseveltian creation; it had hitherto been unknown to American constitutional or statutory law. The practical consequence of the proclamation of the emergency was to call into operation Presidential powers stemming from unrepealed emergency legislation from World War I and even earlier, so that the President might start expanding the peacetime Army and Navy without exciting the populace or incurring the charge that he was warmongering. The Lend Lease Act, the occupation of Iceland, the Atlantic Charter, the initiation of convoys, and the extension of the neutrality patrol almost to the English coast, the "shoot at sight" order,

[22] 290 U.S. 398 (1934).

all skirted the rim of legality, and there can be little question that the destroyer deal violated the Constitution and the statutes, as well as a number of established principles of international law.

In addition to the resurrection of long dormant legislation passed in previous periods of national crisis, new laws were enacted giving the President vast authority. In the immediate preWar period, the Lend Lease Act of March 11, 1941, was perhaps the most important. In the immediate postPearl Harbor period the First and Second War Powers Acts of December 18, 1941, and March 27, 1942, as well as the Emergency Price Control Act of January 30, 1942, added new areas of Presidential power. The Lend Lease Act was probably the broadest delegation of spending power to the executive by the legislature since the barons wrested Magna Carta from King John at Runnymede. As originally enacted and extended it gave the President authority to turn over billions of dollars worth of goods to any country whose defense he regarded as vital to the safety of the United States. Under this Act Edward Stettinius gave away over $50,000,000,000 to some fifty countries, in some of which the Fulbright students and professors have not gotten to the bottom of the local currency credits which the program created even yet. The two War Powers Acts were grab-bags covering such miscellaneous subjects as administrative reorganization for war, censorship of overseas communications, alien property, defense contracts, penalties for priorities violations, trading with the enemy, government property acquisition, and free postage for the armed forces. The Second War Powers Act contained also the sanction for the control and supervision of the national business and industrial establishment; it provided:

> Whenever the President is satisfied that the fulfillment of requirements for the defense of the United States will result in the shortage in supply of any material or any facilities for defense or for private account or for export, the President may allocate such material or facilities in such manner, upon such conditions and to such extent as he shall deem necessary or appropriate in the public interest or to promote the national defense.[23]

The Emergency Price Control Act gave the President, on the finding of necessity, authority to bring any commodity within the price con-

[23]LVI *Stat.* 176.

trol system of the OPA, and to set prices for the commodity in accordance with certain ranges specified in the statute. Rationing, which was of course essential to effective price control in an economy of scarcity, was sanctioned by Title III of the Second War Powers Act cited above. Many other acts, such as the Selective Service Act, conferred important powers on the President, but these were not different in kind from authority exercised in previous emergencies.

Roosevelt expressed his views of the prerogative in a message to the Congress demanding repeal of the prohibition against putting ceilings on food prices until they had reached 100 per cent of parity, embodied in the Emergency Price Control Act of 1942:

> I ask the Congress to take this action by the first of October. Inaction on your part by that date will leave me with an inescapable responsibility to the people of this country to see to it that the war effort is no longer imperiled by threat of economic chaos.
>
> In the event that the Congress should fail to act, and act adequately, I shall accept the responsibility, and I will act.
>
> At the same time that farm prices are stabilized, wages can and will be stabilized also. This I will do.
>
> The President has the power, under the Constitution and under Congressional Acts, to take measures necessary to avoid a disaster which would interfere with the winning of the war . . .
>
> The American people can be sure that I will use my powers with a full sense of my responsibility to the Constitution and to my country. The American people can also be sure that I shall not hesitate to use every power vested in me to accomplish the defeat of our enemies in any part of the world where our own safety demands such defeat.
>
> When the war is won, the powers under which I act automatically revert to the people—to whom they belong.[24]

Roosevelt's words were not idly chosen. He is asking here not for the delegation of legislative powers to the executive, but that Congress in its representative capacity concur in the mode of exercise of powers which the President holds in trust from the people. This is the quintessence of the prerogative, and nothing that Justice Davis in *Ex Parte Milligan* or Chief Justice Hughes in *Home Building and Loan Association v. Blaisdell* say can make anything different of it. Moreover, the powers, in the hands of the President, as Roosevelt makes abun-

[24] Quoted in Rossiter, *op. cit.,* n. 11, p. 268.

dantly clear, are the product of the emergency, and remain with him only for the period of the emergency, whence they revert to the people.

Congress knuckled under, and the President never had occasion to carry his threat into execution. But as Clinton Rossiter has rightly observed:

> Even though this unique assertion of presidential emergency power remained in the form of words and was never transformed into deeds, it is still of considerable significance for the doctrine here expressed that the President's initiative is this nation's ultimate weapon of national salvation. The President's power to act as a dictator in time of crisis may henceforth be regarded as a gift from the sovereign people of the United States![25]

Walter Johnson quotes a Democratic politician to the effect that "Harry Truman, of all the Presidents I have known, could do the big things in the biggest way and the little things in the littlest way."[26] In evaluating his role as Chief of State we are primarily interested in two of the big things he did in a very big way indeed. The first was his commitment of United States forces in Korea in 1950. While public and even general Congressional opinion supported the decision of the President, the specific action undoubtedly skirted the edges of constitutionality and established new benchmarks for the assessment of the Presidential prerogative. Senator Watkins of Utah asked whether the President should not have consulted Congress before ordering the Air Force and the Navy into combat in Korea. Senator Kem of Missouri wanted to know if the President had arrogated to himself the authority to declare war. Senator Taft of Ohio liked nothing about the President's action. He dissented vigorously from the "bungling and inconsistent" policies of the Administration. He thought Acheson should resign since the President's reversal of the Secretary's Far Eastern policies in effect discredited him. He also thought that the Secretary had encouraged the North Koreans to think the United States would not take action in the event of the invasion of South Korea. In short, the Administration had "produced" the Korean crisis. The Senator, moreover, challenged the constitutionality of the President's decision in committing forces in Korea. Even under the United Na-

[25]*Ibid.*, p. 269.
[26]Walter Johnson, *1600 Pennsylvania Avenue*, Little, Brown and Company, Boston, 1960, p. 223.

Unsettled Limits of the American Presidency

tions Charter, he believed, forces could not be committed without prior Congressional authorization. "If it is what it appears to me," he said, "it is a complete usurpation by the President of authority to use the armed forces of this country." But even Taft wound up by saying that if the President had asked him for approval, he would have voted to authorize his actions. Senator Wherry, after demanding Acheson's resignation and calling on the President to consult Congress if any large scale commitment of ground forces in Korea were undertaken, ended up supporting the decision. In the long run, it appears that the President may, under obligations undertaken under the Charter of the United Nations, commit American troops abroad without consulting the Congress. In any case President Truman did, and to a police action that is accounted statistically as the fourth most deadly war in American history.[27]

Truman's second major assertion of the prerogative had a less auspicious outcome. On April 3, 1952, Philip Murray, president of the United Steelworkers of America, called out his men on strike, effective April 9, after management had turned down a wage and benefit adjustment proposal of the Wage Stabilization Board. The President had three alternatives: 1. to invoke the Taft-Hartley law against steelworkers and against his political ally, Murray, who had already postponed the strike for ninety-nine days at the request of the government; 2. to seize the steel mills; 3. to make a deal with management and grant a substantial increase in steel prices. Truman chose the second alternative, and on April 8 ordered the Secretary of Commerce to occupy and operate the mills. The next day he reported his action to the Congress, which maintained a discreet silence. The operators obtained a temporary injunction from the District Court of the District of Columbia on April 30, which was stayed on the same day by the Court of Appeals. The Supreme Court called up the case on certiorari on May 3, bypassing decision by the Court of Appeals, and held the action of the President unconstitutional. The Court split six to three, and the six justices voting against the constitutionality of the seizure all wrote separate opinions; they were all against it, but they could not agree on why they were against it. Chief Justice Vinson wrote a dissent supporting the seizure,

---

[27] The best account of the making of the decision to intervene in Korea is Glenn D. Paige, *The United States Decision to Repel Aggression in Korea*, Harvard University Program in International Relations, Cambridge, 1956, mimeo.

in which Justices Reed and Minton concurred. The six majority opinions may be summarized as follows: 1. Justice Black was against the seizure because he could find no statutory or constitutional grant of power supporting it; 2. Justice Burton was against it because the President could have invoked Taft-Hartley; 3. Justice Frankfurter was against it because it seemed to represent the assertion of an undefined power, of which he could not discern the limitations; 4. Justice Clark was against it because the seizure did not meet the procedural requirements of the sections of the Selective Service Act of 1948 which provided for seizure when producers failed to supply necessary defense material; 5. Justice Jackson was against it because he thought the decision should be made by the Congress; 6. Justice Douglas was against it because he thought it impaired the system of checks and balances. Chief Justice Vinson and Justices Reed and Minton were in favor of the seizure because they thought the President's responsibility to see that the laws were faithfully executed implied the choice, within reason, of the means. "Flexibility as to mode of execution to meet critical situations is a matter of practical necessity . . ."[28]

President Truman, of course, had done exactly what President Roosevelt had done before him. In the seizure of the strikebound Federal Shipbuilding and Air Associates plants in 1941—before Pearl Harbor—the President deliberately sidestepped the inadequate language of Section 9 of the Selective Service Act as well as the Property Requisitioning Act of 1941, and relied upon his independent power to commandeer. The plain fact is that the majority of the Court impaled themselves on the horns of a purely academic dilemma. The United States was at war in 1952. To be sure, war had not been declared—it was that kind of war. But the gravity of the emergency existed without regard to the formality of Congressional action decreeing a state of war. The powers of the President derive from the facts, not from the formalities. And the Congress had plainly recognized the existence of an emergency in its support of the President's commitment of troops in Korea. But Roosevelt's bright new justices were a decade older—and apparently more than a decade wearier in 1952.

President Eisenhower has raised no issue of the prerogative. Richard Neustadt sums things up in these words:

[28]The legal aspects of the steel seizure are thoroughly covered in Alan F. Westin, *The Anatomy of a Constitutional Law Case,* The Macmillan Company, New York, 1958.

Unsettled Limits of the American Presidency

It is natural that Franklin Roosevelt, hungry for the Presidency's power as his birthright, should exemplify the man who helps himself. It is ironic that a Truman, who felt no such hunger and laid claim to no such birthright, still created from his background, and his heroes, and his reading, an image of the office that impelled him toward self-help. It is an equal irony that Eisenhower, hailed by commentators and by voters (and by many intellectuals) as quite uniquely qualified for power in the Presidency, was turned away from self-help by his very qualifications. Only an extraordinary politician could have managed to exploit the opportunities for influence created by the presence of a hero in the White House. But had Eisenhower been a man of politics he never would have come there as the hero that he was. And being what he was, he looked at his presence there through the eyes of an *anti*-politician. There can be little doubt that he exchanged his hero's welcome for much less than its full value in the currency of power. But how could Eisenhower have done otherwise? His image of himself in office dictated the terms of that exchange.[29]

VII

In practically all the momentous decisions of American politics, and in all the vital decisions of national survival, the President stands as a lonely dictator whose lonely word, in the ultimate determination, must decide the issue. And there is nothing that can be done to change in any fundamental way what Dean Rusk has perceptively labelled his "unbearable responsibility."[30] Because the nature of the American Presidency has become so peculiarly the product of modern national, and especially international, political and social organization, there can be no appeal to the familiar devices of a bygone day for mitigating and relieving the President of his massive liability. There was a time when the enhancement of popular sovereignty—the maximization of public participation in decisionmaking—was an effective counterweight to almost any excess in the concentration of political power, but none would today suppose that public participation could significantly improve the quality of the decisionmaking process or relieve the President of the consequences of decisions. Indeed, the relevance of popular participation in the making of decisions of this generation is in inverse

[29] Neustadt, *op. cit.*, n. 7, p. 180.
[30] Dean Rusk, "The President," 38 *Foreign Affairs* 355 (April, 1960).

proportion to the momentousness of the issue. The doctrine of the separation of powers, upon which the Founding Fathers relied so heavily in the framing of the Constitution, can no longer produce much more than impotence before the great crises which this nation, and most nations, must face almost continuously in the modern world. The extension of the franchise—the notion that the cure for democracy is more democracy, which is itself a derivative of a bad translation of the Latin phrase, *similia similibus curantur*—is always a good thing, but it has nothing to contribute to the amelioration of the unbearable responsibility. Nor does the reinforcement of the representative character of governmental institutions seem to be specially relevant to the problem with which we are confronted. Indeed, most of the momentous decisions lie in the area of compulsory bipartisanship, and bipartisanship is a device that minimizes the influences of representative organs since by definition it excludes the Great Debate, except perhaps in Presidential years, and even then not on the floors or in preparation for the decisions of the representative organs.

A good case may be made, of course, for the impossibility of balancing representativeness and efficiency within the context of the Presidential system. From this position some students have found it a short step to the advocacy of parliamentary government—British parliamentary government, that is—and the abandonment of the Presidency as the institution has developed in the United States. Curiously enough, little attention has been given to the possibility that in the United States parliamentary institutions might take a turn similar to those of France rather than those of Great Britain, just as in Latin America, for example, presidential institutions turn out quite differently from the way they operate in the United States. Indeed, the probability is that the admirable characteristics of British parliamentary institutions which so consistently intrigue—and mislead—American students of government derive less from the political mechanics of British governmental arrangements, which we could imitate, than from the character of the British people, which we cannot. An election in Britain returns a party to power; an election in the United States returns people to power, who may succeed in forming a united Congressional party, but are more likely to achieve only a loose agglomeration capable mainly of organizing the houses and capturing the committee chairmanships. And as long as our federal institutions persist, the center of electoral gravity

Unsettled Limits of the American Presidency 287

will not reside in the national party organizations or even within the significant influence of the titular party leaders.

Walter Millis has a rather more realistic view of the situation, which he describes in these words:

> ... Today, every problem has to be elaborately "staffed" by the bureaucracy. In our own democracy, as in totalitarian Russia, government has become a congeries of coalition of vast bureaucratic empires, unavoidably run, as armies must be, by hierarchies of staff. The responsible decisionmaker, at every level, becomes a prisoner of an intricate, interlinked, but insufficiently coordinated staff system. As policy rises toward final formulation, the staff work and staff advice is supposed to be combined and weighed and balanced into an ever closer approximation of the common good, finally presented to the President for his determination.
>
> It is a system with many defects. Responsibility for decisions which are *not* made—often more significant than those which are—is concealed and lost in its intricacies. The ablest younger talents are likely to be stultified and wasted. The good ideas, which often originate near the bottom, undergo a fearful struggle in rising to the top in effective national policy. The interests of the great bureaucratic empires are usually sharply in conflict; but the machinery for combining them into broad policy serving the national interest or the common good is defective or non-existent. It is the executive heads of the empires who form the topmost tiers of Presidential advisers; meeting together in the National Security Council that are supposed to reach the broad and balanced view. But inevitably each is bound by the bureaucratic interests and staff policies of his department; to depart from the policies evolved by it would destroy morale and reduce the departmental work to chaos. The President, carrying a lonely responsibility, sits in a lonely isolation above the clashing bureaucracies with almost no source of broadly independent advice or even of independent information.[31]

A little later he formulates five basic guide lines which he suggests that any inventions or innovations in improving the quality and enhancing the responsibility of the momentous decisions must follow:

> 1. Foreign and military policy must be unitary; this means that in the last analysis it must be dictated by a single governing authority and is beyond *direct* popular control. (It is, of course, subject to a wide

[31] Millis, *op. cit.*, n. 18, pp. 34–35.

variety of popular influences and pressures, but they are disorganized, incoherent, and too often ignorant.)

2. In a free society external policy must, however, be dictated in accordance with the governing authority's best possible estimate of the common good.

3. This estimate will never be more than approximate. But the approximations will be improved to the extent that the ruler is informed, as free as possible from any personal interest or special bias, and capable of weighing the widest possible range of opinions, interests, goals, and political and power relationships.

4. The modern democratic Executive has felt a pressing need to institutionalize this process of approximating the common good and formulating his policy decisions in accordance with it. Historically, parliamentary institutions arose in response to this need on the part of the early national monarchs. In the extraordinary complexity of our time, parliamentary or representative institutions no longer suffice; and the bureaucratic staff system, by which we are now largely governed in fact, has tended to supplement and in a measure to replace them. No doubt the staff system is subject to refinement, but today it seems clearly inadequate to its basic task of ascertaining the common good. If the process is to be satisfactorily institutionalized, some new institutions may be required.

5. To succeed, such institutions cannot look toward introducing more direct popular control into the formulation of external policy. They must be based upon a clearer analysis of the processes by which policy is in fact now formulated, a determination of what and where the weaknesses are, and their eradication.[32]

Millis's essay is entitled "The Constitution and the Common Defense," and he properly addresses his remarks to military and foreign policy decisionmaking. But as he would doubtless be the first to admit, the line between foreign and domestic policy, and between military and civil policy, is getting harder to draw with each passing day. His benchmarks have applicability far beyond the Pentagon and Foggy Bottom.

Concerning the new institutions that may be required more effectively to fulfil the quest for the common good we have an embarrassment of riches. Senator Jackson's Subcommittee on National Policy Machinery of the Senate Committee on Government Operations has

[32]*Ibid.*, pp. 35–36.

stirred up a mare's nest of nostrums and devices, all guaranteed to cure almost any conceivable ailment of the policy process.[33] About the only common ground amongst all the current proposals is a profound disenchantment with the performances of the National Security Council, the Joint Chiefs of Staff, and interdepartmental coordinating committees in general. Some critics, including the present writer, would prefer to shoot the piano player. The NSC, over the years, has had more than its share of the ablest federal administrators in its service at the nonpolitical level. They have not been able to make anything of it, and I am inclined to think that the heavy preponderance of evidence suggests that nobody can make anything of it. Even Senator Jackson, no volunteer for the firing squad, admits that the NSC "is, after all, simply an interdepartmental committee at the Cabinet level. It therefore shares the familiar limitations of the committee system, with its builtin bias toward compromise and lowest common denominator solutions, toward busy-work and, when attendance grows too large, toward speechmaking rather than a real exchange of views." It is equally evident that the Joint Chiefs, as presently constituted, does not compose a military general staff, that it is totally incapable of operating as a major military policy planning body, and that it suffers from precisely the same builtin biases toward compromise and lowest common denominator solutions as does the NSC. It, too, is simply an interdepartmental committee, not even at the Cabinet level.

Some of Senator Jackson's communicants want to patch up the NSC, by sharpening the definition of its functions, encouraging debate rather than concurrence in its proceedings, and emphasizing the primary role of the Secretary of State in the formulation of national security policy. The argument is reminiscent of the patch-it-up, make-do approach to the chaotic financial administration of the federal government adopted in the face of the strictures of the First Hoover Commission in 1949, and probably offers about as much hope of significant improvement. Other commentators want to create a super-Secretary of State—an "Overlord" in the British terminology—to supervise all aspects of foreign relations, political, military, and economic. Still others think a peripatetic Minister of Foreign Affairs of Cabinet rank might permit

[33]"Organizing for National Security," *Interim Report of the Committee on Government Operations, United States Senate, Made by its Sub-Committee on National Policy Machinery* (Washington, D.C., January, 1960).

the Secretary of State to stay at home and devote more time and attention to the infighting. Some hardshell realists think matters might be improved if Defense, State, and the Joint Chiefs would enter into diplomatic relations and exchange Ambassadors. A joint career system for senior military and diplomatic officers is suggested in some quarters. A new and additional Presidential annual report to Congress, on "Requirements and Resources" has found support amongst those who think the Economic Report is worth making. Still other communicants want "think groups" established under more or less independent auspices to perform the functions of Tribal Elders.

Millis,[34] in a more expansive mood, gives some consideration to the revival of the Senate's constitutional "advisory" function, but admits that doing what Washington was unable to accomplish calls for considerable ingenuity. The fact is that what makes the Senate powerful also makes the Senate useless as an advisory council. And in a somewhat exuberant tolerance for "world peace through the rule of law," he even gives house room to the notion of a policy body along the lines of the Supreme Court, which in due course, and with the assistance of an as yet undiscovered John Marshall, might achieve something more than parity as a policy body and reduce the President to the executive secretaryship of a superior power. This, he suggests, undoubtedly with his tongue in his cheek, strains the probabilities. He points also to the Constitutional Council, established in the French Constitution of 1958, which serves a purpose in bridging the gap between "the legislative vote and the executive determination of the common good."

In another vein, he points to the National Academy of Sciences, and suggests an analogous Academy of Political Affairs, composed of the nations' most senior and experienced statesmen and political scientists —former Presidents, Presidential candidates, former Secretaries of State, and nongovernmental experts of similar stature. But the picture of Dwight D. Eisenhower taking advice from Dean Acheson escapes me altogether.

However, Millis does report on the views of George F. Kennan, communicated in a private discussion, in the following words:

> A rather different approach to the whole problem has been advanced. In this view, all such suggestions as have been discussed are attempts

[34]Millis, *op. cit.*, n. 18, pp. 38–41.

to find a unitary solution for what are in fact a series of quite different problems, each requiring its own answer. The inquiry turns around at least three different defects in the existing situation: the want of facilities for providing the President with confidential advice, broadly based and outside the bureaucratic battle; the want of facilities for responsible public debate of foreign policy and the generally low quality, ignorance, and frivolity of such debate as goes on; the want of appropriate means to aid and guide the President in the few greatest, most solemn decisions of state.

To meet the first defect, it is suggested, the President should have a Policy Planning Staff in the White House, on the model of the Policy Planning Staff established in the State Department in the Truman administration. Such a staff should not consist of more than twelve or fifteen people at the outside; these should be free of any particular departmental orientation. They would try to take long-range as well as broad views, to foresee troubles, to devise policies. Their one function would be to assist the President with the independent and unbiased advice which he now has too little means of getting. Their operations would, of course, be completely confidential. Neither the existing White House staff, enmeshed in operating tasks, nor the National Security Council staff system, in general formed out of the departments, can perform this kind of "thinking" function. This proposal is recognizable as a modification of the suggestion, discussed above, of promoting the Secretary of State into a chief Cabinet officer or quasi-prime minister.[35]

I am not a member of Kennan's faction of the party in respect of disengagement and some other substantive aspects of foreign policy, but I am more than happy to find myself following his line of thought in respect of administrative matters. His suggestion puts the problem squarely into the context where it belongs, and the only context within which the major issues we have been discussing can, in my judgment, be solved. In an aide-mémoire which I prepared for Senator Jackson's staff following an extended discussion with them on August 28, 1959, I summarized my own views as follows:

> 1. The Executive Office, which was designed by the Committee on Administrative Management to provide the President with a major source of policy and planning advice responsible directly to him, does not at present contain the elements of policy planning adequate to the requirements of the executive establishment. This situation is due in

[35]*Ibid.*, pp. 43-44.

part to Congressional action in refusing or depriving the President of facilities for policy planning in respect of personnel and manpower and resources allocation policy, and in part to the change in the world position of the United States, which has made defense and foreign relations considerations of prime importance in almost every policy decision.

2. Policy planning in the defense and foreign relations area are presently ineffective in part because they take place at levels subjecting them to service or departmental stresses at the fact-finding and fact-interpreting stages, which result in weak and indecisive staff papers. These staff papers are further emasculated by cabinet committee consideration which mainly reflects the extent to which Secretaries and Agency heads are the prisoners of their subordinates.

3. I doubt very seriously whether foreign policy planning can be conducted within a Department which is responsible for the administration of a limited segment of our international affairs, or whether defense policy planning can be conducted in a "departmental" environment that maximizes service competition, or for that matter can be conducted anywhere except in the office of the Commander-in-Chief.

4. In thinking about the provision of adequate policy planning and coordinating facilities, I visualize the Executive Office reorganized into units headed by responsible directors, with advisory non-statutory cabinet committees as decided by the President, as follows:

(a) *Office of Defense Policy*. The director would be the chairman of the Joint Chiefs, and the staff would be composed in part of service personnel co-opted by the President and in part of such civilian advisers and assistants as he might deem necessary. It would report exclusively to the Commander-in-Chief, and would be responsible for strategic policy planning and assignment of service missions.

(b) *Office of Foreign Policy*. The director would be appointed by the President, and the staff would be composed in part of personnel co-opted by the President from the Department of State and other governmental agencies, and in part of personnel brought in from outside the Government as the President deemed appropriate. It would report exclusively to the President, and would be responsible for foreign policy planning.

(c) *Office of Resources Policy*. The director would be appointed by the President, and the staff would be composed of a permanent technical and administrative group, plus personnel co-opted by the President from other governmental agencies as circumstances required. It would report exclusively to the President, and would be charged with the formulation of policy in respect of national resource application—

i.e., distribution of GNP, including allocation to public and private sectors, policy in respect of stockpiling or substituting of scarce materials, policy in respect of resource utilization and development, etc.

(d) *Office of Economic Policy.* The director would be appointed by the President, and the staff would be composed of a permanent technical and administrative group, plus personnel co-opted by the President from other governmental agencies as circumstances required. It would be charged with the duties of analysis and advice prescribed in the Employment Act of 1946.

(e) *Office of Budget and Administrative Policy.* Continues the functions of the Bureau of the Budget.

(f) *Office of Personnel and Manpower Policy.* To perform functions under personnel and manpower legislation currently under consideration in the Senate.

VIII

The problem of the unsettled limits of the American Presidency arises, in a discussion of the balancing of representativeness and responsibility, almost exclusively within the context of emergency situations. No matter how well the Presidency is staffed, or how adequately the function of advice is conceived and executed, the definition of an emergency and the selection of the method of meeting it is a decision which can be made only by the President himself. There are, of course, all varieties and grades of emergencies. A commonsense test of the gravity of an emergency might involve three elements:

1. Are the foundations of the state threatened?
2. Is the emergency so nearly unique that prior constitutional or statutory authorization is inadequate?
3. Does the emergency arise so suddenly or when the country is so divided that there is too little time or too much risk involved in awaiting the operation of constitutional or legislative processes?[36]

An affirmative answer to all these questions would undoubtedly create the presumption of the necessity for whatever action is necessary to meet the emergency. This action, by definition, can be taken only by the President. He alone commands the requisite firepower. The Congress is incapable within its own resources of bringing physical

[36] In this section I follow closely lines of argument adduced in an as yet unpublished manuscript of my colleague, the late James Hart.

force to bear on any situation. The Court is by nature unable to deal with other than justiciable situations; if the judicial process is invoked in a great emergency through a proper case or controversy the Court may protest or it may sanction, but it cannot be expected to override Presidential action.

In these circumstances the President is securely impaled on the horns of a dilemma. He must either take illegal action to preserve the state, or by inaction incur the risk of destroying the legal order itself. In the best of circumstances he may hope for no more than that legislative or judicial action, or public opinion, will retroactively sanction what he has done. But this does not remove the stain of illegality in the action at the time it was taken. Some students of Presidential power are so sensitive to the exigencies of the rule of law, and so allergic to the notion of Presidential action outside of or in opposition to the law, that they prefer almost any sort of prospective authorization—which in practice must amount to a grant of unlimited discretion to the President to act in what in his discretion he considers a great emergency—which will avoid the commission of an illegal act. Perhaps the classic example of such a prospective authorization is that contained in Article 48 of the Weimar Constitution under color of which von Hindenburg, the Wooden Titan, put the German organic law at the disposal of Adolf Hitler in the consolidation of his totalitarian grip upon the German people.

There is no corresponding provision in the Constitution of the United States of America, although intimations of the fundamental idea involved may perhaps be read into the assertions of Theodore Roosevelt concerning Presidential power, and seem to be implicit in Assistant Attorney General Baldridge's argument in the Steel Seizure Case, in which he observed: ". . . it seems passing strange to say that faced with such a grave situation of national concern there is no power any place in the Government to meet it."

In the debate on the Jay Treaty in 1796 Fisher Ames, in what Channing has called one of the greatest speeches ever made in Congress,[37] designated great emergencies as "extremes." In answer to the question as to what would happen if the treaty should destroy the nation, Ames replied that the Jay Treaty posed no such threat, and added: "Extremes

---

[37] Edward Channing, *History of the United States,* The Macmillan Co., New York, 1908–27, volume IV, pp. 145–146.

Unsettled Limits of the American Presidency

speak for themselves and make their own laws." And at another place in his address he said: "Extremes are not to be supposed, but when they happen they make the law for themselves." It would be difficult to discover a more portentous commentary on the limits of Presidential power.

"Extremes are not to be supposed." Here Ames seems to be saying that not every hard case, not every crisis, nor even every emergency is an extreme. "Extremes speak for themselves." Here he is telling us how to recognize extremes. When they occur men will act upon them, without arguing whether they are in fact extremes or what may legally be done to meet them. The test, in short, is a pragmatic one; there was no effective opposition to Roosevelt's seizure of the Federal Shipbuilding and Air Associates plants in 1941 because men recognized the extreme, but there was effective opposition to Truman's seizure of the steel mills in 1952 because men did not recognize the extreme. "Extremes make their own laws." In the administration of government, and perhaps in human affairs generally, *sui generis* situations do arise which have only this in common, that they compel a choice between breaking the law and saving the nation or obeying the law and destroying the legal order.

The function of law is twofold. It limits, and at the same time it authorizes. But an authorization given to the President to do whatever in his unlimited discretion he regards as necessary to the preservation of the state whenever he in his unlimited discretion considers the life of the state to be endangered, hardly leaves any room at all for the operation of the limitational principle of law. The mere existence of such an authorization, even in the hands of a "Buchanan" President, would be an open invitation to the use of extraordinary powers in ordinary emergencies, and would render inevitable the erosion of law as limitation and of the principle of the rule of law itself. The rule of law, it may be remarked, is an institution of continuing value. It is fundamental to the preservation of an agreed and protected range of human freedom, of justice in the form of equal protection and non-discriminatory government, and of that security which derives from the reasonable predictability of individual obligations and privileges in the social order.

At the same time, it is important to realize that the law was made for man, and not man for the law. It is a means, and not an end. And the very ends to which it is a means are endangered when the life of the nation is threatened. None would suppose that it is more important to preserve the law than to preserve the nation, since such a notion involves an inevitable paradox, and certainly the moral duty of the President to keep within the law ends at the point where the existence of the legal order itself hangs in the balance. The reign of law, moreover, is not an absolute. Only recurring and predictable situations can be brought within the rule of law, and great emergencies do not fall within this definition. Any attempt to save law as authorization in great emergencies by providing virtually unlimited discretion to the President destroys law as limitation altogether. Whatever this may do for the face of the principle of the rule of law, it makes a mockery of its substance.

Great emergencies and legal order stand in an incompatible and mutually exclusive relationship. The frank admission of this incompatibility greatly clarifies the essential problem of the limits of Presidential power. It recognizes the existence of the prerogative, but puts the burden of proof in its invocation squarely upon the President who attempts its exercise. Moreover, it puts claims of power based upon the precedents of Lincoln, Franklin Roosevelt, and others in their proper perspective; they cannot be regarded as legal precedents, and are moral precedents only in the face of a great emergency.[38]

It is not to be supposed that the existence of even a great emergency can make an illegal act legal. Hence the President who invokes the prerogative must contemplate that his record will be stained with illegality unless and until he receives retroactive validation for the acts which he has committed outside the law. In some cases this validation after the fact may be sanctioned by the legislature, in a very few cases perhaps by the courts, and in a certain number only by public opinion or even by history. Dicey tells us that the British Parliament, as a

---

[38]Justice Frankfurter, in his opinion in the *Steel Seizure Case,* attempted to discount the precedents in 1941 by saying that these "isolated instances do not add up either in number, scope, duration or contemporaneous legal justification, to the kind of executive construction of the Constitution revealed in the Midwest Oil Case. Nor do they come to us sanctioned by long-continued acquiescence of Congress giving decisive weight to a construction by the Executive of its powers." But what action in a great emergency would? And by definition great emergencies do not provide reiterative evidence; if they did they would not be emergencies. Justice Jackson likewise attempted a differentiation between the prior unsanctioned seizures and the Truman steel seizure, but without notable success. See Westin, *op. cit.,* n. 28, pp. 147 and 153.

legally sovereign body, may make any act legal which was illegal at the time it was committed. Now the American Congress is not the British Parliament, and is in no sense a sovereign legal body, but it is reasonable to suppose that as long as it does not run afoul of constitutional limitations, such as the interdiction against *ex post facto* laws, it may retrospectively sanction any act of the President which it was within the power of Congress prospectively to authorize.

But this solves only part of the problem. I have previously pointed out that Congress has on occasion appeared to delegate to the President powers which the Congress itself is not authorized to exercise. Every great emergency involves not only executive incursion into the powers of Congress, but executive incursion into the vast range of normally reserved powers and on occasion the invasion of the area which, under our Constitution, the powers of no government are supposed to reach. This is the ultimate area of the prerogative. Congressional approval of acts in this area, even retroactively, may have probative value for the moral judgments of history, but they cannot affect the illegality of the acts themselves. Only history can cleanse this stain.

Corwin tells us that ". . . the blended picture of executive power derivable from the pages of Locke, Montesquieu, and Blackstone is of a broadly discretionary residual power available when all other governmental powers fail . . ."[39] If we may understand the word "power" to mean not legal competence, but rather the residual moral responsibility for doing whatever must be done to preserve the state, the quotation provides us with a very accurate and precise description of Presidential power in great emergencies. Lincoln recognized this responsibility, and its concomitant power, in his message of July 4, 1861, when he accepted the moral obligation to preserve the Union even if he had to break the law in doing it. In the final analysis, this is the only ground upon which Lincoln's conduct in his great emergency, or the conduct of any President in any great emergency, can be brought within the bounds of social approbation.

Comment by Paul H. Appleby:

About the need for improvement in Presidential staff resources there can be no informed disagreement. What to do is very hard to say, however. I have never known planning of systematic sort to be effective in directly influencing programs of our government when "planning" was assigned to anybody or person reporting—even theoretically—to the President from a situation removed from direct operating responsi-

[39] Corwin, *op. cit.*, n. 3, p. 10.

bility. The National Resources Planning Board made important contributions to our public literature, over the long run no doubt has exerted considerable influence in a general way, and may have hastened some specific actions in a shorter run. The Council of Economic Advisors has made extremely useful compilations of data and participated in some useful public discussions. But I believe that in both cases Chief Executives concerned have been concerned almost exclusively to pass their product on to the Congress. I believe this was to have been expected, regardless of the identity of the particular Presidents. Agencies of this kind will have more direct influence on policy if attached at lower levels in the hierarchy at points where control and policy influence is located for coordinating purposes. The Budget Bureau is operationally effective because it has operating responsibilities of a rather crucial sort. Presidents will be better served when the Bureau has some real competition in other staff arms with operating responsibilities to which program planning would be no unharnessed attachment.

Secondly, I have seen two or three examples of special staff at the White House or Executive Office level assigned to single fields—fields coterminous with a single agency. In each instance they resulted chiefly in undermining and confusing responsibility. To serve the man at the head of a pyramid, the supporting staff should have a pyramidal function—seeing everything of some one or more functional kinds throughout the scope of the government or a considerable part thereof. If these staff entities haven't pretty clear coordinating responsibilities, they will be found to have no excuse for being in the programmatic action field.[40]

[40] For comment by David B. Truman, see pp. 467–468.

CHAPTER XVIII

Ethics and the Federal Regulatory Agencies

By LOUIS J. HECTOR

THERE IS today almost unanimous agreement that the federal regulatory agencies face serious ethical problems, that they have failed to cope with these problems, and that something must be done about them. Only the agencies themselves and their most doctrinaire supporters deny this. And even within the agencies there is much unspoken doubt and concern.

There is also today general agreement on the symptoms of these ethical problems of the agencies—undue subservience to the wishes of the regulated industry, or to particularly powerful sections of the industry; acceptance of extensive hospitality and sizable presents from the regulated; discussions of litigated cases, and reception of arguments and factual presentations, in circumstances which cannot be considered judicial; subservience to the views of individuals who exert influence on reappointment or on appropriations; failure to establish general policies with the result that each case is decided on an *ad hoc* basis and need not be related to prior decisions; failure of commissioners to assume personal responsibility for the opinions which are supposed to enunciate the reasons for their decisions; and many others. The catalogue of current complaints is long.

More generally, there are symptoms of a pervasive ethical laxness. The malfeasance exposed by Congressional investigations and the resulting resignations are made even worse by the fact that the resignations are usually forced over strenuous protests of innocence. The calm with which some commissioners, some members of the regulated industries, and even some members of Congress seem to feel that there is nothing seriously wrong with present practices, all indicate a serious misunderstanding of proper governmental standards.

I have heard a commissioner on an important regulatory agency say that he wishes his agency would stop the practice of individual commissioners signing their opinions because this tends to make the commissioners unpopular with the losing parties. I have heard a commissioner of another agency say that if he cannot circulate freely within the regulated industry and talk to anybody about any subject at any time, then he might as well "resign and turn the job over to a bunch of ribbon clerks."

These are not isolated examples. Anyone who has spent much time around the regulatory agencies in recent years—unless he has become hardened to expect the worst—has been disheartened at the general low caliber of the top personnel and the general lack of feeling for ethical problems, or even the simple proprieties.

So we all agree, there is a problem. And we all agree on what the problem is, or at least on what the symptoms of the problem are.

Here agreement ceases.

There are almost as many cures for the ills of the regulatory agencies as there are critics. Let me list just a few of the cures to suggest their diversity:

1. *Detailed written codes of ethics, either passed by Congress or promulgated by the agencies*

Many codes of ethics or principles of practice have been proposed in the past several years. They are all either so general as to be useless or so specific as to be unworkable.

Many agencies have already had for many years broad, highsounding codes or principles of practice. The present troubles show that they have accomplished little or nothing. They could not, since they turn around phrases such as "undue hospitality" and "sway the judgment by attempting to bring pressure or influence," which can be contracted or stretched to suit almost any situation.

The most serious problems of the agencies lie with the commissioners themselves and the commissioners are the ones who interpret these broad phrases in the codes of ethics. I know of no case of a commission in recent years drastically tightening up its own standards or penalizing one of its own members for unethical conduct. Ethical codes which must be policed and interpreted by the same small group that drafts them and to whom they apply, are not likely to be of much effect.

The effort to be more specific in a code of conduct, on the other hand, bogs down in a welter of details and exceptions which reflects the fact that each agency has its own particular types of proceedings, and its own peculiar modes of pressure and improper approach. Seemingly firm principles of conduct, when they are qualified sufficiently to permit general application, turn out to contain so many exceptions that they give no support in practice. They are like stage scenery—firm and strong until you try to lean on them.

The effort to draw up codes of ethics, however, will not stop, and it is good that it will not. For while it does not produce a final product of much value, the process of investigation and study does succeed in driving a lot of game out of the underbrush and does attract general attention to the problems of the agencies. But it is not the answer to those problems.

2. *Appoint better men to the agencies*

This is the opposite of the first approach. It assumes that the whole trouble lies in the character of the men appointed, and that if really good men were appointed there would be no further ethical problems. Those who make this argument point to the great days of various agencies, such as the S.E.C. when it was run by William Douglas and Jerome Frank; the I.C.C. when it was run by Joseph Eastman; the C.A.B. when it was run by Welch Pogue and James Landis.

It is of course true that the present caliber of regulatory agency members is low and that better men would help enormously. But let us look at these golden ages of the agencies more closely. Were they really the result of good men, or of the times and the circumstances?

Upon careful examination, the great days of the agencies turn out to be periods of great enthusiasm immediately following the passage of a new regulatory act or periods of great national crisis, when the commissions were staffed with men excited and passionately devoted to the implementation of the new regulatory scheme or to meeting the crisis. And in the golden age of an agency we almost always find, too, a chairman of great ability and authority who in practice runs the agency almost like a single administrator. As far as I can make out, in the great days of the I.C.C. under Joseph Eastman, Eastman was the I.C.C. Certainly William Douglas and Jerome Frank ran the S.E.C. with a firm hand in the great days of that agency.

If these institutions have really worked effectively only in crises and under special circumstances, it is unrealistic to hope that the mere appointment of better men will make them work under ordinary times. Contrariwise it is too optimistic to expect that men of real ability will accept appointment to boards whose continued failure and ethical snarls imply a basic structural flaw.

We need better men, true, but we need better jobs for them to fill.

3. *Make the regulatory agencies conduct their affairs like courts*

Regulators should act like judges, in other words. This is the perennial approach of a section of the American Bar Association and of a group of Constitutional literalists.

This approach has had its successes over the past twenty years, starting with the report of the Attorney General's Committee in 1941, proceeding down through the Administrative Procedure Act of 1946, and various piecemeal reforms since.

But full judicialization of the work of the regulatory agencies has never really been tried. Exceptions written into the law and pragmatic adjustments made by the agencies have permitted them to go about their regulatory business almost as usual under the blanket of judicial trappings. True, these quasijudicial trappings have caused serious delays, and far more important, a general procedural hypocrisy where agencies talk like courts but don't act like courts; but they have not so far completely stopped the work of regulation.

One of the greatest dangers of the present debate over the regulatory agencies is that it might whip up such a fervor of protest over present procedures that full judicialization would be seriously tried. I know one very distinguished practitioner before the agencies who is resigned to this. It is an alternative we will probably have to exhaust, in his view, even though we know it won't work. For the judicial approach, if taken seriously, would surely kill whatever remaining advantages the agencies now have.

If all of the work of the regulatory agencies is judicialized, then they must become courts in truth and must act like courts. And when they are made into courts we will find a vast amount of necessary regulatory activity which simply will not fit into a judicial scheme: either because it is so unimportant and voluminous that it can only be handled administratively, or because it is the type of multicentered, flexible problem—what Michal Polanyi calls "polycentric"—which can be handled only by prolonged, informal conferences, exchanges of views, and directed staff work.

In the unlikely event that the regulatory agencies were fully judicialized, before very long the great bulk of the regulatory job would have to be taken away from them. Where then would such matters go? To a new independent regulatory agency to start the same problems all over again? Or to an executive agency where they would be handled in the normal executive manner? My own answer is to the executive which is set up to handle such matters. But in either event, the great bulk of the regulatory job would be done outside the judicial framework which is supposed to solve the ethical problems. To achieve increased morality by judicialization of the agencies, therefore, means either to create a hopeless procedural log jam or to increase morality for only a small part of the present regulatory functions.

4. Decrease the judicialization already imposed on the agencies and permit them to operate flexibly

This argument is the classic doctrine, held so widely during the 1930s, that the answer to all governmental regulatory problems is an independent multimember agency which combines executive, judicial, and legislative powers and which because of this very flexibility does an efficient, effective job. Such a program may increase the efficiency of the agencies, though I strongly doubt it, but it is certainly not a solution for their ethical problems. It is just this kind of agency which has got into so much trouble.

I have never been able to understand how the proponents of more informal procedures than we have today are able to argue that this would solve the ethical problems of the agencies, except possibly that the resulting diminution of red tape would encourage men of greater ability to serve on the agencies and these would presumably be men of higher ethical standards. What I suspect is that this line of thought is but another form of harkening back to the golden age of the agencies. The agencies used to work—the argument runs—before all this judicial procedure was imposed upon them; but they don't work now; so the answer to the ethical problems, as to all the other problems of the agencies, is to go back to the way we used to do things. This is often accompanied by side remarks that things aren't really as bad as they are made out, that the present attacks are politically inspired, or that the critics of the agencies don't believe in effective government regulation of business.

One of the greatest problems of the regulatory agencies is the very fact that they are independent bodies responsible to no one and with great flexibility. In this respect, they are almost unique. The legislative branch is elective; it must face periodically the judgment of the American voter. The executive is elective at the top and in its upper reaches, appointive at the pleasure of the elected. While Presidents do not always act swiftly to rid their houses of undue influence and unethical conduct, still they do have this power and when the conduct of their subordinates becomes embarrassing, they exercise it.

The regular judiciary is not elective; it is appointive and it enjoys life tenure. But the judiciary is under the constant scrutiny of a large bar of fellow lawyers and judges. Our courts exist in a public world of judicial morality, elaborated and strengthened over the centuries. Any pattern of favoritism or injudicious procedure is quickly known to a large and vigorous group who will protest loudly.

Contrasted with the publicity in which our courts move, the regulatory agencies work almost in secret. Almost no one except the regulated industry and the bar or the agency understands the complex cases that come before them. The public which is theoretically a part of every agency procedure, is represented only by the staff of the agency, and that staff is not likely to set up a public cry over what they conceive to be the prejudice or unfairness of their superiors. Even Congress, with its Oversight Committee and special investigations, never really comes to grips with the substance of agency action, largely because of the enormous complexity of agency proceedings.

The agencies are in reality their own masters, scarcely responsible to anyone. When an issue is burning, when a legislative policy is newly formulated, when we are in a national crisis, when an agency is staffed with zealous men working hard under the common direction of a forceful chairman—then indeed the multimember regulatory agency with flexible procedures may well do the job. But for everyday governmental purposes, when the crisis has passed or when the enthusiasm of the new legislation has died down, then such agencies become mere power vacuums, where decisions are determined by the competing forces of a few intensive pressures rather than by careful factual investigation and clearly formulated and articulated public policies. In such a circumstance, morality can easily suffer.

In addition to these four general approaches to the ethical problems of the regulatory agencies, we should note the innumerable gimmicks offered to solve the problems—longer tenure, shorter tenure, higher pay, retirement pay for life at the end of a term, judicial robes, and so on. It is my belief, however, that none of this is going to advance us very far toward a solution until we have a clearer view and a clearer general agreement on the nature of the problem. Such a view will show, I believe, that the bipartisan, independent, multimember regulatory agency, contains inherent contradictions which lead to serious moral and ethical problems when too much strain is placed on it.

Of course any vocation, any role in life, poses contradictions which can issue in moral or ethical dilemmas. The legislator has always to face the problem of whether he represents his constituents best by doing what in his judgment is good for them and the nation, or by acting merely as the spokesman for their own particular interests and prejudices. In personal life, a father is called upon constantly to decide whether he should be dictator, counselor, friend, or teacher to his children—all of which roles are necessary and inescapable to fatherhood. We certainly therefore cannot say *a priori* that the independent regulatory agencies cannot work merely because they involve differing activities which lead to differing standards and therefore conflicts of ethics. Such conflicts are the common lot of mankind.

The questions rather are these: How radical are these conflicts? How serious are the ethical dilemmas which they pose? And even should these ethical dilemmas prove very serious indeed, cannot the positive virtues of the independent regulatory agency justify them?

It seems to me sometimes that those who are trying to make sense out of the problems of the regulatory agencies are always battling two opposing dogmas: the first says that the constitutional and moral dilemmas are so great that there should never be any combination of executive, legislative, and judicial power in any agency for any purpose under any circumstances. (It is surprising to find how many lawyers still believe this in their heart of hearts.)

The second dogma says that the independent regulatory agency is the most flexible and efficient instrument of government ever devised, that it is the answer to all complicated government problems, and that if some ethical problems have arisen these are a small price to pay for the marvelous efficiency of this instrument of government. This second view was of course gospel to many of us during the 1930s. It is today frozen into a dogma. It has recently indeed been enshrined in a massive four volume treatise on administrative law. It is a depressing, though salutary, experience to see what one's youthful enthusiasms look like when they are pushed to their logical extreme and embodied in a four volume work replete with footnotes. It is ironic that the independent regulatory agencies—those marvelous instruments of social revolution—are today defended chiefly by the industries they regulate and by the writers of standard legal treatises.

The first job to be done in solving the problems of the regulatory agencies is to avoid these twin dogmas—to root out the lingering traces, if we can, from our own thinking. We must get out from under the mountain of rhetoric and controversy which overlays the subject, and get down to the practical problem of trying to strike a balance between the need for a separation of powers and the requirements of efficient government. We must take a realistic view of human nature and conduct as it develops under prolonged conflict of responsibilities. And today particularly, we must remember the necessity for strong executive direction of all sections of our federal government.

It seems to me that we should ask ourselves these questions:

1. *In what fields do multimember regulatory agencies exercising several different types of governmental power seem to operate both efficiently and ethically?*

We think first, of course, of the many claims commissions of one sort and another which over the years have investigated and adjudicated conflicting private claims in specialized fields. Such agencies rapidly become specialized courts with their own investigatory facilities, deciding cases in accordance with reasonably clear policies. They have historically done an efficient and satisfactory job.

On the other hand, consider the N.L.R.B., an agency which in its youth was a storm center of controversy and criticism. This, too, works well. The Board today administers a statute rendered reasonably clear and precise by amendment and judicial interpretation. It has become a specialized court which has attached to it a specialized investigatory, administrative, and prosecutory staff. However one may feel about recent labor legislation, any criticism must be directed to the legislative policy not to the N.L.R.B. Both labor and management agree generally today, I feel, that the Board does its job ethically and efficiently.

The same is true of the S.E.C. Complex though its work is, it administers a statute whose basic purpose is simple—to compel truth-telling in the securities market—and it has done a good job at this. It has not been as active in investigation and prosecution in recent years as it might have been, but this may reflect a lack of appropriations and a generally tired commission. With a little prodding and a little more money there is no reason why it should not do a good job.

Within the executive branch itself there are countless areas where legislative, executive, and judicial powers are combined. The thousands upon thousands of decisions made under the Social Security Act and under the various veterans acts represent the quasijudicial application of policies developed by the agency itself and then carried out through its administrative instrumentalities. And they do a good job.

In any area where combined executive, legislative, and judicial power —whether or not this is exercised by an "independent" agency—seems to be working efficiently and with no major ethical problems, we should leave it alone. To impose on such agencies a general doctrinaire scheme of separation of powers would be to deprive ourselves of the fruits of all the pragmatic experimentation of our federal government in recent decades.

2. Having seen where agencies exercising combined powers function satisfactorily, let us then ask: Where have they failed to work?

The major failures seem to be the Federal Communications Commission, the Federal Power Commission, the Interstate Commerce Commission, and the Civil Aeronautics Board. Some of their problems briefly sketched are these:

a. These agencies operate under broad multipurposed statutes which require the agency itself to determine general regulatory and economic policy. Over the long run, they have not succeeded in this. The agencies consist of co-equal commissioners who are spared the necessity of hammering out any broad, articulated policies because they are permitted to evolve it case by case as they go along. This has been argued to be a virtue; but in practice it has resulted in a completely *ad hoc* type of procedure and in prolonged conflicts over economic and regulatory policies within the agencies which have made impossible consistent and effective regulation.

b. These multimember commissions are charged not only with formulating policy and deciding specific cases, but have extensive various administrative duties. Every student of the agencies has been appalled to find how much time is taken up at the top level by arguments over administrative details which any one of the commissioners could solve quickly if he were acting alone. They are not solved by the multimember group because each member of the group is constantly thinking of the conflict of policies between himself and the other commissioners and the very important effect that administrative details have on the implementation of those policies.

c. All of these agencies are charged with the duty of promoting the progress and stability of an industry and at the same time policing it. The result is that there has been very little forceful policing. This is a conflict of purpose which when pushed to extremes can well become a serious ethical conflict. How much law violation can an agency overlook because the violation may be helpful to the economic stability of the industry?

d. The commissioners of these agencies are called upon to familiarize themselves in detail with the industry which they regulate, to participate in numerous informal conferences with members of the industry to acquaint themselves with the problems involved, to help meet crises within the industry by flexible, informal government action. And yet these same commissioners from time to time are expected quickly to climb up on a bench, don a judicial mantle, and decide litigated matters between members of the industry or between the industry and the public solely on the basis of a formal record, as if they had never known anyone in the industry or heard anything about it.

Human nature does not fit such a pattern. Every commissioner I have known well, if he took his job seriously, has either tried so hard to be a good administrator that he jeopardized the judicial character of his decisions in litigated cases, or has tried so hard to be a judge that he has failed to acquaint himself in sufficient detail with the industry which he regulates.

3. *Having found out where the trouble spots are, we should then ask ourselves: Why do we not put these areas of regulation under single administrators within the executive branch of the government?*

Is it because these decisions are too important? Certainly the decisions of the F.C.C. on channel allocations are no more important in terms of private rights and interests than are the decisions of the defense establishment on which plane to build or which missile system to adopt. Certainly the location of air routes by the C.A.B. is not of greater importance to the public than the location of highways by the Bureau of Public Roads. The subsidies paid out by the Department of Agriculture exceed many times over all subsidies paid out by any regulatory agency. The Pure Food and Drug Administration within the executive branch of the federal government has a far more delicate public responsibility than any independent regulatory agency. All these jobs have not been always done well within the executive; but they have certainly been done as well as by the independent agencies. And the effect of Presidential oversight and control—to the extent that it exists—has been almost uniformly for the good.

We have a good recent example of how a regulatory job, hopelessly bogged down in the uncertainties of an independent agency, can be accomplished efficiently and fairly by a single administrator. The air safety functions of the C.A.B. were transferred to an executive agency, the F.A.A., on January 1, 1959, and in the year and a half since air safety has made more progress than in the previous decade.

It will be protested that there are certain cases which are so delicate—the allocation of television channels between competing applicants, for instance—that they must be decided by a judicial-like body. This may be. It is my conviction, however, that if we take up each regulatory function in turn and ask the question: "Is it really true that this cannot be done through normal executive procedures?", we will find a very small body of decisions indeed which we must entrust to special courts.

There may be some tasks which Congress and public opinion are not ready to entrust to the executive. In such cases, special courts should be created, or the problems should be given to existing courts.

Such cases should be rare, however, and should be confined to problems which can actually be decided on a truly judicial basis. It is my belief, for instance, that the formulation of an air route pattern can never be accomplished judicially. The allocation of routes to competing applicants perhaps can. Any such matters, if they are going to be judicialized, should be given to courts staffed by men who serve long terms and who have no duties other than judicial ones.

This in brief seems to me the direction of the best current thinking on the regulatory agencies.

Ethical problems in government will always be with us. We need not, however, create agencies which are, by their very organization and conflicting duties, almost occasions of sin. The independent regulatory agency, charged with the duty of promoting and prosecuting a single industry, formulating the general policies to be applied to that industry, and adjudicating cases involving the industry, is just that. Placing these responsibilities in the executive branch and in specialized courts will not solve forever the ethical problems involved in regulation, but it will bring them within the customary machinery of government and make them far more easy to control.

CHAPTER XIX

Congressional-Executive Responsibility

By THOMAS K. FINLETTER

1. Executive-legislative relations are a problem only in countries where there is self-government. Authoritarian countries have no such problem because they do not and cannot have a functioning legislature. They may have the appearance of one but not the reality, because a legislature is the instrument by which representative government, that is self-government, lives.

Self-government in a nation-state cannot be absolute. The town meeting can have absolute self-government because it is small enough. All the adults of a town can take part in the lawmaking. Not so when the government has to deal with bigger areas. The size of the electorate compels the first limitation on absolute self-government which is that the deciding body must be representative, that is, must be a legislature.

But this is only the beginning of the loss of control by the people of the decisionmaking process, as the unit of government grows in size and the problems, domestic and foreign, become more complicated and difficult. These bring about great transfers of power to the Executive, and corresponding reductions in the influence of the people and their representative body. Since 1919, which was the high point of representative democracy in the West, the trend has been strongly toward executive domination and legislative weakness. Representative democracy now exists in only a few of the countries of the world, mainly in the West, and even there the challenges of today's world are so serious that the course is toward ever growing power in the Executive. The "judgment of irrelevance" has been made in many countries against representative democracy, even in its own homeland of Western society.

In a sense Asia and Africa are going in the opposite direction, away from colonialism and toward independence and self-government. This trend though will be spotty. A few of the newly independent countries will work out reasonably good systems of representative rule; but a few only. It looks as though most will have to pass through periods of executive domination. It will take a long time of reducing illiteracy, increasing standards of living, and elementary training in the complicated business of self-government before we can expect anything like functioning legislatures in most of these areas.

2. Russian and Chinese Communism and the resulting world struggle between the Communist and nonCommunist systems are the greatest force working for worldwide executive domination and the world defeat of self-government. In a sense the executive-legislative relationship, in those countries which have a legislature, is the microcosm of the world struggle. There is an interaction between the capacity for self-government in each of the free countries and the struggle of those countries with the Communist menace. The ability of the nonCommunist world to beat back the Communist threat will vary directly with the capacity of the nonCommunist countries to make their institutions of self-government work well.

It therefore seems worthwhile to discuss the executive-legislative relationship in the United States.

3. Such an examination should start from the premise that never before in our history has the United States faced problems as serious as those which now confront it. The combination of the Asian and African revolutions, the population explosion, the hostility and will to dominate of Russia and Communist China, and the existence of weapons of war capable of destroying continents—these, coupled with the responsibility for leadership in which we find ourselves, make it obvious that we very much need the most effective government we can get.

4. Some parts of our machinery of government are far short of this standard.

For example, the lack of responsible debate on national policies.

Debate is the device by which a representative democracy sharpens its policies and brings the wisdom of the community to bear on them.

Debate is at its best when it is responsible, as it is in a parliamentary democracy such as exists in the Scandinavian countries, the United Kingdom, the British Dominions, and some other states. The discussion of issues in a parliamentary democracy is for the highest stakes. If it is convincing enough it can bring about a change of government.

In the American Presidential system, with its fixed four year elections, debate is for almost no stakes at all. Rarely does the discussion in the Senate or House of Representatives bring about important changes in the policies the Administration wants. This is particularly so in matters of foreign relations and defense where, Constitutionally, the President has the dominating role in the decisionmaking. Treaties are but a small part of foreign policy and Congressional control of appropriations and legislation is negative only. On occasion Congress does increase the requested appropriations for defense, but without effect because the Executive will not spend the money Congress is trying to force on him. The President is not likely to allow Congress to use a power, in this case the right to initiate policy, which he conceives of as his under the Constitutional doctrine of the separation of powers. In domestic affairs Congress has more influence, but even there the initiative, by custom, is largely with the Administration and the fact that the President is elected by a nationwide vote gives him the upper hand even in those domestic matters where legislation is necessary. And it must be remembered that the largest part of policy, even in domestic matters, lies in execution and not in new legislation or even in appropriations.

But, this is not to say that public opinion is unimportant. The President and the Administration cannot go much beyond what the public opinion understands and approves. This is the great role of debate—to put both sides of a problem to the people, to insist on explanations of what is proposed and why, to make the Administration justify what it is planning, and if the explanations are good, to get the approval of national opinion for it.

The lack of debate is therefore particularly damaging in a fast moving phase such as the present. Now is the time for decisions which if they are to meet unorthodox conditions must themselves be unorthodox. And unorthodox solutions need explaining, if the people are to like them. Of equal importance, it is often desirable to show by debate of an inadequate proposal that another, and perhaps an unorthodox program, is what the Administration should be working for.

For example: we now need an imaginative foreign aid program and we will not get it without support from public opinion; and we will not have this support unless the policies are explained to the people and they agree that we should have it. Responsible debate is far and away the best way of making the explanation.

We do not have this kind of debate under our system. Speeches may be made on the floors of the Senate and House. Private foreign policy groups may discuss the problem. Magazine articles and books may be written. But none of these gets the arguments over to the people the way responsible debate does in the parliamentary system where the eyes of the nation are on the leaders of the opposing parties in the proceedings in the recognized forum for such a debate—the Legislature—and when the result of the talk may well be a decision which of the two parties is to form the next government.

So, too, with many other important national issues. We have been saddled with policies about Formosa and toward Communist China which many people believe are damaging and indeed dangerous to the United States. Not only has there been no debate, but rational discussion of these subjects has been tabu. Pressure groups and demagogues of the type which have done our country so much damage in recent years (with the help of some well meaning citizens) have put over on the country the peculiar notion that is is wrong even to discuss the Formosa problem or the future of our relations with Communist China. This tabu has lessened somewhat in the past year or so, but it is still there, to the damage of our country. All this would have been much less likely, in fact I do not think it would have been possible, if there had been a forum and a system for responsible debate in our government.

The same can be said of many other issues now confronting the United States government—our Near East policy, Berlin, the future of Germany, disengagement versus status quo in Eastern Europe, the conditions of our relations with Central and South America, and particularly those two great problems of our time: United States military policy and United States policy for the issue of war or peace, of disarmament, of whether we are doing what we should be doing to save this, or the next, generation of Americans from a hydrogen war.

One would have thought that those who are worried about our military policy *vis-à-vis* Russia would have been able to make some dent in public opinion on this issue. The fact is they haven't. Few issues need sharpening, and the public in on them, as much as this one. But for all the able opposition in the Senate and the widespread discussion in the press, our national policy on armaments and on the race for the weapons of the future is about where it would have been if there had been no discussion of the subject at all. The reason is that the debate is not responsible, in the sense I have used it above.

So, too, with the problem of war or peace. Some of us believe there is a great opportunity and a moral responsibility for the United States, acting through its government, to lead in daring and imaginative policies to control the weapons of modern war, and thereby to give mankind a chance to live. Many men in the Congress feel this deeply, including influential members of the Senate. But can they get a debate on this subject going? Can they force the attention of the American people to it? Can they bring American opinion to demand of its government that it do something on this all important business? They cannot. The reason again is that responsible debate does not exist in the American form of government.

5. The reason for this lack of debate, as I have said, is that an American Administration cannot be put out of office except at fixed four year intervals. The right of impeachment practically does not exist; it is too violent a weapon to be useful. Also: the fixed four year term of the Presidential system makes for long periods of power in one party, irrespective of the quality of its leadership or its ability to serve the country. Thus the Republican Party controlled the federal government from 1860 to 1933 with only the Cleveland Administrations and the Bull Moose split and the resulting Wilson victories as the abnormal exceptions. Then, from 1933 came twenty years of the Democratic New Deal—Fair Deal. And—after that we don't yet know the pattern.

There are several reasons for this and some results from it which are not good at this time, when the country needs the best policies and the best men and women in government.

The basic reason for these long periods of one-party rule is that the fixed four year term makes for the avoidance of the issues not responsibly debated from day to day, and the fact that the election will take place on a certain day gives the Administration in office a great advantage. No proper discussion of national issues is possible during the relatively short time between the nominating convention (usually in July) and the election the following November. The election campaign is so heated, is so much of a barnstorming, and is so full of arguments and counterarguments, of slogans and counterslogans, and is so beset by the practitioners of the modern skills of mass persuasion and mass confusion, that it cannot, by any stretching of the facts, be called a serious debate of the policies of the parties or the candidates. The debate of national issues on which the electorate is supposed to give its decision, must take place *before* the nominating convention if it is to take place at all; and as I have said, the American system doesn't provide for such debate at any time.

Recognizing this, the Democratic Party recently tried an innovation for the purpose of getting discussion of national issues in the period between elections. A Democratic Advisory Council was set up, attached to the Democratic National Committee, with the Chairman of the Committee also Chairman of the Council, and with a membership of about twenty-five Democratic leaders, including former President Truman, the Democratic candidates for President and Vice President in 1956 (Adlai E. Stevenson and Senator Estes Kefauver) and several Senators and Governors. The need for some such arrangement was particularly acute in 1957 when the D.A.C. was set up because the federal government was then split between the two parties—the Republicans having the Executive branch and the Democrats both Houses of Congress. As a result the limited debate of our system was even more limited than usual because the Democratic majority in the Congress had all but to abandon its function of opposition, such as it is under our Constitution, and work with the Executive branch to make the government function.

The D.A.C. has done a valuable job of opposition. Its statements have sharpened the issues and have had some effect on the policies themselves. But, good as this opposition is, it is not responsible in the sense in which opposition is responsible in the Parliamentary system and cannot therefore wholly fill this damaging gap in our form of government.

6. The Parliamentary system has avoided these failings of the Presidential system because of a. the great advantage of not having a written Constitution, and b. the skill in the art of self-government of the peoples where the Parliamentary system developed, notably the British.

A written constitution can be changed in minor respects by amendment or by custom but a fundamental arrangement in a written constitution, such as the fixed four year term of the Presidency, cannot be changed either by amendment or by custom. The whole system would have to collapse and a new constitution be adopted as has happened in France, if radical changes are to be made in the structure of government. The amendment for the direct election of Senators is about as far as one can go in formal amendments to the Constitution.

The customary evolution of the British Parliamentary system has made for certain desirable practices which are worth mentioning even though they cannot be brought into our form of government by amendment of our Constitution.

First is this responsible debate we have been talking about. This comes about as the result of the customary right of dissolution—that is, the duty of the Prime Minister when he is defeated on a vote of confidence to advise the Sovereign (who always, because of custom, takes the advice) to form a new government which will have the support of the Commons, or to call a general election for a new Commons. The possibility that a government may be put out of power by a single vote of the Commons produces a three way interplay between the Government, the Opposition, and public opinion, which makes for this responsible debate. This interplay brings about

a. a constructive discussion of public issues;
b. the education of the electorate on such issues;
c. government in accordance with the considered views of the electorate as refined in the debates in the Commons (and to some extent, the Lords).

Such a system can make mistakes but it will not make them because public opinion has not been brought to bear on them or because the government feels that a desirable policy cannot be put into effect because it has not been sufficiently explained to the people—a state of affairs which occurs often in the American system.

The Parliamentary system also trains the future leaders of government. Since the Prime Minister and the Cabinet are chosen from among the Legislature (Commons and Lords), the Commons attracts men and women of the country who want to make government their career; and there they are tested in the full view of national opinion. Their performance in public office, in the back benches, and in Opposition is known and appraised, and when the time comes for filling Cabinet posts, including the top spot of Prime Minister, there is usually little doubt as to who is indicated for office. There is never that improvised and often frivolous choice of candidates for the Presidency and the Cabinet, which happens so much in our system and is a risky and by no means always successful way of choosing the President of the United States and those who are to serve with him in office.

Next: the Parliamentary system is good at the redress of grievances —that is, airing complaints and doing what is necessary to correct the evils which are shown. This was its great historical function. Sometimes it is directed at important national problems, in which case it is but another version of the function of debate in the sharpening of issues. But sometimes it has to do with lesser matters, such as the violation of the rights of some individual or of abuses of power by members of the government, whether of the Executive branch or the Legislature.

This latter also is a valuable function; it plays an important part in maintaining the liberties which the Legislature and the people have fought for over the centuries.

The Presidential system has some devices to protect against abuses by officers of the Executive or Legislative branch but they are not as good as those of the Parliamentary system. The Congressional investigating committees can call attention to derelictions in the Executive branch, and a vote of censure is available to discipline members of the House and Senate. But too often these investigating committees have committed their own abuses; and the vote of censure is too severe a penalty to be effective. Responsible debate for the redress of grievances would have stopped the terrible damage which Senator McCarthy was doing the country long before our system moved in to stop it.

Next: elections in the Parliamentary system are decided more on the issues than in the Presidential system. In the latter, as I said earlier, the fact of the fixed four year term takes the emphasis off the issues and puts it on votecatching appeals. One result is to have the members of the House and Senate elected more on local than on national issues. Another is to have the Presidential choice made not as the result of a preference between different policies of the parties but rather because of the personalities of the rival candidates and the respective party skills (including the amounts of money available) for the business of mass persuasion. It is these factors which have recently brought about the phenomenon of the majority of both Houses of Congress being of a different party than the President even in a Presidential year, a state of affairs previously thought impossible.

7. There are many other differences between the Parliamentary and

Congressional-Executive Responsibility

Presidential systems but these are the most instructive. You will note that all these differences I have discussed have to do with the executive-legislative relationship. Naturally: because this is the point where Authority and Control by the People lock horns.

The British system grew out of a struggle in which the barons, knights, and enfranchised burghers demanded, and got, certain rights from the king. This struggle continued until, with the nineteenth century Reform Acts and the Parliament Act of 1911, the Commons came to represent all the people of the United Kingdom and took over the power of government. The Executive then became the agent of the Legislature—but with one important power of its own which it can use against the Legislature, that is the power of dissolution. Here is a beautiful balance between the two branches of government if one may still regard the Executive as a separate branch. The Legislature is the supreme body, subject only to the people. It can therefore prevent the abuse of authority by the Executive. It cannot abuse its own power; it cannot interfere with strong administration by the Executive when the times call for it; because the Executive's power of dissolution is there to block any such abuse. An election is expensive and it puts the members' seats in jeopardy. Therefore they will not lightly prod the Executive into a dissolution. Also, the electorate will not stand for a frivolous defeat of the government and will not return the members to Commons if they have acted in an irresponsible manner. The result is strong Executive government within a system which debates the issues, brings the people to a considerable extent into the business of government, and at the same time protects their rights and privileges.

The Presidential system gives no such high place to the Legislature. Executive-legislative relations are based on the separation, indeed the conflict, of powers. Madison and others at the Philadelphia Convention of 1788 thought they had set up a blending of the powers, as they called it, rather than the strict separation which Locke and Montesquieu wrote about. But in practice, as the demands for strong federal government grew, reaching their climax in the popular leader Presidents of the twentieth century, the relative power of Congress fell. Congress lacked the indispensable sanction, the power to put the government out of office. From this lessening of the position of Congress came the weaknesses of our system of government. Representative democracy, to be at its best, must put the final authority in the Legislature, subject to the right of the Executive to appeal over the heads of the Legislature to the people.

8. The United States Constitution provides for amendments and there is no Constitutional reason why we could not provide for such a right of dissolution. We could not and would not want to copy the British Parliamentary system but we could make an American version of it. The arrangement would be to give the President (by executive order) and the Congress (by concurrent resolution) each the right to order the dissolution of all three—the Presidency, the House, and the Senate—and to call for an election of all three for a new term of six years—or until another prior dissolution were ordered. This would assure responsible debate, would make the elections more on issues, and would make an American type version of the Parliamentary system. The forms would be different; but the executive-legislative relationship would be in substance the same.[1]

Practically, as I have said, no such amendment is now politically possible. Constitutions don't get amended that way. And I am inclined to think it is a good thing that they don't. Custom is far and away the better method of amendment.

But, you may say, what does one do when custom isn't free to act. Custom can't change the written provisions of the Constitution. Custom can't change the four year term of office for President and the diminished position of the Congress and the lack of responsible debate which came from it. Shouldn't we try for a formal amendment no matter how impossible it seems to get it?

I should like to see such an amendment. I cannot understand why there has been practically no discussion in academic circles of the need for some such change. Perhaps these ideas I have been expressing are wholly wrong. Perhaps there are other changes which should be made which are much better than those I have been talking about. Or perhaps the Constitution is exactly right the way it is. But I don't think anyone will deny that the subject is worth talking about. Surely, with the world the way it is, it is worthwhile looking at our form of government to see whether it is in reasonably good condition to handle the problems which confront it.

[1] I have described this plan in detail in a book called *Can Representative Government Do The Job?*, Reynal and Hitchcock, New York, 1945.

9. One reason for this lack of interest in Constitutional reform is that one worries about any tinkering with the Constitution. Anyone who is familiar with the workings of the United States government at firsthand must be particularly concerned about inadequately thought out changes in the structure of the government.

It may be worthwhile mentioning some examples of reorganization within the Executive branch which show, I think, how subtle and difficult it is to change the structure of government.

My experience with reorganizations in the United States government has not been good: these have had to do with the State Department and the Department of Defense. There was an important reorganization of the State Department at the time I was in it (1941–1944). I will not take the space in this memorandum to go into the details of this reorganization. It is enough to say that until 1943 the structure of the Department was a simple one and that a wholesale revision of it was made in 1943 which added greatly to the number of officials involved with a considerably lessened efficiency in the organization. The basic mistake was the failure to understand that the multiplying of officials with high or medium rank did not necessarily mean either a higher quality in the officials who would occupy these positions or a higher quality of output. Quite the contrary. The State Department reorganization was modelled too much on corporate lines with a resulting denigration of the status of the top ranking officials and the creation of a greater volume of output but with a lower quality. The basic failure was the failure to understand the importance of quality in relation to quantity in output.

Somewhat the same thing happened in the Department of Defense after the enactment of the Act of 1947 which created the separate Air Force. The 1947 Act set up a fairly simple structure with the Secretary of Defense as the chief with three Departments under him (Army, Navy, and Air Force) but with the power of decision in him. If this arrangement had been given a chance, it probably would have worked well. A similar British structure was set up at about the same time and has continued without any change; my impression is that it has been adequate for British needs. However, no sooner had we set up our Department of Defense than we started amending it, with statutes and with reorganization plans. The result is a hodgepodge with no clear theory as to where the power of decision lies and with an abnormal number of Secretaries and Assistant Secretaries in the Department. I understand there are something like twenty-six individuals in the Pentagon with the rank of Secretary or Assistant Secretary. Also, the interrelationship between the four Services, the three Departments, and the top coordinating Department has become so confused and the lines of decision so uncertain that they are in themselves an explanation of the present inadequacy of the Defense program and the great amount of waste in it.

There is no remedy to this except to go back to the most simple structure, a single Department with a single line of authority. Note I say a single Department, not a single Service. The proper lead can be had from the Navy in which there is a single Department with two Services. This formula (one department, several services) can produce the best planning, the best administration, and the best operations.

10. I shall not discuss further these problems of the organization of the Executive branch within itself since this paper is on the broader question of the executive-legislative relationship. I have mentioned them only to show that reorganizations in government are difficult and are not to be undertaken unless the best thought and experience are brought to bear on it. I don't believe the capacity of the American people to organize their government was exhausted in the Philadelphia Convention of 1788 but I do think that, as in 1788, nothing less than the best brains of the country can do the work properly.

We could well start with considerable more concern with this subject in academic circles. Conceivably, if the prestige of academic thinking were to be put back of a Constitutional revision, the people in government would give thought to it. Or, if not that, a good discussion in the academic world might point the way to customary innovations.

11. Custom can do a lot. Custom has already made great changes in the American Constitution, for all that its provisions are rigidly in writing. Indeed the basic concept of the federal government and of the relative powers of the President and the Congress already have been substantially changed by custom.

The original idea was for a federal authority mainly in foreign affairs with domestic matters almost wholly the business of the states. Circumstances, helped by the Supreme Court, brought about customary amendments of these concepts. The authority of the federal government is of a wholly different order from that when the Constitution was written.

The executive-legislative relationship as originally established also has been amended by custom.

The original idea was for a separation of powers, a balancing between the Executive and the Legislature, in which each would check the other so that power would not be abused. The emphasis, except again in foreign matters, was on checking and balancing and the denial of power, all in order not to have abuses of authority such as the men at Philadelphia had seen under the colonial governors and the colonial legislatures of the critical period. Again circumstances, this time helped by some strong Presidents, forced customary amendments. A new type of President grew up.

There were, thus, two concepts of the Presidency. On the one hand were the orthodox Presidents, men who believed in the separation of powers, in checking and balancing, and in working with Congress in common purpose, usually in not too vigorous fashion. Then there were the popular leader Presidents who believed they had a mandate from the people to do what was necessary in the interests of the people. Lincoln was the first, followed by Theodore Roosevelt, Woodrow Wilson, Franklin Roosevelt, and Harry Truman. These men did not believe in being balanced or checked by Congress but, as Wilson said, considered that "the President is at liberty, both in law and conscience, to be as big a man as he can. His office is anything he has the sagacity and force to make it." So believing, these Presidents led the country. They dominated the policymaking power and vastly increased the influence of the President. Occasionally Congress beat them, for the historical struggle is still on, as when the Senate defeated Wilson's effort to have the country play a role in preventing war by collective action. But, on the whole, the popular leaders dominated the Congress.

Now with world problems and demands for American leadership pressing on us as they are, the popular leader President has become standard. No United States government can now function properly under the nineteenth century concept of the President and Congress nicely balanced so that federal power shall be limited.

So, custom can go far in adapting our government to the needs of the country. The important things in determining whether a representative democracy will be as good as it ought to be are the quality of the people in government and in the country, and the policies which they believe in and work for. The substance is more important than the formal structure of government. A perfect Constitution cannot produce a government any better than the people who run it and for whom it is run. And: while a people, through customary action, cannot make any constitution work as well as it should, they can come fairly close to it.

Thus if we look at the history of parliamentary governments after World War I we see that the belief of the time was that this system, which had done so well in the United Kingdom and apparently not too badly in victorious France was to be the model of all the new states of Eastern Europe. We now know that the system failed in all of them. A series of events, many of them beyond the control of the peoples involved, were too much for the new, self-governing constitutions. Even before they were brutalized by the Nazis and by Soviet Russia their parliamentary systems on the British model broke down.[2]

Similarly the American Presidential system spread to nearly all the other republics in this hemisphere. The results have been very different and not always successful—all proving the point that substance counts more than form in these matters.

12. Applying this to the United States, we may generalize that the future of the executive-legislative relationship in this country will vary directly with the success we have in the world struggle of individual freedom versus authoritarianism.

I think it proper to describe the world struggle in this way. To be sure, there is a third force, emerging Asia and Africa, which does not now fit into either category. But the power of the two other world centers (the two Communist empires and Western society—including countries which although not geographically in the West are sympathetically with it) is so great that it seems right to describe the world scene as a struggle between them. It may be that with time, especially if something can be done to prevent hydrogen war and to reduce the excessive influence of modern weapons on the world scene, Asia and Africa will assume a more important relative role than they now do. But for the immediate phase they are only a third force—although a

[2] Arnold John Zurcher, *The Experiment with Democracy in Central Europe*, Oxford University Press, New York, 1933.

most important one which may well become the deciding factor in the world struggle.

This world struggle has considerable influence on the domestic policies and executive-legislative relationship within our own country. The fact of the struggle makes for greater demands on government and therefore for stronger government. It therefore tends to build up executive power and to weaken the legislature in those countries which have functioning legislatures. The problem for many of the countries of the West and of Asia and Africa is whether, granted the demands being made upon them, they are capable of meeting them and at the same time preserving the practices of self-rule which so often seem to interfere with vigorous executive action.

Many countries have already fallen by the way in this regard. And the tendency will be in this direction so long as the conflict continues. If there ever were a final decision in this struggle, the internal arrangements in these countries would follow the major decision. If Communist-Statism wins and becomes the dominating creed of the world, either through force or otherwise, self-government is through and the executive-legislative relationship will be a matter of history only. If Self-Rule wins—and winning would include the acceptance of a diversified world with individual freedom at its best only in the more mature parts of it—then the executive-legislative relationship will continue as an institution with, almost certainly, increasing importance.

13. It follows that the best way to make the American Constitution work and to build a proper executive-legislative relationship is to have the right policies for the present world struggle.

Freedom and self-government will survive only if those who have them can make self-government work well enough i. to defend themselves against physical violence, and ii. to show the world that self-rule can produce as good levels of economic and social wellbeing as the authoritarian forms of government.

I am not arguing that one system or the other must prevail. I have just said that we cannot expect uniformity in the world. Nor do I say that the form of government which is good for us is necessarily good for others. All I am saying is that the peoples who have reached the stage of wanting to govern themselves have got to show that they are capable of protecting themselves in the modern world, of doing this by their own regime of self-government, and that they can do this only by raising the quality of the government which they produce to a considerably higher level than most of them—including the United States—have yet done.

There must be a new insistence on the quality of government we produce, a new impatience and higher standards of the role of the citizen and of the capacity of representative government to govern.

The executive-legislative relationship will be the barometer which will show whether we are winning or losing the battle. If the relationship is such as to insist on strong executive leadership, that is what we are likely to get, and getting it will make us more likely to succeed in the world struggle. And, of course, the reverse is true. A bad or an inadequate executive-legislative relationship which does not bring into government the best we are capable of, will weaken our chances of success. It may even drive us, as it has some other countries already, into taking on the ways of the authoritarians, of getting executive power by denying the legislature and thereby the people, their proper role in government. That way is the road to defeat, either by yielding to the enemy by adopting his ways, or by weakening our strength for the struggle and making us less able to defend ourselves and our way of life. A vigorous peoples' movement, which in governmental terms means a vigorous representative democracy with a well working executive-legislative relationship, is the best way of winning the world conflict.

14. It is beyond the scope of this paper to deal with the substantive problems which the government of the United States will face in the coming decades. We may however generalize to say that the main test is going to be whether the United States is capable of adapting itself to the extraordinarily fast moving problems of this era—whether we are capable of recognizing that this is one of the fastest moving periods of history, of understanding that change is the order of the day, that what is needed of representative government is the ability to anticipate, to shift policies in accordance with the needs which our reason and instinct tell us we have to meet—whether, that is, we are able to adapt our representative democracy—a form of government usually thought of as appropriate for stable and slow moving times—to the incredibly fast moving and dangerous conditions of the present and future. More specifically, the question is whether our slow moving representative type of government is capable of handling the violent

revolutions of today's world which, if not handled, will damage and may destroy our country and our society.

It is not too difficult to identify these revolutions. The most important of them are:

a. The new independence of Asia and Africa and the worldwide spread of the demand for individual rights in all the areas formerly dominated by the Western Powers;
b. The obvious determination of the two Communist empires to achieve military supremacy in this, the fastest moving time of weapons development in all history;
c. The assertion by the two Communist empires that their system of State control can produce standards of living, education, and social wellbeing which cannot be equalled by the free enterprise system or any other system the Western world can develop;
d. The fact that the development of modern weapons has now raised war to such a destructive level that we can no longer afford to continue with a world order in which nation-states have no way of settling disputes other than by war—in short, the necessity to work out at least an embryonic world order which will create a breathing space during which war will not happen, and during this breathing space, to develop a system which will prevent it from happening on any large scale in the future.

These are terrible problems. The mere listing of them makes one despair that any form of government, let alone one committed to the preservation of self-government by the people, will be able to handle them. And yet to handle them is precisely the task which has been put on the United States government. If representative democracy can rise to the level of making a reasonably good try at the solution of these problems, this in itself will force customary changes in the executive-legislative relationship in the United States and in the other leading Western countries of the very highest importance.

CHAPTER XX

The Proper Place of the Political Executive in the Governmental System

By WILLIAM C. FOSTER

BEFORE ATTEMPTING to establish the proper place of the Political Executive in our governmental system it would seem wise to attempt first to describe this special kind of executive and to sort out a few of the tasks at which he will work. I would like to define him as a noncareer executive brought in from private life to head a Government Agency or Department, or to work in a policymaking or top administrative position usually nominated by the President with the advice and consent of the Senate. So the present discussion is confined to the Executive Branch and it generally applies to individuals selected from business or the professions.

Use of such individuals from private life is consistent with our regular process of electing members of the Congress and with quadriennial election of the Chief of the Executive Branch and the Vice President. This periodic exposure of the philosophies and standards and abilities of our legislators and our two top executive leaders to the judgment of the people has demonstrated its wisdom over the 171 years that the system has been operating. It has enriched and protected our democratic process.

Now in order to help the President discharge his tremendous responsibilities, it is essential that he have the right to select as his close executive colleagues those whom he thinks will best be able to help him carry out his task. Such colleagues can be, in some instances, selected from career officials already on the job. These men are familiar with technical methods of our increasingly complicated departments and agencies. Now and then these career officials are utilized successfully. However, I firmly believe that the need for a fresh viewpoint, the knowledge that the individual selected deeply believes in the philosophies and objectives and ideals of the President, are more important in policymaking spots than technical proficiency concerning a particular segment of our governmental machinery.

In addition, even though there is rarely any question of loyalty to the job on the part of career civil servants, close associates of the President must be immediately and fully responsive to the President's own thoughts and aspirations, which is to say loyal to him. With due credit to the professionals in the career service, there would not always be immediate acceptance of, and in fact there might at times be reluctance concerning basic ideas which had a part in the election of the President. The President represents a broad public expression of the will of the people which conceivably may require major change and radical departure from past policies. Such change may appear to entail great risk to those who have been on government rolls a long time. However, our democracy has, by accepting such risks, developed and prospered.

How deeply into the organizational structure use of political executives must penetrate to make the whole institution responsive largely depends on the department. Our present structure has evolved to a large extent by trial and error and the Secretaries of Departments, Deputy Secretaries, Under Secretaries, Assistant Secretaries, Commissioners, Postmaster Generals, Attorney Generals, and the like now number about 1,200 individuals. In a federal employe force of about 2,250,000 people, exclusive of the military, this 1,200 is small in number. To be effective it must be large in influence.

So how has it worked out? What responsibility has the system placed on these political executives, and how has the responsibility been discharged?

First, let us examine some of the areas of responsibility. It seems clear that the political executive, in addition to being fully responsive to the Chief Executive's philosophies and desires, has a further responsibility to disseminate the ideas of the President to all in the executive's agency, to the people of the United States from public platform or by printed word, and, when called upon to do so, to the members and committees of Congress. Support is needed from all these sources in order to make the President's "state of mind" abundantly clear and to have that "state of mind" projected to our people and to the world. The political executive also has a responsibility to his party since the principles of that party have been the basis for the selection of his chief and

Proper Place of Political Executive in Government

the basis for the further approval by the people as a whole of that selection.

These persuasive qualities of the political executive and his more personal loyalties cannot be so readily found among career employees, although there is no intent here to minimize the necessity of using careerists nor to overlook their great contribution. The fact is, however, that for political responsiveness and change the political executive is essential. Perhaps he is the only mechanism which can readily bring change about. Another distinction between career and political executive is that the political one is subject to abrupt and perhaps undeserved removal because of loss of confidence in him by his superiors or simply to make room to pay a political debt. The risk is considerably less for the career officer protected by Civil Service Regulations.

Over the past thirty years, it is true that on several occasions there has been a wholesale and arbitrary change of top executives in both classes, political and career. To this observer, a substantial loss of effectiveness in administration has appeared to ensue at least temporarily each time. However, as I now look back to 1933, to 1948, and to 1953, it becomes clear that by paying this price on the part of the nation and the individual victims, whatever its magnitude, and it is hard to measure, the Executive Branch leadership has been responsive to what the people wanted and has changed national policies sharply in accord therewith.

One element of our national strength lies in the two-party system. Unless we give the new President his opportunity to introduce change in accord with the principle he has espoused, the inertia of officeholders too long on the job, whatever their abilities, may lead to apathy and stagnation. It is recognized that with fresh, vital, courageous leadership on the part of new or reelected Presidents such developments even with much smaller degree of change in high level career and second level political executives, can be designed to retain a great proportion of the values of experience. Human beings being what they are, it is just more difficult to accomplish.

In identifying more clearly the proper place of a political executive in our governmental system it is helpful to look at some of his other characteristics. What are the virtues, or the weaknesses, growing out of the backgrounds which these individuals have?

For one thing, from these differing backgrounds and characteristics come variety, and variety is needed. It is a job of the political executive to analyze the true needs of the President within particular agencies. In addition these executives must inspire their associates to serve the ideals of the President. Too, there are many tough decisions to make. Some of these are different from more conventional ones on the part of career executives who sometimes know too many of the reasons why not, rather than the dominant reason for. The political executive gets things done. He is normally not sympathetic to the committee system so overdone in our government. Committees are essential for exchange of information but they are rarely best for action. But our political executive must, in initiating action, educate people as to why and how, and keep currently advised those who work for him, and those for whom he works, in order to maintain morale. He must be a leader.

His length of stay on the job or the brevity of it, is part of this picture since the very turnover has strength and weakness. In general, it seems clear the political executive should customarily remain for longer than present average periods if he is to carry out the programs for which he has been selected. He should stay long enough to absorb knowledge of the fundamentals, and then have a further period to apply this knowledge. Lacking prior experience this cannot possibly be achieved in major agencies on a basis of only a year or even a year and a half of total service.

The political executive in general has been extremely useful although one can point to instances where he has failed. Sometimes these failures stem from the kind of ethics governing his life. Therefore, in order to have the job done better, and it must be done better, we should give more consideration to the basic character of the man selected. We need to refine and improve the system and part of this refinement and improvement has to do with ethical training of prospective leaders, and the selection of men who live by the right code. It is clear that many dilemmas faced by political executives have grown out of a code which could not stand when subjected to the sometimes great pressures of public office.

What do I have in mind when referring to these strains? There are bound to be numerous conflicts of interest within our government and its agencies. To indicate a simple difference of view, the political executive's personal and family interests are not likely to be in his, or his family's opinion best served by the comparatively low salaries paid by the government. What is the effect of this sort of pressure on an executive's emotional stability? And while it is inappropriate to develop the point in detail here, there certainly is a basic social question to resolve as to whether it is equitable to ask men to devote their whole talent, health, and time to public service when the financial sacrifice can be so great. This requirement also frequently deprives the government of first rate executives who might well have been able to make great and lasting contributions.

In addition to inadequate compensation there are the rigors of attack by the press, by Congressional committees, and by others. The temptation for the political executive to play it the least controversial way is sometimes irresistible because it is pleasanter not to make the fight. The ethics are just as lacking when nothing is done if it is clear the right decision should be to proceed. Career executives too are subject to this, and they face the ethical decision as to whether to remain silent or fight it out. Then there are pressures from party officials who feel that actions taken or policies proposed by the political executive after he becomes more familiar with the issues are prejudicial to statements or principles of the party on which prior public position has been taken. What should the political executive do? If he has the spirit, the strong desire and will to do what he thinks is right, he may alienate support even from his administrative superiors. However, he necessarily must face this kind of challenge since developments within great agencies tend to change one's knowledge of conditions even though past associates may be difficult to divert from preconceived ideas. The paramount guide for the executive is the intent and desire of the President to carry the country along certain lines. There have been cases where political executives have resigned, sometimes voluntarily, sometimes not, because their own beliefs had gradually been crystallized along lines of thought contrary to those of the President.

The political executive takes an oath to support the Constitution of the United States. Such a commitment, however, gives broad scope for differing views on issues and the basic duty of a political executive is to do what in his opinion is right for the interests of the whole people. He must, to be successful as well as true to himself, be responsive to his duty. When his interpretation comes into conflict with the views of his colleagues in the Agency or in the Administration then his ethical dilemma is whether he should attempt to fight for what he believes right in the councils and in public, in opposition to associates and colleagues, while still remaining on the job, or should he resign and take the fight outside? This sort of ethical dilemma arises much more frequently than does the dilemma of temptation from proffered bribes based on money, promise of higher position, or favorable publicity.

Such "payola" or buying of support is not, in my opinion, of frequent occurrence. In fairness it should be said that with rarest exception the political executive has behaved in honest fashion. The few known divergences seem to have been more from stupidity than cupidity and have shown the payoff to be disproportionate to the ultimate punishment of public knowledge and disgrace.

While in the past forty years there has been one use of major bribery in high office covering use of natural resources, most of the cases where acceptance of favors to influence executive action has been charged had to do with such items as refrigerators, fur coats, rugs, or unusual trips or entertainment. Perhaps the failure in these cases to judge wisely what was proper and what was not is a reflection to some extent of our general religious and political principles since in some cases acceptance of the "gift" was actually a matter of degree with no corresponding payoff although the acceptance was clearly wrong.

However, to return to the point, character, integrity, and dependability should be prime considerations in the selection of a political executive. Having these basic foundations one can build on them better skills knowing that with high standards the possibility of venal persuasion will be minimized or nonexistent.

So what does one look for as suitable material for a political executive? One would think that preachers, judges, lawyers, doctors, teachers, bankers, trustees, scientists might well be appropriate sources. Corporate officials, on whom large trustee responsibilities have rested for years, can be helpful, too. Those who have taken oaths of service to interests beyond their own, these are the people who have been trusted by others in the past and presumably would have the right ethics to assume new risks and new pressures without danger of their behaving other than well.

And perhaps there is another aspect that should be examined in addition to professional, business, or financial experience. That is the individual's own record in service to his community. Those who have served their various communities on a voluntary basis with devotion and distinction have been trained in the same general sort of climate to which they will be exposed in the new atmosphere of the political executive.

None of these backgrounds necessarily develops the efficiencies required for a good political executive but at least they provide a sound ethical base to which skills may be added. The new environment will require developing another quality which the political executive must have, namely, the *representativeness* with which he must do his job—representativeness of the people, his party, and the President. He must have more than selfish motivation. He must exhibit selflessness since government service requires taking one out of oneself.

In spite of its less than adequate monetary compensation, such service has rewards in the satisfaction of a contribution to his country, if one has had a successful tour. More concretely there ensue sometimes a substantial broadening of one's character and nature, and the development of new abilities and activities. Many times on return to private life these fit the individual for broader responsibilities. Government service also has the characteristic, in spite of frustrations, of letting one sleep better at night. This has been stated by so many that it is far from a unique phenomenon.

It would seem that in considering how to improve the political executive and the environment in which he works, we should emphasize ways in which to increase the intangible satisfactions while concurrently attempting to reduce some of the frustrations. Some of these latter come from harassment by legislators who do not always confine their activities to legislative functions but feel impelled to intrude into the executive realm. By increasing the prestige of public service it may be possible to reduce the reckless attacks, or perhaps to induce a more charitable approach from such legislators, from the press, and from representatives of other public media. These people have a duty to perform in keeping the public informed but in my opinion many times their duty can be performed with greater thoughtfulness and still not interfere with the spread of useful information.

What then are our conclusions as to the proper place of the political executive in the governmental system? First, that he is an important part of the United States democratic process. Second, that he does experience dilemmas because of his own nature and because of the characteristics of his job. The dilemmas are generated by the opportunities and responsibilities inherent in his policy and decisionmaking importance. But without the political appointee we could not have as much freshness, change, and flexibility as our government needs in this threatening world. He is responsive to changing needs. It is an important way of introducing into the governmental stream the abilities, new ideas, new skills, which are developed in our competitive free enterprise system. I know no better way to encourage and make effective this type of transfusion. Without him we could not so broadly inform the American people of the "state of mind" of the Administration and what is being attempted.

The political executive is more broadly used in the United States than in any other government in the world. It is true that he may sometimes help to create the basis for accusations of inconsistency in external or internal policies because of his constant change.

However, I see no valid reason to change substantially the place of the political executive in our system. I do agree that we should be more careful in his selection, considering the pressure of differing political views and having in mind the importance of the individual's ethics in carrying out the broad responsibilities which he will be given. We know that the executive should be better trained, and always should be supported firmly by his own superior. He should be kept on the job longer. There should be developed ways of increasing his satisfactions and reducing his frustrations. The selection process and its results will automatically be improved with creation of a more persuasive appeal to greater numbers of able people. This should be a function and a responsibility at the level of the President of the United States since good people are the most important raw material in building his record. He should give much more personal attention to it than has been customary.

As one who has done much recruiting of political executives, I know that to get the best people who are needed desperately to do the job, I devoted a very substantial part of personal time to it and did so perhaps more than in comparable agencies. I believe the results paid off.

One way to help achieve top level attention to this matter is for Congress to authorize a truly senior assistant to the President for that purpose. This assistant in turn would have comparable colleagues in each major department. Their task would be solely that of recruiting the best political executives and the very senior career heads of bureaus as well as other specialists. While partisan party considerations would be important for the reasons I have mentioned above, it is my strong belief that with developing understanding of our government's need for the

Proper Place of Political Executive in Government

ablest people as public servants in view of the exigent conditions under which we live, we would also be able to utilize many of our best people on an unpartisan basis. We have done it under war emergency threats in World War I, World War II, and the Korean War. In my opinion the danger to our continued strength and progress which we face today, although perhaps more gradual, is greater than on any of those previous occasions.

With massive responsibilities only good people can reduce the load at the top. They can also reduce the ethical dilemmas which we have discussed because the clashes between conflicting interests do not generate so much pressure when divided into smaller pieces. The right choice is often at least partially indicated before it gets upstairs.

It is perhaps too idealistic to expect that in an economy like ours with its emphasis on material success we will be always able to obtain high principled political executives largely from the ranks of business and the professions. Nonetheless, these sources have been tapped successfully in the past and can be in the future. Government service requires that our leaders make it clear that public good is paramount to private profit. Men rise to this challenge and we can have thousands of potential candidates from which to choose. Part of the national job, therefore, is to elevate the public service to its rightful stature so that more good people accept the challenge and the responsibility. This can be done. It must be done for the continued strength, security, and progress of our country and the free world.

V Modern Organization of Civil-Military Relationships

CHAPTER XXI

The American Military Mind in a Strange New World

By SIDNEY F. GIFFIN

THERE IS of course a military mind in the same sense that there is a legal mind and a scientific mind. The possessors of legal or scientific minds are seldom criticized for having acquired the ethics and the attributes of their professions. In the United States, but also elsewhere, the possession of a military mind has on the contrary been a matter of occasional reproach.

Just prior to Korea, a Chairman of the Joint Chiefs of Staff publicly expressed his alarm concerning inflation should the Louis Johnson defense budget be exceeded. Several leading newspapers applauded his position as welcome evidence that he did *not* possess a military mind. Professional military men were entitled to wonder at the time where, if anywhere, the military mind might be allowed to reside if not in the Chairman of the Joint Chiefs of Staff in his capacity as Chairman.[1]

The military mind is one which understands and accepts the professional military ethic, and it is attained no less hardly than is the legal mind or the scientific mind. It is the product of study, devotion, and tradition. In order to assure its survival, and for no other unique purpose, the people of the United States have long supported the Military Academy at West Point and the Naval Academy at Annapolis, and are now additionally supporting the Air Force Academy at Colorado Springs. In order to mature it, professional education at a graduate level is continued at intervals during most of the officer's career.

It is not proposed here to repeat what, perceptively and at length, Samuel P. Huntington has said about the military mind in *The Soldier and the State*.[2] But some of the qualities which contribute to the profes-

---

[1] Writing for *The Saturday Evening Post*, General Omar N. Bradley subsequently acknowledged having been out of character in this matter.
[2] Harvard University Press, Cambridge, Massachusetts, 1957.

sional military ethic are subject to quick summary. They include, *inter alia,* a high degree of dedication, obedience, loyalty, integrity, devotion to duty, and the conviction of my country right or wrong. These are conservative virtues, not in any political sense but only in that they seek to preserve. In such a sense, the military mind is accordingly a conservative mind and often a cautious mind, possessing a pessimism with regard to human nature which has seldom been disappointed in the short run and never in the long run.

The qualities attached to the military mind are obviously not peculiar to the military, excepting perhaps that they *all* are attributes whereas only some may be the attributes of other disciplines. Moreover, not every quality may be regarded as a virtue for segments of society other than the military. An unquestioning obedience to the commands of authority, for example, might elsewhere be regarded as simple serfdom or mere sheepishness. The criteria of others cannot here be applied to the military, for obedience is cardinal among military qualities. The military mind deserves to be judged in terms of the requirements of a profession which, like other professions, is indispensable to society.

In the practice of his profession, a regular officer in the Armed Forces of the United States is likely to be as obsessed by it as, for example, medical men are obsessed by their profession. These officers yet remain citizens of the United States and members of its society. In most cases, it is three generations from civilian life to civilian life for the military family. The officer is Protestant or Catholic or Jewish. Because he is conservative in the one sense, he is not necessarily so with respect to issues and questions other than those pertaining to his profession. He may favor public power or private power, or he may favor or oppose rapid integration in the schools. He may reflect sectionalism. Nevertheless, he tends to be apolitical in domestic affairs.

Some measure of apoliticality derives from the nomadic nature of military life. But it has been traditional in the Armed Forces of the United States until recently, when with millions in uniform absentee voting has become a virtue, to abstain even from balloting. The small officer corps of an earlier day was so deeply imbued with the principle of civilian ascendancy that it voluntarily refrained from exercising such small measure of political influence as might accrue from aiding in the selection of public officials. During recent years, when absentee voting has been encouraged as a civic duty in the Armed Forces, the officer

American Military Mind in a Strange New World 343

corps has made not the slightest attempt to influence opinion in the Armed Forces respecting political questions or candidates. It will not do so, less because of statutory restraints than because this would be inconsistent with the professional military ethic.

Exception of course exists to this rule. *Pro patria,* the professional military ethic demands support of an adequate military posture. The officer corps is unlikely to consider that any pending posture is as "adequate" as it might be, and this persistent attitude not only encourages lobbying efforts in Washington but may exercise some modest influence on the voting habits of servicemen and women. If this professional bias is taken to suggest that the military mind is not an entirely whole or balanced mind, the indictment has to be accepted. It should be noted that other professions also exhibit the biases of conviction.

The institutions of democracy plainly benefit from a professional military ethic which abjures a participating interest in domestic politics. However, it is solely on the domestic scene that the officer corps demonstrated this attitude. Its apoliticality stops at the water's edge, for the military menaces to American national security lie overseas. Our senior military officers must be intimately concerned, if only in their advisory role, with the interplay of power and politics on the world scale.

They are concerned with this interplay as it has occurred in history, in its unfolding forms, and as it may, however tentatively, be projected into the future. The view they take is not always a small one. From the turn of the century until the appearance of Nicholas J. Spykman and Reinhold Niebuhr, one would be hard put to name an American observer of the relationship between power and politics whose insight approached that of Admiral Alfred T. Mahan. In fact, other than the professional officer corps, no significant segment of American society has consistently throughout our history held what approaches the current "realist" view of world politics.

Until recent decades a realistic American appraisal of power and policy could incorporate considerable optimism, in view of the remarkable good fortune attendant on the geographic position of the United States. With its ocean approaches under British and American control, the country was impregnable at home and might readily bring its military power to bear elsewhere as occasion required. Americans could thus accustom themselves to the idea that their wars would be fought on foreign soil—never at home—and at relatively low cost in blood and treasure.

The officer corps, sharing convictions which were in fact valid, was enabled to rest strategic concepts and doctrine upon a foundation which appeared proof against frustration. Against any likely enemy, the United States could be held inviolate while victory was contrived. This concept held true through both World Wars and the Korean conflict, although the contriving of victory came to involve great cost to the United States and an extensive reliance upon allies.

A similar concept with respect to warfare had previously been able to govern strategic thought in Great Britain. Elsewhere, very different concepts of security had long been thrust upon the military leadership. The communities of Europe, including that of Russia, might plan from time to time on victory in war but could never assure the inviolability of their homelands. Indeed, a persistent Russian concept was deliberately to sacrifice territory in order to exhaust and eventually eject invaders.

The American officer corps today faces, along with the country, the necessity for change in concepts of security which long have ruled all thinking about the security of the United States. The extraordinary redistribution of power which remains as the accomplishment of two great wars had little to do with the necessity for such change. Science and technology bear the responsibility, in having created a nuclear missile offense which will come fully into being when no active military defense can yet cope with it. Whether launched from land, sea, or air, these vicious javelins with their tips of poisoned hydrogen produce a situation in which all concepts of security, for Americans as for other peoples, must for the time being at least be cast with ambiguity.

"We are, as a nation, not accustomed to the frustrations of history."[3] Professional military men are not alone among their countrymen in feeling frustration as a result of the new and deeply disturbing security situation. However, the frustration they feel is likely to be more immediate and personal, because its source touches the area which is their professional concern and responsibility. The bitterness of interservice controversy during the past several years, although not without its uglier aspects, may indeed be symptomatic of this frustration.

The military mind cannot but accept General MacArthur's dictum

[3]Reinhold Niebuhr, *The World Crisis and American Responsibility*, Association Press, New York, 1958, p. 81.

American Military Mind in a Strange New World

that there is no substitute for victory. Yet victory in total nuclear war would have meaning more in terms of the survival of the United States as a self-determining power—and the elimination of the present threat to the integrity of the United States—than in terms of classic military triumph. Total war must therefore be avoided, except as a last resort to protect the national honor, while victory is sought by other means.

The delicacy of the situation raises difficult questions. At what point in cold war and in limited warfare can defeat be accepted by a belligerent capable of raising the limits? At what point in limited military conflict can nuclear weapons be employed? How can the military forces be disposed other than for nuclear warfare when nuclear weapons await in the wings? Can the technical means of sharing, on a NATO basis, responsibility for the employment of nuclear weapons be so devised as to enhance purpose among the Western allies when several among them come to possess nuclear missile capabilities? Is there a means of deterring limited war along with general war? How can we cope with covert and concealed aggression? As one foreign student at an American service school wrote on being asked to criticize the course of instruction: "Many questions. No answers." Or, where answers are offered, they are seldom altogether clear. One thing the military cannot be accused of doing: they are not preparing *solely* to fight the last war.

American military men have persistently sought to deter war without sacrifice of national interest, but never more so than at present. Thus, a ranking Air Force commander says in an interview—"If nuclear war breaks out, SAC has failed in its mission," although he would hasten to add that the Strategic Air Command also has another mission, which is to "win" a war which had not been deterred.

Speaking in Los Angeles sometime after Korea, General MacArthur made the statement: "We are told that we must go on indefinitely as at present. Some say fifty years or more. What is the end? None say. There is no definite objective. We must pass on to those who follow us the search for a final solution." Whether any such thing as a final solution may actually exist, it is plain here that a truly great soldier was anguished because he could discern no immediate path leading to a solution compatible with his character. Henry L. Stimson showed his sympathetic understanding of this frame of mind when he said: "I know the withering effect of limited commitments and I know the regenerative effect of full action."

In truth, the American officer corps shares in full measure "The spiritual problem of modern man, who must find a way of engaging in impossible tasks and not be discouraged when he fails to complete any of them."[4]

It is altogether inconsistent with the professional military ethic that a developing situation of military uncertainty, let alone one of military insecurity, should in any degree be acceptable. The philosophy of the West Point wrestling instructor of a generation back has to rule—"There ain't no holt which can't be broke"—and again, "There's always a guard agin it." The American military mind is compelled to persist in seeking a military solution to the military menace, and if this means a marriage with science our military leaders will be ardent wooers.

In the meantime, until a full military solution is found, the American officer corps has no choice but to hope that a solution which cannot be found in military strategy alone may be available in the grand strategy of the nation, through the admixture of politics and economics with military means. One might anticipate a keen and continuing interest on the part of the military in alliances, bilateral agreements, aid programs, diplomacy, or in any other effort which may give realistic promise of advancing the national security. In response to the challenge of the times, a special sophistication now has to be added to the list of qualities distinguishing the military mind. William W. Kaufmann suggests how special this must be, in saying

> the circumstances call for an intensified effort to increase the military officer's insight into the complexity and delicacy of his problems rather than for a redefinition of the military sphere of competence. This is not to suggest that the military officer should become a political, economic, and social expert as well as a military one. It is meant simply to imply that he should be made increasingly aware of the degree and scope of his functions and responsibilities so that he can solicit and make use of whatever advice may be available from these other realms. What patterns of organization and authority may develop from this expansion in orientation and participation need be of less concern than that the expansion itself should take place, and that it should take place without diluting the traditional military virtues.[5]

[4]*Ibid.*, p. 110.
[5]William W. Kaufmann, *Military Policy and National Security,* Princeton University Press, Princeton, 1956, pp. 264–265.

American Military Mind in a Strange New World 347

As never before in time of peace, military forces of the United States have been maintaining, and must maintain, a kind of alertness very close to that which holds for sensitive areas during wartime. The precarious security situation which renders this necessary makes the United States itself an area of sensitivity. A particular military-civilian relationship has to emerge as a result.

No responsible American would wish to see his civilian compatriots undergoing a state of alert which actually approached that of the military alert forces. This could make of the country what Harold D. Lasswell has described as a "garrison state," and might in time come to defeat Constitutional purposes.

Nonetheless, the lackadaisical attitude which Americans have thus far adopted with respect to practical measures of civil defense can only have, in the long run, a demoralizing effect—even a corrupting effect—on their profoundly concerned professional military men. In an armed and hostile environment, until such time as an active military defense promises substantial success in missile warfare the United States can never again approach invulnerability, but may well be vulnerable in degree as its people adopt or fail to adopt measures of protection.

Very effective measures of protection against any but a direct or close nuclear hit can be taken on a local, and on a family, basis. From the military point of view, the failure to adopt such protective measures, as time goes on and the situation remains serious, could only be regarded as frivolous. Here the words of Woodrow Wilson in May of 1917 are in some sense apropos: "It is not an Army we must train for war; it is a nation." And again, ". . . it must therefore be stressed," says Kaufmann, "that our success in coping with the difficult problems that lie immediately ahead in the realm of military affairs will require a further growth in public sophistication and steadiness about these matters."[6]

Understandably, the American military leadership is likely to accept proposals for the regulation of armaments with something less than enthusiasm. In this regard, military men stand only in the capacity of technicians offering advice to the political leadership. But the relationship existing in the United States between executive and legislative branches makes it plain that this counsel is likely to weigh heavily in the balance.

[6] *Ibid.,* p. 265.

The obvious vested interest of military professionals in an elaborate structure of armed force provides only a superficial explanation for the military attitude toward disarmament. A truer explanation lies in the skepticism, reinforced by history, with which the military mind views suggestions to abjure force unaccompanied by practical suggestions for eliminating such conflicts of interest as have heretofore yielded only to force. It would be disingenuous to pretend that existing conflicts of this nature would not exist should agreement on disarmament be suddenly and magically effected.

Yet the military mind can perceive that armaments themselves constitute at present an extraordinary source of world tension, and that any abatement of tension in a space and missile age might itself lead to other acceptable arrangements. It is thus quite conceivable that honest proposals for measures of real disarmament, accepted by others with the same sincerity as by the United States and subject to reliable mutual checks, would in today's perilous circumstances receive American military endorsement. The military security of the United States is after all the engrossing concern of American military men. If disarmament offered in sober logic the best approach to this end, it is unlikely that any less promising approach could today satisfy the professional military ethic. Accepting this as truth, some measure is thereby provided of the extent to which unparalleled challenge may evoke unparalleled response in military thinking.

But it is the certain duty of American military leaders to endorse no disarmament proposals in which they can discern dangerous pitfalls for the military security of the United States. There are at least three important areas in which dangerous pitfalls may exist. The first of these obviously derives from the unprecedented complexities inherent in the new systems of armaments which must be controlled if control of any armaments is to have meaning.

These systems surpass in technical difficulties of control, almost as much as in their shattering force, the armaments systems on which agreements were sought at Geneva in the twenties and thirties. No student of past attempts at the regulation of armaments can but recall the endless debates concerning, for example, six inch versus eight inch guns on naval cruisers. Technical obstacles to the effective control of modern armaments are formidable indeed, and the military mind should not be regarded as merely captious in being concerned with them.

Again obviously, dangerous pitfalls may exist in respect to the degree of sincerity with which prospective enemies enter upon agreements. Honesty, as the Western world understands the word, apparently plays little part in the Communist approach to problems. But the proprietors of a demonic philosophy must be especially subject to self-interest, and the Communist world is at least equally vulnerable with the West to the new weapons. The possibility exists that the Soviet Union, and even the Chinese Communists, may arrive at a willingness to trade advantages on some reasonable basis of equality. Having in mind their objective of symbolically burying the West, they are unlikely to do so without first exhausting every device of advantage to themselves.

Each Communist disarmament proposal has to be examined in this light, and it is the duty of American leaders, whether military or political, to pursue such examinations. Western negotiators cannot permit an eagerness for the approval of uncommitted peoples, or of their own populations, to lead them into accepting disarmament proposals of a specious or meretricious character. They are entitled to recall that a Khrushchev offer of total disarmament in 1959 is but a repetition of the same offer made by the Soviet Union at Geneva in 1927, concerning which Litvinov cynically remarked that the Soviet Union was perfectly safe in making such a proposal, as the capitalist states could never accept it.

The third pitfall which the control of armaments holds for Americans and other Western democratic peoples is one which totalitarians need not fear but which Western leaders must somehow fend against. This is the fateful enthusiasm of democracy for "total" solutions, the popular eagerness to see millennia in partial concessions. To the military mind, agreements which place ceilings on armaments may be regarded as delusory unless it is understood that ceilings are also floors, for certainly the opposition will maintain forces no less substantial than agreement allows. The fecklessness with which Great Britain and France faced the rise of Mussolini and Hitler is fully illustrative in this connection, but the American record between World Wars was surely no better attuned to reality. Here again the concern of the military leadership, no less than that of the responsible political leadership, has to be for a full realization of public sophistication and steadiness even when—and if—a regulation of armaments becomes practicable.

The United States plainly has crossed so consequential a divide in history that at least one cherished concept of the American past has been abandoned almost without debate of the principle involved. This is the concept, rooted in our colonial heritage and reinforced by the prejudice of European immigrants against conscription, that we should rely on citizen soldiers in a war emergency, maintaining in the meanwhile only a minimum standing force. Today, the most critical war emergency we may face demands substantial standing forces in being, and the American people are maintaining with little complaint combat-ready forces tenfold greater than in any previous between-war period.

Despite every safeguard of civilian control, despite every failsafe device for times of sharp international tension, great and terrible power now resides with the military. American military leaders have specific responsibility for evaluating developments in their military aspects; in order to do so expertly their attention must be confined in large part to acquiring of information and experience quite alien to other echelons of society. It therefore becomes essential that the military profession be maintained as an integral element of the society rather than as something suspected and apart. This is important in order to help assure that the military leadership will act with the real interests of the community in mind, but also to achieve among the American people a considerable understanding and appreciation of the problems with which the military—on their behalf—must contend.

CHAPTER XXII

Representativeness, Efficiency, and the Dual Problem of Civil-Military Relations

By WILLIAM T. R. FOX

GOVERNMENT RESPONSIVE to the value preferences of the governed is representative government. If it is also responsive to changes in the conditions under which the popular mandate is to be executed, representative government can be efficient government. Nowhere has the challenge to representative government called for a more imaginative response to changed conditions than in the civil-military relations of Britain and America. We continue to ask that traditional liberal values be maintained, but we see that the direction from which those values are threatened has changed drastically.

Two or three generations ago the phrase "national security" did not occupy a prominent place in the vocabulary either of statesmen or of students of government. Patterns of civil-military relations in both of the great Englishspeaking democracies were then stabilized on the assumption that a new Cromwell was more of a threat than a new Napoleon and that neither was much of a threat.

"Security" is a word used to describe the efficiency with which the basic values of the self are protected (or are *felt* to be protected); security is not itself one of those values. It follows that "national security" refers to the efficiency with which those values which the nation-state is called upon to maintain are protected. Conventionally, the phrase is used to refer to the efficiency of protection against *external* threat.[1]

For most of the past three centuries the threat, at least in time of peace, was seen as primarily internal. The problem of civil-military relations was thus almost exclusively a problem of maintaining civilian supremacy. A high value was placed on "civil"-izing the domestic political

[1] See H. D. Lasswell and A. Kaplan, *Power and Society*, Yale University Press, New Haven, 1950, p. 61, for a formal definition of security.

process so that the role of legally authorized violence in domestic politics would be restricted to putting down the illegal use of violence.

To meet an external threat, civilian supremacy is not enough. The military over which civilian statesmen are to be supreme has to be strong; and civilian decisions to insure adequate strength cannot be made by ignorant or poorly informed men. These men are not free, however, to choose means to protect the nation-state against external threat which are incompatible with the basic values of the society. In a liberal state, this means that national security is not maintained if military protection of the territory of the state is gained only at the cost of individual freedom.[2] Thus, there are two aspects to the problem of civil-military relations, corresponding to the need to secure liberal values simultaneously against internal and external threats.

Perfect security against either internal or external threats is beyond reach, but the institutions of representative government in many Western countries have been effectively used to enhance individual security from cradle to grave against the hazards of illness, unemployment, ignorance, and arbitrary discrimination. Against the hazards of war and indeed of the corporal dissolution of the society of which the individual is a part his security has in this century been decreased. What adaptations have been made in the traditional civil-military relationship to provide such security as we now enjoy against these increased hazards? To answer this question we must reconstruct the situation prevailing at the end of the nineteenth century, particularly the balance then struck between representativeness and efficiency and the image then prevailing of the role of organized violence in peace and war, and in domestic and world politics. Then we can ask how appropriate have been our responses to the external threat which world war, world revolution, and changes in military technology have made seem so great and so pervasive.

The United States Constitution reflected American fears of large standing armies in peace. Civilian supremacy has for 175 years been both a constitutional precept and a political dogma. This simplistic view of civil-military relations was reinforced by a magnificent unconcern for any threat from abroad. Perhaps the most extravagant assertion of this unconcern was in Abraham Lincoln's Springfield, Illinois, speech in 1837 in which he declared:

[2]See Harold D. Lasswell, *National Security and Individual Freedom*, McGraw-Hill, New York, 1950.

Representativeness, Efficiency, Civil-Military Relations

At what point shall we Americans expect the approach of danger? By what means shall we fortify against it: Shall we expect some trans-Atlantic military giant to step the ocean and crush us at a blow? Never!

All the armies of Europe, Asia, and Africa combined, with all the treasure of the earth (our own excepted) in their military chest, with a Bonaparte for a commander, could not by force take a drink from the Ohio or make a track on the Blue Ridge in a trial of a thousand years.

At what point then is the approach of danger to be expected? I answer, if it ever reach us it must spring up amongst us; it cannot come from abroad. If destruction be our lot we must ourselves be its author and finisher. As a nation of freemen, we must live through all time or die by suicide.[3]

After the Civil War, the land forces of the United States promptly returned to their antebellum status. The Army was small and it was scattered throughout the American West for the last phases of Indian fighting. Even after the Indian fighting ceased, its deployment reflected much less any fear of foreign foe than it did various Congressmen's zeal in keeping a military installation once useful against Indians from being abandoned. Low Army appropriations also reflected the prevailing unconcern for military matters.

True, in the 1880s and 1890s, there was a revival of interest in the Navy; but the result was at first only a coast defense Navy, not yet excited by the visions of the great prophet of sea power, Alfred T. Mahan. Dependence on the Navy and on Coast Artillery reflected a general belief that no large standing army was necessary in peace to prevent defeat in a short war against an overseas foe; and that there would always be time to mobilize and win victory in a long war. There was no fear whatever of immediate North American neighbors.

Military affairs, in the heyday of the dogma of the virtue of a citizen militia, were hardly any more a matter for experts than was civil government.[4] They were a responsibility of citizenship to be shouldered when, as, and if needed. The democratization of arms had gone hand in hand with the democratization of suffrage, for in the prevailing military technology of the nineteenth century one man with one rifle was

---
[3]Quoted in James Reston's "Washington" column, *The New York Times*, February 16, 1958.

[4]The United States Military Academy was established because the special need for engineers was recognized. Army Engineers have, however, been almost as famous for their civil works as for their military works.

regarded as the basic unit of military strength. Men could "vote" with their rifles against an oppressive government almost as readily as they could vote with their ballots for a favored political party.

Events in the War of 1812 and the Mexican War which might have cast doubt on the adequacy of the militia against a foreign foe were conveniently forgotten. Indeed, so long as American security was effectively guaranteed by British sea power and the European balance of power, there was little reason why these events should not be forgotten. As for Britain itself, as the nineteenth century wore on, that country became progressively less able to mount an offensive against a hostile United States. By the end of the century the British government had every reason to want a friendly United States.[5]

If there was little reason to make large preparations for war against a European foe in North America, it seemed absurd to prepare to fight such a foe in Europe. The logic of the policy of "no prior commitment," of never promising in advance to go to the aid of another country, seemed irrefutable. If then there was no danger of defeat in a short war and assured time for democratic virtue and industrial might to repel an invader in a long war, of what use would large-scale peacetime preparations for land warfare have been? This was popular doctrine in England also where the Navy was expected to protect the home islands and what Army there was was fighting (and deterring) small wars throughout the whole of Britain's Asian and African empire. So long as the Army could be safely starved in peacetime and Congress was willing to vote whatever was needed to win in war, one may equally well ask of what use would civilian statesmen with any special military competence have been.

Rising German power in the first decade of the twentieth century caused Britain's reentry into the high politics of the Continent via the Entente Cordiale and the AngloFrench military staff conversations. The second decade saw American intervention in the stalemated First World War. It was still possible for many Americans to believe after 1918, however, that the United States could in any future war of European origin choose to intervene or not as its interests might dictate, and that its interests would ordinarily dictate nonintervention. It was even more widely believed that a new war, in which the United States might

[5] See Lionel Gelber, *The Rise of Anglo-American Friendship, 1895-1905*, Oxford University Press, New York, 1938.

Representativeness, Efficiency, Civil-Military Relations

be called upon to choose intervention, would last long enough for the choice to be made and then for the arms and men to be mobilized to gain victory.

Both world wars had a *Blitzkrieg* opening phase that fell just short of total victory. In both a subsequent United States intervention was decisive in a war of attrition. Thus, prevailing expectations that there would always be time to mobilize, after the crisis of war had occurred, seemed to have been confirmed; but it was only by the slenderest of margins. On the other hand, the pre1914 expectation that a mass army would never be needed except to repel an invasion on our own shores was twice confounded. So also was the forecast, frequently heard in the 1930s, that a democracy could not fight a war against a dictatorship and remain a democracy.[6]

As the genuineness and the immediacy of the threatened overturn of the European order by a fascist dictator became evident in 1940 there was less and less concern expressed that any particular level of defense mobilization was higher than was compatible with the survival of democratic institutions. Pearl Harbor stilled any remaining doubts. From December 7, 1941, on, those who were traditionally concerned about the man on horseback "taking over" had to recognize that the American problem of civil-military relations had been transformed. There had to be security against external threats to American liberties as well as security against internal threats.

Henceforth, even after victory had been won in World War II, it was not enough for civilians to be supreme and to show high politicomilitary competence at the moment of crisis. The Second World War was fought with weapons whose design, development, and production took years, and whose operation required the training of specialists in programs that also took years. The competence had to be demonstrated years in advance.

---

[6] By identifying all forms of massive rearmament with "fascism" the slogan, "You can't fight fascism with fascism," was used to justify isolation and disarmament. Pendleton Herring, *The Impact of War*, Farrar, New York, 1941, argued forcefully on the eve of American participation in World War II that a democratic America could become militarily efficient. Harold D. Lasswell in *National Security and Individual Freedom*, cited *supra*, similarly argued in 1950, when the prospect of protracted high level mobilization had become apparent, that a militarily efficient United States could still promote individual freedom. Both men thought "representativeness" and "efficiency" were compatible, although their difference in emphasis reflects the difference between the unarmed democracy of 1940 and the armed democracy of 1950.

As World War II ended, there was ushered in a new military technology based on atomic weapons in which inter-great power war planning had to be based on the assumption of irretrievably decisive events occurring in the first hours, and a new pattern of world politics in which the nonSoviet world expected the United States government to assume leadership. Thus, long lead times, short reaction times, the expectation of short war, and the responsibility of free world leadership put an unprecedented burden on American civilian leaders during time of peace. Without being able to mobilize the energies spontaneously called forth in an actual war crisis, they had henceforth to evoke a high level of economic sacrifice, keep professional military forces fully equipped and trained in a state of constant readiness, support research on weapons system-evolving with increasing speed and at astronomical cost, maintain a variety of coalition military arrangements, and orchestrate even in peace the variety of economic, psychological, strategy, and military decisions in support of current American policy. Furthermore, not only must the armed forces be in a state of constant readiness but so must the civilian leadership; for the awful decisions that might initiate a two way thermonuclear war may have to be made and executed on extremely short notice.

If unnecessary wars are to be deterred or otherwise avoided, "right" decisions have to be made long before an actual war crisis. If necessary wars, necessary in the sense that the values of our liberal society would be better protected by going to war rather than by avoiding it, "right" decisions have to be made at the instant of crisis, too, but made on the basis of immediately available military power, available only because of earlier timely "right" decisions. Civilian decisions, however much they may reflect devotion to civilian liberal values, can be wrong, even catastrophically wrong, decisions if they also reflect inadequate or even delayed understanding of prevailing conditions.

How well equipped is the civilian leader to make these critical decisions? What access does he have to disinterested expert advice from persons as devoted to the protection of the basic civilian liberal values of our society as himself? How much understanding and discriminating support can he count on from informed levels of public opinion?

We have already referred to some of the characteristics of "the civilian mind," as it existed just before the present era of world wars and technological revolutions and to its preoccupation with the internal threat

Representativeness, Efficiency, Civil-Military Relations

to our values. To what extent need the present internal threat affect a solution to the present problem of civil-military relations?

If the problem of civil-military relations has in most ways been complicated by the course of events in this century, the danger is not that an expanded military threatens civilian control simply by being large. The new military technology is not an all purpose technology. Because it is short on manpower and long on firepower, the armed forces are not equally good for winning foreign wars and putting down domestic insurrection. The Navy was never useful in sailing its ships up on dry land to intimidate the urban populace. Today the Army, Navy, and Air Force are alike in having developed specialized instruments of violence which are singularly inefficient for police action against individuals and dissident small groups in the United States. The armed forces are if anything less useful than in the nineteenth century to a government bent upon suppressing domestic dissent. Furthermore, maintenance of the armed forces at present levels requires the continuing and active support of both the President and Congress. Each year tremendous appropriations must be requested by the President and voted by Congress.

The civilian control which the Founding Fathers had in mind was Congressional control. They were mindful of the charge against King George III in the Declaration of Independence that "He has kept among us, in times of peace, Standing Armies without the Consent of a legislature." That today's Chief Executive finds Congress as often pressing him to ask for more rather than less funds in the name of national defense is but one indication that civilian opinion freely accepts the need for continuing high level peacetime defense mobilization, and that the armed forces would not be the first to feel the impact of any widespread tax fatigue.[7] The internal threat of protracted high level, peacetime defense mobilization to liberal civilian values, if there be one, lies elsewhere.

It is sometimes alleged that the militarization of American life, however unavoidable, has affected basic attitudes so that nonconformity has come to be equated with disloyalty. This may or may not be true. It is an important question and worthy of a separate and careful analysis,

---

[7] The contrast is sharp between the relatively easy acceptance by Congress of Presidential demands for funds for the armed services and the annual difficulty in winning Congressional approval for requests for funds for the foreign aid program.

but it is not a matter of civil-military relations. The record does not show that it is primarily from the professional military men that have come either the intemperate utterances or the arbitrary acts that poison the atmosphere of freedom. If the freedom to "nonconform" is to be protected, as it must be if liberal institutions and values are to be maintained, it is by civilian action in the fields of law and education, not by some change in civil-military relations.

Does the internal threat then perhaps lie in the illiberal value preferences sometimes attributed to the professional soldier? Do his devotion to discipline, his respect for authority, his belief in the virtue of obedience, his frequently expressed distaste for something he calls "politics," his tendency to see critical decisions not as moral choices but as technical problems, etc.—do all these alleged traits taken together make the military expert's advice suspect? The very phrase, civil-military relations, implies that the soldier is somehow out of civil society, very much as the phrase, Soviet-American relations, implies that the Soviet Union is outside the United States. "Civil-military relations" thus almost implies that the user of the phrase would answer that the soldier's advice *is* suspect.

We have already seen that the new era—in which preparedness rather than potential is the effective deterrent and preparedness before the actual crisis of war, rather than mobilization after war begins, is likely to determine the outcome and determine it in short order—requires of statesmen and discriminating opinion elites an understanding of military policy. It also requires, since soldier and statesmen must now work together to elaborate national security policy in peace as well as in war, an understanding on the part of the military of the values of the civil society they are committed to try to conserve. In the exercise of their functional responsibility they must, in the language of the title of this paper, be to some extent "representative" while the civilian leadership must to some extent be "efficient." Just as the night and day distinction between war and peace has been blurred in contemporary world politics, so has the former sharp distinction of requiring representativeness from the statesmen and expertness from the soldier.

The lengthened lead times in preparedness and the critical importance of deterrent strategies in the era of possible thermonuclear war mean that for the Chief Executive to formulate politicomilitary policy there must be a continuous peacetime "concert of judgment" based on a triangular State-Pentagon-Bureau of the Budget relationship and on the deliberations of the National Security Council.[8] Three types of civil-military relations are involved: 1. that between the uniformed subordinates and their civilian superiors within the Department of Defense, 2. that between the officials of the Department of Defense and those of nonmilitary departments, and 3. that between the Department of Defense and the White House. The professional military man in the Pentagon may thus find three not necessarily identical sets of civilian considerations standing between him and the making of Presidential decisions in the politicomilitary field.

As Executive policy in its turn runs the gauntlet of Congressional action, the approval of still a fourth set of civilians with still a fourth set of civilian perspectives is required. Furthermore, though there have been in the past twenty years a series of organizational changes designed to make national security policymaking within the Executive branch more orderly and more rational—the creation of the Joint Chiefs of Staff and the National Security Council and the organization of the three services under a single Department of Defense—there has been no comparable adjustment of Executive-Congressional relations.

It may appear at first sight strange that in spite of this the most dramatic evidences of friction between the civilian and the military have been within the Executive branch.[9] Several explanations are possible. The President is responsible for "whole" policy and the professional soldier is expert in but one of the means, the military, to the attainment of but one of the objectives of national policy, national security. Executive-Congressional relations are "civil-civil" relations no matter how uncivil they may be. Congressional committees invite the expert testimony of the soldier and then urge him to lay bare the dissatisfactions and frustrations he feels as a result of rejected recommendations and reduced budgetary requests. Some military men possibly dissatisfied with the action taken by their civilian superiors may find natural allies in various Congressmen, particularly on committees dealing with military policy and military appropriations and possibly

---

[8] The phrase "concert of judgment" is the title of the first chapter of Arthur MacMahon's *Administration in Foreign Affairs*, University of Alabama Press, 1953, and the first chapter describes the triangular relationship.

[9] See Matthew Ridgway, *Soldier*, Harper and Brothers, New York, 1956; James M. Gavin, *War and Peace in the Space Age*, Harper and Brothers, New York, 1958; and Maxwell Taylor, *The Uncertain Trumpet*, Harper and Brothers, New York, 1959.

also dissatisfied with Executive policy. Thus even though the main choices have already been made within the Executive branch,[10] any Congressional uncooperativeness in ratifying these choices inevitably appears as a friction in the civil-military relationship.

We have already emphasized that under modern conditions of continuing high level external threat the public interest will not be served by viewing the civil and the military as natural enemies. Only if inaction and delay were still tolerable alternatives could one be content with such a relationship. Performance of the security function must rest on the acceptance all round of functional responsibility.[11] There is nothing wrong with civilian-military disagreement if that disagreement is rooted in the particular responsibilities of the contending parties, for the disagreement then clarifies choice and after its resolution positive action can be taken.

Reactions based on some obsolete unfunctional attitudes do not, however, lead either to a rational integration of military and nonmilitary means or a rational shaping of military means to overall national policy objectives. Belief by the military, for example, that "politics" is inherently dirty or belief by the civilian that "the high brass" is straining to "take over" are only gross examples of inherited perspectives which are unfunctional under contemporary conditions of enforced collaboration.

Under prevailing conditions of total diplomacy and possible total war the soldier's indispensable expertise is recognized as never before in peacetime in the Englishspeaking world. At the same time, a new partner in the making of national security policy, the scientist, has won his place in the highest councils of government. As the J. Robert Oppenheimer hearings dramatically and poignantly illustrated,[12] the re-

[10]See S. P. Huntington, "Strategic Planning and the Political Process," *Foreign Affairs*, January, 1960, pp. 285–299.

[11]In the terminology of S. P. Huntington, *The Soldier and the State*, Harvard University Press, Cambridge, Massachusetts, 1957, "functional responsibility" would be described as "objective control," as the control of the military which automatically results from its professional ethic requiring the support of the civilian values of the society which it is professionally serving. I have followed the earlier language of Carl J. Friedrich, "Responsible Government Service Under the Constitution," in *Problems of the American Public Service*, McGraw-Hill, New York, 1935, because I wished to emphasize the need for positive action rather than for "control" to prevent undesired action.

[12]United States Atomic Energy Commission, *In the Matter of J. Robert Oppenheimer*, Transcript of Hearings before Personnel Security Board, April 12, 1954–May 6, 1954,

lation between the politician and the expert in matters of national security is by no means exhausted when one has studied the politician-soldier relationship. The professionalization of the military has made it possible for the responsible senior military officer offering politico-military advice to distinguish in his own mind between the technical military considerations whose relevance he is uniquely equipped to evaluate and his personal political preferences which may or may not be identical with those of his civilian superior. As a professional military man he sees his professional military responsibility as being to clarify the choices of the politician, not to make those choices for him.

On questions of scientific policy with military implications the problem of balancing representativeness and efficiency may be more difficult. Civilian ignorance of new developments in science is even more profound, and prior experience on the part of the professional scientist in making clear when he is "speaking strictly from a scientific point of view" and when he is airing his own policy preference is much less extensive. The case of the scientist, however, throws into relief the transformation of the problem of civil-military relations under twentieth century conditions of persisting external threat.

Purely constitutional solutions of the problem were satisfactory only so long as the external short-run threat was minimal and a deterrent diplomacy could be based on presumed war potential. Now that national security requires the peacetime harnessing and coordination of the resources of the whole society, there can be no solution which is not based on civilian understanding of military problems and a self-conscious awareness by the professional military man of the policy implications of each of the courses of his action which he might plausibly support on wholly technical grounds. The evolution of the curricula in the nation's war colleges reflect this growing awareness and the steps taken to communicate this awareness at least to the group of officers capable of rising to the most critical positions of politico-military responsibility.[13]

However successfully the war colleges and the armed forces' educa-

---

Washington, 1954. See Warner R. Schilling, "The H-Bomb Decision: How to Decide Without Actually Choosing," *Political Science Quarterly*, LXXVI, 1 (March, 1961), 24–46.

[13] See J. W. Masland and L. I. Radway, *Soldiers and Scholars*, Princeton University Press, Princeton, 1957.

tional and training programs generally have prepared the professional soldier for the new civilian-military relationship, the problem is more complex on the civilian side. There is not, and ought not to be, a single, authoritative source of civilian insight on politicomilitary problems in our pluralistic society. Our decentralized system of research, education, and journalism ought to continue to produce a variety of points of view. Only informed civilians can make discriminating response to technically well founded military recommendations, whether they be the soldier's civilian superiors in the Executive branch or the Congressmen with key roles in various Congressional committees. And these in turn must act with the support of disinterested opinion elites across the country whose attitudes have been formed on the basis of a sophisticated treatment of questions of national security policy in the nation's universities and in the nation's press.

CHAPTER XXIII

The Separation of Powers and National Security

By EDWARD L. KATZENBACH, JR.

No MAN, so the saying goes, can serve two masters. God and Mammon, Master Jones and Master Smith create analogous, although not comparable, trials and tribulations for the servant who tries to serve both at once.

Yet the doctrine of the separation of powers in the United States Constitution presupposes such a bifurcation of loyalty on the part of the public servant. Public servants are expected to juggle double allegiance. The Chief Executive and his appointees expect the Civil Servant and the Military to support policy decisions. Congress expects the experts within the Executive Branch to play the role of the disinterested critic. Because expert knowledge and responsibility are set apart, conflicting loyalty has become so much a part of the way of government that it is seldom, indeed almost never, seriously discussed as a central ethical issue. In no other area does this somersaulting ethic create greater frustration and fury than in that of national defense, of military affairs, for here the level of today's economic sacrifice is always at odds with the degree of tomorrow's security.

The problem of conflicting interests has received periodic attention in the Senate, particularly during the course of Senatorial confirmation of Presidential appointees. But the problem has been narrowly conceived in terms of a conflict of financial interest, as an ethical dialogue between positive private financial gain or loss and the need of a guarantee of public integrity. In concrete terms the argument has been centered on the issue of demanding the sale of company shares as a prerequisite to the holding of public office. In practice the legislative efforts thus to insure a high degree of public honesty have never been altogether successful. Five-percenters now accept payola.

An acceptable level of public corruption has been maintained largely through imaginative political appeal to a public conscience temporarily titillated to a point of unusual sensitivity. But while fattening at the public trough is generally regarded as wrong, there is no definition, short of embezzlement and the crudest sort of bribery, which states what actions overstep the bounds of public propriety. "Influence peddling" has never been separated from "candid advice," "unwarranted pressure" from "helpful information." Bribery, friendship, and goodwill are matters on which judgment plays and opinion divides.

This much argued aspect of the problem of the conflict of interest is, however, simplicity itself beside the problem of conflicting loyalties. The ethics of loyalty, given the division between the Executive and the Legislative Branches, and the resultant fracturing of authority and responsibility of both Branches, is a more skittish problem still. Ephemeral and difficult, it is both perennial and serious. The problem of conflicting loyalties is not sufficiently on the public mind to be a part of the public conscience.

Candor is universally proclaimed until its transmutation into criticism. At this point appreciations as to its political value divide. Critics maintain that criticism is the mirror of judgment; policymakers that it is essentially obstructionist. Thus on the national political level the Democratic Party is, in 1960, pleading for another look at "The New Look" in military policy which the Republicans inaugurated eight years ago in the name of national survival. The Republican Party, on the other hand, is taking the position that the Democrats are giving aid and comfort to the enemy by just such criticism. But both Republicans and Democrats stand to gain as well as to lose because of the forthright positions they have taken. The civil servant expert, on the other hand, who publicly disagrees with his political superiors, risks much to gain nothing. For a central aim within any political administration is to force the experts to sing the tune the politicians have called. Diversity is the democratic ideal, unanimity the political reality.

The high hope of the political policymaker is that views contrary to his own will be lost in the high noise level of democracy. He hopes that the frustrated expert will assuage his frustration in private criticism, for he knows that if criticism is registered in Congress, the decibels will mount higher and higher until, perhaps, policy is shattered. Thus the responsible political policymaker seeks to suppress discord and cultivate harmony. The expert, on the other hand, wonders simultaneously just when his conscience will dictate that he come out against agreed upon policy and so run the risk of a ruined career in the national interest.

In short, the separation of powers has created two related ethical problems. The first affects the conscience of the political appointee. It has to do with the acceptable limits of restraints placed on Executive Branch experts appearing before Congress. The second is a problem for the expert, that of the necessity for responsible rebellion.

In theory, there is no reason why this practical problem should ever arise. While it is true that the Military Establishment Act of 1947 provides that the Joint Chiefs of Staff be advisers to Congress as well as to the President and the Secretary of State, the act itself does not seem consonant with the spirit and meaning of the Commander in Chief clause in the Constitution. Clearly the Commander in Chief should be able to command silence. But precedent has shattered prerogative. Today illogical custom has decreed that the appearance of the military and other related experts before the Legislative body is an inalienable part of the notion of civilian control—despite its irrelevance in democracies generally. One might argue that this custom, inaugurated during the great war against militarism, the War of Independence, was not timetried and true, but simply out of date. The argument is irrelevant, however. Political institutions and traditions have remarkable longevity. Learning to live with them is more practical than breaking a lance in an attempt to change them. The problem is to give ethical standards to a fact of life.

Military policy is political policy, political in the sense that within the confines of the national frame of reference the military establishment is considered at once the shield of our security and the apogee of waste and extravagance. Hence, military policy is under simultaneous attack as inadequate, on the one hand, and wasteful on the other, and must be defended by the administration leaders. Basic to this defense is the blockage of the flow of information at some points and its channeling at others. It is understandable then that a major obstruction to Congressional access to information should be the political loyalty of the civilian Pentagon appointees and their attempt to enforce this same political loyalty on military officers.

When Representatives and Senators want information that the military are unwilling to give them because they feel bound by loyalty to their superiors, the gentlemen on Capitol Hill cite a higher law, a greater duty to Country, to Constitution, and to Congress. Under these circumstances the military are encouraged to deny the final authority of the Commander in Chief.

But should the Congress be privy to the disagreement within the Executive Department that may have preceded the final formulation of policy? And if it is not privy, how can it develop contrary information on the basis of which to adopt alternative policy? This problem of developing alternative positions arises in two general areas in defense policy—that in which military and foreign policy overlap, and that in which military demands collide with the national spending ceiling.

Should the advice given the President on a matter of foreign policy be allowed to become Congressional property? Should the military be allowed to voice public disagreement with the Commander in Chief on an issue felt vital to the security of the country? Moreover, and this would seem to be a most important point, when Congressmen speak of freedom to testify, they are generally speaking of public testimony. Congressmen believe that their power to alter thinking in major policy matters comes in large part from an aroused public sentiment—a natural predisposition for a politician. They believe that the press, the fourth estate, is basically the arbiter between the others—the Executive, Legislative, and Judicial—and, as one would expect, their estimate of the role of the press is accurate. Airing policy disagreement is, however, not merely a question of propriety: it runs to the prerogative of command. From this there have arisen questions as politically awkward as they are theoretically titillating.

To whom is the first loyalty of an officer of the United States? Is it to the Commander in Chief, via the Secretaries of the services and via the Secretary of Defense? Is it to the man in the White House who appoints, promotes, and commands? Or is it to the Congress of the United States which confirms that appointment and on which rests a larger responsibility to see that he (or she) is ready to carry out assigned missions?

To put it in proper perspective, it must be noted first of all that the problem is by no means unique to the Department of Defense. Loyalty is the heartbeat of any organization. Loyalty to the Secretary of Agriculture is expected in the Department of Agriculture as is loyalty to the

Secretary of Defense in the Department of Defense. In military matters, the problem of loyalty is often of a different magnitude because of the Pentagon's monopoly of relevant information.

Vividly, if not luridly, a hearing held in 1951 by the Senate Military and Foreign Affairs Committee jointly on the "Military Situation in the Far East," brought this problem, in all its complexity, to the attention of Congress and Executive alike. It was a hearing precipitated by the recall of General of the Army Douglas MacArthur from his post as Supreme Commander of the United Nations Forces in the Korean conflict.

On a number of occasions the General, through letters, particularly through one to the Speaker of the House of Representatives, a civilian admirer, through "taped" broadcasts, press interviews, and an offer to the Chinese "Volunteer" Commander in Chief to talk over an armistice agreement, had embarrassed the Truman Administration. Repeated efforts had been made to get the General to tone down his remarks, but even when he whispered, all the world could hear him. Eventually, and as was inevitable, he was recalled.[1]

There was no open and obvious issue of civilian supremacy for anyone, the central witness at the investigation, General MacArthur, included. But there was an issue closely linked to it, to wit, what information a military man owes and to whom.

Obviously General MacArthur felt that his conduct was justified—just as had young "Billy" Mitchell, the airman, on whose court martial the General had sat some quarter-century before. Both felt that, despite their uniform, they had a patriotic duty to say those things that they thought the Congress and the public had a right to hear. The General's supporters, one of whom was Senator Styles Bridges (Republican, New Hampshire) did everything in their power to defend this position. All maintained that there was a higher loyalty than attention to the admonitions of the dapper World War I artillery major, Harry S. Truman, who happened to be Commander in Chief.

The following colloquy took place over the shining mahogany table

[1]President Eisenhower did not reappoint Admiral Robert B. Carney as Chief of Naval Operations for somewhat analogous reasons—although the reason given was age, despite the fact that the Admiral was only sixty. He, too, had leaked to the press embarrassing beliefs as to the possibilities of a Communist Chinese invasion of Matsu in 1955. (See "Admiral Declines Comment," *New York Herald Tribune*, April 4, 1955, and "Eisenhower Names Burke Chief," *New York Times*, May 26, 1955.)

during the course of these hearings between the then Chairman of the Joint Chiefs of Staff, General of the Army Omar N. Bradley, and Senator Bridges:

> Senator Bridges. If it reaches the time in this country where you think the political decision is affecting what you believe to be basically right militarily, what would you do? . . . Would you speak out, tell the American public? . . . Do you not think that it is your duty, your loyalty to the country to do that?
> General Bradley. No, sir; I don't think so.
> Senator Bridges. Should you not speak out?
> General Bradley. I would; yes, to the constituted authorities; yes.
> Senator Bridges. But would you stop there?
> General Bradley. Yes.[2]

General Bradley was defining "constituted authorities" as those within the Executive Branch. The Chief of Staff of the Army at the time, General J. Lawton Collins, made his definition very specific. "As a military man my Commander in Chief is the President of the United States," he said. "My loyalty is therefore to him. . . ."[3]

Although no administration would or could expect, even within its own ranks, to meet a situation so peculiar as that which pertained during the limited war in Korea with a policy that would be greeted by a solid phalanx of acclaim, any administration must and does expect some degree of homogeneity in publicly expressed sentiments. President Truman expected that General MacArthur might not agree with him, but he also expected the General to give public support at least for the policy he was ordered to carry out. In defense of his outspokenness and general behavior General MacArthur later adduced a political theory which is unique in this country, although common in a country such as France where the military has to encompass political revolution within a doctrine of loyalty. Shortly after his recall the General remarked that he had found:

> in existence a new and heretofore unknown and dangerous concept that the members of our armed forces owe primary allegiance or loyalty to those who temporarily exercise the authority of the Execu-

---

[2] "Military Situation in the Far East," *Hearings before the Senate Committees on Armed Services and Foreign Relations*, 82d Congress, 1st Session, 752, 753 (1951).
[3] *Ibid.*, at 388.

tive Branch of Government rather than to the country and its Constitution which they are sworn to defend. No proposition could be more dangerous.[4]

There is, of course, no doubt whatsoever that no President could tolerate an officer with such a view. This abortive view of Presidential leadership, although most certainly not intended as such by General MacArthur, represents in fact a long step toward anarchy. There remains, however, the problem of defining with precision just where the limits of loyalty can be drawn and how.

A President has a right to expect that advice on military policy, in those cases in which it is virtually synonymous with foreign policy, will be kept from the eyes and ears of the Congress. During the hearings aforementioned, that advice which the military had given the President as to the advisability of entering into the Korean conflict remained locked in confidence. Had Congress the unlimited right to be privy to such advice, a President would hesitate to ask it: for advice not taken could be, as military advice most certainly would be, used against his position by his political enemies.

But this problem of loyalty leads to some most difficult problems both for the military and for Congress—particularly as regards support of the administration budget.

Loyalty is a skittish, intransigent virtue for those at the top of the military structure to honor. It is one on which military men have been marked in their service records year after year, until they reach the high rungs of their hierarchy. Until then the object of loyalty has been easily identifiable in terms of an immediate superior. But at the apex of the military hierarchy loyalty is no longer a single overriding value, but a whole complex of values.

The military chief has a number of equally disagreeable courses of action left open to him when confronted with a directive from President Truman[5] or President Eisenhower[6] that he is expected to support a given budget and hence approve force levels with which he may disagree. He may adopt the philosophy of General Collins quoted above,

---

[4]Quoted in *Washington Post and Times Herald*, March 25, 1952.

[5]"Military Establishment Appropriations Bill for 1948," *Hearings before the House Subcommittee of the Committee on Appropriations*, 80th Congress, 1st Session, 631 (1947).

[6]See *100th Congressional Record* 6621 (1954).

ignore Congress, honor his Commander in Chief, take the position that Executive Branch civilian authority has final responsibility, and that advice therefore should end with his advice to the Secretary of Defense and the President.

For example, a few weeks before the outbreak of war in Korea, the then Chairman of the Joint Chiefs of Staff, General Omar N. Bradley, made a statement which turned out to be intensely embarrassing. For two years within the Administration the General had fought and fought hard for a higher budget.[7] As a matter of fact in April, 1948, as Chief of Staff of the Army, he had joined the Secretary and Chief of Staff of the Air Force in jumping the traces of the President's program when he appeared before the Subcommittee of the House Committee on Appropriations.[8] But in 1950, when the General came before Congress, only a few men like Carl Vinson, Chairman of the House Armed Services Committee, who knows everything, knew how bitter the military were, how deeply disturbed by the skeletonized divisions and squadrons to which they had been reduced. The General's testimony was, therefore, of particular importance. Yet he defended the budget of which he did not, as a military man, approve:

> . . . I go along with the $13,000,000,000 budget. I do not recommend a larger one at this time for various reasons . . . If we had come here and recommended to you a $30,000,000,000 or $40,000,000,000 budget for defense, I think we would be doing a disservice . . .[9]

Later, after the outbreak of war in Korea, he tendered what amounted to a public apology for having let loyalty to the Commander in Chief interfere with the Country's security.[10] Yet when all is said and done, is it possible to avoid recognizing that, given the Separation of Powers and the lack of party discipline which is a concomitant thereof, Executive appointment of "rightminded" officers is a positive necessity?

There is a heavy penalty to be paid for the political bribery of ex-

[7] Walter Millis, *The Forrestal Diaries,* Viking Press, New York, 1951. See generally chapter 10, pp. 382 ff.

[8] "Military Functions, National Military Establishment Appropriation Bill for 1949," *Hearings before the Subcommittee of the House Committee on Appropriations,* 80th Congress, 2d Session, 1224.

[9] "Department of Defense Appropriations for 1951," *Hearings before the Senate Subcommittee on Appropriations,* 81st Congress, 2d Session, 73.

[10] Omar N. Bradley, "A Soldier's Farewell" (as told to Beverly Smith), 12, *Saturday Evening Post,* 8, August 22, 1953, at 63.

perts. If there is dishonesty at the top, dishonesty will run like quicksilver throughout the hierarchy. Is political manipulation so necessary a component of government that the illicit lubricant of dishonesty can be justly used? Department of Defense public relations is in direct need of honest criticism.

Various forms of balderdash and folderol occur in the following composite of on the record public statements of public officials both civilian and military. The end in view, in this case, is public reassurance. The reader may collect the makings of a similar all purpose Pentagon Statement for his own amusement, or disillusionment, over any given three month period:

> Our nation has made great strides in assuring a modern defense; today our security force is the most powerful in our peacetime history; more efficient weapons are being constantly created; the combat power of our divisions, wings and warships has increased; our air force is at the highest state of readiness it has achieved in its ten year history; the combined total of the nation's armed forces represents a dynamic military power of true substance; we have a margin of qualitative superiority over any potential enemy; we have a sufficiency of airpower for the military scheme of things in this air atomic age; our leaders are unanimous in their determination to continue to plan and provide the military posture needed in years to come; what we have now is a sound program.

Surely, the military officer has a responsibility under his oath to the Constitution to speak up against such nonsense as this.

On the other hand, civilian authority has some responsibility to keep military statements reasonably honest as well. Service rivalries continue to be so much a part of an officer's life that he is quite as irresponsible under pressure from his own colleagues as is the civilian from his. Two examples will suffice.

Although the Army did not begin to teach the concept of limited nuclear war in the Command and General Staff School for a surprising length of time after it had become possible to put fissionable material in small enough packages to be used tactically, the Service in the late 1950s finally came, for a short while, to hitch its future to the nuclear star. After it had done so, however, the Army began to put forward its doctrinal position in opposition to that of the United States Air Force with greater and greater forcefulness, and with a heavy admixture of exaggeration. In its fight for scarce dollars—and, incidentally the use of Army testimony here is for the sake of variety, and should in no sense be considered *parti pris*—the Army had to fight the Air Force and its doctrinal position that limited nuclear wars were virtually impossible to keep limited. To further this battle, the Army's Deputy Chief of Staff for Research and Development offered testimony to "prove" that the Air Force's megaton war was unthinkable. The "proof" was deduced by portraying the paralyzingly dreadful effects of radiation as far worse than these were in fact. His testimony before a Congressional Committee was as follows:

> Current planning estimates run on the order of several hundred million deaths that would be either way depending upon which way the winds blew.
> If they blew to the southeast, they would be mostly in the USSR, although they would extend to the Japanese and perhaps down into the Philippine area. If the winds blew the other way, they would extend back into western Europe.[11]

Because this testimony is not untypical of much heavily biased testimony that was being given before Congressional Committees in the early years of the atomic age, and because this particular piece of testimony received worldwide attention, it deserves extended analysis.

In the first place, calling the statement "dishonest" might be considered libelous because of the first two words of the statement, *i.e.*, "current planning." The vagueness of these two words is such that one cannot brand the rest of the statement a lie. But still. . . .

Second, note that the statement may be thought of in a number of contexts. It might have been offered in terms of a preventive war by the United States on the U.S.S.R., by the U.S.S.R. on the U.S.A., and then in terms of a second strike against the U.S.S.R. The statistics might have been thought of in terms of ground or air burst—and there is a great difference between the two in resultant fallout—or the statement might have been made in the context of a counterforce strategy, an attack on enemy military installations, or a spoiling mission against enemy population centers. And finally, the statement could have been

[11] "Study of Airpower," *Hearings before the Senate Subcommittee on the Air Force of the Senate Committee on Armed Services,* 84th Congress, 2d Session, at 861 (Lieutenant General James M. Gavin).

made in the context of weapons which did not then exist, but which might conceivably exist in the future.

Actually, while the statement was not fantasy, it had nothing to do with reality, model 1956. The only context in which the United States would then have had the capability of inflicting "several hundred million deaths" would have been if it had previously decided on preventive war, first against enemy bases and subsequently against enemy populations, using continuing sorties of planes with bombs adjusted for ground bursts in order to achieve the utter devastation of a genuine Carthaginian Peace.

Finally, the fear that surrounds secrecy itself becomes a weapon to be used in controversy. For example, as late as September 16, 1958, the successor to the officer quoted above, likewise a general, made this statement before the American Society for Industrial Security: "However, I say without fear of contradiction that the advanced state of Soviet technology today is due more to Soviet success in espionage and subversion than it is to their scientific apparatus, good as it is." Of course, given his audience, the General was certainly not afraid of contradiction, but that he should utter such a remark, given the repeated statements of United States scientists as to the capabilities of their opposite numbers, is neither more nor less than a gratuitous insult to all without clearance.

However, as unethical as military testimony frequently is, the efforts which are made to keep the military in line may be more serious still in the nuclear age. The methods by which loyalty has, in fact, been enforced have been the same as used in any political situation. Carrot and stick, reward and punishment, temptation and fear, those perennial psychological goads have been used to enforce political discipline on military officers just as they have been, are, and will be on civilian appointees. At the highest echelons the initial obligation which the military officer accepts is the appointment itself. In this, more often than not, there is an initial illusion, for many officers who have never had political affiliations believe that in high posts they are as free as in lower ones to give advice and, whether or not this advice is accepted, to carry out orders. But in fact their new position at the apex of the hierarchy is altogether different from anything in their experience. For here an officer faces a more nearly total responsibility—but to what? Here he is caught between the demands of military security and the support of those other social values represented in the demands of the people's duly elected representatives.

The civilian appointee must assure himself as best he can of the support of the military. For he soon finds out, if he does not already know, that Members of Congress, men with far more experience than he in military affairs, want Pentagon information from the military rather than from him. This being the case he must seek to maximize the likelihood that the military will support before Congress the policy on which he has determined. In a period of cold war, when military problems are a public worry and a political issue, political appointment of the highest ranking officers is inevitably considered a political necessity. Of course, picking the politically adaptable officer is nothing new in United States history. For example, when Henry Stimson, then Secretary of State, went off to the London Disarmament Conference in 1930, he took with him an admiral who, as he himself explained, "did not think as did other admirals."[12] But as the importance of the military increases, so does the desirability, from the Executive point of view, of their political pliability. Recognition of the political inevitability of placing in power military officers whose general orientation is in line with the party in power should add considerably to everyone's understanding of the political process. Only when the military is no longer called upon to testify before Congress will the officer with four or five stars be regarded as an unbiased expert.

Of course, just as promotion to Chairman of the Joint Chiefs is dangled before the Chiefs of the individual services, so promotion to Chief of Staff is dangled before the three star ranks. Where the difficulty has come is further down the hierarchy where promotion is known to come from loyalty to service, and revolt from a given political position taken by the civilian may be rewarded, if not by one administration, at least, perhaps, by the next. Thus the Truman Administration had to cope with dissident officers in the United States Navy, who were ultimately promoted to the highest positions by President Truman's successor, who was at the same time bitterly critical of a group of younger officers in both the Army and Air Force who had leaked information to the press, and thus back to the Congress, or to the Congress and from this source back to the press. These officers, in turn, may

[12] Ernest May, "The Development of Political Military Consultation in the United States," 70, *Political Science Quarterly*, 2, June, 1955, p. 171.

Separation of Powers and National Security

be precisely the ones whom another administration may see decided political advantage in promoting. In short, while political advantage is as much sought after in military circles as in others, the manifestation of it operates in obverse ways, to open as well as to close the channels of communication.

Just as rewards are meted out for good behavior, so punishment is exacted for what is considered bad.

General Matthew B. Ridgway, at one time Chief of Staff in the Eisenhower Administration, complained bitterly that "the pressure brought upon me to make my military judgment conform to the views of higher authority was sometimes subtly, sometimes crudely, applied."[13] Nor are his complaints in any way unusual. In the previous administration much the same complaints were heard from a Chief of Naval Operations, Louis E. Denfield. Despite assurances on the part of the Secretary of the Navy and the Secretary of Defense that they "would do nothing to prevent Congress from exercising its rights, or to deprive American citizens of their constitutional privilege of free speech," Admiral Denfield maintained that in reality "swift vengeance was taken on those whose testimony offended the Secretariat."[14] On one occasion, in Franklin D. Roosevelt's first administration, a Secretary of War, George H. Dern, actually courtmartialed two general staff officers for going to Congress to ask for extra funds.[15] Usually the treatment is more gentle, and the officer in question is simply retired.

There has, as one might expect, been a considerable body of literature on officers' freedom to testify.[16] Of course it can be argued, and frequently is, that since national survival is everyone's business, everyone has an inalienable right to hear the military experts' advice with regard to it. But the Pentagon proposals are, for the most part, the end product of compromise, a long fight and a hard one, and thus are subject to propaganda, misleading generalities, irrelevant statements,

---

[13]Matthew B. Ridgway, "My Battles in War and Peace," *Saturday Evening Post*, January 21, 1956.
[14]Louis E. Denfield, "Why I was Fired," *Colliers*, volume 25, March 18, 1950, p. 14.
[15]See *New York Times*, obituary notice, August 28, 1936.
[16]For example, Demaree Bess, "Are Generals in Politics a Menace?" *Saturday Evening Post*, April 26, 1952, and the author's "Should Our Military Leaders Speak Up?" *New York Times Magazine*, April 15, 1956. See also the very thoughtful letter by Horace M. Kallen in the *New York Times*, September 10, 1950. On the problem generally see Samuel P. Huntington, *The Soldier and the State*, Belknap Press of Harvard University Press, Cambridge, Massachusetts, 1957.

half-truths, and occasionally downright lies when the policy comes before Congress.

Service Secretaries do in fact rewrite the testimony of the military chiefs, and periodically the military are specifically reminded as to what they are supposed to say, or not to say, as the case may be. In the Eisenhower Administration there were two outstanding cases of censorship —one with regard to an article by the Army Chief of Staff, the second with regard to a book by the Commander of the Strategic Air Command.

There is an ideal solution. It should be possible for the Congress to hear disagreement, either between the military, or between the military and the civilians in the Pentagon, or between the Pentagon and the Bureau of the Budget, to listen to the arguments in favor of the proposed solution, and then to make a final judgment on its own. This has been tried in the past—by the Secretary of the Navy under President Wilson, Josephus Daniels, for example. Daniels allowed the General Board of the Navy to make certain recommendations to Congress in 1913, and then he took a contrary position on the grounds that his was the final responsibility. As he said at the time:

> It is not believed that it is dealing honestly with Congress to make large estimates in the expectation that the national legislatures will use the pruning knife. I have reduced the building proposed by the General Board . . . not because of opposition to the progressive ideas of that able body of Naval statesmen, but because it was deemed wise to suggest a budget that will be within the resources of our Government.[17]

Inevitably the President will urge total support. The Congress will always encourage dissent. The President looks upon disagreement amongst those within the Executive Branch with concern and disapproval. Thus in his 1958 State of the Union Message, President Eisenhower pointed to "harmful service rivalries." He was "sure," he said, that "America wants them stopped." But whereas the President was looking, as any President inevitably looks, with civilian eyes at the embarrassment that the military were causing his civilian administration, Congressmen, particularly those on committees dealing directly with the military, tended to look at the problems of the Pentagon through the eyes of the military, whose word they prefer to that of their civilian

---

[17] *Annual Report of the Secretary of the Navy,* Washington, D.C., GPO, 1913, at 11.

superiors. The testimony of the military is the expert testimony which Congressmen seek. This has meaning for them in a way in which the testimony of the short-term Pentagon official simply does not. But more than this, the Congressman out of his own background prefers a federated structure, has respect for the principle of diversity, and has the faith of the politician that controversy is the spark of wisdom and compromise its end.

The problem of Executive Branch coercion of military officers and other Congressional witnesses is, however, only a very small part of the ethical problem which the Separation of Powers has created. The fact that is often overlooked is that the Separation of Powers has caused the fracturing of both the Executive Branch and of Congress.

Despite all of the efforts of succeeding administrations to centralize control of the Executive Branch, it has remained essentially decentralized. Despite the great postwar attempt by Congress to reorganize itself, Congress, too, remains infinitely fractured. Government is divided into invidious policy islands. These islands are always in conflict, and as government becomes larger, their numbers increase.

An interest in government is an interest in policy, seldom an interest in policy administration. Ungracious as it is to suggest this, it frequently seems that recurrent administration and Congressional interest in organization stems more from an interest in creating policy by reorganization than through the medium of it. For example, the Pentagon may be reorganized to save money rather than to see whether more or less should be spent, or a new agency may be set up to focus attention on a given policy rather than to examine it. And each time that the Executive reorganizes, Congress reorganizes as well. Each new administrative cell reproduces itself as if by mitosis. Each new Executive agency begets a new Congressional committee. The Congressional committees may irritate the Executive agency, annoy it with questions, bother it with investigations, and deluge it with suggestions. But for the Executive agency the Congressional committee is always a court of last appeal against an unfriendly Executive Branch decision. As such these Congressional committees represent eternal temptation.

In short, government in these United States is infinitely divided because of the separation of Executive and Legislative. Departments gain autonomy because of a special affinity with a special Congressional committee, and sections of departments have special relations with a subcommittee of the parent committee, and thus beget a degree of autonomy as well. And finally the special program within a special agency sparks the special interest in a Congressional committee chairman, and the program achieves its own individuality with all the perquisites of its particular status.

For the sake of illustration, one might cite the Passport Division of the State Department, which for years was absolved by Congress from meddling Secretaries of State, or the United States Marine Corps which every Marine knows is truly a *Congressional* organization, one in a position to demand an apology in the case of a slur by the Commander in Chief. But perhaps the best illustration lies in that curious segment of the Navy, the Office of the Assistant Chief of the Bureau of Ships for Nuclear Propulsion. The Assistant Chief of this Bureau is Vice Admiral Hyman Rickover, U.S.N. Admiral Rickover has been promoted steadily at Congressional instigation until presently he outranks his nominal superior, the Chief of the Bureau. Not only does the Admiral outrank the Chief, but he enjoys the distinction of being able to write his own budget in very large part. His budget is worked out in private conjunction with the Appropriations Committees of the Congress, outside the control of the Department of the Navy. Furthermore, these committees expect the Admiral, in return for favors thus rendered, to comment on the shipbuilding programs of the Navy as a whole. And this the Admiral is apparently most willing to do.

The point is that the government of the United States is essentially feudal in nature. It consists of great baronies, with all manner of bailiwicks and fiefs within them, each with its own set of overlapping loyalties, responsibilities, and obligations. This being the situation, policy is made by adjustment, and the basis of adjustment is the *case*.

Just as lawyers frequently use the threat of the courts and the expenses of the trial to achieve an adjustment outside them, so the baronies, fiefs, and bailiwicks use the appeal to Congress to achieve compromise decisions.

Again one must resort to illustration. The Department of Health, Education and Welfare decided several years ago to make a case for the closing of post schools on military bases. To make the case it chose to force the closing of a base school close to Washington in segregated Virginia. The Service whose school was subject to the threat did not try, however, to fight out the matter on its merits, but rather went to

Separation of Powers and National Security

Congress with the proposition that if the Department tried to close the school, the Service would order Negro officers with teen age children onto the post—a policy from which it had previously desisted—to test the policy of segregating the children of unsegregated military parents in the public school system. In essence this would force federal judgment as to whether the United States Government should pay the cost of segregated school systems. Congress was informed of this threat. The responsible Committee Chairman warned the Department of Health, Education and Welfare to cease, and there was an end to the matter. Again, the case is merely illustrative. Anyone who has spent a week in the Pentagon has certainly heard the threat of an appeal to Congress at least once. This in turn explains why it is that the United States ship of state is unique in that it leaks outwards and from the top. The leak is part of the ethic of government. So is the withholding of information. Both leakage and secrecy result from and make for the feudality of United States government. The divisions between policy segments were initially created by the doctrine of the Separation of Powers. They ended by destroying that separation in great part and substituting segmented and separated policy units instead. Indeed both the Executive and the Congress have been very careful to keep policy fractured by keeping policy wholes apart. Thus foreign aid has been periodically kept apart from foreign policy, and a civilian agency, the Atomic Energy Commission, spends some 70 per cent of its budget, at a guess, on weapons for the military.

In most cases advice, carefully considered and acted upon, is needed at least if it is contractual rather than generated within the organization itself. Consider, however, the following cases. Case I: One of the Joint Chiefs of Staff commented that the only time he used an advisory agency was when he knew he was right and wanted to prove it to his colleagues by impartial research. Case II: Two generals in the same service disagreed on tactics, and instead of having their disagreement settled, both contracted with advisory groups to build auxiliary data on their individual assumptions. Case III: A group of in-government systems analysts were advised by their chief to contract with outside the government advisers in order to make their work more acceptable. Case IV: A group of outside advisers were handed a study to retype, essentially, so that a given position would bypass an alleged obstructionist in the hierarchy. Case V: A group of distinguished citizens were brought together to give sanction to a report the contents of which they already knew before their study group convened. There is something essentially unsound about a system which has to resort to such devious means to achieve a hearing and gain acceptance.

Of course, the prevalent expectation of exaggeration does much to blunt its effect. In this sense we should be grateful to Madison Avenue. It is a safeguard built into society. But it is a far from satisfactory one, particularly in the military field. Advances in weapons technology make for explosive change. But when one makes a case, one rigidifies a position in a field in which fluidity is absolutely necessary. Hence, compounding exaggeration may be a genuine crime in a nuclear age. Furthermore, because of secrecy and the difficulties of technological access to required data, countercase making is very difficult, and hence direction may be fixed without public debate. For example, it was expected before Korea that A-bombs would be used in another conflict without any detailed thinking as to the danger of this policy in limited war. One might also remark in passing that the situation has been compounded under the present [summer, 1960] administration. It is presently announced policy to use limited-yield atomic weapons in limited war, although the military themselves have largely changed their formerly held positions as to their military and political usefulness. Hence one wonders whether more cannot be done to obviate unethical practices in the casemaking process.

If casemaking is an inevitable byproduct of a fractured governmental organization, and this, in turn, is a direct result of the Separation of Powers, the simple theoretical solution would seem to be the reworking of the Constitution. But the theoretical solution has proved, in practice, to be no solution. Besides there is always a question as to precisely what values are served by reorganization. Certainly British White Papers on National Defense are not always the candid exposé of government policy they are sometimes thought to be.

Obviously the most important quality in the rehabilitation of more honest positiontaking is leadership. Civilian appointees should be willing to stand by their own decisions rather than trying to force the military to take like ones. Second, the civilian appointee should be willing to testify as to exaggerations or distortions by the military under his control. The Senate could help the process immeasurably by pointing out to the new Secretaries just what the problems are in appointment hearings. Indeed in the absence of any formal briefing for Secretaries and given the absence of any training for the position on the part of most appointees, the Senate has an obligation to tell the newly appointed Secretary some of the facts of political life. This it has never attempted to fulfil.

Great effort is needed to effect the dismantling of the barriers to information which presently exist within the classified community. The burden of proof should not be on the need to know, but on the need not to know. There must be an end put to the refusal to communicate. It should be understood that this is genuinely intolerable. The day must come when the gentlemen in the dark blue uniform *will* walk up one flight to see the gentlemen in the light blue, and *can* return with a copy of an Air Force study on the vulnerability of the aircraft carrier—to pick a random example.

Finally the political science fraternity should spend less time explaining the structure of government, and more time with the ethical problems which the Separation of Powers creates. Ethics cannot be legislated; they can only be taught.

In summary, perhaps all that can be said is that national defense is a many faceted political issue. It is, therefore, not one on which, more than another, Congress or public can expect the cold and sober truth. National survival has always been a political issue, and presumably always will be. Moreover, the open society is no less free from the danger of falsehood than the closed society. The difference between the two societies lies rather in the presence of antibodies of truth in the open society which could save it—although, of course, this is by no means guaranteed—and make it prosper. For despite the obfuscation, the general outlines of the true situation are available and can be known if one is willing to give the time and effort. Of course, this is by no means a simple task, for truth must overcome prejudice, an ancient and well entrenched enemy.

Comment by Quincy Wright:
   The problem of separation of powers of government and the integration of different types of expertise are well discussed by William T. R. Fox and Edward L. Katzenbach, Jr., who gave special attention to the problem of civil-military relations. If the Pentagon's expertise, locked in classified documents, is the major basis of foreign policy, how is there to be any democratic control of this aspect of government, most essential for the

people's welfare or even survival? I should like to have seen the following aspect of the question discussed. If nuclear war is mutual suicide, and the expertise of the military is devoted to the problem of winning a war, how will that expertise help us in avoiding extermination? If war is obsolete as a means of national defense, is not the expertise of the diplomat and psychologist what is needed for defense? The problem is not how to win a war but how to prevent a war. This seems to make it all the more necessary that the civilian be on top of the military in policymaking. This principle of democratic government, originally adopted to prevent military takeovers of the government, seems necessary today, in the realm of international relations, to stop the arms race and avoid extermination by nuclear war.

VI. Fusion of Ethics and Organizational Considerations

CHAPTER XXIV

Some Questions on the Measurement and Evaluation of Organization

By KENNETH E. BOULDING

THE CONCEPT of organization is perhaps the most central, and also the most puzzling notion in the scientific view of the universe. The great quest of the scientist is for *ordered structure* in space and time, whether this is in the nucleus, the atom, the molecule, the virus, the gene, the organ, the animal, the human person, or the social organization. An ordered structure capable of behavior and perhaps capable of growth is however precisely what we mean by an organization. All these ordered structures are essentially role structures—open systems with a throughput of components consisting of lower level organizations, in which however the components are forced by the related roles around them to play a certain role in the organizational structure. Thus individual electrons come and go in an atom, but once one is captured it must behave in a certain way until it is lost. Similarly atoms come and go in a molecule, but the molecule remains, molecules come and go in a cell, but the cell remains, cells come and go in a body, but the body remains; persons come and go in an organization, but the organization remains. What "remains" in the midst of all this flux of components is the "role," the "place," and the relations of roles one to another. A role is a hole, an organization is a related and orderly set of holes, and one sometimes catches a fleeting and slightly nightmarish vision of the scientific universe as a set of holes bounded and defined by other holes! The significance of almost anything, like that of a word, is derived largely from its context; everything, however, is the context for other things; context creates itself, *ad infinitum*.

In the processes of the universe we seem to see two apparently opposite, though not essentially contradictory processes at work. One is the constant increase in entropy, that is in "chaos" or "disorder" as work is done and processes are carried out, according to the Second

Law of Thermodynamics. Everything that happens destroys potential, and so makes "happening," which is made possible by potential differences of some kind, less possible. According to this image of the universe all processes in time lead eventually to a universe which is a kind of thin soup of undifferentiated matter and energy, all equally distributed, all at the same temperature, and in which nothing whatever can happen. This gloomy view of the ultimate future may be in process of modification by current controversies among the astronomers, but whatever the outcome of these, whether the universe is a stationary state with continuous creation of hydrogen, as Hoyle supposes, or whether the more conventional views are correct, there is no doubt about the general validity of the increase of entropy with process.

We observe, however, another process at work in the universe which we call "evolution." This is a process by which the population of organizations comes to have more and more complex members in it. The elements evolve in the primordial explosion, at a certain point in time life appears, living forms grow in complexity and culminate in man; man himself forms social organizations which also evolve rapidly toward greater and greater complexity. Here is a process which seems to go in the opposite direction to that of "time's arrow" as measured by entropy. What is happening here is not that entropy is failing to increase, but that entropy itself is getting increasingly *segregated*. There are redistributions of entropy going on, leading to greater organization at some points no doubt at the expense of other points. "Life," as Schroedinger says, "feeds on entropy." In the course of the evolutionary process even though chaos continually increases and "unchaos" diminishes, out of these diminished reserves of order evolution builds increasingly complex castles. The universe on this view is like a rich man continually losing his capital, but in the process transforming his diminishing stock into ever more intricate and differentiated forms.

The first question therefore which I want to raise is whether it would be possible to find a *measure* of the extent of evolution in the *distribution* of entropy. This would be in itself a measure of the degree of organization of the universe or of any part of it, though it would not in itself be an adequate description of organization. No single measure, of course, can describe a complex structure such as an organization. Nevertheless these "indices" which single out certain quantitative aspects are helpful in reducing the complexity of reality to a form which our inadequate minds can grasp. Thus a price index reduces a long list of prices to a single number, and expresses something "important" about the list. Similarly a measure of the degree or quantity of organization, if we had one, would be a useful way of symbolizing something essential and significant in these very complex structures.

It would provide, for instance, a rough measure of the rate of evolution. We have a certain intuitive sense that in the course of evolutionary change "something" is evolving; that there is, in other words, an evolutionary vector, and that it makes sense to say that evolution moves "faster" at some times than at others, or even that it occasionally reverses itself. From the hydrogen atom to the ameba, and from the ameba to man we seem to detect "progress," that is, increase in some quantity which measures progress. It may be that this "upwardness" is an anthropomorphic illusion, and that in some scale of values the retrogression from the ascetic simplicity of the hydrogen atom to the monstrous corruption of mankind may be deplored. It is not the value sign which matters here, however, but the vector, that is, the sense of both direction and magnitude. Few could deny that the process which leads from the hydrogen atom to the ameba to man has both direction and magnitude, and that it would be very useful to have even a rough measure of the magnitude.

Several important problems might be closer to solution if we had a measure of evolutionary change. It is difficult, for instance, to test any theories of the machinery of evolutionary change, whether in biology or in the social sciences, without some measure of the extent of this change. Furthermore a simple measure of the quantity of organization would almost certainly force us to examine higher levels of organizational systems, simply because it would prove unsatisfactory in dealing with the complexities of the higher organizational forms. Consider, for instance, the view that the key to the understanding of the process of evolution is an analysis of the *teaching* process. Here is the one clearly observable process in the universe where the strict laws of conservation do not hold. Energy and matter can only be exchanged: knowledge can be *produced*. When a teacher teaches a class, if the hour has been successful, not only do the students know more as a result of the process, but the teacher frequently knows more, too! Teaching is in no sense an exchange, in which what the student gets the teacher loses. We can break down the teaching process perhaps into two others: the first might be called the *printing* process. It is the process by which a certain structure or organization is imposed on some carrier around it by simple transfer of pattern. The pattern of a page of type imprints itself on many pieces of paper in exactly the same shape. The gene evidently has this property of printing in three dimensions: its self-reproducing quality arises because it can attract to each atom of itself a like atom, which forms a mirror image of the structure, which then exercises the same power of imprinting itself and so reproduces exactly the original pattern of the gene. Similarly a teacher may simply "teach" verbatim something that he knows, like the multiplication table: this is "rote teaching," which results in rote learning.

There is also however a more fundamental process at work: I shall call it, for short, *"inspiring."* This is the process by which the teacher supports and cooperates with a process of internal growth in the mind of the student. This is also the process by which the gene organizes the growth of a phenotype or body quite unlike itself. It is the process also by which ideas and ideologies inspire the growth of cultures and societies. This is clearly a complex and puzzling process, which we understand very imperfectly at present. It has some similarities to the process by which a building is built to follow a blueprint—the blueprint, indeed, might be described as a special case of the "inspiring" process, for the building which it "inspires" is very different from the mere two dimensional plan which maps it. The building of the body, however, or of a society, is inspired by more complex processes than that of the blueprint. The gene seems to be able to change its blueprint in the course of executing it, and society likewise does not develop toward a predetermined end, but according to certain broad principles of change and continuity in a process which is constantly liable to a shift in direction both from conscious images and from unconscious causes.

It is clear that in the "teaching" process we are dealing with something akin to the growth of organization. Knowledge, indeed, can be regarded as a form of organization. In its verbal expression it consists of a structure of related contexts, in each of which any "word" or symbol can play the appropriate role, provided that the code is understood. Thus "house," "domus," "maison," etc., are different words or symbols each of which however plays the same *role* in a language. One despairs, indeed, of ever getting any simple measure of the quantity of knowledge. Nevertheless a measure of the quantity of organization would be of some help here, and might be valuable in testing the "success" of a learning process.

These considerations may seem very abstract and remote from the pressing problems of today. Nevertheless I hope to show that the questions I have raised lie at the heart of most of our major, practical problems. Consider, for instance, the problem of economic development. What we have here is a process of social evolution from an economy at a lower level of organization to one at a higher level. The difference between a rich and a poor society lies mainly in the level of organization which it has attained; rich societies are rich not usually because they are amply endowed with natural resources but because they have learned how to organize themselves into complex processes of production extended through time. Extreme poverty of resource base, of course, like that of the Bushmen or the Eskimos, may condemn any society which lives on it to a low level of organization and a low standard of living. Once these extremes are excluded, however, the level of living, or per capita real income of a society is overwhelmingly a function of its degree of organization. Iceland, which is a fairly well organized society, makes a moderately good living in a most unprepossessing natural environment; there are countries by contrast with fair climates and rich soil "where every prospect pleases" but man ekes out a miserable existence in dire and disorganized poverty.

In the case of economic development we actually possess a rough measure of the degree of attainment of a society and of its rate of progress in the per capita real income. At first sight this seems to be wholly unrelated to the "distribution of entropy" measure which I suggested as a possible index of degree of organization. The relation is a subtle one, but I believe it exists. Consumption is clearly a process which increases entropy: we eat more highly ordered substances than we excrete, automobiles are more highly ordered than scrap iron, clothing is more highly ordered than rags or dust, and so on. Consumption means therefore reducing order to disorder: it is a typically "entropic" process. By contrast production is "anti-entropic." It takes soil and air and water and makes wheat and bread; it takes ore and rock and makes steel and machines; it takes fiber and makes cloth, or cloth and makes clothes. In each case the act of production is that of imposing a greater degree of order in one place, at the cost, however, of greater disorder elsewhere (mine tailings, waste materials, etc.). Production therefore is typical of the evolutionary process in that it segregates entropy and builds up highly ordered, low entropy "products" (commodities) at the cost, no doubt, of producing high entropy "wastes" elsewhere.

Per capita real income is a measure of the rate of production, in some index of units of commodities per unit of time. It is clearly therefore related to the rate at which entropy is being segregated in economic processes. We may ask, however, what about consumption? If all production is consumed, does not the entropy increasing character of consumption just offset the entropy decreasing character of production so that there is no net segregation of entropy or increase in organization? This raises the question whether increase in organization does not come from *accumulation,* that is, from the excess of production over consumption, rather than from production or consumption itself? On this view the rate of progress of a society would be measured by its rate of accumulation rather than by its real income: two societies might have the same real income, but if one consumed less and accumulated more than the other it would be advancing faster.

There is a good deal of truth in this view, especially if we take a broad enough concept of accumulation. There is some confusion of thought here even among economists because of a failure to distinguish between income in the sense of production or consumption, that is, additions to or subtractions from the capital stock, and income in the sense of "use" or enjoyment *of* a capital stock. Thus my enjoyment or use of furniture, houses, clothing, etc. is almost independent of their consumption—that is, the rate at which they wear out. I have argued in an earlier paper[1] that it is this enjoyment or use of a capital stock which is the true measure of human wellbeing, not the rate at which this stock is consumed or produced. Nevertheless there is likely to be a fairly monotonic relation between the amount of use or enjoyment, the total stock which is used or enjoyed, and the rate at which this stock is consumed or produced, especially under fairly constant techniques. We must bear in mind here that the capital stock consists not only of physical objects like furniture, but also of the furniture of our minds and the states of our bodies. Thus the acquisition of memories, the learning of information or skills, and the inculcation of pleasant states of mind is as much capital formation as the building of a dam. When we go to a movie we build a state of mind called "just having

[1]"Income or Welfare," *Review of Economic Studies,* volume 17, 1949–1950, p. 77.

been to a movie." This state depreciates or is consumed just as a chair or a breakfast depreciates, and needs to be restored at suitable intervals.

I do not propose to resolve the question here whether economic organization or welfare can be discussed equally well in its "stock" aspect as capital or in its "flow" aspect as income. I am prepared to argue that both these aspects may be of importance, and that neither can quite be reduced to the other. This dilemma also faces us, we may note, in general evolutionary theory. Is it the "stock" of organisms or species which is significant in measuring the rate of evolution, or is it some rate of "throughput" or metabolism which is most significant? We should not be much interested in a "stock" of things, however complex, which never "did" anything—that is, which had no throughput—evolution is more than the elaboration of skeletal forms. On the other hand, *mere* busyness, mere throughput, mere metabolism is not the sole object of interest either; evolution is not merely the development of vast outputs of slop and enormous appetites and excretions. It is this curious combination of the development of intricate structures which *do* things that are significant to them, or to something, which constitutes the peculiar charm of evolution, and I am not prepared to argue at this point whether this apparent two-dimensionality can be reduced to one dimension or not.

The transformation of a society from a lower level to a higher level of organization is not a process of simple homogeneous growth (indeed, the fashionable term "economic growth" may be quite a misnomer) but is an evolutionary, developmental, and almost embryological process not unlike that of the development of a chicken within (and out of) the egg. The "egg" is the relatively undifferentiated, unorganized subsistence economy of small farmers and craftsmen, without large organizations, without much in the way of complex equipment or formal education. The "chicken" is the developed society, with large and complex organizations, complex accumulations of capital in the form of material, skill and educated and informed intelligence, and an extensive division of labor and differentiation of function. As the chicken grows, it gradually absorbs the "yolk"; subsistence farmers and unskilled laborers get jobs in larger organizations, they get education and skill and they end up as highly differentiated members of complex organizations. One of the problems which a developing society faces which is not usually faced by an embryo is that the "yolk" may revolt and refuse to be absorbed in the chicken: it may even carry the revolt to the point where the chicken is killed and the developmental process stops. Because of this possible resistance the developmental process in society requires a certain identification of the "yolk" with the whole developing society: the undeveloped people must either enjoy vicariously the pleasures of the developing middle class which they themselves are not enjoying, or they must identify themselves with the *hope* that they or their descendants will enjoy the fruits of progress, or they must be coerced into cooperation by the superior power and will of the developing part of society in control of the means of coercion. The first is the British pattern, the second the American, and the third (one fears) the Chinese.

The problem of the measure of the level of organization is quite crucial in the argument of the "cold war" between Communism and capitalist democracy. The Communists claim, in effect, that their system is at a higher level of social evolution, and a higher level of organization, than capitalism, and that it must therefore ultimately triumph, as all higher levels of organization have supposedly triumphed in the evolutionary process. We must beware, incidentally, of a tautology here: if we *define* "higher" by "survival," then of course the higher organism always survives! The "survival of the fittest" slogan is quite empty if fitness is defined as fitness to survive. This underlines the necessity of an independent measure of organization or "fitness" so that the proposition that the fit survive may be *testable* in experience. The Communist claim to be a higher level of organization rests mainly on the assumption that hierarchy is the only organizing instrument. The Communist society is a "one-firm state"—that is, a society organized hierarchically into a single economic organization. It is simply General Motors (or perhaps more realistically, the Pentagon, which is in terms of national income the world's third largest Communist society) expanded to include the whole economy, with the possible exception of a few Nepmen and some surreptitious private trade. A capitalist society by contrast is "ecological" where the Communist society is "organic." A Communist society is a true Leviathan, a vast social whale; a capitalist society is more like a pond with a great multitude of interacting organisms bound together in a system of mutual exchange, or markets.

The biological parallel gives us a certain reason for not accepting the

Communist claim without very careful scrutiny. The key to the problem here is what the economist calls "diminishing returns to scale." In society, as in biology, it by no means always follows that "the bigger the better." Beyond a certain point in the development of a particular type of organism a further increase in size leads to a decline in efficiency, a decline therefore in the "quantity of organization," and a lessened chance, we presume, of survival. Where this point comes at which diminishing returns to scale set in depends on the *type* of organization. Chemical elements seem to show diminishing returns in terms of stability as the atomic number increases, and beyond Bismuth (atomic number eighty-three) no stable (nonradioactive) forms are known. Inorganic molecules form larger structures than the elements, but these rarely exhibit molecular weights above 100. Organic molecules with carbon chains go much farther; cells are much larger organizations again, but again have a limit—no one celled animal reaches more than microscopic dimensions. Differentiation of cells permits the growth of larger organisms: plants get to be quite large, though not very complex: insects achieve great complexity, but cannot break through the size barrier of about three inches in length, and their optimum size seems to be between the ant and the bee. The endoskeleton and the convolution of the lung, the bowels, and the brain permitted the construction of still larger complex forms in the vertebrates, culminating in the mammal, just as the steel frame (an endoskeleton) and air conditioning permits the development of larger buildings than solid walls (exoskeletons) and mere windows permit.

Now, however, the biological parallel, no doubt to our alarm, gives some possible comfort to the Communists. Admitting (which in general Communists do not) the existence of diminishing returns to scale beyond a certain point for *any one form* of organization, do we not see in the evolutionary process the constant transcending of an old size barrier by a new form of organization—the molecule transcending the element, the cell the molecule, the animal the cell, the vertebrate the invertebrate, the mammal the reptile? Can we not argue then that new and more perfect forms of social organization now have enabled us— or shortly will enable us—to transcend the old size barrier and establish, literally, a whale of a society in the Communist state? The question here is crucial to the world's future: it is however an empirical question which cannot be answered *a priori,* but only by studying the organizations themselves. Here again we see how useful would be an acceptable measure of the degree of organization against which we could test the hypothesis that diminishing returns to scale set in at a point far smaller than that of the whole society. It is on this hypothesis, if "returns" are interpreted broadly enough to include all things which are valued by men, not merely commodities, that a market (capitalist) society stands or falls by comparison with an organic (Communist) society.

Somewhere lurking in the wings of this whole argument is, of course, the whole problem of value. The bigger is not necessarily better, the more is not necessarily better, so what *is* better? This unfortunately is a question too important to be left to the philosophers, and too unanswerable to be left to anyone else. The value coordinate is clearly a vector, like organization. We compare two constellations of perceived reality, and we say that one is "better" than the other, that is, is further "out" from some origin of goodness. Insofar as we believe that the evolutionary process carries us not only to more organized systems but also to "better" systems we imply a generally monotonic relationship— which does not, of course, have to be linear—between degree of organization and "goodness." Such a relationship may of course be questioned —indeed even to state it so baldly looks like a reversion to the uncritical Spencerian optimism of the nineteenth century, and one can hardly question that for short, or even for fairly extended periods, evil may clothe itself in organization superior to good. Nevertheless it is surely an implication of the basic long-run optimism of most religious or even secular faiths that the course of evolution toward higher organization is also a movement toward the "good." If this seems homocentric it is at least not surprising in *homines!*

If large and complex constellations of organizations are to be reduced to a one dimensional vector of "goodness" we must have something like a "price system" of valuation coefficients by which the diverse and many dimensional elements of the constellation can be reduced to a single dimension of value. Thus suppose we ask whether a man who is loyal but stupid is "better" or "worse" than a man who is unfaithful but intelligent. The answer we give will clearly depend on the *value weights* which we give to the various qualities. If we give loyalty a low value weight and intelligence a high one, we are likely to rate the intelligent man "better" than the stupid one even if he is unfaithful: if we give loyalty a high value weight by comparison with intelligence the reverse result may obtain. Many of the difficulties of ethical valuation arise because of the absence of a "salient" and clearly agreed upon system of value weights. In economic valuation of course—as in, for instance, the valuation of a heterogeneous constellation of assets in a balance sheet—we have the advantage of a system of value weights given us initially by the structure of relative prices, even though we may modify this considerably in the evaluation process. In ethical valuations we do not have the same advantage, and the difficulties of ethical agreement are a direct result of the absence of an agreed system of value weights.

I would not wish to imply that a measure of organization would automatically yield a system of ethical value weights which would enable us to do perfect "ethical accounting." Nevertheless, because I have some confidence in the generally monotonic character of the relationship between organization and "goodness"—that is, that both generally increase together—I would argue that the development of a workable measure of organization would at least be a first step toward the construction of an ethical calculus. The want of this measure however may impede progress toward the solution of many problems, not only in biology and in the social sciences, but also in ethics.

CHAPTER XXV

Prolegomena to Ethics for Administrators

By NATHAN D. GRUNDSTEIN

I

THE CONTENT of the experience termed moral and the conditions under which administrative activity is associated with the moral and is experienced by the administrator as a moral experience are the concerns of this essay. The moral in administrative experience is not self-evident. Unless it can be made evident, the administrator cannot consciously confront the moral component of his experience. It is not only a matter of "what is a moral decision?"—but also a matter of "when is the administrator confronted with the occasion for a moral decision?" How experiences can be perceived as presenting moral choices for decision by the administrator is one of the threshold problems of constructing an ethics for administrators.

Subjectively experienced morality can appropriately be distinguished from objective morality. The latter is here taken to refer to ideologies of ethics, to the intellectual content of ethical systems categorized in one way or another—*e.g.*, nonutilitarian as opposed to utilitarian ethics or the ethics of motives as opposed to the ethics of consequences of acts. The former—subjectively experienced morality—takes the form of concrete decisions by an individual that are perceived as incorporating deliberately contrived ethical choices. The individualized character of ethical experience is recognized in the "practical or moral environment" to which Dewey has referred, that is, the environment as it appeals to consciousness, as it is affected by the makeup of the agent,[1] and also in the concept of "the moral constitution" ("what one experiences when he submits to the court of his conscience") as elaborated by Edmond N. Cahn.[2]

[1] John Dewey, *Outlines of A Critical Theory of Ethics* (1891 edition, reprinted 1957, Hillary House, New York), p. 99. "Whatever, however near or remote in time and space, an individual's capacities and needs relate him to, is his environment" (p. 100).

[2] Edmond N. Cahn, *The Moral Decision*, Indiana University Press, Bloomington, 1957, p. 16.

Nevertheless, subjectively experienced morality occurs within a social context shaped by the existence of the organization of which the administrator is a part. The moral in the experience of the administrator as a person cannot be dissociated from his role activities, which focus on the creation, design, and maintenance of an organization. Multiple organization memberships only complicate the social contexts supplying the occasions for individualized ethical experiences. An adequate conception of the possibilities implicit in the interplay between the social context of moral experience provided by organizations and the content and conditions of the administrative experience termed moral must also be included among the threshold problems of constructing an ethics for administrators.

The ethical in subjectively experienced morality is capable of being comprehended as a complex of psychosocial processes. These processes represent activity that is generated by the variety of problems connected with the identification, selection, and working out of a demonstrably ethical course of action in situations in which individuals regard organizations both as objects and as instruments.

In law these psychosocial processes have been explained by Cahn as patterned interactions between "the moral constitution" of the individual, "group moral legislation," and the concrete situations providing the occasions for moral deliberation and decisions.[3] Through socialization a group moral standard is internalized by the individual, who proceeds to rework and reshape it within the matrix of his own unique "character, temperament, and intellect (and in the crucible of the 'moral constitution')," and upon the proper occasion he enunciates a deliberately "rephrased moral imperative" which then becomes a part of—but also modifies—the moral order. The individual is not passive and hence never without personal responsibility in the face of a multiplicity of group norms within the community. "When various groups in the community present a number of diverse or opposing attitudes, there is as affirmative an act of personal enterprise and moral commitment in *selecting* one perspective from the available many as in *establishing* a perspective which one believes to be entirely original."[4]

In philosophy, an inclusive explanation of these psychosocial processes

[3]*Ibid.*, pp. 18 *et seq.*
[4]*Ibid.*, p. 305.

was expounded by Dewey.[5] He postulated the individual as being "confronted with institutions" and as having to work out the character of the moral through a response to these institutions. Ethical choice involved an individual reflecting in a critical manner upon "existing morality." The individual was free to inform his conscience of the moral by inquiry into conventional norms, customs, and beliefs within society and the manner of their incorporation into institutions. This right of self-informing ethical inquiry by a person was the *principle of subjective freedom,* which Dewey praised as the contribution of Kant to ethical thought. But it brought to the fore the question of whether or not individual ethical judgments could then be said to have an objective standard. The answer of Dewey was that an ethical standard outside the individual conscience did exist. It was a norm which the individual could extract from social relationships; it was the "ideal embodied in existing customs, ideas, and institutions." Through "reflective intelligence" the individual discovered for himself the inconsistencies at large within the "existing morality." He brought out the moral incongruencies within the social structure. Analysis by the individual also enabled him to extract "the ideal which it pretends to embody," and it is this indigenous ideal which the individual can utilize as a base for criticism of the "existing morality."

For Dewey, the moral was a *willed* end selected by an individual who has a unique thinking-feeling response to an environment which he intends to transform in order to subordinate it to the realization of that chosen end. It is an end that has been judged as desirable (and hence obligatory) in relation to the perceived conditions and requirements of a situation. Feelings unite the individual with the end he has chosen, so the realization of self is possible in activity directed at the attainment of moral ends. To be moral is to be effective in pursuit of the appropriate ends; that is, private self (egoistic) and social self (altruistic) are joined. Dewey was interested in demonstrating that the moral self-satisfaction of the individual and the satisfaction of community needs are reciprocally related. He had, however, to content himself with the assertion that it was a necessary ethical postulate. ". . . in most, if not all cases, the agent acts from a faith that, in realizing his own capacity, he will satisfy the needs of society . . .

[5]Dewey, *supra.*

where such faith is wanting, action becomes halting and character weak."[6]

What has been attempted with respect to the moral or ethical in philosophy and jurisprudence needs to be paralleled in administration, but in a form consistent with its own unique discipline, which aims at building an administrative science. By so doing, the moral or ethical in administration will be envisioned as embracing more than the enumeration of normative constraints on role performance, as going beyond practicing codes of ethics. Insuring that one is conforming with the letter of prescribed norms and is, in this sense, an ethical administrator can exhaust itself in ethical formalism. The moral or ethical in administration is concerned with those organized systems of which the normative is a component of the relationships comprising the system itself. When it is so conceived, ethics for administrators does not stand confined at the periphery of administrative practice but can enter into the field of administration as a competence of the administrator. Moral concepts can be used analytically to deal with the normative component of relationships within an organization. The moral or ethical in administration and the technological or nonnormative need not be put in logical opposition, for administrative competence can be reconceptualized to include within it the effective utilization of the ethical by the administrator. In fact, it is possible to come full circle: the quality and utilization of the technology adopted by an organization—including the design of the organization relationships themselves —may be subjected to a test of technological effectiveness derived from the *normative* rather than from the nonnormative.[7]

That the moral component of organization activity requires a distinct and recognizable competence with respect to the moral by the executive of an organization is the contribution of Chester I. Barnard. His perception of the ways in which the moral enters into organization activity and, above all, its particular significance for the executive function, contributes greatly to the working out of an ethics for administrators that is central, rather than peripheral, to professional management. For Barnard, "Executive positions (a) imply a complex morality, and (b) require a high capacity of responsiiblity, (c) under conditions of activity, necessitating (d) commensurate general and specific technical

[6]*Ibid.*, pp. 127–128.
[7]James C. Worthy, *Big Business and Free Men,* Harper and Brothers, New York, 1959, chapters 5–7.

abilities as a *moral* factor . . . ; in addition there is required (e) the faculty of *creating* morals for others."[8]

Within organizations the moral takes the form of codes, both personal and organizational. Personal (or private) moral codes are the outcome of a complex socialization process which Barnard leaves inexplicit, contenting himself with saying that they "are an active resultant of accumulated (external) influences on persons, evident only from action in concrete conditions."[9] A person does not have internalized within him a single private moral code, but a complex of such codes "arising from different sources of influence and related to several quite diverse types of activities."[10] Organization moral codes differ as between organizations. No attempt is made at a systematic account of their origins. Instead, organization codes are taken as given, as "accruals largely of intangible forces, influences, habitual practice, which must be accepted as a whole."[11]

The moral is subjective. It is associated with "sentiment, feeling, emotion, internal compulsion," rather than with thought which is of a rational or logical or analytical character. The moral functions within the individual as a selection mechanism. It regulates the impulses and desires which lie at the base of personal choice so as to maintain in the ascendancy those which are consistent with individual "propensities of a general and stable character."[12] In view of the existence of a complex of private codes within individuals, different individuals may exhibit variations in their adherence to one or another of these codes under different conditions. There are also possibilities for serious personal difficulties to be associated with choice whenever there is a conflict between codes having "substantially equal validity or power in the subject affected."[13] What is involved in the utilization of the moral as a selection mechanism by the individual is what Barnard calls the quality of responsibility, and his "point is that responsibility is the property of an individual by which whatever morality exists in him becomes effective in conduct."[14]

---

[8] Chester I. Barnard, *The Functions of The Executive,* Harvard University Press, Cambridge, Massachusetts, 1938, p. 272.
[9] *Ibid.,* p. 262.
[10] *Loc. cit.*
[11] *Ibid.,* p. 273.
[12] *Ibid.,* p. 261.
[13] *Ibid.,* p. 264.
[14] *Ibid.,* p. 267.

Executive positions are characterized by moral complexity. These positions impose on the incumbents the necessity of dealing with a complex of organization codes. The higher the rank the greater the moral complexity of the position. The executive must possess the ability "to resolve the moral conflicts implicit" in his position or else he will fail. This ability involves a capacity to discriminate among the factors of a complex situation; a capacity to innovate by recasting the framework of purpose within which conflicts of codes arise; a sensitivity to the moral complexities of a situation, which is tied to the possession by the executive of "an adequate complex of moralities"; and the quality of responsibility developed to a high degree in all of its dimensions.[15]

The moral has both an organizational and an individual function. The endurance of organization is linked by Barnard to the quality of the morality introduced into the system by the executive. Without the "organization morality" created by the executive, cooperative effort disintegrates under the "centrifugal forces of individual interests or motives."[16] The language of Barnard describing what is required of the executive to create moral codes for others is both stirring and apt.

> The creative function as a whole is the essence of leadership. It is the highest test of executive responsibility because it requires for successful accomplishment that element of "conviction" that means identification of personal codes and organization codes in the view of the leader. This is the coalescence that carries "conviction" to the personnel of organization, to that informal organization underlying all formal organization that senses nothing more quickly than insincerity. Without it, all organization is dying, because it is the indispensable element in creating that desire for adherence—for which no incentive is a substitute—on the part of those whose efforts willingly contributed constitute organization.[17]

II

The earlier statement that organizations provide the social context for individualized ethical experiences by administrators points to a path of inquiry which has as its end a more explicit delineation of the

[15]*Ibid.*, pp. 275–278.
[16]*Ibid.*, p. 283.
[17]*Ibid.*, pp. 281–282.

relationship between the two. For this purpose we shall have to think about organization in conceptual terms; we shall have to think of organization in terms of sets of ideas about purposive human relationships which infuse them with pattern and meaning and which, therefore, have an effect upon what is designated moral in the content of administrative experience. Different conceptions of organization open a variety of interpretive frameworks for perceiving the relationships between the subjectively experienced morality of the administrator and the social context in which that experience occurs. These different conceptions of organization also reveal the diverse ways that the moral can be perceived as entering into organization activity. In so doing they provide a variety of bases for assessing the relevance of the ethical to the competence of the administrator.

I discern four primary concepts of organization in contemporary administrative thought. They have not yet emerged as formally stated theoretical models of organization, but they have a solid empirical foundation. I refer to 1. the function (efficiency) model; 2. the value (exchange system) model; 3. the accommodation (incremental decision) model; and 4. the rational (optimizing) model. None of these are analogs, and each attempts an account of organization as a coherent system. It is important to keep in mind that within an enterprise or firm or agency or aggregate of agencies (the formally organized administrative structure of a jurisdiction) more than one system of organization may be in actual or potential existence. Thus, within an organization it may be possible to distinguish by conceptual analysis one or more simultaneously functioning separate systems of organization. It is not *the* organization of the enterprise or agency that is significant, but the *mix* of organization systems.

A. *Ethics for administrators and the functional (efficiency) model of organization*

The functional (efficiency) model has its origins in the body of ideas known generally as scientific management.[18] These ideas were first expounded in systematic fashion by Frederick W. Taylor. They represented an effort to apply scientific method to the problem of organiz-

---

[18]George Filipetti, *Industrial Management In Transition,* revised edition, Richard D. Irwin, Inc., Homewood, 1953, chapters 2 and 3.

ing for the performance of work. All questions of organization were resolvable into technical (nonnormative) questions of fact which were capable of precise solution through the application of a method of analysis assumed to be consistent with the requirements of science to the work involved. The objectives of the organization were determined by the managers and antedated the establishment of the formal organization itself. These objectives were assumed to be translatable into a finite number of logically and explicitly defined functions built upon the rigorous division of labor into specialized tasks. A hierarchical structure provided for the exercise of managerial authority and control throughout the formal organization. The concept of organization was equated with the formal system of structure-function relationships. What was meant by the planning of organization was the design of these structure-function relationships for the efficient performance of work. Cost criteria were incorporated into a calculus for the measurement of productive efficiency. Remuneration for task performance was linked to individual productivity measured in relation to a performance norm.

Within the framework of the assumptions and analytical methods of the functional (efficiency) concept of organization, the design and operation of the formal organization can be understood as presenting the administrator with nonnormative questions of fact rather than with normative questions of value calling for ethical decisions. The task of administration of the organization was conceived in a manner that did not incorporate an ethical competence. It was not that organization activity was immune from ethical (normative) judgment, but that the applicable ethical criteria preceded and were tacitly incorporated into the design of the organization relationships. The pioneers of scientific management thought the formal organization they constructed to meet the requirements of the system for the efficient performance of work was consistent with the person requirements of those who performed the work. Hence moral norms and technological norms were not incongruent in the design of formal organization. Lillian Gilbreth takes pains to establish the congruence of the two in her work on *The Psychology of Scientific Management*. In sum, in the case of the functional (efficiency) concept of organization it is very likely that the decisions of the administrator, to use the language of Barnard, "appear in the

Prolegomena to Ethics for Administrators

guise of technical decisions, and their moral aspects are not consciously appreciated."[19]

The ethical obtrudes upon the administrator from the environment as a challenge to the assumptions tacitly incorporated into the design of the formal organization. These challenges may stress the excluded values and the *costs* (personal and social) arising from their exclusion.[20] They may also take the form of assertions that incorporating different ethical postulates into the design of the organization will provide a more efficient system for the performance of work. Such is the challenge of Worthy, who has contended that the "methods of organization and administration based on concepts of personal liberty are the most efficient for the business enterprise itself."[21] His is a call for a radical revision of the ethical postulates upon which a congruence of interests between system requirements and person requirements should be worked out in the design of organization. In his own words, "the methods and concepts of engineering have proved inappropriate to human organization; . . . particularly unfortunate has been the effort to force man to adapt to the technical organization rather than seeking to adapt the technical organization to man."[22]

B. *Ethics for Administrators and the value (exchange system) model of organization*

Certain findings of the Hawthorne investigation[23] provide a starting point for the examination of the value (exchange system) model of organization. These findings can, in fact, be taken as constituting the origins of this model, the content of which is still in a state of emergence. One of the discoveries of the Hawthorne investigation was that for the employees of the enterprise work can have a significance or meaning independent of and different from that ascribed to it by the managers of the enterprise. The work environment was not only subject to being perceived differently (the phenomenon of differential

---
[19]Barnard, *op. cit.*, p. 281.
[20]Chris Argyris, *Personality and Organization*, Harper and Brothers, New York, 1957.
[21]Worthy, *op. cit.*, p. 54.
[22]*Ibid.*, p. 67.
[23]F. J. Roethlisberger, William J. Dickson, *Management and The Worker*, Harvard University Press, Cambridge, Massachusetts, 1939.

perception, so that there was no necessary correspondence between the work environment as a postulated external reality and individual perceptions of that environment), but it was also the object of ascribed meanings. In this manner the work environment became infused with varied patterns of significance which had the function of making it meaningful to the person participant in that environment.

The elements comprising the work environment were not perceived as neutral objects, but as symbolizing a complex of social relationships in which the person perceiver was involved and to which were ascribed meanings having their source in the feelings, sentiments, and goals of the person. Within organizations, therefore, the experienced reality of individuals is a socially influenced psychological construct (a psychosocial reality) and this is the reality that is being administered by the executive of an organization. It is a reality that has a logic of its own. It supplies the person with an internally consistent rationale for purposes of action with reference to the work environment. Thus the Hawthorne investigators could identify the existence of an "ideological organization" within the enterprise. Two contrasting rationales (or "ideological organizations") were denominated the "logic of efficiency" —which was characterized by the existence of an economic calculus of costs—and the "logic of sentiments"—which was characterized by a noneconomically determined calculus of costs. The first was described as rational and the second as nonlogical. Each was the basis for a distinct type of social aggregate and control system within the enterprise; each influenced the motivations and response of the individual toward work; each performed a different function within an organization; each was socially manipulable; and potentially each could stand in opposition to the other.

The advance that was effected by Barnard grows out of, 1. his rescue of "organization" as a concept to explain a system of human activity from the morass of hopelessly intricate person subjectivity, and 2. his innovation of the theory of the economy of incentives to explain "the contributions of personal efforts which constitute the energies of organizations."[24] Barnard prevented organization from getting "lost" in the "mind" of each unique person participant in organization activity. The sharp and persistent focus on the coordinated *activities* of those engaged in purposive behavior enabled Barnard to establish the ex-

[24]Barnard, *op. cit.*, p. 139.

ternal, impersonal, relational character of organization.[25] And his invention of the "dual personality—an organization personality and an individual personality"—buttressed the separation of organization from the subjective and personal.[26] Organization as a *system* remains external to the person participants, but with respect to which subjective feelings are possible without altering its character as a *system of coordinated activities*.

The theory of incentives is related to the primary notion of individual acts as constituting the raw material of organization. What persons can contribute in the way of effort is visualized as a potential rather than as a fixed content of acts. Incentives are inducements offered by the organization to secure contributions of individual efforts from persons. Though not usually thought out in terms of an explicit calculus of choice, "the net satisfactions which induce a man to contribute his efforts to an organization result from the positive advantages as against the disadvantages which are entailed."[27] To the extent that attitudes and motives of a person can be psychologically influenced, the inducement value of incentives can be altered through persuasion. Inducements vary in imputed worth as between persons, and the same person may impute different worth to identical incentives at different times.

Organizations with different purposes encounter different paradoxes in the design of a scheme of incentives. Industrial organizations are limited by the inherent weakness of material incentives. The long-range survival of political organizations is rooted in "ideal benefactions and community satisfactions," but the everyday necessities require the employment of "personal prestige and material rewards" as incentives. The latter, though an inferior kind of inducement, tend, because of inherent limitations, "to destroy the vital idealism upon which political organization is based."[28]

No one kind of incentive is adequate in any type of organization. Every scheme of incentives is unstable and represents "the final residual of all the conflicting forces involved in organization."[29] Both the material and the nonmaterial incentives can and should be utilized to differentiate between the gradations of value to the organization of par-

[25] *Ibid.*, pp. 72 *et seq.*
[26] *Ibid.*, p. 88.
[27] *Ibid.*, p. 140.
[28] *Ibid.*, p. 157.
[29] *Ibid.*, p. 159.

ticular persons or person contributions. In short, the economy of incentives can be stated as a problem in organization costs—the costs of the various inducements in relation to the worth of the desired services.

At this point we confront the value (exchange system) concept of organization. There is a series of transactions going on over time between the individual and the organization, by which an exchange is effected between the services of the individual required by the organization and the inducements produced by the organization that are offered as a return. What is the process by which a calculus of value is worked out and value assigned to the components entering into the exchange? Are transactions between the individual and the organization the only transactions going on, or is there a much more complex system of bargaining in existence between participants within the organization? What is the social apparatus through which the transactions are negotiated? Is there something analogous to a market in operation within organizations which governs the determination of the value of contributions and the distribution of values among organization contributors? What variations in exchange systems will result from differences in the occupational and social composition of the organization personnel, particularly from the presence of personnel for whom professional norms constitute the dominant moral code? How does the administrator function as a creator, arbiter, bargainer, and allocator of values?

Ralph M. Stogdill[30] has applied the value (exchange system) concept to group achievement. The network of transactions between individual and group is visualized as an input-output system. Individual member inputs are "performances, expectations, and interactions" with others of the group. The output of the group is a specific productivity and group integration and morale. Each party to the transaction pays a cost for the desired values which are the object of the exchange. Neither party is fully cognizant of the costs paid by the other. The cost to the group is the time and effort which the group must subtract from task performance in order to meet a varied range of primary and secondary values that are within individual expectations as group members. The individual member costs are "reckoned in terms of the time and effort they devote to the group, the dues they pay, the illnesses

[30]Ralph Melvin Stogdill, *Individual Behavior and Group Achievement*, Oxford University Press, New York, 1959.

Prolegomena to Ethics for Administrators

and accidents they suffer in the performance of their duties, the frustrations and disappointments they experience, the freedom of self-determination they surrender, and the subordination of personal loyalties and goals to the welfare of the group."[31] It is not by an objective economic calculus but by a feeling judgment of the relative equity of the distribution of rewards within the group, which is cast up against a subjective calculus of personal costs and returns, that the individual decides whether or not he is satisfied with group membership. The formal organization required for task performance necessarily incorporates a differential valuation of member contributions and the problem here is to minimize the resulting dissatisfactions. It is impossible for the group to satisfy the expectations of each member to the maximum degree. At the same time, the group has a way of constricting the demands made upon the group by an individual for the satisfaction of his personal expectations.

> A member's loyalty to a group appears to be determined by some ratio between the personal cost he has to pay to support the group and the magnitude of the discrepancy between his expectations and the outcomes he experiences in the group. When this ratio becomes so unbalanced that the member feels cheaply valued or that his interests are betrayed, he may also feel inclined to let the organization suffer whatever reverses may be in store for it.[32]

M. Dalton's study of *Men Who Manage* illuminates the process of emergence and distribution of values within organizations and provides an explanation of the social aggregates through which value oriented transactions take place. He offers an interpretation of the significance of these transactions to the manager and of the function of the manager in the exchange of values going on between organization participants. Now what I am going to say about Dalton's study is often more implicit than explicit in the content of his book. He does not attempt a formal theory of organization. He views organization "as a shifting set of contained and ongoing counter phases of action."[33] These "counter phases of action" are represented by opposing tendencies contained in the polarities of formal and informal behavior within an organization. Nevertheless, there is an interplay between the two

[31] *Ibid.*, p. 379.
[32] *Ibid.*, p. 382.
[33] Melville Dalton, *Men Who Manage,* John Wiley and Sons, Inc., New York, 1959, p. 4.

which is not random.[34] At the root of all behavior are the claims of individuals upon the organization which they seek to realize by diverse means.

The better to comprehend Dalton's study I have conceptualized it (in diagrammatic form) as follows:

I. Organization Expressed as Static Polar States

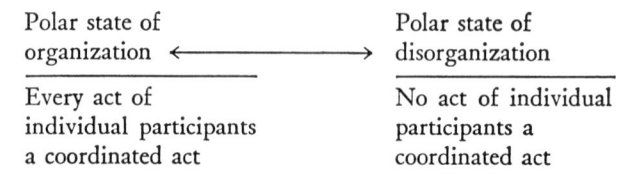

Polar state of organization ←————→	Polar state of disorganization
Every act of individual participants a coordinated act	No act of individual participants a coordinated act

II. Organization Expressed as Tendencies Toward Polar States

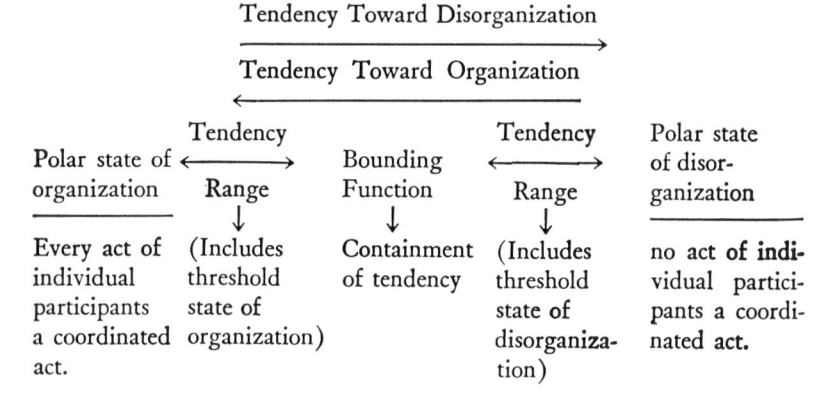

Tendency Toward Disorganization →

Tendency Toward Organization ←

Polar state of organization	Tendency ←——→ Range	Bounding Function	Tendency ←——→ Range	Polar state of disorganization
Every act of individual participants a coordinated act.	↓ (Includes threshold state of organization)	↓ Containment of tendency	↓ (Includes threshold state of disorganization)	no act of individual participants a coordinated act.

The diagrams are intended to make explicit the idea of organization (and, by implication, the idea of disorganization) which is left rather inchoate by Dalton, and to focus attention on the "bounding function." The latter is central to an understanding of the function of the moral in organization behavior as elaborated by Dalton. As polar states, both organization and disorganization are ideal possibilities. They are never completely realized; they are realized only in degree over time. I have postulated the existence of threshold states as compatible with the notion of contained but shifting "counter phases of

[34]*Ibid.*, pp. 226 *et seq.*

action" exhibiting tendencies toward one polar state or the other. What are the necessary conditions for each polar state to exist and how does this relate to the "bounding function"? Resort to a third diagram will help to clarify what I infer from Dalton's study as the answer.

III. The "Bounding Function" and the polar states of organization and disorganization

necessary condition for the polar state of organization	Bounding Function	necessary condition for the polar state of disorganization
Tendency Range ⟷		⟷ Tendency Range
Existence of an appropriate system of transactions for the exchange of person-organization values	Autocorrective Value Distribution Process within organization over time ↓	Absence of an appropriate system of transactions for the exchange of person-organization values
Total congruence of individual and group goals with organization goals	Cliques as constituting the organized "market" governing transactions comprising the value exchange system ↓ High level horizontal aggressive clique as the moral arbiter and value allocator	Total incongruence of individual and group goals with organization goals

The social processes which constitute a system for exchanging and distributing values within a firm are detailed by Dalton. He elaborates the rationale and the informal structure supporting an ongoing organization pattern of value oriented transactions. These transactions take place in a firm characterized by the existence within it of "systems of opposition" in active conflict that grow out of contradictions indigenous to the work environment and the (inappropriate) modes of operating followed by personnel of the firm. What sustains the "systems of opposition" are the actual or potential contradictions present in the planned and unplanned factors making for change—"the firm's demand for efficiency, the impatience of personnel for promotion, the clash of extremists in theory and practice, the differences among organized interests, and the variations in ability among executives to deal with confusion."[35]

In the case of efficiency claims, for example, the control systems based upon an economic calculus of rationality and devised by the upper level management to reduce production costs, have the effect of creating cost pressures upon operating unit heads. These pressures, in turn, induce the operating unit heads at times to cooperate with each other in evasive behavior intended to nullify the formal controls as ideally visualized by the management,[36] and at times to oppose each other in a competitive search for organization means whereby the adverse incidence of the cost pressures could be shifted.[37] The upper level management values designed into the control systems were sensitive to production costs and insensitive to intermediate management's personal and social structure costs. As to these latter costs, Dalton observes that "there are operating costs in the broad sense that include use of funds to meet the demands of daily personal relations—*the maintenance of a good fellowship structure as well as material equipment.* The financial costs of keeping social mechanisms in repair merge with those of the physical."[38] A whole complex of unforeseen and unintended exchanges of favors and services springs into existence, and its object is to insure the maintenance within the organization of the values excluded by the official control system.

Cliques are the particular informal social structure through which contradictions within the organization are manipulated to secure specific ends for clique members. "Cliques may work for moral as well as immoral ends. Whether or not we are able to preach what we practice, the organization will fall apart without sustaining action by some clique."[39] All cliques are built around an exchange of services between their members, but cliques can be differentiated in terms of status re-

[35]Dalton, *supra*, p. 52.
[36]*Ibid.*, pp. 47–48.
[37]*Ibid.*, pp. 37 *et seq.*
[38]*Ibid.*, p. 47.
[39]*Ibid.*, p. 52.

Prolegomena to Ethics for Administrators 413

lations between members, in terms of the "equality" of the exchange as between members, and in terms of their function as resistors or supporters of organization change.[40] The "corrective" clique within the firm is "a high level horizontal aggressive clique."[41] It is a changesupporting clique with a continuity of membership arising from a history of "cooperative victories in getting favors and outwitting others."[42] It has a repertoire of "correctives" for containing and restricting deviant cliques,[43] and the application of these correctives constitutes the bounding function, without which a state of disorganization would result.

> ... almost never would an able executive be discharged for clique activity. Higher managers value these skills as necessary for cutting a way through or around chaotic situations. Public relations and equalitarian ideology may require denial, but top managers are more disposed to pardon than punish occasional excesses of the social skill required for organizational coherence and action.[44]

There is an intertwining of the individual (personal) and organizational (social) significance of the moral experience of the administrator. Viewed as a social skill, a competence with respect to the moral is a competence that enables the resolution of a host of normatively based and socially supported claims upon the organization. The presence of internal conflict, the absence of authoritative guidance, and ambiguity surrounding the values involved, enhance its importance as a social skill. It is valuable for what it can contribute to the maintenance of the organization. As such, it is perceived as a fitting object of reward. The most precious of the rewards that the organization can give is career advancement. Variable competence with respect to the moral as a social skill operates in fact as a differential selection mechanism within organization, separating the effective from the ineffective managers.[45]

The rewarding by organization of moral competence as a social skill means the encouragement of those who are capable of developing

---
[40]*Ibid.*, pp. 57 *et seq.*
[41]*Ibid.*, p. 65.
[42]*Ibid.*, p. 61.
[43]*Ibid.*, p. 65.
[44]*Ibid.*, p. 67.
[45]Dalton, *supra*, chapter 9, *passim*.

an appropriate social character. By social character I mean a social self suited to what organization roles seem to require. The development of an appropriate social character is, in turn, related to the individualized complex of emotive orientations and cognitive capabilities that are usually designated as personality. The latter appears to operate as a limiting factor on the ability of some persons to develop the social character requisite for managerial effectiveness. For the individual administrator it is all that is comprehended within the struggle between what personality permits and social character demands that is the domain of subjectively experienced morality. It is the domain within which occurs the interplay of the existential and social reality dimensions of organization experience. I think we can best visualize that subjective experience as a struggle to construct a personal calculus of costs for matching the two in action under conditions in which the supreme and unaffordable cost is the destruction of an adequate self-image or, stated differently, a sense of the loss of self-integrity.

Happily, not every moral decision involves a confrontation of self. Barnard has put the ordeal of the executives when it does: "To do something that is required obviously for the good of organization but which conflicts with deep personal codes—such as the sense of what is honest —destroys personal probity; but not to do it destroys organization cohesiveness and efficiency."[46] When a confrontation of self is involved in a moral decision, the requisite of "creative morality" stands as an ideal norm by which the administrator can evaluate his own calculus of costs. What is left open by concentrating exclusively upon moral competence as a social skill is the quality of the organization morality (as expressed in particular organization codes) that emerges from the decisions of those who are adjudged effective managers and who function as moral arbiters within the organization.

C. *Ethics for Administrators and the Accommodation (Incremental Decision) Model of Organization*

Here interest is focused on public agencies. The questions of ethical significance for the administrator relate to the adaptation of organization structure and decision processes to environmental factors and its

[46] Barnard, *supra*, p. 280.

Prolegomena to Ethics for Administrators

effect upon the social product contributed by organization to society. The assumption is that with respect to public agencies and the environment within which they function, organization cannot be regarded as a sharply bounded system. With the accommodation (incremental decision) model of organization, the implications of a characterizing relationship between an organization and its environment are the main concern.

The concept of the incremental decision has been elaborated by Lindblom.[47] It is the product of a specific process or method for arriving at decisions involving the solution of complex social problems for purposes of making policy choices. It stands in contrast to the formalized concept of the rational decision process, not only as a method but as descriptive of what in practice most public administrators really do. Lindblom has described the first "as the method of successive limited comparisons" and the second as "the rational-comprehensive method."[48] Characteristically, the former is "continually building out from the current situation, step-by-step and by small degrees; the latter starting from fundamentals anew each time, building on the past only as experience is embodied in a theory, and always prepared to start completely from the ground up."[49]

The method of the incremental decision provides a way for reducing complex problems to manageable proportions; for simplifying them to a point where, by reason of the agreement thereby attained on either the objectives to be achieved or the policies to be followed, action is possible. The problem simplification inherent in the method of the incremental decision represents not only a realistic concession to inescapable cognitive and informational limitations on choice (the "bounded rationality" of Simon),[50] but also an effort to be realistic by concentrating on policies that are politically relevant. As such, the method is a response to a view of social change processes in a democratic society. The view is that policies change "almost entirely through incremental adjustments."[51] The nonincremental policies ignored by the adminis-

---

[47]Charles E. Lindblom, "The Science of 'Muddling Through,'" volume 19, number 2, *Public Administration Review*, spring, 1959, p. 79.
[48]*Ibid.*, p. 81.
[49]*Loc. cit.*
[50]James G. March and Herbert A. Simon, *Organizations*, John Wiley and Sons, New York, 1958, chapter 6.
[51]Lindblom, *supra*, p. 84.

trator are not feasible politically and so may be put to one side as irrelevant. What results is a simplified analysis which, in the opinion of Lindblom, is not "capricious" because it is "achieved by concentrating on policies that differ only incrementally."[52]

The values or objectives excluded by the process of simplification do not end in the dust heap of social neglect. Individuals are free to join together around any value of common interest. In effect there is a social division of labor with respect to the pursuit of social interests. It is a plausible contention that what results is "a more comprehensive regard for the values of the whole society than any attempt at intellectual comprehensiveness."[53] Political and administrative adjustments between incremental decisions are more easily made, for it is easier both to predict incremental changes and to correct the adverse consequences of such changes. Viewed over time, the process of making policy by incremental decisions "is a process of successive approximation to some desired objectives in which what is desired itself continues to change under reconsideration."[54]

It is essential to keep in mind that what we have to consider here is the interlocking of two components. The first is a distinctive method of decision, the "successive limited comparisons" approach of the incremental decision. The second is a compatible system of organization, which I have categorized as the accommodation model of organization. In all likelihood empirical inquiry will disclose a number of variants of the model in actual existence, but there has been a detailed and comprehensive disclosure of the processes and structure of one such system. I refer to the recent comprehensive study by Sayre and Kaufman of the system by which New York City is governed.[55] Their exploration of contestant strategies for the shaping of governmental decisions provides an in-depth version of the accommodation model of organization as it exists in New York City.

Sayre and Kaufman describe the agencies of administration as operating within a political environment in which no segment of the electorate is dominant and in which there is incessant competition for electorate support. All leadership, administrative and otherwise, feels the press of inadequate decisionmaking power, either for the decisions

[52] *Ibid.*, p. 85.
[53] *Loc. cit.*
[54] *Ibid.*, p. 86.
[55] Wallace S. Sayre and Herbert Kaufman, *Governing New York City*, Russell Sage Foundation, New York, 1960.

Prolegomena to Ethics for Administrators

they wish to make or over the decisions of others. In consequence, all leaders are preoccupied with building alliances, effecting settlements with "allies or competitors," and bargaining for a more advantageous position wherever a center of decisions exists. "Every decision of importance is consequently the product of mutual accommodation." There is a profusion of decision centers. These decision centers consist of a "core group" (those invested with formal authority) and "satellite groups" (the influencers). Neither group exhibits a "solid internal unity." All core groups seek to effect coalitions with portions of their respective satellite groups; otherwise decisions cannot withstand the opposition that may emanate from within the satellite groups. At the same time, satellite groups are seeking to effect alliances with each other and thus are also engaged in a continuous process of bargaining. Furthermore, "bargaining and accommodation" characterize relations between decision centers, who may be regarded as being in competition with one another. In short, "mutual accommodation" is the system's only "ubiquitous and invariant" feature. "Every program and policy represents a compromise among the interested participants."[56]

Only the exploitation of the opportunities that are an outgrowth of the contradictions unavoidably produced by the incessant maneuvering of a welter of organized and contending participant-claimants enable the executive of a line agency to retain some control of his agency's policies and programs. "He must be a manipulator, or he will become an instrument in the hands of others and possibly pay high costs as a consequence."[57] The energies of the line executive go into the formulation of strategies—strategies for agency control, environmental support, and the prevention of attacks upon the agency. Innovative action is itself dependent upon strategies for securing the particular equipoise of forces that will permit it. Innovation is the "small increment" of activity left over after the "customary routine [and] strategies for survival" are attended to. "The strategies available to them discourage departures from routine, introduction of extensive alterations, experiments in program method, for the strategies are most effective within the established framework. The path of innovation is rocky, twisting, and full of pitfalls."[58]

For the accommodation model, bargaining decisions are the char-

[56]*Ibid.*, pp. 709–714 *passim.*
[57]*Ibid.*, pp. 250–251.
[58]*Ibid.*, p. 304 and pp. 250–264 *passim.*

acteristic type of decision; just as for the rational (optimizing) model, the analytic decisions are the characteristic type. It is this factor that invests the accommodation model with a distinctive significance when it is viewed from the standpoint of subjectively experienced morality.

The "incremental decision" is a phrase which aptly describes the social product of a method of decision at a point in time in relation to some implied continuum of social change over time. The method of decision may be consistent with a consciously selected, professionally defensible technique of policy choice (the method of successive limited comparisons) or it may be no more than expedient decisionmaking (compromise bargaining which lacks an external policy referent). Both methods of decision represent processes of accommodation by the administrator to perceived constraints imposed by an external sociocultural reality, and as such both may result in an "incremental decision." But the latter as the product of expedient accommodation may be nondirectional (meaningless) in relation to a continuum of social change over time.

The difference between having the analytic decisions typically fix the range for bargaining choices, and having the bargaining decisions typically fix the range for analytically determined choices bears directly upon the subjectively experienced morality of the administrator. The individual can be perceived as a self-conscious resource of an organization who cannot escape assessing his vocational life commitments in terms of a personal calculus of life costs and returns that takes into account the worth assigned by him to the social product (the net social gain) accruing from the activity of the organization over time. The social product of a system over time in which he was a participant enters into the appraisal by the individual administrator of the worthwhileness for him of the investment of his life in the activities of that system. For the system to be ineffective (no net social gain), or to be effective only in relation to inappropriate ends (again no net social gain), is to block the realization of the moral as a subjective individual experience. Thus the accommodation model has within it a potentiality whereby the possibilities for denigration of the motivation underlying the professionalism of the individual administrator are increased.

From the standpoint of subjectively experienced morality, inquiry into the accommodation model focuses on the moral effects upon the individual administrator of tendency and net social gain over time that is manifested by organization activity. The social rationality assumed for the accommodation model becomes obscure in actual operation. The bargaining processes of accommodation encompass a complex of contingent factors that are not amenable to a high degree of control; initiating and maintaining the social relationships that will permit organization activity can exhaust the energies of the administrator; there are no adequate measures of social change and hence of net social gain over time resulting from accommodation decision processes; and in the absence of operationally adequate concepts of social costs, a postulate of economizing behavior on the part of the participants remains sterile.

The barganing over organization programs and objectives is experienced by the administrator as a discovery of personal beliefs and values. That discovery emerges as a conscious calculus of what personal costs the administrator is willing to pay for the attainment of social goals through organization activities. The administrator forms a conception of himself as a cost to be included in the calculus by which the costs of social change are computed. The individual administrator cannot escape deciding how far he will identify with social goals, and the incidence of personal costs that he chooses to assume for their attainment is a measure of his identification with them. The potential danger in the processes of accommodation is the imposition, or threatened imposition, of personal costs upon the administrator that are perceived by him as excessive.

CHAPTER XXVI

The Ethical Challenge of Modern Administration

By ORDWAY TEAD

IT IS PRECISELY by the development of his administrative skills that Man preserves and extends his freedom. The complexity of modern society and the omnipresence of large-scale organizations not only provide an opportunity for the fullest development of the responsible self; they actually place a premium on the exercise of a greater measure of personal responsibility by more people than ever before.[1]

One of the most pervasive realities of modern American life is administration—the fact, the process, and the responsibility. The word as here used will be equated with management and with executive labors of a general, high level directive nature. Wherever we turn in the conduct of our highly organized society there are those who administer or manage and those whose labors or activities are administered or directed. This is true of government at all levels, of business and industry, of educational systems, schools, colleges, and universities, of hospitals, churches, prisons, and numerous philanthropic agencies of social amelioration. We literally live and move and have our being in frameworks supervised by administrators.

There are common problems of basic function in most if not in all organizations. There is the explicit work of carrying out the designated purposes—the producing of that sought to be realized. There is the work of financial measure, evaluation, and control. There is the distributive, informing, selling, public relations role. There is the role of motivation, stimulation, and morale building among those who are members or employes. There is the integrative or coordina-

---

[1] See Harlan Cleveland, "Dinosaurs and Personal Freedom," *The Saturday Review*, February 28, 1959.

tive assignment of tying together all the several functional activities for the assured fulfilment of the avowed purpose.

Stated in other terms administration includes the planning, organizing, initiating, directing, overseeing, coordinating, and evaluating of the ongoing enterprise. Broadly viewed there are two separable types of managerial activity. One has to do with the technical process, the technological implementing, of the explicit purpose of the organization. The other has to do with the continuing and inspiriting relating of the personnel of the agency to the effective doing of the assigned job. Obviously the process and the personnel phases of management often interweave. But the application of human energy to the purposes in hand constitutes a distinct operation and calls for special and definite skills. Indeed it is in this phase of management that the ethical problem becomes explicitly posed.

I shall confine myself in this paper to the generic problem. This is not a discussion of business morals. Indeed to do justice to the numerous aspects of business ethics would take me further afield than is possible, urgently important though the issues are.[2] If I can within the framework of all organizations with their varying purposes identify the ethical responsibilities typically imposed, I will have traversed an area of both breadth and depth which I believe has practical utility.

I propose, therefore, to look first at administration in a *democratic* society with its own special and unique frame of reference and see what criteria or norms of managerial conduct are implicit in this democratic frame. I propose second to consider how ethical sensibility in these directions and under these conditions is to be encouraged and cultivated.

Our democratic American society stands for certain declared moral and ethical intentions and aims. For example, each person is autonomous, an end in himself with purposes of self-fulfilment, growth, and self-actualization which are not to be denied. Self-respecting,

---

[2] A thoughtful, admirable, and useful introductory discussion is Chester I. Barnard's lecture, "Elementary Conditions of Business Morals," published by the Committee on the Barbara Weinstock Lectures, University of California, Berkeley, 1958.

A summary discussion of the business aspects of this problem is to be found in Marquis W. Childs and Douglass Cater, *Ethics in a Business Society,* Harper and Brothers, New York, 1954.

In *Business and Religion* edited by Edward C. Bursk, Harper and Brothers, 1959, the views of a number of prominent businessmen are given.

The Ethical Challenge of Modern Administration

self-responsible personalities take precedence over ends of all organizational dominances. The "organization man," as he has been described, represents a distortion of values. But in any formal organization the individual has a limited freedom within which he has to assume the responsibilities of work and functional usefulness. He should be provided freedom to be creative in his own unique way and to assume responsibility for the function he is assigned to perform. The consent of the governed is an essential condition in a true picture in all our multifarious organizations. Participation in decision-making in those matters which affect one's personal destiny and fulfilment is a required democratic attribute. Communication is a responsive, reciprocal process is an imperative requirement so that personal involvement shall be informed and affirmative. Equality of opportunity to realize one's own potential is an intrinsic condition. The leadership which our society and its organizations require is one of persuasive appeal and stimulation—not of authoritarianism. It has to do with establishing a valid case on behalf of some common purpose to which the individual can with integrity ally himself. The authority which administration has rightfully to exercise is one characterized by an informed, tactful, collaborative appeal in which power is exercised cooperatively and not unilaterally.

In short, the strategy is one of dealing with wholesome, healthy, well personalities who are assumed to prefer to be productive rather than destructive or lazy, to be friendly rather than hostile, to be cooperative rather than antagonistic, to be interested rather than bored.

And the underlying condition of the use of this strategy is that the basic terms and conditions of employment or membership shall be in line with current standards recognized by all concerned as basically fair, honorable, and constructive.

What is at stake is the reconciliation of organizations and their purposes with personalities and their purposes, desires, rights, and obligations. The ideal end result is that the person in association with the organization finds himself in one or more of his major interests fulfilled and realized in satisfying ways. And not the least of the tasks of administration is to be concerned to bring this reconciliation to pass. It is preeminently in this aspect that administration becomes a moral act and an ethical mandate.

I

It thus has to do with a variety of implementing managerial tasks which have to be consciously in mind to this end. These tasks can be identified in a variety of ways and one is in the now somewhat familiar provision of the features of what has come to be called the personnel function. This may be summarily suggested in the following terms as having bearing upon ethical concerns.

The purposes of the organization with which the individual proposes to become associated should become clear to him by virtue of some explicit communication. It is not, depending on the context, that one can tolerably accept a mere job, or become a perfunctory student, a passive patient, or a nominal affiliate. Any administration is presumably infused with a purpose and as such it has to interpret the organization to prospective newcomers with some widened appeal at once persuasive and explicit. This means that in the introductory process the individual should be assigned a place in which his unique talents are relevant to the specific task that he is being asked to assume. Appropriate selection and placement are imperative. The introductory process also has an orientation phase including often some training effort and some familiarity with the expectations upon the new member as to standards of action, personal relationships, and group participations. This process should also include clear information and implicit recognition or acceptance by the new member as to the "terms and conditions" of the relationship. In matters of employment this will usually require knowledge of the agreed terms of the "labor contract." This, of course, may be the product of collective bargaining or, less desirably, of managerial determination by fiat. But it is important at this point that the accusation of exploitation with respect to these terms shall not be justified. The terms of the contract of employment itself are thus infused with ethical implication. And if this contract derives from free negotiation among bargaining equals, the assumption has been generally accepted that a "fair" and temporarily acceptable bargain has been reached. The question, however, as to what precisely is implied by equal bargaining power is not permanently or wholly clear in its ethical aspects. We traverse here an area where the size and strength of the respective bargaining agencies are complicating and shifting factors of some ambiguity.

A consideration for health and physical wellbeing of the personnel also comes within this purview. This often extends to what is now referred to as "fringe benefits," having to do with the provisions for illness, disability, dismissal, vacations, old age, etc.

It may thus be said that explicit assumption of a personnel function by administration underscores the need for an ethical outlook which considers people as ends as they pursue the several purposive requirements.

II

But beyond the field of personnel administration there is a complex of broader interrelationships. I propose to consider briefly the following related phases of the managerial task: leadership, authority, communication, participation, creativity, representation, negotiation, and consent. All administration has to be dynamically concerned with these several processes and their end results. And unless they are clearly viewed as to their intrinsic, substantive quality, ethical sensibility will remain inadequate to the complexities of the task. All of these are areas of moral significance.

III

Leadership is a controversial concept. But I shall try to interpret what I mean when I say that democratic, face to face leadership is at the heart of ethical accountability. I oppose this, of course, to authoritarian leadership in which the leader's objectives and purposes are uncritically advanced as the sole alternative, and to which passive loyalty is the required end and criterion of leading success. In the democratic concept the role of the leader has to do with loyalty to purposes which the led come to accept after objective scrutiny concerning whether they contribute to their own individual purposes of self-actualization and fulfilment. "He redeemeth our life from destruction" becomes the descriptive dictum for the democratic leader. He hopefully transcends for and with the led the futility of meaninglessness, lack of direction and goal, absence of personal significance and of opportunity for creative expression.

That the administrator can and should be the leader in this sense is not only realistic but is wholly practical, especially if we leave to each manager to interpret according to his own temperament, character, and ingenuity how he will go about standing symbolically for leadership, stimulation, heartening focus upon a worthy corporate end.

IV

There is a proper ethical role also for the exercise of *authority*. Authority can be of several kinds. It can be the exercise of arbitrary power usurpation; it can stem from position and status, of knowledge and expertise, or of the total participative outcome of consultation with the appropriate shared sources of wider knowledge. In this last interpretation there is thus the authority of collaborative understanding resulting from a listening attitude, of group devotion and true leadership influence in the sense just defined.

In the assignment of management the expectation of achievement and purposive performance is high, not to say imperative. The manager is responsible to secure the intended results. And in the ethical sense the ways by which these results are achieved are crucial.

What are the consequences of this exercise of authority on all involved? Are favorable outcomes reasonably assured? Have all the modifying factors been adequately evaluated? These are questions about authority which the executive should raise and try to answer in advance in the light of the fullest information and consultation. Authority can be wisely and desirably exercised when the one who exercises it can say in effect—the numerous alternate consequences have been appraised in the light of the best knowledge available from all sources; and this specific exercise of authority seems the most desirable one. Among the desired outcomes, of course, should be the beneficent effect of the decision in the long look on the condition and prospects of employe or member personalities in happy reconciliation with sound corporate results.

V

Communication is another ambiguous concept. Indeed much that now passes for communication is only the self-satisfied reaction of the executive that he has *told* others as effectively as he knows how.

The Ethical Challenge of Modern Administration

But communication is soundly measured by one test only—namely, the effective response. The question has to be answered—has communication (through whatever medium conveyed) resulted in a *change* in the total reaction of those to whom it is addressed? The response may come in terms of alterations in attitudes, skills, or behavior. And it can even be positive or negative as long as it is consciously explicit and overt. Failure to agree is often as important to managerial comprehension as is a successful outcome. Either result is informative to the communicator in terms of "feedback," for either result leaves him more fully aware of what he has to cope with as future data in the resolving of his problem.

Perhaps as important a resultant as any in true communication is the reaction upon the managerial person that he now reappraises the elements of a situation more realistically. On the part of the executive there has to be *listening* as well as utterance. Only thus can there come the sense of fuller command of the subtler aspects of that with which the communication is concerned.

Communication is important ethically because it involves purposeful changes in persons—alterations of thought or conduct which may have favorable or adverse consequences on the personalities of those who are virtually required to listen. And the possible consequences have to be prospectively weighed even in the initial decision to attempt to communicate.

The gadgets of communication are numerous, and the larger the organization the more mechanical, impersonal, and indirect they are likely to become. "To go before the constituency" in personal confrontation should therefore usually be the preferred means dictated by ingenuity and courage, so that reactions can be immediate, direct, and capable of a vivid evaluation. Good communication is thus a teaching process toward good learning, by which is also meant that the learner is coming to think, feel, act, and express *differently*. Without this difference in the potential of response there has been no learning; and by the same token there has been no fulfilment of communication. The nearer the point, seat, or source of communication to the felt concern of those being consulted, the better it can be. And this further involves the skill of lesser managers and supervisors down the line as interpreters, sounding boards, and listening posts for top management.

The ethical mandate to bear in mind here is that any pietistic assumption that the will and need to communicate assure the fact of a true mutuality of response and understanding, is a false not to say dangerous assumption. Communication is a personal and human fact with a personalized and knowable result. It cannot be left to *devices* to do what *only persons can do with and to each other* wherever there are intentions of goodwill which have become reciprocal. At its ultimate, ethical best, communication approaches communion. It advances unity of intention and purpose.

VI

I consider *participation* next because I am referring to the voluntary efforts of the groups at interest to get a basis of collaboration. The need to communicate about how best to realize purposes is thus jointly acknowledged and can thus be willingly brought into being. Devoluted small groups of similarly functioning individual members become the key to the best participative action. "What do we all know about how best to do this specific assignment?" becomes the question before the house. "Let all of us involved in getting results pool our best experience and ideas to achieve maximum productivity or performance on behalf of the end in view"—in genuine participation this has become the sincere affirmation of the directive agents of management.

Various processes of participation are of value in forwarding ends of efficient performance all the way down through the managerial hierarchy. Worker or member participation has thus to be organized, shared, given approval, guaranteed security against jealousies, and rewarded. This is the basic democratic method by which the actual work processes, standards, and conditions will secure the interest and allegiance of the generality of participants. It can also be the organized channel through which the encouragement of individual creativity can well function.

VII

If it is assumed, as I shall assume, that the desire for the satisfactions of personal *creativity* is one of the dominant human drives, there has to be provision for the instrumentalities of its encouragement. The opportunity to be creative has to be structured cooperatively. And this, as much experience has shown, can bring remarkably beneficial results both in improved performance and in self-fulfilment.

Here again, however, there has to be the initiative of administration to bring this to pass; and this task becomes a vital ethical assignment. In any completely satisfactory way this aim is not easy to achieve, for there is still work in the world at which even the moron may feel stultified. But that this creative fulfilment is an ethical end to be striven for is undeniable. Some types of organization will probably find it easier than others to approach nearest to this goal. Educational agencies, for example, should fulfil this need and desire of the creative student far more completely than is now usually the fact; but to achieve this result there must be a fuller grasp and application of the psychology of learning by both teacher and student.

VIII

I highlight the fact of the value of the principle of *representation* because there will be plenty of occasions in which pure democracy is impractical and indeed undesirable. The ethical prescription here is that within organizations the several groups which may correctly view their interests and their contributions from differing angles have the right and the responsibility to have those interests voiced in a representative way in councils where common policies and problems are being considered. Identify disparate functional interests, see that they themselves choose their own effective representatives; provide regular occasions of participative conference; supply full opportunity for access to all relevant facts and opinions—all this is the prescription for achieving a satisfactory use of representation in achieving co-ordinative unity.

IX

Negotiation, too, is usually conducted on some representative basis. The underlying relationship of the individual to the organization may on periodic occasions bring into play the process of group or collective negotiative dealings. In industry and in other employing agencies we speak of this as the effort to reach agreement upon "the terms and conditions of employment." And increasingly the ethical imperative of a collective bargaining process is being recognized. This usually entails, moreover, a condition of approximately equal bargaining power, howsoever brought about. And the negotiative process to achieve this end has to be periodically reviewed in all its supplementary conditions to be sure that this equality is being attained. So-called "right to work" laws, for example, have a seemingly valid ethical purpose. But if they seriously impair the equal collective dealing basis and actually work to bring back into operation a purely individual bargaining relationship, the result will be not equalized negotiation but the old master and servant relation. To preserve the equal bargaining power as a reality seems an ethical obligation.

X

Implicit in these several concepts is the requirement and some method for the *consent of the governed,* which is integral to the democratic purpose. There are to be sure varying degrees of consent. Sumner H. Slichter used to refer to the fact of the institutional presence of "antagonistic cooperation"; there is passive consent, uninformed and nominal consent. And there is the true consent of a knowledgeable participation in relevant decisions with a positive and understanding concurrence in the matter at issue. It would seem to be ethically required that on most of the larger issues of policy and practice there be this informed, willing, and interested consent in well administered organizations—and on a greatly enlarged volume of problems. This has become the condition in the absence of which morale, genuine cooperation, creative participation, and a legitimate institutional loyalty will not be realized.

XI

I would reemphasize in relation to this ethical challenge the reality of the existence of what is known as *conflict of interest.* Such conflicts are inescapable, are continuing or recurring, are to a point—creative. And they imply and require some capacity on the part of the institutional leaders to be patient enough to guide the agency through and

The Ethical Challenge of Modern Administration

beyond such humanly natural tensions to a deepened sense of common intention and cooperative purpose.

One reason for elaborating upon participation, negotiation, representation, and consent is to make clear that it is through the honest confrontation of the reality of conflicts of interest by administrators that they will be brought to invoke measures which will enable the organization to work through and transcend its disparate internal outlooks to a creative, fruitful reconciliation of the interests of the several claimants for consideration. Differing groups immersed in differing duties will have differing views as to how to fulfil those duties in relation to the total organizational purpose. The sooner and the more consistently administrators realize this fundamental truth, the more affirmatively will they work for arrangements and agencies of conference from whose deliberations greater unity can be brought.

For there is still the perennial danger and the temptation upon the executive leader to believe that "father knows best" and that the affirmation of his paternal concern and the claim that he is presiding over a "big happy family," will shortchange the participative democratic process. Such a conviction of the importance of "sweetness and light" fails to bring into the open the perennial conflict of interests; but this truth sounds to many executives heterodox and subversive rather than fructifying, which in fact it is or can be.

XII

The larger and the more complex the institution, the greater is the need for this kind of acknowledgment to the end that organized representative means will be employed to offset sheer size with the internal agencies planned to bring about devolution, reconciliation, and unification. The administrator's task obviously gains in magnitude with the size of the corporate group. But it also becomes different in kind in the need for this devolution, for a structuring of representative, participative, coordinating bodies to share the burden of supplying information, making lesser decisions and assuming some measure of authority and accountability. The task of running a one room school is patently poles apart from that of being president of Harvard University. And the ethical mandate upon the administrator in the latter case requires wide general and technical knowledge, cooperative skill, tact and patience, and ethical sensibility of a high order. In all the larger administrative responsibilities a governmental or bureaucratic superstructure can frustrate the administrator, unless these mandates of democratic consultation are heeded.

XIII

I come, therefore, in conclusion to raise briefly the question as to the possibilities of cultivating ethical sensibility. It seems to me that the components looking toward this cultivation include at least the following:

1. The administrator must gain a full grasp and knowledge of the problems of his field as to which the ethical complexities are conceivably entailed in the kinds of human and morally consequential dealings and decisions required. Identification of these as possible aspects of an educational training program are practical possibilities.

2. The administrator should come to have a conscious awareness of, a sympathy with, and eagerness to make use of, those approaches and methods broadly referred to here as *democratic*. He should be strongly predisposed to democratic or shared outlooks. He had better realize all that it can mean operationally for ethical good to want authority *with* others and not *over* others. Every aspect of the democratic aspiration and process should become a well nigh religious passion with him albeit directed by reflective judgment.

3. He should know which aspects of his program and policies are means and which are ends, what the organization needs to fulfil its purposes, and at the same time in what ways the individuals from sweepers to trustees are having genuine scope for personality expression and creative fulfilment.

4. He should have a permissive view of the basic wholesomeness of personality and of the psychological drives and satisfactions which healthymindedness seems to require to give play to on behalf of the fulfilment of the whole man.

5. Somehow he should see all this as related to the fundamental moral mandate upon him to act responsibly as a son of man and hopefully as a son of the God Who presides over, originates, and wills the human scene, subject to wide human latitude.

6. He had better have gotten some predisposition in these several di-

rections by his earlier exposures in education—in liberal arts colleges and in graduate schools of administration. And if these institutions are not doing what they should along these several lines the ethical mandate is that the time to begin is now.

These several requirements are easy to state. They are harder to come by: nor is there any royal road to such goals. Initial aptitude, humility of outlook, conscious self-cultivation—these are stronger assets than the popular "executive development courses" which constitute a strong movement in corporate business management today. What issues have to be raised and puzzled over, what sensitivities have to be encouraged, what philosophical predilections in the broad areas of political science, social psychology, and the administrative arts have to be favored as illuminating the problems which will be faced—all of this has to be made articulate. But application to the personal case, the facing of delicate issues in individual and group confrontation, the ability with courage, humility, and tolerance to bear the brunt—these are largely to be learned the hard way, namely, in the maelstrom of administrative action where the price of mistakes can hopefully be improved learning.

I would offer every encouragement to executive development courses as our industrial corporations are recently extending them. But they must be broad, liberal, patient; and they are no substitute for early training, basic character, and vision. We do unquestionably do better than ever in our society today with the ethical encounters of administrators. But we have a long way to go and much reiteration is necessary about the constituent elements of the ethical implications entailed and the basic principle for their resolution.

The reward of all this is great. The reward is the harmonizing of our practices with our American professions. The reward will be in terms of finer personality, greater productivity, improved social harmony, and democratic consistency. The reward has to do with self-actualization, with the rightful personal freedoms and the creative opportunities opened out by administration at all levels of the operative hierarchy.

I agree with Cleveland:

> In a world of large scale organization everybody is expected to understand and practice the art of administration. Those who do so effectively will experience a sense of freedom—not in the interstices, but right in the middle of things.[3]

[3]*Op. cit.*

Ethics and Bigness

Comment by Paul H. Appleby:

Pretensions to face to face relationships over too deep a hierarchal spread fool only the executives who pretend to them. As organizations become larger, top management performance must rely ever more on face to face leadership of subexecutives by exemplifying to and stimulating in those subexecutives effective face to face leadership. I would tie this same thought to an emphasis on going beyond "listening" to "questioning." Listening by itself may get too exclusively certain forms of acquiescence and grievance from subordinates. Knowing how to ask good questions, and doing it often, is highly useful—not to say essential. In the same connection I emphasize Ordway Tead's remarks about conflicts of interest and relate them to structural arrangements. One of the purposes of structure is to achieve unity; another is to cause issues to emerge at about the places where they should be handled.

Similarly, I would draw together Tead's remark about "every aspect of democratic aspiration and process" and the concluding part of his sentence, "There will be plenty of occasions in which pure democracy is impracticable and indeed undesirable." The point could well be emphasized and elucidated further. I recall the chairman of a sociology department who insisted in a mimeographed memorandum that "only a sociologist has any right to influence the conduct of a sociology department." By the same reasoning, sociologists would have no "right" to influence anything but sociology departments. There is need to advance thought about different applications of the democratic spirit in government and nongovernment, in a large nation, and in local communities.

Finally, I note a partial exception to the word "still" in this clause ". . . for there is still work in the world at which even the moron may feel stultified." I agree essentially; in the large I think there has been a progressive diminution in this kind of work. But with the new "want creation" phenomenon in our economy of abundance we may be experiencing an increase in activities that demean employes and employment. Production of the doodads and phonies advertised through a good many television hours—and the very advertising of them—makes the activities of a lot of people wasteful and ridiculous.

CHAPTER XXVII

Irresponsibility as an Article of Faith

By DON K. PRICE

I

EARLY IN 1960, a television comedy team was taking part in a spectacular review of "The Fabulous Fifties." The skit showed a vapid stenographer and a junior executive gossiping at the office water cooler about the recent frauds in television quiz shows, and their exposure by a Congressional investigation. The junior executive dismissed as unimportant all other public issues in his indignation over this one, with the clinching argument, "It's a *moral* issue." The stenographer agreed: "To me," she said, "that's always more important than a real issue."

Students of government are apt to be a little too impatient with the set of ideas that is summed up in this bit of dialogue—especially those of us who are troubled by an obvious threat to our national survival, and who see less emotional energy being expended in an effort to cope with the problem than in a morbid self-concern with the state of our political piety. That is not the way, we may well believe, to get along in a world which is being shaken by a harddriving and fanatical ideology. Yet we cannot dispose of our own political consciences so easily. In our way of thinking, we have to reconcile somehow our system of political power with our system of ethics. This is at the heart of our notions about political responsibility.

The point at which our standards of political responsibility raise the most acute and difficult issues is at the pivot of our political system: the relationship between the legislature and the executive. We are currently seeing issues raised in this touchy area in a number of difficult ways. How can we enforce standards of honesty and fair play in the federal regulatory commissions, which Congress has protected from discipline by the President in its effort to protect them against improper influence? How can the President get candid advice on issues of national security from his principal military and scientific counsellors without insulating them from a proper degree of questioning by the Congress and the press? How can the Congress make sure that our governmental machinery for the determination of military and foreign policy is properly constituted without destroying the ability of the President to use it in a flexible and responsible manner?

Most of the general formulas for improving our system of legislative-executive relations have accordingly turned on one of two ideas. The first has been that our traditional institutions are basically unsound, and that a reform in our Constitutional system or our party system must be the first step toward real improvement. The second is that the main difficulties come because we fail to enforce our present Constitutional prohibitions against the encroachment of one branch of government on the other. The first formula is to abolish the separation of powers; the second is to try to make it effective.

Of the two approaches, I generally hold with the second. But both of them, in their conventional forms, seem inadequate. We generally make too much of gadgets in our political and administrative thinking, and when we shift our attention to the ethical basis of politics we think in terms of a negative and naïve morality. And this way of thinking betrays us because, at the core of our system of constitutional responsibility, our main difficulties come not from having a system that is too primitive, but one that is too sophisticated; not from being more corrupt in our political motives than other peoples, but from being too perfectionist in our approach to politics. We are not going to solve the specific issues in our legislative-executive relations immediately, but it would pay us to try to get our general ideas straight, to try to understand the ways in which our traditional ethical ideas have affected our political and administrative institutions, and to see whether we can discover an approach that will be both morally valid and effective in practice.

II

Let us begin by taking a brief look at the two main approaches to this problem that have been customary in the past.

The first approach is to reform the Constitutional or party system, or both together. It usually includes two related proposals.

One is the proposal for the adoption of a parliamentary or cabinet system. It is based on the belief that the root of the trouble lies in our Constitutional separation of powers; under such a system, the argument runs, deadlocks cannot be settled by appeal to the people; the remedy is to give one of the two branches more influence or control over the election of the other. This proposal takes two opposite forms: some advocate the election of the chief executive by the Congress, hoping to find our salvation in legislative supremacy; others propose to give the President the right to dissolve a recalcitrant Congress and appeal to the electorate, in order to assure more effective executive leadership.

The other proposal, which sometimes goes along with the first, is a plea for more effective party discipline: only more tightly organized parties, with more consistent philosophies and more disciplinary authority over members of Congress, can prevent the stalemates and inconsistencies that plague American politics.

The inconsistencies spring, of course, from the difficulty of reconciling diverse sectional and class and other special interests within any coherent system. What will make people rise above these special interests to join in a common interest? The advocates of the parliamentary-plus-party system have usually assumed either that the possibility of the legislature turning the executive out of office (or vice versa) will force the contending factions to team up into two responsible parties: or else they have assumed that the existence of two disciplined parties will lead to a demand for a procedure by which deadlocks can be resolved, and an appeal made to the electorate. But the question whether a change in the formal machinery of government is a necessary prerequisite for the creation of coherent and disciplined parties, or vice versa, is a source of some uncertainty.

And that uncertainty is compounded when we look at various experiments with the formal unification of powers outside the classic setting of the Palace of Westminster. Why did not the formal unification of powers in the Third and Fourth Republics of France bring about the same party discipline, the same coherence of policy, and the same sense of responsibility as in the United Kingdom? The French example suggests that legislators, when faced with the possibility of dissolution, may prefer not to face up to the potential issue; their recourse may be to agree to divide and destroy power, rather than to unify it in a responsible manner.

Or consider the only major experiment in the United States (since the Articles of Confederation) with a system of unification of powers. The city manager (or council manager) plan is now the most widespread form of municipal government for cities of all sizes except the very smallest and the very largest, and it unifies powers thoroughly in the council, which appoints the city manager and can dismiss him at will. And under this scheme we do not always find an issue presented to the voters between two clearcut systems of policy, which are expected to be administered with no regard for politics; the most frequent electoral issue is whether the council is a mere rubber stamp under the dictation of the manager, or whether the manager is a spineless politician who tolerates interference with his administration by the council members. And more than a few councils have come to power on the basis of a plan to keep the administration weak and divided, in order to parcel out pieces of it among themselves.

Under a system of formal unification of powers, it is evident that an electorate and a legislature can be led to evade their responsibility and to live in a political morass of divided authority and unresolved conflicts, rather than to rise to a higher level of responsibility and consistency. The institutional machinery is important, tremendously important, but it alone is obviously not enough.

Those who have come to that conclusion (or started with it) have generally turned to the second general approach to the reform of legislative-executive relations: the enforcement of our Constitutional separation of powers, which is usually confused by encroachment in one direction or another. This approach sometimes takes extreme forms. Some argue that for decades the President has been encroaching on the Constitutional powers of the Congress, and that executive initiative in legislation and leadership in politics constitute a dictatorial threat to the traditions of the Republic. On the other hand, some say that the solution of our problems demands more unified administration, and any attempts by members of Congress or Congressional committees to meddle with problems of organization or administration are obviously motivated by a low greed for political influence. These generalizations will not get us anywhere, partly because executive leadership in policy, and legislative support and control of administration, are both part of our national tradition and virtually required by our

Constitution. But equally important, they are not helpful because they are based on a wrong reading of the source of the conflict.

Members of Congress and government administrators squabble over their jurisdictional boundaries, no doubt, because of natural selfishness and low motives. But such motives are relatively easy to compromise. The more difficult squabbles come when both sides are motivated by high principle. Every trade has its *deformation professionelle,* and there are fairly clear general distinctions between the ethical attitudes of the legislator and the administrator. To oversimplify greatly, members of Congress are men of high principle whose basic ideals are patriotism and individual justice, who are forced to respond most directly to pressures from local interests. Their professional habits induce them to think in terms of individual cases, not general policy, and their temptation is political power. On the other hand, the top government administrator has come up through a technical or managerial career; his professional ethics require a concern for the maintenance of standards of performance; the problems that cross his desk are national in scope, and can be dealt with only in terms of general policy; the pressure on him is to get his job done, and his temptation is to expand his agency's importance, and his own with it.

General ethical principles, of course, might lead the politician and the administrator to surmount their characteristic conflicts by rising above narrow and parochial and specialized interests to a higher scale of values, to a more general common interest in national welfare. This works, but only up to a point. Let us invent a hypothetical illustration: a Congressman from Nevada is on the House Committee on Research, and that Committee hears that the Federal Institute of Biology is proposing to build a $10,000,000 molecular invigorator. If the Congressman is an old fashioned patronage politician, he may cause the Institute a lot of trouble by pressing the Institute to locate the new installation in his home district, to give all the jobs to deserving Democrats—no, in Nevada it would probably be Republicans. But if he is more enlightened, he may have risen to the level of putting the broad program of the Administration, or of his party, ahead of his baser political instincts; in this case, he will be for the new facility, wherever it may best be located, as a major step toward advancing our basic science and keeping up with the Russians. Unless he is against it because he is convinced that government spending is threatening the basis of our free enterprise economy, which is the only sure bastion of liberty in a Marxistridden world. Either way, of course, he can fit nicely into the picture of those who would like to see the government controlled by a disciplined party under a parliamentary system.

Unfortunately for our scheme, however, moral advancement does not always stop there. Our Congressman may decide that it is up to him, as a member of the Committee, to examine the scientific and administrative experts and think for himself. Then the fat is in the fire. Sometimes this process results, curiously enough, in his discovery that sound national policy and pure patriotism require the molecular invigorator to be located in the part of the country where it would do most to restore prosperity to a distressed area, and at the same time be near a particular combination of transportation facilities and cheap labor—a combination of criteria that would put it inevitably in the Eleventh Congressional District of Nevada, as anyone but a prejudiced bureaucrat could see. Or if he does not make such a fortuitous discovery, he may find that a particular group of bureaucratic scientists is pushing a type of facility that will greatly favor the advancement of socialized medicine, and it is only his own crusading spirit that can identify the right type, manufactured by the right company, and thus save the Administration (it could even be his own party's) from being deceived by its disloyal subordinates.

The more conscientious, thoughtful, and hardworking the Congressman, the more he may want to make up his mind regardless of party discipline or Administration leadership. This step to a higher level of value—higher for anyone who gives priority to independent truth and scorns political compromise—makes party conformity and the coordination of policy difficult.

On the Executive side, some similar steps can be identified. The distinguished scientist who is Research Director of the Institute, if he is a cheap politician, may simply want to build his invigorator anywhere that will produce him the highest appropriation. (In that case, if he deals with the most influential Congressman, he may get his money quickly, for such are sometimes the rewards of lack of virtue.) If he dutifully takes his program to the Administration for coordination, as hierarchical principles and a concern for broad policy require, he may get his appropriation, or he may not, and in the latter case virtue has to be its own reward. But if his vision is broad, his imagination lofty and unselfish, and his appreciation of the importance of biology to the national security and the welfare of civilization adequately developed, he cannot take No from any shortsighted lout in the Budget Bureau (obviously the President himself couldn't have been properly informed on an issue of such importance). So the higher morality requires him to connive with the Congressman—even the one who wants that molecular invigorator for his own district.

At this point, of course, coordination of policy has been thoroughly destroyed, and the higher morality satisfied. (In the past, some historians and theologians say, the highest and purest and most zealous morality has had a way of turning back down into the lowest actions.) But this kind of thing—this flouting of central authority not for low motives but for high—is hard to deal with, especially because issues of policy get mixed up with issues of organization and procedure: the Congressman may decide his vote not on the substance of policy, but to establish a principle with respect to the procedure by which his Committee may hold the Institute accountable; the Research Director may fail to explain his real line of reasoning to the Congress out of a fear of legislative encroachment on his authority. This kind of complication is frustrating to those who wish to substitute some more responsible form of government, some more effective system of party discipline, for our present can of worms in Washington. For reformers can win if they are opposed only by those who are generally recognized as unethical, but a reform is bound to be difficult if it calls for changes in habits that are highly esteemed by the community.

Walter Bagehot, who wrote the first classic study of Cabinet government in England, observed that it worked well because the English were a deferential people, who did not seek to pry behind the façade of the Crown—the apparent power—to inquire into the working of the Cabinet—the effective power. He thought the same system could work in republics, if the mechanism were faithfully copied. Perhaps it can. But the record suggests that, once the voters become self-conscious about their relationship to the government, and their ability to control its inner workings, they may never be content again to direct their attention only to policy issues. The British government and civil service still carry on under the protecting shadow of monarchical tradition. But we wandered out of that Garden of Eden when we found that the form of government itself was something we could decide for ourselves. Having tasted that knowledge, it seems hard to go back to a system where our politicians look only at policy, and our administrators are in charge of administration.

But, having reached this stage of self-consciousness, if we cannot go back can we go ahead? Can any new set of ideas give us the basis for a more responsible pattern of legislative-executive relationships? Do we have to cling to notions that condemn us to political frustration, in a time that calls for responsible action? If we are to get at such questions, we may have to look back at the way in which we grew up, in the United States, with some ethical attitudes toward government that make difficult a responsible set of legislative-executive relations. How, in short, did political irresponsibility come so dangerously close to becoming an article of popular faith in America?

III

We may usefully consider the responsibility of any system of government, particularly its system of legislative-executive relations, by looking at two of its phases, as long as we keep in mind that they are two phases of the same thing: responsibility for political leadership, and administrative responsibility.

Responsible political leadership requires not only a responsible structure, but also a set of common assumptions and loyalties. Among these assumptions two are especially important.

One is the general belief that the affairs of government and politics should be the highest concern of the most respected citizens, and that some of them should always be ready and willing to seek public office. Policy is not something that can be determined in advance by an ideological code, and if the leaders of government do not personally command high respect, politics not only becomes a scramble of selfish interests—it degenerates into a contest in which the contenders change the rules of the game for their own ends and bribe the umpire. Since in fact decisions made by government, even in the weakest nations, have profound effects on private interests, it is necessary to have men in high office who have moral authority and respect in their own right, if they are not to be controlled by irresponsible forces from outside.

In the first years of the American Republic, we were ruled by the

Federalist Establishment, by the rich and wellborn, by the elders of New England and the vestrymen of Virginia. We did not yet think of politics as involving so much of a conflict of interest that our political conscience was uneasy about entrusting rule to men of large affairs. Indeed, the clearsighted but cynical Hamilton believed as a matter of principle that we should imitate the British constitution as it was, "bottomed on corruption," because its very elements of corruption— its amalgam of economic and political interests—gave it stability and strength. (Or so Jefferson charged in his *Anas*.) But several political currents were against such a union of economic and political power.

One was the current that began with John Adams. His staunch Puritanism expected the worse of human nature, and favored a conservative constitution, but one whose prime value was liberty.[1] John Quincy Adams, with his interest in science as well as the Scriptures, hoped for a strong national government for the encouragement of technology and industry, but he was elbowed aside by the advancing agrarian democracy of the new West. Meanwhile in New England, Transcendental and Unitarian idealism became too detached, and the doctrine of the evangelistic sects too perfectionist, to draw men into active political leadership. None of them really believed that worldly power was respectable. They were deeply concerned with public problems, but neither antislavery agitation nor the prohibition crusade was designed to lead men into positions of political responsibility. With the general drift away from active political involvement of the New England aristocracy, it is symbolically altogether too appropriate that Charles Francis Adams served with honor in appointive but not elective office, and the next generation of the family produced *The Degradation of the Democratic Dogma* and the weary disillusion of *The Education of Henry Adams*. When Henry Adams finally decided to give up his dislike of bankers and join his friends in accepting the gold standard, the old Puritan ethic succumbed at last to Alexander Hamilton.

Jefferson, like John Adams, was shocked by Hamilton's cynical pref-

---

[1] John Adams's general outlook on politics and politicians may be inferred from his youthful diary, one entry of which reads as follows: "May 30, 1760, Friday. Rose early. Several Country Towns, within my observation, have at least a dozen Taverns and Retailers. Here the Time, the Money, the Health and the Modesty, of most that are young and of many old, are wasted; here Diseases, vicious Habits, Bastards and Legislators, are frequently begotten." L. H. Butterfield, editor in chief, *The Diary and Autobiography of John Adams*, Belknap Press of Harvard University Press, 1961.

erence for a corrupt connection between economic and political power; but his formula for dispensing with that connection was not Puritan morality but the generous idealism of the Enlightenment. His secular approach was typified by the effort to protect government against control by ecclesiastical as well as economic power; many of the early state constitutions forbade ministers of religion to hold public office. But Jefferson's Deism and the tolerant skepticism of his contemporaries gave way throughout the South and West to the revivalism of the evangelistic churches; they shared his preference for the simple agrarian virtues; they shared his distaste for the complex problems of political power; but they inherited none of his traditional, almost Roman, belief in the duty of the citizen to accept the burdens of public office. And in the South they found themselves committed, less than a quarter-century after Jefferson died and Jackson left the White House, to a fundamentalist defense of King Cotton and his slave system.

The leaders of the evangelistic churches disliked ecclesiastical power, or any other power that might interfere with their freedom. Their ancestors had suffered under a combination of royal and episcopal authority; they were eager, in their search for spiritual perfection, to do without organized authority of any kind. Today there are fundamentalist sects that get financial support from men of great wealth because they oppose the government and encourage the personal qualities that make for a docile labor force. A century ago, however, it was religion that was still, perhaps, the moving force; the business corporations that came along pleading for absolute independence from political interference were riding the ideological coat tails of the free churches that had at last shaken loose from government support and control, including such nuisances as compulsory oaths and legal tithes.

The free churches of the frontier supplied much of the democratic idealism which (combined, of course, with the practical interests of the uplanders and backwoodsmen) began to look with suspicion on men of wealth in high office, at the same period, and for the same reason, that it moved most of our state capitals away from the largest cities to minor country towns. The contempt of many of the rich and well educated for politics began at least in part as a reaction against the popular prejudice that—until recently—rejected them as candidates for public office.

In their reaction against the cynicism of Hamilton, perfectionists

Irresponsibility as an Article of Faith

of both the sophisticated Transcendental and the backwoods evangelistic varieties forgot the balanced view (like James Madison's) that had characterized the period of the Founding Fathers. In their passion to protect politics against corruption by economic forces, they attempted to separate politics entirely from economics. This was an idealistic error much like the notion that international affairs could be conducted entirely without regard to armed force. By keeping military power separated in peacetime from policy calculations of a responsible nature, idealists made war more likely, and less subject to policy restraints when it occurred. In a similar way, by denying the connections between governmental and business affairs—a connection that can never be free of selfish motives—idealists made it impossible to develop within government a restrained and balanced set of policies for the encouragement, support, and control of business. The shift from the mixed system of public and private enterprises of the early part of the nineteenth century to pure *laissez faire* did not bring less corruption, but more. The Cumberland Road and the Erie Canal involved nothing like the flagrant graft of the Credit Mobilier and the railway land grants.

The temptation to deny the influence of materialistic motives on human activity is as pervasive in politics as in personal affairs. In our politics, it has continued most strongly in the agrarian myth: the Jeffersonian notion of the inherent moral superiority of the rural voter, a traditional prejudice which has buttressed the grossly unfair overrepresentation of rural areas in our State legislatures, which in turn profoundly influences the distribution of power in party organizations and in the Congress. And this rural power, which on agricultural issues deals the cards frankly for the economic benefit of the farmer, lines up most often on industrial issues in support of the more conservative wing of business.

How do these attitudes show up in contemporary relations between the legislature and executive? Two examples are obvious. The agrarian ideal held that public office should be undertaken only out of a sense of duty, and not corrupted by extravagant salaries. The result of this perfectionist view is that Congress sets the salary of political executives who are charged with economic decisions vast enough to dwarf the largest corporations, at levels far below those of industrial management. Consequently, since modern ideas do not make it possible to substitute monastic ideals for a personnel policy, this leads inevitably to an Executive Branch in which the positions of top responsibility tend to be reserved for the very rich.

But then we do not like to see the very rich making governmental decisions affecting their interests, and we press Congress to pass laws about it. The result is a great todo over minor aspects of the problem, such as the forced sale of stock by great industrialists whose particular stock is less of a temptation than their prejudices accumulated from a lifetime of association; or such as rules to forbid regulatory officials from accepting petty favors when they are obviously less tempted by current entertainment than by the possibility of a future career in the business they are regulating.

In more recent years, the motive of protecting politics from corruption by business has had much less force than the passion of business, even when accepting public subsidies, to reassert its independence of government. This is largely, no doubt, a pragmatic and not an idealistic passion. But not entirely; indeed, ordinary selfishness would not account for the doctrinaire fervor of some of the arguments for the independence of business from government. This fervent belief in the inherent superiority of business over government leads to the notion that money spent by a private company in making consumer goods, no matter how frivolous their purpose, is a contribution to a dynamic and productive economy, while money spent by government for education or advanced research is a drain on the system.

But this notion is now giving way to a more subtle one: it is not so much where the money comes from that counts, but who spends it. The taint on tax money can be purified by putting it in the hands of personnel who are not carried on a government payroll. The old business prejudice against bureaucrats started with a wholesome respect for the thrifty man who did his own work, made his own way, ran his risks, and did not depend on influence or authority for his prosperity. The prejudice remains, even in fields where it is getting harder and harder to do without influence, or to accept the risks. Many of the new functions of government, paid for entirely out of tax funds, are being administered not by government officials but by private corporations under contract: the atomic energy and space programs are the best examples, but the practice has been spreading piecemeal in others.

The contractual system has been a brilliant improvisation, and may constitute a most significant addition to our governmental system. But it will do so only if we work out a more sensible basis of distinguishing between the kinds of operations that should be kept within government and those that should be administered privately, and in the latter case, a better system of enforcing responsibility for the use of public funds. For the trouble with the system is that it has spread not in response to rational calculation, but as a means of evading irrelevant ethical prejudices. The executive agencies invented and developed the contractual system, but they did so as a sort of gamesmanship to avoid the popular prejudices that play on the Congress. To spend billions through contracts with private corporations does not involve much increase in the number of government officials. Once the money is out of the hands of officials who are by definition potentially corrupt, and in the hands of businessmen who are by definition efficient, a Congressional committee need no longer feel responsible for the way in which the dollars are spent. In the legislative oversight of public expenditures, the Jeffersonian or Puritan passion for austerity need not follow the dollars past the boundary of the civil service; beyond that point, responsibility becomes more tolerant of the compromises that become necessary as economic and political, materialistic and idealistic, considerations are mixed.

The first difficulty that America faces in developing a more responsible system of legislative-executive relations is that we have not quite accepted, in some of the important segments of our society, the primary assumption which is the foundation of responsibility for policy—that the most respected citizens of the nation will themselves consider political leadership their most important calling. That assumption has remained a living tradition throughout our history in some parts of our society—in some of the southern and border states the lawyer in politics has always retained high general prestige. But in the major industrial and metropolitan regions the general attitude of the professional and business classes has been predominantly antipolitical, to such an extent as to give weight to the argument that we have no real conservative tradition in America. The natural position of a conservative should be to sustain a strong government, all the more so in an era when the main international threat is from a movement that threatens the institutions of private property and traditional ethics alike. Perhaps we are becoming more mature in this respect; the proportion of men of wealth among those who in 1959 were considered possibilities for the

Presidency shows that the very rich can no longer consider their wealth a handicap to political popularity.

The second assumption that is essential as a basis for a responsible system of policy determination is that political leaders must be prepared, and the structure of government must encourage them, to subordinate their specialized or partisan beliefs or interests, on matters of major concern, to the development of some more general consensus. And this usually means compromise, a word that carries a connotation of something less than high moral principle.

The various Protestant churches that put their stamp on popular ethical thought during the early nineteenth century in the United States varied widely in the effect of their teaching on the morality of compromise. At one extreme, there were the sects which thought of the church as required to withdraw from the world in order to assure the salvation of its members. Most of these sects were founded on rigid and conservative dogma, like the Mennonites or the Primitive Baptists. They did not see their members as having an obligation to help solve the practical problems of the broader community; a few even objected on predestinarian principle to efforts to convert others to their own beliefs.

But even the more liberal theologies of the popular evangelistic denominations, or for that matter the extremely liberal theology of those who led the movement toward the Social Gospel, did little to teach the ethical necessity of political compromise. For whenever the liberal theologian seized on a social issue, he made it a peculiar and unique crusade; he carried over into politics the disposition of his fundamentalist ancestors to select a particular aspect of doctrine and make it serve as a distinction from all other sects. He was usually for bringing to a prompt end some specific social evil; he was against war, or slavery, or alcohol, or prostitution. With Thoreau, he would disavow civil obligations rather than yield his moral position. The pessimistic sectarians had held that man could be saved only by withdrawing him entirely from the world; the nineteenth century optimists thought the job could be done if he could only be protected against a few specific social maladies. The competition among the sects of either type was not calculated to produce the urbane, tolerant, somewhat cynical ecclesiastical leader, such as those found so frequently in the established Church of England. Nor did it teach an ethical approach which justified a lay politician in

Irresponsibility as an Article of Faith

compromising his own principles in order to take part in a workable majority.

The basic ethical attitudes that set the traditions of the modern parliamentary tradition in Great Britain took form just before the more rigid views of the later Victorian period became fashionable, and well before the newer intolerance of the radical political factions. That old tolerant view was best summed up in the plea of Lord Melbourne, who as Prime Minister told his Cabinet that it didn't matter what they said as long as they all said the same thing. It is not hard to imagine an American political leader of the period thinking that way, or acting accordingly; it is a little hard to imagine him saying something like this without being shamefaced about it. For this degree of tolerance and compromise were in harmony with that other remark attributed to Lord Melbourne, speaking as a relic of the skeptical eighteenth century made uncomfortable by the new evangelism of the nineteenth: "Things have come to a pretty pass when religion is allowed to invade the sphere of private life."

The kind of unity that developed within the two parties of the classic period of Cabinet Government was not a unity of political theory or doctrine. There was nothing in either the Conservative or Liberal doctrine anywhere nearly so finespun and systematic as the doctrine of any one of a dozen German or French parties. But a political leader was simply supposed to subordinate his views for the sake of agreement with his colleagues, and to maintain for Her Majesty a majority Government; this form of self-discipline was accounted as admirable as that of the career official who for the sake of Her Majesty's Civil Service loyally administered policies with which he disagreed. The mutual tolerance that is the foundation of this system was shaken for a time by the logic of socialism; the existence of an Opposition Party committed to Marxist doctrine seemed to stretch too far the loyalty of the politician and the civil servant alike. But the willingness of the Tories to sacrifice the purity of *laissez-faire* economics is now rivalled by the eagerness of Labour to explain away its commitment to a rigid principle of public ownership.

In France and Germany, it has been harder to establish the idea that compromise of party principle is ethically desirable in order to constitute an effective and responsible majority. This idea was in Great

Britain the great enemy of a multiplicity of parties. But it is very different from the idea that there is a single set of principles that ought to prevail, and a single party to support them. For it assumes that the principles the party embodies at any one time are only compromises, and thus not deserving of ultimate moral sanctions, and that the party that is the majority today may become the minority tomorrow. Even when a nation rejects the mystique of absolutism, it may still not be ready to accept such a notion, and may need to turn to a single leader as the rallying point of loyalty. For the idea of compromise that is at the basis of a responsible two-party system involves a good supply of an intellectual quality which at worst may look like cynicism, or at best like genuine humility, a belief that any human system of thought is based on imperfections, and that it is impious to try to give it absolute authority.

In the United States it is a commonplace to observe that we do not have two well disciplined parties. Each is only a conglomeration of local interests, which unites mainly for the purpose of trying to elect the President. Some reformers would like to avoid the dilemma between the British and the old Continental approach—to have a two-party system, and yet have each party based on a real ideological unity. Some such reformers are not very much interested in both parties; they want their own party unified in doctrine, without losing members; they see it as truly embodying the general will, if it could only eliminate its internal dissent and still keep a majority—much like the comfortable lady in Helen Hokinson's cartoon who remarked to her husband over the breakfast newspaper, "But if you can't trust the Republicans to be nonpartisan whom can you trust?"

But this is not the general attitude in the United States. Our rival sects have become more tolerant. Our moral perfectionists have become less confident. And a new wing of theological opinion, by admitting the imperfectibility of man, is led to conclude that power and responsibility involve moral dilemmas in which compromise is inevitable. If we in the United States have difficulty accepting compromise as a justifiable basis for political action, it is no longer because there are too many William Lloyd Garrisons among us to offer moral objections to it. It may be a sign of the temper of the times that a novel (*Advise and Consent*), at the top of the best seller list early in 1960, sympathetically portrays the moral dilemmas of the practising politician in the United

Irresponsibility as an Article of Faith

States Senate. Indeed, it goes so far in this direction that the reader may well conclude that politics has no content whatever, and politicians exist only to scheme for power.

Nor do we seem in any danger of committing ourselves to irreconcilable economic ideologies. Marxism never had a real mass appeal, and it has lost most of its minority following among the intellectuals; at the other extreme, the faith in pure private enterprise among business leaders has been so tempered by a willingness to accept subsidies that its profession has become more of a perfunctory ritual than a crusade.

It is no longer the sectarians or the socialists, but the scientists who give us an uneasy conscience about the compromises that are necessary for responsible government. Their testimony on public issues carries weight partly because they have proved their ability to shake the world with their discoveries, and partly because they have a profound moral conviction of the essential rightness of their approach, and the discipline which serves it. But like anyone else, a scientist tends to see mainly the aspects which can be dealt with by his particular discipline. And on the other aspects of the problem, he is likely to be guided (again like anyone else) by his moral convictions or his own interests, and is rather more likely than others to despise the compromises made by politicians or administrators.

So today, when an issue hits the headlines, the tendency of the Congress and of the Executive Branch alike is to appoint a special committee of scientists to tell it what to do, or set up a special research project (maybe even one manned by social scientists) to give it the answers. This tendency has led to a situation in which each political party has a committee of scientists supporting or formulating its position, and a research project is required to buttress any respectable minority or majority report from a Congressional committee. So, for example, we have one school of scientists telling us that atomic fallout imperils the future of the human race, and another reassuring us that it is a trivial threat, which can readily be accepted in view of the needs of national defense.

Now this is obviously not the fault of science, or of the scientists as scientists. For most scientists realize better than laymen the way in which practical problems or political issues are complexes including moral and economic and emotional, as well as technological or scientific components. But there is a very great difficulty in the frequent public assumption that the way to solve a complex political problem is by public debate and legislation on the policy issue, with the decision guided mainly by the scientific data. The difficulty is not only that the scientists are likely to be as intolerant of political compromise as were the professional moralists of a couple of generations ago. It lies mainly in the fact that the scientists and engineers have made government generally such a complex business that we can no longer judge the responsibility of a system of legislative-executive relations by its handling of policy issues after they reach the stage of public debate.

As a result, compromise is a necessary but not a sufficient condition for the creation of a consensus representing a true national interest. It is no longer any more possible for a President or a Senator to bring forth a new important policy by presenting his isolated individual ideas to the electorate than it is feasible for a Commander in Chief to mount a white horse and lead troops into battle. For policy is created by a complex process of staff work, in which science as well as politics may play an important role. Its success depends not merely on the brilliance of debate, but on years of patient work; many of the problems over which politicians agonize in public today could have been solved satisfactorily only by beginning work at least ten years ago.

In these circumstances, the role of the elected legislator must be not merely one of protesting against executive mistakes, and not merely one of debating general issues of political philosophy, those were his major functions in an era of negative government, a simpler and happier era when the welfare of the individual depended mainly on protection against oppression and the national defense on the volunteer militia. When those were the problems, it was possible to be confident that responsibility could be enforced by having the legislature concerned only with policy in the broad sense; by judicious compromises on issues that any intelligent layman could understand, it could create something like a national consensus. This model worked in the United Kingdom, for example, by virtue of requiring the House of Commons to choose between one Cabinet and another; it was essential to the discipline of the system that the House not maintain specialized committees which might amend the policy of the government, and thus confuse responsibility.

But the choice which such a system puts before the legislature and the people is an oversimplified choice between two oversimplified philosophies, neither of which may be relevant to the real problems facing the government, both of which may be sweeping all the real issues under the rug. That system, it is true, made the ethical choices for both the legislator and the administrator in Great Britain more simple than does the complex and diffuse systems of legislative-executive relations in America; provided they were willing to accept the political compromises engineered by the Cabinet, their duty to support (or loyally oppose) Her Majesty's Government in the House, and to administer its policies in Her Majesty's Civil Service, was clearcut.

Most of the advocates of some form of parliamentary government for the United States find it hard to face the issue of what to do about Congressional committees. To leave them with their independent review of policy, under a parliamentary system in which Congress could unseat the President or a Prime Minister, would invite the irresponsibility of the French Third Republic, rather than the discipline of the House of Commons. Yet it is a sound instinct that sees in the Congressional committees and their exercise of independent judgment, an essential role for the future, even if they involve Congressmen in moral dilemmas between party regularity and their own independent judgment, and put civil servants and military officers sometimes in the position of choosing between their personal opinions and their obligations to their superiors. The perfectionist standards of the moralist and the scientist will have to adjust, no doubt, to the habits of political compromise and discipline in order to make effective government possible. But given the dangers of putting too great influence in a centralized bureaucracy, civilian or military, and of permitting it to conceal the shortcomings in its own processes and organization, we may want to let our public officials, like everyone else, learn to live with a few moral dilemmas rather than solve them automatically by reference to authority.

To sum up, the way we go about looking for political leadership in the United States is still influenced by ethical attitudes carried over from the perfectionist thinking of the midnineteenth century. We are not yet prepared to consider public office the highest calling of the citizen, and we are still inclined on principle to take care of great public issues by leaving them to private advisers to decide, and private institutions to administer. We have learned a great deal about the moral necessity of compromise and tolerance, but we have hardly begun to appreciate that superficial compromise is not the chief end to be desired in a technologically demanding world. We still hardly understand that our institutional machinery for policy determination has to produce not merely verbal and philosophical agreement, but the highest possible degree of technical and administrative effectiveness, to meet the problems of the future. And this brings us to the second phase of political responsibility—administrative responsibility.

IV

Some of our most cherished traditional ideas make it hard for us to swallow the notion that our administrative arrangements are at the heart of our policy problem. Many liberals prefer to write high principles and an expanded moral responsibility into law, and take it for granted that someone will work out the details. And many conservatives prefer to believe that administration has nothing to do with policy; that the sole function of the public service is to be neutral in such matters, and carry out efficiently what Congress has legislated. Some liberals seem to believe that the voice of the people should be a purely spiritual force—to think that patriotism and civic spirit should provide an adequate motive power to carry out public policy and that attention to the necessary means implies a distrust of either charismatic leadership or the Spirit of Progress—much as the Antimissionary Baptist thinks that to make an organized effort at conversion is a sign of lack of faith in predestination. The conservative, on the other hand, is afraid of creating an efficient machinery of government, lest it result in an aggrandizement of government at the expense of private interests. Unfortunately, the two positions, in practical terms, arrive at the same end.

In such matters we are the victims of a double double-standard.

The first of the two double standards is the distinction which our popular attitudes make between government, which we tend to put on a moral pedestal and then distrust when we detect its moral lapses, and private institutions, especially business, in which we characteristically assume that the end justifies the means. A case in which a television station bribes a government regulatory agency by excessive hospitality, for example, is automatically considered a proof of the natural sinfulness of politics; it normally leads to a clamor for a more rigid code of ethics for government; it rarely occurs to anyone to suggest that the private business concerned ought at least not be permitted to deduct the costs of such hospitality from its income for tax purposes.

On the positive side, this double standard is desirable for the government; it is obviously good to maintain ethical standards for government on as high a plane as possible. But there is a negative side to this double standard: the basic trouble in the government-business relationship often comes because a weak organization is dealing with a strong one, and the government is usually the weaker in terms of the strength of its career personnel, and the discipline and cohesion of its hierarchy. In such a situation, to expect that the stronger organization, when large interests are at stake, would not influence the personnel of the weaker one is to ask for a moral impossibility.

But why, then, is our government the weaker contestant in such issues, when by definition it commands sovereign and superior power? To answer this question we must go into the ethical attitudes toward administrative organization and personnel that developed in American nineteenth century democracy. During the period when the Federalist aristocracy was collapsing as the ruling party, and its leadership was passing to the democracy of the new West and the new urban political machines of the East, a new form was being given to the administrative structure of our governmental institutions, which had come to be the object of almost religious veneration by the American people. And there were curious parallels, to say the least, between the main developments in governmental and religious institutions.

In the decades just after the churches of Massachusetts and Connecticut lost their established status, the great revivals of the 1830s and 1840s combined with the general democratic spirit to favor the growth of those Protestant churches with the less highly organized hierarchies. Laud's maxim had been, "No bishop, no King"; the American frontier in effect retorted, "No King, no bishop." The Episcopalians were outdistanced by the Methodists, and among the Calvinist denominations the Princeton Presbyterians lost ground to the backwoods Baptists.

In both cases, whether or not episcopacy was involved, the change was certainly in the direction of less hierarchical authority. And at the same time identical currents were at work in political organization. Alexander Campbell helped lead a losing fight in the Virginia Constitutional Convention of 1829 for the repeal of the property qualification for voting, against James Madison, James Monroe, and John Marshall. But in the nation, in the long run, he was on the winning side. The long ballot—providing for the direct election of administrative officers rather than their appointment by the chief executive—was adopted generally in state constitutions and city charters in this period; the federal government was saved from a similar weakening of its hierarchical structure only by the rigidity of its Constitution, but informally the same objective was almost accomplished by the growing control of Congressional committees over federal bureaus and agencies.

What happened to the hierarchical principle was also happening to the career principle. The churches with clergies that could be ordained only after formal training lost members rapidly in competition with those that relied on the enthusiasm rather than the education of their ministers. The "priesthood of all believers" was made a working principle in the evangelistic sects of the frontier, and in the layman's activities in the cities. This was the period when the same distrust of the educated élites led to the admission of lawyers to the bar without formal training, and led to the principle of rotation in office through political spoils in the federal as well as the state and local governments. The political equivalent of the "priesthood of all believers" was Jackson's dictum that the duties of public office were simple enough so that they could be entrusted to any citizen of good moral character. And this attitude prevailed in military as well as civilian affairs; we went into the Civil War with much of the Army on both sides made up of regiments that elected their own officers, and that in many respects remained under the orders of the state governors rather than the President and his generals.

The reform of the spoils system beginning in the late nineteenth century owed something to the moral zeal of the reformers. It owed even more, perhaps, in the federal government to the professional ethics of the scientists and technicians. A civil works engineer, a public health doctor, a land surveyor, a soil or food chemist—workers in such fields, with the support of their professional colleagues outside the government, were able to insist on the gradual adoption of technical standards for the recruitment and promotion of technical personnel. The scientists had joined with the dissenting sects in the Enlightenment and the eighteenth century revolutions against the forces of royal and ecclesiastical authority. In the nineteenth century, however, their respect for education and professional standards led them to take a vigorous line in advocating a more thoroughly trained career service in many of the executive departments of government. The moral reformers remained mainly negative in their aims; they were interested in prohibiting patronage and corruption among the great mass of routine employes, and this emphasis had continued to characterize the efficiency and economy wing of government reform ever since. But the professional ethics of the scientists and engineers made them more interested in positive policy objectives than in the prevention of patronage, and most of all made them want trained men of professional competence in the top jobs.

This ethical impulse was bounded, generally, by the limits of a technical program; a public health doctor, for example, typically cared little about the work of bureaus other than the Public Health Service. Indeed, he tended to look on any effort from above to coordinate his program with others as no better than the old fashioned partisan corruption. The scientist in government was for high career standards within his speciality, and was for furthering his specialized program, but he retained all the popular distrust of a top hierarchy. His professional ethics led him to object to a coordinated Executive Branch with a strong administrative career system at the top; the British administrative proverb that "the expert should be on tap but not on top" has frequently been quoted by scholars, but rarely applied by administrators in America.

In a sense, then, each specialized bureau of government was politically on its own; if it had political support, the professional groups concerned could insist on its having high standards for its top personnel. If its policies were unpopular, its political opponents would often find it more effective, and cheaper, to cripple or control its administration rather than to oppose the policies themselves. And this, I suspect, largely accounts for the wide differences in the rate of growth and in administrative standards between the agricultural programs of the federal government and those which dealt with urban and industrial problems. The Department of Agriculture very early became a strong organization with high educational standards for its career personnel, for the farmers backed its programs and wanted them to be well run. The corresponding agencies dealing with urban and industrial problems were fought at every step in their development by corporate interests that feared government regulation and competition, and that employed most of the experts who worked outside the universities.

The professional ethics of the scientist who worked in various agricultural fields supported the development of governmental programs; in other fields, they were more likely to look on government from the same point of view as industrial management. Similarly, the lawyers in and out of Congress who were interested in the regulation of public utilities and business found it desirable to set up those regulatory functions in independent commissions, with little or no responsibility to the President; in the field of agriculture, the same kinds of regulatory functions have been entrusted to the Department of Agriculture.

The moral prejudices against hierarchy and professionalism which were planted deep in our traditions by the evangelical churches more than a century ago have been carried over—with surprisingly little modification to meet the demands of the new technology—in the attitudes which Congress maintains toward the executive branch. We find it hard to admit the need for a government service as a corporate entity; we are so afraid of the restrictions that it may put on free democratic policy decisions that we refuse to admit that only an effective government service can formulate effective alternative policies for legislative action, or carry out whatever policy is finally decided.

If we wonder why more young men and women do not show an interest in careers of public service, this may be the reason: we maintain, as a working article of faith, that it is wrong to offer them an organized career in public service. At a time when every major industrial corporation concerns itself above all things with the recruitment, development, and promotion of its career executives, we still, on principle, in much of our legislation try to deny the corporate nature of our civil service. Our practice is actually much better than our theory, but the theory of our civil service is still that the young administrator, no matter how well prepared for his job, has no right to expect career advancement, or to hold his rank as a matter of right if his superiors decide to transfer him to another set of duties. Nor is he encouraged to develop esprit de corps by a system in which many members of Congress will not admit the responsibility of the political head of a department for the policies developed by its staff, but insist on criticizing and exposing the position of the career officials as well.

This is true, at least, in those fields in which we think we can still afford the luxury of a choice—and this brings us to the second of our two double standards: the contrast between the military and civilian career systems and executive hierarchies. In the early days of the Republic, we were especially afraid of the military profession and its influence on political decisions; the stubborn opposition to the creation of military academies or later of the General Staff, and President Wilson's indignation at learning that the Staff had actually prepared war plans, are cases in point. But under the pressure of necessity, we have quite properly dismissed these fears. If you look at any of the ways in which an organization as such is strengthened and made effective, you will see a tremendous difference between what Congress will permit the military services, and what it will permit the civil service.

Compare, for example, the effort that is spent on the recruitment and training of military officers with that spent for the same purposes by the civil service. An elaborate system of undergraduate academies and staff colleges for the military officers, supplemented by extensive funds to send them to civilian universities for advanced training; by contrast, in spite of recent marked changes for the better, very small provisions for similar civilian purposes. Or consider the comparative degree of freedom of the military agencies to adjust their internal organization without regard to legislative action; the President has been denied a renewal of his statutory reorganization power, but special reorganization power has been given by law to the Secretary of Defense. Or consider the amount and quality of staff agencies available to the President and the heads of civilian departments; in any interdepartmental conference in Washington involving both military and civilian interests, everyone takes it for granted that the military delegation will come with elaborate staff support and heavily documented positions, while the typical civilian department will be able to muster only one grade twelve civilian for every three brigadier generals. It is like an antitrust case in which you expect to see a junior attorney from Justice overmatched by a full battery of Wall Street counsel.

There is waste and extravagance in every branch of human effort, no doubt, and it ought to be prevented whenever the effort to prevent it can save as much as it costs. But the variations in our standards of economizing show our real character—like the man who saves on the education of his children in order to buy a color television set. We—

the newspapers and the general run of voters as well as the Congressmen—see nothing amiss when an executive of a defense industry rides up to a Congressional hearing in a chauffeur driven limousine. But if that limousine carries a general, we are likely to think the taxpayers' money is being wasted. And if it carries a civil servant we are morally affronted.

The example, of course, is itself of no importance. But the moral attitudes that it represents carry over and apply to things that are important: the expenditures that are necessary in an organization if it is to make itself into a trained and disciplined service, rather than an irresponsible collection of dissatisfied individuals. And for these, Congress is on principle willing to pay what is necessary to build an effective missile plant or military service—but not to build a responsible civil service.

One result of this kind of economy is probably the waste of a lot of money, for an untrained and uncontrolled service is never worth what it costs. But there is a probable result that is much more frightening. Our policies are shaped in part by the competition of our political parties. But that competition can operate only on the issues which the voters and legislators can understand, and on alternatives of which they are aware. This is moderately effective in a field like agriculture, where most of the issues can be understood by the well educated voter, and in any case he and his Congressman can choose among a great many expert advisers carrying on studies openly in a variety of independent institutions. But policies are shaped, too, by the competition of various types of expert staffs, working within the framework of their various jurisdictional interests and the limitations of their professional points of view. And this competition may become the controlling force in any field which is highly technical in nature, in which most of the experts work in secret, and in which the main opportunity of the layman—even the responsible political executive—to determine the outcome is not by arguing with it at the end, but at the outset by defining the basic assumptions on which it is begun, and by choosing the staffs to do the job. All these things tend to be true in the fields of military and international affairs on which our future depends so heavily.

If you put a mule and a rabbit in a double harness, you can guess which will run away with the wagon. And if, under our present double standard, you put military and civilian staffs both to work on any problem (*e.g.,* disarmament), you may guess the outcome. On the one side, a large staff of old pros, dedicated by years of training and discipline to the strengthening of their profession, and with good reason suspicious that irresponsible political civilians may make softheaded decisions that would leave them holding the bag. On the other side, a series of short term and improvised staffs, made up largely of part time and volunteer workers, who submit reports and recommendations but do not have continuing authority to help carry those reports into effect. If we should be led into trouble by having too large a military proportion in our policy mix, it would not be the fault of the mythical military mind. It would be hard to find a less militaristic type than the American career officer. It would more probably be the fault of the popular American attitudes which do not encourage Congress to take (and pay for) the steps necessary to develop a civil service that is able to pull its share of the load when teamed up with the military departments.

If we fail to provide an adequate career civil service, the most dangerous result is not managerial inefficiency, but a lack of democratic control over the formulation of national policy. For democratic control can no longer be guaranteed merely by the possibility of displacing one set of top politicians in favor of another—though that possibility is a necessary ultimate sanction. That was a plausible formula in the days when the principal decisions of policy were relatively simple, and when made took effect immediately. But it is inadequate on issues in which the potential choices have to be opened up, and the potential solutions invented by lengthy and highly technical staff work.

There is no danger that any single staff within the American government will have a monopoly on knowledge and competence with respect to any issue. (An exception might once have been necessary for military affairs, but not today in view of the great variety of industrial and other staffs financed outside the government by the military departments.) The danger is the opposite: that we fail to provide a top civil service with enough stability of tenure and dedication of purpose to provide the President and the Congress with alternative bases of decisions to those put forward by private interests. Or by the military services.

The main problems with which administrative officials at this level must deal are neither problems of managing particular bureaus efficiently, nor of dealing with the scientific content of the programs of these particular bureaus. They are instead the problems of making the programs of the several bureaus knit together effectively, and their policies harmonize. This cannot be done either by the bureau chiefs who think in terms of their own programs, or by the Congressional committees that are similarly specialized in their interests. As the studies of Senator Jackson's Subcommittee have been suggesting, we are just beginning to appreciate the complexities of the machinery for the integration of national policy. From the point of view of the general national interest, the selfishness of private property is no longer the main obstacle, and public ownership is no solution; the real problem is how to transcend the ethical attitudes that are interested only in particular segments of government policy and to create a new unity among them.

This requires some sophisticated techniques that we are just beginning to learn, but those techniques are less important than the ability and motivation of the people who must apply them. But for this purpose we do not require a corps of selfless geniuses; we could afford to settle, for the time being, for a general career corps of top civilians as systematically trained, as well paid, and as highly motivated toward their understanding of the public interest as the staff officers of the military services themselves.

If we are going to create such a service, Congress must in the end do the job. The President can take the lead in this as in any other matter, but the Congress must take the action before the President can carry it out. And it is by no means hopeless to expect it will do so. For Congress is rarely given credit for its constructive accomplishments, or for rising above its natural jealousy of the Executive Branch in the national interest. The provision of a more responsible system of government by the strengthening of the Presidency, over the decades since Woodrow Wilson wrote *Congressional Government,* is itself an accomplishment of the Congress. The establishment of a civil service system, the budget system, the annual economic report, the executive reorganization plan technique, and through it the creation of the Executive Office of the President—all required Congressional action at the outset, and continued Congressional support for their effectiveness. It is a remnant of our political immaturity that we do not give Congress praise for work it accomplishes by effective delegation to the Executive Branch, when we have learned to give the President credit for what he does by delegation to his subordinates.

When we as a nation imagined that *vox populi* should speak through Congress without being corrupted by recommendations from a self-interested bureaucracy, it was at the period when we thought that a man's ideals could be pure and untainted by material concerns. We have learned since then that such idealism is self-defeating in matters of personal ethics; perhaps we have learned the same lesson in politics and administration, and are about ready to act on our new knowledge.

If we do, and add to a strong Presidency the supporting career public services the Executive Departments require, the function of the Congress itself will be heightened in importance and interest. In its function of holding the President and the Executive Branch accountable under the ground rules of the American Constitution, the Congress has one great asset: because it is not responsible for the tenure of the Executive, it is free to amend or modify the Executive's proposals in its best judgment without creating governmental crises. The continuous tension between Congress and the President that this type of scrutiny provides is a healthy one—provided the process of review is based on proposals from a responsible executive, and is conducted responsibly by the Congress.

At the Constitutional and political level, Congress has done well to create the main outlines of a responsible Presidency. At the administrative level, it now needs to set up a more responsible civil service. If it does not do so, its scrutiny of the Executive is likely to take the form, all too often, of the exposure of minor offenses or the enforcement of minor economies within the Departments. But in this period of crisis, Congress has a higher role than that of a federal house detective. A board of directors of a bank ought not to take satisfaction in catching its cashier in embezzlement; it ought to prefer to choose cashiers who are honest. And the Congress, if it creates a career service of a higher order of quality, will find it possible to rise above the enforcement of negative virtues and devote its time to the more challenging policy issues that a more competent administration would raise. As voters, we would be taking a narrow view of ethics if we should try to keep our political leaders absorbed in exposing payola, and let them fail to provide the vigorous and effective government which alone can assure us freedom and justice in a turbulent world.

V

The essential problem of general ethics, I suppose, is to reconcile the demands of absolute moral principles, or absolute love, with the dilemmas of everyday existence. In our legislative-executive relationship, which is the balance point of our Constitutional system, we similarly have to reconcile the demands of absolute democracy with the practical necessities of an executive authority and administrative system that can make effective the purposes of democracy. To achieve the proper balance between the two demands—or some way of transcending them for the benefit of both—is the essence of political responsibility.

Any approach which ignores the practical necessities of executive authority and administrative system leads to irresponsibility. We were pretty far down that road at one time, with our late nineteenth century habit of administration by Congressional committees, and our early twentieth century doctrine of the initiative and referendum. The worst danger of anarchic irresponsibility, of course, is that it leads in emergencies to an irrational swing in the other direction, toward the irresponsibility of totalitarianism.

The notion of strengthening responsibility by changing the institutional mechanism of legislative-executive relations—typically, by imitating the parliamentary system—could be applied so as to lead us toward either extreme; as indicated above, some of its variations would merely let the legislature elect and dismiss the executive, while others would let a popularly elected President dissolve the Congress and appeal to the electorate. The former would destroy the one element in our system that has, over the past half-century, begun to provide coherence and responsibility in both policy and administration. The latter is a far more sophisticated idea, but to be effective it would require a more drastic reduction in the ability of the Congress to amend policy proposals than we are likely to want.

For in our national political tradition, objection to this idea comes less from the lower motives in our political past, than from the higher;

not from the lack of innocence that is represented in corruption, but the loss of innocence that is represented in political self-consciousness. Our independent religious sectarians and our early scientists joined in an awareness of the need for democracy to act, not merely by legislating, or by granting or withholding appropriations, but by determining the organization and administrative system of the government. It is not, fundamentally, the separation of powers that complicates the responsibilities of our legislators and executives, and subjects them to ethical dilemmas; it is the loss of political innocence that came with the republican revolution—the unwillingness of the electorate to leave the organization and personnel of government to be controlled by traditional authority and by a career service organized under its shelter.

With that loss, of course, came a decline in political morals; every politician was tempted not merely to propose policies in the interest of the nation but to use the personnel of government for purposes of patronage; not to debate issues in terms of their intrinsic merit, but to defeat them by sabotaging, or to control them by detaching and domineering, the relevant pieces of the government establishment. But self-consciousness can bring self-knowledge and responsibility, as well as depravity. The Congress, since the Civil War, has supported a series of Presidents in gradually strengthening the Presidency as a responsible pivot of our legislative-executive system. And it has taken the first steps—but needs to go much further and faster—in establishing a more effective system of career personnel, at a level of competence adequate to meet the responsibilities of the decades ahead. As it does so, it will surely retain—and it will be wise to do so—its system of specialized committees for the review and amendment of Executive policy, even at the cost of some degree of coherence and symmetry.

The very success of technology is the strongest argument against technocracy. Policy can be developed only with the aid of scientists and administrators which makes it all the more necessary to put them in a responsible relationship to elected legislators and elected executives. The most effective source of public criticism of a policy that is developed in scientific depth will be legislative committees that explore in specialized depth, and that are free to propose detailed changes without requiring a change in the basic policy of the government.

This process can be abused, but it can also be useful. The tensions that it sets up are probably creative, in the long run. Complete ethical self-satisfaction, on the part of either legislator or administrator, is probably a sign of partisan or bureaucratic smugness; if committee amendment of policy causes a few inconsistencies and ethical dilemmas, it may, in spite of the ulcers that it produces, be a healthy process. At the moment, however, we are probably overdoing it; in the immediate future, we need, I think, to call on the Congress to introduce a substantially greater measure of discipline in holding its own committees responsible, in keeping them from encroaching on jobs that they would do well to leave to the executive and in insisting that the President supply the policy leadership that our system expects of him.

But if Congress does so, that is no reason why it should go on indefinitely toward a system of suppressing the diversity of committee review of executive policy. We are unlikely to err unduly in that direction; all our habits of thought are against it. And the variety of political views that our pluralistic system makes possible may enable us, even in an era of fanatic nationalism, to escape the idea that the welfare of a single country is the only and ultimate good. We are going to need strong measures of self-protection for a long time, but the dizzying successes of our scientists force us to look ahead to a time when the present degree of international anarchy will be intolerable. Or it may be so already.

But no matter whether we stick with our present formal system of legislative-executive relations or devise another, the basic ideas that have made irresponsibility an article of political faith in the United States are obsolete. We will not discharge our ethical obligations in political affairs merely by believing in freedom, or by devising a better Constitutional formula; this planet has become too troubled a place for a nation, especially a very rich nation, to find a hermitage. Our existence, to say nothing of our welfare, calls for the dedication of a higher order of ability to both the political and the administrative responsibilities of government, a greater awareness of the moral dilemmas that are involved in public responsibility, and a greater willingness to place our bets—in money, in effort, and in organization—on the development of the professional career service that we need. Some cynic has remarked that in politics it ain't what you pray for that you believe in, it's what you bet on. In our fix, we had better be doing some of both.

Irresponsibility as an Article of Faith

Comment by Paul H. Appleby:

I confine my comments on this interesting and stimulating paper to the point on which I am in disagreement—Don K. Price's major stress on the need for "a government service as a corporate entity." While most of what he says about this I can agree with (with an exception I deem important to be addressed in a moment), I think this particular reform too slight to serve our needs by itself. I doubt that any single reform could make enough difference, even if more monumental changes than I think feasible were in fact attainable. As is so often true, I think the medicine required would be a mixture—some of this, some of that, and a dash or two of several other things.

Surely it is highly important to pay much more attention to proper staffing of top career posts than is now done. Price is eminently correct in calling for an end to Congressional efforts to fix responsibility on career subordinates instead of on their political chiefs. (This might be not too hard to achieve. The principal requirement would be for President and Department heads to insist that *they* were responsible, that they must be held accountable.) Surely, too, the disparity between military and civilian staff resources, and between civilian and private rewards for attorneys and other staff personnel cry loudly for remedy. These and other steps designed to strengthen career staff would be helpful, if not enough so as to end our principal worries about governmental effectiveness.

The exception I would note is to Price's argument for practices under which career executives would hold their rank as a matter of right, regardless of their assignments. The argument seems to rest on the zeal of American industry in the past decade or two in recruiting and developing executive personnel. But American industry does not guarantee executive rank regardless of assignment, nor is it likely to do so. Nor does governmental experience seem convincing. New York State, the British, French, and Indian governments are about as sticky as any in maintaining executive rank once attained. Surely the French governmental performance before de Gaulle, and the New York State civil service performance, do not shame the United States national civilian civil service. This itself would suggest the importance of other factors. Furthermore, France, India, and Britain do on occasion demote. In the case of France, demotion and abandonment of any tenure claim comes most clearly and regularly at the very point where Price seems to seek guaranteed status—at the level of a careerist who is a chief aide to a Minister. It is my opinion that insured rank would be damaging, not helpful, and that there are other and better ways of providing the elements of security which Price seems to have in mind.

Perhaps I should say that I think radical Constitutional changes infeasible and most of those proposed inappropriate here. I am with Price in feeling that we have to rely largely on improved practice and statutes in an acceleration of the evolutionary course we have long pursued. But I am alerted to the verge of alarm by his remark about "generally holding with" the idea of trying to make the separation of powers "effective." For want of explanation I withhold expressions of anguish.

Comment by David B. Truman:

Although the papers by Rowland Egger, Don K. Price, and Stephen K. Bailey are assigned to different subtopics in the scheduled discussion, an important theme runs, sometimes clearly and sometimes only by implication, through all of them. It is one of critical urgency for democracy in America, but it is not irrelevant to that system in other settings.

Both Egger and Price approach this theme, or suggest it, through their wholesome skepticism concerning the capacity of mere structural or organizational changes to solve the problem they both address, how to produce viable and effective public policy in the contemporary setting without loss of the freedom implicit in representativeness. Neither would be so foolish as to suggest with Lincoln Steffens that formal governmental machinery is of no consequence, but both argue persuasively that any given structure may produce quite different results, depending on the environment in which it is operating. (The more sweeping the change, perhaps, the greater the range of possibilities, since any existing system with a tolerable degree of stability contains within it unnoticed and unplanned elements that tend to limit the variety of outcomes of which it is capable. Some things are unlikely to occur in British politics not because the system is parliamentary but because it is British; the destructive potentialities in a presidential system have been realized less conspicuously in the United States than in societies that apparently have lacked the political resources for keeping them in check.)

Both Egger and Price, the latter most explicitly, suggest that the immediate American problem is more fundamental than governmental structure. It is the deeply moral problem of a political society that is strongly antipolitical and thus antigovernmental, one in which the obligations of political leadership are avoided and in which, partly as a consequence, the often tragic dilemmas of public responsibility are not understood. Thus the question that can be put to Egger's four concluding proposals, beyond that of their administrative workability, is whether the conditions exist in which the society can produce Presidents capable of using such machinery and, more important, in which the society will respond to those initiatives when they are taken. Devices for the planning of policy are likely to be fruitless in a society that lacks, especially in its more privileged segments, a respect for and an understanding of the arts of governing.

Price's reference to the often unnoticed persistence in the "backward" South of a high regard for the career in politics should produce more than passing reflection. As anyone who has observed the regional distribution of high political craftsmanship in the Congress will recognize, the most "advanced" sections of the country are those in which the political career is least valued and in which the arts of governing are least respected. As Bailey's moving essay suggests, through much of the society the profound respectability of assuming responsibility for the often insoluble ethical dilemmas of governing is not granted, even among the most sophisticated.

Facing these dilemmas, as Bailey eloquently testifies, is the real burden of public office. How they are faced, however, is not primarily dependent on whether "the most respected citizens of the nation will themselves consider political leadership their most important calling," as Price argues. Whether they assume leadership in this way or not may be of less consequence, given the apparent limits on the utility of the amateur in such affairs, than that the most respected citizens regard those who do accept the burden of political leadership as being engaged in *the society's* most important calling. This, it seems to me, is "the foundation of responsibility for policy," to use Price's phrase, the indispensable obligation of the chief beneficiaries of the system if it, and they, are to survive.

APPENDIX I

First Lyman Bryson Lecture: Ethics and Politics

By RICHARD McKEON

LYMAN BRYSON is commemorated in the subject of this lecture as well as in the title of the series, for problems of ethics and politics were at the center of his inquiry and thought. I remember Lyman Bryson as a man of wisdom and as a man of his times. He had made the insights of other men and other ages his own, and he sought new knowledge to treat new problems. But he knew that old problems take new turns, and that new problems acquire lengthening histories in the adjustments of innovation and tradition; and he reminded us that familiar words are put to novel uses and misuses, and that new words are used to express thoughts and distinctions which are not as unaccustomed as the terminology we devise for them.

I have chosen "Ethics and Politics" as my subject because the relation between individual behavior and group action raises problems which men have considered since the beginning of recorded thought and action and which, nonetheless, assume forms today which have never been faced before. The title "Ethics and Politics" might have been applied to selections from the works of Confucius, Plato, or Kautilya. We still treat the problems which the ancients discussed, sometimes borrowing, sometimes rejecting, sometimes forgetting what they said. Yet the problems of the ancients are not our problems. They have been transformed by changes in circumstances, attitudes, institutions, language, and science. We assume that we know what is right and wrong in fact and action when we accumulate evidence of growing evils or oppose actions of men or operations of organizations and ideologies; but we are uncertain of the criteria of good and evil, right and wrong, when we turn to the consideration of what should be done and how the means at our disposal should be used. We apply conceptions of right and wrong to the actions of groups, peoples, and nations; our conceptions of right and wrong, in turn, reflect the customs and values of the groups to which we belong and of the groups that surround them and elicit our loyalty and opposition.

The ethics of individuals, of communities, and of interactions among communities, cultures, and nations cannot be separated from each other, and we have not learned how to relate them. We distinguish what is from what ought to be and call them facts and values respectively; yet what we think is the case is colored or even determined by the values we accept, and in practical problems, preferences are facts. We must judge changes in human life and in societies and nations by standards of right and wrong; yet our ideas of right and wrong and our conceptions of the individual and society must be adjusted to the changed circumstances of the modern world, which become, in that adjustment, changes in what we are able to do and what might be done to us, in our aspirations and our fears.

The problems of ethics and politics are in part problems of improving action in accordance with recognized criteria and in part problems of improving criteria in application to understood opportunities and dangers. In one respect they are old problems, for it is no recent discovery that the behavior of individuals and the customs and laws of communities are interrelated. In another respect they are new, for changes in knowledge and technology, in institutions and organizations, in powers and rights, and in communication and understanding have totally changed the nature and potentialities of individuals and communities. Our conceptions of right and wrong, and of values in general as they are applied in the relation of individuals and community and in the relation of communities with each other, depend as never before on recognition of realizable aspirations and imposable sanctions. It is therefore all the more important to distinguish the ways in which we decide what is right and what is wrong from the ways in which we seek to advance the right as we conceive it and to combat the wrong. The first are persistent problems: the ways in which right and wrong are distinguished recur in the changed circumstances of different ages and cultures. The second are emergent problems: the ways in which distinctions of right and wrong are used effectively depend on circumstances and conditions. The distinctions we use have a varied history; but our circum-

First Lyman Bryson Lecture: Ethics and Politics

stances and problems are in many respects unique and the ways in which the distinctions are practicable and applicable are without precise precedent.

In the distinction of right and wrong two possibilities have presented themselves from the beginning: either men must discover and recognize common values which should govern individual lives and social institutions, or they must establish social and political institutions which permit them to cultivate different values in their own lives and to agree on common courses of action without necessarily agreeing on the reasons for them. There were unitary and pluralistic views of ethics and politics in antiquity, and both have persisted through history to the present. The circumstances of the present, however, have introduced ambiguities and paradoxes which obscure the distinctions between them. There is no more agreement today than in the past concerning what is the good life for man or the common good for the communities of men. It is argued plausibly that there are common goods which are sought by different cultures, religions, and polities, and it is concluded, therefore, *either* that the clarification of what is common would improve the lives and the relations of men, *or* that social, economic, and political changes would remove the forces in society that impede their attainment of the good. It is argued no less plausibly that such ideological agreement is neither possible nor desirable, and it is concluded, therefore, that happiness, progress, knowledge, and justice depend on the free cultivation of differences and that agreement concerning practical affairs should concentrate on the consequences for which men may be held accountable rather than on intentions, beliefs, and doctrines imputed to them.

These ambiguities and paradoxes underlie the oppositions between Communist and Western conceptions of ethics and politics. Classical Communist analyses foresee a time when political and other forms of coercion will be unnecessary and a new morality will emerge in the classless society after the state has withered away. Until the new ethics emerges and the need of politics disappears, a political dictatorship must determine the values, including the moral values, by which men live. The classical formulations of Western democracy treat man as a political and social animal who adjusts politics to ethics by establishing democratic institutions in which political power is exercised by the governed and human liberties are acquired by individuals. A new ethics is gradually emerging as individual rights—moral, economic, and cultural—and political, civil, and social rights are extended more broadly to more men and eventually to all men. In the cold war operations of unitary and pluralistic views of ethics and politics, it becomes difficult to distinguish ethical purposes from power manipulations; and the dangers of oppression and conformism, of domination and aggression, are detected in all the relations of men and communities.

These paradoxes and ambiguities are not limited, however, to the large ideological oppositions of the modern world. They appear in the discussion of ethical issues within the tradition in which the problems of ethics and politics are found in the relations of free men and democratic institutions. The issues which we raise about fundamental questions of right and wrong tend to fall into similar ideological oppositions. Our only available means to clarify basic criteria seem to be simple distinctions, like the opposition between tradition and innovation, internal and external, real and apparent, in which either of the opposed terms may be presented as the basis for improvement or as the cause of degeneration.

If standards are sought we ask how the traditional values embodied in our religions and in our constitution can be given renewed effectiveness in the decisions of men and of society; or we ask how the new knowledge and the new methods of science can be applied in solving social and political problems and in moral therapy. The relations between tradition and innovation are complex, yet they are set in simple opposition because tradition becomes inoperative through the accretion of unconsidered innovations, and innovation is impeded by adherence to outmoded traditions.

If the causes which determine men's actions are sought, they are found in the interaction of internal urges and external influences which fix the objectives men think they should seek and the restrictions they think they must impose. Cultivation of common values constitutes the community and contributes to the growth of the individual, but conformism is our most widely recognized cause of loss of individuality and impoverishment of community life; creative spontaneity develops values for the individual and for society, but erratic eccentricity expresses individual frustration and undermines common understanding.

First Lyman Bryson Lecture: Ethics and Politics

If the oppositions of values are sought, they are found in the differences between the real goods which men could achieve and the apparent goods which they in fact pursue or profess to want. We have new means to cure psychological aberrations and personality defects, as well as new persuaders to implant ideas and wants; we have new reasons for recognizing the dangers of deciding what is really good for other men and also the dangers of tolerating their irresponsible pursuit of what they want.

The persistent problems of ethics and politics may be schematized about two issues which were raised by ancient thinkers and which are still alive in contemporary discussion: whether the principles of ethics and the principles of politics are the same or are distinct and interrelated, and whether ethics and politics have a natural foundation or are the result of conventional agreement and arbitrary institution. Some philosophers have held that the behavior of individuals and societies should be judged in the same way; others have held that they present different problems and should be judged by different methods and according to different criteria. Some philosophers have argued that men desire things because they are good or seem to be good; others have argued that men call things good because they desire them. The combinations of these basic conceptions yield four views of the relation of ethics and politics which have recurred in many forms and applications.

All four views were developed by the philosophers of ancient Greece. Both Plato and Aristotle held that the virtues and the state have natural foundations but they differed concerning the relation of ethics and politics. Plato found the same principles for ethics and politics; like the principles of science they were eternal Ideas. The search of Socrates for the moral virtue of justice in man, as Plato presented it in the *Republic,* was by way of justice "writ large" in the state, and it led to the discovery of the same cardinal virtues in the individual and in the state, both dependent on the transcendental Idea of the Good. Aristotle found different principles for ethics and politics in the characters of men and in the institutions of states. He laid the foundations of the practical "science" of politics and divided it into two interdependent parts; the part concerned with the virtues of individual men was called "ethics," and the part concerned with the constitutions of states was called "politics" in the narrow sense. He argued that the characters of men are influenced by the communities in which they are raised and live, and that the constitutions of states are determined by the circumstances under which they are formed and by the character of their citizens. He raised questions concerning the relation of the good man and the good citizen and found that they are the same only in a good state. The ancient Sophists and Atomists held that virtue and the state have conventional foundations, and both schools developed a theory of "social compact." Protagoras described man as "by nature a political animal," as Aristotle did later, but Protagoras argued that the constitutions and laws of different people, their languages, religions, and moral codes are based on convention or law (*nomos*), not on nature. Democritus found the criteria of choice and avoidance in the emotions; the "pleasant" therefore differs from man to man, but the good and the true are the same for all men, and the rule of good men is needed if the state is to be well managed.

These four patterns of the relation of ethics and politics influence thought and action in two ways. The persistent problems of ethics and politics arise from the fact that in any age controversial differences arise concerning how the basic principles of human action are to be determined: by wisdom or insight into universal values, by prudence in distinguishing and relating private actions and public functions, by power imposing laws and implanting moral customs, or by knowledge removing the influence of emotions and ignorance which distort or impede action in accordance with the laws of nature and human nature. The emergent problems of ethics and politics, on the other hand, arise from the fact that in any age each of these opposed theories has concrete meanings in the actual circumstances and in the ordinary language of people who must make decisions in which they take into account, whatever their attitudes and philosophies, the values, institutions, power, and science of the men with whom they deal. Changes in circumstances and attitudes determine the ways in which basic questions of right and wrong are treated in thought and action by fixing the language in which they are stated and the conditions under which they arise.

Our histories and the facts we allege become part of the controversy concerning basic questions of ethics and politics rather than accounts of the complex situation in which problems arise and must be understood and resolved. In taking account of oppositions we also take sides, and we write many histories which expound different stories of the evolution of values, institutions, power, and knowledge. The basic issues are obscured because the history from which we take our allegations of fact traces the development of one view of ethics and politics, and the emergent problems are simplified because we give preeminence to chosen sets of conditioning influences.

In the history of the West, we usually mark off three stages in the evolution of the conceptions and operations of ethics and politics: philosophic ideas and distinctions were worked out in antiquity; the spread of Christianity after the third century brought revealed truths and the precepts of a divine covenant to bear on human actions and purposes; the growth of science after the seventeenth century provided new knowledge relevant to behavior and society and new instrumentalities of action and production. The history of these periods can be treated in terms which clarify the basic issues raised in the emergent conditions and institutions, or it can be treated in terms which make the emergent problems steps toward a sounder conception of ethics and politics contained in the historian's position on basic issues. Our ancient histories enter into the ancient controversies—we discover discrepancies of theory and practice, that the ancients talked about democracy and freedom, but they tolerated slavery, despised manual and banausic labor, discriminated against barbarians, and that their illiberalism in practice, despite their invention and use of liberal language prepared for totalitarianism and the closed society. Our medieval histories enter into the controversies concerning knowledge and belief—we simplify theological consideration of transcendent values and the many phases of theological use of philosophic theories and we forget that thought and action were also influenced by the development of canon law and the Scholastic method in which opposed positions were treated in disputation, by cosmological and biological speculation which contributed to the formation of the medieval theory of popular sovereignty, and by the growth of secular and ecclesiastical institutions and of theories of human, natural, and divine law.

The distinction of basic issues of right and wrong from emergent issues in the past is relevant to our present problems because we continue to use, and to dispute about, philosophic distinctions and religious beliefs. But a like distinction in the issues of the modern period is at the center of our problems. The development of ethics and politics since the seventeenth century has been an exploration of the ethics of free men and the politics of democratic institutions, and our theories and actions have been conditioned by the development of science, of democracy, and of organizations designed to extend and apply knowledge, freedom, and power. Present means of action and modes of communication are radically different from those available when deliberate efforts were first made to apply science to ethics and politics; the problems they are applied to are likewise different from those considered by ancient philosophers and medieval theologians and jurists. Moreover, the persistent problems of how right is distinguished from wrong have become more difficult as we have developed new powers of action and enlarged responsibilities. The basic issues of right and wrong cannot be stated in isolation from the emergent problems, since the particular language and conditioning circumstances in which problems are discussed and encountered affect criteria as well as issues. Nonetheless, an examination of the different ways in which problems of ethics and politics have been treated should disclose patterns of appeal to principles and of allegation of fact which are the patterns of ethics and politics adapted to practical application and factual interpretation. To understand how questions are raised is to understand what is at issue and what is required of solutions. Three stages can be distinguished in the treatment of ethics and politics since the seventeenth century which are marked off by the aspects of "democracy" used in successive formulations of issues of right and wrong.

The first stage was part of the scientific revolution and was set forth in many treatises in the seventeenth and the first half of the eighteenth century. Philosophers proposed, or tried, to apply the methods of the natural sciences to human nature, passions, and understanding, to behavior, ethics, law, and the state. The subject of inquiry was man and the state. In the common language of that inquiry, they were related by terms like "power" and all the basic positions concerning ethics and politics were expressed in analysis of power exercised in sovereignty and in virtue, and determined by natural law and by social compact. Philosophers as different as Hobbes, Spinoza, and Locke repeat slightly variant forms of the same formulas, such as, that power is right, and that things are not desired because they are good but are called "good" because they are desired or are thought to cause pleasure. Yet in the development of their scientific analyses, these common phrases take on different meanings. Spinoza found a natural basis for ethics in the perfection of man which can be advanced by the development of reason and "adequate ideas," and he developed a pluralistic separation of ethics, politics, and religion, concerned respectively with the pursuit of individual perfection, the exercise of power and freedom, and the cultivation of piety and obedience. Each of these three processes is endangered when it is confused with the other two. Hobbes and Locke found only conventional bases for ethics, but Hobbes developed a unitary, and Locke a pluralistic, conception of ethics and politics: according to Hobbes, good and evil in the commonwealth, like right and wrong, and mine and thine, depend on the will of the sovereign; according to Locke, moral good and evil consist in the conformity or disagreement of our voluntary actions to some law dependent on the will and power of the lawmaker, but there are three kinds of law, and moral law is distinct from divine law and civil law. Divine law is the measure of *sin* and *duty;* civil law is the measure of *crime* and *innocence;* and moral law or the law of opinion or reputation is the measure of *virtue* and *vice*.

In the course of the seventeenth century, democracy assumed a new importance among familiar forms of government enumerated in antiquity. Spinoza argued that democracy is of all forms of government "the most natural and the most consonant with individual liberty." Hobbes, who was no advocate of democracy, argued that democracy is first in order of time and institution, since to establish any form of government by social compact requires the agreement of the great multitude. Locke finds the beginning of political societies in the social compact which, by the consent of all, makes "that community one body, with power to act as one body, which is only by the will and determination of the majority." He therefore adds the warning that by "commonwealth" he means "not a democracy, or any form of government, but any independent community." This notion of the priority of democracy and the acknowledgment that governments are based on the consent of the people became an assumption that was usually granted, though variously interpreted, in the issues of later stages of the determination of right and wrong.

The second stage of the treatment of ethics and politics was part of the democratic revolution initiated in the latter half of the eighteenth century. Controversy and action were oriented, not to the nature of man and of the state, but to rights of men and of parties, orders, factions, or classes. In the common language of debate and revolution, the discussion of power became the projection of "institutions," and all the basic positions concerning ethics and politics were expressed in constitutional devices to reconcile common good with private interests, and to adjust sovereignty of law to checks and balance of powers. The change in the language of the discussion is marked sharply: "democracy" and "aristocracy" are ancient words, but "democrat" and "aristocrat" were not used before the 1780s. The change in fact to which the coinage of those words corresponded is found in political institutions: the world had become more "aristocratic" and more "democratic," for the new aristocracy was not the same as the old nobility, but was larger and exercised more extensive political powers; and constituted bodies—parliaments, diets, "orders," or "estates" in the various European countries had assumed political powers as associations of people with the same occupation, function, interest, or manner of life.

The change of problems in this new orientation is apparent in the deliberations of the American Constitutional Convention in 1787. The Convention embodied the sovereignty of the people. Its function was to set up the institutions of government in recognition of the principle that governments are instituted among men, deriving their just powers from the consent of the governed. But the delegates did not think that the functions of the government instituted by the people could or should be exercised under the exclusive control of the people: some of them argued that their present evils were due to an excess of democracy; some were fearful of the tyranny of the many as well as of the few; and they sought to protect the people both from their rulers and from their own transient impressions by the methods of electing the two houses of Congress and the President and by the balance of legislative, executive, and judicial powers. The oppositions of aristocrats and democrats were continued in the statements of the parties that grew up under the new Constitution, and when Emerson wrote his essay on "Politics" he could still find the chief distinction between the parties of his time in the fact that "one has the best cause, and the other contains the best men."

First Lyman Bryson Lecture: Ethics and Politics

John Stuart Mill's lifelong examination of the merits and defects of democracy reveals the same changed problems. He was fearful of the tyranny of the majority and of the degradation of representative bodies under democratic rule, but he was also convinced that there are two criteria of any form of government: the degree to which it takes advantage of the existing good qualities of its citizens, and the degree to which it increases and enhances their qualities. The development of his conception of democracy is part of the opposition of liberals and conservative political parties, and the opposition of parties, was related to the opposition of philosophic schools. The Whigs, like Burke and Macaulay, were empiricists, and the Tories, like Coleridge and Carlyle, were intuitionists. Mill argued for the superiority of the school of experience, but he also argued that it was not necessary to agree on the criteria of moral distinctions in order to agree on decisions of right and wrong.

Mill differentiates two stages in the discussion of liberty which are parallel to the two stages in the relations of ethics and politics. At the first stage, liberty meant protection against the tyranny of the political rulers; after the institution of self-rule in democratic republics, such limitation of power might seem unnecessary, but it was discovered that protection was needed against the tyranny of the magistrate and the tyranny of prevailing opinion and feeling. The first stage was concerned with the relation of ruler and ruled. The second stage, after the institution of democratic republics, was concerned with the relation of individual and society. Our experience in the hundred years since Mill sketched this history shows the need to add a third stage and to understand more fully what has happened, for advances in democracy are marked by *agreements* concerning ways in which *differences* may be cultivated and may contribute to security and progress. The problems of the earlier stages do not disappear but are transformed in the later stages. The relation of ruler and ruled was transformed when men ceased to think of rulers as an independent power but instead derived the power of ruling from the ruled. The problem of the tyranny of rulers became a constitutional problem. The relation of individual and society involved both the constitutional problems of the frame of government determined by the powers of individuals and society and the institutional problem of the exercise of power by individuals and parties within the frame of government.

The problem of the tyranny of magistrates and of public opinion became an institutional problem. It has become increasingly difficult, however, to differentiate the individual and society. Much of John Dewey's political philosophy was devoted to an effort to formulate a new individualism free from the errors of the old and to discover the public and state among the numerous nongovernmental associations which affect public interest. The dangers of political tyranny and of the tyranny of common opinion still exist, but both have been transformed into the more inclusive problem of the tyranny of the operator and the persuader.

The third stage of the relation of ethics and politics is part of the organizational revolution of our times. We still talk about the nature of man and of the state and about the rights of men and the interests of parties and classes, but what we say about them derives its practical meaning from considerations of communities, peoples, and mankind, and from the forces that move them to action. In the common language of planning and propaganda, the discussion of "power" and of "institutions" has become an analysis of "facts" and of "contexts" and "conditions" which determine our views about what men think and how they will act. All the basic positions concerning ethics and politics are expressed in programs to reconcile cultivation of traditional values with use of new means to satisfy needs and wants and to adjust acquisition of new freedoms with construction of more inclusive organizations.

The change in the language of the discussion is marked sharply. The major moral and political oppositions which led to the Second World War were stated in terms of an opposition between democratic and antidemocratic theories and societies. In the major oppositions since 1945 both sides in the major controversies present their systems as democratic. The oppositions are not lessened by the resultant ambiguity, but the common use of the word "democracy" is more than a propaganda device. Methods of mass communication give the term "democracy" an immediate value which it did not have twenty years ago, for communication and organization have diversified the practicable senses in which governments and societies depend on the consent of the people. Yet we treat the problems of "democracy" alternatively by using the oppositions borrowed from the past to show that "mass democracy" or "parliamentary democracy" is or is not true democracy, and by examining the facts of present operation in education, the development of technology and science, or the increase of the gross national product to discover similarities which make it possible for one system to imitate the other or which make either in some respect attractive to uncommitted people.

Problems of ethics and politics appear in three guises in contemporary discussions of action as they apply to the lives of individuals, to the actions of governments and organizations, and to the relations of peoples and nations. In all three guises they are stated in paradoxes and ambiguities in which our language is poorly adapted to the facts. Our language continues simple oppositions which are not simply applicable, and it is better suited to negative use in disapproval of action or criticism of omission than to positive use beyond the context of controversy; our accomplishments depend on innovations for which we have not invented a suitable language and which are distorted into subjects for controversy by our accustomed distinctions.

If one seeks analysis of the moral influence of the community and the public on the individual, one finds an extensive anxietyridden literature about conformism, materialism, mass culture, and anti-intellectualism, but almost no treatment of the ways in which the organizations of modern life have provided new patterns for exercise of responsibility, for attitudes of understanding, and for commitment to the good of others and new opportunities for the cultivation of cultural values. If one seeks analysis of the actions of governments and organizations, one finds abundant news of disclosures, official and unofficial, of moral defects in what is done by representatives of the government, businessmen, trade union officials, professional men, educators, and purveyors of entertainment and culture, for which the proposed remedy is to arouse public opinion, to enforce an existing law, or to pass a new law. Only occasionally does news or inquiry throw light on the new operations which institutions have undertaken under present conditions and which suggests a need to reexamine our conceptions of those institutions or to reconsider the functions they should exercise. If one seeks analysis of the relations of communities, peoples, and nations, one learns about new nationalisms and blocs—economic, political, military, and cultural—which fragment and distort common objectives, about tensions, aggressions, and suppressions, which impede or prevent cooperation, or about alignments and controversies in which predetermined lines of interest forestall any consideration of what is desirable or right.

The basic patterns of ethics and politics appear both in the controversies of an age and in the facts about which the oppositions center. Paradoxes arise for the relations of professed objectives and reported factual situations. These discrepancies may be used to impede action or to provide a guide for action, and the ethical problem in the relations of men is to effect the transition from static opposition to cooperative action. In the ethical problems within communities and between communities in our times, the recurrent proposed programs tend to reflect the basic patterns of ethics and politics: there are those who hold that all such problems are fundamentally problems of insight and understanding and that our sensitivity to values has lagged behind our technical and material powers; there are those who hold that they are fundamentally problems of knowledge and that our sciences of man and of society have not kept pace with our sciences of nature; there are those who hold that they are fundamentally problems of power and that the distribution of rights, powers, and technical and practical knowhow will rectify the evils of concentrated power; there are those who hold that they are fundamentally political problems and that the establishment of sanctions and the constitution of agencies to enforce them will provide the equitable framework within which understanding, knowledge, and power may develop without manipulation or violence.

The efforts to describe our times repeat the same paradoxes. The twentieth century has made notable advances and has suffered deplorable retrogressions in each of these dimensions of moral problems: advances in mutual understanding and toleration, regressions in undisguised prejudice and institutionalized discrimination; advances in the satisfaction of needs by technology and by technical cooperation, regressions in exclusivisms and multidimensional nationalisms; advances in the elaboration and extension of human rights and freedoms, regressions in more systematic forms of suppression, slavery, and conformity; advances in provisions for self-government and the rule of law, regressions in dictatorships and suppressive controls.

The same patterns indicate the considerations which operate in the solution of moral problems when the relevant facts are recognized to include the aspirations of men. Statements of the problems of ethics and politics must take into account conceptions of values, means for their realization, rights reserved to individuals and groups for free, autonomous, spontaneous action, and the customs and laws of the communities in which men live. The older problems of the ethics of free men and the politics of democratic communities continue in our more recent formulation of these problems. We still have constitutional problems of providing a framework for discussion and action, based on the consent of the governed, in which the pursuit of ideal ends is protected by checks and balances of powers; but we find paradoxes in the operation of tradition and innovation in our constitutional history since constitutional provisions are basic rules governing action which are modified by interpretation and amendment. We still have institutional problems in the activities of parties and factions to produce consensus and cleavage on policies which serve as hypotheses concerning how the ends we seek are to be accomplished; but we find paradoxes in the operation of internal and external influences in these activities since our parties have not coincided with either ideological or class differences. We have assimilated constitutional and institutional problems to organizational problems of what to do and how to do it; but we find paradoxes in the operation of real and apparent ends in the multiplication of associations which require, in the place of distinctions between government and governed and between individual and society, a distinction of public and private applicable to the actions of individuals and of associations, governmental and nongovernmental. The real becomes apparent, and the apparent real, through manipulation and misstatement.

The problems of ethics and politics of our times are problems of giving proper weight to what men seek and what they should seek, their real and their apparent goods, in circumstances in which men are increasingly aware both that means are available to advance the happiness of men and the security and progress of society and that the pursuit of any sought good is always in some sense a real good, even when it is, in another sense, dubious or spurious and when it interferes with the attainment of other goods which are desirable in themselves and essential to the good originally sought. The problem of how we determine what is right is not a metaphysical speculation for idle moments or public conferences. It is stated concretely in three recurrent dilemmas of practical action.

The first is the dilemma which results from our success in devising new means of satisfying wants and needs and in discovering new values and providing a wider extension of established values. It might be expected that increased success in satisfying needs and in raising standards of living would make possible the cultivation of other values. Yet progress in technology seems to bring with it the evils of delinquency, materialism, and mass culture, and unwanted "higher values" seem to be palliatives to conceal or disguise social injustice.

The second is the dilemma which results from the development of new possibilities of rights and freedoms and from the institution of new means of participating in self-government. It might be expected that the acquisition and use of rights of self-determination and self-government would increase the rights and freedoms of individuals. Yet the operation of "democratic" institutions seems to bring with it a fear of individual deviation, spontaneity, or eccentricity, and the actions of "individualists" seem to transform democratic institutions into despotic instrumentalities.

The third is the dilemma which results from the increase in our knowledge and in our power. It might be expected that the freedoms on which knowledge and effective power are based would be broadened with the increase of knowledge and skills. Yet the freedoms we cultivate have little relation to the advancement of knowledge or the good, and our applications of knowledge have little clear effect on the extension of freedoms.

These are dilemmas which are useful in assessing controversial oppositions because they indicate the reasons why either of the opposed programs may lead to undesirable results. They are also useful, however, in forming policy and planning courses of action because they indicate the diverse considerations which must be taken into account. Such considerations do not settle controversies; but they clarify what is involved in differentiating right from wrong, and they provide means of coming to agreement about actions to be undertaken despite continuing differences concerning basic analyses. The three dilemmas differ in kind, and each raises issues in the persistent problems of ethics and politics.

The problem of how needs may be satisfied and values may be achieved is part of the long history of discussion in which wisdom or divine revelation is pitted against science or technical skill as means of determining what is good and of achieving it. However the supposed opposition is resolved, this problem in its present form emphasizes the need in moral problems to have means by which to recognize what is good as well as means by which to procure what is wanted.

The problem of how freedoms are preserved and the rule of law established is part of the long history of discussion in which right or freedom is pitted against law or obligation as means of determining ends and of achieving them. However the supposed opposition is resolved, this problem in its present form emphasizes the need in moral problems to consider public and private objectives and to secure both.

The problem of how criteria of value can be brought into operation without denial of freedom and how the exercise of freedom can lead to improvement in the life of the individual and in the common lot of society is part of the long discussion of the relation of the good to natural bases and to arbitrary customs. However the supposed opposition is resolved, this problem in its present form emphasizes the need in moral problems to begin with actual desires and felt needs and yet to take into account the possible passage from what is desired to what is in some communicable sense desirable. The three problems therefore provide a framework for the discussion of individual liberty, of national policy, and of cooperation of peoples in which the issues of right and wrong may be clarified by reference to values, knowledge, power, and institutions, without ideological or partisan commitment to a doctrinaire view of their structure and interrelations.

APPENDIX II

Report on the Conference on Science, Philosophy and Religion

THE FIFTEENTH CONFERENCE held at the Men's Faculty Club of Columbia University from August 27 to 30, 1956 considered "Aspects of Human Equality: Equality of Opportunity," basing its discussion on working papers developed at The Institute on Ethics which met at the Lake Mohonk Mountain House, Mohonk, New York, June 4 to 18, and at The Jewish Theological Seminary of America, June 18 to 29. During 1958 and 1959 Conference Fellows collaborated with those of the Institute in various approaches to study of ethics, including a seminar, "One World—One Ethics?" The program of these sessions, held at the Columbia Men's Faculty Club, from August 31 to September 2, 1959, is on pages 513–521.

At the business meeting of August 31, 1960, the following officers were elected:

Louis Finkelstein, president
*Lyman Bryson, honorary president, and chairman of the executive committee
Richard P. McKeon, First Lyman Bryson Lecturer
Clarence H. Faust, Second Lyman Bryson Lecturer, and vice president
John LaFarge, S.J., vice president
Harold D. Lasswell, vice president, and chairman of the executive committee
Jessica Feingold, executive vice president

It was agreed that general reorganization, including changes in the list of Fellows (given in the 1960 program on pages 505–506) should be studied in the light of plans to stimulate discussions with scholars in other parts of the world. Continuing the tradition begun at Amherst in 1944 and followed at Lake Mohonk annually or oftener from 1946 through 1956, such plans have been the subject of study at meetings at New York University's Gould House, February 20–22, 1959, Lake

*deceased

Mohonk Mountain House, June 26-28, 1959, and January 6-8, 1961, and in New York City, February 20, 1959, April 16, 1959, and June 14 and November 11, 1960. A seminar to be held at the Columbia Men's Faculty Club from August 29 through 31, 1961, will explore with thinkers from Latin America the theme, "Considerations for an International Conference on the Ethics of Mutual Involvement." Other proposals and criticisms of the Conference generally will be welcome.

April 3, 1961

CONTRIBUTORS TO "ETHICS AND BIGNESS"*

ROBERT C. ANGELL, *The University of Michigan*, professor of sociology and director, college honors program; author, *The Moral Integration of American Cities, Free Society and Moral Crisis*, and others

PAUL H. APPLEBY, *Maxwell Graduate School of Citizenship and Public Affairs, Syracuse University*, dean emeritus

STEPHEN K. BAILEY, *Maxwell Graduate School of Citizenship and Public Affairs, Syracuse University*, professor of political science; author, *Congress Makes a Law*, and others

KENNETH E. BOULDING, *The University of Michigan*, professor of economics; author, *Principles of Economic Policy, The Skills of the Economist*, and others

JAMES MACGREGOR BURNS, *Williams College*, professor of political science; author, *Congress on Trial, Roosevelt: The Lion and the Fox, John Kennedy: A Political Profile*, and others

HARLAN CLEVELAND, Assistant Secretary of State; formerly *Maxwell Graduate School of Citizenship and Public Affairs, Syracuse University*, dean; Conference on Science, Philosophy and Religion, co-chairman, 1960; The Institute for Religious and Social Studies, lecturer, 1960; The Institute on Ethics, executive committee, member; co-editor, *The Art of Overseasmanship*; co-author, *The Overseas Americans*, and others

KARL K. DARROW, *American Physical Society, Columbia University*, secretary; author, *Atomic Energy, Introduction to Contemporary Physics: Renaissance of Physics*, and others

ROBERT J. DWYER, *Catholic Diocese of Reno*, bishop; author, *Gentile Comes to Utah*, papers and articles in *"Thought," "America," "Commonweal," "Social Order," "Liturgical Arts,"* and others

ROWLAND EGGER, *University of Virginia*, professor of political science and chairman, Woodrow Wilson department and department of foreign affairs; author, *Organization of Peace at the Administrative Level, Research, Education and Regionalism* (with Weldon Cooper), and others

THOMAS K. FINLETTER, *Council on Foreign Relations*, director; Secretary of the Air Force, 1950–1953; *Coudert Brothers*, partner; Conference on Science, Philosophy and Religion, program committee, member, 1960; The Institute for Religious and Social Studies, faculty seminar, chairman; The Institute on Ethics, executive committee, member; author, *Power and Policy, Foreign Policy: The Next Phase*, and others

DAVID FINN, *Ruder and Finn, Incorporated*, president; The Jewish Theological Seminary of America, board of directors, member; Conference on Science, Philosophy and Religion, program committee, member, 1960; contributor to *Management Methods* and the *Harvard Business Review*; author, *Public Relations and Management*

WILLIAM C. FOSTER, *Olin Mathieson Chemical Corporation*, director and vice president in charge of public affairs; Committee on Economic Development, member; Federal City Council of Washington, president

WILLIAM T. R. FOX, *Columbia University*, professor of international relations

SIDNEY F. GIFFIN, *United States Air Force*, brigadier general; Office of Armed Forces Information and Education, Department of Defense, director

NATHAN D. GRUNDSTEIN, *Graduate School of Public and International Affairs, University of Pittsburgh*, professor

LOUIS J. HECTOR, *Hector, Faircloth and Rutledge*, Miami, Florida, attorney; Civil Aeronautics Board, former member

C. M. HERZFELD, *Heat Division, National Bureau of Standards*, chief; University of Maryland, professor of physics

F. ERNEST JOHNSON, *Teachers College, Columbia University*, professor emeritus of edu-

*Position generally based on list of August, 1960.

cation; *Conference on Science, Philosophy and Religion,* co-chairman, 1960; *The Institute for Religious and Social Studies,* course chairman; *The Institute on Ethics,* executive committee, member; author, *The Social Gospel Re-Examined;* editor, *World Order: Its Intellectual and Cultural Foundations, Foundations of Democracy, Wellsprings of the American Spirit, American Education and Religion, Religious Symbolism, Religion and Social Work, Patterns of Faith in America Today, Patterns of Ethics in America Today,* and others

EDWARD L. KATZENBACH, JR., *Institute of Defense Analyses,* consultant; *National Academy of Sciences,* consultant; *Cambridge Air Force Research Center,* Hanscom Field, consultant; author of numerous articles and reviews

HAROLD D. LASSWELL, *Yale University,* Edward J. Phelps professor of law and political science; *Conference on Science, Philosophy and Religion,* chairman, 1960; *The Institute for Religious and Social Studies,* trustee; *The Institute on Ethics,* executive committee, member; author, *Ethics, World Revolution of Our Time, The Policy Sciences: Recent Developments in Scope and Method* (with Daniel Lerner), and others

ROBERT LEE, *Union Theological Seminary,* assistant professor of church and community; *The Institute for Religious and Social Studies,* moderator, 1960–1961; author, *Social Sources of Church Unity: An Interpretation of Unitive Movements in American Protestantism, Protestant Churches in the Brooklyn Heights, Upper Manhattan: A Community Study of Washington Heights,* and others

WAYNE A. R. LEYS, *Roosevelt University,* professor of philosophy and dean of the graduate division; author, *Ethics for Policy Decisions, Philosophy and the Public Interest* (with Charner Perry), and others

ROBERT B. LIVINGSTON, *National Institute of Mental Health and National Institute of Neurological Diseases and Blindness,* director of basic research

BERNARD MANDELBAUM, *The Jewish Theological Seminary of America,* provost and associate professor of homiletics; *Conference on Science, Philosophy and Religion,* program committee, member, 1960; *The Institute for Religious and Social Studies,* faculty seminar, member; contributor to the *Mordecai M. Kaplan Jubilee Volumes, The American Academy of Jewish Research Annual,* and others

EUGENE J. MCCARTHY, *United States Senator from Minnesota*

RICHARD MCKEON, *The University of Chicago,* Charles F. Grey distinguished service professor of philosophy and Greek; *Conference on Science, Philosophy and Religion,* program committee, member, 1960, First Lyman Bryson Lecturer; *The Institute on Ethics,* executive committee, member; author, *The Philosophy of Spinoza, Freedom and History,* and others; co-editor, 12th and 13th Conference symposia

TALCOTT PARSONS, *Harvard University,* professor of sociology; author, *Essays in Sociological Theory, Structure and Process in Modern Societies,* and others

JAMES A. PERKINS, *Carnegie Corporation of New York,* vice-president

CHARNER PERRY, *The University of Chicago,* professor of philosophy and chairman of the department of philosophy; editor, *"Ethics," "The Philosophy of American Democracy,"* author, *Philosophy and the Public Interest* (with Wayne A. R. Leys), and others

DON K. PRICE, *Graduate School of Public Administration, Harvard University,* dean and professor of government; *President's advisory committee on government organization,* member; author, *The Political Economy of American Foreign Policy, Government and Science,* and others

DAVID W. SILVERMAN, *Conservative Synagogue of Riverdale, New York,* rabbi; *The Institute for Religious and Social Studies,* faculty seminar, member

DONALD E. STOKES, *Survey Research Center, University of Michigan*

Contributors to "Ethics and Bigness"

ALAN M. STROOCK, *The Jewish Theological Seminary of America*, board of directors, chairman

CHARLES P. TAFT, *Taft and Lavercombe*, member; *Cincinnati City Council*, member; author, *Why I Am for the Church, Democracy in Politics and Economics,* and others

ORDWAY TEAD, *Harper and Brothers*, vice president, director, and editor of social and economic books; *Conference on Science, Philosophy and Religion,* executive committee, member; author, *The Climate of Learning, Administration: Its Purpose and Performance;* co-author, *Trustees, Teachers, Students, Character Building and Higher Education,* and others

DAVID B. TRUMAN, *Columbia University*, professor of government

QUINCY WRIGHT, *University of Virginia*, professor of international law; *Conference on Science, Philosophy and Religion,* fellow; author, *Contemporary International Relations; A Balance Sheet, International Law and the United Nations,* and others

PAUL N. YLVISAKER, *Public Affairs Program, The Ford Foundation,* director

PUBLICATIONS OF THE CONFERENCE ON SCIENCE, PHILOSOPHY AND RELIGION

Science, Philosophy and Religion, A Symposium, 1941. (The papers prepared for the meetings held in New York City on September 9, 10, and 11, 1940.) Out of print.

Science, Philosophy and Religion, Second Symposium, 1942. (The papers prepared for the meetings held in New York City on September 8, 9, 10, and 11, 1941.)

Science, Philosophy and Religion, Third Symposium, 1943. (The papers prepared for the meetings held in New York City on August 27, 28, 29, 30, and 31, 1942.) Out of print.

Approaches to World Peace, Fourth Symposium, 1944. (The papers prepared for the meetings held in New York City on September 9, 10, 11, 12, and 13, 1943.) Out of print.

Approaches to National Unity, Fifth Symposium, 1945. (The papers prepared for the meetings held in New York City on September 7, 8, 9, 10, and 11, 1944.) Out of print.

Approaches to Group Understanding, Sixth Symposium, 1947. (The papers prepared for the meetings held in New York City on August 23, 24, 25, 26, and 27, 1945.)

Conflicts of Power in Modern Culture, Seventh Symposium, 1947. (The papers prepared for the meetings held in Chicago on September 9, 10, and 11, 1946.) Out of print.

Learning and World Peace, Eighth Symposium, 1948. (The papers prepared for the meetings held in Philadelphia on September 7, 8, 9, and 10, 1947.)

Goals for American Education, Ninth Symposium, 1950. (The papers prepared for the meetings held in New York City on September 7, 8, 9, and 10, 1948.)

Perspectives on a Troubled Decade: Science, Philosophy and Religion, 1939–1949, Tenth Symposium, 1950. (The papers prepared for the meetings held in New York City on September 6, 7, 8, and 9, 1949.)

Foundations of World Organization: A Political and Cultural Appraisal, Eleventh Symposium, 1952. (The papers prepared for the meetings held in New York City on September 5, 6, 7, and 8, 1950.)

Freedom and Authority in Our Time, Twelfth Symposium, 1953. (The papers prepared for the meetings held in New York City on September 4, 5, 6, and 7, 1951.)

Symbols and Values: An Initial Study, Thirteenth Symposium, 1954. (The papers prepared for the meetings held in New York City on September 2, 3, 4, and 5, 1952.)

Symbols and Society, Fourteenth Symposium, 1955. (The papers prepared for the meetings held in Cambridge, Massachusetts, on August 30 and 31, and September 1 and 2, 1954.)

Aspects of Human Equality, Fifteenth Symposium, 1957. (The papers prepared for the meetings held in New York City, on August 29, 30, and 31, and September 1, 1955.)

Program

SIXTEENTH CONFERENCE ON SCIENCE, PHILOSOPHY AND RELIGION IN THEIR RELATION TO THE DEMOCRATIC WAY OF LIFE

"CHALLENGES TO TRADITIONAL ETHICS: GOVERNMENT, POLITICS, AND ADMINISTRATION"

HAROLD D. LASSWELL, CHAIRMAN
HARLAN CLEVELAND and F. ERNEST JOHNSON, CO-CHAIRMEN

MONDAY, TUESDAY, WEDNESDAY, and THURSDAY
AUGUST 29, 30, 31, and SEPTEMBER 1, 1960

THE JEWISH THEOLOGICAL SEMINARY OF AMERICA
Northeast Corner of Broadway and 122nd Street
New York City
Telephone: RIverside 9-8000

The Setting: The Changing Conditions and Prospects
of Political Success
(Section I)

Papers by[1]

ROBERT C. ANGELL
HANNAH ARENDT
MAX GLUCKMAN
W. W. KULSKI
HAROLD D. LASSWELL
DANIEL LERNER
MICHAL POLANYI
BENJAMIN I. SCHWARTZ
GUY WINT

As preparation for the entire Conference it is expected that discussion of this material will not be limited to any given session.

All sessions not otherwise indicated will be held in the Auditorium, Teachers Institute-Unterberg Memorial Building, The Jewish Theological Seminary of America.

1. For convenient identification the papers in Section I are mimeographed on gray paper, those in Section II on orange, Section III on blue, Section IV on pink, Section V on green, and Section VI on yellow.

MONDAY, AUGUST 29
9:00 a.m.

Planning Meeting
Chairmen and Program Committee

HAROLD D. LASSWELL, *Chairman*

    STUART GERRY BROWN
    HARLAN CLEVELAND
    GERSON D. COHEN
    CLARENCE H. FAUST
    JESSICA FEINGOLD
    LOUIS FINKELSTEIN
    THOMAS K. FINLETTER
    DAVID FINN
    SIMON GREENBERG
    HUDSON HOAGLAND
    F. ERNEST JOHNSON
    JOSEPH F. KAUFFMAN
    JOHN LaFARGE, S.J.
    R. M. MacIVER
    BERNARD MANDELBAUM
    LAURENCE C. McHUGH, S.J.
    RICHARD P. McKEON

Program

JOHN P. PLAMENATZ
SEYMOUR SIEGEL

12:00 noon

Luncheon Meetings
Session Chairmen and Paper Writers in Session Groups

            Dining Hall
            Louis M. Brush
            Memorial Dormitory

3:00 p.m.

GENERAL SESSION

CLARENCE H. FAUST, *Chairman*

Discussion of[2]
Modern Big-scale Organizations:
The Consequences for Moral Responsibility
(Section II)

based on papers by

KENNETH E. BOULDING
HARLAN CLEVELAND
KARL K. DARROW
ROBERT J. DWYER
CHARLES M. HERZFELD
ROBERT LEE
ROBERT B. LIVINGSTON[3]
TALCOTT PARSONS
JAMES A. PERKINS
DAVID W. SILVERMAN
ORDWAY TEAD

2. Papers available in mimeographed form. All oral discussion off the record.
3. Text not received before program in press, August 15.

8:30 p.m.

GENERAL SESSION

HARLAN CLEVELAND, *Chairman*

Discussion of[2]
The Balancing of Representativeness and Efficiency
(Section III)

based on papers by

STEPHEN K. BAILEY
ROWLAND A. EGGER
THOMAS K. FINLETTER
WILLIAM C. FOSTER
WILLIAM T. R. FOX
SIDNEY F. GIFFIN
LOUIS J. HECTOR
EDWARD L. KATZENBACH, JR.
DON K. PRICE
BERNARD SCHWARTZ
PAUL N. YLVISAKER

TUESDAY, AUGUST 30
10:00 a.m.

GENERAL SESSION

HARLAN CLEVELAND, *Chairman*

Discussion of[2]
The Balancing of Representativeness and Efficiency
(Section III—Continued)

2:30 p.m.

GENERAL SESSION

THOMAS K. FINLETTER, *Chairman*

Discussion of[2]
"Ethics" in Practical Politics

in the United States of America
(Section IV)

based on papers by

JAMES MACGREGOR BURNS
DAVID FINN
WAYNE A. R. LEYS
EUGENE J. MCCARTHY
DONALD E. STOKES
CHARLES P. TAFT

8:30 p.m.

THE FIRST LYMAN BRYSON LECTURE
"Ethics and Politics"
by RICHARD P. MCKEON

Tribute to Lyman Bryson
by HARLOW SHAPLEY

LOUIS FINKELSTEIN, *Chairman*

Horace Mann Auditorium
Teachers College
Columbia University
(Broadway, 120–121 Sts.)

WEDNESDAY, AUGUST 31
9:30 a.m.

GENERAL SESSION

JOHN LAFARGE, S.J., *Chairman*

Discussion of[2]
The Interplay of the Great Traditions and Political Conduct
(Section V)

based on papers by

SALO W. BARON
BEN ZION BOKSER
GEORGE E. GORDON CATLIN
JOHN R. CONNERY, S.J.

CLARENCE H. FAUST[3]
MUSLIH FER[3]
ASAF A. A. FYZEE
RICHARD A. GARD
HUMAYUN KABIR[3]
WILLIAM H. LAZARETH
K. SATCHIDANANDA MURTY
CATHERINE SCHAEFER
ROGER L. SHINN
ARTHUR F. WRIGHT

1:00 p.m.

Luncheon Business Meeting of the Fellows of the Conference on Science, Philosophy and Religion, to transact necessary business of the corporation, including election of officers

Dining Hall

3:00 p.m.

GENERAL SESSION

SIMON GREENBERG, *Chairman*

Discussion of[2]
The Interplay of the Great Traditions and Political Conduct
(Section V—Continued)

THURSDAY, SEPTEMBER 1
10:00 a.m.

GENERAL SESSION

HAROLD D. LASSWELL, *Chairman*

Discussion of[2]
Suggested Principles of Ethical Conduct
in Government, Politics, and Administration
(Section VI)

Program

based on papers by

RAYMOND ARON
URIE BRONFENBRENNER
NATHAN D. GRUNDSTEIN
JEROME HALL
HARRY W. JONES
EUGEN KOGON[3]
MYRES S. McDOUGAL
HARALD OFSTAD
CHARNER PERRY
HARRY B. PRICE
JOHN P. PLAMENATZ
EDWARD A. SHILS[3]
RUTH STRANG

1:00 p.m. to 4 p.m.

LUNCHEON AND GENERAL SUMMARY SESSION

JOSEPH F. KAUFFMAN, *Chairman*

Dining Hall

CONFERENCE ON SCIENCE, PHILOSOPHY AND RELIGION*

Officers

Louis Finkelstein, *The Jewish Theological Seminary of America*—president
**Lyman Bryson, *Teachers College, Columbia University*—honorary president, and chairman of the executive committee
Richard P. McKeon, *The University of Chicago*—Third Conference on Science, Philosophy and Religion Lecturer
Clarence H. Faust, *Fund for the Advancement of Education, The Ford Foundation*—vice president
John LaFarge, S.J., *"America"*—vice president
Jessica Feingold, *The Institute for Religious and Social Studies*—executive vice president

---

Executive Committee

CONFERENCE ON SCIENCE, PHILOSOPHY AND RELIGION LECTURERS
R. M. MacIver, *Columbia University*
Richard P. McKeon
Harlow Shapley, *Harvard University*

**Lyman Bryson
Harlan Cleveland, *Maxwell Graduate School of Citizenship and Public Affairs, Syracuse University*
Thurston N. Davis, S.J., *"America"*
Clarence H. Faust
Jessica Feingold
Louis Finkelstein
Hudson Hoagland, *Worcester Foundation for Experimental Biology*
F. Ernest Johnson, *Teachers College, Columbia University*
John LaFarge, S.J.
Harold D. Lasswell, *Yale University*
I. I. Rabi, *Columbia University*
Wendell M. Stanley, *University of California at Berkeley*
Ordway Tead, *Harper and Brothers*
M. L. Wilson, *The Ford Foundation*

Fellows

Thomas Ritchie Adam, *New York University*
William F. Albright, *The Johns Hopkins University*
Robert Bierstedt, *The City College of New York*
Van Wyck Brooks
**Lyman Bryson
Harry J. Carman, *Columbia College, Columbia University*
Harlan Cleveland
Stewart G. Cole
William G. Constable, *Museum of Fine Arts, Boston*
Norman Cousins, *"The Saturday Review"*

*As of November 18, 1958
**Deceased

Thurston N. Davis, S.J.
Karl W. Deutsch, *Yale University*
Hoxie N. Fairchild, *Hunter College of the City of New York*
Clarence H. Faust
Louis Finkelstein
A. Durwood Foster, *Pacific School of Religion*
Lawrence K. Frank
Philipp G. Frank, *Institute for the Unity of Science*
Charles Frankel, *Columbia University*
Simon Greenberg, *The Jewish Theological Seminary of America*
Caryl P. Haskins, *Carnegie Institution of Washington*
Charles W. Hendel, *Yale University*
Hudson Hoagland
Albert Hofstadter, *Columbia University*
F. Ernest Johnson
Robert B. Johnson, *National Conference of Christians and Jews*
**Clyde Kluckhohn, *Harvard University*
John LaFarge, S.J.
Harold D. Lasswell
Dorothy D. Lee, *Harvard University*
R. M. MacIver
Jacques Maritain, *Princeton University*
Robert J. McCracken, *The Riverside Church*
Richard P. McKeon
Margaret Mead, *American Museum of Natural History*
Henry A. Murray, *Harvard University*
John Courtney Murray, S.J., *Woodstock College*
Ernest Nagel, *Columbia University*
John U. Nef, *The University of Chicago*
F. S. C. Northrop, *Yale University*
Peter H. Odegard, *University of California at Berkeley*
J. Robert Oppenheimer, *Institute for Advanced Study*
Harry A. Overstreet, *The City College of New York*
Anton C. Pegis, *Pontifical Institute of Mediaeval Studies, Toronto*
Gerald B. Phelan, *St. Michael's College, Toronto*
Liston Pope, *The Divinity School, Yale University*
I. I. Rabi
Roy W. Sellars, *University of Michigan*
Harlow Shapley
George N. Shuster, *Center for the Study of Democratic Institutions*
Wendell M. Stanley
Donald C. Stone, *Graduate School of Public and International Affairs, University of Pittsburgh*
Ordway Tead
M. L. Wilson
Quincy Wright, *University of Virginia*

PARTICIPANTS IN PROGRAM***

Robert C. Angell, *The University of Michigan*
Paul H. Appleby, *Maxwell Graduate School of Citizenship and Public Affairs, Syracuse University*
Hannah Arendt
Raymond Aron, *University of the Sorbonne*
Stephen K. Bailey, *Maxwell Graduate School of Citizenship and Public Affairs, Syracuse University*
Helen E. Baker, *General Department of United Church Women, National Council of Churches*
Salo W. Baron, *Columbia University*
Ben Zion Bokser, *The Jewish Theological Seminary of America*
Kenneth E. Boulding, *University of Michigan*
Urie Bronfenbrenner, *Cornell University*
Dyke Brown, *The Ford Foundation*
Stuart Gerry Brown, *Maxwell Graduate School of Citizenship and Public Affairs, Syracuse University*
James MacGregor Burns, *Williams College*
Donald R. Campion, S.J., *"America"*
Harry J. Carman, *Columbia College, Columbia University*
William L. Cary, *Law School, Columbia University*
George E. Gordon Catlin, *McGill University*
William P. Clancy, *Church Peace Union*
Gordon R. Clapp, *Development and Resources Corporation*
Harlan Cleveland, *Maxwell Graduate School of Citizenship and Public Affairs, Syracuse University*
H. Van B. Cleveland, *John Hancock Mutual Life Insurance Company*
Gerson D. Cohen, *The Jewish Theological Seminary of America*
Stewart G. Cole
John R. Connery, S.J., *Chicago Province of the Society of Jesus*
Karl K. Darrow, *American Physical Society, Columbia University*
Robert J. Dwyer, *Bishop, Catholic Diocese of Reno*
Rowland A. Egger, *University of Virginia*
Erik H. Erikson, *Harvard University*
Clarence H. Faust, *The Ford Foundation*
Jessica Feingold, *The Institute for Religious and Social Studies, The Jewish Theological Seminary of America*
Muslih Fer, *The Public Administration Institute of Turkey and the Middle East*
Louis Finkelstein, *The Jewish Theological Seminary of America*
Thomas K. Finletter, *Secretary of the Air Force, 1950–1953*
David Finn, *Ruder and Finn, Incorporated*
A. Durwood Foster, *Pacific School of Religion*
William C. Foster, *Olin Mathieson Chemical Corporation*
William T. R. Fox, *Columbia University*
Philipp G. Frank, *Institute for the Unity of Science*
Asaf A. A. Fyzee, *University of Jammu and Kashmir*
Richard A. Gard, *Yale University*
Sidney F. Giffin, *United States Air Force*
J. Gordon Gilkey, Jr., *The Riverside Church*
Max Gluckman, *Victoria University of Manchester*

***Writers of papers and comments and those expected to attend, as of August 15.

Simon Greenberg, *The Jewish Theological Seminary of America*
Nathan D. Grundstein, *Graduate School of Public and International Affairs, University of Pittsburgh*
Cameron P. Hall, *Department of the Church and Economic Life, National Council of Churches*
Jerome Hall, *Indiana University*
Abram L. Harris, *The University of Chicago*
Louis J. Hector, *Hector, Faircloth and Rutledge*
Charles M. Herzfeld, *Heat Division, National Bureau of Standards*
Hudson Hoagland, *Worcester Foundation for Experimental Biology*
F. Ernest Johnson, *Teachers College, Columbia University*
Robert B. Johnson, *The Field Foundation*
Harry W. Jones, *Columbia University*
Humayun Kabir, *Minister, Scientific Research and Cultural Affairs, Government of India*
Edward L. Katzenbach, Jr., *Institute of Defense Analyses*
Joseph F. Kauffman, *The Jewish Theological Seminary of America*
Solon T. Kimball, *Teachers College, Columbia University*
Eugen Kogon, *"Frankfurter-Hefte"*
W. W. Kulski, *Maxwell Graduate School of Citizenship and Public Affairs, Syracuse University*
John LaFarge, S.J. *"America"*
Harold R. Landon, *Cathedral Church of St. John the Divine*
Harold D. Lasswell, *Yale University*
William H. Lazareth, *Philadelphia Lutheran Seminary*
Robert Lee, *Union Theological Seminary*
Daniel Lerner, *Massachusetts Institute of Technology*
Harold C. Letts, *Division of Christian Life and Work, National Council of Churches*
Wayne A. R. Leys, *Roosevelt University*
Robert B. Livingston, *National Institute of Mental Health*
R. M. MacIver, *Columbia University*
Bernard Mandelbaum, *The Jewish Theological Seminary of America*
William W. Marvel, *Carnegie Corporation of New York*
Eugene J. McCarthy, *United States Senate*
James McClellan, *Teachers College, Columbia University*
Myres S. McDougal, *Yale University*
Laurence C. McHugh, S.J., *"America"*
Richard P. McKeon, *The University of Chicago*
Sterling M. McMurrin, *University of Utah*
Joost A. M. Meerloo, *Columbia Presbyterian Medical Center*
K. Satchidananda Murty, *Andhra University*
N. A. Nikam, *Mysore University*
Harald Ofstad, *University of Stockholm*
Stanley Parry, C.S.C., *University of Notre Dame*
Talcott Parsons, *Harvard University*
James A. Perkins, *Carnegie Corporation of New York*
Charner Perry, *The University of Chicago*
John P. Plamenatz, *Nuffield College, Oxford University*
Michal Polanyi, *Merton College, Oxford University*
Don K. Price, *Graduate School of Public Administration, Harvard University*
Harry B. Price, *United Nations Technical Assistance Program*

Participants in Program

Jon L. Regier, *Division of Home Missions, National Council of Churches*
Ira De A. Reid, *Haverford College*
Nina Ridenour, *Ittleson Family Foundation*
Meryl Ruoss, *Department of the Urban Church, National Council of Churches*
Edward T. Sandrow, *Rabbinical Assembly of America*
Catherine Schaefer, *National Catholic Welfare Conference for United Nations Affairs*
Benjamin I. Schwartz, *Harvard University*
Bernard Schwartz, *The Law School, New York University*
Harlow Shapley, *Harvard University*
Franklin Sherman, *School of Religion, State University of Iowa*
Edward A. Shils, *Committee on Social Thought, The University of Chicago*
Roger L. Shinn, *Union Theological Seminary*
Seymour Siegel, *The Jewish Theological Seminary of America*
David W. Silverman, *Conservative Synagogue of Riverdale*
Walter A. Stewart, *New York Psychoanalytic Institute*
Donald E. Stokes, *Survey Research Center, University of Michigan*
Ruth Strang, *Teachers College, Columbia University*
Lewis L. Strauss, *The Library Corporation, The Jewish Theological Seminary of America*
Charles P. Taft, *Taft and Lavercombe*
Ordway Tead, *Harper and Brothers*
John L. Thomas, S.J., *Institute of Social Order, St. Louis University*
Warren Weaver, *Alfred P. Sloan Foundation*
R. Norris Wilson, *Department of Church World Service, National Council of Churches*
Guy Wint, *St. Antony's College, Oxford University*
Arthur F. Wright, *Yale University*
Quincy Wright, *University of Virginia*
Paul N. Ylvisaker, *Public Affairs Program, The Ford Foundation*

PAPERS DISCUSSED AT PREVIOUS CONFERENCE MEETINGS

Science, Philosophy and Religion, A Symposium, 1941. (The papers prepared for the meetings held in New York City on September 9, 10, and 11, 1940.) Out of print.

Science, Philosophy and Religion, Second Symposium, 1942. (The papers prepared for the meetings held in New York City on September 8, 9, 10, and 11, 1941.)

Science, Philosophy and Religion, Third Symposium, 1943. (The papers prepared for the meetings held in New York City on August 27, 28, 29, 30, and 31, 1942.) Out of print.

Approaches to World Peace, Fourth Symposium, 1944. (The papers prepared for the meetings held in New York City on September 9, 10, 11, 12, and 13, 1943.) Out of print.

Approaches to National Unity, Fifth Symposium, 1945. (The papers prepared for the meetings held in New York City on September 7, 8, 9, 10, and 11, 1944.) Out of print.

Approaches to Group Understanding, Sixth Symposium, 1947. (The papers prepared for the meetings held in New York City on August 23, 24, 25, 26, and 27, 1945.) Out of print.

Conflicts of Power in Modern Culture, Seventh Symposium, 1947. (The papers prepared for the meetings held in Chicago on September 9, 10, and 11, 1946.) Out of print.

Learning and World Peace, Eighth Symposium, 1948. (The papers prepared for the meetings held in Philadelphia on September 7, 8, 9, and 10, 1947.)

Goals for American Education, Ninth Symposium, 1950. (The papers prepared for the meetings held in New York City on September 7, 8, 9, and 10, 1948.)

Perspectives on a Troubled Decade: Science, Philosophy and Religion, 1939–1949, Tenth Symposium, 1950. (The papers prepared for the meetings held in New York City on September 6, 7, 8, and 9, 1949.)

Foundations of World Organization: A Political and Cultural Appraisal, Eleventh Symposium, 1952. (The papers prepared for the meetings held in New York City on September 5, 6, 7, and 8, 1950.)

Freedom and Authority in Our Time, Twelfth Symposium, 1953. (The papers prepared for the meetings held in New York City on September 4, 5, 6, and 7, 1951.)

Symbols and Values: An Initial Study, Thirteenth Symposium, 1954. (The papers prepared for the meetings held in New York City on September 2, 3, 4, and 5, 1952.)

Symbols and Society, Fourteenth Symposium, 1955. (The papers prepared for the meetings at Harvard University, August 30 and 31, September 1 and 2, 1954.)

Aspects of Human Equality, Fifteenth Symposium, 1956. (The papers prepared for the meetings held in New York City on August 29, 30, and 31, and September 1, 1955.)

Published by
THE CONFERENCE ON SCIENCE, PHILOSOPHY AND RELIGION
3080 Broadway
New York 27, New York

Distributed by
HARPER & BROTHERS

Program

"ONE WORLD—ONE ETHICS?"

MEETING OF THE FELLOWS
OF THE CONFERENCE ON
SCIENCE, PHILOSOPHY AND RELIGION
IN THEIR RELATION TO THE
DEMOCRATIC WAY OF LIFE

LYMAN BRYSON, Honorary President
LOUIS FINKELSTEIN, President

MONDAY, TUESDAY, and WEDNESDAY
AUGUST 31, SEPTEMBER 1, and 2, 1959

THE MEN'S FACULTY CLUB
COLUMBIA UNIVERSITY
400 WEST 117th STREET
NEW YORK CITY

All sessions will be held on the
Third Floor of The Men's Faculty Club

MONDAY, AUGUST 31
12:00 p.m.

                Luncheon Meeting
           Chairmen and Paper Writers

                                                Long Room

2:30 p.m.

GENERAL SESSION

Lyman Bryson, *Chairman*

Discussion of*
Can a common ethical denominator be drawn
from the traditional ethical systems?

Prepared discussants
Clarence H. Faust
Simon Greenberg
John LaFarge, S.J.

8:30 p.m.

GENERAL SESSION

Discussion of*
The relationship between contemporary
religious systems and ethical practices

based on papers by
John C. Bennett
K. Satchidananda Murty
John L. Thomas, S.J.
Isadore Twersky

TUESDAY, SEPTEMBER 1
10:00 a.m.

GENERAL SESSION

Daniel Lerner, *Chairman*

Discussion of*
International aspects of ethical problems in areas
not commonly considered foreign operations—

*Papers available in mimeographed form. All oral discussion off the record.

agriculture, anti-trust laws, currency, education, employment, immigration, taxation, etc.— Usually approached solely on the national level

> based on papers by
> Joost A. M. Meerloo
> Walter J. Ong, S.J.
> David McCord Wright

12:30

Luncheon Business Meeting of the Fellows of the Conference on Science, Philosophy and Religion, to transact necessary business of the corporation, including election of officers

> Long room

2:30 p.m.

GENERAL SESSION

Harry J. Carman, *Chairman*

Discussion of*
Ethical problems in areas commonly considered foreign operations: ethics of influence across international lines

> based on papers by
> Harlan Cleveland
> Richard P. McKeon

WEDNESDAY, SEPTEMBER 2
8:30 a.m. Breakfast Meeting

GENERAL SUMMARY SESSION
and
Discussion of
The World Academy of Ethics

CONFERENCE ON SCIENCE, PHILOSOPHY AND RELIGION**

Officers

Louis Finkelstein, *The Jewish Theological Seminary of America*—president
Lyman Bryson, *Teachers College, Columbia University*—honorary president, and chairman of the executive committee
Richard P. McKeon, *The University of Chicago*—Third Conference on Science, Philosophy and Religion Lecturer
Clarence H. Faust, *Fund for the Advancement of Education, The Ford Foundation*—vice president
John LaFarge, S.J., *"America"*—vice president
Jessica Feingold, *The Institute for Religious and Social Studies*—executive vice president

---

Sixteenth Conference

"Challenges to Traditional Ethics: Government, Politics, and Administration"

August 29—September 2, 1960

Harold D. Lasswell, *The Law School, Yale University*—Chairman
Harlan Cleveland, *Maxwell Graduate School of Citizenship and Public Affairs, Syracuse University*—co-chairman
F. Ernest Johnson, *Teachers College, Columbia University*—co-chairman

---

Executive Committee

CONFERENCE ON SCIENCE, PHILOSOPHY AND RELIGION LECTURERS
R. M. MacIver, *Columbia University*
Richard P. McKeon
Harlow Shapley, *Harvard University*

Lyman Bryson
Harlan Cleveland
Thurston N. Davis, S.J., *"America"*
Clarence H. Faust
Louis Finkelstein
Hudson Hoagland, *Worcester Foundation for Experimental Biology*
F. Ernest Johnson
John LaFarge, S.J.
Harold D. Lasswell
I. I. Rabi, *Columbia University*
Wendell M. Stanley, *University of California at Berkeley*
Ordway Tead, *Harper and Brothers*
M. L. Wilson, *The Ford Foundation*

Fellows

Thomas Ritchie Adam, *New York University*
William F. Albright, *The Johns Hopkins University*
Robert Bierstedt, *The City College of New York*
Van Wyck Brooks

**As of November 18, 1958

Lyman Bryson
Harry J. Carman, *Columbia College, Columbia University*
Harlan Cleveland
Stewart G. Cole
William G. Constable, *Museum of Fine Arts, Boston*
Norman Cousins, *"The Saturday Review"*
Thurston N. Davis, S.J.
Karl W. Deutsch, *Yale University*
Hoxie N. Fairchild, *Hunter College of the City of New York*
Clarence H. Faust
Louis Finkelstein
A. Durwood Foster, *Pacific School of Religion*
Lawrence K. Frank
Philipp G. Frank, *Institute for the Unity of Science*
Charles Frankel, *Columbia University*
Simon Greenberg, *The Jewish Theological Seminary of America*
Caryl P. Haskins, *Carnegie Institution of Washington*
Charles W. Hendel, *Yale University*
Hudson Hoagland
Albert Hofstadter, *Columbia University*
F. Ernest Johnson
Robert B. Johnson, *National Conference of Christians and Jews*
Clyde Kluckhohn, *Harvard University*
John LaFarge, S.J.
Harold D. Lasswell
Dorothy D. Lee, *Harvard University*
R. M. MacIver
Jacques Maritain, *Princeton University*
Robert J. McCracken, *The Riverside Church*
Richard P. McKeon
Margaret Mead, *American Museum of Natural History*
Henry A. Murray, *Harvard University*
John Courtney Murray, S.J., *Woodstock College*
Ernest Nagel, *Columbia University*
John U. Nef, *The University of Chicago*
F. S. C. Northrop, *Yale University*
Peter H. Odegard, *University of California at Berkeley*
J. Robert Oppenheimer, *Institute for Advanced Study*
Harry A. Overstreet, *The City College of New York*
Anton C. Pegis, *Pontifical Institute of Mediaeval Studies, Toronto*
Gerald B. Phelan, *St. Michael's College, Toronto*
Liston Pope, *The Divinity School, Yale University*
I. I. Rabi
Roy W. Sellars, *University of Michigan*
Harlow Shapley
George N. Shuster, *Hunter College of the City of New York*
Wendell M. Stanley
Donald C. Stone, *Graduate School of Public and International Affairs, University of Pittsburgh*
Ordway Tead
M. L. Wilson
Quincy Wright, *The University of Chicago*

PARTICIPANTS IN PROGRAM***

Thomas Ritchie Adam
Ruth Nanda Anshen, *"World Perspectives"*
S. B. Bapat, *The United Nations*
Roland H. Bainton, *Yale University*
John C. Bennett, *Union Theological Seminary*
Roy Blough, *Columbia University*
Courtney C. Brown, *Columbia University*
Lyman Bryson
Donald R. Campion, S.J., *"America"*
Harry J. Carman
H. Van B. Cleveland, *John Hancock Mutual Life Insurance Company*
Harlan Cleveland
Gerson D. Cohen, *The Jewish Theological Seminary of America*
Stewart G. Cole
William G. Constable
Norman Cousins
Robert A. Dahl, *Yale University*
Henry David, *Columbia University*
Moshe Davis, *The Jewish Theological Seminary of America*
Thurston N. Davis, S.J.
Halbert L. Dunn, *United States Department of Health, Education, and Welfare*
Richard Eells, *General Electric Company*
Rowland A. Egger, *University of Virginia*
Clarence H. Faust
Jessica Feingold
Louis Finkelstein
David Finn, *Ruder and Finn*
Philipp G. Frank
Charles Frankel
Simon Greenberg
Hudson Hoagland
Albert Hofstadter
F. Ernest Johnson
Robert B. Johnson
Harry W. Jones, *Columbia University*
Wolfe Kelman, *The Rabbinical Assembly of America*
Isaac Klein, *Temple Emanuel, Buffalo*
David C. Kogen, *The Jewish Theological Seminary of America*
W. W. Kulski, *Maxwell Graduate School of Citizenship and Public Affairs, Syracuse University*
John LaFarge, S.J.
Daniel Lerner, *Massachusetts Institute of Technology*
R. M. MacIver
Bernard Mandelbaum, *The Jewish Theological Seminary of America*
Laurence C. McHugh, *"America"*
Richard P. McKeon
Sterling M. McMurrin, *University of Utah*
Joost A. M. Meerloo, *Columbia University*
K. Satchidananda Murty, *Andhra University, India*
Waldemar A. Nielsen, *The Ford Foundation*

***Writers of papers and comments, and those expected to attend as of August 10th.

Walter J. Ong, S.J., *Saint Louis University*
Charner M. Perry, *The University of Chicago*
David M. Potter, *Yale University*
Nina Ridenour, *Ittleson Family Foundation*
William Ruder, *Ruder and Finn*
Joseph J. Schwab, *The University of Chicago*
Harlow Shapley
George N. Shuster
Seymour Siegel, *The Jewish Theological Seminary of America*
Ralph Simon, *Congregation Rodfei Zedek, Chicago*
Phillips Talbot, *American Universities Field Staff*
Howard C. Taylor, Jr., *College of Physicians and Surgeons, Columbia University*
Ordway Tead
John L. Thomas, S.J., *Saint Louis University*
Kenneth W. Thompson, *The Rockefeller Foundation*
Willard L. Thorp, *Amherst College*
Isadore Twersky, *Harvard University*
U Thant, *Permanent Representative of Burma to the United Nations*
Preston Valien, *Fisk University*
Charles W. Wegener, *The University of Chicago*
Christopher Wright, *Council for Atomic Age Studies, Columbia University*
David McCord Wright, *McGill University*

PAPERS DISCUSSED AT PREVIOUS CONFERENCE MEETINGS

Science, Philosophy and Religion, A Symposium, 1941. (The papers prepared for the meetings held in New York City on September 9, 10, and 11, 1940.) Out of print.

Science, Philosophy and Religion, Second Symposium, 1942. (The papers prepared for the meetings held in New York City on September 8, 9, 10, and 11, 1941.)

Science, Philosophy and Religion, Third Symposium, 1943. (The papers prepared for the meetings held in New York City on August 27, 28, 29, 30, and 31, 1942.) Out of print.

Approaches to World Peace, Fourth Symposium, 1944. (The papers prepared for the meetings held in New York City on September 9, 10, 11, 12, and 13, 1943.) Out of print.

Approaches to National Unity, Fifth Symposium, 1945. (The papers prepared for the meetings held in New York City on September 7, 8, 9, 10, and 11, 1944.) Out of print.

Approaches to Group Understanding, Sixth Symposium, 1947. (The papers prepared for the meetings held in New York City on August 23, 24, 25, 26, and 27, 1945.) Out of print.

Conflicts of Power in Modern Culture, Seventh Symposium, 1947. (The papers prepared for the meetings held in Chicago on September 9, 10, and 11, 1946.) Out of print.

Learning and World Peace, Eighth Symposium, 1948. (The papers prepared for the meetings held in Philadelphia on September 7, 8, 9, and 10, 1947.)

Goals for American Education, Ninth Symposium, 1950. (The papers prepared for the meetings held in New York City on September 7, 8, 9, and 10, 1948.)

Perspectives on a Troubled Decade: Science, Philosophy and Religion, 1939–1949, Tenth Symposium, 1950. (The papers prepared for the meetings held in New York City on September 6, 7, 8, and 9, 1949.)

Foundations of World Organization: A Political and Cultural Appraisal, Eleventh Symposium, 1952. (The papers prepared for the meetings held in New York City on September 5, 6, 7, and 8, 1950.)

Freedom and Authority in Our Time, Twelfth Symposium, 1953. (The papers prepared for the meetings held in New York City on September 4, 5, 6, and 7, 1951.)

Symbols and Values: An Initial Study, Thirteenth Symposium, 1954. (The papers prepared for the meetings held in New York City on September 2, 3, 4, and 5, 1952.)

Symbols and Society, Fourteenth Symposium, 1955. (The papers prepared for the meetings at Harvard University, August 30 and 31, September 1 and 2, 1954.)

Aspects of Human Equality, Fifteenth Symposium, 1956. (The papers prepared for the meetings held in New York City on August 29, 30, and 31, and September 1, 1955.)

Published by
THE CONFERENCE ON SCIENCE, PHILOSOPHY AND RELIGION
3080 Broadway
New York 27, New York

Distributed by
HARPER & BROTHERS

Index

Aaronides, 214n
Academic organization, xviii-xix
  moral judgments in, 85-98
  see also Universities
Accommodation model, of organization, 403, 414-419
Accountants' codes, 8
Acheson, Dean, 282-283, 290
Ackerman, J. Emory, 195n
Action:
  ethics of, 22, 37, 59
  guides for, 484-487
Activism, 150-153, 158-160, 162-163, 165
Acton, Lord, 34-35, 36
Adam, Thomas Ritchie, 505, 517, 519
Adams, Charles Francis, 269, 443
Adams, Henry, 443
Adams, James Luther, 209n
Adams, John, 443
Adams, John Quincy, 266, 443
Administration:
  academic, 97-98
  and authority, 425, 426, 432
  Catholic, 173-177, 178-185
  concept of, 421-422
  in Judaism, 221, 231-232
  Protestant, 199, 211
  and responsibility, policy, 454-466, 468
  scientific, 111-115, 119, 121
  see also Executive organization
Administrative Procedures Act, 11, 302
Administrators, ethics for, 9-10, 12, 397-419, 421-434, 439-442
Adventures of Tom Sawyer, The (Mark Twain), 21
Advice, scientific, 113-114
Advise and Consent (Drury), 58, 450-451
Advisory agencies, 379-380
AFL-CIO Codes of Ethical Practices, The, 8n, 19
Africa, 311-312, 324-325, 327
Agriculture, Department of, xl, 309, 457, 458
Air Force, Department of the, xxxvii, 321-322
Albright, William F., 505, 517
Altgeld, John Peter, 273
"America," 505, 507, 508, 517, 519

American Association of Theological Schools, 193
American Baptist Convention, 190
American Bar Association, 302
American Bible Society, 193
American Cancer Society, xxvii
American Friends Service Committee, lxiv, 193
American Institute of Managemeint, 190
American Jewish Year Book, 220
American Museum of Natural History, 506
American Society for Industrial Security, 373
American Society for Political and Legal Philosophy, 11n
American Society for Public Administration, 9
Ames, Fisher, 294-295
Amherst College, 489
Amish groups, 204
Amrine, M., 112n
Anabaptists, 159
Anas (Jefferson), 443
Anderson, Ind., Church of God in, 205-207
Andhra University, 508, 519
Angell, Robert C., lxiv-lxv, 197, 491, 497, 507
Annapolis, Naval Academy at, 341
Anshen, Ruth Nanda, 519
Appleby, Paul H., xviii, xlv-xlvi, liv, 4n, 9n, 16, 36-37, 297-298, 434, 467, 491, 507
Applied research, 106-107, 117-118, 120
Appointments, Presidential, 301-302, 329-331, 336, 363, 365, 370, 374-376, 380-381
Aquinas, St. Thomas, 149
Arabian American Oil Company, xxxi-xxxii
Arendt, Hannah, xxi, 14n, 16, 497, 507
Argyris, Chris, 405n
Aristocracy, 480
Aristotle, 45, 74, 149, 475-476
Armies, peacetime, 350, 352-353
  see also Military
Arminian Theology, 152, 155, 158, 160
Army Department, 321-322

523

Index

Aron, Raymond, 503, 507
Arthur, Chester A., 272
Articles of Confederation, 438
Asia, 311-312, 324-325, 327
Assemblies of God, 194
Association of the Bar of the City of New York, 51, 58n
Atlantic Charter, 279
Atomic Energy Commission, 379
Atomists, 476
Attwood, William, xli
Aubert, Roger, 177n
Authoritarianism, vs. freedom, 311, 324-327
Authority, and administration, 425, 426, 432
Authority relationships, 85-90

Bagehot, Walter, 441
Bailey, Stephen K., xviii, 21-37, 467, 468, 491, 500, 507
Bainton, Roland H., 519
Baker, Helen E., 507
Baldridge, Holmes, Assistant Attorney General, 294
Bales, Robert F., 154n
Ballinger investigation, 6n
Banfield, Edward C., 61n
Bapat, S. B., 519
Baptists, 151
Bargaining processes, 417-419, 424-425, 430
Barnard, Chester I., 400-402, 404-405, 406-407, 414, 422n
Barnes, Roswell P., 209
Barnett, J. D., 4n, 18
Baron, Salo W., 215n, 501, 507
Barry, David W., 209
Basic research, 100, 103, 106-107, 111, 114, 117-118, 120
Bazedon, David T., xxvi, xxviii
Becker, Carl, 34
Becker, Howard, 204n
Behavioral sciences, 157
Bellah, Robert N., 141n
Bendix, Reinhard, 208n
Bennett, John C., 514, 519
Benton, Thomas H., 268
Berelson, Bernard R., 63n
Berle, Adolf A., Jr., xxvi, xxvii-xxviii, xxix, xxxviii
Bess, Demaree, 375n

Bierstedt, Robert, 505, 517
Bill of Rights, 217
Bishops, Catholic, 179
Black, Hugo L., 284
Blackstone, Sir William, 297
Blaine, James G., 272
Blake, William, 74
Blau, J. L., 226n
Blizzard, Samuel W., 200n-201n
Blough, Roy, 519
Board members, university, 88-89
Bokser, Ben Zion, 501, 507
Boston, Mass., 42
Boulding, Kenneth E., xix, 187, 192, 203, 232, 385-395, 491, 499, 507
Bradley, Omar N., 341n, 368, 370
Brandeis, Louis, 6n
Brewer, Earl D. C., 205n
Bribery, 24-27, 334, 364
Bridges, Styles, 367-368
Bright, John, 263
Brodbeck, Arthur J., 166n
Bronfenbrenner, Urie, 503, 507
Brooks, Van Wyck, ix, 505, 517
Brown, Courtney C., 519
Brown, Dyke, 507
Brown, Stuart Gerry, 498, 507
Brownlow, Louis, 266-267
Brownson, Orestes, 170
Brunner, Emil, 14n, 17, 189
Bryson, Lyman, 489, 505, 513, 514, 517, 518, 519
    First Lecture, xx, 471-487, 501
Buchan, John, 21
Buchanan, James, 269
Buchanan, Scott, 133n
Buddhist University, xl
Budget Bureau, 298
Bull Moose split, 315
Bulletin of the Atomic Scientists, 102
Burdick, Eugene, 166n
Bureaucracy, liii-liv, lx
    and Protestantism, 198-199, 200-202, 208-209
Bureau of Public Roads, 309
Burgess, Joseph, 27
Burghardt, Walter J., S.J., 183n
Burke, Edmund, 481
Burma, xl
Burns, James MacGregor, xviii, 39-44, 491, 501, 507
Bursk, Edward C., 422n

Index

Burton, Harold H., 284
Business:
  and ethical standards, 46-48, 422, 446, 454-455
  political attitudes of, 55-56
  and religious administration, 190-191, 221, 224
  stereotype of, 251-252
Butterfield, L. H., 443n

Cahn, Edmond N., 397-398
Calhoun, John Caldwell, 267-268
California, 268
California, University of, 505, 506, 517, 518
Callender and Charlesworth, 6n, 18
Calvin, John, 153
Calvinism, 147-151, 154-156, 158, 159, 160
Cambridge Air Force Research Center, 492
Campbell, Alexander, 455
Campbell, Angus, 67n, 68n
Campbell, Ernest Q., 209
Campion, Donald R., S.J., 507, 519
Camus, A., 116
Candidates, political, 40-44
Can Representative Government Do the Job? (Finletter), 320n
Cantors Assembly of America, 221n
Capitalism, society of, 392, 394
Career service, *see* Civil Service
Carey, John L., 8n, 17
Carlyle, Thomas, 481
Carman, Harry J., 505, 507, 515, 518, 519
Carnegie Corporation of N.Y., 492, 508
Carnegie Institution of Washington, 506
Carney, Robert B., 367n
Cary, William L., 507
Case, Francis, 6n
Cater, Douglass, 422n
Caterpillar Tractor Company, xxiv
Catholicism, *see* Roman Catholicism
Catlin, George E. Gordon, 501, 507
Cavendish, Henry, 103
Cavert, Samuel McCrea, 194n
Censorship, of military, 375-376
Census of Religious Bodies (1926), 195
Center for the Study of Democratic Institutions, 506
Central Intelligence Agency, xl
Chaco War, 261
Chandler, Zach, 272

Change, tempo of, xlix
Channing, Edward, 294
Charisma, 208-210, 213-214
Cherokee Nation, 267
Chesterton, G. K., 24
Chicago, University of, 492, 505, 506, 508, 509
Childs, Marquis W., 422n
China, Communist, 312, 314, 349, 392
Christian Century, 192
Christian Missionary Alliance, 205
Christiani, Léon, 174n
Christianity:
  and American religious organization, 141-160, 163-167
  and the Roman Empire, 214-215
  and secularism, 184-185
  spread of, 477
Church:
  concepts of, 154-155, 189-190
  the local, 200-204
  membership in, 142-143, 149, 153
  role of, 145-147, 150, 152-153
  and State, 141, 144, 147, 155, 166, 171-172, 176, 185, 217
Church and Modern Society, The (Ireland), 169
Church of God, Anderson, Ind., 205-207
Church of the Nazarene, 205
Church Peace Union, 193, 507
Churchill, Winston, 22
Cincinnati, Ohio, 53, 56
City:
  and the metropolis, 235-236
  population, and government, 66-67, 438
  and urban renewal, 245-257
City College of N.Y., 505, 506, 517, 518
City manager plans, 438
Civil Aeronautics Board, 301, 307, 309, 491
Civil defense, 347
Civilian Conservation Corps, 277
Civil-military relationships:
  and the military mind, 341-350, 358
  problems of, 351-362
  and separation of power, 363-382
Civil Service, 329-331, 332, 333, 363, 364
  ideals of, 9n
  standards for, 457-463, 465-466, 467
  system of, 458-463
Civil Service Commission, 9n, 11
Civil War, 353, 456

Claims commissions, 306
Clancy, William P., 507
Clapp, Gordon R., 9n, 18, 507
Clark, Tom C., 284
Clay, Henry, 268
Clear, Val, 205-206, 207
Cleveland Citizens League, 53-54
Cleveland, Grover, 272-273, 315
Cleveland, H. van B., 507, 519
Cleveland, Harlan, xviii, xxiii-xlvi, 421n, 433, 491, 497, 498, 499, 500, 505, 507, 515, 517, 518, 519
Cliques, in organization, 411, 412-413
Code of Procedure in Placement of Rabbis, 228-229
Code of Rabbinic Ethics, 230
Codes of Ethics, 3-16, 300-301, 401-402
Cohen, Gerson D., 498, 507, 519
Cold war, 345, 380, 392, 474
Cole, Stewart G., 505, 507, 518, 519
Coleridge, Samuel Taylor, 481
Collins, J. Lawton, 368, 369
Columbia Broadcasting System, xxxi
Columbia Presbyterian Medical Center, 508
Columbia University, 489, 490, 491, 493, 505, 506, 507, 508, 509, 517, 518, 519
Commission on Jewish Education, 222
Commissions, independent, 49-50, 299-310, 458
Committee system, 332, 451
see also Congressional committees
Common Law, 155
Communication:
  and administration, 423, 424, 425-428
  problems of, xlvii-lxv
Communism, 349, 392-394, 473
  and the Church, 177, 182, 184
  and world struggle, 312, 324-327
Community:
  as Church problem, 188, 203
  and the individual, 398-399
  influence of, 483-485
  in Judaism, 216-219
  "moral," 158-159
Competitive system, 59, 79-80
Compromise, and government, 448-454
Compromise of 1850, 269
Conference on Ethics of Mutual Involvement, 490

Conference on Science, Philosophy and Religion:
  goals of, ix-xi
  membership, 505-506, 517-518
  publications of, 495-496, 511-512, 521-522
  report on, 489-490
  Sixteenth, summarized, xiv-xxi
  contributors to, 491-493
  participants in, 507-509, 519-520
  program of, 497-503
Conflict:
  and mankind, 125-126
  of moral codes, 401-402
Conflict of interest, 4-16, 49-51, 57-58, 90-93, 363-364, 430-431, 434, 443, 446
Confucius, 471
Congar, Yves Marie Joseph, 181n
Congregation, in Judaism, 214-215, 217, 218, 222-224, 231-232
Congregationalists, 151, 163
Congress, U.S., 48, 49, 261-263, 270ff., 304, 309, 316, 319-320, 363, 365-366, 374-376
  accomplishments of, 462-463
  and ethical attitudes, 439-441, 453
  and military control, 357, 359
  see also Legislative-executive
Congressional committees, 262, 288-289, 372, 377-378, 451, 453, 456, 464, 466
  investigations by, 5-6, 45, 299, 318, 333, 335
Congressional Government (Wilson), 462
Conkling, Roscoe, 272
Connecticut, 21-36, 455
Connery, John R., S.J., xxi, 501, 507
Consent, degrees of, 425, 430, 431
Conservative Judaism, 218, 219-232
Conservative Synagogue of Riverdale, 509
Constable, William G., 505, 518, 519
Constitution, U.S., lvi, 259ff., 286, 296n, 316, 317, 333, 352, 363, 365, 456, 480
  First Amendment, 141, 217
  and revision, xix-xx, 320-324, 325, 380, 436-439, 463, 466, 467
  Tenth Amendment, 279
Constitutional Convention (1787), 480

Index

Contract system, government, xxxv-xl, 102-103, 111, 446-447
Coolidge, Calvin, 276
Cooper, Weldon, 491
Cooperation, and pluralistic society, xviii, xlvii-lxv
Copeland, M. T., 8n, 17
Cornell University, 507
Corruption, 363-364, 370-371, 443, 445-446, 456-457
  attitudes toward, 45-46, 53
  and local government, 24-35
Corwin, Edward S., 260, 270, 297
Council of Economic Advisors, 298
Council of the Four Lands, 215-217
Council manager plans, 438
Council of Trent, 174
Counter-Reformation, Catholic, 174-176
Courts:
  as institutions, liii, lx
  in Judaism, 215-217
  regulatory agencies as, 302-303
  see also Judicial branch
Cousins, Norman, 505, 518, 519
Covenant, conception of, 148, 151
Creativity:
  and administration, 423, 425, 428-429
  freedom for, xviii, 106-120, 129-130
  scientific, 128-131
Criticism, public, 79-80
Cuba, 273
Cultural orientation, American values in, 157-167
Curley, James M., 42
Curtiss-Wright Corporation, 261
Custom:
  power of, 322-324
  and social cooperation, xlviii, lxii
Cuyahoga County, Ohio, 55-56

Dahl, Robert A., 519
Dalton, Melville, 409-413
Daniels, Josephus, 376
Dansette, Adrien, 184n
Darrow, Karl K., xviii, 99-104, 491, 499, 507
David, Henry, 519
Davies, W. D., 209n
Davis, Moshe, 218n, 519
Davis, Thurston N., S.J., 505, 506, 517, 518, 519

Debate:
  on national policy, 312-316, 317
  public, 451-452
Decisionmaking:
  in government laboratory, 107-108, 112-115
  metropolitan, 235-257
  and the people, 285-286, 311, 313
  and public administration, 9, 22-23, 37
  systems of, xxx
  the term, xxiv
Declaration of Independence, 357
Defense, Department of, xxxv, xxxvii, 321-322, 359, 366-367, 371, 491
Defense, Secretary of, 86
De Gaulle, Charles, 467
Delany, William, 61n
Democracy:
  and administration, 36-37, 286-288, 422-433, 434
  and Catholicism, 169-172
  development of, 478-487
  effectiveness for, 464-466, 467-468
  and the electorate, 62-63, 72
  problems of, 311-327
  science in, 131-137
  and social cooperation, xlviii-xlix
  and "total" solutions, 349-350
  and war, 355
Democratic Advisory Council, 316
Democratic National Committee, 316
Democratic Party, 315-316, 364
Democritus, 476
Denfield, Louis E., 375
Denominational pluralism, 141-143, 147, 166-167
Denominations, Protestant, 194, 204-208
Dern, George H., 375
Desqueyrat, André, 182n
Deutsch, Karl W., 506, 518
Development and Resources Corporation, 507
Dewey, John, xlviii, 397, 399-400, 482
DeWitt, N. W., 14n, 17
Dickson, William J., 405n
Dilliard, Irving, 5n, 17
Dimock, Marshall, xxxii-xxxiii
Diogenes, 24
Disarmament, 348-349, 355
Disciples of Christ, 205, 207
Divine Law, 150-151

Index

Donham, W. B., 4n, 18
Douglas, Paul H., 3, 58
　committees, 4, 6n, 50-51
Douglas, William, 284, 301
Douglass, Truman B., 209
Drinker, H., 8n, 17
Dugger, R., 6n, 18
Duhamel, Georges, 100
Dukhbors, 204
Dunkards, 204
Dunn, Halbert L., 519
Dushkin, A., 222n
Dwyer, Robert J., xix, 169-185, 491, 499, 507

Eastman, Joseph, 301
Ecclesiastical structure, 192-211
Economic Cooperation Administration, xl
Economic growth:
　and the government, xxxviii-xxxix, 443-448, 451
　of society, 389-394
Economic policy, proposed office of, 293
Economics, classical, 157
Edict of Milan, 173
Education, 125, 429, 432-433
　and Catholic Church, 172, 178, 185
　and government aid, xxxix
　and government evaluation, 65-66, 70, 71
　in Judaism, 220, 221-222, 224, 225
　Protestant, 198-199
Educators Assembly of America, 221n
Edwards, Jonathan, 156
Eells, Richard, 519
Egger, Rowland A., xvii, xix, 259-297, 491, 500, 507, 519
Eisenhower, Dwight D., 284-285, 290, 367n, 369, 374-375, 376
Elections:
　and campaigns, 30, 40-42, 49, 55-56
　process of, 315-316, 320, 329, 331
Electoral research, 63-70
Ellis, John Tracy, 171n
Emancipation Proclamation, 271
Emergency Price Control Act, 280-281
Emerson, Ralph Waldo, xxxii, 480
Emmerich, H., 9n, 17
Encyclopaedia of Social Sciences, 45
Engelman, U. Z., 222n

England, Protestant, 164
　see also Great Britain
Enlightenment, the, xlviii, 157, 161, 444
Entente Cordiale, 354
Entropy, process of, 385-386, 389-391
Episcopalians, 163
Erikson, Erik H., 507
Established Church, concept of, 142, 147
Ethic of Power, The, ii, xxi
Ethical problems:
　in academic structures, xviii-xix, 85-98
　and metropolitan diversity, 235-239
　and organization, 422-434
　and politics, 471-487
　of regulatory agencies, 299-310
　from separation of powers, 365, 381
Ethical sensibility, 432-433
Ethics:
　for administrators, 397-419
　business, 46-48, 422
　Christian, 156
　and the elected official, 21-37, 239
　and government evaluation, 63-64
　guides for, 115-121
　of loyalty, 363-364
　of mutual involvement, 490
　military, 341-346, 360n
　official standards for, 3-16, 45-51, 300-301
　of opinion management, 73-81
　and political responsibility, 332-337, 363, 435-468
　and practical politics, 39-44, 53-60
　professional, 5-10, 46-48, 105-121, 230, 456-458
　public and private relationship, xviii, xxiii-xlvi
　and scientific secrecy, 102
　traditional, challenge to, xiii-xiv
　and value weights, xix, 394-395
Ethics and Bigness, contributors to, 491-493
Ethics Committee, Rabbinical Assembly, 229-230
Ethics for Policy Decisions (Leys), 15n
Europe, 324, 344, 354
Evangelistic churches, 443, 444-445, 448
Evolution, process of, 386-394
Ewing, Thomas, 269
Exchange system, of organization, 403, 405-414

Index

Executive-legislative relationships, 311-327, 359-360, 364-382
   improvement of, 435-466
   and separation of power, 48, 259-263, 264-266, 297
Executive organization, government, xix, 292-293, 321-322
   appointed officials in, 329-337
   metropolitan, 235-257
   Presidency in, 259-298
   and regulatory agencies, 49-50, 299-310
Executives, *see* Administrators; Presidency
Ex Parte Merryman, 271
Ex Parte Milligan, 270, 281

Faculty, university, 86-93, 97-98, 106-107
Fairchild, Hoxie N., 506, 518
Faust, Clarence H., xxi, 489, 498, 499, 502, 505, 506, 507, 514, 517, 518, 519
Febronianism, 176
Federal Aviation Agency, 309
Federal Bureau of Investigation, xl
Federal Communications Commission, xxxi, 307, 309
Federal Council of Churches, 193, 205
Federal Creed of Service, 9n
Federal Housing Administration, xxxvii
Federal Power Commission, 307
Federal Shipbuilding and Air Associates plants, 284, 295
Federal Theology, 151
Federalist Papers, lvi, 45, 269
Feingold, Jessica, xx-xxi, 489, 498, 505, 507, 517, 519
Fer, Muslih, xxi, 502, 507
Filipetti, George, 403n
Fillmore, Millard, 269
Finances, *see* Funds
Finkelstein, Louis, ix, xx, 215n, 489, 498, 501, 505, 506, 507, 513, 517, 518, 519
Finletter, Thomas K., xix, 311-327, 491, 498, 500, 507
Finn, David, xviii, 73-80, 491, 498, 501, 507, 519
Fletcher, J., 8n, 17
Fliche, Augustin, 174n, 175n, 177n
Ford, John Cuthbert, S.J., 184n

Ford Foundation, xxvii, xl, 51, 493, 505, 507, 509, 517, 519
Ford Motor Company, xxxiv
Foreign Missions Conference in North America, 193
Foreign policy, lxv, 292, 313-315
   see also Policy
Formosa, 314
Foster, A. Durwood, 506, 507, 518
Foster, William C., xix, 329-337, 491, 500, 507
Fox, William T. R., xix, 351-362, 381, 491, 500, 507
France, 175-176, 182, 286, 290, 317, 324, 349, 437, 449, 467
Franck report, 112
Frank, Jerome, 301
Frank, Lawrence K., 506, 518
Frank, Philipp G., 506, 507, 518, 519
Frankel, Charles, 519
Frankfurter, Felix, 284, 296n
Franklin, Benjamin, 157
Freedom:
   vs. authoritarianism, 311, 324-327
   creative, xviii, 106-120, 129-130
   and the organization, 423
   preservation of, 486-487
   of religion, 141, 151
French Revolution, 175-176
Freud, Sigmund, 151
Friedrich, Carl J., 11n, 360n, 189n
Fulbright, J. W., 45, 280
Functional model, of organization, 403-405
Fundraising, and Standards, 223
Funds:
   church, 193, 195
   military, 357, 370, 375
   research, 101, 102-103
Fyzee, Asaf A. A., 502, 507

Gard, Richard A., 502, 507
Garfield, James A., 272
Gavin, James M., 359n, 372n
Gelasius I, St., Pope, 172
Gelber, Lionel, 354n
General Electric Company, xxxiv, xxxvi, 519
Geneva Conferences, 348, 349
George III, King, 357

Germany, 354, 449
Gibbons, Cardinal, 170
Giffin, Sidney F., xix, 341-350, 491, 500, 507
Gifts, acceptance of, 7, 58, 299, 334
Gilbreth, Lillian, 404
Gilkey, J. Gordon, Jr., 507
Ginzberg, Louis, 215n
Glazer, Nathan, 229n
Gluckman, Max, 497, 507
Goal-pluralism, 159-160
God:
 Kingdom of, 148-150, 158-160
 Word of, 232
Goldin, Judah, 215n
"Goodness," and organization, 394-395
Gospel Trumpet, 206
Gough, J. W., 265
Government:
 attitudes toward, xviii, 47-48, 57, 61-72, 442-466
 and ethical problems, xiv-xv, 3-16, 45-51
 institutions of, 480-481
 local, 21-36, 53-55, 235-257
 political executive in, 329-337
 as power phenomenon, 4
 and Presidential authority, 259-298
 and private organizations, xxv, xxviii-xxix, xxxii-xl, xlv-xlvi
 and science, 105-121, 123, 134-137
 and the secular spirit, 184-185
 size of, 48
Government service, *see* Civil Service; Public service
Grace, access to, 151-152, 158
Graham, Father Robert A., S.J., 171-172
Grant, Ulysses S., 272
Great Britain, 177, 286, 296-297, 312, 316-321, 324, 344, 349, 351, 354, 392, 437, 441, 449-450, 452-453, 467, 468
Greenberg, Ephraim, 229n
Greenberg, Simon, 498, 502, 506, 508, 514, 518, 519
Group achievement, and value concept, 408-409
Group conflict, and politics, 62, 66
Grundstein, Nathan D., xix, 397-419, 491, 503, 508
Guide to Congregational Standards, 227
Guttman, Louis, 64n

Hales, Edward Elton Young, 177n
Hall, Cameron P., 508
Hall, Jerome, 503, 508
Hamilton, Alexander, 45, 260, 443, 444
Hancock, John, Mutual Life Insurance Co., 507, 519
Hand, Learned, 4-5
Handlin, Oscar, 219n
Handy, Robert T., 202
Hanna, Mark, 273
Harbrecht, Paul, S.J., xxvi
Harding, Warren G., 276
Harnack, Adolf von, 146n, 209n
Harper and Brothers, 493, 505, 509
Harris, Abram L., 508
Harrison, Paul, 188
Harrison, William Henry, 268, 273
Hart, James, 293n
Harvard University, 492, 505, 506, 507, 509, 517, 518
Haskins, Caryl P., 506, 518
Hatch Act, 11-12
Haverford College, 509
Hawthorne investigation, 405-406
Hayes, Rutherford B., 272
Health, Education and Welfare, Department of, 378-379, 519
Hecker, Father Isaac, 170
Hector, Faircloth and Rutledge, 491, 508
Hector, Louis J., xvii, xix, 299-310, 491, 500, 508
Heermance, E. L., 8n, 17
Hendel, Charles W., 506, 518
Herberg, Will, 143n
Herring, Pendleton, 355n
Hertzberg, Arthur, 226n
Herzfeld, Charles M., xviii, 105-121, 491, 499, 508
Hierarchical principle, 455-456, 458
Hierarchy, academic, 85-90
Hindenburg, Paul von, 294
Hitler, Adolf, 294, 349
Hoagland, Hudson, 498, 505, 506, 508, 517, 518, 519
Hobbes, Thomas, 151, 157, 478-479
Hocedez, Edgar, 178n
Hofstadter, Albert, 506, 518, 519
Home Building and Loan Assoc. v. Blaisdell, 278-279, 281
Homrighauson, E., 14n, 18
Honesty, standards of, 3-4, 8, 16

Index

Hoosac Mills case, 277-278
Hoover Commission, First, 289
Hoover, Herbert, 276
Houser, T. V., 8n, 17
House of Representatives, 313, 314, 318
  see also Congress
Hudnut, W. H., 200n
Hughes, Charles E., 278, 281
Human behavior, study of, 157
Hunter College, 506
Huntington, Samuel P., 341, 360n, 375n
Huntoon, R. D., 121
Hutterian Brethren, 204
Hyman, Sydney, 263n

Iceland, 279
Ideas, adaptation of, 127-128
Ideology:
  and science, 116-117
  and society, l-lxiv
Incentives, theory of, 407-408
Incremental decision, 403, 414-419
Independent commissions, 49-50, 299-310, 458
India, 467
Indiana University, 508
Individual:
  and ethical choice, 398-400
  in the organization, 408-414, 418-419, 422-425, 432
Individualism, and religious values, 153-157, 158-161
Industry:
  and regulatory agencies, 299, 308-310
  and scientific research, 102, 103
  see also Business
Institute for Advanced Study, 506, 508
Institute for Religious and Social Studies, The, x, 191, 192, 505, 507
Institute for the Unity of Science, 506, 507, 518
Institute of Defense Analyses, 492, 508
Institute on Ethics, The, 489, 491, 492
Institutionalization:
  process of, 206-207
  and value system, 146-147, 149, 151-167
Institutions:
  democratic, 288-293, 297-298, 473-474, 478-487
  role of, 123-126

Institutions (Cont.)
  safeguards for, 134-137
  of societies, xviii, li-lxiv
Interchurch Center, The, 193
Internal Revenue Service, 6n
International City Managers' Association, 9
International Missionary Council, 193
International relations, lxv, 292, 313-315
Interstate Commerce Commission, 301, 307
Inter-University Case Committee, 10n
Intuitionists, 12-13
Investigations:
  Congressional, 5-6, 45, 299, 318, 333, 335
  of officials, 11
Iowa, State University of, 509
Ireland, John, 169-170, 171, 185
Irish Catholicism, 164, 182
Islam, 144
Israel, State of, 165
Italy, 177
Ittleson Family Foundation, 509

Jackson, Andrew, 266-268, 269, 444, 456
Jackson, Henry M., 288-289, 291, 462
Jackson, Robert H., 284, 296n
Jacobson, Gershom, 223n
Jammu and Kashmir, University of, 507
Janowitz, Morris, 61n
Jarry, Eugene, 175n
Javits, Jacob K., 3, 6n
Jay Treaty, 294
Jefferson, Thomas, 157, 266, 269, 443-444
Jehovah's Witnesses, 204-205
Jesuits, 146n, 164, 174-175, 176, 507
Jette, Marie Henri, 176n
Jewish Law, 148-149
Jewish Theological Seminary of America, The, ix-x, xx, 225-228, 489, 491, 492, 493, 497, 498, 505, 506, 507, 508, 509, 519
John XXIII, Pope, 182
Johns Hopkins University, 505, 517
Johnson, Andrew, 272
Johnson, F. Ernest, xx, 195n, 491-492, 497, 498, 505, 506, 508, 517, 518, 519
Johnson, Louis, 341
Johnson, Robert B., 506, 508, 518, 519
Johnson, Walter, 282

532   Index

Joint Chiefs of Staff, 289-290, 359, 365, 374, 379
Jones, Harry W., 503, 508, 519
Joseph, Chief Rabbi Jacob, 218
Josephism, 176
Journet, Charles, 179n
Judaism:
  in American religious organization, 143-144, 148-149, 163-167
  and the Conference, x
  Conservative, 218, 219-232
  organizational patterns of, 213-232
  Orthodox, 165, 218, 221, 222, 225
  JudeoChristian tradition, 115-116, 148, 167, 184
Judicial branch, government, 48-49, 304
  and separation of power, 259-263
Judicialization, and regulatory agencies, 302-305, 308

Kabir, Humayun, 502, 508
Kallen, Horace M., 375n
Kant, Immanuel, 33, 399
Kaplan, A., 351n
Kaplan, Mordecai M., 217n
Katzenbach, Edward L., Jr., xix, 363-382, 492
Kauffman, Joseph F., 498, 503, 508
Kaufman, Herbert, 416-417
Kaufmann, Ezekiel, 214n
Kaufmann, William W., 346, 347
Kautilya, 471
Keating, Kenneth B., 6n
Kefauver, Estes, 316
Kelly, Gerald, S.J., 184n
Kelman, Wolfe, 519
Kem, James Preston, Senator, 282
Kennan, George F., 290-291
Kennedy, John F., 58n
Kentucky, 54
Khrushchev, N., 349
Kickbacks, 27-29
Kimball, Solon T., 508
Kingsley, Donald, 6n, 17
Kingsley, J., 9n, 17
Kintner, Robert, xxxi
Kirchheimer, O., 11n, 17
Klein, Rabbi Isaac, 228n, 519
Kluckhohn, Clyde, 506, 518
Kogen, David C., 519
Kogon, Eugen, 503, 508

Kohn, Eugene, 226n
Korean War, 282-283, 284, 337, 344, 367-368, 369, 370
Kornhauser, William, 166n
Kulski, W. W., 497, 508, 519

Lacordaire, Jean, 169
LaFarge, John, S.J., 489, 498, 501, 505, 506, 508, 514, 517, 518, 519
Laity, Catholic, 180-181, 185
Lake Mohonk Mountain House, 489-490
Lambie, Morris, 237
LaMennais, Felicité Robert de, 169
Landis, B. Y., 7n, 18
Landis, James, 301
Landon, Harold R., 508
Large-scale organization, and ethical problems, xiv-xviii
Lasswell, Harold D., 347, 351n, 352n, 355n, 489, 492, 497, 498, 502, 505, 506, 508, 517, 518
Latin America, 177-178, 183, 286, 490
Latourette, Kenneth Scott, 176n
Laud, William, 455
Law:
  and Christian ethics, 155-156
  ethical force of, 50-51
  rule of, 487
  and the Presidency, 294-297
Lazareth, William H., 502, 508
Lazarsfeld, Paul F., 63n
Leadership:
  and administration, 423, 425-426
  charismatic, 208-210, 211
  collective, xxx, xxxv-xl, xlvi
  in Judaism, 223-224
  and political responsibility, 442-454, 468
  Protestant, 198-199
Lecler, Joseph, 175n
Lee and Yang, 119
Lee, Robert, xix, 187-211, 219n, 492, 499, 508
Lefever, E., 14n, 17
Leflon, Jean, 176n
Legislative branch, see Congress, U.S.
Legislative-executive relationships, 311-327, 359-360, 364-382
  improvement of, 435-466
  and separation of power, 48, 259-263, 264-266, 297
Leibrecht, W., 209n
Lend Lease Act, 279, 280

Index

Leo XIII, Pope, 169, 178
Lerner, Daniel, 497, 508, 515, 519
Letts, Harold C., 508
Lever Act, 276
Levites, 214n
Leys, Wayne A. R., xviii, 3-19, 44, 51, 80-81, 492, 501, 508
Liberty, concepts of, 481
  see also Freedom
Lies, ethics of, 59-60
Lilienthal, David, 9n, 17
Lincoln, Abraham, xxxv, 269-272, 275,
Lindblom, Charles E., 415, 416 296, 297, 323, 352-353
Lindemann, Klaus A., 61n
Litvinov, M. M., 349
Livingston, Robert B., xviii, 123-137, 492, 499, 508
Lobbying, xxxiii-xxxiv
Locke, John, 156, 157, 264-265, 297, 319, 478-479
London Disarmament Conference (1930), 374
Look Magazine, xli
Loth, David, 6n, 17
Loubser, Johannes J., 141n
Louis XIV, King, 175
Lowrie, Walter, 209n
Loyalty, conflicts of, 90-93, 363-373
Loyalty oaths, 11-12
Luther, Martin, 203
Lutheranism, 147, 151, 156, 163
Lynch, William F., S.J., 183n

MacArthur, Douglas, 344-345, 367, 368-369
Macaulay, Thomas, 481
Machiavelli, N., 151, 157
MacIver, R. M., l, lix, 498, 505, 506, 508, 517, 518, 519
MacMahon, Arthur, 359n
McAvoy, Thomas Timothy, C.S.C., 170n, 171n
McCarthy, Eugene J., xviii, 45-51, 492, 501, 508
McCarthy, Joseph, 62, 262, 318
McClellan, James, 508
McCracken, Robert J., 506, 518
McDougal, Myres S., 503, 508
McGill, B., 6n, 18
McGill University, 507
McGraw Edison Company, xxxiv

McHugh, Laurence C., S.J., 498, 508, 519
McKeon, Richard P., xx, 116, 471-487, 489, 492, 498, 501, 505, 506, 508, 515, 517, 518, 519
McKinley, William, 273
McMurrin, Sterling M., 508, 519
McPhee, William N., 63n
Madison Avenue, role of, xviii, 73-75
Madison, James, 239, 266, 319, 445, 456
Mahan, Alfred T., 343, 353
Maimonides, Moses, 214n
Maislen, George, 221n
Man:
  basic wants of, xliii-xlv
  concepts of, 35-36, 473-476, 479-487
  and world order, 123-130
Mandelbaum, Bernard, 37, 492, 498, 508, 519
Manning, Bayless, 58n
March, James G., 415n
Maritain, Jacques, 506, 518
Markets, system of, li-lii, lx
Marshall, John, 262, 456
Martin, Victor, 174n, 175n, 177n
Marx, Karl, 157
Marxism, 451
Maryland, University of, 491
Masland, J. W., 361n
Massachusetts, 455
Massachusetts Institute of Technology, 508, 519
Mathieson, Olin, Chemical Corp., 491, 507
May, Ernest, 374n
Mayer, Milton, 78
Mead, Margaret, 506, 518
Medical codes, 8
Meerloo, Joost A. M., 508, 515, 519
Melbourne, William, Lord, 449
Melchoir Bonnet, Bernardine, 176n
Membership:
  Church, 142-143, 149, 153
  Jewish congregations, 231-232
Men Who Manage (Dalton), 409-413
Mennonites, 143, 448
Mergers, Protestant, 194-195, 196-197
Merit system, 55
Methodist Church, 194, 205
Metropolis:
  characteristics of, 235-239
  decisionmaking in, 239-257
Mexican War, 268, 354
Mexico, 275

534   Index

Meyers v. United States, 260
Michels, Robert, 208
Michigan, University of, 491, 492, 506, 507, 509, 518
   Survey Research Center, xviii, 63-70
Middletown, Conn., 21-36
Midwest Oil case, 296n
Military Assistance Advisory Groups, xxxvii
Military-civil relationships, 459-461
   and the military mind, 341-350, 358
   and organization, 459-461
   problems of, 351-362
   and separation of powers, 363-382
Military Establishment Act (1947), 365
Mill, John Stuart, 481
Miller, Perry, 151n
Millis, Walter, 273n, 287-288, 290, 291, 370n
Milton, George Fort, 263, 277n
Minister, roles of, 200-203, 209-210
Minorities:
   and government evaluation, 65, 71
   in metropolitan areas, 237-238, 243, 252-257
Minton, Sherman, 284
Mission Covenant, 205
Misunderstanding of the Church (Brunner), 189
Mitchell, "Billy," 367
Modernist movement, 170
Mohonk, *see* Lake Mohonk
Monroe, James, 456
Montesquieu, 297, 319
Monypenny, P., 9n, 18
Moral codes, 3-16, 300-301, 401-402
Moral judgments, *see* Ethical problems
Moral law, 148-149
Moral Man and Immoral Society (Niebuhr), 58
Mores, institutional, 119-121
Morningside Heights, N.Y., 193
Morse, Hermann N., 209
Morton, Oliver P., 272
Moses, 213, 214n
Mosher, W., 9n, 17
Mott, John R., 208
Muckraking, 5-6
Municipal government, *see* City
Murray, Henry A., 506, 518
Murray, John Courtney, S.J., 506, 518

Murray, Philip, 283
Murty, K. Satchidananda, 502, 508, 514, 519
Mussolini, B., 349
Mysore University, 508
Myths, and society, l-lxiv

Nagel, Ernest, 506, 518
Napoleon, 176
National Academy of Sciences, 290, 492
National Association of Synagogue Administrators, 221n
National Broadcasting Company, xxxi, xlii
National Bureau of Standards, 107n, 508
National Catholic Welfare Conference, 171, 172n, 509
National Conference of Christians and Jews, 193, 506
National Council of Churches, 193-194, 197, 199, 200, 507, 508
National Evangelical Association, 193
National Federation of Jewish Men's Clubs, 221n
National Industrial Recovery Act, 277
National Institute of Mental Health, 492, 508
National Labor Relations Board, 306-307
National policy, *see* Policy
National Resources Planning Board, 298
National security, 351-352, 356-362
   and the military, 343-350
   and separation of powers, 363-382
National Security Council, 287, 289, 291, 359
National Women's League, 221n
Natural Law, 149-150, 155-156, 161, 185, 477, 478
Navy Department, 321-322, 378
Nazarenes, 194
Nef, John U., 506, 518
Negotiation, and administration, 425, 429-430, 431
Negroes, 238, 252-257
Neustadt, Richard E., xvii, 262n, 284-285
Newbigin, Lesslie, 208-209
New Deal, Democratic, 315
New England, 443
New England Congregationalists, 151
Newton, Sir Isaac, 156
New York City, 55, 416

Index

New York Psychoanalytic Institute, 509
New York State, 467
New York Times, xxxiv
New York University, 489, 505, 509, 517
Niebuhr, H. Richard, 190, 200-201, 204n
Niebuhr, Reinhold, 58, 343, 344n, 346n
Nielsen, Waldemar A., 519
Nikam, N. A., 508
Niles, D. T., 189
Noland, A., 118n
North Atlantic Treaty Organization, 345
Northrop, F. S. C., 506, 518
Notre Dame University of, 508
Nottingham, Elizabeth, 191, 204n
Nuclear war, 314, 324, 327, 344-345, 347, 356, 358, 371-373, 380, 382
Nucleation process, 197-198
Nullification doctrine, 267-268

Occupational ethics, 5-10
O'Connell, Daniel, 169
Odegard, Peter H., 45, 506, 518
Officer corps, 342-344, 346
see also Military
Ofstad, Harald, 503, 508
Ohio, 54-55
Olney, Richard, 273
O'Neil, C. William, Governor, 54
O'Neil, John, 183n
"One World—One Ethics?", 489
program of, 513-515
Ong, Walter J., S.J., 515, 520
Open Door policy, 273
Opinion, *see* Public opinion
Oppenheimer, J. Robert, 360-361, 506, 518
Oregon, 268
Organization:
concepts of, 385, 403-419
and ethical challenge, 422-434
measurement of, 385-395
and moral codes, 400-402
"Organization man," 423
Organizational dilemma:
and Judaism, 222
and Protestantism, 187-211
Organizational revolution, xix, 187, 192-210, 231-232, 482
Organizational Revolution, The (Boulding), 192

Orthodox Judaism, 165, 218, 221, 222, 225
Overstreet, Harry A., 506, 518
Ownership, xxvi
Oxford University, 508, 509
Oxnam, G. Bromley, 209

Pacific School of Religion, 506, 507, 518
Page, Charles H., 200
Paige, Glenn D., 283n
Paine, Thomas, 74
Papacy, authority of, 173, 174-176, 178-179
Parkins, Roswell, 58n
Parliament Act (1911), 319
Parliamentary system, 286, 288, 312, 314, 316-320, 324, 449-450, 468
proposal of, 436-437, 453, 464
Parry, Stanley, C.S.C., 508
Parsons, Talcott, xix, 141-167, 492, 499, 508
Participation, and administration, 423, 425, 428, 431
Partisanship, ethics of, 80-81
Party system, xviii, 29-30, 39-44
attitudes toward, 69
and ethical challenges, 53-60
and reform proposals, 436-438
strength of, 331
Patent rights, 102
Patronage, 55
Paul, Apostle, 191-192
Pearson, Hesketh, 27n
Pegis, Anton C., 506, 518
Pendleton Act, 272
Pennsylvania, 274
Pentagon, as a society, 392
see also Military
Pentecostal groups, 205
Perfectionism, 13-15
Perkins, James A., xviii-xix, 85-98, 492, 499, 508
Perry, Charner, xviii, xlvii-lxv, 11n, 492, 503, 508, 520
Personal competence, sense of, 67-68, 71
Personal ethics, xviii, xxiii-xlvi
Personnel function, 301-302, 329-330, 336, 424-425
Pettigrew, Thomas F., 209
Phelan, Gerald B., 506, 518
Philadelphia Convention (1788), 319, 322

Philadelphia Lutheran Seminary, 508
Philosophical ethics, 12-16
Physical sciences, 128
Physics, contemporary, 99-104
Pierce, Franklin, 269
Pike, James A., 208
Pitcher, Alvin, 217n
Pittsburgh, University of, 491, 506, 508
Pius VI, Pope, 176
Pius VII, Pope, 176
Pius IX, Pope, 178
Pius X, St., Pope, 182
Pius XI, Pope, 181
Pius XII, Pope, 183
Placement Commission, Rabbinical Assembly, 229
Plamenatz, John P., 499, 503, 508
Plato, 7, 80, 236, 471, 475
Pluralistic society, cooperation in, xviii, xlvii-lxv
Pogue, Welch, 301
Poland, 216, 279
Polanyi, Michal, xxi, 303, 497, 508
Policy, national:
 and debate, 312-315
 planning of, 290-293, 297-298
 responsibility for, 364-366, 381-382, 447-466, 468
Policy choices, by incremental decision, 415-418
Political action, by corporations, xxxiii-xxxiv
Political campaigns:
 conduct of, 40-42, 49, 55-56
 financing of, 30, 41
Political democracy, basis for, 157
Political efficacy, sense of, 67-69, 71
Political organization, xviii
 attitudes toward, 61-72
 ethical problems in, 21-37, 39-44, 53-60, 435-436, 471-487
 the executive in, 329-337
 and incentive theory, 407
 and the military, 342-343, 361-362
 norms of conduct in, 3-16, 45-51
 and public relations, 73-81
Political parties, *see* Party system
"Politics" (Emerson), 480
Polk, James Knox, 268, 269
Pontifical Institute of Mediaeval Studies, 506

Pope, Liston, 204n, 506, 518
Potter, David M., 520
Pound, Roscoe, 155n
Pourrat, Pierre P., 175n
Power:
 corporate diffusion of, xxx
 effect of, 34-35, 36-37
 government diffusion of, xxxv-xl, xlvi
 of science, 128-129
 and world policy, 343-350
Powers, separation of, *see* Separation
Practical ethics, 219, 221, 223, 230
Preclin, Edmond, 175n
Predestination, doctrine of, 147, 149, 151-152
Prerogative, Presidential, 265-271, 273, 276, 281, 282-284, 296
Presbyterians, 163
Presidency, system of, 312-320, 468
 and appointments, 301-302, 329-331, 336, 363, 365, 370, 374-376, 380-381
 and civil-military relations, 357, 358-360
 as Commander-in-Chief, 365-366, 368-370
 concepts of, 323
 unsettled limits of, 259-298
 see also Executive
President, university, 86-87, 89-90, 96-97
Presidential Power (Neustadt), xvii
Press, as ethical force, 49, 50
Pressures:
 adjustment of, 97-98
 management of, 73-81
Price, Don K., xix-xx, 435-468, 492, 500, 508
Price, Harry B., 503, 508
Prichard, H. A., 12n, 17
Priesthood, 145-146, 179-180
Primitive Baptists, 448
Princeton University, 506, 518
Principles, and institutions, lxi, lxiii-lxiv
Private enterprise, and the public, xxv-xxxiv
 see also Business
Professional ethics, 5-10, 46-48, 105-121, 230, 456-458
Professionalism, 133
Professors, university, 86-93, 97-98, 106-107
Property Requisitioning Act, 284

Index

Prophecy, in Judaism, 213-214
Protagoras, 476
Protestantism, 177, 182, 448, 455
   in American religious organization, 143-144, 146-160, 163-167
   organizational dilemma of, 187-211, 219n
Psychology, and religious thought, 151
Psychology of Scientific Management, The (Gilbreth), 404
Public Administration Institute of Turkey and the Middle East, 507
Public Administration Review, 3
Public agencies, and organization, 414-419
   see also Regulatory agencies
Public executive, the term, xxiv-xxv, xxxii-xxxiv, xlvi
   see also Administrators
Public interest, 5-16, 448-449
   concepts of, xli-xliii
   diversity in, 235-257
   and the metropolis, 235-239, 246-247
   and party politics, 29-30, 36
   and the private agency, 248-249
Public opinion, 313-315, 317, 329
   force of, 50
   management of, 73-81
Public relations, xxxi, xxxiv, 73-81
Public service:
   and ethical problems, 21-37, 239, 332-337, 453
   ethical standards for, 3-16, 45-51
   position of, 248-249, 337
   salaries in, 54-56
   see also Civil Service
Pullman strike, 273
Pure Food and Drug Administration, 309
Puritanism, 151, 153, 155-157, 159, 443-444

Rabbi, role of, 214, 225, 227-230, 231
Rabbinic Judaism, 214-215
Rabbinical Assembly of America, 219, 225-230, 232, 509, 519
Rabi, I. I., 505, 506, 517, 518
Radway, L. I., 361n
Rand Corporation, xxxvii
Rational model, of organization, 403, 418
Rationalism, 157

Realism, 13-15
Reasoning, common patterns of, lvi-lxii, lxiv
Reconstruction Finance Corporation, 6n, 45
Redford, E. S., 10n, 17
Reece, B. Carroll, xxix
Reed, Stanley F., 284
Reese, W. L., 219n
Reform Acts, British, 319
Reform Judaism, 163, 165, 218, 221, 222, 225, 231
Reform movements, 53
Reformation, Protestant, 146-147, 151, 159, 174
Regier, Jon L., 509
Regulatory agencies, federal, 49-50, 458
   ethical problems of, 299-310
Reid, Ira De A., 509
Religion:
   and government, 443-445, 455
   and long-range goals, xix, 163-167, 183-185, 210-211, 232
   role of, xiii, xvii-xviii
   and science, 115-116
   status of, 199
Religion and Society (Nottingham), 190
Religious orders, 145-146, 174-175, 179-180
Religious organization, xix
   in American society, 141-167
   and the Catholic Church, 169-185
   in Judaism, 213-232
   and Protestantism, 187-211
Religious Newswriters Association, 193
Religious Research Association, 193
Representation, and administration, 425, 429, 431
Representative government, *see* Democracy
Republican Party, 272, 315, 316, 364
Republic (Plato), 475
Rerum Novarum, 178
Research:
   applied, 106-107, 117-118, 120
   basic, 100, 103, 106-107, 111, 114, 117-118, 120
   big-scale scientific, 99-104, 131-137
   contract, 102-103, 111
   government, 105-121
   world view for, 124-137

Residence, and government evaluation, 66-67
Resources policy, 292-293
Reston, James, 353n
Rickover, Hyman, 378
Ridenour, Nina, 509, 520
Ridgway, Matthew B., 359n, 375
Right and wrong, conceptions of, 471-474, 476-487
Riverside Church, The, 506, 507
Robson, W. A., 262n
Roethlisberger, F. J., 405n
Role structures, 385
Role-theory, 80-81
Roman Catholicism:
  in American religious organization, 143-150, 152-156, 163-167
  institutionalized church of, 188
  and modern society, 169-185
Roman Empire, and the Jews, 214-215
Roosevelt, Franklin D., 43, 276-282, 284, 285, 295, 296, 323, 375
Roosevelt, Theodore, 263, 265-266, 273-275, 294, 323
Roosevelt University, 492, 508
Rosmini, 169
Ross, W. D., 12n, 17
Rossiter, Clinton, 264, 281n, 282
Roth, Cecil, 215n, 216
Rousseau, Jean Jacques, 33, 80
Routtenberg, Max J., 224n, 226n
Ruder and Finn, Inc., 491, 507
Ruder, William, 520
Ruoss, Meryl, 509
Rural populations, 66-67, 445
Rusk, Dean, 285
Russell, Bertrand, 75
Russia, *see* Soviet Russia

St. George, Katherine, 6n
St. Michael's College, Toronto, 506, 518
Salaries:
  academic, 103
  government, 54-56, 332-333, 445-446
Salesmanship, 76-78
Sandrow, Edward T., 509
Sanhedrin, the, 215, 216
Saturday Review, 505
Savery, G. M., 193n
Sayre, W., 9n, 19, 416-417
Scandinavian countries, 312

Schaefer, Catherine, 502, 509
Schechter, Solomon, 220-221
Schilling, Warner R., 361n
Schlesinger, A. M., Jr., 109n
Schneider, Herbert W., 199
School system, *see* Education
Schott, John, 201n
Schubert, Glendon, Jr., 14n, 19
Schwab, Joseph J., 520
Schwartz, Benjamin I., 497, 509
Schwartz, Bernard, xxi, 6n, 17, 500, 509
Science:
  and ethics, 478-479
  and government, 451-453, 457, 465
  and the military, 345-346
  and national security, 360-361
  and Puritanism, 156-157
  and world issues, 123-137
Science Commission, proposal for a, 136-137
Scientific management, 403-404
Scientific organization, xviii
  and big-scale research, 99-104, 131-137
  decisionmaking in, 123, 133-137
  in the government laboratory, 105-121
Scott, Winfield, 267, 268
Sears, Roebuck & Company, xxvi, xxxi
Second Temple, 214, 215
Secrecy:
  government, 379, 381
  scientific, 102
Secretaries, Cabinet, 380-381
Sect groups, 194, 204-208, 448
Secular Institutes, 146, 181
Secularism, 143-144
  and the Catholic Church, 172, 181-185
  definition of, 184
Securities and Exchange Commission, 277, 301, 307
Selective Service Acts, 281, 284
Self-government, structure of, 311-327
  see also Democracy
Self-selling ideas, 78-80
Sellars, Roy W., 506, 518
Selznick, Philip, 188-189, 211
Senate Military and Foreign Affairs Committee, 367
Senate, U.S., 313, 314, 318, 363, 380-381
  see also Congress, U.S.
Separation of powers:
  doctrine of, 259-263, 286, 313, 319, 323

Index

Separation of powers (Cont.)
   effectiveness for, 436-466, 467
   and legislative-executive relation, 48, 259-263, 264-266, 297
   and national security, 363-382
   and regulatory agencies, 305-307
Seventh Day Adventists, 205
Shakespeare, William, 74
Shapley, Harlow, 501, 505, 506, 509, 517, 518, 519
Shaw, George Bernard, 27
Sherman, Franklin, 509
Shils, Edward A., xxi, 503, 509
Shinn, Roger L., 502, 509
Shrader, Wesley, 200n
Shuster, George N., 506, 518, 520
Sick Chicken Case, 278
Sidgewick, Henry, lxii
Siegel, Seymour, 499, 509, 520
Silverman, David W., xix, 213-232, 492, 499, 509
Simon, Herbert A., 415
Simon, Ralph, 520
Sittler, Joseph, 201n
Sklare, Marshall, 217n, 226n
Slichter, Sumner H., 430
Sloan, Alfred P., Foundation, 509
Smith, Beverly, 370n
Smith, Fred, 36
Smith, Harold D., 4n, 17
Smith, T. V., 14n, 18
Snead, Sam, xlii
Snell, Bertrand H., 277
Social character, 413-414
Social compact, 476, 478
Social groups:
   and government evaluation, 65, 71-72
   metropolitan, 237-238, 252-257
Social integration, 124
Social linkages, lxiv-lxv
Social sciences, 128
Social Security Act, 307
Social structure, American, 165-167
Society:
   and the creative scientist, 115-117, 120, 126-137
   evolution of, 389-394
   and opinion management, 78-81
   secular, and religion, 144-150, 152-167
Society of Jesus, 146n, 164, 174-175, 176, 507

Sociology, of science, 118-119
Socrates, xlviii, 475
Sohm, Rudolf, 209n
Soldier and the State, The (Huntington), 341
Sophists, 476
Sorbonne, University of, 507
South, the, 444, 445, 447, 468
South Carolina Nullificationists, 267-268, 278
Southern Baptist Convention, 194
Soviet Russia, 133, 287, 312, 314, 324, 344, 349, 372, 373
Spinoza, B., 478-479
Spoils system, reform of, 456-457
Spykman, Nicholas J., 343
Stahl, O., 9n, 17
Stamp, Josiah C., 4n, 19, 262
Stanley, Wendell M., 505, 506, 517, 518
Stanton, Edwin M., 271
Stanton, Frank, xxxi
State, and church, 141, 144, 147, 155, 166, 171-172, 176, 185, 217
State Department, 321, 378
   Secretary, role of, 289-290, 291
State government, salaries in, 54-55
Steel Seizure Case, 294, 295, 296n
Steffens, Lincoln, 5n-6n, 18, 57, 468
Stein, Harold, 10n, 18
Stettinius, Edward, 280
Stevenson, Adlai E., x-xi, 316
Stewart, Walter A., 509
Stimson, Henry L., 345, 374
Stockholm, University of, 508
Stogdill, Ralph M., 408-409
Stokes, Donald E., xviii, 61-72, 492, 501, 509
Stone, Donald C., 506, 518
Stone, J., 8n, 18
Storey, Robert, 8n, 18
Strang, Ruth, xvi, 503, 509
Strategic Air Command, 345
Strauss, Lewis L., 509
Stroock, Alan M., ix-xi, 493
Structure:
   ecclesiastical, 199-211
   in Judaism, 224-225, 227-228
   purposes of, 434, 468
   of research organization, 105-115
Students, university, 93-97

Subjective morality, 397-398, 403, 419-420
Suburbs, and metropolitan government, 241-242, 244-246, 255
Subversives, investigations for, 11-12
Sunday School Movement, 193
Supreme Court, U.S., 261-263, 269 ff., 283-284, 290, 294, 322
Survival, of mankind, 123-128
Synagogue:
    and administration, 231
    ideals of, 224-225
Syracuse University, 491, 505, 507, 508, 519

Taft, Charles P., xviii, 53-60, 493, 501, 509
Taft, Robert, 55-56, 282-283
Taft, William Howard, 260, 274-275
Taft-Hartley Law, 283-284
Taft and Lavercombe, 493, 509
Talbot, Phillips, 520
Talmud, the, 214n, 215
Taney, Roger, 271
Taubes, Jacob, 189
Tax-exempt foundations, xxvii, xxix-xxx, xxxii
Tax exemption, for religious groups, 141
Taylor, Frederick W., 403
Taylor, Howard C., Jr., 520
Taylor, Maxwell, 359n
Taylor, O. H., 161n
Taylor, Zachary, 268-269
Teachers' codes, 8
Teaching process, 387-389
Tead, Ordway, xix, 421-434, 493, 499, 505, 506, 509, 517, 518, 519
Teapot Dome scandal, 6n
Technology, and science, 129-130, 137
Television networks, xxxi
Temple Emanuel, Buffalo, 519
Temple, William, 208
Tenure of Office Act, 273
Testem Benevolentiae, 170
Texas, 6n, 268
Thant, U, 520
Thomas, John L., S.J., 509, 514, 520
Thomism, 150
Thompson, Kenneth W., 520
Thoreau, Henry, 448
Thorp, Willard L., 520
Torah, the, 217, 220, 227

Tories, 481
Totalitarianism, vs. freedom, 311, 324-327
Towl, A., 8n, 17
Transcendentalism, 443, 445
Trent Affair, 269
Troeltsch, Ernst, 142-143, 144-145, 153, 204n
Truman, David B., 37, 298, 467-468, 493
Truman, Harry S., 63, 282-285, 291, 295, 316, 323, 367, 368, 369, 374
Trumbull, W. M., 8n, 18
Trustees, university, 88-89
Tufari, Paul, S.J., 146n
Tufts, James H., xlviii
Twain, Mark, 21
Twersky, Isadore, 514, 520
Tyler, John, 268

Union Theological Seminary, 492, 508, 509, 518
Unitarianism, 163, 443
United Nations, 508, 519
    Charter, 282-283
    Relief and Rehabilitation Adm., xxxix
United States:
    and the Catholic Church, 164, 170-172, 185
    and civil-military relations, 351-362
    and decisionmaking, in science, 133-137
    ethical demands of, 4-6
    government attitudes of, 312-327, 442-454, 455-457
    Judaism in, 217-232
    morality in, 46-48
    and Protestant organization, 187-211
    religious organization in, 141-167
    social structure of, 165-167
    and world politics, 343-350
United States Air Force, 357, 371-372, 374
United States Air Force Academy, 341
United States Army, 353, 357, 371-372, 374
United States v. Curtiss-Wright Export Corporation, 261-262
United States Marine Corps, 378
United States Military Academy, 353n
United States Naval Academy, 341
United States Navy, 353, 357, 374, 376
United Steelworkers of America, 283
United Synagogue of America, 219, 220-225, 227, 229n

Index

United Synagogue Youth, 221n
Universalism, 158
Universities:
    moral judgments in, 85-98
    salaries, 103
    and scientific research, xxxii, 102-103, 106-107, 111, 117
Urban population, and government evaluation, 66-67
Urban renewal, 248-257
Urs von Balthasar, Hans, 184n
Utah, University of, 508, 519
Utilitarianism, 12, 15n, 157

Valien, Preston, 520
Value model, of organization, 403, 405-414
Value weights, 394-395
Values:
    conflicting, 85, 93-97, 131-133
    criteria of, 471-487
    institutionalized, 146-147, 149, 151-167
    and promotion practices, 77-80
Van Buren, Martin, 268, 269
Van Doren, Charles, xxiii-xxiv, xxxi, xli
Van Doren, Mark, xxiii, xli
Van Dusen, H. P., 194n
Victoria University of Manchester, 507
Vincent, George C., 201n
Vinson, Carl, 283-284, 370
Virginia Constitutional Convention, 455
Virginia, University of, 491, 493, 506, 507, 509
Visser't Hooft, W. A., 209
Von Wiese, Leopold, 204n
Voting:
    by military, 342-343
    rates of, 62-63, 70

Wade, Ben, 272
Wade-Davis Bill, 271-272
Waldo, Dwight, 9, 18
War:
    American responses to, 352-358, 361
    cold, 345, 380, 392, 474
    nuclear, 314, 324, 327, 344-345, 347, 356, 358, 371-373, 380, 382
    or peace, 314-315
    and scientific research, 101-102, 112
War colleges, 361-362

War of 1812, 354
War powers, 269, 271, 275-276, 278-281
War Powers Acts, 280, 281
Warner, D. S., 205-206
Warren, Lindsay, 50-51
Washington, George, 266
Washington State Chapter, American Society for Public Administration, 9
Weaver, J. C., 111n
Weaver, Warren, 509
Weber, Max, lvi, 142-143, 145, 147, 153, 155, 156, 161n, 166, 188, 208, 209n, 210, 214n
Wegener, Charles W., 520
Weimar Constitution, 294
Wiener, P. P., 118n
Wesley, John, 161n
West:
    and Communism, 349
    ethical concepts of, 473-474, 477
Westchester, N.Y., 224
Westin, Alan F., 284n, 296n
West Point, Military Academy at, 341
West Virginia, 272
Wherry, Kenneth Spicer, Senator, 283
Whigs, 481
Whitley, Oliver Read, 205n
Willbern, Y., 10n, 19
Williams College, 491, 507
Wilson, Charles, xxxii, xxxiv
Wilson, Henry, 272
Wilson, M. L., 505, 506, 517, 518
Wilson, R. Norris, 509
Wilson vs. New, 278
Wilson, Woodrow, 9, 19, 244, 275-276, 315, 323, 347, 376, 459, 462
Wint, Guy, 497, 509
Wisdom, standards of, 3-4, 10-16
Woodstock College, 506
Worcester Foundation for Experimental Biology, 505, 508, 517
World Academy of Ethics, 515
World Council of Churches, 193
World politics:
    and the military, 345-350
    new pattern of, 356
    and science, 123-137
World War I, 218, 275, 279, 337, 344, 354
World War II, 128, 279-281, 337, 344, 355-356, 482

Worthy, James C., 400n, 405
Wright, Arthur F., 502, 509
Wright, Christopher, 520
Wright, David McCord, 515, 520
Wright, Deil, 61n
Wright, Quincy, 381-382, 493, 506, 509, 518

Yale University, 492, 505, 506, 507, 508, 509
Yearbook, Church of God, 206, 207
Yinger, J. Milton, 197, 204n

Ylvisaker, Paul N., xix, 235-257, 493, 500, 509
Young Ireland movement, 170
Young Men's Christian Association, 193
Young People's League, 221n
Young People's Society for Christian Endeavor, 193
Young Women's Christian Association, 193
Yugoslavia, xxxviii

Zurcher, Arnold John, 324n